Read, **Reason**, Write

AN ARGUMENT TEXT AND READER

ELEVENTH EDITION

Dorothy U. Seyler

Mc
Graw
Hill
Education

READ, REASON, WRITE: AN ARGUMENT TEXT AND READER, ELEVENTH EDITION

Published by McGraw-Hill Education, 2 Penn Plaza, New York, NY 10121. Copyright © 2015 by McGraw-Hill Education. All rights reserved. Printed in the United States of America. Previous editions © 2012, 2010, and 2008. No part of this publication may be reproduced or distributed in any form or by any means, or stored in a database or retrieval system, without the prior written consent of McGraw-Hill Education, including, but not limited to, in any network or other electronic storage or transmission, or broadcast for distance learning.

Some ancillaries, including electronic and print components, may not be available to customers outside the United States.

This book is printed on acid-free paper.

5 6 7 8 9 0 DOC/DOC 1 0 9 8 7 6 5

ISBN: 978-0-07-803621-7
MHID: 0-07-803621-6

Senior Vice President, Products & Markets: *Kurt L. Strand*
Vice President, General Manager, Products & Markets: *Michael Ryan*
Vice President, Content Production & Technology Services: *Kimberly Meriwether David*
Managing Director: *David S. Patterson*
Director: *Susan Gouijnstook*
Brand Manager: *Claire Brantley*
Executive Director of Development: *Lisa Pinto*
Director, Content Production: *Terri Schiesl*
Lead Content Project Manager: *Jane Mohr*
Buyer: *Jennifer Pickel*
Cover Designer: *Studio Montage, St. Louis, MO.*
Cover Image: © *Shaun Lowe/Getty Images*
Media Project Manager: *Jennifer Bartell*
Compositor: *Laserwords Private Limited*
Typeface: *10/12 Palatino*
Printer: *R. R. Donnelley*

All credits appearing on page or at the end of the book are considered to be an extension of the copyright page.

Library of Congress Cataloging-in-Publication Data

Seyler, Dorothy U.
  Read, reason, write : an argument text and reader / Dorothy U. Seyler.—Eleventh ed.
    pages cm
  ISBN 978-0-07-803621-7 (acid-free paper) — ISBN 0-07-803621-6 (acid-free paper)
  1. English language—Rhetoric. 2. Persuasion (Rhetoric) 3. College readers.
4. Report writing. I. Title.
  PE1408.S464 2014
  808'.0427—dc23
                                                              2013040964

The Internet addresses listed in the text were accurate at the time of publication. The inclusion of a website does not indicate an endorsement by the authors or McGraw-Hill Education, and McGraw-Hill Education does not guarantee the accuracy of the information presented at these sites.

www.mhhe.com

Brief Contents

Contents

New to the Eleventh Edition

This new edition continues the key features of previous editions while adding new material that will make it even more helpful to both students and instructors. Significant changes include the following.

- **New essays.** Both the student essay in MLA style and the student essay in APA are new. The first is longer and focuses on the interesting topic of genetically modified foods; the second, written for a sociology course, is presented in full.

- **New coverage**. There is **new material on paraphrasing** in Chapter 1 and **new material on preparing an annotated bibliography** in Chapter 12.

- **More visuals**. There are more visuals throughout the text, consistent with the increased use of visuals in all our media today.

- **Streamlined content.** The new edition is more streamlined, without any loss of significant coverage or readings.

- **New readings**. With thirty readings in the instructional chapters and forty-six readings in the anthology chapters, this edition has a total of seventy-six readings. In addition there are now nine student essays and the literature in the Appendix. Fifty-one of the readings are new, and some readings from the tenth edition are in new places, paired with new readings, providing a fresh perspective.

- **Enhanced coverage of documentation**. Two of the new readings are rather lengthy studies, complete with documentation, offering students further examples of documentation, supporting the four student essays that contain documentation.

- **Focus on current issues that are relevant to students**. Of the eight chapters in the anthology section, all have new readings, and most have a new focus. For example, the chapter on education in this edition concentrates entirely on issues relating to colleges, issues of cost and value to students as well as the purpose of higher education. The sports chapter examines the Penn State scandal and doping in sports, especially in cycling. The final chapter is still about America, this time looking to the future through the prism of past and present problems and successes.

Features of
Read, Reason, Write

These are among the features that have made *Read, Reason, Write* a best-selling text for so many editions.

- An emphasis on good reading skills for effective arguing and writing.
- Instruction, models, and practice in understanding reading context and analyzing elements of style.
- Instruction, models, and practice in writing clear, accurate summaries.
- Focus on argument as contextual: written (or spoken) to a specific audience with the expectation of counterarguments.
- Explanations and models of various types of arguments that bridge the gap between an understanding of logical structures and the ways we actually write arguments.
- Presentation of Aristotelian, Toulmin, and Rogerian models of argument as useful guides to analyzing the arguments of others and organizing one's own arguments.
- In-depth coverage of induction, deduction, analogy, and logical fallacies.
- Guidelines and revision boxes throughout the text that provide an easy reference for students.
- Instruction, models, and practice in finding and evaluating sources and in composing and documenting researched papers.
- A rich collection of readings, both timely and classic, that provides examples of the varied uses of language and strategies for argument.
- A brief but comprehensive introduction to reading and analyzing literature, found in the Appendix.

Let Connect Composition Help Your Students Achieve Their Goals

McGraw-Hill's solutions are proven to improve student performance. Powered by a four-year student subscription to Connect Composition Plus Essentials 3.0, *Read, Reason, Write* offers **LearnSmart Achieve**, a groundbreaking adaptive learning resource that individualizes writing instruction and helps improve student writing.

LearnSmart Achieve combines a continuously adaptive learning plan with learning resources that focus students on building proficiency in the language and critical processes of composition. Learning resources include contextualized grammar and writing lessons, videos, animations, and interactive exercises. Students are also provided with immediate feedback on their work and progress. A built-in time-management tool keeps students on track to ensure they achieve their course goals.

LearnSmart Achieve represents the goals of individual instructors and writing programs and provides valuable reports related to progress, achievement, and students who may be at risk. With LearnSmart Achieve, instructors can have the confidence of knowing—and the data that demonstrates—that their students, however diverse, are moving toward their highest course expectations: better prepared, confident thinkers and writers with transferable skills. See the next page for more details on what you will find in LearnSmart Achieve.

McGraw-Hill's **Digital Success Academy** offers a wealth of online training resources and course creation tips to help get you started. Go to connectsuccessacademy.com.

LearnSmart Achieve provides instruction and practice for your students in the following areas.

UNIT	TOPIC	
THE WRITING PROCESS	The Writing Process Generating Ideas Planning and Organizing	Writing a Rough Draft Revising Proofreading, Formatting, and Producing Texts
CRITICAL READING	Reading to Understand Literal Meaning Evaluating Truth and Accuracy in a Text	Evaluating the Effectiveness and Appropriateness of a Text

THE RESEARCH PROCESS	Developing and Implementing a
	   Research Plan
	Evaluating Information and Sources
		Integrating Source Material into
		   a Text
		Using Information Ethically
		   and Legally

REASONING AND ARGUMENT	Developing an Effective Thesis or Claim
	Using Evidence and Reasoning to
	   Support a Thesis or Claim
		Using Ethos (Ethics) to Persuade
		   Readers
		Using Pathos (Emotion) to Persuade
		   Readers
		Using Logos (Logic) to Persuade
		   Readers

MULTILINGUAL WRITERS	Helping Verbs, Gerunds and Infinitives, and Phrasal Verbs Nouns, Verbs, and Objects Articles	Count and Noncount Nouns Sentence Structure and Word Order Subject-Verb Agreement Participles and Adverb Placement
GRAMMAR AND COMMON SENTENCE PROBLEMS	Parts of Speech Phrases and Clauses Sentence Types Fused (Run-on) Sentences Comma Splices Sentence Fragments Pronouns	Pronoun-Antecedent Agreement Pronoun Reference Subject-Verb Agreement Verbs and Verbals Adjectives and Adverbs Dangling and Misplaced Modifiers Mixed Constructions Verb Tense and Voice Shifts
PUNCTUATION AND MECHANICS	Commas Semicolons Colons End Punctuation Apostrophes Quotation Marks Dashes	Parentheses Hyphens Abbreviations Capitalization Italics Numbers Spelling
STYLE AND WORD CHOICE	Wordiness Eliminating Redundancies Sentence Variety Coordination and Subordination	Faulty Comparisons Word Choice Clichés, Slang, and Jargon Parallelism

LearnSmart Achieve can be assigned by units and/or topics.

Let the Customizable Resources of Create Help You to Achieve Your Course's Goals

Your courses evolve over time—shouldn't your course material evolve as well? With McGraw-Hill CREATE, you can easily arrange and customize material from a variety of sources, including your own. You can choose your format (print or electronic) and what you want from:

- Chapters of *Read, Reason, Write*—choose only those chapters that you cover.
- A range of additional selections from other McGraw-Hill collections such as *The Ideal Reader* (800 readings by author, genre, mode, theme, and discipline) and many more.
- Your own resources, such as syllabi, institutional information, study guides, assignments, diagrams, artwork, student writing, art, photos, and more.

Go to www.mcgrawhillcreate.com and register today.

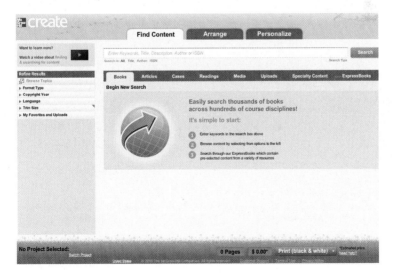

From the Author

I have written in previous prefaces to *Read, Reason, Write* that being asked to prepare a new edition is much like being asked back to a friend's home. Although you count on it, you are still delighted when the invitation comes. I am happy that the tenth edition kept old friends and made new ones as well and that once again I am writing a preface, this time to the eleventh edition. *Read, Reason, Write* is now almost 30 years old! Over all of these years, the text has grown in size—most books have—but also in stature within the teaching community and in its value to students. Of course, even though I have retired from full-time teaching, like fine wine neither this text nor I am getting older—only better.

Although some important new material strengthens the eleventh edition, the essential character of *Read, Reason, Write* remains the same. This text still unites instruction in critical reading and analysis, argument, and research strategies with a rich collection of readings that provide both practice for these skills and new ideas and insights for readers. A key purpose of *Read, Reason, Write* remains the same: to help students develop into better writers of the kinds of papers they are most often required to write, both in college and in the workplace, that is, summaries, analyses, reports, arguments, and documented essays. To fulfill this key purpose, the text must do more than offer instruction and opportunities for practice; it must also show students how these skills connect in important ways. Through all of its years, this text has been committed to showing students how reading, analytic, argumentative, and research skills are interrelated and how these skills combine to develop each student's critical thinking ability.

About the Author

Dorothy Seyler is Professor Emerita of English at Northern Virginia Community College. A Phi Beta Kappa graduate of the College of William and Mary, Dr. Seyler holds advanced degrees from Columbia University and the State University of New York at Albany. She taught at Ohio State University, the University of Kentucky, and Nassau Community College before moving with her family to Northern Virginia.

She is the author of *Introduction to Literature* (second edition), *Doing Research* (second edition), *The Reading Context* and *Steps to College Reading* (both in their third editions), and *Patterns of Reflection* (seventh edition). In 2007 Dr. Seyler was elected to membership in the Cosmos Club in Washington, DC for "excellence in education."

Professor Seyler has published articles in professional journals and popular magazines. She is currently working on a narrative nonfiction book about early-nineteenth-century explorer William John Bankes. She enjoys tennis and golf, traveling, and writing about both sports and travel.

Acknowledgments

No book of value is written alone. I am pleased to acknowledge the contributions of others in shaping this text. My thanks are due—as always—to the library staff at the Annandale Campus of Northern Virginia Community College who over the years helped me find needed information. I would also like to thank all of the students whose essays grace this text. They should be proud of the skill and effort they put into their writing. And I am indebted to Erik Neilson of the University of Richmond and Michael Hughes of Virginia Tech University for providing me with the student essays from their colleges, giving me a nice "stack" from which to choose the new essays for this edition. I appreciate the input of many reviewers over the years.

My former editor Steve Pensinger needs to be remembered for steering me through four editions. I am also grateful to Tim Julet and Alexis Walker for guidance through the fifth edition and to Chris Narozny, developmental editor of the sixth edition. My hat's off to Lisa Moore, executive editor for the sixth and seventh editions; to Christopher Bennem, sponsoring editor for the eighth, ninth, and tenth editions. Last, but not least, my thanks go to past developmental editors Joshua Feldman, Phil Butcher, Janice Wiggins-Clarke, and to my current developmental editor Susan Messer. I have been blessed with a chorus of voices enriching this text through my wonderful journey with this book: May you all live long and prosper!

I'll close by once again dedicating *Read, Reason, Write* to my daughter Ruth who, in spite of her own career and interests, continues to give generously of her time, reading possible essays for each new edition and listening patiently to my endless debates about changes. And for all students who use my text: May you understand that it is the liberal education that makes continued growth of the human spirit both possible and pleasurable.

Dorothy U. Seyler

Professor Emerita

Northern Virginia Community College

Critical Reading and Analysis

Writers and Their Sources

READ: What is the situation in the photo? Who are the two figures, where are they, and how do they differ?

REASON: What ideas are suggested by the photo?

REFLECT/WRITE: Why might this visual have been chosen for Chapter 1?

"Are you happy with your new car?" Oscar asks.

"Oh, yes, I love my new car," Rachel responds.

"Why?" queries Oscar.

"Oh, it's just great—and dad paid for most of it," Rachel exclaims.

"So you like it because it was cheap," Oscar says. "But, wasn't your father going to pay for whatever car you chose?"

"Well, yes—within reason."

"Then why did you choose the Corolla? Why is it so great?"

Rachel ponders a moment and then replies: "It's small enough for me to feel comfortable driving it, but not so small that I would be frightened by trucks. It gets good mileage, and Toyota cars have a good reputation."

"Hmm. Maybe I should think about a Corolla. Then again, I wouldn't part with my Miata!" Oscar proclaims.

A simple conversation, right? In fact, this dialogue represents an **argument.** You may not recognize it as a "typical" argument. After all, there is no real dispute between Oscar and Rachel—no yelling, no hurt feelings. But in its most basic form, an argument is a *claim* (Rachel's car is great) supported by *reasons* (the car's size, mileage, and brand). Similar arguments could be made in favor of this car in other contexts. For instance, Rachel might have seen (and been persuaded by) a television or online Toyota advertisement, or she might have read an article making similar claims in a magazine such as *Consumer Reports.* In turn, she might decide to develop her argument into an essay or speech for one of her courses.

READING, WRITING, AND THE CONTEXTS OF ARGUMENT

Arguments, it seems, are everywhere. Well, what about this textbook, you counter. Its purpose is to inform, not to present an argument. True—to a degree. But textbook authors also make choices about what is important to include and how students should learn the material. Even writing primarily designed to inform says to readers: Do it my way! Well, what about novels, you "argue." Surely they are not arguments. A good point—to a degree. The ideas about human life and experience we find in novels are more subtle, more indirect, than the points we meet head-on in many arguments. Still, expressive writing presents ideas, ways of seeing the world. It seems that arguments can be simple or profound, clearly stated or implied. And we can find them in much—if not most—of our uses of language.

You can accept this larger scope of argument and still expect that in your course on argument and critical thinking you probably will not be asked to write a textbook or a novel. You might, though, be asked to write a summary or a style analysis, so you should think about how those tasks might connect to the world of argument. Count on this: You will be asked to write! Why work on your writing skills? Here are good answers to this question:

- Communication skills are the single most important skill sought by employers.
- The better writer you become, the better reader you will be.

- The more confident a writer you become, the more efficiently you will handle written assignments in all your courses.
- The more you write, the more you learn about who you are and what really matters to you.

You are about to face a variety of writing assignments. Always think about what role each assignment asks of you. Are you a student demonstrating knowledge? A citizen arguing for tougher drunk-driving laws? A scholar presenting the results of research? A friend having a conversation about a new car? Any writer—including you—will take on different roles, writing for different audiences, using different strategies to reach each audience. There are many kinds of argument and many ways to be successful—or unsuccessful—in preparing them. Your argument course will be challenging. This text will help you meet that challenge.

RESPONDING TO SOURCES

If this is a text about *writing* arguments, why does it contain so many readings? (You noticed!) There are good reasons for the readings you find here:

- College and the workplace demand that you learn complex information through reading. This text will give you lots of practice.
- You need to read to develop your critical thinking skills.
- Your reading will often serve as a basis for writing. In a course on argument, the focus of attention shifts from you to your subject, a subject others have debated before you. You will need to understand the issue, think carefully about the views of others, and only then join in the conversation.

To understand how critical thinkers may respond to sources, let's examine "The Gettysburg Address," Abraham Lincoln's famous speech dedicating the Gettysburg Civil War battlefield. We can use this document to see the various ways writers respond—in writing—to the writing of others.

THE GETTYSBURG ADDRESS | ABRAHAM LINCOLN

Fourscore and seven years ago our fathers brought forth on this continent a new nation, conceived in liberty and dedicated to the proposition that all men are created equal. Now we are engaged in a great civil war, testing whether that nation, or any nation so conceived and so dedicated, can long endure. We are met on a great battlefield of that war. We have come to dedicate a portion of that field as a final resting place for those who here gave their lives that that nation might live. It is altogether fitting and proper that we should do this. But, in a larger sense, we cannot dedicate—we cannot consecrate—we cannot hallow—this ground. The brave men, living and dead, who struggled here have consecrated it far above our poor power to add or to detract.

The world will little note nor long remember what we say here, but it can never forget what they did here. It is for us, the living, rather to be dedicated here to the unfinished work which they who fought here have thus far so nobly advanced. It is rather for us to be here dedicated to the great task remaining before us—that from these honored dead we take increased devotion to that cause for which they gave the last full measure of devotion; that we here highly resolve that these dead shall not have died in vain; that this nation, under God, shall have a new birth of freedom; and that government of the people, by the people, for the people shall not perish from the earth.

What Does It Say?   THE RESPONSE TO CONTENT

Instructors often ask students to *summarize* their reading of a complex chapter, a supplementary text, or a series of journal articles on library reserve. Frequently, book report assignments specify that summary and evaluation be combined. Your purpose in writing a summary is to show your understanding of the work's main ideas and of the relationships among those ideas. If you can put what you have read into your own words and focus on the text's chief points, then you have command of that material. Here is a sample restatement of Lincoln's "Address":

> Our nation was initially built on a belief in liberty and equality, but its future is now being tested by civil war. It is appropriate for us to dedicate this battle-field, but those who fought here have dedicated it better than we. We should dedicate ourselves to continue the fight to maintain this nation and its princi-ples of government.

Sometimes it is easier to recite or quote famous or difficult works than to state, more simply and in your own words, what has been written. The ability to summarize reflects strong writing skills. For more coverage of writing summa-ries, see pages 10–13. (For coverage of paraphrasing, a task similar to summary, see pp. 18–20.)

How Is It Written?
How Does It Compare
with Another Work?   THE ANALYTIC RESPONSE

Summary requirements are often combined with analysis or evaluation, as in a book report. Most of the time you will be expected to *do something* with what you have read, and to summarize will be insufficient. Frequently you will be asked to analyze a work—that is, to explain the writer's choice of style (or the work's larger rhetorical context). This means examining sentence patterns, organization, metaphors, and other techniques selected by the writer to convey attitude and give force to ideas. Developing your skills in analysis will make you both a better reader and a better writer.

Many writers have examined Lincoln's word choice, sentence structure, and choice of metaphors to make clear the sources of power in this speech.* Analyzing Lincoln's style, you might examine, among other elements, his effective use of *tricolon:* the threefold repetition of a grammatical structure, with the three points placed in ascending order of significance.

> Lincoln uses two effective tricolons in his brief address. The first focuses on the occasion for his speech, the dedication of the battlefield: "we cannot dedicate—we cannot consecrate—we cannot hallow. . . ." The best that the living can do is formally dedicate; only those who died there for the principle of liberty are capable of making the battlefield "hallow." The second tricolon presents Lincoln's concept of democratic government, a government "of the people, by the people, for the people." The purpose of government—"for the people"—resides in the position of greatest significance.

A second type of analysis, a comparison of styles of two writers, is a frequent variation of the analytic assignment. By focusing on similarities and differences in writing styles, you can see more clearly the role of choice in writing and may also examine the issue of the degree to which differences in purpose affect style. One student, for example, produced a thoughtful and interesting study of Lincoln's style in contrast to that of Martin Luther King Jr.:

> Although Lincoln's sentence structure is tighter than King's and King likes the rhythms created by repetition, both men reflect their familiarity with the King James Bible in their use of its cadences and expressions. Instead of saying eighty-seven years ago, Lincoln, seeking solemnity, selects the biblical expression "Fourscore and seven years ago." Similarly, King borrows from the Bible and echoes Lincoln when he writes "Five score years ago."

Is It Logical?
Is It Adequately Developed?
Does It Achieve Its Purpose?　　THE EVALUATION RESPONSE

Even when the stated purpose of an essay is "pure" analysis, the analysis implies a judgment. We analyze Lincoln's style because we recognize that "The Gettysburg Address" is a great piece of writing and we want to see how it achieves its power. On other occasions, evaluation is the stated purpose for close reading and analysis. The columnist who challenges a previously published editorial has analyzed the editorial and found it flawed. The columnist may fault the editor's logic or lack of adequate or relevant support for the editorial's main idea. In each case the columnist makes a negative evaluation of the editorial, but that judgment is an informed one based on the columnist's knowledge of language and the principles of good argument.

Part of the ability to judge wisely lies in recognizing each writer's (or speaker's) purpose, audience, and occasion. It would be inappropriate to assert

---

* See, for example, Gilbert Highet's essay, "The Gettysburg Address," in *The Clerk of Oxenford: Essays on Literature and Life* (New York: Oxford UP, 1954), to which I am indebted in the following analysis.

that Lincoln's address is weakened by its lack of facts about the battle. The historian's purpose is to record the number killed or to analyze the generals' military tactics. Lincoln's purpose was different.

> As Lincoln reflected upon this young country's being torn apart by civil strife, he saw the dedication of the Gettysburg battlefield as an opportunity to challenge the country to fight for its survival and the principles upon which it was founded. The result was a brief but moving speech that appropriately examines the connection between the life and death of soldiers and the birth and survival of a nation.

These sentences begin an analysis of Lincoln's train of thought and use of metaphors. The writer shows an understanding of Lincoln's purpose and the context in which he spoke.

How Does It Help Me to Understand Other Works, Ideas, Events?

THE RESEARCH RESPONSE

Frequently you will read not to analyze or evaluate but rather to use the source as part of learning about a particular subject. Lincoln's address is significant for the Civil War historian both as an event of that war and as an influence on our thinking about that war. "The Gettysburg Address" is also vital to the biographer's study of Lincoln's life or to the literary critic's study either of famous speeches or of the Bible's influence on English writing styles. Thus Lincoln's brief speech is a valuable source for students in a variety of disciplines. It becomes part of their research process. Able researchers study it carefully, analyze it thoroughly, place it in its proper historical, literary, and personal contexts, and use it to develop their own arguments.

To practice reading and responding to sources, study the following article by Deborah Tannen. The exercises that follow will check your reading skills and your understanding of the various responses to reading just discussed. Use the prereading questions to become engaged with Tannen's essay.

WHO DOES THE TALKING HERE? | DEBORAH TANNEN

Professor of linguistics at Georgetown University, Deborah Tannen writes popular books on the uses of language by "ordinary" people. Among her many books are *Talking from 9 to 5* (1994) and *I Only Say This Because I Love You* (2004). Here she responds to the debate over who talks more, men or women.

PREREADING QUESTIONS What is the occasion for Tannen's article—what is she responding to? Who does most of the talking in your family—and are you okay with the answer?

It's no surprise that a one-page article published this month in the journal *Science* inspired innumerable newspaper columns and articles. The study, by Matthias Mehl and four colleagues, claims to lay to rest, once and for all, the

1

stereotype that women talk more than men, by proving—scientifically—that women and men talk equally.

2   The notion that women talk more was reinforced last year when Louann Brizendine's "The Female Brain" cited the finding that women utter, on average, 20,000 words a day, men 7,000. (Brizendine later disavowed the statistic, as there was no study to back it up.) Mehl and his colleagues outfitted 396 college students with devices that recorded their speech. The female subjects spoke an average of 16,215 words a day, the men 15,669. The difference is insignificant. Case closed.

3   Or is it? Can we learn who talks more by counting words? No, according to a forthcoming article surveying 70 studies of gender differences in talkativeness. (Imagine—70 studies published in scientific journals, and we're still asking the question.) In their survey, Campbell Leaper and Melanie Ayres found that counting words yielded no consistent differences, though number of words per speaking turn did. (Men, on average, used more.)

4   This doesn't surprise me. In my own research on gender and language, I quickly surmised that to understand who talks more, you have to ask: What's the situation? What are the speakers using words for?

5   The following experience conveys the importance of situation. I was addressing a small group in a suburban Virginia living room. One man stood out because he talked a lot, while his wife, who was sitting beside him, said nothing at all. I described to the group a complaint common among women about men they live with: At the end of a day she tells him what happened, what she thought and how she felt about it. Then she asks, "How was your day?"—and is disappointed when he replies, "Fine," "Nothing much" or "Same old rat race."

6   The loquacious man spoke up. "You're right," he said. Pointing to his wife, he added, "She's the talker in our family." Everyone laughed. But he explained, "It's true. When we come home, she does all the talking. If she didn't, we'd spend the evening in silence."

7   The "how was your day?" conversation typifies the kind of talk women tend to do more

Who is the most passive figure in this group?

of: spoken to intimates and focusing on personal experience, your own or others'. I call this "rapport-talk." It contrasts with "report-talk"—giving or exchanging information about impersonal topics, which men tend to do more.

Studies that find men talking more are usually carried out in formal experi- 8 ments or public contexts such as meetings. For example, Marjorie Swacker observed an academic conference where women presented 40 percent of the papers and were 42 percent of the audience but asked only 27 percent of the questions; their questions were, on average, also shorter by half than the men's questions. And David and Myra Sadker showed that boys talk more in mixed-sex classrooms—a context common among college students, a factor skewing the results of Mehl's new study.

Many men's comfort with "public talking" explains why a man who tells his 9 wife he has nothing to report about his day might later find a funny story to tell at dinner with two other couples (leaving his wife wondering, "Why didn't he tell me first?").

In addition to situation, you have to consider what speakers are doing with 10 words. Campbell and Ayres note that many studies find women doing more "affiliative speech" such as showing support, agreeing or acknowledging others' comments. Drawing on studies of children at play as well as my own research of adults talking, I often put it this way: For women and girls, talk is the glue that holds a relationship together. Their best friend is the one they tell everything to. Spending an evening at home with a spouse is when this kind of talk comes into its own. Since this situation is uncommon among college students, it's another factor skewing the new study's results.

Women's rapport-talk probably explains why many people think women 11 talk more. A man wants to read the paper, his wife wants to talk; his girlfriend or sister spends hours on the phone with her friend or her mother. He concludes: Women talk more.

Yet Leaper and Ayres observed an overall pattern of men speaking more. 12 That's a conclusion women often come to when men hold forth at meetings, in social groups or when delivering one-on-one lectures. All of us—women and men—tend to notice others talking more in situations where we talk less.

Counting may be a start—or a stop along the way—to understanding gen- 13 der differences. But it's understanding when we tend to talk and what we're doing with words that yields insights we can count on.

Source: *Washington Post*, July 15, 2007, copyright Deborah Tannen. Reprinted by permission.

QUESTIONS FOR READING AND REASONING

1. What was the conclusion of the researchers who presented their study in *Science*?
2. Why are their results not telling the whole story, according to Tannen? Instead of counting words, what should we study?

3. What two kinds of talk does Tannen label? Which gender does the most of each type of talking?
4. What is Tannen's main idea or thesis?

QUESTIONS FOR REFLECTION AND WRITING

5. How do the details—and the style—in the opening and concluding paragraphs contribute to the author's point? Write a paragraph answer to this question. Then consider: Which one of the different responses to reading does your paragraph illustrate?
6. Do you agree with Tannen that understanding how words are used must be part of any study of men and women talking? If so, why? If not, how would you respond to her argument?
7. "The Gettysburg Address" is a valuable document for several kinds of research projects. For what kinds of research would Tannen's essay be useful? List several possibilities and be prepared to discuss your list with classmates.

WRITING SUMMARIES

Preparing a good summary is not easy. *A summary briefly restates, in your own words, the main points of a work in a way that does not misrepresent or distort the original.* A good summary shows your grasp of main ideas and your ability to express them clearly. You need to condense the original while giving all key ideas appropriate attention. As a student you may be assigned a summary to

- show that you have read and understood assigned works;
- complete a test question;
- have a record of what you have read for future study or to prepare for class discussion; or
- explain the main ideas in a work that you will also examine in some other way, such as in a book review.

When assigned a summary, pay careful attention to word choice. Avoid judgment words, such as "Brown then proceeds to develop the *silly* idea that. . . ." Follow these guidelines for writing good summaries.

GUIDELINES for Writing Summaries

1. **Write in a direct, objective style, using your own words.** Use few, if any, direct quotations, probably none in a one-paragraph summary.
2. **Begin with a reference to the writer (full name) and the title of the work, and then state the writer's thesis.** (You may also want to include where and when the work was published.)

3. **Complete the summary by providing other key ideas.** Show the reader how the main ideas connect and relate to one another.

4. **Do not include specific examples, illustrations, or background sections.**

5. **Combine main ideas into fewer sentences than were used in the original.**

6. **Keep the parts of your summary in the same balance as you find in the original.** If the author devotes about 30 percent of the essay to one idea, that idea should get about 30 percent of the space in your summary.

7. **Select precise, accurate verbs to show the author's relationship to ideas.** Write Jones *argues*, Jones *asserts*, Jones *believes*. Do not use vague verbs that provide only a list of disconnected ideas. Do *not* write Jones *talks about*, Jones *goes on to say*.

8. **Do not make any judgments about the writer's style or ideas.** Do *not* include your personal reaction to the work.

EXERCISE: Summary

With these guidelines in mind, read the following two summaries of Deborah Tannen's "Who Does the Talking Here?" (see pp. 8–9). Then answer the question: What is flawed or weak about each summary? To aid your analysis, (1) underline or highlight all words or phrases that are inappropriate in each summary, and (2) put the number of the guideline next to any passage that does not adhere to that guideline.

SUMMARY 1

I really thought that Deborah Tannen's essay contained some interesting ideas about how men and women talk. Tannen mentioned a study in which men and women used almost the same number of words. She goes on to talk about a man who talked a lot at a meeting in Virginia. Tannen also says that women talk more to make others feel good. I'm a man, and I don't like to make small talk.

SUMMARY 2

In Deborah Tannen's "Who Does the Talking Here?" (published July 15, 2007), she talks about studies to test who talks more—men or women. Some people think the case is closed—they both talk about the same number of words. Tannen goes on to say that she thinks people use words differently. Men talk a lot at events; they use "report-talk." Women use "rapport-talk" to strengthen relationships; their language is a glue to maintain relationships. So just counting words does not work. You have to know why someone is speaking.

Although we can agree that the writers of these summaries have read Tannen's essay, we can also find weaknesses in each summary. Certainly the second summary is more helpful than the first, but it can be strengthened by eliminating some details, combining some ideas, and putting more focus on Tannen's main idea. Here is a much-improved version:

REVISED SUMMARY

In Deborah Tannen's essay "Who Does the Talking Here?" (published July 15, 2007), Tannen asserts that recent studies to determine if men or women do the most talking are not helpful in answering that question. These studies focus on just counting the words that men and women use. Tannen argues that the only useful study of this issue is one that examines how each gender uses words and in which situations each gender does the most talking. She explains that men tend to use "report-talk" whereas women tend to use "rapport-talk." That is, men will do much of the talking in meetings when they have something to report. Women, on the other hand, will do more of the talking when they are seeking to connect in a relationship, to make people feel good. So, if we want to really understand the differences, we need to stop counting words and listen to what each gender is actually doing with the words that are spoken.

At times you may need to write a summary of a page or two rather than one paragraph. Frequently, long reports are preceded by a one-page summary. A longer summary may become part of an article-length review of an important book. Or instructors may want a longer summary of a lengthy or complicated article or text chapter. The following is an example of a summary of a lengthy article on cardiovascular health.

SAMPLE LONGER SUMMARY

In her article "The Good Heart," Anne Underwood (*Newsweek*, October 3, 2005) explores recent studies regarding heart disease that, in various ways, reveal the important role that one's attitudes have on physical health, especially the health of the heart. She begins with the results of a study published in the *New England Journal of Medicine* that examined the dramatic increase in cardiovascular deaths after an earthquake in Los Angeles in 1994. People who were not hurt by the quake died as a result of the fear and stress brought on by the event. As Underwood explains in detail, however, studies continue to show that psychological and social factors affect coronaries even more than sudden shocks such as earthquakes. For example, according to Dr. Michael Frenneaux, depression "at least doubles an otherwise healthy person's heart-attack risk." A Duke University study showed that high levels of hostility also raised the risk of death by heart disease. Another study showed that childhood traumas can increase heart disease risks by 30 to 70 percent. Adults currently living under work and family stress also increase their risks significantly.

How do attitudes make a difference? A number of studies demonstrate that negative attitudes, anger, and hostile feelings directly affect the chemistry of the body in ways that damage blood vessels. They also can raise blood pressure. Less directly, people with these attitudes and under stress often eat more, exercise less, and are more likely to smoke. These behaviors add to one's risk. Some physicians are seeking to use this information to increase the longevity of heart patients. They are advising weight loss and exercise, yoga and therapy, recognizing, as Underwood concludes, that "the heart does not beat in isolation, nor does the mind brood alone."

Observe the differences between the longer summary of Anne Underwood's article and the paragraph summary of Deborah Tannen's essay:

- Some key ideas or terms may be presented in direct quotation.
- Results of studies may be given in some detail.
- Appropriate transitional and connecting words are used to show how the parts of the summary connect.
- The author's name is often repeated to keep the reader's attention on the article summarized, not on the author of the summary.

ACTIVE READING: USE YOUR MIND!

Reading is not about looking at black marks on a page—or turning the pages as quickly as we can. Reading means constructing meaning, getting a message. We read with our brains, not our eyes and hands! This concept is often underscored by the term *active reading*. To help you always achieve active reading, not passive page turning, follow these guidelines.

GUIDELINES for Active Reading

1. **Understand your purpose in reading.** Do not just start turning pages to complete an assignment. Think first about your purpose. Are you reading for knowledge on which you will be tested? Focus on your purpose as you read, asking yourself, "What do I need to learn from this work?"

2. **Reflect on the title before reading further.** Titles are the first words writers give us. Take time to look for clues in a title that may reveal the work's subject and perhaps the writer's approach or attitude as well. Henry Fairlie's title "The Idiocy of Urban Life," for example, tells you both Fairlie's subject (urban or city living) and his position (urban living is idiotic).

3. **Become part of the writer's audience.** Not all writers have you and me in mind when they write. As an active reader, you need to "join" a writer's audience by learning about the writer, about the time in which the piece was written, and about the writer's expected audience. For readings in this text you are aided by introductory notes; study them.

4. **Predict what is coming.** Look for a writer's main idea or purpose statement. Study the work's organization. Then use this information to anticipate what

is coming. When you read "There are three good reasons for requiring a dress code in schools," you know the writer will list *three* reasons.

5. **Concentrate.** Slow down and give your full attention to reading. Watch for transition and connecting words that show you how the parts of a text connect. Read an entire article or chapter at one time—or you will need to start over to make sense of the piece.

6. **Annotate as you read.** The more senses you use, the more active your involvement. That means marking the text as you read (or taking notes if the material is not yours). Underline key sentences, such as the writer's thesis. Then, in the margin, indicate that it is the thesis. With a series of examples (or reasons), label them and number them. When you look up a word's definition, write the definition in the margin next to the word. Draw diagrams to illustrate concepts; draw arrows to connect example to idea. Studies have shown that students who annotate their texts get higher grades. Do what successful students do.

7. **Keep a reading journal.** In addition to annotating what you read, you may want to develop the habit of writing regularly in a journal. A reading journal gives you a place to note impressions and reflections on your reading, your initial reactions to assignments, and ideas you may use in your next writing.

EXERCISE: Active Reading

Read the following essay, studying the annotations that are started for you. As you read, add your own notes. Then test your active reading by responding to the questions that follow the essay.

THE RISE OF THE NEW GROUPTHINK | SUSAN CAIN

A graduate of Princeton and Harvard Law and former corporate attorney, Susan Cain thought about her preference for reading and small groups over public speaking and decided to write on the subject. Her book *Quiet: The Power of Introverts in a World That Can't Stop Talking* (2012) is the result. The following article, drawn from ideas for her book, appeared January 15, 2012.

Topic.

1   Solitude is out of fashion. Our companies, our schools and our culture are in thrall to an idea I call the New Groupthink, which holds that creativity and achievement come from an oddly gregarious place. Most of us now work in teams, in offices without walls, for managers who prize people skills above all else. Lone geniuses are out. Collaboration is in.

Author seems to disagree?

2   But there's a problem with this view. Research strongly suggests that people are more creative when they enjoy privacy and freedom from interruption. And the most spectacularly creative people in many fields are often introverted, according to studies by the psychologists Mihaly Csikszentmihalyi and Gregory Feist. They're extroverted enough to exchange and advance ideas, but see themselves as independent and individualistic. They're not joiners by nature.

One explanation for 3 these findings is that introverts are comfortable working alone—and solitude is a catalyst to innovation. As the influential psychologist Hans Eysenck observed, introversion fosters creativity by "concentrating the mind on the tasks in hand, and preventing the dissipation of energy on social and sexual matters unrelated to work." In other words, a person sitting quietly under a tree in the backyard, while everyone else is clinking glasses on the patio, is more likely to have an apple land on his head. (Newton was one of the world's great introverts: William Wordsworth described him as "A mind for ever/ Voyaging through strange seas of Thought, alone.")

Solitude has long been associated with creativity and transcendence. 4 "Without great solitude, no serious work is possible," Picasso said. A central narrative of many religions is the seeker—Moses, Jesus, Buddha—who goes off by himself and brings profound insights back to the community.

Culturally, we're often so dazzled by charisma that we overlook the quiet 5 part of the creative process. Consider Apple. In the wake of Steve Jobs's death, we've seen a profusion of myths about the company's success. Most focus on Mr. Jobs's supernatural magnetism and tend to ignore the other crucial figure in Apple's creation: a kindly, introverted engineering wizard, Steve Wozniak, who toiled alone on a beloved invention, the personal computer.

Rewind to March 1975: Mr. Wozniak believes the world would be a better 6 place if everyone had a user-friendly computer. This seems a distant dream—most computers are still the size of minivans, and many times as pricey. But Mr. Wozniak meets a simpatico band of engineers that call themselves the Homebrew Computer Club. The Homebrewers are excited about a primitive new machine called the Altair 8800. Mr. Wozniak is inspired, and immediately begins work on his own magical version of a computer. Three months later, he unveils his amazing creation for his friend, Steve Jobs. Mr. Wozniak wants to give his invention away free, but Mr. Jobs persuades him to co-found Apple Computer.

The story of Apple's origin speaks to the power of collaboration. 7 Mr. Wozniak wouldn't have been catalyzed by the Altair but for the kindred spirits of Homebrew. And he'd never have started Apple without Mr. Jobs.

But it's also a story of solo spirit. If you look at how Mr. Wozniak got the 8 work done—the sheer hard work of creating something from nothing—he did it alone. Late at night, all by himself.

Intentionally so. In his memoir, Mr. Wozniak offers this guidance to aspir- 9 ing inventors:

"Most inventors and engineers I've met are like me . . . they live in their 10 heads. They're almost like artists. In fact, the very best of them are artists. And artists work best alone. . . . I'm going to give you some advice that might be hard to take. That advice is: Work alone . . . Not on a committee. Not on a team."

11   And yet The New Groupthink has overtaken our workplaces, our schools and our religious institutions. Anyone who has ever needed noise-canceling headphones in her own office or marked an online calendar with a fake meeting in order to escape yet another real one knows what I'm talking about. Virtually all American workers now spend time on teams and some 70 percent inhabit open-plan offices, in which no one has "a room of one's own." During the last decades, the average amount of space allotted to each employee shrank 300 square feet, from 500 square feet in the 1970s to 200 square feet in 2010.

12   Our schools have also been transformed by the New Groupthink. Today, elementary school classrooms are commonly arranged in pods of desks, the better to foster group learning. Even subjects like math and creative writing are often taught as committee projects. In one fourth-grade classroom I visited in New York City, students engaged in group work were forbidden to ask a question unless every member of the group had the very same question.

13   The New Groupthink also shapes some of our most influential religious institutions. Many mega-churches feature extracurricular groups organized around every conceivable activity, from parenting to skateboarding to real estate, and expect worshipers to join in. They also emphasize a theatrical style of worship—loving Jesus out loud, for all the congregation to see. "Often the role of a pastor seems closer to that of church cruise director than to the traditional roles of spiritual friend and counselor," said Adam McHugh, an evangelical pastor and author of "Introverts in the Church."

14   Some teamwork is fine and offers a fun, stimulating, useful way to exchange ideas, manage information and build trust.

15   But it's one thing to associate with a group in which each member works autonomously on his piece of the puzzle; it's another to be corralled into endless meetings or conference calls conducted in offices that afford no respite from the noise and gaze of co-workers. Studies show that open-plan offices make workers hostile, insecure and distracted. They're also more likely to suffer from high blood pressure, stress, the flu and exhaustion. And people whose work is interrupted make 50 percent more mistakes and take twice as long to finish it.

16   Many introverts seem to know this instinctively, and resist being herded together. Backbone Entertainment, a video game development company in Emeryville, Calif., initially used an open-plan office, but found that its game developers, many of whom were introverts, were unhappy. "It was one big warehouse space, with just tables, no walls, and everyone could see each other," recalled Mike Mika, the former creative director. "We switched over to cubicles and were worried about it—you'd think in a creative environment that people would hate that. But it turns out they prefer having nooks and crannies they can hide away in and just be away from everybody."

17   Privacy also makes us productive. In a fascinating study known as the Coding War Games, consultants Tom DeMarco and Timothy Lister compared the work of more than 600 computer programmers at 92 companies. They found that people from the same companies performed at roughly the same level—but that there was an enormous performance gap between organizations. What

distinguished programmers at the top-performing companies wasn't greater experience or better pay. It was how much privacy, personal workspace and freedom from interruption they enjoyed. Sixty-two percent of the best performers said their workspace was sufficiently private compared with only 19 percent of the worst performers. Seventy-six percent of the worst programmers but only 38 percent of the best said that they were often interrupted needlessly.

Solitude can even help us learn. According to research on expert performance by the psychologist Anders Ericsson, the best way to master a field is to work on the task that's most demanding for you personally. And often the best way to do this is alone. Only then, Mr. Ericsson told me, can you "go directly to the part that's challenging to you. If you want to improve, you have to be the one who generates the move. Imagine a group class—you're the one generating the move only a small percentage of the time." 18

Conversely, brainstorming sessions are one of the worst possible ways to stimulate creativity. The brainchild of a charismatic advertising executive named Alex Osborn who believed that groups produced better ideas than individuals, workplace brainstorming sessions came into vogue in the 1950s. "The quantitative results of group brainstorming are beyond question," Mr. Osborn wrote. "One group produced 45 suggestions for a home appliance promotion, 56 ideas for a money-raising campaign, 124 ideas on how to sell more blankets." 19

But decades of research show that individuals almost always perform better than groups in both quality and quantity, and group performance gets worse as group size increases. The "evidence from science suggests that business people must be insane to use brainstorming groups," wrote the organizational psychologist Adrian Furnham. "If you have talented and motivated people, they should be encouraged to work alone when creativity or efficiency is the highest priority." 20

The reasons brainstorming fails are instructive for other forms of group work, too. People in groups tend to sit back and let others do the work; they instinctively mimic others' opinions and lose sight of their own; and, often succumb to peer pressure. The Emory University neuroscientist Gregory Berns found that when we take a stance different from the group's, we activate the amygdala, a small organ in the brain associated with the fear of rejection. Professor Berns calls this "the pain of independence." 21

The one important exception to this dismal record is electronic brainstorming, where large groups outperform individuals; and the larger the group the better. The protection of the screen mitigates many problems of group work. This is why the Internet has yielded such wondrous collective creations. Marcel Proust called reading a "miracle of communication in the midst of solitude," and that's what the Internet is, too. It's a place where we can be alone together—and this is precisely what gives it power. 22

MY point is not that man is an island. Life is meaningless without love, trust and friendship. 23

And I'm not suggesting that we abolish teamwork. Indeed, recent studies suggest that influential academic work is increasingly conducted by teams rather than by individuals. (Although teams whose members collaborate remotely, from separate universities, appear to be the most influential of all.) The problems we face in science, economics and many other fields are more 24 complex than ever before, and we'll need to stand on one another's shoulders if we can possibly hope to solve them.

25   But even if the problems are different, human nature remains the same. And most humans have two contradictory impulses: we love and need one another, yet we crave privacy and autonomy.

26   To harness the energy that fuels both these drives, we need to move beyond the New Groupthink and embrace a more nuanced approach to creativity and learning. Our offices should encourage casual, cafe-style interactions, but allow people to disappear into personalized, private spaces when they want to be alone. Our schools should teach children to work with others, but also to work on their own for sustained periods of time. And we must recognize that introverts like Steve Wozniak need extra quiet and privacy to do their best work.

27   Before Mr. Wozniak started Apple, he designed calculators at Hewlett-Packard, a job he loved partly because HP made it easy to chat with his colleagues. Every day at 10 a.m. and 2 p.m., management wheeled in doughnuts and coffee, and people could socialize and swap ideas. What distinguished these interactions was how low-key they were. For Mr. Wozniak, collaboration meant the ability to share a doughnut and a brainwave with his laid-back, poorly dressed colleagues—who minded not a whit when he disappeared into his cubicle to get the real work done.

QUESTIONS FOR READING AND REASONING

1. What does Cain mean by the "new groupthink"? Where do we find this phenomenon and how do we recognize it?

2. According to research, what kinds of people are most creative? What environment is most conducive to productivity and creativity?

3. What is Cain's thesis—the claim of her argument?

4. How does she support her claim? List specific details of her support.

QUESTIONS FOR REFLECTION AND WRITING

5. How does Cain qualify her claim in the final five paragraphs? What makes this an effective conclusion to her essay?

6. What is the most interesting piece of information or concept, for you, in Cain's argument? Why? Write a journal entry—four or five sentences at least—in response to this question.

USING PARAPHRASE

Paraphrasing's goal is the same as summary's: An accurate presentation of the information and ideas of someone else. Unlike summary, we paraphrase an entire short work. This can be a poem (see p. 539 for a paraphrase of a poem) or a complex section of prose that needs a simpler (but often longer than the original) restatement so that we are clear about its meaning. We paraphrase short but complex pieces; we summarize an entire essay or chapter or book.

Writers also use paraphrasing to restate *some* of the information or ideas from a source as part of developing their own work. They do this extensively in a researched essay, but they may also paraphrase parts of a source to add support to their discussion—or to be clear about another writer's ideas that they will evaluate or challenge in some way.

Think, for a moment, about the writing process. Writers use many kinds of experiences to develop their work. Formal researched essays contain precise documentation and may use summary, paraphrase, and direct quotations, but they rarely include personal references. Today, however, writers may blend styles and strategies—in personal essays and researched essays, for example—rather than keeping them distinct. And some scholars today also write books for nonspecialists. In these books—or articles—documentation is placed only at the back, a more informal style is used, and personal experiences may be included to engage readers. Journalists, too, often blend personal experience and informal styles while drawing on one or more sources to develop and support their ideas. Among the readings in this text you will find a few personal essays and scholarly essays as well as works demonstrating a blending of styles and strategies. This blending can be confusing for college students. Make sure that you always understand what kind of work you are expected to produce in each class, for every assignment.

Now, to illustrate paraphrase, suppose you don't want to summarize Lincoln's entire speech, but you do want to use his opening point as a lead-in to commenting on our own times. You might write:

> Lincoln's famous speech at the dedication of the Gettysburg battlefield begins
> with the observation that our nation was initially built on a belief in liberty
> and equality, but the country's future had come to a point of being tested. We
> are not actually facing a civil war today, but we are facing a culture war, a war
> of opposing values and beliefs, that seems to be tearing our country apart.

Paraphrasing—putting Lincoln's idea into your own words—is a much more effective opening than quoting Lincoln's first two sentences. It's his idea that you want to use, not his language. Observe three key points:

1. The idea is Lincoln's but the word choice is entirely different. Resist the urge to borrow any of Lincoln's phrases—that would be quoting and would require quotation marks—and that does not serve your purpose.
2. You still give credit to Lincoln for the idea.
3. Summary, paraphrasing, and quoting all share this one characteristic: You let readers know that you are using someone else's information or ideas.

EXERCISE: Paraphrase

1. Find several examples of paraphrasing in Cain's essay.
2. Assume that you are writing an essay on the disadvantages of brainstorming. Paraphrase the ideas in Cain's paragraph 20 to use in this assumed essay.

3. For an essay on the value of solitude in our too-bustling world, evaluate the following two paragraphs that use some of the material from Cain's paragraphs 3 and 4.

PARAPHRASE 1

Introverts have no trouble with solitude. Most adults are socialized to want close friends and family connections, but introverts are also content to have time alone to read, think, and create. What extroverts must learn is that no serious work is possible without solitude. Newton and other insightful people use their solitude as a catalyst for innovation, even, as Susan Cain notes, for transcendence.

PARAPHRASE 2

Introverts have no trouble with solitude. Most adults are socialized to want close friends and family connections, but introverts are also content to have time alone to read, think, and create. In her essay "The Rise of the New Groupthink," Susan Cain worries that today's emphasis on group projects fostered in open office spaces will not provide the solitude that can lead to new ideas. Yet, as Cain observes, it is often those who are given opportunities to think and work by themselves who provide us with new insights and new inventions.

ACKNOWLEDGING SOURCES INFORMALLY

As you have seen in the summaries and paraphrases above, even when you are not writing a formally documented paper, you must identify each source by author. What follows are some of the conventions of writing to use when writing about sources.

Referring to People and Sources

Readers in academic, professional, and business contexts expect writers to follow specific conventions of style when referring to authors and to various kinds of sources. Study the following guidelines and examples and then mark the next few pages for easy reference—perhaps by turning down a corner of the first and last pages.

References to People

*   In a first reference, give the person's full name (both the given name and the surname): *Ellen Goodman, Robert J. Samuelson.* In second and subsequent references, use only the last name (surname): *Goodman, Samuelson.*
*   Do not use Mr., Mrs., or Ms. Special titles such as President, Chief Justice, or Doctor may be used in the first reference with the person's full name.
*   Never refer to an author by her or his first name. Write *Tannen*, not *Deborah*; *Lincoln*, not *Abraham*.

References to Titles of Works

Titles of works must *always* be written as titles. Titles are indicated by capitalization and by either quotation marks or italics.

Guidelines for Capitalizing Titles

- The first and last words are capitalized.
- The first word of a subtitle is capitalized.
- All other words in titles are capitalized except
  — Articles (*a, an, the*).
  — Coordinating conjunctions (*and, or, but, for, nor, yet, so*).
  — Prepositions (*in, for, about*).

Titles Requiring Quotation Marks

Titles of works published within other works—within a book, magazine, or newspaper—are indicated by quotation marks.

ESSAYS	"Who Does the Talking Here?"
SHORT STORIES	"The Story of an Hour"
POEMS	"To Daffodils"
ARTICLES	"Choose Your Utopia"
CHAPTERS	"Writers and Their Sources"
LECTURES	"Crazy Mixed-Up Families"
TV EPISODES	"Pride and Prejudice" (one drama on the television show *Masterpiece Theatre*)

Titles Requiring Italics

Titles of works that are separate publications and, by extension, titles of items such as works of art and websites are in italics.

PLAYS	*A Raisin in the Sun*
NOVELS	*War and Peace*
NONFICTION BOOKS	*Read, Reason, Write*
BOOK-LENGTH POEMS	*The Odyssey*
MAGAZINES AND JOURNALS	*Wired*
NEWSPAPERS	*Wall Street Journal*
FILMS	*The Wizard of Oz*
PAINTINGS	*The Birth of Venus*
TELEVISION PROGRAMS	*Star Trek*
WEBSITES	*worldwildlife.org*
DATABASES	*ProQuest*

Read the following article and respond by answering the questions that follow. Observe, as you read, how the author refers to the various sources he uses to develop his article and how he presents material from those sources. We will use this article as a guide to handling quotations.

THE FUTURE IS NOW: IT'S HEADING RIGHT AT US, BUT WE NEVER SEE IT COMING

JOEL ACHENBACH

A former humor columnist and currently a staff writer for the *Washington Post,* Joel Achenbach also has a regular blog on *washingtonpost.com.* His books include anthologies of his columns and *Captured by Aliens: The Search for Life and Truth in a Very Large Universe* (2003). The following article was published April 13, 2008.

PREREADING QUESTIONS What is nanotechnology? What do you think will be the next big change—and what field will it come from?

1   The most important things happening in the world today won't make tomorrow's front page. They won't get mentioned by presidential candidates or Chris Matthews[1] or Bill O'Reilly[2] or any of the other folks yammering and snorting on cable television.

2   They'll be happening in laboratories—out of sight, inscrutable and unhyped until the very moment when they change life as we know it.

3   Science and technology form a two-headed, unstoppable change agent. Problem is, most of us are mystified and intimidated by such things as biotechnology, or nanotechnology, or the various other -ologies that seem to be threatening to merge into a single unspeakable and incomprehensible thing called biotechnonanogenomicology. We vaguely understand that this stuff is changing our lives, but we feel as though it's all out of our control. We're just hanging on tight, like Kirk and Spock when the Enterprise starts vibrating at Warp 8.

4   What's unnerving is the velocity at which the future sometimes arrives. Consider the Internet. This powerful but highly disruptive technology crept out of the lab (a Pentagon think tank, actually) and all but devoured modern civilization—with almost no advance warning. The first use of the word "internet" to refer to a computer network seems to have appeared in this newspaper on Sept. 26, 1988, in the Financial section, on page F30—about as deep into the paper as you can go without hitting the bedrock of the classified ads.

5   The entire reference: "SMS Data Products Group Inc. in McLean won a $1,005,048 contract from the Air Force to supply a defense data network internet protocol router." Perhaps the unmellifluous compound noun "data network internet protocol router" is one reason more of us didn't pay attention. A couple of months later, "Internet"—still lacking the "the" before its name—finally elbowed its way to the front page when a virus shut down thousands of computers. The story referred to "a research network called Internet," which "links as many as 50,000 computers, allowing users to send a variety of information to each other." The scientists knew that computer networks could

---

[1] Political talk-show host on MSNBC.—Ed.

[2] Radio and television talk-show host on the FOX News Channel.—Ed.

SPEED BUMP. By permission of Dave Coverly and Creators Syndicate, Inc.

be powerful. But how many knew that this Internet thing would change the way we communicate, publish, sell, shop, conduct research, find old friends, do homework, plan trips and on and on?

Joe Lykken, a theoretical physicist at the Fermilab research center in Illinois, tells a story about something that happened in 1990. A Fermilab visitor, an English fellow by the name of Tim Berners-Lee, had a new trick he wanted to demonstrate to the physicists. He typed some code into a little blank box on the computer screen. Up popped a page of data.   6

Lykken's reaction: *Eh.*   7

He could already see someone else's data on a computer. He could have the colleague e-mail it to him and open it as a document. Why view it on a separate page on some computer network?   8

But of course, this unimpressive piece of software was the precursor to what is known today as the World Wide Web. "We had no idea that we were seeing not only a revolution, but a trillion-dollar idea," Lykken says.   9

Now let us pause to reflect upon the fact that Joe Lykken is a very smart guy—you don't get to be a theoretical physicist unless you have the kind of brain that can practically bend silverware at a distance—and even he, with that giant cerebral cortex and the billions of neurons flashing and winking, saw the proto-Web and harrumphed. It's not just us mortals, even scientists don't always grasp the significance of innovations. Tomorrow's revolutionary technology may be in plain sight, but everyone's eyes, clouded by conventional thinking, just can't detect it. "Even smart people are really pretty incapable of envisioning a situation that's substantially different from what they're in," says Christine Peterson, vice president of Foresight Nanotech Institute in Menlo Park, Calif.   10

So where does that leave the rest of us?   11

In technological Palookaville.   12

Science is becoming ever more specialized; technology is increasingly a series of black boxes, impenetrable to but a few. Americans' poor science literacy means that science and technology exist in a walled garden, a geek ghetto. We are a technocracy in which most of us don't really understand   13 what's happening around us. We stagger through a world of technological and medical miracles. We're zombified by progress.

14   Peterson has one recommendation: Read science fiction, especially "hard science fiction" that sticks rigorously to the scientifically possible. "If you look out into the long-term future and what you see looks like science fiction, it might be wrong," she says. "But if it doesn't look like science fiction, it's definitely wrong."

15   That's exciting—and a little scary. We want the blessings of science (say, cheaper energy sources) but not the terrors (monsters spawned by atomic radiation that destroy entire cities with their fiery breath).

16   Eric Horvitz, one of the sharpest minds at Microsoft, spends a lot of time thinking about the Next Big Thing. Among his other duties, he's president of the Association for the Advancement of Artificial Intelligence. He thinks that, sometime in the decades ahead, artificial systems will be modeled on living things. In the Horvitz view, life is marked by robustness, flexibility, adaptability. That's where computers need to go. Life, he says, shows scientists "what we can do as engineers—better, potentially."

17   Our ability to monkey around with life itself is a reminder that ethics, religion and old-fashioned common sense will be needed in abundance in decades to come. . . . How smart and flexible and rambunctious do we want our computers to be? Let's not mess around with that Matrix business.

18   Every forward-thinking person almost ritually brings up the mortality issue. What'll happen to society if one day people can stop the aging process? Or if only rich people can stop getting old?

19   It's interesting that politicians rarely address such matters. The future in general is something of a suspect topic . . . a little goofy. Right now we're all focused on the next primary, the summer conventions, the Olympics and their political implications, the fall election. The political cycle enforces an emphasis on the immediate rather than the important.

20   And in fact, any prediction of what the world will be like more than, say, a year from now is a matter of hubris. The professional visionaries don't even talk about predictions or forecasts but prefer the word "scenarios." When Sen. John McCain, for example, declares that radical Islam is the transcendent challenge of the 21st century, he's being sincere, but he's also being a bit of a soothsayer. Environmental problems and resource scarcity could easily be the dominant global dilemma. Or a virus with which we've yet to make our acquaintance. Or some other "wild card."

21   Says Lykken, "Our ability to predict is incredibly poor. What we all thought when I was a kid was that by now we'd all be flying around in anti-gravity cars on Mars."

22   Futurists didn't completely miss on space travel—it's just that the things flying around Mars are robotic and take neat pictures and sometimes land and sniff the soil.

23   Some predictions are bang-on, such as sci-fi writer Arthur C. Clarke's declaration in 1945 that there would someday be communications satellites orbiting the Earth. But Clarke's satellites had to be occupied by repairmen who would maintain the huge computers required for space communications. Even

in the late 1960s, when Clarke collaborated with Stanley Kubrick on the screenplay to *2001: A Space Odyssey*, he assumed that computers would, over time, get bigger. "The HAL 9000 computer fills half the spaceship," Lykken notes.

Says science-fiction writer Ben Bova, "We have built into us an idea that 24 tomorrow is going to be pretty much like today, which is very wrong."

The future is often viewed as an endless resource of innovation that will 25 make problems go away—even though, if the past is any judge, innovations create their own set of new problems. Climate change is at least in part a consequence of the invention of the steam engine in the early 1700s and all the industrial advances that followed.

Look again at the Internet. It's a fantastic tool, but it also threatens to dis- 26 perse information we'd rather keep under wraps, such as our personal medical data, or even the instructions for making a fission bomb.

We need to keep our eyes open. The future is going to be here sooner 27 than we think. It'll surprise us. We'll try to figure out why we missed so many clues. And we'll go back and search the archives, and see that thing we should have noticed on page F30.

QUESTIONS FOR READING AND REASONING

1. What is Achenbach's subject? What is his thesis? Where does he state it?
2. What two agents together are likely to produce the next big change?
3. Summarize the evidence Achenbach provides to support the idea that we don't recognize the next big change until it is here.
4. If we want to try to anticipate the next big change, what should we do?
5. What prediction did Arthur C. Clarke get right? In what way was his imagination incorrect? What can readers infer from this example?
6. Are big changes always good? Explain.
7. How does Achenbach identify most of his sources? He does not identify Chris Matthews or Bill O'Reilly in paragraph 1. What does this tell you about his expected audience?

PRESENTING DIRECT QUOTATIONS: A GUIDE TO FORM AND STYLE

Although most of your papers will be written in your own words and style, you will sometimes use direct quotations. Just as there is a correct form for references to people and to works, there is a correct form for presenting borrowed material in direct quotations. Study the guidelines and examples and then mark these pages, as you did the others, for easy reference.

Reasons for Using Quotation Marks

We use quotation marks in four ways:

- To indicate dialogue in works of fiction and drama
- To indicate the titles of some kinds of works
- To indicate the words that others have spoken or written
- To separate ourselves from or call into question particular uses of words

The following guidelines apply to all four uses of quotation marks, but the focus will be on the third use.

A Brief Guide to Quoting

1. *Quote accurately.* Do not misrepresent what someone else has written. Take time to compare what you have written with the original.
2. *Put all words taken from a source within quotation marks.* (To take words from a source without using quotation marks is to plagiarize, a form of stealing punished in academic and professional communities.)
3. *Never change any of the words within your quotation marks.* Indicate any deleted words with ellipses [spaced periods (. . .)]. If you need to add words to make the meaning clear, place the added words in [square brackets], not (parentheses).
4. *Always make the source of the quoted words clear.* If you do not provide the author of the quoted material, readers will have to assume that you are calling those words into question—the fourth reason for quoting. Observe that Achenbach introduces Joe Lykken in paragraph 6 and then uses his last name or "he" through the next three paragraphs so that readers always know to whom he is referring and quoting.
5. *When quoting an author who is quoted by the author of the source you are using, you must make clear that you are getting that author's words from your source, not directly from that author.*
   For example:

ORIGINAL:	"We had no idea that we were seeing not only a revolution, but a trillion-dollar idea."
INCORRECT:	Referring to his first experience with the World Wide Web, Lykken observed: "We had no idea that we were seeing . . . a revolution."
CORRECT:	To make his point about our failure to recognize big changes when they first appear, Achenbach quotes theoretical physicist Joe Lykken's response to first seeing the World Wide Web: "We had no idea that we were seeing . . . a revolution."

6. *Place commas and periods inside the closing quotation mark—even when only one word is quoted:* Unable to anticipate big changes coming from modern science, we are, Achenbach observes, in "technological Palookaville."

7. *Place colons and semicolons outside the closing quotation mark:* Achenbach jokingly explains our reaction to the complexities of modern technologies in his essay "The Future Is Now": "We're zombified by progress."

8. *Do not quote unnecessary punctuation.* When you place quoted material at the end of a sentence you have written, use only the punctuation needed to complete your sentence.

ORIGINAL:	The next big change will be "happening in laboratories—out of sight, inscrutable, and unhyped."
INCORRECT:	Achenbach explains that we will be surprised by the next big change because it will, initially, be hidden, "happening in laboratories—."
CORRECT:	Achenbach explains that we will be surprised by the next big change because it will, initially, be hidden, "happening in laboratories."

9. *When the words you quote are only a part of your sentence, do not capitalize the first quoted word, even if it was capitalized in the source.* **Exception:** You introduce the quoted material with a colon.

INCORRECT:	Achenbach observes that "The future is often viewed as an endless resource of innovation."
CORRECT:	Achenbach observes that "the future is often viewed as an endless resource of innovation."
ALSO CORRECT:	Achenbach argues that we count too much on modern science to solve problems: "The future is often viewed as an endless resource of innovation."

10. *Use single quotation marks (the apostrophe key on your keyboard) to identify quoted material within quoted material:* Achenbach explains that futurists "prefer the word 'scenarios.'"

11. *Depending on the structure of your sentence, use a colon, a comma, or no punctuation before a quoted passage.* A colon provides a formal introduction to a quoted passage. (See the example in item 9.) Use a comma only when your sentence requires it. Quoted words presented in a "that" clause are not preceded by a comma.

ORIGINAL:	"What's unnerving is the velocity at which the future sometimes arrives."
CORRECT:	"What's unnerving," Achenbach notes, "is the velocity at which the future sometimes arrives."
ALSO CORRECT:	Achenbach observes that we are often unnerved by "the velocity at which the future sometimes arrives."

12. *To keep quotations brief, omit irrelevant portions. Indicate missing words with ellipses.* For example: Achenbach explains that "we want the blessings of science . . . but not the terrors." Some instructors want the ellipses placed

in square brackets—[. . .]—to show that you have added them to the original. Modern Language Association (MLA) style does not require the square brackets unless you are quoting a passage that already has ellipses as part of that passage. The better choice would be not to quote that passage.

13. *Consider the poor reader.*
   - Always give enough context to make the quoted material clear.
   - Do not put so many bits and pieces of quoted passages into one sentence that your reader struggles to follow the ideas.
   - Make sure that your sentences are complete and correctly constructed. Quoting is never an excuse for a sentence fragment or distorted construction.

> **NOTE:** All examples of quoting given above are in the present tense. We write that "Achenbach notes," "Achenbach believes," "Achenbach asserts." Even though his article was written in the past, we use the present tense to describe his ongoing ideas.

FOR READING AND ANALYSIS

As you read the following article, practice active reading, including annotating each essay. Concentrate first on what the author has to say, but also observe the organization of the essay and the author's use of quotations and references to other authors and works.

FIVE LEADERSHIP LESSONS FROM JAMES T. KIRK | ALEX KNAPP

Currently Social Media editor at *Forbes* magazine and popular blogger, Alex Knapp has been a freelance writer and editor for many years. He holds a law degree from the University of Kansas and focuses, in his writing, on the future of technology and culture.

PREREADING QUESTIONS What lessons might Captain Kirk have to offer to businesspeople who read *Forbes* magazine? How might these lessons have value to you as a college student?

1   Captain James T. Kirk is one of the most famous Captains in the history of Starfleet. There's a good reason for that. He saved the planet Earth several times, stopped the Doomsday Machine, helped negotiate peace with the Klingon Empire, kept the balance of power between the Federation and the Romulan Empire, and even managed to fight Nazis. On his five-year mission commanding the U.S.S. Enterprise, as well as subsequent commands,

James T. Kirk was a quintessential leader, who led his crew into the unknown and continued to succeed time and time again.

Kirk's success was no fluke, either. His style of command demonstrates a keen understanding of leadership and how to maintain a team that succeeds time and time again, regardless of the dangers faced. Here are five of the key leadership lessons that you can take away from Captain Kirk as you pilot your own organization into unknown futures.

1. NEVER STOP LEARNING

"You know the greatest danger facing us is ourselves, an irrational fear of the unknown. But there's no such thing as the unknown— only things temporarily hidden, temporarily not understood."

Captain Kirk may have a reputation as a suave ladies man, but don't let that exterior cool fool you. Kirk's reputation at the Academy was that of a "walking stack of books," in the words of his former first officer, Gary Mitchell. And a passion for learning helped him through several missions. Perhaps the best demonstration of this is in the episode "Arena," where Kirk is forced to fight a Gorn Captain in single combat by advanced beings. Using his own knowledge and materials at hand, Kirk is able to build a rudimentary shotgun, which he uses to defeat the Gorn.

If you think about it, there's no need for a 23rd Century Starship Captain to know how to mix and prepare gunpowder if the occasion called for it. After all, Starfleet officers fight with phasers and photon torpedoes. To them, gunpowder is obsolete. But the same drive for knowledge that drove Kirk to the stars also caused him to learn that bit of information, and it paid off several years later.

In the same way, no matter what your organization does, it helps to never stop learning. The more knowledge you have, the more creative you can be. The more you're able to do, the more solutions you have for problems at your disposal. Sure, you might never have to face down a reptilian alien on a desert planet, but you never know what the future holds. Knowledge is your best key to overcoming whatever obstacles are in your way.

2. HAVE ADVISORS WITH DIFFERENT WORLDVIEWS

"One of the advantages of being a captain, Doctor, is being able to ask for advice without necessarily having to take it."

Kirk's closest two advisors are Commander Spock, a Vulcan committed to a philosophy of logic, and Dr. Leonard McCoy, a human driven by compassion and scientific curiosity. Both Spock and McCoy are frequently at odds with each other, recommend different courses of action and bringing very different types of arguments to bear in defense of those points of view. Kirk sometimes goes with one, or the other, or sometimes takes their advice as a springboard to developing an entirely different course of action.

9   However, the very fact that Kirk has advisors who have a different world-view not only from each other, but also from himself, is a clear demonstration of Kirk's confidence in himself as a leader. Weak leaders surround themselves with yes men who are afraid to argue with them. That fosters an organizational culture that stifles creativity and innovation, and leaves members of the organization afraid to speak up. That can leave the organization unable to solve problems or change course. Historically, this has led to some serious disasters, such as *Star Wars Episode I: The Phantom Menace.*

10   Organizations that allow for differences of opinion are better at developing innovation, better at solving problems, and better at avoiding groupthink. We all need a McCoy and a Spock in our lives and organizations.

3. BE PART OF THE AWAY TEAM

11   *"Risk is our business. That's what this starship is all about. That's why we're aboard her."*

12   Whenever an interesting or challenging mission came up, Kirk was always willing to put himself in harm's way by joining the Away Team. With his boots on the ground, he was always able to make quick assessments of the situation, leading to superior results. At least, superior for everyone with a name and not wearing a red shirt. Kirk was very much a hands-on leader, leading the vanguard of his crew as they explored interesting and dangerous situations.

13   When you're in a leadership role, it's sometimes easy to let yourself get away from leading Away Team missions. After all, with leadership comes perks, right? You get the nice office on the higher floor. You finally get an assistant to help you with day to day activities, and your days are filled with meetings and decisions to be made, and many of these things are absolutely necessary. But it's sometimes easy to trap yourself in the corner office and forget what life is like on the front lines. When you lose that perspective, it's that much harder to understand what your team is doing, and the best way to get out of the problem. What's more, when you're not involved with your team, it's easy to lose their trust and have them gripe about how you don't understand what the job is like.

14   This is a lesson that was actually imprinted on me in one of my first jobs, making pizzas for a franchise that doesn't exist anymore. Our general manager spent a lot of time in his office, focused on the paperwork and making sure that we could stay afloat on the razor-thin margins we were running. But one thing he made sure to do, every day, was to come out during peak times and help make pizza. He didn't have to do that, but he did. The fact that he did so made me like him a lot more. It also meant that I trusted his decisions a lot more. In much the same way, I'm sure, as Kirk's crew trusted his decisions, because he knew the risks of command personally.

4. PLAY POKER, NOT CHESS

"Not chess, Mr. Spock. Poker. Do you know the game?"   15

In one of my all-time favorite *Star Trek* episodes, Kirk and his crew face 16 down an unknown vessel from a group calling themselves the "First Federation." Threats from the vessel escalate until it seems that the destruction of the *Enterprise* is imminent. Kirk asks Spock for options, who replies that the *Enterprise* has been playing a game of chess, and now there are no winning moves left. Kirk counters that they shouldn't play chess they should play poker. He then bluffs the ship by telling them that the *Enterprise* has a substance in its hull called "corbomite" which will reflect the energy of any weapon back against an attacker. This begins a series of actions that enables the *Enterprise* crew to establish peaceful relations with the First Federation.

I love chess as much as the next geek, but chess is often taken too seri- 17 ously as a metaphor for leadership strategy. For all of its intricacies, chess is a game of defined rules that can be mathematically determined. It's ultimately a game of boxes and limitations. A far better analogy to strategy is poker, not chess. Life is a game of probabilities, not defined rules. And often understanding your opponents is a much greater advantage than the cards you have in your hand. It was knowledge of his opponent that allowed Kirk to defeat Khan in *Star Trek II by* exploiting Khan's two-dimensional thinking. Bluffs, tells, and bets are all a big part of real-life strategy. Playing that strategy with an eye to the psychology of our competitors, not just the rules and circumstances of the game, can often lead to better outcomes than following the rigid lines of chess.

5. BLOW UP THE ENTERPRISE

"'All I ask is a tall ship and a star to steer her by.' You could feel the wind 18 *at your back in those days. The sounds of the sea beneath you, and even if you take away the wind and the water it's still the same. The ship is yours. You can feel her. And the stars are still there, Bones."*

One recurring theme in the original *Star Trek* series is that Kirk's first love is 19 the *Enterprise.* That love kept him from succumbing to the mind-controlling spores in "This Side of Paradise," and it's hinted that his love for the ship kept him from forming any real relationships or starting a family. Despite that love, though, there came a point in *Star Trek III: The Search For Spock,* where Captain Kirk made a decision that must have pained him enormously—in order to defeat the Klingons attacking him and save his crew, James Kirk destroyed the *Enterprise.* The occasion, in the film, was treated with the solemnity of a funeral, which no doubt matched Kirk's mood. The film ends with the crew returning to Vulcan on a stolen Klingon vessel, rather than the *Enterprise.* But they returned victorious.

We are often, in our roles as leaders, driven by a passion. It might be a 20 product or service, it might be a way of doing things. But no matter how much that passion burns within us, the reality is that times change. Different products are created. Different ways of doing things are developed. And there will come times in your life when that passion isn't viable anymore. A time when it no longer makes sense to pursue your passion. When that happens, no matter how painful it is, you need to blow up the *Enterprise.* That is, change what isn't working and embark on a new path, even if that means having to live in a Klingon ship for awhile.

FINAL TAKEAWAY:

21   In his many years of service to the Federation, James Kirk embodied several leadership lessons that we can use in our own lives. We need to keep exploring and learning. We need to ensure that we encourage creativity and innovation by listening to the advice of people with vastly different opinions. We need to occasionally get down in the trenches with the members of our teams so we understand their needs and earn their trust and loyalty. We need to understand the psychology of our competitors and also learn to radically change course when circumstances dictate. By following these lessons, we can lead our organizations into places where none have gone before.

QUESTIONS FOR READING

1. What is Knapp's subject?
2. What does the first point—never stop learning—reveal about Kirk's academy behavior?
3. What does having advisors with differing views reveal about a leader?
4. Explain what the author means by destroying the *Enterprise* as a leadership strategy.

QUESTIONS FOR REASONING AND ANALYSIS

5. Knapp appears to use just a simple list as his structure. What other structure does the author use?
6. Knapp clearly loved the *Star Trek* TV series. How does he guide readers who may not have grown up watching Captain Kirk?
7. The author argues that leaders should play poker, not chess. Explain his view of life and the point of his game analogy.

QUESTIONS FOR REFLECTION AND WRITING

8. The *Star Trek* series has been one of the most popular and long running. If you have not watched this series, has Knapp's essay piqued your interest in Captain Kirk and encouraged you to seek out the reruns? Why or why not?
9. Which of the five lessons seems most easily applied to college students? Why? Explain your choice.
10. Which of the five lessons seems least applicable to college students? Why? Now, you are one of Captain Kirk's advisors. What good advice can you find in the lesson that has been put at the bottom of the list?

1. Write a one-paragraph summary of Alex Knapp's essay. Be sure that your summary clearly states the author's main idea, the claim of his argument. Take your time and polish your word choice.

2. Read actively and then prepare a one-and-a-half-page summary of Patricia B. Strait's "When Societies Collide," (pp. 500–11). Your readers want an accurate and balanced but much shorter version of the original because they will not be reading the original article. Explain not only what the writer's main ideas are but also how the writer develops her essay. That is, what kind of research supports the article's thesis? Pay close attention to your word choice.

3. A number of years ago, before the first Kindle, Bill Gates argued that e-books will replace paper books. What are the advantages of e-books? What are the advantages of paper books? Are there any disadvantages to either type of book? Which do you prefer? How would you argue for your preference?

GOING ONLINE

Select one futuristic idea that interests you—robots in the home, cars that don't need drivers, artificial intelligence, a moon colony, or whatever else captures your imagination—and see what you can learn about it online. Be prepared to share your information in a class discussion, or consider exploring your topic in an essay.

Responding Critically to Sources

READ: What is the situation? Who is hiding under the bed?

REASON: Whom do we expect to be under the bed? What strategy has been used?

REFLECT/WRITE: What makes this cartoon clever?

In some contexts, the word *critical* carries the idea of harsh judgment: "The manager was critical of her secretary's long phone conversations." In other contexts, the term means to evaluate carefully. When we speak of the critical reader or critical thinker, we have in mind someone who reads actively, who thinks about issues, and who makes informed judgments. Here is a profile of the critical reader or thinker:

TRAITS OF THE CRITICAL READER/THINKER

- **Focused on the facts.**
  Give me the facts and show me that they are relevant to the issue.
- **Analytic.**
  What strategies has the writer/speaker used to develop the argument?
- **Open-minded.**
  Prepared to listen to different points of view, to learn from others.
- **Questioning/skeptical.**
  What other conclusions could be supported by the evidence presented?
  How thorough has the writer/speaker been?
  What persuasive strategies are used?
- **Creative.**
  What are some entirely different ways of looking at the issue or problem?
- **Intellectually active, not passive.**
  Willing to analyze logic and evidence.
  Willing to consider many possibilities.
  Willing, after careful evaluation, to reach a judgment, to take a stand on issues.

EXAMINING THE RHETORICAL CONTEXT OF A SOURCE

Reading critically requires preparation. Instead of "jumping into reading," begin by asking questions about the work's rhetorical context. Rhetoric is about the *art of writing* (or *speaking*). Someone has chosen to shape a text in a particular way at this time for an imagined audience to accomplish a specific goal. The better you understand all of the decisions shaping a particular text, the better you will understand that work. And, then, the better you will be able to judge the significance of that work. So, try to answer the following five questions before reading. Then complete your answers while you read—or by doing research and thinking critically after you finish reading.

Who Is the Author?

Key questions to answer include:

- *Does the author have a reputation for honesty, thoroughness, and fairness?* Read the biographical note, if there is one. Ask your instructor about the author or learn about the author in a biographical dictionary or online. Try *Book Review Digest* (in your library or online) for reviews of the author's books.
- *Is the author writing within his or her area of expertise?* People can voice opinions on any subject, but they cannot transfer expertise from one subject area to another. A football player endorsing a political candidate is a citizen with an opinion, not an expert on politics.
- *Is the author identified with a particular group or set of beliefs? Does the biography place the writer or speaker in a particular institution or organization?* For example, a member of a Republican administration may be expected to favor a Republican president's policies. A Roman Catholic priest may be expected to take a stand against abortion. These kinds of details provide hints, but you should not decide, absolutely, what a writer's position is until you have read the work with care. Be alert to reasonable expectations but avoid stereotyping.

What Type—or Genre—of Source Is It?

Are you reading a researched and documented essay by a specialist—or the text of a speech delivered the previous week to a specific audience? Is the work an editorial—or a letter to the editor? Does the syndicated columnist (such as Dave Barry, who appears later in this chapter) write humorous columns? Is the cartoon a comic strip or a political cartoon from the editorial page of a newspaper? (You will see both kinds of cartoons in this text.) Know what kind of text you are reading before you start. That's the only way to give yourself the context you need to be a good critical reader.

What Kind of Audience Does the Author Anticipate?

Understanding the intended audience helps you answer questions about the depth and sophistication of the work and a possible bias or slant.

- *Does the author expect a popular audience, a general but educated audience, or a specialist audience of shared expertise? Does the author anticipate an audience that shares cultural, political, or religious values?* Often you can judge the expected audience by noting the kind of publication in which the article appears, the publisher of the book, or the venue for the speech. For example, *Reader's Digest* is written for a mass audience, and *Psychology Today* for a general but more knowledgeable reader. By contrast, articles in the *Journal of the American Medical Association* are written by physicians and research scientists for a specialized reader. (It would be inappropriate, then, for a general reader to complain that an article in *JAMA* is not well written because it is too difficult.)

- *Does the author expect an audience favorable to his or her views? Or with a "wait and see" attitude? Or even hostile?* Some newspapers and television news organizations are consistently liberal whereas others are noticeably conservative. (Do you know the political leanings of your local paper? Of the TV news that you watch? Of the blogs you choose?) Remember: All arguments are "slanted" or "biased"—that is, they take a stand. That's as it should be. Just be sure to read or listen with an awareness of the author's particular background, interests, and possible stands on issues.

What Is the Author's Primary Purpose?

Is the work primarily informative or persuasive in intent? Designed to entertain or be inspiring? Think about the title. Read a book's preface to learn of the author's goals. Pay attention to tone as you read.

What Are the Author's Sources of Information?

Much of our judgment of an author and a work is based on the quality of the author's choice of sources. So always ask yourself: Where was the information obtained? Are sources clearly identified? Be suspicious of those who want us to believe that their unnamed "sources" are "reliable." Pay close attention to dates. A biography of King George III published in 1940 may still be the best source. An article urging more development based on county population statistics from the 1990s is no longer reliable.

> **NOTE:** None of the readings in this textbook were written for publication in this textbook. They have all come from some other context. To read them with understanding you must identify the original context and think about how that should guide your reading.

EXERCISES: Examining the Context

1. For each of the following works, comment on what you might expect to find. Consider author, occasion, audience, and reliability.
   a. An article on the Republican administration, written by a former campaign worker for a Democratic presidential candidate.
   b. A discussion, published in the Boston *Globe,* of the New England Patriots' hope for the next Super Bowl.
   c. A letter to the editor about conservation, written by a member of the Sierra Club. (What is the Sierra Club? Check out its website.)
   d. A column in *Newsweek* on economics. (Look at the business section of this magazine. Your library has it.)
   e. A 1988 article in *Nutrition Today* on the best diets.

f.   A biography of Benjamin Franklin published by Oxford University Press.

g.   A *Family Circle* article about a special vegetarian diet written by a physician. (Who is the audience for this magazine? Where is it sold?)

h.   A *New York Times* editorial written after the Supreme Court's striking down of Washington, DC's handgun restrictions.

i.   A speech on new handgun technology delivered at a convention of the National Rifle Association.

j.   An editorial in your local newspaper titled "Stop the Highway Killing."

2.   Analyze an issue of your favorite magazine. Look first at the editorial pages and the articles written by staff, then at articles contributed by other writers. Answer these questions for both staff writers and contributors:

a.   Who is the audience?

b.   What is the purpose of the articles and of the entire magazine?

c.   What type of article dominates the issue?

3.   Select one environmental website and study what is offered. The EnviroLink Network (www.envirolink.org) will lead you to many sites. Write down the name of the site you chose and its address (URL). Then answer these questions:

a.   Who is the intended audience?

b.   What seems to be the primary purpose or goal of the site?

c.   What type of material dominates the site?

d.   For what kinds of writing assignments might you use material from the site?

ANALYZING THE STYLE OF A SOURCE

Critical readers read for implication and are alert to tone or nuance. When you read, think not only about *what* is said but also about *how* it is said. Consider the following passage:

> Bush's stupid "war"—so much for the Congress declaring war—drags on, costing unhappy taxpayers billions, while the "greatest army in the world" cannot find the real villain hiding somewhere in a cave.

This passage observes that the Iraq War continues, costing much money, while the United States still has not found the perpetrator of 9/11. But, it actually says more than that, doesn't it? Note the writer's attitude toward Bush, the war, and the U.S. military.

How can we rewrite this passage to make it more favorable? Here is one version produced by students in a group exercise:

> President Bush continues to defend the war in Iraq—which Congress never declared but continues to fund—in spite of the considerable cost to stabilize that country and the region. Meanwhile more troops will be needed to finally capture bin Laden and bring him to justice.

The writers have not changed their view that the Iraq War is costing a lot and that so far we have failed to capture bin Laden. But, in this version neither Bush nor the military is ridiculed. What is the difference in the two passages? Only the word choice.

Denotative and Connotative Word Choice

The students' ability to rewrite the passage on the war in Iraq to give it a positive attitude tells us that, although some words may have similar meanings, they cannot always be substituted for one another without changing the message. Words with similar meanings have similar *denotations.* Often, though, words with similar denotations do not have the same connotations. A word's *connotation* is what the word suggests, what we associate the word with. The words *house* and *home,* for example, both refer to a building in which people live, but the word *home* suggests ideas—and feelings—of family and security. Thus the word *home* has a strong positive connotation. *House* by contrast brings to mind a picture of a physical structure only because the word doesn't carry any "emotional baggage."

We learn the connotations of words the same way we learn their denotations—in context. Most of us, living in the same culture, share the same connotative associations of words. At times, the context in which a word is used will affect the word's connotation. For example, the word *buddy* usually has positive connotations. We may think of an old or trusted friend. But when an unfriendly person who thinks a man may have pushed in front of him says, "Better watch it, *buddy,*" the word has a negative connotation. Social, physical, and language contexts control the connotative significance of words. Become more alert to the connotative power of words by asking what words the writers could have used instead.

> **NOTE:** Writers make choices; their choices reflect and convey their attitudes. *Studying the context in which a writer uses emotionally charged words is the only way to be sure that we understand the writer's attitude.*

EXERCISES: Connotation

1. For each of the following words or phrases, list at least two synonyms that have a more negative connotation than the given word.
    a. child
    b. persistent
    c. thin
    d. a large group
    e. scholarly
    f. trusting
    g. underachiever
    h. quiet
2. For each of the following words, list at least two synonyms that have a more positive connotation than the given word.
    a. notorious
    b. fat
    c. politician
    d. old (people)
    e. fanatic
    f. reckless
    g. drunkard
    h. cheap

3. Read the following paragraph and decide how the writer feels about the activity described. Note the choice of details and the connotative language that make you aware of the writer's attitude.

> Needing to complete a missed assignment for my physical education class, I dragged myself down to the tennis courts on a gloomy afternoon. My task was to serve five balls in a row into the service box. Although I thought I had learned the correct service movements, I couldn't seem to translate that knowledge into a decent serve. I tossed up the first ball, jerked back my racket, swung up on the ball—clunk—I hit the ball on the frame. I threw up the second ball, brought back my racket, swung up on the ball—ping—I made contact with the strings, but the ball dribbled down on my side of the net. I trudged around the court, collecting my tennis balls; I had only two of them.

4. Write a paragraph describing an activity that you liked or disliked without saying how you felt. From your choice of details and use of connotative language, convey your attitude toward the activity. (The paragraph in exercise 3 is your model.)

5. Select one of the words listed below and explain, in a paragraph, what the word connotes to you personally. Be precise; illustrate your thoughts with details and examples.

a. nature
b. mother
c. romantic
d. geek
e. playboy
f. artist

COLLABORATIVE EXERCISES: On Connotation

1. List all of the words you know for *human female* and for *human male*. Then classify them by connotation (positive, negative, neutral) and by level of usage (formal, informal, slang). Is there any connection between type of connotation and level of usage? Why are some words more appropriate in some social contexts than in others? Can you easily list more negative words used for one sex than for the other? Why?

2. Some words can be given a different connotation in different contexts. First, for each of the following words, label its connotation as positive, negative, or neutral. Then, for each word with a positive connotation, write a sentence in which the word would convey a more negative connotation. For each word with a negative connotation, write a sentence in which the word would suggest a more positive connotation.

a. natural
b. old
c. committed
d. free
e. chemical
f. lazy

3. Each of the following groups of words might appear together in a thesaurus, but the words actually vary in connotation. After looking up any words whose connotation you are unsure of, write a sentence in which each word is used

correctly. Briefly explain why one of the other words in the group should not be substituted.

a. brittle, hard, fragile

b. quiet, withdrawn, glum

c. shrewd, clever, cunning

d. strange, remarkable, bizarre

e. thrifty, miserly, economical

Tone

We can describe a writer's attitude toward the subject as positive, negative, or (rarely) neutral. Attitude is the writer's position on, or feelings about, his or her subject. The way that attitude is expressed—the voice we hear and the feelings conveyed through that voice—is the writer's *tone*. Writers can choose to express attitude through a wide variety of tones. We may reinforce a negative attitude through an angry, somber, sad, mocking, peevish, sarcastic, or scornful tone. A positive attitude may be revealed through an enthusiastic, serious, sympathetic, jovial, light, or admiring tone. We cannot be sure that just because a writer selects a light tone, for example, the attitude must be positive. Humor columnists such as Dave Barry often choose a light tone to examine serious social and political issues. Given their subjects, we recognize that the light and amusing tone actually conveys a negative attitude toward the topic.

COLLABORATIVE EXERCISES: On Tone

With your class partner or in small groups, examine the following three paragraphs, which are different responses to the same event. First, decide on each writer's attitude. Then describe, as precisely as possible, the tone of each paragraph.

1. It is tragically inexcusable that this young athlete was not examined fully before he was allowed to join the varsity team. The physical examinations given were unbelievably sloppy. What were the coach and trainer thinking of not to insist that each youngster be examined while undergoing physical stress? Apparently they were not thinking about our boys at all. We can no longer trust our sons and our daughters to this inhuman system so bent on victory that it ignores the health—indeed the very lives—of our children.

2. It was learned last night, following the death of varsity fullback Jim Bresnick, that none of the players was given a stress test as part of his physical examination. The oversight was attributed to laxness by the coach and trainer, who are described today as being "distraught." It is the judgment of many that the entire physical education program must be reexamined with an eye to the safety and health of all students.

3. How can I express the loss I feel over the death of my son? I want to blame someone, but who is to blame? The coaches, for not administering more rigorous physical checkups? Why should they have done more than other coaches have done before or than other coaches are doing at other schools? My son, for not telling me that he felt funny after practice? His teammates, for not telling the coaches that my son said he did not feel well? Myself, for not knowing that

something was wrong with my only child? Who is to blame? All of us and none of us. But placing blame will not return my son to me; I can only pray that other parents will not have to suffer so. Jimmy, we loved you.

■ ■

Level of Diction

In addition to responding to a writer's choice of connotative language, observe the *level of diction* used. Are the writer's words primarily typical of conversational language or of a more formal style? Does the writer use slang words or technical words? Is the word choice concrete and vivid or abstract and intellectual? These differences help to shape tone and affect our response to what we read. Lincoln's word choice in "The Gettysburg Address" (see pp. 4–5) is formal and abstract. Lincoln writes "on this continent" rather than "in this land," "we take increased devotion" rather than "we become more committed." Another style, the technical, will be found in some articles in this text. The social scientist may write that "the child . . . is subjected to extremely punitive discipline," whereas a nonspecialist, more informally, might write that "the child is controlled by beatings or other forms of punishment."

One way to create an informal style is to choose simple words: *land* instead of *continent.* To create greater informality, a writer can use contractions: *we'll* for *we will.* There are no contractions in "The Gettysburg Address."

NOTE: In your academic and professional writing, you should aim for a style informal enough to be inviting to readers but one that, in most cases, avoids contractions or slang words.

Sentence Structure

Attitude is conveyed and tone created primarily through word choice, but sentence structure and other rhetorical strategies are also important. Studying a writer's sentence patterns will reveal how they affect style and tone. When analyzing these features, consider the following questions:

1. *Are the sentences generally long or short, or varied in length?*
Are the structures primarily:

- *Simple* (one independent clause)
  In 1900 empires dotted the world.
- *Compound* (two or more independent clauses)
  Women make up only 37 percent of television characters, yet women make up more than half of the population.
- *Complex* (at least one independent and one dependent clause)
  As nations grew wealthier, traditional freedom wasn't enough.

Sentences that are both long and complex create a more formal style. Compound sentences joined by *and* do not increase formality much because such sentences are really only two or more short, simple patterns hooked together.

On the other hand, a long "simple" sentence with many modifiers will create a more formal style. The following example, from an essay on leadership by Michael Korda, is more complicated than the sample compound sentence above:

- *Expanded simple sentence*
  [A] leader is like a mirror, reflecting back to us our own sense of purpose, putting into words our own dreams and hopes, transforming our needs and fears into coherent policies and programs.

In "The Gettysburg Address" three sentences range from 10 to 16 words, six sentences from 21 to 29 words, and the final sentence is an incredible 82 words. All but two of Lincoln's sentences are either complex or compound-complex sentences. By contrast, in "The Future Is Now," Joel Achenbach includes a paragraph with five sentences. These sentences are composed of 7, 11, 3, 11, and 19 words each. All five are simple sentences.

2.   *Does the writer use sentence fragments (incomplete sentences)?*

Although many instructors struggle to rid student writing of fragments, professional writers know that the occasional fragment can be used effectively for emphasis. Science fiction writer Bruce Sterling, thinking about the "melancholic beauty" of a gadget no longer serving any purpose, writes:

- Like Duchamp's bottle-rack, it becomes a found objet d'art. A metallic fossil of some lost human desire. A kind of involuntary poem.

The second and third sentences are, technically, fragments, but because they build on the structure of the first sentence, readers can add the missing words *It becomes* to complete each sentence. The brevity, repetition of structure, and involvement of the reader to "complete" the fragments all contribute to a strong conclusion to Sterling's paragraph.

3.   *Does the writer seem to be using an overly simplistic style? If so, why?*

Overly simplistic sentence patterns, just like an overly simplistic choice of words, can be used to show that the writer thinks the subject is silly or childish or insulting. In one of her columns, Ellen Goodman objects to society's over-simplifying of addictions and its need to believe in quick and lasting cures. She makes her point with reference to two well-known examples—but notice her technique:

- Hi, my name is Jane and I was once bulimic but now I am an exercise guru . . .
- Hi, my name is Oprah and I was a food addict but now I am a size 10.

4.   *Does the writer use parallelism (coordination) or antithesis (contrast)?*

When two phrases or clauses are parallel in structure, the message is that they are equally important. Look back at Korda's expanded simple sentence. He coordinates three phrases, asserting that a leader is like a mirror in these three ways:

- Reflects back our purpose
- Puts into words our dreams
- Transforms our needs and fears

Antithesis creates tension. A sentence using this structure says "not this" but "that." Lincoln uses both parallelism and antithesis in one striking sentence:

- The world will little note nor long remember
    <u>what</u> we say here,
but it [the world] can never forget
    <u>what</u> they did here.

Metaphors

When Korda writes that a leader is like a mirror, he is using a *simile*. When Lincoln writes that the world will not remember, he is using a *metaphor*—actually *personification*. Metaphors, whatever their form, all make a comparison between two items that are not really alike. The writer is making a *figurative comparison*, not a literal one. The writer wants us to think about some ways in which the items are similar. Metaphors state directly or imply the comparison; similes express the comparison using a connecting word; personification always compares a nonhuman item to humans. The exact label for a metaphor is not as important as

- recognizing the use of a figure of speech,
- identifying the two items being compared,
- understanding the point of the comparison, and
- grasping the emotional impact of the figurative comparison.

> **REMEMBER:** Pay attention to each writer's choice of metaphors. Metaphors reveal much about feelings and perceptions of life. And, like connotative words, they affect us emotionally even if we are not aware of their use. Become aware. Be able to "open up"—explain—metaphors you find in your reading.

EXERCISE: Opening Up Metaphors

During World War II, E. B. White, the essayist and writer of children's books, defined the word *democracy* in one of his *New Yorker* columns. His definition contains a series of metaphors. One is: Democracy "is the hole in the stuffed shirt through which the sawdust slowly trickles." We can open up or explain the metaphor this way:

> Just as one can punch a hole in a scarecrow's shirt and discover that there is only sawdust inside, nothing to be impressed by, so the idea of equality in a democracy "punches" a hole in the notion of an aristocratic ruling class and reveals that aristocrats, underneath, are ordinary people, just like you and me.

Here are two more of White's metaphors on democracy. Open up each one in a few sentences.

> Democracy is "the dent in the high hat."
> Democracy is "the score at the beginning of the ninth."

Organization and Examples

Two other elements of writing, organization and choice of examples, also reveal attitude and help to shape the reader's response. When you study a work's organization, ask yourself questions about both placement and volume. Where are these ideas placed? At the beginning or end—the places of greatest emphasis—or in the middle, suggesting that they are less important? With regard to volume, ask yourself, "What parts of the discussion are developed at length? What points are treated only briefly?" *Note:* Sometimes simply counting the number of paragraphs devoted to the different parts of the writer's subject will give you a good understanding of the writer's main idea and purpose in writing.

Repetition

Well-written, unified essays will contain some repetition of key words and phrases. Some writers go beyond this basic strategy and use repetition to produce an effective cadence, like a drum beating in the background, keeping time to the speaker's fist pounding the lectern. In his repetition of the now-famous phrase "I have a dream," Martin Luther King Jr. gives emphasis to his vision of an ideal America. In the following paragraph, a student tried her hand at repetition to give emphasis to her definition of liberty:

> Liberty is having the right to vote and not having other laws which restrict
> that right; it is having the right to apply to the university of your choice
> without being rejected because of race. Liberty exists when a gay man has
> the right to a teaching position and is not released from the position when
> the news of his orientation is disclosed. Liberty exists when a woman who
> has been offered a job does not have to decline for lack of access to day
> care for her children, or when a 16-year-old boy from a ghetto can get an
> education and is not instead compelled to go to work to support his
> needy family.

These examples suggest that repetition generally gives weight and seriousness to writing and thus is appropriate when serious issues are being discussed in a forceful style.

Hyperbole, Understatement, and Irony

These three strategies create some form of tension to gain emphasis. Hyperbole overstates:

- "I will love you through all eternity!"

Understatement says less than is meant:

- Coming in soaking wet, you say, "It's a bit damp outside."

Irony creates tension by stating the opposite of what is meant:

- To a teen dressed in torn jeans and a baggy sweatshirt, the parent says, "Dressed for dinner, I see."

Quotation Marks, Italics, and Capital Letters

Several visual techniques can also be used to give special attention to certain words. A writer can place a word or phrase within quotation marks to question its validity or meaning in that context. Ellen Goodman writes, for example:

- I wonder about this when I hear the word "family" added to some politician's speech.

Goodman does not agree with the politician's meaning of the word *family*. The expression *so-called* has the same effect:

- There have been restrictions on the Tibetans' so-called liberty.

Italicizing a key word or phrase or using all caps also gives additional emphasis. Dave Barry, in an essay satirizing "smart" technology, uses all caps for emphasis:

- Do you want appliances that are smarter than you? Of course not. Your appliances should be DUMBER than you, just like your furniture, your pets and your representatives in Congress.

Capitalizing words not normally capitalized has the same effect of giving emphasis. As with exclamation points, writers need to use these strategies sparingly, or the emphasis sought will be lost.

EXERCISES: Recognizing Elements of Style

1. Name the technique or techniques used in each of the following passages. Then briefly explain the idea of each passage.
   a. We are becoming the tools of our tools. (Henry David Thoreau)
   b. The bias and therefore the business of television is to *move* information, not collect it. (Neil Postman)
   c. If guns are outlawed, only the government will have guns. Only the police, the secret police, the military. The hired servants of our rulers. Only the government—and a few outlaws. (Edward Abbey)
   d. Having read all the advice on how to live 900 years, what I think is that eating a tasty meal once again will surely doom me long before I reach 900 while not eating that same meal could very well kill me. It's enough to make you reach for a cigarette! (Russell Baker)
   e. If you are desperate for a quick fix, either legalize drugs or repress the user. If you want a civilized approach, mount a propaganda campaign against drugs. (Charles Krauthammer)
   f. Oddly enough, the greatest scoffers at the traditions of American etiquette, who scorn the rituals of their own society as stupid and stultifying, voice respect for the customs and folklore of Native Americans, less industrialized people, and other societies they find more "authentic" than their own. (Judith Martin)

g. Text is story. Text is event, performance, special effect. Subtext is ideas. It's motive, suggestions, visual implications, subtle comparisons. (Stephen Hunter)

h. This flashy vehicle [the school bus] was as punctual as death: seeing us waiting at the cold curb, it would sweep to a halt, open its mouth, suck the boy in, and spring away with an angry growl. (E. B. White)

2. Read the following essay by Dave Barry. Use the questions that precede and follow the essay to help you determine Barry's attitude toward his subject and to characterize his style.

NOW THAT IT'S ALL OVER, LET'S EAT! | DAVE BARRY

A humor columnist for the *Miami Herald* for many years, Dave Barry is syndicated in more than 150 newspapers. He is a Pulitzer Prize winner for his humor columns and is the author of a number of books, including *Dave Barry's Complete Guide to Guys* (2000), a laugh-out-loud look at what guys are thinking, and not thinking, and, with Ridley Pearson, a series of illustrated books for young readers 10 and up. The following column appeared September 6, 2012.

PREREADING QUESTIONS What is Barry's purpose in writing? What does he want to accomplish—besides being funny?

After many standing ovations and much shouting of "whoo," the 1 Democrats have wrapped up their convention and are heading home, except for Bill Clinton, who is expected to conclude his remarks sometime around Halloween.

So now both major political parties have presented their visions for 2 America's future, which can be summarized as follows:

THE DEMOCRATIC VISION: If we elect Mitt Romney and Paul Ryan, the 3 nation is going straight down the toilet.

THE REPUBLICAN VISION: If we reelect Barack Obama and Joe Biden, 4 the nation is going straight down the toilet.

And now, at last, the time has come for us, the American people—having 5 been presented with these two starkly contrasting philosophies of government at a critical time in our nation's history—to watch football. But first let's take a few minutes to look back on the two conventions, and see what observations we can make.

OBSERVATION ONE: The atmosphere sometimes produces weather.   6

You'd think that two political parties teeming with highly informed 7 geniuses eager to run the country would already be aware of this fact, but apparently they are not, since the Republicans scheduled their convention in Florida during hurricane season, and the Democrats scheduled their big night for an outdoor stadium in North Carolina in the summer. I am not suggesting here that these geniuses are stupid.

No, wait, I am suggesting that.   8

9   OBSERVATION TWO: Street protests are ineffective, by which I mean stupid.

10   For two weeks now, I have watched protesters shouting. They never talk; they always shout, often through bullhorns—at the police, at the media, at each other, at civilian passersby, and sometimes at nothing. I do not believe any of these protesters changed anybody's mind about anything, because— follow me closely—normal people do not like to be shouted at.

11   Normal people also are not inclined to listen receptively to arguments presented by anybody dressed as a giant vagina, or a giant anything else. One night in Tampa, as I was walking to my rental car, a convertible pulled up, and in the back seat, riding parade style, were two people wearing full-body furry pink pig costumes. They told me that they were riding around Tampa at night dressed as pigs to persuade people to stop eating meat. As they explained their views, my reaction was not to think, "They're right! I shall become a vegetarian"! My reaction was a combination of, "These people are insane," and "I could go for some barbecue."

12   OBSERVATION THREE: Political conventions are not as much fun as they used to be.

13   By "fun," I mean, yet again, stupid, but this time in a good way. I'm talking about the days when almost all the delegates wore giant ridiculous hats, and people got off-message, and unscripted things happened, including the occasional fistfight, and the schedule got so screwed up that the presidential nominee had to deliver his acceptance speech at 3:30 a.m. in a haze of cigarette smoke and tear gas.

14   I'm talking about the days when every convention featured "favorite son" candidates—politicians who had absolutely no chance to win, but their state delegations nominated them anyway, purely so they could have big pointless fun celebrations on the convention floor. I still vividly remember watching, on TV, the 1968 Republican convention, during which the Hawaii delegation nominated Sen. Hiram Fong, thereby setting off a wondrously entertaining 20-minute demonstration—a joyful conga line of people weaving around the floor wearing leis and waving signs that said "HI HI Hiram!"

15   That could never happen today. For one thing, Hiram is dead. (Although I would still vote for him.) But the main reason is that nothing remotely frivolous or spontaneous is allowed to happen at conventions anymore. This means that almost all the "excitement" comes from judging how well or poorly a given speaker executed a given speech. Inside the convention bubble, everybody gets very worked up about this; much of what passes for journalism consists of journalists declaring, with journalistic certainty, how a given speaker made them feel.

16   Anyway, the conventions are over. We won't go through this again for another four years. And we have no way of knowing where the nation will be then.

17   No, wait, we do: the toilet.

18   I don't know about you, but I'm ready for some football.

Source: *Miami Herald*, September 6, 2012. Reprinted by permission of Tribune Media Services.

1. Humor is not a subject; it may be a purpose or a strategy. What is Barry's subject?
2. What is his claim—that is, what point does he want to make about his subject?
3. How would you describe the essay's tone? Does a nonserious tone exclude the possibility of a degree of serious purpose? Explain your answer.

4. What passage in Barry's column do you find the funniest? Why?
5. What specific strategies does Barry use to create tone and convey attitude? List, with examples, as many as you can.

WRITING ABOUT STYLE

What does it mean to "do a style analysis"? A style analysis answers the question "How is it written?" Let's think through the steps in preparing a study of a writer's choice and arrangement of language.

Understanding Purpose and Audience

A style analysis is not the place for challenging the ideas of the writer. A style analysis requires the discipline to see how a work has been put together *even if you disagree with the writer's views*. You do not have to agree with a writer to appreciate his or her skill in writing.

If you think about audience in the context of your purpose, you should conclude that a summary of content does not belong in a style analysis. Why? Because we write style analyses for people who have already read the work. Remember, though, that your reader may not know the work in detail, so give examples to illustrate the points of your analysis.

Planning the Essay

First, organize your analysis according to elements of style, not according to the organization of the work. Scrap any thoughts of "hacking" your way through the essay, commenting on the work paragraph by paragraph. This approach invites summary and means that you have not selected an organization that supports your purpose in writing. Think of an essay as like the pie in Figure 2.1. We could divide the pie according to key ideas—if we were summarizing. But we can also carve the pie according to elements of style, the techniques we have discussed in this chapter. This is the general plan you want to follow for your essay.

Choose those techniques you think are most important in creating the writer's attitude and discuss them one at a time. Do not try to include the entire pie; instead, select three or four elements to examine in detail. If you were asked to write an analysis of the Dave Barry column, for example, you might select his

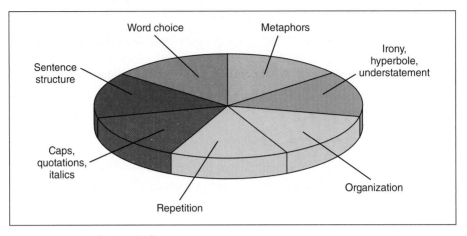

FIGURE 2.1 **Analyzing Style**

use of quotation marks, hyperbole, and irony. These are three techniques that stand out in Barry's writing.

Drafting the Style Analysis

If you were to select three elements of style, as in the Dave Barry example above, your essay might look something like this:

Paragraph 1: Introduction	1. Attention-getter 2. Author, title, publication information of article/book 3. Brief explanation of author's subject 4. Your thesis—that you will be looking at style
Paragraph 2: First body paragraph	Analysis of quotation marks. (See below for more details on body paragraphs.)
Paragraph 3: Second body paragraph	1. Topic sentence that introduces analysis of hyperbole 2. Three or more examples of hyperbole 3. Explanation of how each example connects to the author's thesis—that is, how the example of hyperbole works to convey attitude. This is your analysis; don't forget it!

Paragraph 4: Third body paragraph	Analysis of irony—with same three parts as listed above.

Paragraph 5: Conclusion	Restate your thesis: We can understand Barry's point through a study of these three elements of his style.

A CHECKLIST FOR REVISION

When revising and polishing your draft, use these questions to complete your essay.

☐ Have I handled all titles correctly?

☐ Have I correctly referred to the author?

☐ Have I used quotation marks correctly when presenting examples of style? (Use the guidelines in Chapter 1 for these first three questions.)

☐ Do I have an accurate, clear presentation of the author's subject and thesis?

☐ Do I have enough examples of each element of style to show my readers that these elements are important?

☐ Have I connected examples to the author's thesis? That is, have I shown my readers how these techniques work to develop the author's attitude?

To reinforce your understanding of style analysis, read the following essay by Ellen Goodman, answer the questions that follow, and then study the student essay that analyzes Goodman's style.

IN PRAISE OF A SNAIL'S PACE | ELLEN GOODMAN

Author of *Close to Home* (1979), *At Large* (1981), and *Keeping Touch* (1985), collections of her essays, Ellen Goodman began as a feature writer for the Boston *Globe* in 1967 and was a syndicated columnist from 1976 until her retirement in 2009. The following column was published August 13, 2005.

PREREADING QUESTIONS Why might someone write in praise of snail mail? What does Goodman mean by "hyperactive technology"?

CASCO BAY, Maine—I arrive at the island post office carrying an artifact 1 from another age. It's a square envelope, handwritten, with a return address that can be found on a map. Inside is a condolence note, a few words of memory and sympathy to a wife who has become a widow. I could have sent these words far more efficiently through e-mail than through this "snail mail." But I am among those who still believe that sympathy is diluted by two-thirds when it arrives over the Internet transom.

2   I would no more send an e-condolence than an e-thank you or an e-wedding invitation. There are rituals you cannot speed up without destroying them. It would be like serving Thanksgiving dinner at a fast-food restaurant.

3   My note goes into the old blue mailbox and I walk home wondering if slowness isn't the only way we pay attention now in a world of hyperactive technology.

4   Weeks ago, a friend lamented the trouble she had communicating with her grown son. It wasn't that her son was out of touch. Hardly. They were connected across miles through e-mail and cell phone, instant-messaging and text-messaging. But she had something serious to say and feared that an e-mail would elicit a reply that said: I M GR8. Was there no way to get undivided attention in the full in-box of his life? She finally chose a letter, a pen on paper, a stamp on envelope.

5   How do you describe the times we live in, so connected and yet fractured? Linda Stone, a former Microsoft techie, characterizes ours as an era of "continuous partial attention." At the extreme end are teenagers instant-messaging while they are talking on the cell phone, downloading music and doing homework. But adults too live with all systems go, interrupted and distracted, scanning everything, multi-technological-tasking everywhere.

Are we having fun yet?

We suffer from the illusion, Stone says, that we can expand our personal 6 bandwidth, connecting to more and more. Instead, we end up overstimulated, overwhelmed and, she adds, unfulfilled. Continuous partial attention inevitably feels like a lack of full attention.

But there are signs of people searching for ways to slow down and listen 7 up. We are told that experienced e-mail users are taking longer to answer, freeing themselves from the tyranny of the reply button. Caller ID is used to find out who we don't have to talk to. And the next "killer ap," they say, will be e-mail software that can triage the important from the trivial.

Meanwhile, at companies where technology interrupts creativity and 8 online contact prevents face-to-face contact, there are no e-mail-free Fridays. At others, there are bosses who require that you check your BlackBerry at the meeting door.

If a ringing cell phone once signaled your importance to a client, now that 9 client is impressed when you turn off the cell phone. People who stayed connected 10 ways, 24-7, now pride themselves on "going dark."

"People hunger for more attention," says Stone, whose message has been 10 welcomed even at a conference of bloggers. "Full attention will be the aphrodisiac of the future."

Indeed, at the height of our romance with e-mail, "You've Got Mail" was 11 the cinematic love story. Now e-mail brings less thrill—"who will be there?" And more dread—"how many are out there?" Today's romantics are couples who leave their laptops behind on the honeymoon.

As for text-message flirtation, a young woman ended hers with a man who 12 wrote, "C U L8R." He didn't have enough time to spell out Y-O-U?

Slowness guru Carl Honore began "In Praise of Slowness" after he found 13 himself seduced by a book of condensed classic fairy tales to read to his son. One-minute bedtime stories? We are relearning that paying attention briefly is as impossible as painting a landscape from a speeding car.

It is not just my trip to the mailbox that has brought this to mind. I come 14 here each summer to stop hurrying. My island is no Brigadoon: WiFi is on the way, and some people roam the island with their cell phones, looking for a hot spot. But I exchange the Internet for the country road.

Georgia O'Keeffe once said that it takes a long time to see a flower. No 15 technology can rush the growth of the leeks in the garden. All the speed in the Internet cannot hurry the healing of a friend's loss. Paying attention is the coin of this realm.

Sometimes, a letter becomes the icon of an old-fashioned new fashion. 16 And sometimes, in this technological whirlwind, it takes a piece of snail mail to carry the stamp of authenticity.

1. What has Goodman just done? How does this action serve the author as a lead-in to her subject?
2. What is Goodman's main idea or thesis?
3. What examples illustrate the problem the author sees in our times? What evidence does Goodman present to suggest that people want to change the times?
4. What general solutions does Goodman suggest?

5. How do the details at the beginning and end of the essay contribute to Goodman's point? Write a paragraph answer to this question. Then consider: Which one of the different responses to reading does your paragraph illustrate?
6. The author describes our time as one of "continuous partial attention." Does this phrase sum up our era? Why or why not? If you agree, do you think this is a problem? Why or why not?
7. For what kinds of research projects would this essay be useful? List several possibilities to discuss with classmates.

STUDENT ESSAY

A Convincing Style

James Goode

Ellen Goodman's essay, "In Praise of a Snail's Pace," is not, of course, about snails. It is about a way of communicating that our society has largely lost or ignored: the capability to pay full attention in communications and relationships. Her prime example of this is the "snail mail" letter, used for cards, invitations, and condolences. Anything really worth saying, she argues, must be written fully and sent by mail to make us pay attention. Goodman's easy, winning style of word choice and metaphor persuades us to agree with her point, a point also backed up by the logic of her examples.

"In Praise of a Snail's Pace" starts innocently. The author is merely taking a walk to the post office with a letter, surely nothing unusual. But as Goodman describes her letter, she reveals her belief that "snail mail" is a much more authentic way of sharing serious tidings than a message that "arrives over the

Internet transom." The letter, with its "square" envelope and "handwritten" address, immediately sounds more personal than the ultramodern electronic message. The words have guided the reader's thinking. Goodman also describes our times as "connected yet fractured" and us as living in a world of "continuous partial attention." "Being connected" becomes synonymous by the end of the essay with "not paying attention." Word choice is crucial here. The author creates in the reader's mind a dichotomy: be fast and false, or slow down and mean it.

Goodman's metaphors make a point, too. "A picture is worth a thousand words" and the pictures created by the words here further the fast/slow debate. The idea that sending an e-condolence would be "like serving Thanksgiving dinner at a fast-food restaurant" gives an instant image of the worthlessness of an e-mail condolence note. The mother trying to get attention in the "full in-box" of her son's life shows us that a divided and distracted brain answering five hundred e-mails cannot be expected to concentrate on any of them. Again, trying to pay attention briefly is just as impossible as "painting a landscape from a speeding car." The "tyranny" of the reply button must be overcome by our "going dark." Getting away from our electronic world, Goodman reasons, helps us restore meaning to what we do.

But while the reader listens to clever words and paints memorable mind pictures, any resistance is worn away with a steady stream of examples. From the author mailing an envelope to Georgia O'Keeffe's remark that it takes a long time to see a flower, example after example supports her view. The mother wishing for the total attention of her son and the office workers' turning off cell phones and computers have already been mentioned. Linda Stone, a former Microsoft techie and a credible authority on modern communications and their effects on users, is quoted several times. Goodman notes with excellent effect that Stone's message has been received even at a conference of bloggers—if the most connected group out there supports this, why shouldn't everyone else? The author herself comes to an island every year to escape the mad hurry of the business world by wandering country roads. These examples build until the reader is convinced that snail mail is the mark of authenticity and connectedness.

"In Praise of a Snail's Pace" is a thoughtful essay that takes aim at the notion that one person can do it all and still find meaning. The "connected" person is in so much of a hurry that he or she must not be really interested in much of anything. By showing "interrupted and distracted" readers that "no technology can rush the growth of the leeks in the garden," the author makes a convincing case for the real effectiveness of written mail. Whether through word choice, metaphor, or example, Ellen Goodman's message comes through: Slow down and send some "snail mail" and be really connected for once.

ANALYZING TWO OR MORE SOURCES

Scientists examining the same set of facts do not always draw the same conclusions; neither do historians and biographers agree on the significance of the same documents. How do we recognize and cope with these disparities? As critical readers we analyze what we read, pose questions, and refuse to believe everything we find in print or online. To develop these skills in recognizing differences, instructors frequently ask students to contrast the views of two or more writers. In psychology class, for example, you may be asked to contrast the views of Sigmund Freud and John B. Watson on child development. In a communications course, you may be asked to contrast the moderator styles of two talk-show hosts. We can examine differences in content or presentation, or both. Here are guidelines for preparing a contrast of sources.

GUIDELINES for Preparing a Contrast Essay

- **Work with sources that have something in common.** Think about the context for each, that is, each source's subject and purpose. (There is little sense in contrasting a textbook chapter, for example, with a TV talk show because their contexts are so different.)
- **Read actively to understand the content of the two sources.** Tape films, radio, or TV shows so that you can listen/view them several times, just as you would read a written source more than once.

- **Analyze for differences, focusing on your purpose in contrasting.** If you are contrasting the ideas of two writers, for example, then your analysis will focus on ideas, not on writing style. To explore differences in two news accounts, you may want to consider all of the following: the impact of placement in the newspaper/magazine, accompanying photographs or graphics, length of each article, what is covered in each article, and writing styles. Prepare a list of specific differences.
- **Organize your contrast.** It is usually best to organize by points of difference. If you write first about one source and then about the other, the ways that the sources differ may not be clear for readers. Take the time to plan an organization that clearly reveals your contrast purpose in writing. To illustrate, a paper contrasting the writing styles of two authors can be organized according to the following pattern:

Introduction: Introduce your topic and establish your purpose to contrast styles of writer A and writer B.

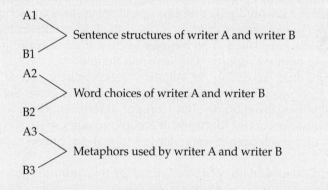

Conclusion: Explain the effect of the differences in style of the writers.

- **Illustrate and discuss each of the points of difference for each of the sources.** Provide examples and explain the impact of the differences.
- **Always write for an audience who may be familiar with your general topic but not with the specific sources you are discussing.** Be sure to provide adequate context (names, titles of works, etc.).

EXERCISE: Analyzing Two Sources

Whenever two people choose to write on the same topic, there are bound to be differences in choice of specifics and emphasis—as well as differences in political, social, or philosophical perspective. So, we need to read widely and not settle for only one source for our information. When reading newspapers, journals of opinion, and blogs, we need to become aware of the "leaning" or "slant" of each source.

Read the following two articles on the taking of hostages at an Algerian oil field by jihadists and the death of some hostages and some kidnappers when Algerian armed forces sought to free the hostages, an event that was covered by all news outlets as the story unfolded. Analyze each article for possible differences on the following points: impact of any visuals, length of treatment, differences in key points about the story, differences in how the issue is framed—in the context provided—and differences in style and tone.

Bring detailed notes to class for discussion, or write an analysis that contrasts the two articles on several key points of difference.

ALGERIAN HOSTAGE CRISIS HEIGHTENS AS SCORES ARE REPORTED DEAD
ARTHUR BRIGHT

This article was posted January 17, 2013, by the *Christian Science Monitor* at CSMonitor.com.

1   Dozens of hostages, both Algerian and foreign, have reportedly escaped the natural gas field in eastern Algeria that Islamic militants seized on Monday, but as the hostage situation enters its second day, an estimated 35 hostages and 15 hostage-takers were killed in an airstrike as they tried to move from one plant location to another, reports Al Jazeera and Reuters.

2   Reuters reports that according to Algerian news sources, some 30 Algerians and 15 foreigners have escaped the natural gas field in the Sahara Desert near the Algerian-Libyan border. But scores of Algerians and dozens of foreigners remain hostages of the "Battalion of Blood" militant group, according to statements that the hostages were allowed to make in phone calls to news outlets.

3   An unidentified hostage who spoke to France 24 television said prisoners were being forced to wear explosive belts. Their captors were heavily armed and had threatened to blow up the plant if the Algerian army tried to storm it.

4   Two hostages, identified as British and Irish, spoke to Al Jazeera television and called on the Algerian army to withdraw from the area to avoid casualties.

5   "We are receiving care and good treatment from the kidnappers. The (Algerian) army did not withdraw and they are firing at the camp," the British man said. "There are around 150 Algerian hostages. We say to everybody that negotiations is a sign of strength and will spare many any loss of life."

6   Reuters adds that US, French, and British officials did not confirm the numbers of their respective citizens who were being held by the terrorist group.

7   Although the raid on the field comes just days after the start of France's intervention in Mali, it is unlikely the attack was a spur-of-the-moment response to events in Mali. Helima Croft, a Barclays Capital senior geopolitical strategist, told the *New York Times* that "this type of attack had to have advanced planning. It's not an easy target of opportunity."

HOSTAGES REPORTEDLY DEAD IN ALGERIAN OIL FIELD SIEGE | JAMIE DETTMER

The kidnapping of oil workers—including several Americans—on Algerian soil by jihadists has apparently ended in tragedy.

This article also appeared on January 17, 2013, posted at *The Daily Beast*.

1   At least half-a-dozen Western oil workers including Americans held hostage since Wednesday by heavily armed al-Qaeda-linked Islamists at a natural gas complex in eastern Algeria died today when Algerian government forces mounted an attack to free them, say the militants holding them.

2   Amid confusing reports, the casualties at the sprawling Amenas gas complex 800 miles southeast of Algiers are being put at anything from six hostages to 34, including Algerian workers. Several captors, including the kidnappers' ground leader, Abou El Baraa, are said to have died, too, in the mission mounted by Algerian security forces that involved low-flying helicopter assaults.

A private security source working for oil companies in Algeria told *The Daily Beast* the operation to retake the facility was "messy." He added: "The Algerian soldiers were firing pretty indiscriminately. This wasn't a surgical operation."

3   A spokesman for the British Foreign Office confirmed an "ongoing military operation" against the hostage takers but couldn't verify whether there'd been casualties. Nor would he comment on reports that about 15 foreign hostages had escaped earlier from the gas field near the Libyan border that's run by BP, the Norwegian company Statoil, and Algeria's state oil agency.

4   The Algerian operation mounted to break the Sahara Desert siege came as security experts started to pin down the motives behind the seizing of the gas field by militants loyal to the notorious one-eyed Jihadist warlord, Mokhtar Belmokhtar, who is nicknamed variously "The Uncatchable"—he has been reported killed several times—or "Mr. Marlboro" for his involvement in cigarette smuggling that has helped to finance his operations.

5   Militants seized the facility on Wednesday, saying the attack was in response to France's military intervention in neighboring Mali, where French Foreign legionnaires have joined Malian government troops in halting advances by Islamists who have taken over much of northern Mali.

6   But terrorism analysts say Belmokhtar had more than one objective in mind when he ordered his fighters in a well-planned operation to seize the facility and secure Western hostages, including boosting his own standing among jihadists after he was recently passed over for promotion within al-Qaeda.

7   An Algerian native with a storied two-decade history of armed militancy, Belmokhtar was one of the leading figures of al-Qaeda in the Islamic Maghreb (AQIM) and commanded a highly effective cell of fighters in north Mali until October, when Yahya Abou El Hamame was appointed over him as AQIM's "Emir of the Sahel."

8   "He has a reputation as an autonomous operator," says Stephen Ellis of the African Studies Center at the University of Leiden in The Netherlands. "He is well known as going his own way both when it comes to his criminal and smuggling activities and his militancy. In the Sahel the various jihadist groups are very fissiparous. They split and re-form regularly only to split again."

Mokhtar Belmokhtar

9   Some of the differences that cause division are not only connected to disputes over terrorism strategy or ideology. Leaders clash over the spoils that can be made—from ransoms paid for the release of Western hostages to the distribution of profits from smuggling guns, drugs, and tobacco.

10   Following his being passed over for promotion, Belmokhtar left the al-Qaeda franchise to set up his own jihadi outfit, naming it Khaled Abu-al-Abbas Brigaed or al-Muwaqqu'un bil-Dima (Those Who Sign in Blood).

. . .

11   One of his associates, Oumar Ould Hamaha, told the Associated Press in the autumn that they were leaving al-Qaeda "so that we can better operate in the field. . . . We want to enlarge our zone of operation throughout the entire Sahara, going from Niger through to Chad and Burkina Faso."

12   Born in Ghardaia, Algeria, in 1972, Belmokhtar traveled to Afghanistan as a 19-year-old to join training camps run by jihadists, returning in 1992 to his homeland, joining first Algeria's Islamic Armed Group (GIA) then helping to set up the Salafist Group for Preaching and combat (GSPC) that subsequently merged with al-Qaeda.

13   Belmokhtar is reported to be in alliance now with another former AQIM fighter Hamadou Ould Khairou, a Mauritanian that U.S. security sources say is involved in the drug trade.

. . .

14   "In my opinion, even if Belmokhtar uses the slogan of the French attack in Mali, this is not his real intention," said Ely Karmon, a Senior Research Scholar at the Institute for Counter-Terrorism at the Interdisciplinary Center in Herzliya, Israel. "It is motivated by money."

15   Last month, the Signed-in-Blood brigade warned against the West trying to halt the Islamist takeover of northern Mali. "We will respond forcefully; we promise we will follow you to your homes and you will feel pain and we will attack your interests," warned the group.

FOR READING AND ANALYSIS

THE "F WORD" | FIROOZEH DUMAS

Born in Iran, Firoozeh Dumas moved to California when she was seven, returned to Iran with her family for two years, and then came back to California. She attended the University of California at Berkeley, married, and has three children. Initially she started to write stories for her children. These were developed into *Funny in Farsi: A Memoir of Growing Up Iranian in America* (2003), from which the following excerpt is taken. *Laughing Without an Accent* was followed in 2008.

PREREADING QUESTIONS Based on her title, what did you first think this work would be about? How does the information above help you to adjust your thinking?

My cousin's name, Farbod, means "Greatness." 1

When he moved to America, all the kids called him "Farthead." My brother 2 Farshid ("He Who Enlightens") became "Fartshit." The name of my friend Neggar means "Beloved," although it can be more accurately translated as "She Whose Name Almost Incites Riots." Her brother Arash ("Giver") initially couldn't understand why every time he'd say his name, people would laugh and ask him if it itched.

All of us immigrants knew that moving to America would be fraught with 3 challenges, but none of us thought that our names would be such an obstacle. How could our parents have ever imagined that someday we would end up in a country where monosyllabic names reign supreme, a land where "William" is shortened to "Bill," where "Susan" becomes "Sue," and "Richard" somehow evolves into "Dick"? America is a great country, but nobody without a mask and a cape has a *z* in his name. And have Americans ever realized the great scope of the guttural sounds they're missing? Okay, so it has to do with linguistic roots, but I do believe this would be a richer country if all Americans could do a little tongue aerobics and learn to pronounce "kh," a sound more commonly associated in this culture with phlegm, or "gh," the sound usually made by actors in the final moments of a choking scene. It's like adding a few new spices to the kitchen pantry. Move over, cinnamon and nutmeg, make way for cardamom and sumac.

Exotic analogies aside, having a foreign name in this land of Joes and Marys 4 is a pain in the spice cabinet. When I was twelve, I decided to simplify my life by adding an American middle name. This decision serves as proof that sometimes simplifying one's life in the short run only complicates it in the long run.

My name, Firoozeh, chosen by my mother, means "Turquoise" in Persian. 5 In America, it means "Unpronounceable" or "I'm Not Going to Talk to You Because I Cannot Possibly Learn Your Name and I Just Don't Want to Have to Ask You Again and Again Because You'll Think I'm Dumb or You Might Get Upset or Something." My father, incidentally, had wanted to name me Sara. I do wish he had won that argument.

To strengthen my decision to add an American name, I had just finished 6 fifth grade in Whittier, where all the kids incessantly called me "Ferocious." That summer, my family moved to Newport Beach, where I looked forward to starting a new life. I wanted to be a kid with a name that didn't draw so much attention, a name that didn't come with a built-in inquisition as to when and why I had moved to America and how was it that I spoke English without an accent and was I planning on going back and what did I think of America?

7   My last name didn't help any. I can't mention my maiden name, because:

8   "Dad, I'm writing a memoir."

9   "Great! Just don't mention our name."

10   Suffice it to say that, with eight letters, including a z, and four syllables, my last name is as difficult and foreign as my first. My first and last name together generally served the same purpose as a high brick wall. There was one exception to this rule. In Berkeley, and only in Berkeley, my name drew people like flies to baklava. These were usually people named Amaryllis or Chrysanthemum, types who vacationed in Costa Rica and to whom lentils described a type of burger. These folks were probably not the pride of Poughkeepsie, but they were refreshingly nonjudgmental.

11   When I announced to my family that I wanted to add an American name, they reacted with their usual laughter. Never one to let mockery or good judgment stand in my way, I proceeded to ask for suggestions. My father suggested "Fifi." Had I had a special affinity for French poodles or been considering a career in prostitution, I would've gone with that one. My mom suggested "Farah," a name easier than "Firoozeh" yet still Iranian. Her reasoning made sense, except that Farrah Fawcett was at the height of her popularity and I didn't want to be associated with somebody whose poster hung in every postpubescent boy's bedroom. We couldn't think of any American names beginning with F, so we moved on to J, the first letter of our last name. I don't know why we limited ourselves to names beginning with my initials, but it made sense at that moment, perhaps by the logic employed moments before bungee jumping. I finally chose the name "Julie" mainly for its simplicity. My brothers, Farid and Farshid, thought that adding an American name was totally stupid. They later became Fred and Sean.

12   That same afternoon, our doorbell rang. It was our new next-door neighbor, a friendly girl my age named Julie. She asked me my name and after a moment of hesitation, I introduced myself as Julie. "What a coincidence!" she said. I didn't mention that I had been Julie for only half an hour.

13   Thus I started sixth grade with my new, easy name and life became infinitely simpler. People actually remembered my name, which was an entirely refreshing new sensation. All was well until the Iranian Revolution, when I found myself with a new set of problems. Because I spoke English without an accent and was known as Julie, people assumed I was American. This meant that I was often privy to their real feelings about those "damn I-raynians." It was like having those X-ray glasses that let you see people naked, except that what I was seeing was far uglier than people's underwear. It dawned on me that these people would have probably never invited me to their house had they known me as Firoozeh. I felt like a fake.

14   When I went to college, I eventually went back to using my real name. All was well until I graduated and started looking for a job. Even though I had graduated with honors from UC–Berkeley, I couldn't get a single interview. I was guilty of being a humanities major, but I began to suspect that there was more to

my problems. After three months of rejections, I added "Julie" to my résumé. Call it coincidence, but the job offers started coming in. Perhaps it's the same kind of coincidence that keeps African Americans from getting cabs in New York.

Once I got married, my name became Julie Dumas. I went from having an identifiably "ethnic" name to having ancestors who wore clogs. My family and non-American friends continued calling me Firoozeh, while my coworkers and American friends called me Julie. My life became one big knot, especially when friends who knew me as Julie met friends who knew me as Firoozeh. I felt like those characters in soap operas who have an evil twin. The two, of course, can never be in the same room, since they're played by the same person, a struggling actress who wears a wig to play one of the twins and dreams of moving on to bigger and better roles. I couldn't blame my mess on a screen writer; it was my own doing.

I decided to untangle the knot once and for all by going back to my real name. By then, I was a stay-at-home mom, so I really didn't care whether people remembered my name or gave me job interviews. Besides, most of the people I dealt with were in diapers and were in no position to judge. I was also living in Silicon Valley, an area filled with people named Rajeev, Avishai, and Insook.

Every once in a while, though, somebody comes up with a new permutation and I am once again reminded that I am an immigrant with a foreign name. I recently went to have blood drawn for a physical exam. The waiting room for blood work at our local medical clinic is in the basement of the building, and no matter how early one arrives for an appointment, forty coughing, wheezing people have gotten there first. Apart from reading *Golf Digest* and *Popular Mechanics*, there isn't much to do except guess the number of contagious diseases represented in the windowless room. Every ten minutes, a name is called and everyone looks to see which cough matches that name. As I waited patiently, the receptionist called out, "Fritzy, Fritzy!" Everyone looked around, but no one stood up. Usually, if I'm waiting to be called by someone who doesn't know me, I will respond to just about any name starting with an *F*. Having been called Froozy, Frizzy, Fiorucci, and Frooz and just plain "Uhhhh . . . ," I am highly accommodating. I did not, however, respond to "Fritzy" because there is, as far as I know, no *t* in my name. The receptionist tried again, "Fritzy, Fritzy DumbAss." As I stood up to this most linguistically original version of my name, I could feel all eyes upon me. The room was momentarily silent as all of these sick people sat united in a moment of gratitude for their own names.

Despite a few exceptions, I have found that Americans are now far more willing to learn new names, just as they're far more willing to try new ethnic foods. Of course, some people just don't like to learn. One mom at my children's school adamantly refused to learn my "impossible" name and instead settled on calling me "F Word." She was recently transferred to New York where, from what I've heard, she might meet an immigrant or two and, who knows, she just might have to make some room in her spice cabinet.

1. What happened when the author changed her name to Julie?
2. What happened when she sought a job after college, using her original name?
3. When did she decide to use only her original name?
4. When Dumas is called at the medical clinic, what does she think the other patients are feeling?

5. Although this essay may not have the "feel" of an argument, it nonetheless makes a point. What is Dumas's claim?
6. What has changed in America since her arrival as a young girl? Is the change complete? What would she like to see Americans learn to do?
7. What writing strategies are noteworthy in creating her style? Illustrate with examples.

8. How much effort do you make to pronounce names correctly? Why is it important to get a person's name right?
9. Have you had the experience of Americans impatient with the pronunciation of your name—or just refusing to get it right? If so, what has been your response?
10. What might be some of the reasons Americans have trouble with the pronunciation of ethnic names—whether the names belong to foreign nationals or to ethnic Americans? Reflect on possible causes.
11. What are the advantages of facing the world with humor?

LOVE TO READ, KIDS? YOUR TIME IS ALMOST UP | ALEXANDRA PETRI

A graduate of Harvard University, Alexandra Petri writes the ComPost blog, a "lighter take" on current issues, and is an op-ed columnist for the *Washington Post*. She wrote for the *Harvard Crimson* while at college and has appeared on Boston's Comedy Studio and Comedy Connection. The following column was published December 8, 2012.

PREREADING QUESTIONS Does the author's title make you curious about her subject? What do you expect her to be writing about?

1   Forget *The Catcher in the Rye.*

2   New Common Core standards (which affect 46 states and the District) will require that, by 2014, 70 percent of high school seniors' reading assignments be nonfiction. Some suggested texts include "FedViews" by the Federal Reserve Bank of San Francisco, the EPA's "Recommended Levels of Insulation" and "Invasive Plant Inventory" by California's Invasive Plant Council.

Forget *Huckleberry Finn* and *Moby Dick.* Bring out the woodchipping 3
manuals!

I like reading. I love reading. I always have. I read recreationally still. I read 4
on buses, in planes, while crossing streets. My entire apartment is covered in
books. And now, through some strange concatenation of circumstances, I
write for a living.

And it's all because, as a child, my parents took the time to read me 4
"Recommended Levels of Insulation."

Oh. "Recommended Levels of Insulation." That was always my favorite, 6
although "Invasive Plant Inventory" was a close second. (What phrases in literature or life will ever top the rich resonance of its opening line? "The
Inventory categorizes plants as High, Moderate, or Limited, reflecting the level
of each species' negative ecological impact in California. Other factors, such
as economic impact or difficulty of management, are not included in this
assessment." "Call me Ishmael" has nothing on it!)

"It is important to note that even Limited species are invasive and should 7
be of concern to land managers," I frequently tell myself in moments of crisis.
"Although the impact of each plant varies regionally, its rating represents
cumulative impacts statewide." How true that is, even today.

My dog-eared copy of "Recommended Levels of Insulation" still sits on 8
my desk. That was where I first learned the magic of literature.

"Insulation levels are specified by R-Value. R-Value is a measure of insula- 9
tion's ability to resist heat traveling through it." What authority in that
sentence!

And then came the table of insulation values. I shudder every time that 10
table appears. It is one of the great villains in the history of the English language. Uriah Heep and Captain Ahab can't hold a candle to it. In fact, I do not
know who these people are. I have never read about them.

I do remember curling up with "Recommended Levels of Insulation" and 11
reading it over and over again. It was this that drove me to pursue writing as a
career—the hope one day of crafting a sentence that sang the way "Drill holes
in the sheathing and blow insulation into the empty wall cavity before install-
ing the new siding" sings.

Look, I was an English major, so I may be biased. But life is full of enough 12
instruction manuals.

The best way to understand what words can do is to see them in their 13
natural habitat, not constrained in the dull straitjackets of legalese and regula-
tionish and manualect. It's like saying the proper way of encountering puppies
is in puppy mills. Words in regulations and manuals have been mangled and
tortured and bent into unnatural positions, and the later you have to discover
such cruelty, the better.

The people behind the core have sought to defend it, saying that this 14
change is not meant to supplant literature. This increased emphasis on nonfiction would not be a concern if the core worked the way it was supposed to,
with teachers in other disciplines like math and science assigning the hard
technical texts that went along with their subjects.

15   But teachers worry that this will not happen. Principals seem to be having trouble comprehending the requirement themselves. Besides, the other teachers are too busy, well, teaching their subjects, to inflict technical manuals on their students, and they may expect the English department to pick up the slack. Hence the feared great Purge of Literature.

16   The core has good intentions, but it will be vital to make sure the execution is as good, or we will head down the road usually paved with good intentions. There, in the ninth circle, students who would otherwise have been tearing through Milton and Shakespeare with great excitement are forced to come home hugging manuals of Exotic Plants.

17   All in all, this is a great way to make the kids who like reading hate reading.

QUESTIONS FOR READING

1. What event has prompted Petri to write?
2. How does the author describe the language of manuals?
3. How do the Core creators defend the new requirements?
4. What does Petri think will happen?

QUESTIONS FOR REASONING AND ANALYSIS

5. What is Petri's thesis—that is, the claim of her argument?
6. How would you describe the essay's tone? Is it appropriate to say that there is more than one? Explain.
7. Analyze the author's style: What strategies does she use? Are they effective? Why or why not?

QUESTIONS FOR REFLECTING AND WRITING

8. What is your reaction to the new Core standards? Is it important for students to know how to read nonfiction? Are manuals a good choice to develop this skill? Explain your views.
9. Should students read great works of literature throughout middle and high school? If yes, why? If no, why not?

SUGGESTIONS FOR DISCUSSION AND WRITING

1. Analyze the style of one of the essays from Section 5 of this text. Do not comment on every element of style; select several elements that seem to characterize the writer's style and examine them in detail. Remember that style analyses are written for an audience familiar with the work, so summary is not necessary.

2. Many of the authors included in this text have written books that you will find in your library. Select one that interests you, read it, and prepare a review of it that synthesizes summary, analysis, and evaluation. Prepare a review of about 300 words; assume that the book has just been published.

3. Choose two newspaper and/or magazine articles that differ in their discussion of the same person, event, or product. You may select two different articles on a person in the news, two different accounts of a news event, an advertisement and a *Consumer Reports* analysis of the same product, or two reviews of a book or movie. Analyze differences in both content and presentation and then consider why the two accounts differ. Organize by points of difference and write to an audience not necessarily familiar with the articles.

4. Choose a recently scheduled public event (the Super Bowl, the Olympics, a presidential election, the Academy Award presentations, the premiere of a new television series) and find several articles written before and several after the event. First compare articles written after the event to see if they agree factually. If not, decide which article appears to be more accurate and why. Then examine the earlier material and decide which was the most and which the least accurate. Write an essay in which you explain the differences in speculation before the event and why you think these differences exist. Your audience will be aware of the event but not necessarily aware of the articles you are studying.

The World of Argument

CHAPTER 3

Understanding the Basics of Argument

CUL DE SAC   *BY RICHARD THOMPSON*

READ: What is the situation? What is the reaction of the younger children? What does the older boy try to do?

REASON: Why is the older boy frustrated?

REFLECT/WRITE: What can happen to those who lack scientific knowledge?

In this section we will explore the processes of thinking logically and analyzing issues to reach informed judgments. Remember: Mature people do not need to agree on all issues to respect one another's good sense, but they do have little patience with uninformed or illogical statements masquerading as argument.

CHARACTERISTICS OF ARGUMENT

Argument Is Conversation with a Goal

When you enter into an argument (as speaker, writer, or reader), you become a participant in an ongoing debate about an issue. Since you are probably not the first to address the issue, you need to be aware of the ways that the issue has been debated by others and then seek to advance the conversation, just as you would if you were having a more casual conversation with friends. If the time of the movie is set, the discussion now turns to whose car to take or where to meet. If you were to just repeat the time of the movie, you would add nothing useful to the conversation. Also, if you were to change the subject to a movie you saw last week, you would annoy your friends by not offering useful information or showing that you valued the current conversation. Just as with your conversation about the movie, you want your argument to stay focused on the issue, to respect what others have already contributed, and to make a useful addition to our understanding of the topic.

Argument Takes a Stand on an Arguable Issue

A meaningful argument focuses on a debatable issue. We usually do not argue about facts. "Professor Jones's American literature class meets at 10:00 on Mondays" is not arguable. It is either true or false. We can check the schedule of classes to find out. (Sometimes the facts change; new facts replace old ones.) We also do not debate personal preferences for the simple reason that they are just that—personal. If the debate is about the appropriateness of boxing as a sport, for you to declare that you would rather play tennis is to fail to advance the conversation. You have expressed a personal preference, interesting perhaps, but not relevant to the debate.

Argument Uses Reasons and Evidence

Some arguments merely "look right." That is, conclusions are drawn from facts, but the facts are not those that actually support the assertion, or the conclusion is not the only or the best explanation of those facts. To shape convincing arguments, we need more than an array of facts. We need to think critically, to analyze the issue, to see relationships, to weigh evidence. We need to avoid the temptation to "argue" from emotion only, or to believe that just stating our opinion is the same thing as building a sound argument.

Argument Incorporates Values

Arguments are based not just on reason and evidence but also on the beliefs and values we hold and think that our audience may hold as well. In a reasoned debate, you want to make clear the values that you consider relevant to the argument. In an editorial defending the sport of boxing, one editor wrote that boxing "is a sport because the world has not yet become a place in which the qualities that go into excellence in boxing [endurance, agility, courage] have no value" (*Washington Post,* February 5, 1983). But James J. Kilpatrick also appeals to values when he argues, in an editorial critical of boxing, that we should not want to live in a society "in which deliberate brutality is legally authorized and publicly applauded" (*Washington Post,* December 7, 1982). Observe, however, the high level of seriousness in the appeal to values. Neither writer settles for a simplistic personal preference: "Boxing is exciting," or "Boxing is too violent."

Argument Recognizes the Topic's Complexity

Much false reasoning (the logical fallacies discussed in Chapter 6) results from a writer's oversimplifying an issue. A sound argument begins with an understanding that most issues are terribly complicated. The wise person approaches such ethical concerns as abortion or euthanasia or such public policy issues as tax cuts or trade agreements with the understanding that there are many philosophical, moral, and political issues that complicate discussions of these topics. Recognizing an argument's complexity may also lead us to an understanding that there can be more than one "right" position. The thoughtful arguer respects the views of others, seeks common ground when possible, and often chooses a conciliatory approach.

THE SHAPE OF ARGUMENT: WHAT WE CAN LEARN FROM ARISTOTLE

Still one of the best ways to understand the basics of argument is to reflect on what the Greek philosopher Aristotle describes as the three "players" in any argument: the *writer* (or *speaker*), the *argument itself,* and the *reader* (or *audience*). Aristotle also reminds us that the occasion or "situation" (*kairos*) is important in understanding and evaluating an argument. Let's examine each part of this model of argument.

Ethos (about the Writer/Speaker)

It seems logical to begin with *ethos* because without this player we have no argument. We could, though, end with the writer because Aristotle asserts that this player in any argument is the most important. No argument, no matter how logical, no matter how appealing to one's audience, can succeed if the audience rejects the arguer's credibility, his or her *ethical* qualities.

Think how often in political contests those running attack their opponent's character rather than the candidate's programs. Remember the smear campaign against Obama—he is (or was) a Muslim and therefore unfit to be president, the first point an error of fact, the second point an emotional appeal to voters' fears. Candidates try these smear tactics, even without evidence, because they understand that every voter they can convince of an opponent's failure of *ethos* is a citizen who will vote for them.

Many American voters want to be assured that a candidate is patriotic, religious (but of course not fanatic!), a loyal spouse, and a loving parent. At times, we even lose sight of important differences in positions as we focus on the person instead. But, this tells us how much an audience values their sense of the arguer's credibility. During his campaign for reelection, after the Watergate break-in, Nixon was attacked with the line "Would you buy a used car from this guy?" (In defense of used-car salespeople, not all are untrustworthy!)

Logos (about the Logic of the Argument)

Logos refers to the argument itself—to the assertion and the support for it. Aristotle maintains that part of an arguer's appeal to his or her audience lies in the logic of the argument and the quality of the support provided. Even the most credible of writers will not move thoughtful audiences with inadequate evidence or sloppy reasoning. Yes, "arguments" that appeal to emotions, to our needs and fantasies, will work for some audiences—look at the success of advertising, for example. But, if you want to present a serious claim to critical readers, then you must pay attention to your argument. Paying attention means not only having good reasons but also organizing them clearly. Your audience needs to see *how* your evidence supports your point. Consider the following argument in opposition to the war on Iraq.

> War can be justified only as a form of self-defense. To initiate a war, we need to be able to show that our first strike was necessary as a form of self-defense. The Bush administration argued that Iraq had weapons of mass destruction and intended to use them against us. Responding to someone's "intent" to do harm is always a difficult judgment call. But, in this case, there were no weapons of mass destruction so there could not have been any intent to harm the United States, or at least none that was obvious and immediate. Thus we must conclude that this war was not the right course of action for the United States.

You may disagree (many will) with this argument's assertion, but you can respect the writer's logic, the clear connecting of one reason to the next. One good way to strengthen your credibility is to get respect for clear reasoning.

Pathos (about Appeals to the Audience)

Argument implies an audience, those whose views we want to influence in some way. Aristotle labels this player *pathos*, the Greek word for both passion and suffering (hence *pathology*, the study of disease). Arguers need to be aware of their audience's feelings on the issue, the attitudes and values that will affect their response to the argument. There are really two questions arguers must answer: "How can I engage my audience's interest?" and "How can I engage their sympathy for my position?"

Some educators and health experts believe that childhood obesity is a major problem in the United States. Other Americans are much more focused on the economy—or their own careers. Al Gore is passionately concerned about the harmful effects of global warming; others, though increasingly fewer, think he lacks sufficient evidence of environmental degradation. How does a physician raise reader interest in childhood obesity? How does Gore convince doubters that we need to reduce carbon emissions? To prepare an effective argument, we need always to plan our approach with a clear vision of how best to connect to a specific audience—one which may or may not agree with our interests or our position.

Kairos (about the Occasion or Situation)

While *ethos, logos,* and *pathos* create the traditional three-part communication model, Aristotle adds another term to enhance our understanding of any argument "moment." The term *kairos* refers to the occasion for the argument, the situation that we are in. What does this moment call for from us? Is the lunch table the appropriate time and place for an argument with your coworker over her failure to meet a deadline that is part of a joint project? You have just received a 65 on your history test; is this the best time to e-mail your professor to protest

Personal confrontation at a business meeting: Not cool.

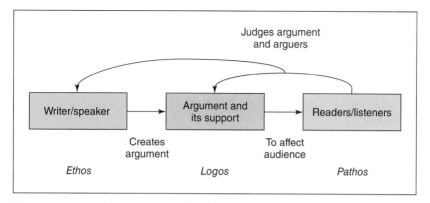

FIGURE 3.1 Aristotelian Structure of Argument

the grade? Would the professor's office be the better place for your discussion than an e-mail sent from your BlackBerry minutes after you have left class?

The concept of *kairos* asks us to consider what is most appropriate for the occasion, to think through the best time, place, and genre (type of argument) to make a successful argument. This concept has special meaning for students in a writing class who sometimes have difficulty thinking about audience at all. When practicing writing for the academic community, you may need to modify the language or tone that you use in other situations.

We argue in a specific context of three interrelated parts, as illustrated in Figure 3.1.

We present support for an assertion to a specific audience whose expectations and character we have given thought to when shaping our argument. And we present ourselves as informed, competent, and reliable so that our audience will give us their attention.

THE LANGUAGE OF ARGUMENT

We could title this section the *languages* of argument because arguments come in visual language as well as in words. But visual arguments—cartoons, photos, ads—are almost always accompanied by some words: figures speaking in bubbles, a caption, a slogan (Nike's "Just Do It!"). So we need to think about the kinds of statements that make up arguments, whether those arguments are legal briefs or cartoons, casual conversations or scholarly essays. To build an argument we need some statements that support other statements that present the main idea or claim of the argument.

- Claims: usually either inferences or judgments, for these are debatable assertions.
- Support: facts, opinions based on facts (inferences), or opinions based on values, beliefs, or ideas (judgments) or some combination of the three.

Let's consider what kinds of statements each of these terms describes.

Facts

Facts are statements that are verifiable. Factual statements refer to what can be counted or measured or confirmed by reasonable observers or trusted experts.

> There are twenty-six desks in Room 110.
>
> In the United States about 400,000 people die each year as a result of smoking.

These are factual statements. We can verify the first by observation—by counting. The second fact comes from medical records. We rely on trusted record-keeping sources and medical experts for verification. By definition, we do not argue about the facts. Usually. Sometimes "facts" change, as we learn more about our world. For example, only in the last thirty years has convincing evidence been gathered to demonstrate the relationship between smoking and various illnesses of the heart and lungs. And sometimes "facts" are false facts. These are statements that sound like facts but are incorrect. For example: Nadel has won more Wimbledon titles than Federer. Not so.

Inferences

Inferences are opinions based on facts. Inferences are the conclusions we draw from an analysis of facts.

> There will not be enough desks in Room 110 for upcoming fall-semester classes.
>
> Smoking is a serious health hazard.

Predictions of an increase in student enrollment for the coming fall semester lead to the inference that most English classes scheduled in Room 110 will run with several more students per class than last year. The dean should order new desks. Similarly, we infer from the number of deaths that smoking is a health problem; statistics show more people dying from tobacco than from AIDS, or murder, or car accidents, causes of death that get media coverage but do not produce nearly as many deaths.

Inferences vary in their closeness to the facts supporting them. That the sun will "rise" tomorrow is an inference, but we count on its happening, acting as if it is a fact. However, the first inference stated above is based not just on the fact of twenty-six desks but on another inference—a projected increase in student enrollment—and two assumptions. The argument looks like this:

FACT:	There are twenty-six desks in Room 110.
INFERENCE:	There will be more first-year students next year.
ASSUMPTIONS:	1. English will remain a required course.
	2. No additional classrooms are available for English classes.
CLAIM:	There will not be enough desks in Room 110 for upcoming fall-semester classes.

This inference could be challenged by a different analysis of the facts supporting enrollment projections. Or, if additional rooms can be found, the dean will not need to order new desks. Inferences can be part of the support of an argument, or they can be the claim of an argument.

Judgments

Judgments are opinions based on values, beliefs, or philosophical concepts. (Judgments also include opinions based on personal preferences, but we have already excluded these from argument.) Judgments concern right and wrong, good and bad, better or worse, should and should not:

> No more than twenty-six students should be enrolled in any English class.
>
> Cigarette advertising should be eliminated, and the federal government should develop an antismoking campaign.

NOTE: Placing such qualifiers as "I believe," "I think," or "I feel" in an assertion does not free you from the need to support that claim. The statement "I believe that President Bush was a great president" calls for an argument based on evidence and reasons.

To support the first judgment, we need to explain what constitutes overcrowding, or what constitutes the best class size for effective teaching. If we can support our views on effective teaching, we may be able to convince the college president that ordering more desks for Room 110 is not the best solution to an increasing enrollment in English classes. The second judgment also offers a solution to a problem, in this case a national health problem. To reduce the number of deaths, we need to reduce the number of smokers, either by encouraging smokers to quit or nonsmokers not to start. The underlying assumption: Advertising does affect behavior.

EXERCISE: Facts, Inferences, and Judgments

Compile a list of three statements of fact, three inferences, and three judgments. Try to organize them into three related sets, as illustrated here:

- Smoking is prohibited in some restaurants.
- Secondhand smoke is a health hazard.
- Smoking should be prohibited in all restaurants.

We can classify judgments to see better what kind of assertion we are making and, therefore, what kind of support we need to argue effectively.

FUNCTIONAL JUDGMENTS (guidelines for judging how something or someone works or could work)

Tiger Woods is the best golfer to play the game.

Antismoking advertising will reduce the number of smokers.

AESTHETIC JUDGMENTS (guidelines for judging art, literature, music, or natural scenes)

The sunrise was beautiful.

The Great Gatsby's structure, characters, and symbols are perfectly wedded to create the novel's vision of the American dream.

ETHICAL JUDGMENTS (guidelines for group or social behavior)

Lawyers should not advertise.

It is discourteous to talk during a film or lecture.

MORAL JUDGMENTS (guidelines of right and wrong for judging individuals and for establishing legal principles)

Taking another person's life is wrong.

Equal rights under the law should not be denied on the basis of race or gender.

Functional and aesthetic judgments generally require defining key terms and establishing criteria for the judging or ranking made by the assertion. How, for example, do we compare golfers? On the amount of money won? The number of tournaments won? Or the consistency of winning throughout one's career? What about the golfer's quality and range of shots? Ethical and moral judgments may be more difficult to support because they depend not just on how terms are defined and criteria established but on values and beliefs as well. If taking another person's life is wrong, why isn't it wrong in war? Or is it? These are difficult questions that require thoughtful debate.

EXERCISES: Understanding Assumptions, Facts, False Facts, Inferences, and Judgments

1. Categorize the judgments you wrote for the previous exercise (p. 77) as either aesthetic, moral, ethical, or functional. Alternatively, compile a list of three judgments that you then categorize.
2. For each judgment listed for exercise 1, generate one statement of support, either a fact or an inference or another judgment. Then state any underlying assumptions that are part of each argument.
3. Read the following article and then complete the exercise that follows. This exercise tests both careful reading and your understanding of the differences among facts, inferences, and judgments.

YOUR BRAIN LIES TO YOU | SAM WANG and SANDRA AAMODT

Dr. Samuel S. H. Wang is a professor of molecular biology and neuroscience at Princeton, where he manages a research lab. Dr. Sandra Aamodt, former editor of *Nature Neuroscience*, is a freelance science writer. Drs. Wang and Aamodt are the authors of *Welcome to Your Brain: Why You Lose Your Car Keys but Never Forget How to Drive and Other Puzzles of Everyday Life* (2008). The following article appeared on June 27, 2008, in the *New York Times*.

1 False beliefs are everywhere. Eighteen percent of Americans think the sun revolves around the earth, one poll has found. Thus it seems slightly less egregious that, according to another poll, 10 percent of us think that Senator Barack Obama, a Christian, is instead a Muslim. The Obama campaign has created a Web site to dispel misinformation. But this effort may be more difficult than it seems, thanks to the quirky way in which our brains store memories—and mislead us along the way.

2 The brain does not simply gather and stockpile information as a computer's hard drive does. Current research suggests that facts may be stored first in the hippocampus, a structure deep in the brain about the size and shape of a fat man's curled pinkie finger. But the information does not rest there. Every time we recall it, our brain writes it down again, and during this re-storage, it is also reprocessed. In time, the fact is gradually transferred to the cerebral cortex and is separated from the context in which it was originally learned. For example, you know that the capital of California is Sacramento, but you probably don't remember how you learned it.

3 This phenomenon, known as source amnesia, can also lead people to forget whether a statement is true. Even when a lie is presented with a disclaimer, people often later remember it as true.

4 With time, this misremembering only gets worse. A false statement from a non-credible source that is at first not believed can gain credibility during the months it takes to reprocess memories from short-term hippocampal storage to longer-term cortical storage. As the source is forgotten, the message and its implications gain strength. This could explain why, during the 2004 presidential campaign, it took some weeks for the Swift Boat Veterans for Truth campaign against Senator John Kerry to have an effect on his standing in the polls.

5 Even if they do not understand the neuroscience behind source amnesia, campaign strategists can exploit it to spread misinformation. They know that if their message is initially memorable, its impression will persist long after it is debunked. In repeating a falsehood, someone may back it up with an opening line like "I think I read somewhere" or even with a reference to a specific source.

6 In one study, a group of Stanford students was exposed repeatedly to an unsubstantiated claim taken from a Web site that Coca-Cola is an effective paint thinner. Students who read the statement five times were nearly one-third more likely than those who read it only twice to attribute it to *Consumer Reports* (rather than *The National Enquirer*, their other choice), giving it a gloss of credibility.

7   Adding to this innate tendency to mold information we recall is the way our brains fit facts into established mental frameworks. We tend to remember news that accords with our worldview, and discount statements that contradict it.

8   In another Stanford study, 48 students, half of whom said they favored capital punishment and half of whom said they opposed it, were presented with two pieces of evidence, one supporting and one contradicting the claim that capital punishment deters crime. Both groups were more convinced by the evidence that supported their initial position.

9   Psychologists have suggested that legends propagate by striking an emotional chord. In the same way, ideas can spread by emotional selection, rather than by their factual merits, encouraging the persistence of falsehoods about Coke—or about a presidential candidate.

10   Journalists and campaign workers may think they are acting to counter misinformation by pointing out that it is not true. But by repeating a false rumor, they may inadvertently make it stronger. In its concerted effort to "stop the smears," the Obama campaign may want to keep this in mind. Rather than emphasize that Mr. Obama is not a Muslim, for instance, it may be more effective to stress that he embraced Christianity as a young man.

11   Consumers of news, for their part, are prone to selectively accept and remember statements that reinforce beliefs they already hold. In a replication of the study of students' impressions of evidence about the death penalty, researchers found that even when subjects were given a specific instruction to be objective, they were still inclined to reject evidence that disagreed with their beliefs.

12   In the same study, however, when subjects were asked to imagine their reaction if the evidence had pointed to the opposite conclusion, they were more open-minded to information that contradicted their beliefs. Apparently, it pays for consumers of controversial news to take a moment and consider that the opposite interpretation may be true.

13   In 1919, Justice Oliver Wendell Holmes of the Supreme Court wrote that "the best test of truth is the power of the thought to get itself accepted in the competition of the market." Holmes erroneously assumed that ideas are more likely to spread if they are honest. Our brains do not naturally obey this admirable dictum, but by better understanding the mechanisms of memory perhaps we can move closer to Holmes's ideal.

Source: Originally appeared in the *New York Times*, June 27, 2008. Reprinted by permission of the authors.

Label each of the following sentences as F (fact), FF (false fact), I (inference), or J (judgment).

_____ 1. Campaigns have trouble getting rid of misinformation about their candidate.

_____ 2. When we reprocess information we may get the information wrong, but we always remember the source.

_____ 3. The Obama campaign should stress that he became a Christian as a young man.

_____ 4. Most of us remember information that matches our view of the world.

_____ 5. When students were told to be objective in evaluating evidence, they continued to reject evidence they disagreed with.

_____ 6. Coke is an effective paint thinner.

_____ 7. True statements should be accepted and false statements rejected.

_____ 8. Justice Holmes was wrong about the power of truth to spread more widely than falsehood.

_____ 9. The more we understand about the way the world works, the better our chances of separating truth from falsehood.

_____ 10. Americans do not seem to understand basic science.

THE SHAPE OF ARGUMENT: WHAT WE CAN LEARN FROM TOULMIN

British philosopher Stephen Toulmin adds to what we have learned from Aristotle by focusing our attention on the basics of the argument itself. First, consider this definition of argument: *An argument consists of evidence and/or reasons presented in support of an assertion or claim that is either stated or implied.* For example:

CLAIM:	We should not go skiing today
GROUNDS:	because it is too cold.
GROUNDS:	Because some laws are unjust,
CLAIM:	civil disobedience is sometimes justified.
GROUNDS:	It's only fair and right for academic institutions to
CLAIM:	accept students only on academic merit.

The parts of an argument, Toulmin asserts, are actually a bit more complex than these examples suggest. Each argument has a third part that is not stated in the preceding examples. This third part is the "glue" that connects the support—the evidence and reasons—to the argument's claim and thus fulfills the logic of the argument. Toulmin calls this glue an argument's *warrants*. These are the principles or assumptions that allow us to assert that our evidence or reasons—what Toulmin calls the *grounds*—do indeed support our claim. (Figure 3.2 illustrates these basics of the Toulmin model of argument.)

CLAIM:	Academic institutions should accept students only on academic merit.
GROUNDS:	It is only fair and right.
WARRANT:	(1) Fair and right are important values. (2) Academic institutions are only about academics.

FIGURE 3.2 **The Toulmin Structure of Argument**

Look again at the sample arguments to see what warrants must be accepted to make each argument work:

CLAIM:	We should not go skiing today.
GROUNDS:	It is too cold.
WARRANTS:	When it is too cold, skiing is not fun; the activity is not sufficient to keep one from becoming uncomfortable. AND: Too cold is what is too cold for me.
CLAIM:	Civil disobedience is sometimes justified.
EVIDENCE:	Some laws are unjust.
WARRANTS:	To get unjust laws changed, people need to be made aware of the injustice. Acts of civil disobedience will get people's attention and make them aware that the laws need changing.
CLAIM:	Academic institutions should accept students only on academic merit.
EVIDENCE:	It is fair and right.
WARRANTS:	Fair and right are important values. AND: Academic institutions are only about academics.

Warrants play an important role in any argument, so we need to be sure to understand what they are. Note, for instance, the second warrant operating in the first argument: The temperature considered uncomfortable for the speaker will also be uncomfortable for her companions—an uncertain assumption. In the second argument, the warrant is less debatable, for acts of civil disobedience usually get media coverage and thus dramatize the issue. The underlying assumptions in the third example stress the need to know one's warrants. Both warrants will need to be defended in the debate over selection by academic merit only.

COLLABORATIVE EXERCISE: Building Arguments

With your class partner or in small groups, examine each of the following claims. Select two, think of one statement that could serve as evidence for each claim, and then think of the underlying assumption(s) that complete each of the arguments.

1.   Professor X is not a good instructor.
2.   Americans need to reduce the fat in their diets.
3.   Tiger Woods is a great golfer.
4.   Military women should be allowed to serve in combat zones.
5.   College newspapers should be free of supervision by faculty or administrators.

Toulmin was particularly interested in the great range or strength or probability of various arguments. Some kinds of arguments are stronger than others because of the language or logic they use. Other arguments must, necessarily, be heavily qualified for the claim to be supportable. Toulmin developed his language to provide a strategy for analyzing the degree of probability in a given argument and to remind us of the need to qualify some kinds of claims. You have already seen how the idea of warrants, or assumptions, helps us think about the "glue" that presumably makes a given argument work. Taken together, Toulmin terms and concepts help us analyze the arguments of others and prepare more convincing arguments of our own.

Claims

A claim is what the argument asserts or seeks to prove. It answers the question "What is your point?" In an argumentative speech or essay, the claim is the speaker's or writer's main idea or thesis. Although an argument's claim "follows" from reasons and evidence, we often present an argument—whether written or spoken—with the claim stated near the beginning of the presentation. We can better understand an argument's claim by recognizing that we can have claims of fact, claims of value, and claims of policy.

Claims of Fact

Although facts usually support claims, we do argue over some facts. Historians and biographers may argue over what happened in the past, although they are more likely to argue over the significance of what happened. Scientists also argue over the facts, over how to classify an unearthed fossil, or whether the fossil indicates that the animal had feathers. For example:

> **CLAIM:**   The small, predatory dinosaur *Deinonychus* hunted its prey in packs.

This claim is supported by the discovery of several fossils of *Deinonychus* close together and with the fossil bones of a much larger dinosaur. Their teeth have also been found in or near the bones of dinosaurs that have died in a struggle.

Assertions about what will happen are sometimes classified as claims of fact, but they can also be labeled as inferences supported by facts. Predictions about a future event may be classified as claims of fact:

> **CLAIM:**   The United States will win the most gold medals at the 2012 Olympics.

> **CLAIM:**   I will get an A on tomorrow's psychology test.

What evidence would you use to support each of these claims? (And, did the first one turn out to be correct?)

Claims of Value

These include moral, ethical, and aesthetic judgments. Assertions that use such words as *good* or *bad, better* or *worse,* and *right* or *wrong* will be claims of value. The following are all claims of value:

> **CLAIM:**   Roger Federer is a better tennis player than Andy Roddick.

> **CLAIM:**   *Adventures of Huckleberry Finn* is one of the most significant American novels.

CLAIM:	Cheating hurts others and the cheater too.
CLAIM:	Abortion is wrong.

Arguments in support of judgments demand relevant evidence, careful reasoning, and an awareness of the assumptions one is making. Support for claims of value often include other value statements. For example, to support the claim that censorship is bad, arguers often assert that the free exchange of ideas is good and necessary in a democracy. The support is itself a value statement.

Claims of Policy

Finally, claims of policy are assertions about what should or should not happen, what the government ought or ought not to do, how to best solve social problems. Claims of policy debate, for example, college rules, state gun laws, or federal aid to Africans suffering from AIDS. The following are claims of policy:

CLAIM:	College newspapers should not be controlled in any way by college authorities.
CLAIM:	States should not have laws allowing people to carry concealed weapons.
CLAIM:	The United States must provide more aid to African countries where 25 percent or more of the citizens have tested positive for HIV.

Claims of policy are often closely tied to judgments of morality or political philosophy, but they also need to be grounded in feasibility. That is, your claim needs to be doable, to be based on a thoughtful consideration of the real world and the complexities of public policy issues.

Grounds (or Data or Evidence)

The term *grounds* refers to the reasons and evidence provided in support of a claim. Although the words *data* and *evidence* can also be used, note that *grounds* is the most general term because it includes reasons or logic as well as examples or statistics. We determine the grounds of an argument by asking the question "Why do you think that?" or "How do you know that?" When writing your own arguments, you can ask yourself these questions and answer by using a *because* clause:

CLAIM:	Smoking should be banned in restaurants because
GROUNDS:	secondhand smoke is a serious health hazard.
CLAIM:	Federer is a better tennis player than Roddick because

GROUNDS:	1. he was ranked number one longer,
	2. he won more tournaments than Roddick, and
	3. he won more major tournaments than Roddick.

Warrants

Why should we believe that your grounds do indeed support your claim? Your argument's warrants answer this question. They explain why your evidence really is evidence. Sometimes warrants reside in language itself, in the meanings of the words we are using. If I am *younger* than my brother, then my brother must be *older* than I am. In a court case attempting to prove that Jones murdered Smith, the relation of evidence to claim is less assured. If the police investigation has been properly managed and the physical evidence is substantial, then Smith may be Jones's murderer. The prosecution has—presumably beyond a reasonable doubt—established motive, means, and opportunity for Smith to commit the murder. In many arguments based on statistical data, the argument's warrant rests on complex analyses of the statistics—and on the conviction that the statistics have been developed without error.

Still, without taking courses in statistics and logic, you can develop an alertness to the "good sense" of some arguments and the "dubious sense" of others. You know, for example, that good SAT scores are a predictor of success in college. Can you argue that you will do well in college because you have good SATs? No. We can determine only a statistical probability. We cannot turn probabilities about a group of people into a warrant about one person in the group. (In addition, SAT scores are only one predictor. Another key variable is motivation.)

What is the warrant for the Federer claim?

CLAIM:	Federer is a better tennis player than Roddick.
GROUNDS:	The three facts listed above.
WARRANT:	It is appropriate to judge and rank tennis players on these kinds of statistics. That is, the better player is one who has held the number-one ranking for the longest time, has won the most tournaments, and also has won the most major tournaments.

Backing

Standing behind an argument's warrant may be additional *backing*. Backing answers the question "How do we know that your evidence is good evidence?" You may answer this question by providing authoritative sources for the data used (for example, the Census Bureau or the U.S. Tennis Association). Or, you may explain in detail the methodology of the experiments performed or the surveys taken. When scientists and social scientists present the results of their research, they anticipate the question of backing and automatically provide a detailed explanation of the process by which they acquired their evidence. In criminal trials, defense attorneys challenge the backing of the prosecution's argument. They question the handling of blood samples sent to labs for DNA testing, for instance. The defense attorneys want jury members to doubt the *quality* of the evidence.

This discussion of backing returns us to the point that one part of any argument is the audience. To create an effective argument, ask yourself: Will my warrants and backing be accepted? Is my audience likely to share my values, religious beliefs, or scientific approach? If you are speaking to a group at your church, then backing based on the religious beliefs of that church may be effective. If you are preparing an argument for a general audience, then using specific religious assertions as warrants or backing probably will not result in an effective argument.

Qualifiers

Some arguments are absolute; they can be stated without qualification. *If I am younger than my brother, then he must be older than I am.* Most arguments need some qualification; many need precise limitations. If, when playing bridge, I am dealt eight spades, then my opponents and partner together must have five spade cards—because there are thirteen cards of each suit in a deck. My partner *probably* has one spade but *could* be void of spades. My partner *possibly* has two or more spades, but I would be foolish to count on it. When bidding my hand, I must be controlled by the laws of probability. Look again at the smoking-ban claim. Observe the absolute nature of both the claim and its support. If secondhand smoke is indeed a health hazard, it will be that in *all* restaurants, not just in some. With each argument ask what qualification is needed for a successful argument.

Sweeping generalizations often come to us in the heat of a debate or when we first start to think about an issue. For example: *Gun control is wrong because it restricts individual rights.* But on reflection surely you would not want to argue against all forms of gun control. (Remember: An unqualified assertion is understood by your audience to be absolute.) Would you sell guns to felons in jail or to children on the way to school? Obviously not. So, let's try the claim again, this time with two important qualifiers:

> **QUALIFIED**   Adults without a criminal record should not be restricted
> in the
>
> **CLAIM:**   purchase of guns.

Others may want this claim further qualified to eliminate particular types of guns or to control the number purchased or the process for purchasing. The gun-control debate is not about absolutes; it is all about which qualified claim is best.

Rebuttals

Arguments can be challenged. Smart debaters assume that there are people who will disagree with them. They anticipate the ways that opponents can challenge their arguments. When you are planning an argument, you need to think about how you can counter or rebut the challenges you anticipate. Think of yourself as an attorney in a court case preparing your argument *and* a defense of the other attorney's challenges to your argument. If you ignore the important role of rebuttals, you may not win the jury to your side.

USING TOULMIN'S TERMS TO ANALYZE ARGUMENTS

Terms are never an end in themselves; we learn them when we recognize that they help us to organize our thinking about a subject. Toulmin's terms can aid your reading of the arguments of others. You can "see what's going on" in an argument if you analyze it, applying Toulmin's language to its parts. Not all terms will be useful for every analysis because, for example, some arguments will not have qualifiers or rebuttals. But to recognize that an argument is *without qualifiers* is to learn something important about that argument.

First, here is a simple argument broken down into its parts using Toulmin's terms:

GROUNDS:	Because Dr. Bradshaw has an attendance policy,
CLAIM:	students who miss more than seven classes will
QUALIFIER:	most likely (last year, Dr. Bradshaw did allow one student, in unusual circumstances, to continue in the class) be dropped from the course.
WARRANT:	Dr. Bradshaw's syllabus explains her attendance policy, a
BACKING:	policy consistent with the concept of a discussion class that depends on student participation and consistent with the attendance policies of most of her colleagues.
REBUTTAL:	Although some students complain about an attendance policy of any kind, Dr. Bradshaw does explain her policy and her reasons for it the first day of class. She then reminds students that the syllabus is a contract between them; if they choose to stay, they agree to abide by the guidelines explained on the syllabus.

This argument is brief and fairly simple. Let's see how Toulmin's terms can help us analyze a longer, more complex argument. Read actively and annotate the following essay while noting the existing annotations using Toulmin's terms. Then answer the questions that follow the article.

THE THREAT TO FREE SPEECH AT UNIVERSITIES | GREG LUKIANOFF

An attorney, Greg Lukianoff holds degrees from American University and Stanford Law School. He is the president of the Foundation for Individual Rights in Education (FIRE), a regular columnist at *Huffington Post,* and the author of *Unlearning Liberty: Campus Censorship and the End of the American Debate* (2012). The following argument was published January 6, 2012.

PREREADING QUESTIONS Are there good reasons to have campus speech codes? Are there problems with speech codes?

Toulmin's Terms

1   Activists embarked on a campaign in the 1980s to eradicate hurtful, bigoted and politically incorrect speech by enacting speech codes at universities across the country. Although the movement presented itself as a forward-thinking way to make campuses welcoming, the initiative stood in stark contrast to the celebrated "free speech movement" of the 1960s, whose proponents understood that vague exceptions to free speech were inevitably used by those in power to punish opinions they dislike or disagree with. And unfortunately the effort gained momentum as prestigious institutions passed speech codes.

Rebutted—universities wrongly motivated

Claim implied in word choice

2   The legal fig leaf upon which the speech-codes movement relied was the concept of "hostile work environment" harassment. Because civil rights laws, chief among them Title IX, banned sexual discrimination on campuses, harassment jurisprudence—sometimes combined with other tenuous rationales—became the primary legal tool universities used to formulate speech codes.

Grounds

3   Courts, however, understood that merely naming a restriction a "harassment" code did not inoculate it from First Amendment scrutiny. In nearly a dozen courtroom losses between 1989 and 2010, harassment-based speech codes have been defeated at campuses from the University of Michigan to Stanford. Amazingly, these defeats have not slowed the spread of these codes. The Foundation for Individual Rights in Education (FIRE), of which I am president, conducts an extensive annual study of campus speech codes; our 2012 report found that 65 percent of nearly 400 top colleges maintain codes that prohibit substantial amounts of clearly protected speech.

4   Overly broad harassment codes remain the weapon of choice on campus to punish speech that administrators dislike. In a decade fighting campus censorship, I have seen harassment defined as expressions as mild as "inappropriately directed laughter" and used to police students for references to a student government candidate as a "jerk and a fool" (at the University of Central Florida in 2006) and a factually verifiable if unflattering piece on Islamic extremism in a conservative student magazine (at Tufts University in 2007). Other examples abound. Worryingly, such broad codes and heavy-handed

Warrant

enforcement are teaching a generation of students that it may be safer to keep their mouths shut when important or controversial issues arise. Such illiberal lessons on how to live in a free society are poison to freewheeling debate and thought experimentation and, therefore, to the innovative thinking that both higher education and our democracy need.

The Education Department's Office for Civil Rights (OCR), which enforces Title IX on college campuses, tried in 2003 to put a stop to the "government made me do it" excuse for speech codes. It issued a letter to every college receiving federal funds—so, virtually all—making clear that harassment requires a serious pattern of discriminatory behavior, not just mere offense. Since then, the number of campus speech codes has slowly begun to decline. *— Grounds (5)*

But last year the OCR backpedaled. The agency issued a 19-page letter in April dictating to colleges the procedures they must follow in sexual harassment and assault cases. Among its many troubling points, including a requirement that sexual harassment cases be adjudicated using the lowest possible standard of evidence allowable in court, is the fact that the letter makes no mention of the First Amendment or free speech. This ignores the role that vague and broad definitions of harassment have played in justifying campus speech codes and censorship over the past few decades. By mandating so many procedural steps colleges must take to respond to allegations of sexual harassment while simultaneously failing to mandate a consistent, limited and constitutional definition of harassment, the OCR encourages those on campus who are already inclined to use such codes to punish speech they simply dislike. *— Rebuttal (6)*

Rather than proffer shifting rules, the OCR should end the threat of harassment-based campus speech codes once and for all. The Supreme Court offered its only guidance on the thorny issue of student-on-student harassment in the 1999 case *Davis v. Monroe County Board of Education.* The justices recognized the necessity of carefully defining what constitutes "harassment" in the educational context, lest everyday interactions be rendered a federal offense. The court defined harassment as discriminatory conduct, directed at an individual, that is "so severe, pervasive, and objectively offensive" that "victim-students are effectively denied equal access to an institution's resources and opportunities." *— Backing, with claim in paragraph 8 (7)*

This definition, if applied fairly, poses little threat to free speech and effectively prohibits real harassment *— (8)*

This week, FIRE and a broad coalition of organizations (the Tully Center for Free Speech at Syracuse University, National Coalition Against Censorship, the Heartland Institute, National Association of Scholars, Alliance Defense Fund Center for Academic Freedom, Feminists for Free Expression, Woodhull Sexual Freedom Alliance, American Booksellers Foundation for Free Expression, Accuracy in Academia, and the American Council of Trustees and Alumni) are writing to the OCR to request that it publicly affirm the *Davis* standard as the controlling definition for harassment on campus. *— Backing-support for claim (9)*

By simply following the Supreme Courts guidance, the OCR would assure that serious harassment is punished on campus while free speech is robustly protected. In one move, OCR could rid campuses of a substantial portion of all speech codes while protecting institutions from losing still more First Amendment lawsuits. Most important, by recognizing the *Davis* standard, the OCR would send a message that free speech and free minds are essential to— not incompatible with—the development of creative, critical and innovative thinkers on our nations campuses. *— Claim restated (10) / Warrant*

Source: *Washington Post*, January 6, 2012. Reprinted by permission of the author.

QUESTIONS FOR READING

1.   What is Lukianoff's subject? (Free speech is not sufficiently precise as an answer.)

2.   What is the legal basis for colleges' speech codes? How has this law been challenged in the past?

3.   Explain the shifting positions of the Office of Civil Rights; what does the author want this office to do now?

QUESTIONS FOR REASONING AND ANALYSIS

4.   What is Lukianoff's claim?

5.   What is his primary support? (Add a "because" clause to his claim to find his grounds.)

6.   Review the author's comments about college authorities—those he holds responsible for speech codes. What, in Lukianoff's view, is their reason for wanting speech codes? Does the author provide evidence for this warrant? Is support needed?

QUESTIONS FOR REFLECTION AND WRITING

7.   Reflect on the author's position that codes let colleges punish views they don't like. Is this the only reason for speech codes? Do you agree that it is the primary motivation of college officials?

8.   Lukianoff asserts that it is possible to punish "serious harassment" on campus without restricting free speech. How should colleges do this? (One student's free speech is often another's perceived insult.) What suggestions do you have for writing clear guidelines for students that will define the author's desired balance?

9.   How can colleges create a sense of community with mutual respect while still embracing the free exchange of ideas?

Toulmin's terms can help you to see what writers are actually "doing" in their arguments. Just remember that writers do not usually follow the terms in precise order. Indeed, you can find both grounds and backing in the same sentence, or claim and qualifiers in the same paragraph, and so on. Still, the terms can help you to sort out your thinking about a claim you want to support. Now use your knowledge of argument as you read and analyze the following arguments.

FOR ANALYSIS AND DEBATE

CHEERING FREE SPEECH | JEFFREY MATEER AND ERIN LEU

Jeff Mateer is General Counsel of Liberty Institute, overseeing the legal team in the organization's commitment to the support of religious liberty. His law degree is from Southern Methodist University, and he is admitted to the bar in Texas. Erin Leu, a graduate of Harvard Law School, was an attorney at Liberty and represented the Kountze cheerleaders. She is now an associate with a law firm in the Dallas area. Their article was published November 5, 2012.

PREREADING QUESTIONS Once you read the opening sentence, can you appreciate the title's clever play with words? What do you expect the essay to be about?

Cheerleaders in Kountze, Tex., recently learned an invaluable lesson about the 1 Constitution and the importance of individual expression without government censorship. Ironically, it's a lesson they had to watch a court teach their school district.

Controversy arose this fall when the cheerleaders at Kountze High School 2 decided to model good sportsmanship by replacing the often-violent messages on their banners, such as "Scalp the Indians," with encouraging religious messages. The only complaints came from an antireligion advocacy group more than 1,000 miles away. In response, the Kountze superintendent issued an unlawful directive banning all such religious speech.

The cheerleaders sued their school district to preserve their rights to free 3 speech and religious expression. Their cause gained international support, from tens of thousands of individuals across six continents. Texas Gov. Rick Perry and state Attorney General Greg Abbott spoke out, applauding the students for standing up for their rights and denouncing government hostility toward religion.

Two weeks ago a Texas court issued a temporary injunction allowing the 4 cheerleaders to display their banners for at least the remainder of the season. Free speech prevailed, reminding us of the well-established principle that students do not shed their constitutional rights to freedom of speech or expression at the schoolhouse gate.

People from all political persuasions should be celebrating this decision. 5 Many are mistakenly arguing, however, that the outcome is incorrect because the Supreme Court struck down school-sponsored prayer at football games in the 2000 case *Santa Fe v. Doe.* But *Santa Fe* recognized that "there is a crucial difference between *government* speech endorsing religion, which the Establishment Clause forbids, and *private* speech endorsing religion, which the Free Speech and Free Exercise Clauses protect."

In *Santa Fe,* the court held that a school policy that created a majoritarian 6 election on religion and explicitly encouraged prayer created government speech. Conversely, in this case, both Texas law and the school's policies affirm that when students speak at school events, including football games, they are engaging in private speech and their views do not reflect the position of the school. Indeed, the policies at issue in *Kountze* create a forum for student speech and require the school district to remain neutral toward all viewpoints. *Santa Fe* involved government speech; Kountze involves private student speech.

The Kountze cheerleaders alone decide what message to place on their 7 banners. The team is student-run, with school officials present only to monitor safety. Each week two cheerleaders take turns leading the team, including choosing whether to create banners and, if so, what messages they should bear. The supplies to create the banners are paid for with private funds, as are the cheerleaders' uniforms, further demonstrating the private nature of their speech.

In *Santa Fe,* the court stated that: "By no means do [the Religion Clauses] 8 impose a prohibition on all religious activity in our public schools. . . . Indeed, the common purpose of the Religion Clauses is to secure religious liberty." When football players or cheerleaders are on the field in uniform, they do not become agents of the state. No one would argue that high school football players are prohibited from praying together. In the same manner, just because cheerleaders wear uniforms and are on school property does not mean that they become instruments of the school or that they must surrender their right to free speech.

9   High school students' rights to free speech should be robustly protected. These students are nearly adults; they are about to enter college, military service or the workforce. Schools should be teaching students about the First Amendment and the free marketplace of ideas, including that other individuals may advocate for messages with which they disagree, instead of censoring speech that some might find offensive. As the Supreme Court has stated: "The vigilant protection of constitutional freedoms is nowhere more vital than in the community of American schools."

10   This is because "[t]he Nation's future depends upon leaders trained through wide exposure to that robust exchange of ideas which discovers truth out of a multitude of tongues, [rather] than through any kind of authoritative selection."

11   We better serve our students by educating them about our country's commitment to free expression rather than shutting out certain views. Otherwise, our schools do a great disservice to students and fail to prepare them to be citizens of our free society.

12   Nonetheless, the character of the Kountze cheerleaders should give us hope for the future. With young adults like these ready to respectfully stand for our Constitution, our freedoms are more secure.

Source: *Washington Post*, November 5, 2012. Reprinted by permission of the authors.

QUESTIONS FOR READING

1. What is the situation that led to this essay? What did the cheerleaders do?
2. What was the court's ruling? The authors write that Texas law has supported the cheerleaders, but is this case closed?

QUESTIONS FOR REASONING AND ANALYSIS

3. What is the authors' claim? What grounds (reasons/evidence) do they provide?
4. Mateer and Leu agree with the court's ruling that football players can pray on the field. They argue that the cheerleaders' religious signs are not the same. How do they defend the similarity?
5. Study the final four paragraphs; what makes them an effective conclusion? How are the authors "defining" the issue in these paragraphs?

QUESTIONS FOR REFLECTION AND WRITING

6. The core of this argument is that the cheerleaders' signs are private speech because they do not represent the school. Do you agree with their position? If you agree, how would you add to their discussion? If you disagree, how would you challenge it?
7. If you were the judge making the final ruling on this case, how would you rule? Why?

HOW CAN WE BAN INSULTS AGAINST JEWS BUT NOT MUSLIMS?

WILLIAM SALETAN

A graduate of Swarthmore College, William Saletan writes about science, technology, and politics for the online magazine *Slate*. He has published several books, including *Bearing Right: How Conservatives Won the Abortion War* (2004). The following article was posted September 28, 2012.

PREREADING QUESTIONS Does your college have rules against hate speech? Are such rules consistent with First Amendment rights?

How can we ban hate speech against Jews while defending mockery of 1 Muslims? Jews have too much influence over U.S. foreign policy. Gay men are too promiscuous. Muslims commit too much terrorism. Blacks commit too much crime.

Each of those claims is poorly stated. Each, in its clumsy way, addresses a 2 real problem or concern. And each violates laws against hate speech. In much of what we call the free world, for writing that paragraph, I could be jailed.

Libertarians, cultural conservatives, and racists have complained about 3 these laws for years. But now the problem has turned global. Islamic governments, angered by an anti-Muslim video that provoked protests and riots in their countries, are demanding to know why insulting the Prophet Mohammed is free speech but vilifying Jews and denying the Holocaust isn't. And we don't have a good answer.

If we're going to preach freedom of expression around the world, we have 4 to practice it. We have to scrap our hate-speech laws.

Muslim leaders want us to extend these laws. At this week's meeting of the 5 U.N. General Assembly, they lobbied for tighter censorship. Egypt's president said freedom of expression shouldn't include speech that is "used to incite hatred" or "directed towards one specific religion." Pakistan's president urged the "international community" to "criminalize" acts that "endanger world security by misusing freedom of expression." Yemen's president called for "international legislation" to suppress speech that "blasphemes the beliefs of nations and defames their figures." The Arab League's secretary-general proposed a binding "international legal framework" to "criminalize psychological and spiritual harm" caused by expressions that "insult the beliefs, culture and civilization of others."

President Obama, while condemning the video, met these proposals with 6 a stout defense of free speech. Switzerland's president agreed: "Freedom of opinion and of expression are core values guaranteed universally which must be protected." And when a French magazine published cartoons poking fun at Mohammed, the country's prime minister insisted that French laws protecting free speech extend to caricatures.

This debate between East and West, between respect and pluralism, isn't 7 a crisis. It's a stage of global progress. The Arab spring has freed hundreds of millions of Muslims from the political retardation of dictatorship. They're taking responsibility for governing themselves and their relations with other countries. They're debating one another and challenging us. And they should, because we're hypocrites.

Pakistani activists of the hard line Sunni party Jamaat-e-Islami (JI) burn a U.S. flag during a protest against an anti-Islam movie in Peshawar on September 18, 2012. Police used tear gas to disperse a crowd of more than 2,000 protesters trying to reach the US consulate in northwest Pakistan as fresh demonstrations erupted against an anti-Islam film.

8   From Pakistan to Iran to Saudi Arabia to Egypt to Nigeria to the United Kingdom, Muslims scoff at our rhetoric about free speech. They point to European laws against questioning the Holocaust. Monday on CNN, Iranian President Mahmoud Ahmedinejad needled British interviewer Piers Morgan: "Why in Europe has it been forbidden for anyone to conduct any research about this event? Why are researchers in prison? . . . Do you believe in the freedom of thought and ideas, or no?" On Tuesday, Pakistan's U.N. ambassador, speaking for the Organization of Islamic Cooperation, told the U.N. Human Rights Council:

9   We are all aware of the fact that laws exist in Europe and other countries which impose curbs, for instance, on anti-Semitic speech, Holocaust denial, or racial slurs. We need to acknowledge, once and for all, that Islamophobia in particular and discrimination on the basis of religion and belief are contemporary forms of racism and must be dealt with as such. Not to do so would be a clear example of double standards. Islamophobia has to be treated in law and practice equal to the treatment given to anti-Semitism.

10   He's right. Laws throughout Europe forbid any expression that "minimizes," "trivializes," "belittles," "plays down," "contests," or "puts in doubt" Nazi crimes. Hungary, Poland, and the Czech Republic extend this prohibition to communist atrocities. These laws carry jail sentences of up to five years. Germany adds two years for anyone who "disparages the memory of a deceased person."

Hate speech laws go further. Germany punishes anyone found guilty of 11 "insulting" or "defaming segments of the population." The Netherlands bans anything that "verbally or in writing or image, deliberately offends a group of people because of their race, their religion or beliefs, their hetero- or homo-sexual orientation or their physical, psychological or mental handicap." It's illegal to "insult" such a group in France, to "defame" them in Portugal, to "degrade" them in Denmark, or to "expresses contempt" for them in Sweden. In Switzerland, it's illegal to "demean" them even with a "gesture." Canada punishes anyone who "willfully promotes hatred." The United Kingdom outlaws "insulting words or behavior" that arouse "racial hatred." Romania forbids the possession of xenophobic "symbols."

What have these laws produced? Look at the convictions upheld or accepted 12 by the European Court of Human Rights. Four Swedes who distributed leaflets that called homosexuality "deviant" and "morally destructive" and blamed it for AIDS. An Englishman who displayed in his window a 9/11 poster proclaiming, "Islam out of Britain." A Turk who published two letters from readers angry at the government's treatment of Kurds. A Frenchman who wrote an article disputing the plausibility of poison gas technology at a Nazi concentration camp.

Look at the defendants rescued by the court. A Dane "convicted of aiding 13 and abetting the dissemination of racist remarks" for making a documentary in which three people "made abusive and derogatory remarks about immigrants and ethnic groups." A man "convicted of openly inciting the population to hatred" in Turkey by "criticizing secular and democratic principles and openly calling for the introduction of Sharia law." Another Turkish resident "convicted of disseminating propaganda" after he "criticized the United States' intervention in Iraq and the solitary confinement of the leader of a terrorist organization." Two Frenchmen who wrote a newspaper article that "portrayed Marshal Pétain in a favorable light, drawing a veil over his policy of collaboration with the Nazi regime."

Beyond the court's docket, you'll find more prosecutions of dissent. A 14 Swedish pastor convicted of violating hate-speech laws by preaching against homosexuality. A Serb convicted of discrimination for saying, "We are against every gathering where homosexuals are demonstrating in the streets of Belgrade and want to show something, which is a disease, like it is normal." An Australian columnist convicted of violating the Racial Discrimination Act by suggesting that "there are fair-skinned people in Australia with essentially European ancestry . . . who, motivated by career opportunities available to Aboriginal people or by political activism, have chosen to falsely identify as Aboriginal."

My favorite case involves a Frenchman who sought free-speech protection 15 under Article 10 of the European Convention on Human Rights:

Denis Leroy is a cartoonist. One of his drawings representing the attack on 16 the World Trade Centre was published in a Basque weekly newspaper . . . with a caption which read: "We have all dreamt of it . . . Hamas did it." Having been sentenced to payment of a fine for "condoning terrorism," Mr Leroy argued that his freedom of expression had been infringed.

The Court considered that, through his work, the applicant had glorified the 17 violent destruction of American imperialism, expressed moral support for the perpetrators of the attacks of 11 September, commented approvingly on the violence perpetrated against thousands of civilians and diminished the dignity of the victims. Despite the newspaper's limited circulation, the Court observed that the drawing's publication had provoked a certain public reaction, capable of stirring up violence and of having a demonstrable impact on public order in the Basque Country. The Court held that there had been no violation of Article 10.

18   How can you justify prosecuting cases like these while defending cartoonists and video makers who ridicule Mohammed? You can't. Either you censor both, or you censor neither. Given the choice, I'll stand with Obama. "Efforts to restrict speech," he warned the U. N., "can quickly become a tool to silence critics and oppress minorities."

19   That principle, borne out by the wretched record of hate-speech prosecutions, is worth defending. But first, we have to live up to it.

QUESTIONS FOR READING

1. What event has led to Saletan's article?
2. Which groups/countries want to extend hate speech laws? Which countries have defended free speech?
3. What is the Muslim world's view of the West's "commitment" to free speech?

QUESTIONS FOR REASONING AND ANALYSIS

4. What is Saletan's claim? (Be precise; he isn't just taking a position on hate speech laws.)
5. What evidence does the author provide? What is especially significant about the ruling on the cartoonist Leroy?
6. Examine Saletan's opening paragraphs; what makes his opening effective?

QUESTIONS FOR REFLECTION AND WRITING

7. Were you aware of the extent of hate speech laws in the West? Are you surprised? Should you be more surprised by the inconsistency in rulings? Reflect on these questions.
8. Has Saletan convinced you that we do not practice what we preach? Why or why not? If you disagree, how would you refute Saletan?
9. Is it possible to understand hate speech restrictions in Western Europe relative to the Holocaust? Is it possible to understand and still oppose prosecution of someone who wants to argue that there was no Holocaust? Is it possible to legislate against ignorance or stupidity? Reflect on these questions.

1. Compare the style and tone of Mateer/Leu's and Saletan's essays. Has each one written in a way that works for the author's approach to this issue? Be prepared to explain your views or develop them into a comparative analysis of style.

2. Reread and study the essay "Your Brain Lies to You" (pp. 79–80) and then analyze the argument's parts, using Toulmin's terms.

GOING ONLINE

Another issue on college campuses is student drinking. Should colleges find ways to crack down on underage student alcohol use and binge drinking? You may be able to offer some answers to this question based on your knowledge and experience. You may also want to go online for some statistics about college drinking and health and safety risks. Drawing on both experience and data, what claim can you support?

CHAPTER 4

Writing Effective Arguments

READ: Who are the figures in the painting? What are they doing?

REASON: What details in the painting help to date the scene?

REFLECT/WRITE: What is significant about the moment captured in this painting?

The basics of good writing remain much the same for works as seemingly different as the personal essay, the argument, and the researched essay. Good writing is focused, organized, and concrete. Effective essays are written in a style and tone that are suited to both the audience and the writer's purpose. These are sound principles, all well known to you. But how, exactly, do you achieve them when writing argument? This chapter will help you answer that question.

KNOW YOUR AUDIENCE

Too often students plunge into writing without thinking much about audience, for, after all, their "audience" is only the instructor who has given the assignment, and their purpose is to complete the assignment and get a grade. These views of audience and purpose are likely to lead to badly written arguments. First, if you are not thinking about readers who may disagree with you, you may not develop the best defense of your claim. Second, you may ignore your essay's needed introductory material on the assumption that the instructor, knowing the assignment, has a context for understanding your writing. To avoid these pitfalls, use the following questions to sharpen your understanding of audience.

Who Is My Audience?

If you are writing an essay for the student newspaper, your audience consists—primarily—of students, but do not forget that faculty and administrators also read the student newspaper. If you are preparing a letter-to-the-editor refutation of a recent column in your town's newspaper, your audience will be the readers of that newspaper—that is, adults in your town. Some instructors give assignments that create an audience such as those just described so that you will practice writing with a specific audience in mind.

If you are not assigned a specific audience, imagine your classmates, as well as your instructor, as part of your audience. In other words, you are writing to readers in the academic community. These readers are intelligent and thoughtful, expecting sound reasoning and convincing evidence. From diverse cultures and experiences, these readers also represent varied values and beliefs. Do not confuse the shared expectations of writing conventions with shared beliefs.

What Will My Audience Know about My Topic?

What can you expect a diverse group of readers to know? Whether you are writing on a current issue or a centuries-old debate, you must expect most readers to have some knowledge of the issues. Their knowledge does not free you from the responsibility of developing your support fully, though. In fact, their knowledge creates further demands. For example, most readers know the main arguments on both sides of the abortion issue. For you to write as if they do not—and thus to ignore the arguments of the opposition—is to produce an argument that probably adds little to the debate on the subject.

On the other hand, what some readers "know" may be little more than an overview of the issues from TV news—or the emotional outbursts of a family member. Some readers may be misinformed or prejudiced, but they embrace their views enthusiastically nonetheless. So, as you think about the ways to develop and support your argument, you will have to assess your readers' knowledge and sophistication. This assessment will help you decide how much background information to provide or what false facts need to be revealed and dismissed.

Where Does My Audience Stand on the Issue?

Expect readers to hold a range of views, even if you are writing to students on your campus or to an organization of which you are a member. It is not true, for instance, that all students want coed dorms or pass/fail grading. And, if everyone already agrees with you, you have no reason to write. An argument needs to be about a topic that is open to debate. So:

- Assume that some of your audience will probably never agree with you but may offer you grudging respect if you compose an effective argument.
- Assume that some readers do not hold strong views on your topic and may be open to convincing, if you present a good case.
- Assume that those who share your views will still be looking for a strong argument in support of their position.
- Assume that if you hold an unpopular position your best strategy will be a conciliatory approach. (See p. 103 for a discussion of the conciliatory argument.)

How Should I Speak to My Audience?

Your audience will form an opinion of you based on how you write and how you reason. The image of argument—and the arguer—that we have been creating in this text's discussion is of thoughtful claims defended with logic and evidence. However, the heated debate at yesterday's lunch does not resemble this image of argument. Sometimes the word *persuasion* is used to separate the emotionally charged debate from the calm, intellectual tone of the academic argument. Unfortunately, this neat division between argument and persuasion does not describe the real world of debate. The thoughtful arguer also wants to be persuasive, and highly emotional presentations can contain relevant facts in support of a sound idea. Instead of thinking of two separate categories—argument and persuasion—think instead of a continuum from the most rigorous logic to extreme flights of fantasy. Figure 4.1 suggests this continuum with some kinds of arguments placed along it.

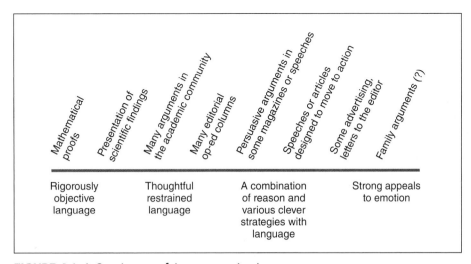

FIGURE 4.1 A Continuum of Argumentative Language

Where should you place yourself along this continuum of language? You will have to answer this question with each specific writing context. Much of the time you will choose "thoughtful, restrained language" as expected by the academic community, but there may be times that you will use various persuasive strategies. Probably you will not select "strong appeals to emotion" for your college or workplace writing. Remember that you have different roles in your life, and you use different *voices* as appropriate to each role. Most of the time, you will want to use the serious voice you normally select for serious conversations with other adults. This is the voice that will help you establish your credibility, your *ethos.*

As you learned in Chapter 2, irony is a useful rhetorical strategy for giving one's words greater emphasis by actually writing the opposite of what you mean. Many writers use irony effectively. Irony catches our attention, makes us think, and engages us with the text. Sarcasm is not quite the same as irony. Irony can cleverly focus on life's complexities. Sarcasm is more often vicious than insightful, relying on harsh, negative word choice. Probably in most of your academic work, you will want to avoid sarcasm and think carefully about using any strongly worded appeal to your readers' emotions. Better to persuade your audience with the force of your reasons and evidence than to lose them because of the static of nasty language. But the key, always, is to know your audience and understand how best to present a convincing argument to that specific group.

UNDERSTAND YOUR WRITING PURPOSE

There are many types or genres of argument and different reasons for writing—beyond wanting to write convincingly in defense of your views. Different types of arguments require different approaches, or different kinds of evidence. It helps to be able to recognize the kind of argument you are contemplating.

What Type (Genre) of Argument Am I Preparing?

Here are some useful ways to classify arguments and think about their support.

- **Investigative paper similar to those in the social sciences.** If you are asked to collect evidence in an organized way to support a claim about advertising strategies or violence in children's TV programming, then you will be writing an investigative essay. You will present evidence that you have gathered and analyzed to support your claim.

- **Evaluation.** If your assignment is to explain why others should read a particular book or take a particular professor's class, then you will be preparing an evaluation argument. Be sure to think about your criteria: What makes a book or a professor good? Why do you dislike Lady Gaga? Is it her music—or her lifestyle?

- **Definition.** If you are asked to explain the meaning of a general or controversial term, you will be writing a definition argument. What do we mean by *wisdom*? What are the characteristics of *cool*? A definition argument usually requires both specific details to illustrate the term and general ideas to express its meaning.

- **Claim of values.** If you are given the assignment to argue for your position on euthanasia, trying juveniles as adults, or the use of national identification cards, recognize that your assignment calls for a position paper, a claim based heavily on values. Pay close attention to your warrants or assumptions in any philosophical debate.

- **Claim of policy.** If you are given a broad topic: "What should we do about _____?" and you have to fill in the blank, your task is to offer solutions to a current problem. What should we do about childhood obesity? About home foreclosures? These kinds of questions are less philosophical and more practical. Your solutions must be workable.

- **Refutation or rebuttal.** If you are given the assignment to find a letter to the editor, a newspaper editorial, or an essay in this text with which you disagree, your job is to write a refutation essay, a specific challenge to a specific argument. You know, then, that you will repeatedly refer to the work you are rebutting, so you will need to know it thoroughly.

What Is My Goal?

It is also helpful to consider your goal in writing. Does your topic call for a strong statement of views (i.e., "These are the steps we must take to reduce childhood obesity")? Or, is your goal an exploratory one, a thinking through of possible answers to a more philosophical question ("Why is it often difficult to separate performance from personality when we evaluate a star?")? Thinking about your goal as well as the argument's genre will help to decide on the kinds of evidence needed and on the approach to take and tone to select.

Will the Rogerian or Conciliatory Approach Work for Me?

Psychologist Carl Rogers asserts that the most successful arguments take a conciliatory approach. The characteristics of this approach include

- showing respect for the opposition in the language and tone of the argument,
- seeking common ground by indicating specific facts and values that both sides share, and
- qualifying the claim to bring opposing sides more closely together.

In their essay "Euthanasia—A Critique," authors Peter A. Singer and Mark Siegler provide a good example of a conciliatory approach. They begin their essay by explaining and then rebutting the two main arguments in favor of euthanasia. After stating the two arguments in clear and neutral language, they write this in response to the first argument:

> We agree that the relief of pain and suffering is a crucial goal of medicine. We question, however, whether the care of dying patients cannot be improved without resorting to the drastic measure of euthanasia. Most physical pain can be relieved with the appropriate use of analgesic agents. Unfortunately, despite widespread agreement that dying patients must be provided with necessary analgesia, physicians continue to underuse analgesia in the care of dying patients because of the concern about depressing respiratory drive or creating addiction. Such situations demand better management of pain, not euthanasia.

In this paragraph the authors accept the value of pain management for dying patients. They go even further and offer a solution to the problem of suffering among the terminally ill—better pain management by doctors. They remain thoughtful in their approach and tone throughout, while sticking to their position that legalizing euthanasia is not the solution.

Consider how you can use the conciliatory approach to write more effective arguments. It will help you avoid "overheated" language and maintain your focus on what is doable in a world of differing points of view. There is the expression that "you can catch more flies with honey than with vinegar." Using "honey" instead of "vinegar" might also make you feel better about yourself.

MOVE FROM TOPIC TO CLAIM TO POSSIBLE SUPPORT

When you write a letter to the editor of a newspaper, you have chosen to respond to someone else's argument that has bothered you. In this writing context, you already know your topic and, probably, your claim as well. You also know that your purpose will be to refute the article you have read. In composition classes, the context is not always so clearly established, but you will usually be given some guidelines with which to get started.

Selecting a Topic

Suppose that you are asked to write an argument that is in some way connected to First Amendment rights. Your instructor has limited and focused your topic choice and purpose. Start thinking about possible topics that relate to freedom of speech and censorship issues. To aid your topic search and selection, use one or more invention strategies:

- Brainstorm (make a list).
- Freewrite (write without stopping for ten minutes).
- Map or cluster (connect ideas to the general topic in various spokes, a kind of visual brainstorming).
- Read through this text for ideas.

Your invention strategies lead, let us suppose, to the following list of possible topics:

> Administrative restrictions on the college newspaper
> Hate speech restrictions or codes
> Deleting certain books from high school reading lists
> Controls and limits on alcohol and cigarette advertising
> Restrictions on violent TV programming
> Dress codes/uniforms

Looking over your list, you realize that the last item, dress codes/uniforms, may be about freedom but not freedom of speech, so you drop it from consideration. All of the other topics have promise. Which one do you select? Two considerations should guide you: interest and knowledge. First, your argument is likely to be more thoughtful and lively if you choose an issue that matters to you. But, unless you have time for study, you are wise to choose a topic about which you already have some information and ideas. Suppose that you decide to write about television violence because you are concerned about violence in American society and have given this issue some thought. It is time to phrase your topic as a tentative thesis or claim.

Drafting a Claim

Good claim statements will keep you focused in your writing—in addition to establishing your main idea for readers. Give thought both to your position on the issue and to the wording of your claim. *Claim statements to avoid:*

- Claims using vague words such as *good* or *bad.*

VAGUE:	TV violence is bad for us.
BETTER:	We need more restrictions on violent TV programming.

- Claims in loosely worded "two-part" sentences.

UNFOCUSED:	Campus rape is a serious problem, and we need to do something about it.

BETTER:	College administrators and students need to work together to reduce both the number of campus rapes and the fear of rape.

- Claims that are not appropriately qualified.

OVERSTATED:	Violence on television is making us a violent society.
BETTER:	TV violence is contributing to viewers' increased fear of violence and insensitivity to violence.

- Claims that do not help you focus on your purpose in writing.

UNCLEAR PURPOSE:	Not everyone agrees on what is meant by violent TV programming.

(Perhaps this is true, but more important, this claim suggests that you will define violent programming. Such an approach would not keep you focused on a First Amendment issue.)

BETTER:	Restrictions on violent TV programs can be justified.

(Now your claim directs you to the debate over restrictions of content.)

Listing Possible Grounds

As you learned in Chapter 3, you can generate grounds to support a claim by adding a "because" clause after a claim statement. We can start a list of grounds for the topic on violent TV programming in this way:

We need more restrictions on violent television programming *because*

- Many people, including children and teens, watch many hours of TV (get stats).
- People are affected by the dominant activities/experiences in their lives.
- There is a connection between violent programming and desensitizing and fear of violence and possibly more aggressive behavior in heavy viewers (get detail of studies).
- Society needs to protect young people.

You have four good points to work on, a combination of reasons and inferences drawn from evidence.

Listing Grounds for the Other Side or Another Perspective

Remember that arguments generate counterarguments. Continue your exploration of this topic by considering possible rebuttals to your proposed grounds. How might someone who does not want to see restrictions placed on television programming respond to each of your points? Let's think about them one at a time:

We need more restrictions on violent television programming because

1. *Many people, including children and teens, watch many hours of TV.*

Your opposition cannot really challenge your first point on the facts, only its relevance to restricting programming. The opposition might argue that if parents think their children are watching too much TV, they should turn it off. The restriction needs to be a family decision.

2. *People are affected by the dominant activities/experiences in their lives.*

It seems common sense to expect people to be influenced by dominant forces in their lives. Your opposition might argue, though, that many people have the TV on for many hours but often are not watching it intently for all of that time. The more dominant forces in our lives are parents and teachers and peers, not the TV. The opposition might also argue that people seem to be influenced to such different degrees by television that it is not fair or logical to restrict everyone when perhaps only a few are truly influenced by their TV viewing to a harmful degree.

3. *There is a connection between violent programming and desensitizing and fear of violence and possibly more aggressive behavior in heavy viewers.*

Some people are entirely convinced by studies showing these negative effects of violent TV programming, but others point to the less convincing studies or make the argument that if violence on TV were really so powerful an influence, most people would be violent or fearful or desensitized.

4. *Society needs to protect young people.*

Your opposition might choose to agree with you in theory on this point—and then turn again to the argument that parents should be doing the protecting. Government controls on programming restrict adults, as well as children, whereas it may only be some children who should watch fewer hours of TV and not watch adult "cop" shows at all.

Working through this process of considering opposing views can help you see

- where you may want to do some research for facts to provide backing for your grounds,
- how you can best develop your reasons to take account of typical counter-arguments, and
- if you should qualify your claim in some ways.

Planning Your Approach

Now that you have thought about arguments on the other side, you decide that you want to argue for a qualified claim that is also more precise:

> To protect young viewers, we need restrictions on violence in children's programs and ratings for prime-time adult shows that clearly establish the degree of violence in those shows.

This qualified claim responds to two points of the rebuttals. Our student hasn't given in to the other side but has chosen to narrow the argument to emphasize the protection of children, an area of common ground.

Next, it's time to check some of the articles in this text or go online to get some data to develop points 1 and 3. You need to know that 99 percent of homes have at least one TV; you need to know that by the time young people graduate from high school, they have spent more time in front of the TV than in the classroom. Also, you can find the average number of violent acts by hour of TV in children's programs. Then, too, there are the various studies of fearfulness and aggressive behavior that will give you some statistics to use to develop the third point. Be sure to select reliable sources and then cite the sources you use. *Citing sources is not only required and right; it is also part of the process of establishing your credibility and thus strengthening your argument.*

Finally, how are you going to answer the point about parents controlling their children? You might counter that in theory this is the way it should be—but in fact not all parents are at home watching what their children are watching, and not all parents care enough to pay attention. However, all of us suffer from the consequences of those children who are influenced by their TV watching to become more aggressive or fearful or desensitized. These children grow up to become the adults the rest of us have to interact with, so the problem becomes one for the society as a whole to solve. If you had not disciplined yourself to go through the process of listing possible rebuttals, you may not have thought through this part of the debate.

DRAFT YOUR ARGUMENT

Many of us can benefit from a step-by-step process of invention—such as we have been exploring in the last few pages. In addition, the more notes you have from working through the Toulmin structure, the easier it will be to get started on your draft. Students report that they can control their writing anxiety when they generate detailed notes. A page of notes that also suggests an organizational strategy can remove that awful feeling of staring at a blank computer screen.

In the following chapters on argument, you will find specific suggestions for organizing the various kinds of arguments. But you can always rely on one of these two basic organizations, regardless of the specific genre:

PLAN 1: ORGANIZING AN ARGUMENT

Attention-getting opening (why the issue is important, or current, etc.)

Claim statement

Reasons and evidence in order from least important to most important

Challenge to potential rebuttals or counterarguments

Conclusion that reemphasizes claim

PLAN 2: ORGANIZING AN ARGUMENT

Attention-getting opening

Claim statement (or possibly leave to the conclusion)

Order by arguments of opposing position, with your challenge to each

Conclusion that reemphasizes (or states for the first time) your claim

GUIDELINES for Drafting

- **Try to get a complete draft in one sitting so that you can "see" the whole piece.**
- **If you can't think of a clever opening, state your claim and move on to the body of your essay.** After you draft your reasons and evidence, a good opening may occur to you.
- **If you find that you need something more in some parts of your essay, leave space there as a reminder that you will need to return to that paragraph later.**
- **Try to avoid using either a dictionary or thesaurus while drafting.** Your goal is to get the ideas down. You will polish later.
- **Learn to draft at your computer.** Revising is so much easier that you will be more willing to make significant changes if you work at your PC. If you are handwriting your draft, leave plenty of margin space for additions or for directions to shift parts around.

REVISE YOUR DRAFT

If you have drafted at the computer, begin revising by printing a copy of your draft. Most of us cannot do an adequate job of revision by looking at a computer screen. Then remind yourself that revision is a three-step process: rewriting, editing, and proofreading.

Rewriting

You are not ready to polish the writing until you are satisfied with the argument. Look first at the total piece. Do you have all the necessary parts: a claim, support, some response to possible counterarguments? Examine the order of your reasons and evidence. Do some of your points belong, logically, in a different place? Does the order make the most powerful defense of your claim? Be willing to move whole paragraphs around to test the best organization. Also reflect on the argument itself. Have you avoided logical fallacies? Have you qualified statements when appropriate? Do you have enough support? The best support?

Consider development: Is your essay long enough to meet assignment requirements? Are points fully developed to satisfy the demands of readers? One key to development is the length of your paragraphs. If most of your paragraphs are only two or three sentences, you have not developed the point of each paragraph satisfactorily. It is possible that some paragraphs need to be combined because they are really on the same topic. More typically, short paragraphs need further explanation of ideas or examples to illustrate ideas. Compare the following paragraphs for effectiveness:

First Draft of a Paragraph from an Essay on Gun Control

One popular argument used against the regulation of gun ownership is the need of citizens, especially in urban areas where the crime rate is higher, to possess a handgun for personal protection, either carried or kept in the home. Some citizens may not be aware of the dangers to themselves or their families when they purchase a gun. Others, more aware, may embrace the myth that "bad things only happen to other people."

Revised Version of the Paragraph with Statistics Added

One popular argument used against the regulation of gun ownership is the need of citizens, especially in urban areas where the crime rate is higher, to possess a handgun for personal protection, whether it is carried or kept in the home. Although some citizens may not be aware of the dangers to themselves or their families when they purchase a gun, they should be. According to the Center to Prevent Handgun Violence, from their web page "Firearm Facts," "guns that are kept in the home for self-protection are 22 times more likely to kill a family member or friend than to kill in self-defense." The Center also reports that guns in the home make homicide three times more likely and suicide five times more likely. We are not thinking straight if we believe that these dangers apply only to others.

A quick trip to the Internet has provided this student with some facts to support his argument. Observe how he has referred informally but fully to the source of his information. (If your instructor requires formal MLA documentation in all essays, then you will need to add a Works Cited page and give a full reference to the website. See pp. 318–329.)

Editing

Make your changes, print another copy, and begin the second phase of revision: editing. As you read through this time, pay close attention to unity and coherence, to sentence patterns, and to word choice. Read each paragraph as a separate unit to be certain that everything is on the same subtopic. Then look at your use of transition and connecting words, both within and between paragraphs. Ask yourself: Have you guided the reader through the argument using appropriate connectors such as *therefore, in addition, as a consequence, also,* and so forth?

Read again, focusing on each sentence, checking to see that you have varied sentence patterns and length. Read sentences aloud to let your ear help you find awkward constructions or unfinished thoughts. Strive as well for word choice that is concrete and specific, avoiding wordiness, clichés, trite expressions, or incorrect use of specialized terms. Observe how Samantha edited one paragraph in her essay "Balancing Work and Family":

Draft Version of Paragraph   ?   agr

Women have come a long way in equalizing themselves, but inequality within marriages do exist. One reason for this can be found in the media. Just last week America turned on their televisions to watch a grotesque dramatization of skewed priorities. On *Who Wants to Marry a Millionaire,* a panel of

Vague reference.

Wordy.

Short sentences.

Vague reference.

women vied for the affections of a millionaire who would choose one of them to be his wife. This show said that women can be purchased. Also that men must provide and that money is worth the sacrifice of one's individuality. The show also suggests that physical attraction is more important than the building of a complete relationship. Finally, the show says that women's true value lies in their appearance. This is a dangerous message to send to both men and women viewers.

Edited Version of Paragraph

Although women have come a long way toward equality in the workplace, inequality within marriages can still be found. The media may be partly to blame for this continued inequality. Just last week Americans watched a grotesque dramatization of skewed priorities. On *Who Wants to Marry a Millionaire*, a panel of women vied for the affections of a millionaire who would choose one of them to be his wife. Such displays teach us that women can be purchased, that men must be the providers, that the desire for money is worth the sacrifice of one's individuality, that physical attraction is more important than a complete relationship, and that women's true value lies in their appearance. These messages discourage marriages based on equality and mutual support.

Samantha's editing has eliminated wordiness and vague references and has combined ideas into one forceful sentence. Support your good argument by taking the time to polish your writing.

A Few Words about Words and Tone

You have just been advised to check your word choice to eliminate wordiness, vagueness, clichés, and so on. Here is a specific checklist of problems often found in student papers with some ways to fix the problems:

- *Eliminate clichés.* Do not write about "the fast-paced world we live in today" or the "rat race." First, do you know for sure that the pace of life for someone who has a demanding job is any faster than it was in the past? Using time effectively has always mattered. Also, clichés suggest that you are too lazy to find your own words.
- *Avoid jargon.* In the negative sense of this word, *jargon* refers to nonspecialists who fill their writing with "heavy-sounding terms" to give the appearance of significance. Watch for any overuse of "scientific" terms such as *factor* or *aspect,* or other vague, awkward language.
- *Avoid language that is too informal for most of your writing contexts.* What do you mean when you write: "*Kids* today watch too much TV"? Alternatives include *children, teens, adolescents.* These words are less slangy and more precise.
- *Avoid nasty attacks on the opposition.* Change "those jerks who are foolish enough to believe that TV violence has no impact on children" to language that explains your counterargument without attacking those who

may disagree with you. After all, you want to change the thinking of your audience, not make them resent you for name-calling.

- *Avoid all discriminatory language.* In the academic community and the adult workplace, most people are bothered by language that belittles any one group. This includes language that is racist or sexist or reflects negatively on older or disabled persons or those who do not share your sexual orientation or religious beliefs. Just don't do it!

Proofreading

You also do not want to lose the respect of readers because you submit a paper filled with "little" errors—errors in punctuation, mechanics, and incorrect word choice. Most readers will forgive one or two little errors but will become annoyed if they begin to pile up. So, after you are finished rewriting and editing, print a copy of your paper and read it slowly, looking specifically at punctuation, at the handling of quotations and references to writers and to titles, and at those pesky words that come in two or more "versions": *to, too,* and *two; here* and *hear; their, there,* and *they're;* and so forth. If instructors have found any of these kinds of errors in your papers over the years, then focus your attention on the kinds of errors you have been known to make.

Refer to Chapter 1 for handling references to authors and titles and for handling direct quotations. Use a glossary of usage in a handbook for homonyms (words that sound alike but have different meanings), and check a handbook for punctuation rules. Take pride in your work and present a paper that will be treated with respect. What follows is a checklist of the key points for writing good arguments that we have just examined.

A CHECKLIST FOR REVISION ▪▪▪▪▪▪▪▪▪▪▪▪▪▪▪▪▪▪▪▪▪▪▪▪▪▪▪▪

- ☐ Have I selected an issue and purpose consistent with assignment guidelines?
- ☐ Have I stated a claim that is focused, appropriately qualified, and precise?
- ☐ Have I developed sound reasons and evidence in support of my claim?
- ☐ Have I used Toulmin's terms to help me study the parts of my argument, including rebuttals to counterarguments?
- ☐ Have I taken advantage of a conciliatory approach and emphasized common ground with opponents?
- ☐ Have I found a clear and effective organization for presenting my argument?
- ☐ Have I edited my draft thoughtfully, concentrating on producing unified and coherent paragraphs and polished sentences?
- ☐ Have I eliminated wordiness, clichés, jargon?
- ☐ Have I selected an appropriate tone for my purpose and audience?
- ☐ Have I used my word processor's spell-check and proofread a printed copy with great care? ▪▪▪▪▪▪▪▪▪▪▪▪▪▪▪▪▪▪▪▪▪▪▪▪▪▪▪▪

FOR ANALYSIS AND DEBATE

FIVE MYTHS ABOUT TORTURE AND TRUTH | DARIUS REJALI

A professor of political science at Reed College, Iranian-born Darius Rejali is a recognized expert on the causes and meaning of violence, especially on torture, in our world. His book *Torture and Democracy* (2007) has won acclaim and resulted in frequent interview sessions for Rejali. His latest book is *Spirituality and the Ethics of Torture* (2009). The following essay appeared on December 16, 2007, in the *Washington Post*.

PREREADING QUESTIONS Can you think of five myths about torture? What do you expect Rejali to cover in this essay?

1   *So the CIA did indeed torture Abu Zubaida, the first al-Qaeda terrorist suspect to have been waterboarded. So says John Kiriakou, the first former CIA employee directly involved in the questioning of "high-value" al-Qaeda detainees to speak out publicly. He minced no words last week in calling the CIA's "enhanced interrogation techniques" what they are.*

2   *But did they work? Torture's defenders, including the wannabe tough guys who write Fox's "24," insist that the rough stuff gets results. "It was like flipping a switch," said Kiriakou about Abu Zubaida's response to being waterboarded. But the al-Qaeda operative's confessions—descriptions of fantastic plots from a man who intelligence analysts were convinced was mentally ill— probably didn't give the CIA any actionable intelligence. Of course, we may never know the whole truth, since the CIA destroyed the videotapes of Abu Zubaida's interrogation. But here are some other myths that are bound to come up as the debate over torture rages on.*

3   **1. Torture worked for the Gestapo.** Actually, no. Even Hitler's notorious secret police got most of their information from public tips, informers and interagency cooperation. That was still more than enough to let the Gestapo decimate anti-Nazi resistance in Austria, Czechoslovakia, Poland, Denmark, Norway, France, Russia and the concentration camps.

4   Yes, the Gestapo did torture people for intelligence, especially in later years. But this reflected not torture's efficacy but the loss of many seasoned professionals to World War II, increasingly desperate competition for intelligence among Gestapo units and an influx of less disciplined younger members. (Why do serious, tedious police work when you have a uniform and a whip?) It's surprising how unsuccessful the Gestapo's brutal efforts were. They failed to break senior leaders of the French, Danish, Polish and German resistance. I've spent more than a decade collecting all the cases of Gestapo torture "successes" in multiple languages; the number is small and the results pathetic, especially compared with the devastating effects of public cooperation and informers.

5   **2. Everyone talks sooner or later under torture.** Truth is, it's surprisingly hard to get anything under torture, true or false. For example, between 1500

and 1750, French prosecutors tried to torture confessions out of 785 individuals. Torture was legal back then, and the records document such practices as the bone-crushing use of splints, pumping stomachs with water until they swelled and pouring boiling oil on the feet. But the number of prisoners who said anything was low, from 3 percent in Paris to 14 percent in Toulouse (an exceptional high). Most of the time, the torturers were unable to get any statement whatsoever.

And such examples could be multiplied. The Japanese fascists, no strangers to torture, said it best in their field manual, which was found in Burma during World War II: They described torture as the clumsiest possible method of gathering intelligence. Like most sensible torturers, they preferred to use torture for intimidation, not information.   6

3. People will say anything under torture. Well, no, although this is a favorite chestnut of torture's foes. Think about it: Sure, someone would lie under torture, but wouldn't they also lie if they were being interrogated without coercion?   7

In fact, the problem of torture does not stem from the prisoner who *has* information; it stems from the prisoner who doesn't. Such a person is also likely to lie, to say anything, often convincingly. The torture of the informed may generate no more lies than normal interrogation, but the torture of the ignorant and innocent overwhelms investigators with misleading information. In these cases, nothing is indeed preferable to anything. Anything needs to be verified, and the CIA's own 1963 interrogation manual explains that "a time-consuming delay results"—hardly useful when every moment matters.   8

Intelligence gathering is especially vulnerable to this problem. When police officers torture, they know what the crime is, and all they want is the confession. When intelligence officers torture, they must gather information about what they don't know.   9

4. Most people can tell when someone is lying under torture. Not so—and we know quite a bit about this. For about 40 years, psychologists have been testing police officers as well as normal people to see whether they can spot lies, and the results aren't encouraging. Ordinary folk have an accuracy rate of about 57 percent, which is pretty poor considering that 50 percent is the flip of a coin. Likewise, the cops' accuracy rates fall between 45 percent and 65 percent—that is, sometimes less accurate than a coin toss.   10

Why does this matter? Because even if torturers break a person, they have to recognize it, and most of the time they can't. Torturers assume too much and reject what doesn't fit their assumptions. For instance, Sheila Cassidy, a British physician, cracked under electric-shock torture by the Chilean secret service in the 1970s and identified priests who had helped the country's socialist opposition. But her devout interrogators couldn't believe that priests would ever help the socialists, so they tortured her for another week until they finally became convinced. By that time, she was so damaged that she couldn't remember the location of the safe house.   11

12   In fact, most torturers are nowhere near as well trained for interrogation as police are. Torturers are usually chosen because they've endured hardship and pain, fought with courage, kept secrets, held the right beliefs and earned a reputation as trustworthy and loyal. They often rely on folklore about what lying behavior looks like—shifty eyes, sweaty palms and so on. And, not surprisingly, they make a lot of mistakes.

13   **5. You can train people to resist torture.** Supposedly, this is why we can't know what the CIA's "enhanced interrogation techniques" are: If Washington admits that it waterboards suspected terrorists, al-Qaeda will set up "waterboarding-resistance camps" across the world. Be that as it may, the truth is that no training will help the bad guys.

14   Simply put, nothing predicts the outcome of one's resistance to pain better than one's own personality. Against some personalities, nothing works; against others, practically anything does. Studies of hundreds of detainees who broke under Soviet and Chinese torture, including Army-funded studies of U.S. prisoners of war, conclude that during, before and after torture, each prisoner displayed strengths and weaknesses dependent on his or her own character. The CIA's own "Human Resources Exploitation Manual" from 1983 and its so-called Kubark manual from 1963 agree. In all matters relating to pain, says Kubark, the "individual remains the determinant."

15   The thing that's most clear from torture-victim studies is that you can't train for the ordeal. There is no secret knowledge out there about how to resist torture. Yes, there are manuals, such as the IRA's "Green Book," the anti-Soviet "Manual for Psychiatry for Dissidents" and "Torture and the Interrogation Experience," an Iranian guerrilla manual from the 1970s. But none of these volumes contains specific techniques of resistance, just general encouragement to hang tough. Even al-Qaeda's vaunted terrorist-training manual offers no tips on how to resist torture, and al-Qaeda was no stranger to the brutal methods of the Saudi police.

16   And yet these myths persist. "The larger problem here, I think," one active CIA officer observed in 2005, "is that this kind of stuff just makes people feel better, even if it doesn't work."

Source: *Washington Post*, June 28, 2008. Reprinted by permission of the author.

QUESTIONS FOR READING

1. What context for his discussion does the author provide in the opening two paragraphs?
2. What worked better than torture for the Gestapo? What led to an increase in torture in the Gestapo?
3. What do the data show about getting people to speak by torturing them?
4. Who are the people most likely to lie under torture?
5. Why are interrogators not very good at recognizing when the tortured are lying?

QUESTIONS FOR REASONING AND ANALYSIS

6. What structure does the author use? What kind of argument is this?
7. What is Rejali's position on torture, the claim of his argument?
8. What grounds does he present in support of his claim?
9. Describe Rejali's style; how does his style of writing help his argument?

QUESTIONS FOR REFLECTION AND WRITING

10. Which of the five discussions has surprised you the most? Why?
11. Has the author convinced you that all five myths lack substance? Why or why not? If you disagree, how would you refute Rejali?
12. Why do intelligence and military personnel continue to use harsh interrogation strategies even though the evidence suggests that what, if anything, they learn will not be useful? Ponder this question.

TORTURE IS WRONG—BUT IT MIGHT WORK | M. GREGG BLOCHE

A law professor at Georgetown University, Gregg Bloche is also a physician. His MD and JD degrees are both from Yale University. Bloche specializes in medical ethics, health care law, and human rights law. Widely published, he is the author of *The Hippocratic Myth* (2011). His essay on torture appeared on May 29, 2011.

PREREADING QUESTIONS Has Bloche intrigued you with his title? What do you expect his position to be?

Torture, liberals like me often insist, isn't just immoral, it's ineffective. We like this proposition because it portrays us as protectors of the nation, not wusses willing to risk American lives to protect terrorists. And we love to quote seasoned interrogators' assurances that building rapport with the bad guys will get them to talk. 1

But the killing of Osama bin Laden four weeks ago has revived the old debate about whether torture works. Could it be that "enhanced interrogation techniques" employed during the George W. Bush administration helped find bin Laden's now-famous courier and track him to the terrorist in chief's now-infamous lair? 2

Sen. John McCain (R-Ariz.) and current administration officials say no. Former attorney general Michael Mukasey and former vice president Dick Cheney say yes. 3

The idea that waterboarding and other abuses may have been effective in getting information from detainees is repellant to many, including me. It's 4 contrary to the meme many have embraced: that torture doesn't work because people being abused to the breaking point will say anything to get the brutality to stop—anything they think their accusers want to hear.

5   But this position is at odds with some behavioral science, I've learned. The architects of enhanced interrogation are doctors who built on a still-classified, research-based model that suggests how abuse can indeed work.

6   I've examined the science, studied the available paper trail and interviewed key actors, including several who helped develop the enhanced interrogation program and who haven't spoken publicly before. This inquiry has made it possible to piece together the model that under-girds enhanced interrogation.

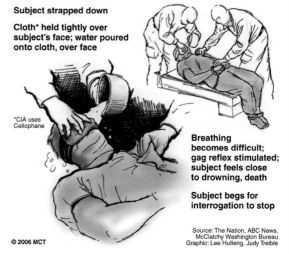

What is water-boarding?

Water-boarding is a harsh interrogation method that simulates drowning and near death; origins traced to the Spanish Inquisition.

Subject strapped down

Cloth* held tightly over subject's face; water poured onto cloth, over face

*CIA uses Cellophane

Breathing becomes difficult; gag reflex stimulated; subject feels close to drowning, death

Subject begs for interrogation to stop

© 2006 MCT

Source: The Nation, ABC News, McClatchy Washington Bureau
Graphic: Lee Hulteng, Judy Treible

7   This model holds that harsh methods can't, by themselves, force terrorists to tell the truth. Brute force, it suggests, stiffens resistance. Rather, the role of abuse is to induce hopelessness and despair. That's what sleep deprivation, stress positions and prolonged isolation were designed to do. Small gestures of contempt—facial slaps and frequent insults—drive home the message of futility. Even the rough stuff, such as "walling" and waterboarding, is meant to dispirit, not to coerce.

8   Once a sense of hopelessness is instilled, the model holds, interrogators can shape behavior through small rewards. Bathroom breaks, reprieves from foul-tasting food and even the occasional kind word can coax broken men to comply with their abusers' expectations.

9   Certainly, interrogators using this approach have obtained false confessions. Chinese interrogators did so intentionally, for propaganda purposes, with American prisoners during the Korean War. McCain and other critics of "torture-lite" cite this precedent to argue that it can't yield reliable information. But the same psychological sequence—induction of hopelessness, followed by rewards to shape compliance—can be used to get terrorism suspects to tell the truth, or so the architects of enhanced interrogation hypothesize.

10   Critical to this model is the ability to assess suspects' truthfulness in real time. To this end, CIA interrogators stressed speedy integration of intelligence from all sources. The idea was to frame questions to detect falsehoods; interrogators could then reward honesty and punish deceit.

It's been widely reported that the program was conceived by a former Air 11 Force psychologist, James Mitchell, who had helped oversee the Pentagon's program for training soldiers and airmen to resist torture if captured. That Mitchell became the CIA's maestro of enhanced interrogation and personally water-boarded several prisoners was confirmed in 2009 through the release of previously classified documents. But how Mitchell got involved and why the agency embraced his methods remained a mystery.

The key player was a clinical psychologist turned CIA official, Kirk Hubbard, 12 I learned through interviews with him and others. On the day 19 hijackers bent on mass murder made their place in history, Hubbard's responsibilities at the agency included tracking developments in the behavioral sciences with an eye toward their tactical use. He and Mitchell knew each other through the network of psychologists who do national security work. Just retired from the Air Force, Mitchell figured he could translate what he knew about teaching resistance into a methodology for breaking it. He convinced Hubbard, who introduced him to CIA leaders and coached him through the agency's bureaucratic rivalries.

Journalistic accounts have cast Mitchell as a rogue who won a CIA con- 13 tract by dint of charisma. What's gone unappreciated is his reliance on a research base. He had studied the medical and psychological literature on how Chinese interrogators extracted false confessions. And he was an admirer of Martin Seligman, the University of Pennsylvania psychologist who had developed the concept of "learned helplessness" and invoked it to explain depression.

Mitchell, it appears, saw connections and seized upon them. The despair 14 that Chinese interrogators tried to instill was akin to learned helplessness. Seligman's induction of learned helplessness in laboratory animals, therefore, could point the way to prison regimens capable of inducing it in people. And—this was Mitchell's biggest conceptual jump—the Chinese way of shaping behavior in prisoners who were reduced to learned helplessness held a broader lesson.

To motivate a captive to comply, a Chinese interrogator established an 15 aura of omnipotence. For weeks or months, the interrogator was his prisoner's sole human connection, with monopoly power to praise, punish and reward. Rapport with the interrogator offered the only escape from despair. This opened possibilities for the sculpting of behavior and belief. For propaganda purposes, the Chinese sought sham confessions. But Mitchell saw that behavioral shaping could be used to pursue other goals, including the extraction of truth.

Did the methods Mitchell devised help end the hunt for bin Laden? Have 16 they prevented terrorist attacks? We'll never know. Not only are counterterrorism operations shrouded in secrecy, but it's impossible to prove or disprove claims that enhanced interrogation works better than other methods when prisoners are intent on saying nothing.

Scientific study of this question would require random sorting of suspects 17 into groups that receive either torture-lite or conventional forms of interrogation. To frame this inquiry is to show why it can't be carried out: It would violate international law and research ethics. The CIA, Hubbard told me, conducted no such study for this reason.

18   So we're left with the unsavory possibility that torture-lite works—and that it may have helped find bin Laden. It does no good to point out, as some human rights advocates have, that the detainees who yielded information about his courier did so after the abuse stopped. The model on which enhanced interrogation is based can account for this. The detainees' cooperation could have ensued from hopelessness and despair, followed by interrogators' adroit use of their power to punish and reward.

19   This possibility poses the question of torture in a more unsettling fashion, by denying us the easy out that torture is both ineffective and wrong. We must choose between its repugnance to our values and its potential efficacy. To me, the choice is almost always obvious: Contempt for the law of nations would put us on a path toward a more brutish world. Conservatives are fond of saying, on behalf of martial sacrifice, that freedom isn't free. Neither is basic decency.

Source: *Washington Post*, May 29, 2011. Reprinted by permission of the author.

QUESTIONS FOR READING

1. What argument is embraced by those who are opposed to the use of torture?
2. What did Bloche learn about the purpose of "enhanced interrogation"? How is it used as part of a process for getting information?
3. What must interrogators assess for this model to work? How do they try to do this?
4. Why can we not know for certain if torture works?

QUESTIONS FOR REASONING AND ANALYSIS

5. What is Bloche's claim? (Be careful; it is not a simple statement.)
6. What grounds does he present in support of his claim?
7. Study the author's introduction; what does he gain by announcing his position on torture in his opening paragraph?
8. Study Bloche's conclusion: Why is deciding on one's position more difficult now? What does Bloche mean by his final sentence?

QUESTIONS FOR REFLECTION AND WRITING

9. Has Bloche convinced you that the issue of using enhanced interrogation has become more complex? Why or why not? If you disagree with the author, how would you refute him?
10. Both Bloche and Rejali discuss the issue of interrogators needing to assess what, if any, good information they may be getting from interrogation. What does this tell you about the task of intelligence gathering? Ponder this issue for class discussion or writing.

1. Do Rejali and Bloche hold opposing viewpoints on the use of torture—or are their differences more that of approach and focus? Read each author again and then write an analysis of their differences in style, approach to the issue, and position on the issue.

2. Reflect on what you have learned about torture from Rejali and Bloche and then consider: What may be the greatest "unknown" part of the equation in the use of interrogation as a strategy for finding people who have broken the law? Or, put another way, what do you see as the biggest problem to assuring success from questioning people under pressure to get intelligence from them?

3. Should the debate over enhanced interrogation procedures be about effectiveness or ethics? And, if it should be about effectiveness, then how much evidence is needed to defend torture on the grounds that it works? Ponder these questions.

GOING ONLINE

The debate over the use of enhanced interrogation techniques and of hidden sites abroad continues. Bloche mentions several studies in his discussion. Go online and see what more you can learn about this debate. Ponder this question: Why do some continue these strategies when studies fail to confirm that they work?

CHAPTER 5

Reading, Analyzing, and Using Visuals and Statistics in Argument

READ: This photo is of Princess Cottage, built in 1855 on Union Beach, NJ, as it looked after Hurricane Sandy (Fall 2012). The cottage has since been torn down.

REASON: What is your initial reaction to this photo? How does it make you feel? What does it make you think about?

REFLECT/WRITE: There are many images of the hurricane's destruction; why would someone select this image for publication?

We live in a visual age. Many of us go to movies to appreciate and judge the film's visual effects. The Internet is awash in pictures and colorful icons. Perhaps the best symbol of our visual age is *USA Today,* a paper filled with color photos and many tables and other graphics as a primary way of presenting information. *USA Today* has forced the more traditional papers to add color to compete. We also live in a numerical age. We refer to the events of September 11, 2001, as 9/11—without any disrespect. This chapter brings together these markers of our times as they are used in argument—and as argument. Finding statistics and visuals used as part of argument, we also need to remember that cartoons and advertisements are arguments in and of themselves.

RESPONDING TO VISUAL ARGUMENTS

Many arguments bombard us today in visual forms. These include photos, political cartoons, and advertising. Most major newspapers have a political cartoonist whose drawings appear regularly on the editorial page. (Some comic strips are also political in nature, at least some of the time.) These cartoons are designed to make a political point in a visually clever and amusing way. (That is why they are both "cartoons" and "political" at the same time.) Their uses of irony and caricatures of known politicians make them among the most emotionally powerful, indeed stinging, of arguments.

Photographs accompany many newspaper and magazine articles, and they often tell a story. Indeed some photographers are famous for their ability to capture a personality or a newsworthy moment. So accustomed to these visuals today, we sometimes forget to study photographs. Be sure to examine each photo, remembering that authors and editors have selected each one for a reason.

Advertisements are among the most creative and powerful forms of argument today. Remember that ads are designed to take your time (for shopping) and your money. Their messages need to be powerful to motivate you to action. With some products (what most of us consider necessities), ads are designed to influence product choice, to get us to buy brand A instead of brand B. With other products, ones we really do not need or which may actually be harmful to us, ads need to be especially clever. Some ads do provide information (car X gets better gas mileage than car Y). Other ads (perfume ads, for example) take us into a fantasy land so that we will spend $50 on a small but pretty bottle. Another type of ad is the "image advertisement," an ad that assures us that a particular company is top-notch. If we admire the company, we will buy its goods or services.

Here are guidelines for reading visual arguments. You can practice these steps with the exercises that follow.

GUIDELINES for Reading Photographs

- **Is a scene or situation depicted?** If so, study the details to identify the situation.
- **Identify each figure in the photo.**
- **What details of scene or person(s) carry significance?**
- **How does the photograph make you feel?**

GUIDELINES for Reading Political Cartoons

- **What scene is depicted?** Identify the situation.
- **Identify each of the figures in the cartoon.** Are they current politicians, figures from history or literature, the "person in the street," or symbolic representations?
- **Who speaks the lines in the cartoon?**
- **What is the cartoon's general subject?** What is the point of the cartoon, the claim of the cartoonist?

GUIDELINES for Reading Advertisements

- **What product or service is being advertised?**
- **Who seems to be the targeted audience?**
- **What is the ad's primary strategy?** To provide information? To reinforce the product's or company's image? To appeal to particular needs or desires? For example, if an ad shows a group of young people having fun and drinking a particular beer, to what needs/desires is the ad appealing?
- **Does the ad use specific rhetorical strategies such as humor, understatement, or irony?**
- **What is the relation between the visual part of the ad (photo, drawing, typeface, etc.) and the print part (the text, or copy)?** Does the ad use a slogan or catchy phrase? Is there a company logo? Is the slogan or logo clever? Is it well known as a marker of the company? What may be the effect of these strategies on readers?
- **What is the ad's overall visual impression?** Consider both images and colors used.

EXERCISES: Analyzing Photos, Cartoons, and Ads

1. Analyze the photo on page 123, using the guidelines previously listed.
2. Review the photos that open Chapters 1, 4, 5, 8, 10, 19, and 22. Select the one you find most effective. Analyze it in detail to show why you think it is the best.

3. Analyze the cartoon below using the guidelines listed previously. You may want to jot down your answers to the questions to be well prepared for class discussion.

4. Review the cartoons that open Chapters 2, 3, 6, 7, 9, 15, 16, 17, 20, and 21. Select the one you find most effective. Analyze it in detail to show why you think it is the cleverest.

5. Analyze the ads on pages 124–26, again using the guidelines listed above. After answering the guideline questions, consider these as well: Will each ad appeal effectively to its intended audience? If so, why? If not, why not?

the river of life

·····································

Retracing a historic journey to help fight malaria.

···

In 1858, Scottish missionary David Livingstone embarked on a historic journey along the Zambezi River in southern Africa. On that trip, malaria claimed the life of Livingstone's wife, Mary Livingstone himself also later died from the disease.

Today, 150 years later, malaria remains a threat. Over one million people, mostly children and pregnant women, die from malaria each year. About 40 percent of the global population is vulnerable to the disease.

But an unprecedented global action—by governments and corporations, NGOs and health organizations—has been mobilized against malaria. And this combined effort is yielding results:

• Across Africa, people are receiving anti-malarial medications, as well as bed nets and insecticides that protect against the mosquitoes that transmit the disease.

Photo by Helge Bendl

• In Rwanda, malaria cases are down by 64 percent, and deaths by 66 percent. Similar results are seen in Ethiopia and Zambia. And in Mozambique, where 9 out of 10 children had been infected, that number is now 2 in 10.

• Scientists are expanding the pipeline of affordable, effective anti-malarial medicines, while also making progress on discovering a vaccine.

April 25 is World Malaria Day. As part of that event, a team of medical experts will retrace Livingstone's journey along the Zambezi, the "River of Life." As part of the Roll Back Malaria Zambezi Expedition, they will travel 1,500 miles in inflatable boats through Angola, Namibia, Botswana, Zambia, Zimbabwe and Mozambique.

By exposing the difficulties of delivering supplies to remote areas, the expedition will demonstrate that only a coordinated, cross-border action can beat back the disease, and turn the lifeline of southern Africa into a "River of Life" for those threatened by malaria.

ExxonMobil is the largest non-pharmaceutical private-sector contributor to the fight against malaria. But our support is more than financial. We are actively partnering with governments and agencies in affected countries, enabling them to combat malaria with the same disciplined, results-based business practices that ExxonMobil employs in its global operations.

Livingstone once said, "I am prepared to go anywhere, provided it be forward." The communities burdened by this disease cannot move forward until malaria is controlled and, someday, eradicated. We urge everyone to join in this global effort.

For more information, visit www.zambezi-expedition.org and www.rollbackmalaria.org.

ExxonMobil
Taking on the world's toughest energy challenges.™

FOR STRONGER TEETH CHEW ORBIT
Orbit is now accepted by the American Dental Association

ADA
Accepted
American
Dental
Association ®

The ADA Council on Scientific Affairs' Acceptance of Orbit is based on its finding that the physical action of chewing Orbit sugar-free gum for 20 minutes after eating, stimulates saliva flow, which helps to prevent cavities by reducing plaque acids and strengthening teeth.

**Your business side. Your creative side.
Inspire both. Introducing Avid's new editing lineup.**

Quality, performance and value. A new way of thinking. A new way of doing business.
Take a closer look at **Avid.com/NewThinkingScript.**

READING GRAPHICS

Graphics—photographs, diagrams, tables, charts, and graphs—present a good bit of information in a condensed but also visually engaging format. Graphics are everywhere: in textbooks, magazines, newspapers, and the Internet. It's a rare training session or board meeting that is conducted without the use of graphics to display information. So, you want to be able to read graphics and create them, when appropriate, in your own writing. First, study the chart below that illustrates the different uses of various visuals. General guidelines for reading graphics follow. The guidelines will use Figure 5.1 to illustrate points. Study the figure repeatedly as you read through the guidelines.

Understanding How Graphics Differ

Each type of visual serves specific purposes. You can't use a pie chart, for example, to explain a process; you need a diagram or a flowchart. So, when reading graphics, understand what each type can show you. When preparing your own visuals, select the graphic that will most clearly and effectively present the particular information you want to display.

TYPE	PURPOSE	EXAMPLE
Diagram	show details demonstrate process	drawing of knee tendons photosynthesis
Table	list numerical information	income of U.S. households
Bar chart	comparative amounts of related numbers	differences in suicide rates by age and race
Pie chart	relative portions of a whole	percentages of Americans by educational level
Flowchart	steps in a process	purification of water
Graph	relationship of two items	income increases over time
Map	information relative to a geographical area	locations of world's rain forests

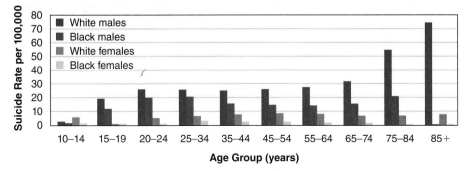

FIGURE 5.1 Differences in Suicide Rate According to Race, Gender, and Age
(Source: Data from the U.S. Bureau of the Census, 1994)

GUIDELINES for Reading Graphics

1. **Locate the particular graphic referred to in the text and study it at that point in your reading.** Graphics may not always be placed on the same page as the text reference. Stop your reading to find and study the graphic; that's what the writer wants you to do. Find Figure 5.1 on the previous page.

2. **Read the title or heading of the graphic.** Every graphic is given a title. What is the subject of the graphic? What kind of information is provided? Figure 5.1 shows differences in suicide rates by race, gender, and age.

3. **Read any notes, description, and the source information at the bottom of the graphic.** Figure 5.1 came from the U.S. Bureau of the Census for 1994. Critical questions: What is this figure showing me? Is the information coming from a reliable source? Is it current enough to still be meaningful?

4. **Study the labels—and other words—that appear as part of the graphic.** You cannot draw useful conclusions unless you understand exactly what is being shown. Observe in Figure 5.1 that the four bars for each age group (shown along the horizontal axis) represent white males, black males, white females, and black females, in that order, for each age category.

5. **Study the information, making certain that you understand what the numbers represent.** Are the numerals whole numbers, numbers in hundreds or thousands, or percentages? In Figure 5.1 we are looking at suicide *rates per 100,000 people* for four identified groups of people at different ages. So, to know exactly how many white males between 15 and 19 commit suicide, we need to know how many white males between 15 and 19 there are (or were in 1994) in the United States population. The chart does not give us this information. It gives us *comparative rates* per 100,000 people in each category and tells us that almost 20 in every 100,000 white males between 15 and 19 commit suicide.

6. **Draw conclusions.** Think about the information in different ways. Critical questions: What does the author want to accomplish by including these figures? How are they significant? What conclusions can you draw from Figure 5.1? Answer these questions to guide your thinking:

   a. Which of the four compared groups faces the greatest risk from suicide over his or her lifetime? Would you have guessed this group? Why or why not? What might be some of the causes for the greatest risk to this group?

   b. What is the greatest risk factor for increased suicide rate—race, gender, age, or a combination? Does this surprise you? Would you have guessed a different factor? Why?

   c. Which group, as young teens, is at greatest risk? Are you surprised? Why or why not? What might be some of the causes for this?

Graphics provide information, raise questions, explain processes, engage us emotionally, make us think. Study the various graphics in the exercises that follow to become more expert in reading and responding critically to visuals.

EXERCISES: Reading and Analyzing Graphics

1. Study the pie charts in Figure 5.2 and then answer the following questions.
   a. What is the subject of the charts?
   b. In addition to the information within the pie charts, what other information is provided?
   c. Which group increases by the greatest relative amount? How would you account for that increase?
   d. Which figure surprises you the most? Why?
2. Study the line graph in Figure 5.3 and then answer the following questions.
   a. What two subjects are treated by the graph?
   b. In 2000 what percentage of men's income did women earn?
   c. During which five-year period did men's incomes increase by the greatest amount?
   d. Does the author's prediction for the year 2005 suggest that income equality for women will have taken place?
   e. Are you bothered by the facts on this graph? Why or why not?
3. Study the table in Figure 5.4 and then answer the following questions.
   a. What is being presented and compared in this table?
   b. What, exactly, do the numerals in the second line represent? What, exactly, do the numerals in the third line represent? (Be sure that you understand what these numbers mean.)
   c. For the information given in lines 2, 3, 4, and 5, in which category have women made the greatest gains on men?
   d. See if you can complete the missing information in the last line. Where will you look to find out how many men and women were single parents in 2000? (In 2010?)
   e. Which figure surprises you the most? Why?
4. Maps can be used to show all kinds of information, not just the locations of cities, rivers, or mountains. Study the map in Figure 5.5 and then answer the questions that follow.
   a. What, exactly, does the map show? Why does it not "look right"?
   b. How many electoral votes did each candidate win?
   c. How are the winning states for each candidate clustered? What conclusions can you draw from observing this clustering?
   d. What advice would you give to each party to ensure that party's presidential win in 2016?
   e. How would the map look if it were drawn to show population by state? Would the red states look bigger or smaller?

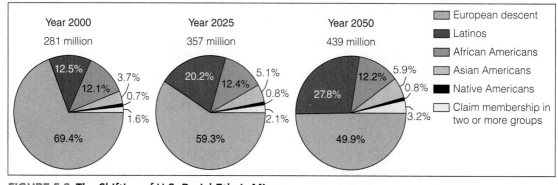

FIGURE 5.2 The Shifting of U.S. Racial-Ethnic Mix (Source: James M. Henslin, *Essentials of Sociology: A Down-to-Earth Approach*, 9th Edition, Figure 9.11 (p. 241), © 2011. Reprinted by permission of Pearson Education, Inc., Upper Saddle River, NJ.)

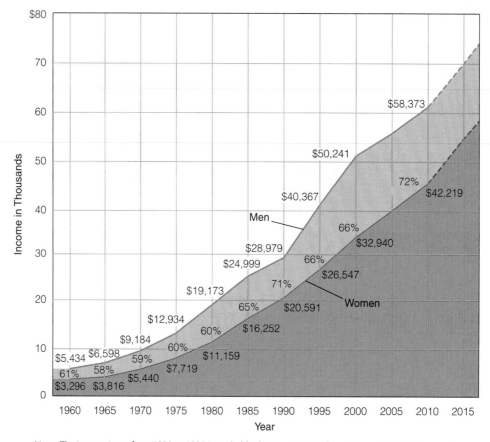

Note: The income jump from 1990 to 1995 is probably due to a statistical procedure. The 1995 source (for 1990 income) uses "median income," while the 1997 source (for 1995 income) merely says "average earnings." How the "average" is computed is not stated. Broken lines indicate the author's estimates.

FIGURE 5.3 The Gender Gap Over Time: What Percentage of Men's Income Do Women Earn? (Source: James M. Henslin, *Essentials of Sociology: A Down-to-Earth Approach*, 9th Edition, Figure 10.8 (p. 264), © 2011. Reprinted by permission of Pearson Education, Inc., Upper Saddle River, NJ.)

	1970		2000	
	MEN	**WOMEN**	**MEN**	**WOMEN**
Estimated life expectancy	67.1	74.1	74.24	79.9
% high school graduates	53	52	87	88
% of BAs awarded	57	43	45	55
% of MAs awarded	60	40	45	55
% of PhDs awarded	87	13	61	39
% in legal profession	95	5	70	30
Median earnings	$26,760	$14,232	$35,345	$25,862
Single parents	1.2 million	5.6 million	n/a	n/a

FIGURE 5.4 Men and Women in a Changing Society (Sources: for 1970: *1996 Statistical Abstract*, U.S. Dept. of Commerce, Economics and Statistics Administration, Bureau of the Census. 2000 data: National Center for Education Statistics http://nces.ed.gov/fastfacts)

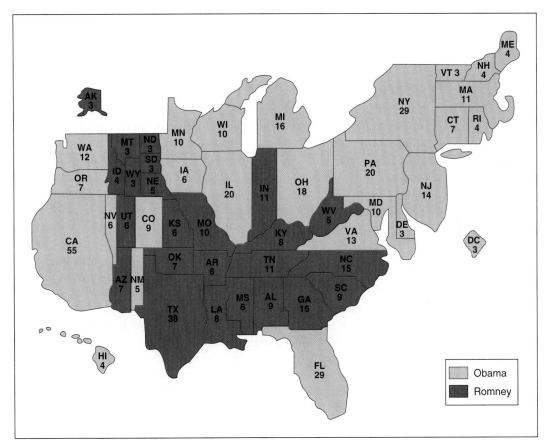

Note: **States drawn in proportion to number of electoral votes. Total electoral votes: 538** (Source: Based on a map that originally appeared in *New York Times*, November 5, 2002. Reprinted by permission of NYT Graphics. From O'Connor and Sabato, *American Government* © 2002; published by Allyn and Bacon, Boston, MA Copyright © 2002 by Pearson Education. Updated for the 2012 election by the author.)

FIGURE 5.5 Electoral Votes per State for the 2012 Presidential Election

THE USES OF AUTHORITY AND STATISTICS

Most of the visuals you have just studied provide a way of presenting statistics—data that many today consider essential to defending a claim. One reason you check the source information accompanying graphics is that you need to know—and evaluate—the authority of that source. When a graphic's numbers have come from the Census Bureau, you know you have a reliable source. When the author writes that "studies have shown . . . ," you want to become suspicious of the authority of the data. All elements of the arguments we read—and write—affect a writer's credibility.

Judging Authorities

We know that movie stars and sports figures are not authorities on soft drinks and watches. But what about *real* authorities? When writers present the opinions or research findings of authorities as support for a claim, they are saying to readers that the authority is trustworthy and the opinions valuable. But what they are asserting is actually an assumption or warrant, part of the glue connecting evidence to claim. Remember: Warrants can be challenged. If the "authority" can be shown to lack authority, then the logic of the argument is destroyed. Use this checklist of questions to evaluate authorities:

☐ *Is the authority actually an authority on the topic under discussion?* When a famous scientist supports a candidate for office, he or she speaks as a citizen, not as an authority.

☐ *Is the work of the authority still current?* Times change; expertise does not always endure. Galileo would be lost in the universe of today's astrophysicists. Be particularly alert to the dates of information in the sciences in general, in genetics and the entire biomedical field, in health and nutrition. It is almost impossible to keep up with the latest findings in these areas of research.

☐ *Does the authority actually have legitimate credentials?* Are the person's publications in respected journals? Is he or she respected by others in the same field? *Just because it's in print does not mean it's a reliable source!*

☐ *Do experts in the field generally agree on the issue?* If there is widespread disagreement, then referring to one authority does not do much to support a claim. This is why you need to understand the many sides of a controversial topic before you write on it, and you need to bring knowledge of controversies and critical thinking skills to your reading of argument. This is also why writers often provide a source's credentials, not just a name, unless the authority is quite famous.

☐ *Is the authority's evidence reliable, so far as you can judge, but the interpretation of that evidence seems odd, or seems to be used to support strongly held beliefs?* Does the evidence actually connect to the claim? A respected authority's work can be stretched or manipulated in an attempt to defend a claim that the authority's work simply does not support.

EXERCISES: Judging Authorities

1. Jane Goodall has received worldwide fame for her studies of chimpanzees in Gombe and for her books on those field studies. Goodall is a vegetarian. Should she be used as an authority in support of a claim for a vegetarian diet? Why or why not? Consider:
   a. Why might Goodall have chosen to become a vegetarian?
   b. For what arguments might Goodall be used as an authority?
   c. For what arguments might she be used effectively for emotional appeal?
2. Suppose a respected zoologist prepares a five-year study of U.S. zoos, compiling a complete list of all animals at each zoo. He then updates the list for each of the five years, adding births and deaths. When he examines his data, he finds that deaths are one and one-half times the number of births. He considers this loss alarming and writes a paper arguing for the abolishing of zoos on the grounds that too many animals are dying. Because of his reputation, his article is published in a popular science magazine. How would you evaluate his authority and his study?
   a. Should you trust the data? Why or why not?
   b. Should you accept his conclusions? Why or why not?
   c. Consider: What might be possible explanations for the birth/death ratio?

Understanding and Evaluating Statistics

There are two useful clichés to keep in mind: "Statistics don't lie, but people lie with statistics" and "There are lies, damned lies, and statistics." The second cliché is perhaps a bit cynical. We don't want to be naïve in our faith in numbers, but neither do we want to become so cynical that we refuse to believe any statistical evidence. What we do need to keep in mind is that when statistics are presented in an argument they are being used by someone interested in winning that argument.

Some writers use numbers without being aware that the numbers are incomplete or not representative. Some present only part of the relevant information. Some may not mean to distort, but they do choose to present the information in language that helps their cause. There are many ways, some more innocent than others, to distort reality with statistics. Use the following guidelines to evaluate the presentation of statistical information.

GUIDELINES for Evaluating Statistics

- **Is the information current and therefore still relevant?** Crime rates in your city based on 2000 census data probably are no longer relevant, certainly not current enough to support an argument for increased (or decreased) police department spending.

- **If a sample was used, was it randomly selected and large enough to be significant?** Sometimes in medical research, the results of a small study are publicized to guide researchers to important new areas of study. When these results are reported in the press or on TV, however, the small size of the study is not always made clear. Thus one week we learn that coffee is bad for us, the next week that it is okay.
- **What information, exactly, has been provided?** When you read "Two out of three chose the Merit combination of low tar and good taste," you must ask yourself "Two-thirds of how many altogether?"
- **How have the numbers been presented?** And what is the effect of that presentation? Numbers can be presented as fractions, whole numbers, or percentages. Writers who want to emphasize budget increases will use whole numbers—billions of dollars. Writers who want to de-emphasize those increases select percentages. Writers who want their readers to respond to the numbers in a specific way add words to direct their thinking: "a *mere* 3 percent increase" or "the *enormous* $5 billion increase."

EXERCISES: Reading Tables and Charts and Using Statistics

1. Figure 5.6, a table from the Census Bureau, shows U.S. family income data from 1980 to 2009. Percentages and median income are given for all families and then, in turn, for white, black, Asian, and Hispanic families. Study the data and then complete the exercises that follow.

   a. In a paper assessing the advantages of a growing economy, you want to include a paragraph on family income growth to show that a booming economy helps everyone, that "a rising tide lifts all boats." Select data from the table that best support your claim. Write a paragraph beginning with a topic sentence and including your data as support. Think about how to present the numbers in the most persuasive form.

   b. Write a second paragraph with the topic sentence "Not all Americans have benefited from the boom years" or "A rising tide does not lift all boats." Select data from the table that best support this topic sentence and present the numbers in the most persuasive form.

   c. Exchange paragraphs with a classmate and evaluate each other's selection and presentation of evidence.

2. Go back to Figure 5.1 (p. 127) and reflect again on the information that it depicts. Then consider what conclusions can be drawn from the evidence and what the implications of those conclusions are. Working in small groups or with a class partner, decide how you want to use the data to support a point.

3. Figure 5.7 (p. 136), another table from the Census Bureau, presents mean earnings by highest degree earned. First, be sure that you know the difference between mean and median (which is the number used in Figure 5.6). Study the data and reflect on the conclusions you can draw from the statistics. Consider: Of the various groups represented, which group most benefits from obtaining a college degree—as opposed to having only a high school diploma?

Year	Number of families (1,000)	Percent distribution							Median income (dollars)
		Under $15,000	$15,000 to $24,999	$25,000 to $34,999	$35,000 to $49,999	$50,000 to $74,999	$75,000 to $99,999	$100,000 and over	
ALL FAMILIES [1]									
1990	66,322	8.7	9.4	10.3	15.6	22.5	14.6	19.1	54,369
2000 [2]	73,778	7.0	8.6	9.3	14.3	19.8	15.1	26.2	61,063
2008	78,874	8.4	9.2	9.9	13.7	19.3	14.2	26.0	61,521
2009 [3]	76,867	8.7	9.1	10.0	13.8	19.4	13.5	25.6	60,088
WHITE									
1990	56,803	6.6	8.7	10.0	15.8	23.3	15.4	20.4	56,771
2000 [2]	61,330	5.7	7.9	9.0	14.2	20.1	15.8	27.7	63,849
2008 [4, 5]	64,183	6.9	8.5	9.5	13.4	19.8	15.0	27.5	65,000
2009 [3, 4, 5]	64,145	7.2	8.4	9.5	13.8	19.9	14.1	27.0	62,545
BLACK									
1990	7,471	23.9	14.7	12.5	14.4	17.5	8.8	8.2	32,946
2000 [2]	8,731	15.7	14.0	12.8	15.8	16.7	10.3	13.0	40,547
2008 [4, 5]	9,359	18.2	14.4	12.8	15.3	16.6	9.8	13.4	39,879
2009 [3, 4, 5]	9,367	18.0	14.5	13.3	15.2	16.4	10.6	12.1	38,409
ASIAN AND PACIFIC ISLANDER									
1990	1,536	8.1	7.8	8.2	11.6	21.2	15.0	28.5	64,969
2000 [2]	2,962	6.2	6.4	6.4	11.7	17.3	15.5	37.0	75,393
2008 [4, 7]	3,494	7.7	7.2	7.6	12.8	16.0	13.0	36.6	73,578
2009 [3, 4, 7]	3,592	6.9	7.0	7.9	10.4	17.7	12.3	37.7	75,027
HISPANIC ORIGIN [8]									
1990	4,961	17.0	16.3	13.6	17.3	19.1	8.5	8.2	36,034
2000 [2]	8,017	12.8	14.6	13.0	18.1	19.4	10.5	12.0	41,469
2008	10,503	15.5	14.6	14.1	16.8	17.2	9.6	12.5	40,466
2009 [3]	10,422	15.2	14.7	14.3	16.0	17.9	9.5	12.4	39,730

[**Constant dollars based on CPI-U-RS deflator. Families as of March of following year, (66,322 represents 66,322,000).** Based on Current Population Survey, Annual Social and Economic Supplement (ASEC); see text, this section, Section 1, and Appendix III. For data collection changes over time, see <http://www.census.gov/hhes/www/income/data/historical/history.html>. For definition of median, see Guide to Tabular Presentation]

[1] Includes other races not shown separately.   [2] Data reflect implementation of Census 2000-based population controls and a 28,000 household sample expansion to 78,000 households.   [3] Median income is calculated using $2,500 income intervals. Beginning with 2009 income data, the Census Bureau expanded the upper income intervals used to calculate medians to $250,000 or more. Medians falling in the upper open-ended interval are plugged with "$250,000." Before 2009, the upper open-ended interval was $100,000 and a plug of "$100,000" was used.   [4] Beginning with the 2003 Current Population Survey (CPS), the questionnaire allowed respondents to choose more than one race. For 2002 and later, data represent persons who selected this race group only and excludes persons reporting more than one race. The CPS in prior years allowed respondents to report only one race group. See also comments on race in the text for Section 1.   [5] Data represent White alone, which refers to people who reported White and did not report any other race category.   [6] Data represent Black alone, which refers to people who reported Black and did not report any other race category.   [7] Data represent Asian alone, which refers to people who reported Asian and did not report any other race category. [8] People of Hispanic origin may be any race.

Source: U.S. Census Bureau, *Income, Poverty and Health Insurance Coverage in the United States: 2009*, Current Population Reports, P60-238, and Historical Tables—Table F-23, September 2010. See also <http://www.census.gov/hhes/www/income/income.html> and <http://www.census.gov/hhes/www/income/data/historical/families/index.html>.

FIGURE 5.6 Money Income of Families—Percent Distribution by Income Level in Constant (2009) Dollars: 1980 to 2009.

WRITING THE INVESTIGATIVE ARGUMENT

The first step in writing an investigative argument is to select a topic to study. Composition students can write successful investigative essays on the media, on campus issues, and on various local concerns. Although you begin with a topic—not a claim—since you have to gather evidence before you can see what

Characteristic	Total persons	Mean earnings by level of highest degree (dol.)							
		Not a high school graduate	High school graduate only	Some college, no degree	Associate's	Bachelor's	Master's	Professional	Doctorate
All persons [1] . . .	**42,469**	**20,241**	**30,627**	**32,295**	**39,771**	**58,665**	**73,738**	**127,803**	**103,054**
Age:									
25 to 34 years old. . . .	35,595	19,415	30,627	31,392	35,544	45,662	58,997	86,440	74,628
35 to 44 years old. . . .	49,356	24,728	27,511	39,606	42,489	66,346	80,583	136,366	108,147
45 to 54 years old. . . .	51,956	23,725	36,090	44,135	45,145	69,548	86,532	146,808	112,134
55 to 64 years old. . . .	50,372	24,537	34,583	42,547	42,344	59,670	75,372	149,184	110,895
65 years old and over .	37,544	19,395	28,469	29,602	33,541	44,147	45,138	95,440	95,585
Sex:									
Male.	50,180	23,036	35,468	39,204	47,572	69,479	90,954	150,310	114,347
Female	33,797	15,514	24,304	23,340	33,432	43,689	58,534	89,897	83,706
White [2].	43,337	20,457	31,429	33,119	40,632	57,762	73,771	127,942	104,533
Male.	51,287	23,353	36,416	40,352	48,521	71,286	81,776	149,149	115,497
Female	34,040	15,187	24,615	25,537	33,996	43,309	58,036	89,526	85,682
Black [2].	33,362	18,938	25,970	29,129	33,734	47,799	60,067	102,328	82,510
Male.	37,553	21,829	30,723	33,969	41,142	55,655	68,890	(B)	(B)
Female	29,831	15,644	22,954	25,433	29,464	42,567	54,523	(B)	(B)
Hispanic [3].	29,565	19,816	25,998	29,836	33,783	49,017	71,322	79,220	88,435
Male.	32,279	21,588	28,908	35,089	38,768	58,570	80,737	(B)	89,968
Female	25,713	16,170	21,473	24,281	29,785	39,568	61,843	(B)	(B)

[In dollars. For persons 18 years old and over with earnings. Persons as of March 2010. Based on Current Population Survey; see text, Section 1 and Appendix III. For definition of mean, see Guide to Tabular Presentation]

B Base figure too small to meet statistical standards for reliability of a derived figure. [1] Includes other races not shown separately. [2] For persons who selected this race group only. [3] Persons of Hispanic origin may be any race.

Source: U.S. Census Bureau, Current Population Survey, unpublished data, <http://www.census.gov/population/www/socdemo/educ-attn.html>.

FIGURE 5.7 Mean Earnings by Highest Degree Earned: 2009

it means, you should select a topic that holds your interest and that you may have given some thought to before choosing to write. For example, you may have noticed some clever ads for jeans or beer, or perhaps you are bothered by plans for another shopping area along a major street near your home. Either one of these topics can lead to an effective investigative, or inductive, argument.

Gathering and Analyzing Evidence

Let's reflect on strategies for gathering evidence for a study of magazine ads for a particular kind of product (the topic of the sample student paper that follows).

- Select a time frame and a number of representative magazines.
- Have enough magazines to render at least twenty-five ads on the product you are studying.
- Once you decide on the magazines and issues to be used, pull *all* ads for your product. Your task is to draw useful conclusions based on adequate data objectively collected. You can't leave some ads out and have a valid study.

- Study the ads, reflecting on the inferences they allow you to draw. The inferences become the claim of your argument. You may want to take the approach of classifying the ads, that is, grouping them into categories by the various appeals used to sell the product.

More briefly, consider your hunch that your area does not need another shopping mall. What evidence can you gather to support a claim to that effect? You could locate all existing strip or enclosed malls within a 10-mile radius of the proposed new mall site, visit each one, and count the number and types of stores already available. You may discover that there are plenty of malls but that the area really needs a grocery store or a bookstore. So instead of reading to find evidence to support a claim, you are creating the statistics and doing the analysis to guide you to a claim. Just remember to devise objective procedures for collecting evidence so that you do not bias your results.

Planning and Drafting the Essay

You've done your research and studied the data you've collected; how do you put this kind of argument together? Here are some guidelines to help you draft your essay.

GUIDELINES for Writing an Investigative Argument

- **Begin with an opening paragraph that introduces your topic in an interesting way.** Possibilities include beginning with a startling statistic or explaining what impact the essay's facts will have on readers.
- **Devote space early in your paper to explaining your methods or procedures, probably in your second or third paragraph.** For example, if you have obtained information through questionnaires or interviews, recount the process: the questions asked, the number of people involved, the basis for selecting the people, and so on.
- **Classify the evidence that you present.** Finding a meaningful organization is part of the originality of your study and will make your argument more forceful. It is the way you see the topic and want readers to see it. If you are studying existing malls, you might begin by listing all of the malls and their locations. But then do not go store by store through each mall. Rather, group the stores by type and provide totals.
- **Consider presenting evidence in several ways, including in charts and tables as well as within paragraphs.** Readers are used to visuals, especially in essays containing statistics.
- **Analyze evidence to build your argument.** Do not ask your reader to do the thinking. No data dumps! Explain how your evidence *is* evidence by discussing the connection between facts and the inferences they support.

Analyzing Evidence: The Key to an Effective Argument

This is the thinking part of the process. Anyone can count stores or collect ads. What is your point? How does the evidence you have collected actually support your claim? You must guide readers through the evidence. Consider this example:

In a study of selling techniques used in computer ads in business magazines, a student, Brian, found four major selling techniques, one of which he classifies as "corporate emphasis." Brian begins his paragraph on corporate emphasis thus:

> In the technique of corporate emphasis, the advertiser discusses the whole range of products and services that the corporation offers, instead of specific elements. This method relies on the public's positive perception of the company, the company's accomplishments, and its reputation.

Brian then provides several examples of ads in this category, including an IBM ad:

> In one of its eight ads in the study, IBM points to the scientists on its staff who have recently won the Nobel Prize in physics.

But Brian does not stop there. He explains the point of this ad, connecting the ad to the assertion that this technique emphasizes the company's accomplishments:

> The inference we are to draw is that IBM scientists are hard at work right now in their laboratories developing tomorrow's technology to make the world a better place in which to live.

Preparing Graphics for Your Essay

Tables, bar charts, and pie charts are particularly helpful ways to present statistical evidence you have collected for an inductive argument. One possibility is to create a pie chart showing your classification of ads (or stores or questions on a questionnaire) and the relative amount of each item. For example, suppose you find four selling strategies. You can show in a pie chart the percentage of ads using each of the four strategies.

Computers help even the technically unsophisticated prepare simple charts. You can also do a simple table. When preparing graphics, keep these points in mind:

- Every graphic must be referred to in the text at the appropriate place—where you are discussing the information in the visual. Graphics are not disconnected attachments to an argument. They give a complete set of data in an easy-to-digest form, but some of that data must be discussed in the essay.
- Every graphic (except photographs) needs a label. Use Figure 1, Figure 2, and so forth. Then, in the text refer to each graphic by its label.
- Every graphic needs a title. Always place a title after Figure 1 (and so forth), on the same line, at the top or bottom of your visual.

• In a technically sophisticated world, hand-drawn graphics are not acceptable. Underline the graphic's title line, or place the visual within a box. (Check the tool bar at the top of your screen.) Type elements within tables. Use a ruler or compass to prepare graphics, or learn to use the graphics programs in your computer.

A CHECKLIST FOR REVISION

☐ Have I stated a claim that is precise and appropriate to the data I have collected?

☐ Have I fully explained the methodology I used in collecting my data?

☐ Have I selected a clear and useful organization?

☐ Have I presented and discussed enough specifics to show readers how my data support my conclusions?

☐ Have I used graphics to present the data in an effective visual display?

☐ Have I revised, edited, and proofread my paper?

STUDENT ESSAY

BUYING TIME

Garrett Berger

Chances are you own at least one wristwatch. Watches allow us immediate access to the correct time. They are indispensable items in our modern world, where, as the saying is, time is money. Today the primary function of a wristwatch does not necessarily guide its design; like clothes, houses, and cars, watches have become fashion statements and a way to flaunt one's wealth.

Introduction connects to reader.

To learn how watches are being sold, I surveyed all of the full-page ads from the November issues of four magazines. The first two, *GQ* and *Vogue*, are well-known fashion magazines. *The Robb Report* is a rather new magazine that caters to the overclass. *Forbes* is of course a well-known financial magazine. I was rather surprised at the number of advertisements I found. After surveying 86 ads, marketing 59 brands, I have concluded that today watches are being sold through five main strategies: DESIGN/BRAND appeal, CRAFTSMANSHIP, ASSOCIATION, FASHION appeal, and EMOTIONAL appeal. The percentage of ads using each of these strategies is shown in Figure 1.

Student explains his methodology of collecting ads. Paragraph concludes with his claim.

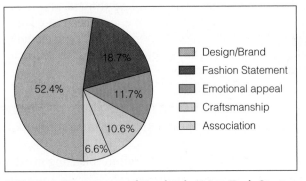

FIGURE 1 Percentage of Total Ads Using Each Strategy

Discussion of first category.

In most DESIGN/BRAND appeal ads, only a picture and the brand name are used. A subset of this category uses the same basic strategy with a slogan or phrases to emphasize something about the brand or product. A Mont Blanc ad shows a watch profile with a contorted metal link band, asking the question "Is that you?" The reputation of the name and the appeal of the design sell the watch. Rolex, perhaps the best-known name in high-end watches, advertises, in *Vogue,* its "Oyster Perpetual Lady-Datejust Pearlmaster." A close-up of the watch face showcases the white, mother-of-pearl dial, sapphire bezel, and diamond-set band. A smaller, more complete picture crouches underneath, showing the watch on its side. The model name is displayed along a gray band that runs near the bottom. The Rolex crest anchors the bottom of the page. Forty-five ads marketing 29 brands use the DESIGN/BRAND strategy. A large picture of the product centered on a solid background is the norm.

Discussion of second category.

CRAFTSMANSHIP, the second strategy, focuses on the maker, the horologer, and the technical sides of form and function. Brand heritage and a unique, hand-crafted design are major selling points. All of these ads are targeted at men, appearing in every magazine except *Vogue.* Collector pieces and limited editions were commonly sold using this strategy. The focus is on accuracy and technical excellence. Pictures of the inner works and cutaways, technical information, and explanations of movements and features are popular. Quality and exclusivity are all-important.

Detailed examples to illustrate second category.

A Cronoswiss ad from *The Robb Report* is a good example. The top third pictures a horologer, identified as "Gerd-R Lange, master watchmaker and founder of Cronoswiss in Munich," directly below. The middle third of the ad shows a watch, white-faced with a black leather band. The logo and slogan appear next to the watch. The bottom third contains copy beginning with the words "My watches are a hundred years behind the times." The rest explains what that statement means. Mr. Lange apparently believes that technical perfection in horology has already been attained. He also offers his book, *The Fascination of Mechanics,* free of charge along with the "sole distributor for North America" at the bottom. A "Daniel Roth" ad from the same magazine displays the name across the top of a white page; toward the top, left-hand corner a gold buckle and black band lead your eye to the center, where a gold watch with a transparent face displays its inner works exquisitely. Above and to the right, copy explains the exclusive and unique design accomplished by inverting the movement, allowing it to be viewed from above.

The third strategy is to sell the watch by establishing an ASSOCIATION with an object, experience, or person, implying that its value and quality are beyond question. In the six ads I found using this approach, watches are associated with violins, pilots, astronauts, hot air balloons, and a hero of the free world. This is similar to the first strategy, but relies on a reputation other than that of the maker. The watch is presented as being desirable for the connections created in the ad.

Discussion of third category.

Parmigiani ran an ad in *The Robb Report* featuring a gold watch with a black face and band illuminated by some unseen source. A blue-tinted violin rises in the background; the rest of the page is black. The brief copy reads: "For those who think a Stradivarius is only a violin. The Parmigiani Toric Chronograph is only a wristwatch." "The Moon Watch" proclaims an Omega ad from *GQ*. Inset on a white background is a picture of an astronaut on the moon saluting the American flag. The silver watch with a black face lies across the lower part of the page. The caption reads: "Speedmaster Professional. The first and only watch worn on the moon." Omega's logo appears at the bottom. Figure 2 shows another Omega use of this strategy.

WATER IS MICHAEL PHELPS' NATURAL ELEMENT.
PLANET OCEAN IS HIS CHRONOGRAPH.

FIGURE 2 Example of Association Advertising

The fourth strategy is to present the watch simply as a FASHION statement. In this line of attack, the ads appeal to our need to be current, accepted, to fit in and be like everyone else, or to make a statement, setting us apart from others as hip and cool. The product is presented as a necessary part of our wardrobes. The watch is fashionable and will send the "right" message. Design and style are the foremost concerns; "the look" sells the watch.

Discussion of fourth category.

Techno Marine has an ad in *GQ* which shows a large close-up of a watch running down the entire length of the left side of the page. Two alternate color schemes are pictured on the right, separating small bits of copy. At the bottom on the right are the name and logo. The first words at the top read: "Keeping time—you keep your closet up to the minute, why not your wrist? The latest addition to your watch wardrobe should be the AlphaSport." Longines uses a similar strategy in *Vogue.* Its ad is divided in half lengthwise. On the left is a black-and-white picture of Audrey Hepburn. The right side is white with the Longines' logo at the top and two ladies' watches in the center. Near the bottom is the phrase "Elegance is an Attitude." Retailers appear at the bottom. The same ad ran in *GQ,* but with a man's watch and a picture of Humphrey Bogart. A kind of association is made, but quality and value aren't the overriding concerns. The point is to have an elegant attitude like these fashionable stars did, one that these watches can provide and enhance.

The fifth and final strategy is that of EMOTIONAL appeal. The ads using this approach strive to influence our emotional responses and allege to influence the emotions of others towards us. Their power and appeal are exerted through the feelings they evoke in us. Nine out of ten ads rely on a picture as the main device to trigger an emotional link between the product and the viewer. Copy is scant; words are used mainly to guide the viewer to the advertiser's desired conclusions.

Discussion of fifth category.

A Frederique Constant ad pictures a man, wearing a watch, mulling over a chess game. Above his head are the words "Inner Passion." The man's gaze is odd; he is looking at something on the right side of the page, but a large picture of a watch superimposed over the picture hides whatever it is that he is looking at. So we are led to the watch. The bottom third is white and contains the maker's logo and the slogan "Live your Passion." An ad in *GQ* shows a man holding a woman. He leans against a rock; she reclines in his arms. Their eyes are closed, and both have peaceful, smiling expressions. He is wearing a Tommy Hilfiger watch. The ad spans two pages; a close-up of the watch is presented on the right half of the second page. The only words are the ones in the logo. This is perhaps one of those pictures that are worth a thousand words. The message is he got the girl because he's got the watch.

Strong conclusion; the effect of watch ads.

Even more than selling a particular watch, all of these ads focus on building the brand's image. I found many of the ads extremely effective at conveying their messages. Many of the better-known brands favor the comparatively simple DESIGN/BRAND appeal strategy, to reach a broader audience. Lesser-known, high-end makers contribute many of the more specialized strategies. We all count and mark the passing hours and minutes. And society places great importance on time, valuing punctuality. But these ads strive to convince us that having "the right time" means so much more than "the time."

FOR READING AND ANALYSIS

EVERY BODY'S TALKING | JOE NAVARRO

Joe Navarro spent more than twenty-five years in the FBI, specializing in counterintelligence and profiling. He is recognized as an authority on nonverbal messages, especially given off by those who are lying, and he continues to consult to government and industry. He has also turned his expertise to poker and has published, with Marvin Karlines, *Read 'Em and Reap* (2006), a guide to reading the nonverbal messages from poker opponents. The following essay appeared in the *Washington Post* on June 24, 2008.

PREREADING QUESTIONS What does the term "counterintelligence" mean? How much attention do you give to body language messages from others?

Picture this: I was sailing the Caribbean for three days with a group of friends and their spouses, and everything seemed perfect. The weather was beautiful, the ocean diaphanous blue, the food exquisite; our evenings together were full of laughter and good conversation.

Things were going so well that one friend said to the group, "Let's do this again next year." I happened to be across from him and his wife as he spoke those words. In the cacophony of resounding replies of "Yes!" and "Absolutely!" I noticed that my friend's wife made a fist under her chin as she grasped her necklace. This behavior stood out to me as powerfully as if someone had shouted, "Danger!"

I watched the words and gestures of the other couples at the table, and everyone seemed ecstatic—everyone but one, that is. She continued to smile, but her smile was tense.

Her husband has treated me as a brother for more than 15 years, and I consider him the dearest of friends. At that moment I knew that things between him and his wife were turning for the worse. I did not pat myself on the back for making these observations. I was saddened.

For 25 years I worked as a paid observer. I was a special agent for the FBI specializing in counterintelligence—specifically, catching spies. For me, observing human behavior is like having software running in the background, doing its job—no conscious effort needed. And so on that wonderful cruise, I made a "thin-slice assessment" (that's what we call it) based on just a few significant behaviors. Unfortunately, it turned out to be right: Within six months of our return, my friend's wife filed for divorce, and her husband discovered painfully that she had been seeing someone else for quite a while.

When I am asked what is the most reliable means of determining the health of a relationship, I always say that words don't matter. It's all in the language of the body. The nonverbal behaviors we all transmit tell others, in real time, what we think, what we feel, what we yearn for or what we intend.

Now I am embarking on another cruise, wondering what insights I will have about my travel companions and their relationships. No matter what, this promises to be a fascinating trip, a journey for the mind and the soul. I am with a handful of dear friends and 3,800 strangers, all headed for Alaska; for an observer it does not get any better than this.

While lining up to board on our first day, I notice just ahead of me a couple who appear to be in their early 30s. They are obviously Americans (voice, weight and demeanor).

Not so obvious is their dysfunctional relationship. He is standing stoically, shoulders wide, looking straight ahead. She keeps whispering loudly to him, but she is not facing forward. She violates his space as she leans into him. Her face is tense and her lips are narrow slivers each time she engages him with what clearly appears to be a diatribe. He occasionally nods his head but avoids contact with her. He won't let his hips near her as they start to walk side by side. He reminds me of Bill and Hillary Clinton walking toward the Marine One helicopter immediately after the Monica Lewinsky affair: looking straight ahead, as much distance between them as possible.

TORSO	ARMS	HANDS AND FINGERS	FEET AND LEGS
LEANING AWAY FROM SOMEONE: Means we dislike or disagree with them. **LEANING TOWARD SOMEONE:** Means we like or agree with them.	**FINGERTIPS SPREAD APART ON A SURFACE:** A display of confidence and authority.	**THUMBS UP:** A good indication of positive thoughts.	**JIGGLING/KICKING FOOT:** Indicates discomfort.
SPLAYING OUT: A sign of comfort becomes a territorial or dominance display when there are serious issues being discussed.	**ARMS AKIMBO:** Establishes dominance or communicates there are 'issues.'	**STEEPLING:** (FINGERTIP TO FINGERTIP) A powerful display of confidence.	**CROSSING LEGS:** Indicates we are comfortable.
CROSSED ARMS: Suddenly crossing arms tightly is a sign of discomfort.	**ARMS BEHIND THE BACK:** Says "don't draw near" —keeps people at bay.	**NECK TOUCHING:** Indicates emotional discomfort, doubt or insecurity.	**TOE POINTS UPWARD:** Signals a good mood.

Illustrations by Peter Arkle. Reprinted by permission.

10   I think everyone can decipher this one from afar because we have all seen situations like this. What most people will miss is something I have seen this young man do twice now, which portends poorly for both of them. Every time she looks away, he "disses" her. He smirks and rolls his eyes, even as she stands beside him. He performs his duties, pulling their luggage along; I suspect he likes to have her luggage nearby as a barrier between them. I won't witness the dissolution of their marriage, but I know it will happen, for the research behind this is fairly robust. When two people in a relationship have contempt for each other, the marriage will not last.

When it comes to relationships and courtship behaviors, the list of useful 11 cues is long. Most of these behaviors we learned early when interacting with our mothers. When we look at loving eyes, our own eyes get larger, our pupils dilate, our facial muscles relax, our lips become full and warm, our skin becomes more pliable, our heads tilt. These behaviors stay with us all of our lives.

I watched two lovers this morning in the dining room. Two young people, 12 perhaps in their late 20s, mirror each other, staring intently into each other's eyes, chin on hand, head slightly tilted, nose flaring with each breath. They are trying to absorb each other visually and tactilely as they hold hands across the table.

Over time, those who remain truly in love will show even more indicators 13 of mirroring. They may dress the same or even begin to look alike as they adopt each other's nonverbal expressions as a sign of synchrony and empathy. They will touch each other with kind hands that touch fully, not with the fingertips of the less caring.

They will mirror each other in ways that are almost imperceptible; they will 14 have similar blink rates and breathing rates, and they will sit almost identically. They will look at the same scenery and not speak, merely look at each other and take a deep breath to reset their breathing synchrony. They don't have to talk. They are in harmony physically, mentally and emotionally, just as a baby is in exquisite synchrony with its mother who is tracing his every expression and smile.

As I walk through the ship on the first night, I can see the nonverbals of 15 courtship. There is a beautiful woman, tall, slender, smoking a cigarette outside. Two men are talking to her, both muscular, handsome, interested. She has crossed her legs as she talks to them, an expression of her comfort. As she holds her cigarette, the inside of her wrist turns toward her newfound friends. Her interest and comfort with them resounds, but she is favoring one of them. As he speaks to her, she preens herself by playing with her hair. I am not sure he is getting the message that she prefers him; in the end, I am sure it will all get sorted out.

At the upscale lounge, a man is sitting at the bar talking animatedly to the 16 woman next to him and looking at everyone who walks by. The woman has begun the process of ignoring him, but he does not get it. After he speaks to her a few times, she gathers her purse and places it on her lap. She has turned slightly away from him and now avoids eye contact. He has no clue; he thinks he is cool by commenting on the women who pass by. She is verbally and nonverbally indifferent.

The next night it is more of the same. This time, I see two people who just 17 met talking gingerly. Gradually they lean more and more into each other. She is now dangling her sandal from her toes. I am not sure he knows it. Perhaps he sees it all in her face, because she is smiling, laughing and relaxed. Communication is fluid, and neither wants the conversation to end. She is extremely interested.

18   All of these individuals are carrying on a dialogue in nonverbals. The socially adept will learn to read and interpret the signs accurately. Others will make false steps or pay a high price for not being observant. They may end up like my friend on the Caribbean cruise, who missed the clues of deceit and indifference.

19   This brings me back to my friend and his new wife, who are on this wonderful voyage. They have been on board for four days, and they are a delight individually and together. He lovingly looks at her; she stares at him with love and admiration. When she holds his hand at dinner, she massages it ever so gently. Theirs is a strong marriage. They don't have to tell me. I can sense it and observe it. I am happy for them and for myself. I can see cues of happiness, and they are unmistakable. You can't ask for more.

Source: *Washington Post*, June 24, 2008. Reprinted by permission of the author.

QUESTIONS FOR READING

1.   What is Navarro's subject? (Do not answer "taking cruises"!)
2.   What clues are offered to support the conclusion that the two cruise couples' relationships are about to dissolve?
3.   What are the nonverbal messages that reveal loving relationships?
4.   What nonverbal messages should the man in the lounge be observing?

QUESTIONS FOR REASONING AND ANALYSIS

5.   What is Navarro's claim?
6.   What kind of evidence does he provide?
7.   How do the illustrations contribute to the argument? What is effective about the author's opening?

QUESTIONS FOR REFLECTION AND WRITING

8.   Has the author convinced you that nonverbal language reveals our thoughts and feelings? Why or why not?
9.   Can you "read" the nonverbal language of your instructors? Take some time to analyze each of your instructors. What have you learned? (You might also reflect on what messages you may be sending in class.)

For all investigative essays—inductive arguments—follow the guidelines in this chapter and use the student essay as your model. Remember that you will need to explain your methods for collecting data, to classify evidence and present it in several formats, and also to explain its significance for readers. Just collecting data does not create an argument. Here are some possible topics to explore:

1. Study print ads for one type of product (e.g., cars, cosmetics, cigarettes) to draw inferences about the dominant techniques used to sell that product. Remember that the more ads you study, the more support you have for your inferences. You should study at least twenty-five ads.

2. Study print ads for one type of product as advertised in different types of magazines clearly directed to different audiences to see how (or if) selling techniques change with a change in audience. (Remember: To demonstrate no change in techniques can be just as interesting a conclusion as finding changes.) Study at least twenty-five ads, in a balanced number from the different magazines.

3. Select a major figure currently in the news and conduct a study of bias in one of the newsmagazines (e.g., *Time, U.S. News & World Report,* or *Newsweek*) or a newspaper. Use at least eight issues of the magazine or newspaper from the last six months and study all articles on your figure in each of those issues. To determine bias, look at the amount of coverage, the location (front pages or back pages), the use of photos (flattering or unflattering), and the language of the articles.

4. Conduct a study of amounts of violence on TV by analyzing, for one week, all prime-time programs that may contain violence. (That is, eliminate sitcoms and decide whether you want to include or exclude news programs.) Devise some classification system for types of violence based on your prior TV viewing experience before beginning your study—but be prepared to alter or add to your categories based on your viewing of shows. Note the number of times each violent act occurs. You may want to consider the total length of time (per program, per night, per type of violent act) of violence during the week you study. Give credit to any authors in this text or other publications for any ideas you borrow from their articles.

5. As an alternative to topic 4, study the number and types of violent acts in children's programs on Saturday mornings. (This and topic 4 are best handled if you can record and then replay the programs several times.)

6. Conduct a survey and analyze the results on some campus issue or current public policy issue. Prepare questions that are without bias and include questions to get information about the participants so that you can correlate answers with the demographics of your participants (e.g., age, gender, race, religion, proposed major in college, political affiliation, or whatever else you think is important to the topic studied). Decide whether you want to survey students only or both students and faculty. Plan how you are going to reach each group.

CHAPTER 6

Learning More about Argument: Induction, Deduction, Analogy, and Logical Fallacies

PEARLS BEFORE SWINE   **BY STEPHAN PASTIS**

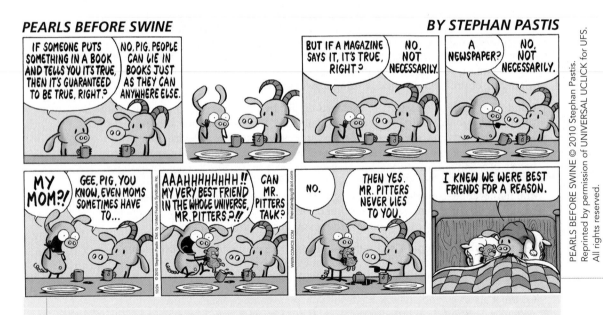

READ: What is the situation? What are Pig's reactions to what he is told?

REASON: Who are the only creatures who can never lie? What is Pig's solution to what he has been told? Are we invited to accept Pig's solution?

REFLECT/WRITE: What makes the cartoon amusing? What is its more serious message?

You can build on your knowledge of the basics of argument, examined in Chapter 3, by understanding some traditional forms of argument: induction, deduction, and analogy. It is also important to recognize arguments that do not meet the standards of good logic.

INDUCTION

Induction is the process by which we reach inferences—opinions based on facts, or on a combination of facts and less debatable inferences. The inductive process moves from particular to general, from support to assertion. We base our inferences on the facts we have gathered and studied. In general, the more evidence, the more convincing the argument. No one wants to debate tomorrow's sunrise; the evidence for counting on it is too convincing. Most inferences, though, are drawn from less evidence, so we need to examine these arguments closely to judge their reasonableness.

The pattern of induction looks like this:

EVIDENCE: There is the dead body of Smith. Smith was shot in his bedroom between the hours of 11:00 P.M. and 2:00 A.M., according to the coroner. Smith was shot by a .32-caliber pistol. The pistol left in the bedroom contains Jones's fingerprints. Jones was seen, by a neighbor, entering the Smith home at around 11:00 the night of Smith's death. A coworker heard Smith and Jones arguing in Smith's office the morning of the day Smith died.

CLAIM: Jones killed Smith.

The facts are presented. The jury infers that Jones is a murderer. Unless there is a confession or a trustworthy eyewitness, the conclusion is an inference, not a fact. This is the most logical explanation. The conclusion meets the standards of simplicity and frequency while accounting for all of the known evidence.

The following paragraph illustrates the process of induction. In their book *Discovering Dinosaurs*, authors Mark Norell, Eugene Gaffney, and Lowell Dingus answer the question "Did dinosaurs really rule the world?"

> For almost 170 million years, from the Late Triassic to the end of the Cretaceous, there existed dinosaurs of almost every body form imaginable: small carnivores, such as *Compsognathus* and *Ornitholestes*, ecologically equivalent to today's foxes and coyotes; medium-sized carnivores, such as *Velociraptor* and the troödontids, analogous to lions and tigers; and the monstrous carnivores with no living analogs, such as *Tyrannosaurus* and *Allosaurus*. Included among the ornithischians and the elephantine sauropods are terrestrial herbivores of diverse body form. By the end of the Jurassic, dinosaurs had even taken to the skies. The only habitats that dinosaurs did not dominate during the Mesozoic were aquatic. Yet, there were marine representatives, such as the primitive toothed bird *Hesperornis*. Like penguins, these birds were flightless, specialized for diving, and probably had to return to land to reproduce. In light of this broad morphologic diversity [number of

body forms], dinosaurs did "rule the planet" as the dominant life form on
Earth during most of the Mesozoic [era that includes the Triassic, Jurassic, and
Cretaceous periods, 248 to 65 million years ago].

Observe that the writers organize evidence by type of dinosaur to demonstrate
the range and diversity of these animals. A good inductive argument is based
on a sufficient volume of *relevant* evidence. The basic shape of this inductive
argument is illustrated in Figure 6.1.

CLAIM:	Dinosaurs were the dominant life form during the Mesozoic era.
GROUNDS:	The facts presented in the paragraph.
ASSUMPTION (WARRANT):	The facts are representative, revealing dinosaur diversity.

FIGURE 6.1 The Shape of an Inductive Argument

COLLABORATIVE EXERCISE: Induction

With your class partner or in small groups, make a list of facts that could be used to
support each of the following inferences:

1. Fido must have escaped under the fence during the night.
2. Sue must be planning to go away for the weekend.
3. Students who do not hand in all essay assignments fail Dr. Bradshaw's English class.
4. The price of Florida oranges will go up in grocery stores next year.
5. Yogurt is a better breakfast food than bread.

DEDUCTION

Although induction can be described as an argument that moves from particular to general, from facts to inference, deduction cannot accurately be described
as the reverse. Deductive arguments are more complex. *Deduction is the reasoning process that draws a conclusion from the logical relationship of two assertions, usually one broad judgment or definition and one more specific assertion, often an inference.*
Suppose, on the way out of American history class, you say, "Abraham Lincoln
certainly was a great leader." Someone responds with the expected question
"Why do you think so?" You explain: "He was great because he performed
with courage and a clear purpose in a time of crisis." Your explanation contains
a conclusion and an assertion about Lincoln (an inference) in support. But
behind your explanation rests an idea about leadership, in the terms of deduction, *a premise.* The argument's basic shape is illustrated in Figure 6.2.

CLAIM:	Lincoln was a great leader.
GROUNDS:	1. People who perform with courage and clear purpose in a crisis are great leaders.
	2. Lincoln was a person who performed with courage and a clear purpose in a crisis.
ASSUMPTION (WARRANT):	The relationship of the two reasons leads, logically, to the conclusion.

FIGURE 6.2 The Shape of a Deductive Argument

Traditionally, the deductive argument is arranged somewhat differently from these sentences about Lincoln. The two reasons are called *premises;* the broader one, called the *major premise,* is written first and the more specific one, the *minor premise,* comes next. The premises and conclusion are expressed to make clear that assertions are being made about categories or classes. To illustrate:

MAJOR PREMISE: All people who perform with courage and a clear purpose in a crisis are great leaders.

MINOR PREMISE: Lincoln was a person who performed with courage and a clear purpose in a crisis.
———————————
CONCLUSION: Lincoln was a great leader.

If these two premises are correctly, that is, logically, constructed, then the conclusion follows logically, and the deductive argument is *valid.* This does not mean that the conclusion is necessarily *true.* It does mean that if you accept the truth of the premises, then you must accept the truth of the conclusion, because in a valid argument the conclusion follows logically, necessarily. How do we know that the conclusion must follow if the argument is logically constructed? Let's think about what each premise is saying and then diagram each one to represent each assertion visually. The first premise says that all people who act a particular way are people who fit into the category called "great leaders":

The second premise says that Lincoln, a category of one, belongs in the category of people who act in the same particular way that the first premise describes:

If we put the two diagrams together, we have the following set of circles, demonstrating that the conclusion follows from the premises:

We can also make negative and qualified assertions in a deductive argument. For example:

PREMISE: No cowards can be great leaders.

PREMISE: Falstaff was a coward.

CONCLUSION: Falstaff was not a great leader.

Or, to reword the conclusion to make the deductive pattern clearer: No Falstaff (no member of this class) is a great leader. Diagramming to test for validity, we find that the first premise says no A's are B's:

The second premise asserts all C's are A's:

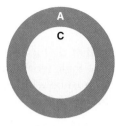

Put together, we see that the conclusion follows necessarily from the premises: No C's can possibly be members of class B.

Some deductive arguments merely look right, but the two premises do not lead logically to the conclusion that is asserted. We must read each argument carefully or diagram each one to make certain that the conclusion follows from the premises. Consider the following argument: *Unions must be communistic because they want to control wages.* The sentence contains a conclusion and one reason, or premise. From these two parts of a deductive argument we can also determine the unstated premise, just as we could with the Lincoln argument: *Communists want to control wages.* If we use circles to represent the three categories of people in the argument and diagram the argument, we see a different result from the previous diagrams:

Diagramming the argument reveals that it is invalid; that is, it is not logically constructed because the statements do not require that the union circle be placed inside the communist circle. We cannot draw the conclusion we want from any two premises, only from those that provide a logical basis from which a conclusion can be reached.

We must first make certain that deductive arguments are properly constructed or valid. But suppose the logic works and yet you do not agree with the claim? Your complaint, then, must be with one of the premises, a judgment or inference that you do not accept as true. Consider the following argument:

MAJOR PREMISE:	(All) dogs make good pets.
MINOR PREMISE:	Fido is a dog.
CONCLUSION:	Fido will make a good pet.

This argument is valid. (Diagram it; your circles will fit into one another just as with the Lincoln argument.) However, you are not prepared to agree, necessarily, that Fido will make a good pet. The problem is with the major premise. For the argument to work, the assertion must be about *all* dogs, but we know that not all dogs will be good pets.

When composing a deductive argument, your task will be to defend the truth of your premises. Then, if your argument is valid (logically constructed), readers will have no alternative but to agree with your conclusion. If you disagree with someone else's logically constructed argument, then you must show why one of the premises is not true. Your counterargument will seek to discredit one (or both) of the premises. The Fido argument can be discredited by your producing examples of dogs that have not made good pets.

A deductive argument can serve as the core of an essay, an essay that supports the argument's claim by developing support for each of the premises. Since the major premise is either a broad judgment or a definition, it will need to be defended on the basis of an appeal to values or beliefs that the writer expects readers to share. The minor premise, usually an inference about a particular situation (or person), would be supported by relevant evidence, as with any inductive argument. You can see this process at work in the Declaration of Independence. Questions follow the Declaration to guide your analysis of this famous example of the deductive process.

THE DECLARATION OF INDEPENDENCE

In Congress, July 4, 1776
The unanimous declaration of the thirteen
United States of America

1 When in the course of human events, it becomes necessary for one people to dissolve the political bands which have connected them with another, and to assume among the powers of the earth, the separate and equal station to which the Laws of Nature and of Nature's God entitle them, a decent respect

to the opinions of mankind requires that they should declare the causes which impel them to the separation.

We hold these truths to be self-evident, that all men are created equal, that they are endowed by their Creator with certain unalienable rights, that among these are life, liberty and the pursuit of happiness. That to secure these rights, governments are instituted among men, deriving their just powers from the consent of the governed. That whenever any form of government becomes destructive of these ends, it is the right of the people to alter or to abolish it, and to institute new government, laying its foundation on such principles and organizing its powers in such form, as to them shall seem most likely to effect their safety and happiness. Prudence, indeed, will dictate that governments long established should not be changed for light and transient causes; and accordingly all experience hath shown, that mankind are more disposed to suffer, while evils are sufferable, than to right themselves by abolishing the forms to which they are accustomed. But when a long train of abuses and usurpations, pursuing invariably the same object evinces a design to reduce them under absolute despotism, it is their right, it is their duty, to throw off such government, and to provide new guards for their future security. Such has been the patient sufferance of these Colonies; and such is now the necessity which constrains them to alter their former systems of government. The history of the present King of Great Britain is a history of repeated injuries and usurpations, all having in direct object the establishment of an absolute tyranny over these States. To prove this, let facts be submitted to a candid world. 2

He has refused his assent to laws, the most wholesome and necessary for the public good. 3

He has forbidden his Governors to pass laws of immediate and pressing importance, unless suspended in their operation till his assent should be obtained; and when so suspended, he has utterly neglected to attend to them. 4

He has refused to pass other laws for the accommodation of large districts of people, unless those people would relinquish the right of representation in the Legislature, a right inestimable to them and formidable to tyrants only. 5

He has called together legislative bodies at places unusual, uncomfortable, and distant from the depository of their public records, for the sole purpose of fatiguing them into compliance with his measures. 6

He has dissolved representative houses repeatedly, for opposing with manly firmness his invasions on the rights of the people. 7

He has refused for a long time, after such dissolutions, to cause others to be elected; whereby the legislative powers, incapable of annihilation, have returned to the people at large for their exercise; the State remaining in the meantime exposed to all the dangers of invasion from without and convulsions within. 8

He has endeavoured to prevent the population of these States; for that purpose obstructing the laws of naturalization of foreigners; refusing to pass others to encourage their migration hither, and raising the conditions of new appropriations of lands. 9

10   He has obstructed the administration of justice, by refusing his assent to laws for establishing judiciary powers.

11   He has made judges dependent on his will alone, for the tenure of their offices, and the amount and payment of their salaries.

12   He has erected a multitude of new offices, and sent hither swarms of officers to harass our people, and eat out their substance.

13   He has kept among us, in times of peace, standing armies without the consent of our legislatures.

14   He has affected to render the military independent of and superior to the civil power.

15   He has combined with others to subject us to a jurisdiction foreign to our constitution, and unacknowledged by our laws; giving his assent to their acts of pretended legislation:

16   For quartering large bodies of armed troops among us:

17   For protecting them, by a mock trial, from punishment for any murders which they should commit on the inhabitants of these States:

18   For cutting off our trade with all parts of the world:

19   For imposing taxes on us without our consent:

20   For depriving us, in many cases, of the benefits of trial by jury:

21   For transporting us beyond seas to be tried for pretended offences:

22   For abolishing the free system of English laws in a neighbouring Province, establishing therein an arbitrary government, and enlarging its boundaries so as to render it at once an example and fit instrument for introducing the same absolute rule into these Colonies:

23   For taking away our Charters, abolishing our most valuable laws, and altering fundamentally the forms of our governments:

24   For suspending our own Legislatures, and declaring themselves invested with power to legislate for us in all cases whatsoever.

25   He has abdicated government here, by declaring us out of his protection and waging war against us.

26   He has plundered our seas, ravaged our coasts, burnt our towns, and destroyed the lives of our people.

27   He is at this time transporting large armies of foreign mercenaries to complete the works of death, desolation and tyranny, already begun with circumstances of cruelty and perfidy scarcely paralleled in the most barbarous ages, and totally unworthy the head of a civilized nation.

28   He has constrained our fellow citizens taken captive on the high seas to bear arms against their country, to become the executioners of their friends and brethren, or to fall themselves by their hands.

29   He has excited domestic insurrections amongst us, and has endeavoured to bring on the inhabitants of our frontiers, the merciless Indian savages, whose known rule of warfare, is an undistinguished destruction of all ages, sexes, and conditions.

30   In every stage of these oppressions we have petitioned for redress in the most humble terms; our repeated petitions have been answered only by repeated injury. A prince whose character is thus marked by every act which may define a tyrant is unfit to be the ruler of a free people.

Nor have we been wanting in attention to our British brethren. We have 31 warned them from time to time of attempts by their legislature to extend an unwarrantable jurisdiction over us. We have reminded them of the circumstances of our emigration and settlement here. We have appealed to their native justice and magnanimity, and we have conjured them by the ties of our common kindred to disavow these usurpations, which would inevitably interrupt our connections and correspondence. They too have been deaf to the voice of justice and of consanguinity. We must, therefore, acquiesce in the necessity, which denounces our separation, and hold them, as we hold the rest of mankind, enemies in war, in peace friends.

We, therefore, the Representatives of the United States of America, in 32 General Congress assembled, appealing to the Supreme Judge of the world for the rectitude of our intentions, do, in the name, and by the authority of the good people of these Colonies, solemnly publish and declare, That these United Colonies are, and of right ought to be Free and Independent States; that they are absolved from all allegiance to the British Crown, and that all political connection between them and the State of Great Britain, is and ought to be totally dissolved; and that as Free and Independent States, they have full power to levy war, conclude peace, contract alliances, establish commerce, and to do all other acts and things which Independent States may of right do. And for the support of this declaration, with a firm reliance on the protection of Divine Providence, we mutually pledge to each other our lives, our fortunes, and our sacred honor.

QUESTIONS FOR ANALYSIS

1. What is the Declaration's central deductive argument? State the argument in the shape illustrated above: major premise, minor premise, conclusion. Construct a valid argument. If necessary, draw circles representing each of the three terms in the argument to check for validity. (*Hint:* Start with the claim "George III's government should be overthrown.")

2. Which paragraphs are devoted to supporting the major premise? What kind of support has been given?

3. Which paragraphs are devoted to supporting the minor premise? What kind of support has been given?

4. Why has more support been given for one premise than the other?

EXERCISES: Completing and Evaluating Deductive Arguments

Turn each of the following statements into valid deductive arguments. (You have the conclusion and one premise, so you will have to determine the missing premise that would complete the argument. Draw circles if necessary to test for validity.) Then decide which arguments have premises that could be supported. Note the kind of support that might be provided. Explain why you think some arguments have insupportable premises. Here is an example:

PREMISE:	All Jesuits are priests.
PREMISE:	No women are priests.
CONCLUSION:	No women are Jesuits.

Since the circle for women must be placed outside the circle for priests, it must also be outside the circle for Jesuits. Hence the argument is valid. The first premise is true by definition; the term *Jesuit* refers to an order of Roman Catholic priests. The second premise is true for the Roman Catholic Church, so if the term *priest* is used only to refer to people with a religious vocation in the Roman Catholic Church, then the second premise is also true by definition.

1. Mrs. Ferguson is a good teacher because she can explain the subject matter clearly.
2. Segregated schools are unconstitutional because they are unequal.
3. Michael must be a good driver because he drives fast.
4. The media clearly have a liberal bias because they make fun of religious fundamentalists.

ANALOGY

The argument from analogy is an argument based on comparison. Analogies assert that since A and B are alike in several ways, they must be alike in another way as well. The argument from analogy concludes with an inference, an assertion of a significant similarity in the two items being compared. The other similarities serve as evidence in support of the inference. The shape of an argument by analogy is illustrated in Figure 6.3.

   Although analogy is sometimes an effective approach to an issue because clever, imaginative comparisons are often moving, analogy is not as rigorously logical as either induction or deduction. Frequently, an analogy is based on only two or three points of comparison, whereas a sound inductive argument presents many examples to support its conclusion. Further, to be convincing, the points of comparison must be fundamental to the two items being compared. An argument for a county leash law for cats developed by analogy with dogs may cite the following similarities:

GROUNDS:	A has characteristics 1, 2, 3, and 4.
	B has characteristics 1, 2, and 3.
CLAIM:	B has characteristic 4 (as well).
ASSUMPTION	If B has three characteristics in common with A, it must have
(WARRANT):	the key fourth characteristic as well.

FIGURE 6.3 **The Shape of an Argument by Analogy**

- Cats are pets, just like dogs.
- Cats live in residential communities, just like dogs.
- Cats can mess up other people's yards, just like dogs.
- Cats, if allowed to run free, can disturb the peace (fighting, howling at night), just like dogs.

Does it follow that cats should be required to walk on a leash, just like dogs? If such a county ordinance were passed, would it be enforceable? Have you ever tried to walk a cat on a leash? In spite of legitimate similarities brought out by the analogy, the conclusion does not logically follow because the arguer is overlooking a fundamental difference in the two animals' personalities. Dogs can be trained to a leash; most cats (Siamese are one exception) cannot be so trained. Such thinking will produce sulking cats and scratched owners. But the analogy, delivered passionately to the right audience, could lead community activists to lobby for a new law.

Observe that the problem with the cat-leash-law analogy is not in the similarities asserted about the items being compared but rather in the underlying assumption that the similarities logically support the argument's conclusion. A good analogy asserts many points of comparison and finds likenesses that are essential parts of the nature or purpose of the two items being compared. The best way to challenge another's analogy is to point out a fundamental difference in the nature or purpose of the compared items. For all of their similarities, when it comes to walking on a leash, cats are *not* like dogs.

EXERCISES: Analogy

Analyze the following analogies. List the stated and/or implied points of comparison and the conclusion in the pattern illustrated in Figure 6.3. Then judge each argument's logic and effectiveness as a persuasive technique. If the argument is not logical, state the fundamental difference in the two compared items. If the argument could be persuasive, describe the kind of audience that might be moved by it.

1. College newspapers should not be under the supervision or control of a faculty sponsor. Fortunately, no governmental sponsor controls the *New York Times*, or we would no longer have a free press in this country. We need a free college press, too, one that can attack college policies when they are wrong.
2. Let's recognize that college athletes are really professional and start paying them properly. College athletes get a free education, and spending money from boosters. They are required to attend practices and games, and—if they play football or basketball—they bring in huge revenues for their "organization." College coaches are also paid enormous salaries, just like professional coaches, and often college coaches are tapped to coach professional teams. The only difference: The poor college athletes don't get those big salaries and huge signing bonuses.
3. Just like any business, the federal government must be made to balance its budget. No company could continue to operate in the red as the government does and expect to be successful. A constitutional amendment requiring a balanced federal budget is long overdue.

LOGICAL FALLACIES

A thorough study of argument needs to include a study of logical fallacies because so many "arguments" fail to meet standards of sound logic and good sense. Why do people offer arguments that aren't sensible?

Causes of Illogic

Ignorance

One frequent cause for illogical debate is a lack of knowledge of the subject. Some people have more information than others. The younger you are, the less you can be expected to know about complex issues. On the other hand, if you want to debate a complex or technical issue, then you cannot use ignorance as an excuse. Instead, read as much as you can, listen carefully to discussions, ask questions, and select topics about which you have knowledge or will research before writing.

Egos

Ego problems are another cause of weak arguments. Those with low self-esteem often have difficulty in debates because they attach themselves to their ideas and then feel personally attacked when someone disagrees with them. Remember: Self-esteem is enhanced when others applaud our knowledge and thoughtfulness, not our irrationality.

Prejudices

The prejudices and biases that we carry around, having absorbed them "ages ago" from family and community, are also sources of irrationality. Prejudices range from the worst ethnic, religious, or sexist stereotypes to political views we have adopted uncritically (Democrats are all bleeding hearts; Republicans are all rich snobs) to perhaps less serious but equally insupportable notions (if it's in print, it must be right). People who see the world through distorted lenses cannot possibly assess facts intelligently and reason logically from them.

A Need for Answers

Finally, many bad arguments stem from a human need for answers—any answers—to the questions that deeply concern us. We want to control our world because that makes us feel secure, and having answers makes us feel in control. This need can lead to illogic from oversimplifying issues.

Based on these causes of illogic, we can usefully divide fallacies into (1) oversimplifying the issue and (2) ignoring the issue by substituting emotion for reason.

Fallacies That Result from Oversimplifying

Errors in Generalizing

Errors in generalizing include overstatement and hasty or faulty generalization. All have in common an error in the inductive pattern of argument. The inference drawn from the evidence is unwarranted, either because too broad a generalization is made or because the generalization is drawn from incomplete or incorrect evidence.

Overstatement occurs when the argument's assertion is unqualified—referring to all members of a category. Overstatements often result from stereotyping, giving the same traits to everyone in a group. Overstatements are frequently signaled by words such as *all, every, always, never,* and *none.* But remember that assertions such as "children love clowns" are understood to refer to "all children," even though the word *all* does not appear in the sentence. It is the writer's task to qualify statements appropriately, using words such as *some, many,* or *frequently,* as appropriate.

Overstatements are discredited by finding only one exception to disprove the assertion. One frightened child who starts to cry when the clown approaches will destroy the argument. Here is another example:

- Lawyers are only interested in making money.

  (What about lawyers who work to protect consumers, or public defenders who represent those unable to pay for a lawyer?)

Hasty or faulty generalizations may be qualified assertions, but they still oversimplify by arguing from insufficient evidence or by ignoring some relevant evidence. For example:

- Political life must lead many to excessive drinking. In the last six months the paper has written about five members of Congress who either have confessed to alcoholism or have been arrested on DUI charges.

  (Five is not a large enough sample from which to generalize about *many* politicians. Also, the five in the newspaper are not a representative sample; they have made the news because of their drinking.)

Forced Hypothesis

The *forced hypothesis* is also an error in inductive reasoning. The explanation (hypothesis) offered is "forced," or illogical, because either (1) sufficient evidence does not exist to draw any conclusion or (2) the evidence can be explained more simply or more sensibly by a different hypothesis. This fallacy often results from not considering other possible explanations. You discredit a forced hypothesis by providing alternative conclusions that are more sensible than or just as sensible as the one offered. Consider this example:

- Professor Redding's students received either A's or B's last semester. He must be an excellent teacher.

  (The grades alone cannot support this conclusion. Professor Redding could be an excellent teacher; he could have started with excellent students; he could be an easy grader.)

Non Sequitur

The term *non sequitur,* meaning literally "it does not follow," could apply to all illogical arguments, but the term is usually reserved for those in which the conclusions are not logically connected to the reasons. In a hasty generalization, for example, there is a connection between support (five politicians in the news) and conclusion (many politicians with drinking problems), just not a convincing connection. With the *non sequitur* there is no recognizable connection, either because (1) whatever connection the arguer sees is not made clear to others or because (2) the evidence or reasons offered are irrelevant to the conclusion. For example:

- Donna will surely get a good grade in physics; she earned an A in her biology class.

   (Doing well in one course, even one science course, does not support the conclusion that the student will get a good grade in another course. If Donna is not good at math, she definitely will not do well in physics.)

Slippery Slope

The *slippery slope* argument asserts that we should not proceed with or permit A because, if we do, the terrible consequences X, Y, and Z will occur. This type of argument oversimplifies by assuming, without evidence and usually by ignoring historical examples, existing laws, or any reasonableness in people, that X, Y, and Z will follow inevitably from A. This kind of argument rests on the belief that most people will not want the final, awful Z to occur. The belief, however accurate, does not provide a sufficiently good reason for avoiding A. One of the best-known examples of slippery slope reasoning can be found in the gun-control debate:

- If we allow the government to register handguns, next it will register hunting rifles; then it will prohibit all citizen ownership of guns, thereby creating a police state or a world in which only outlaws have guns.

   (Surely no one wants the final dire consequences predicted in this argument. However, handgun registration does not mean that these consequences will follow. The United States has never been a police state, and its system of free elections guards against such a future. Also, citizens have registered cars, boats, and planes for years without any threat of their confiscation.)

False Dilemma

The *false dilemma* oversimplifies by asserting only two alternatives when there are more than two. The either–or thinking of this kind of argument can be an effective tactic if undetected. If the arguer gives us only two choices and one of those is clearly unacceptable, then the arguer can push us toward the preferred choice. For example:

- The Federal Reserve System must lower interest rates, or we will never pull out of the recession.

   (Clearly, staying in a recession is not much of a choice, but the alternative may not be the only or the best course to achieve a healthy economy. If interest rates go too low, inflation can result. Other options include the government's creating new jobs and patiently letting market forces play themselves out.)

False Analogy

When examining the shape of analogy, we also considered the problems with this type of argument. (See pp. 160–61.) Remember that you challenge a false analogy by noting many differences in the two items being compared or by noting a significant difference that has been ignored.

Post Hoc Fallacy

The term *post hoc*, from the Latin *post hoc, ergo propter hoc* (literally, "after this, therefore because of it") refers to a common error in arguments about cause. One oversimplifies by confusing a time relationship with cause. Reveal the illogic of *post hoc* arguments by pointing to other possible causes:

- We should throw out the entire city council. Since the members were elected, the city has gone into deficit spending.

  (Assuming that deficit spending in this situation is bad, was it caused by the current city council? Or did the current council inherit debts? Or is the entire region suffering from a recession?)

EXERCISES: Fallacies That Result from Oversimplifying

1. Here is a list of the fallacies we have examined so far. Make up or collect from your reading at least one example of each fallacy.
   a. Overstatement
   b. Stereotyping
   c. Hasty generalization
   d. Forced hypothesis
   e. *Non sequitur*
   f. Slippery slope
   g. False dilemma
   h. False analogy
   i. *Post hoc* fallacy

2. Explain what is illogical about each of the following arguments. Then name the fallacy represented. (Sometimes an argument will fit into more than one category. In that case name all appropriate terms.)
   a. Everybody agrees that we need stronger drunk-driving laws.
   b. The upsurge in crime on Sundays is the result of the reduced rate of church attendance in recent years.
   c. The government must create new jobs. A factory in Illinois has laid off half its workers.
   d. Steve has joined the country club. Golf must be one of his favorite sports.
   e. Blondes have more fun.
   f. You'll enjoy your Volvo; foreign cars never break down.
   g. Gary loves jokes. He would make a great comedian.
   h. The economy is in bad shape because of the Federal Reserve Board. Ever since it expanded the money supply, the stock market has been declining.
   i. Either we improve the city's street lighting, or we will fail to reduce crime.
   j. DNA research today is just like the study of nuclear fission. It seems important, but it's just another bomb that will one day explode on us. When will we learn that government must control research?

   k. To prohibit prayer in public schools is to limit religious practice solely to internal belief. The result is that an American is religiously "free" only in his or her own mind.

   l. Professor Johnson teaches in the political science department. I'll bet she's another socialist.

   m. Coming to the aid of any country engaged in civil war is a bad idea. Next we'll be sending American troops, and soon we'll be involved in another Vietnam.

   n. We must reject affirmative action in hiring or we'll have to settle for incompetent employees.

Fallacies That Result from Avoiding the Real Issue

There are many ways to divert attention from the issue under debate. Of the six discussed here, the first three try to divert attention by introducing a separate issue or "sliding by" the actual issue. The following three divert by appealing to the audience's emotions or prejudices. In the first three the arguer tries to give the impression of good logic. In the last three the arguer charges forward on emotional manipulation alone.

Begging the Question

To assume that part of your argument is true without supporting it is to *beg the question*. Arguments seeking to pass off as proof statements that must themselves be supported are often introduced with such phrases as "the fact is" (to introduce opinion), "obviously," and "as we can see." For example:

- Clearly, lowering grading standards would be bad for students, so a pass/fail system should not be adopted.

  (Does a pass/fail system lower standards? No evidence has been given. If so, is that necessarily bad for students?)

Red Herring

The *red herring* is a foul-smelling argument indeed. The debater introduces a side issue, some point that is not relevant to the debate:

- The senator is an honest woman; she loves her children and gives to charities.

  (The children and charities are side issues; they do not demonstrate honesty.)

Straw Man

The *straw man* argument attributes to opponents incorrect and usually ridiculous views that they do not hold so that their position can be easily attacked. We can challenge this illogic by demonstrating that the arguer's opponents do not hold those views or by demanding that the arguer provide some evidence that they do:

- Those who favor gun control just want to take all guns away from responsible citizens and put them in the hands of criminals.

  (The position attributed to proponents of gun control is not only inaccurate but actually the opposite of what is sought by gun-control proponents.)

Ad Hominem

One of the most frequent of all appeals to emotion masquerading as argument is the *ad hominem* argument (literally, argument "to the man"). When someone says that "those crazy liberals at the ACLU just want all criminals to go free," or a pro-choice demonstrator screams at those "self-righteous fascists" on the other side, the best retort may be silence, or the calm assertion that such statements do not contribute to meaningful debate.

Common Practice or Bandwagon

To argue that an action should be taken or a position accepted because "everyone is doing it" is illogical. The majority is not always right. Frequently, when someone is defending an action as ethical on the ground that everyone does it, the action isn't ethical and the defender knows it isn't. For example:

- There's nothing wrong with fudging a bit on your income taxes. After all, the superrich don't pay any taxes, and the government expects everyone to cheat a little.

  (First, not everyone cheats on taxes; many pay to have their taxes done correctly. And if it is wrong, it is wrong regardless of the number who do it.)

Ad Populum

Another technique for arousing an audience's emotions and ignoring the issue is to appeal *ad populum*, "to the people," to the audience's presumed shared values and beliefs. Every Fourth of July, politicians employ this tactic, appealing to God, mother, apple pie, and "traditional family values." Simply reject the argument as illogical.

- Good, law-abiding Americans must be sick of the violent crimes occurring in our once godly society. But we won't tolerate it anymore; put the criminals in jail and throw away the key.

  (This does not contribute to a thoughtful debate on criminal justice issues.)

EXERCISES: Fallacies That Result from Ignoring the Issue

1. Here is a list of fallacies that result from ignoring the issue. Make up or collect from your reading at least one example of each fallacy.
   a. Begging the question
   b. Red herring
   c. Straw man

      d. *Ad hominem*

      e. Common practice or bandwagon

      f. *Ad populum*

2. Explain what is illogical about each of the following arguments. Then name the fallacy represented.

      a. Gold's book doesn't deserve a Pulitzer Prize. She had been married four times.

      b. I wouldn't vote for him; many of his programs are basically socialist.

      c. Eight out of ten headache sufferers use Bayer to relieve headache pain. It will work for you, too.

      d. We shouldn't listen to Colman McCarthy's argument against liquor ads in college newspapers because he obviously thinks young people are ignorant and need guidance in everything.

      e. My roommate Joe does the craziest things; he must be neurotic.

      f. Since so many people obviously cheat the welfare system, it should be abolished.

      g. She isn't pretty enough to win the contest, and besides she had her nose "fixed" two years ago.

      h. Professors should chill out; everybody cheats on exams from time to time.

      i. The fact is that bilingual education is a mistake because it encourages students to use only their native language and that gives them an advantage over other students.

      j. Don't join those crazy liberals in support of the American Civil Liberties Union. They want all criminals to go free.

      k. Real Americans understand that free-trade agreements are evil. Let your representatives know that we want American goods protected. ■ ■

EXERCISE: Analyzing Arguments

Examine the following letter to the editor by Christian Brahmstedt that appeared in the *Washington Post* on January 2, 1989. If you think it contains logical fallacies, identify the passages and explain the fallacies.

Help Those Who Help, Not Hurt, Themselves

1   In the past year, and repeatedly throughout the holiday season, the *Post* has devoted an abnormally large share of newsprint to the "plight" of the vagrants who wander throughout the city in search of free handouts: i.e., the "homeless."

2   As certain as taxes, the poor shall remain with civilization forever. Yet these "homeless" are certainly not in the same category as the poor. The poor of civilization, of which we have all been a part at one time in our lives, are proud and work hard until a financial independence frees them from the category.

The "homeless" do not seek work or pride. They are satisfied to beg and survive on others' generosity.

The best correlation to the "homeless" I have witnessed are the gray squirrels on Capitol Hill. After feeding several a heavy dose of nuts one afternoon, I returned the next day to see the same squirrels patiently waiting for a return feeding. In the same fashion, the "homeless" are trained by Washington's guilt-ridden society to continue begging a sustenance rather than learning independence. 3

The *Post* has preached that these vagrants be supported from the personal and federal coffers—in the same manner as the squirrels on Capitol Hill. This support is not helping the homeless; it is only teaching them to rely on it. All of our parents struggled through the depression as homeless of a sort, to arise and build financial independence through hard work. 4

The "homeless" problem will go away when, and only when, Washingtonians refuse to feed them. They will learn to support themselves and learn that society demands honest work for an honest dollar. 5

It would be better for Washington citizens to field their guilt donations to the poor, those folks who are holding down two or more jobs just to make ends meet, rather than throwing their tribute to the vagrants on the sewer grates. The phrase "help those who help themselves" has no more certain relevance than to the "homeless" issue. 6

Source: © *The Washington Post*.

FOR READING AND ANALYSIS

DECLARATION OF SENTIMENTS | ELIZABETH CADY STANTON

Elizabeth Cady Stanton (1815–1902) was one of the most important leaders of the women's rights movement. Educated at the Emma Willard Seminary in Troy, New York, Stanton studied law with her father before her marriage. At the Seneca Falls Convention in 1848 (the first women's rights convention), Stanton gave the opening speech and read her "Declaration of Sentiments." She founded and became president of the National Women's Suffrage Association in 1869.

PREREADING QUESTION As you read, think about the similarities and differences between this document and the Declaration of Independence. What significant differences in wording and content do you find?

1   When, in the course of human events, it becomes necessary for one portion of the family of man to assume among the people of the earth a position different from that which they have hitherto occupied, but one to which the laws of nature and of nature's God entitle them, a decent respect to the opinions of mankind requires that they should declare the causes that impel them to such a course.

Elizabeth Cady Stanton and her daughter, Harriot. from a daguerreotype 1856.

2   We hold these truths to be self-evident: that all men and women are created equal; that they are endowed by their Creator with certain inalienable rights; that among these are life, liberty, and the pursuit of happiness; that to secure these rights governments are instituted, deriving their just powers from the consent of the governed. Whenever any form of government becomes destructive of these ends, it is the right of those who suffer from it to refuse allegiance to it, and to insist upon the institution of a new government, laying its foundation on such principles, and organizing its powers in such form, as to them shall seem most likely to effect their safety and happiness. Prudence, indeed, will dictate that governments long established should not be changed for light and transient causes; and accordingly all experience hath shown that mankind are more disposed to suffer, while evils are sufferable, than to right themselves by abolishing the forms to which they were accustomed. But when a long train of abuses and usurpations, pursuing invariably the same object evinces a design to reduce them under absolute despotism, it is their duty to throw off such government, and to provide new guards for their future security. Such has been the patient sufferance of the women under this government, and such is now the necessity which constrains them to demand the equal station to which they are entitled.

3   The history of mankind is a history of repeated injuries and usurpations on the part of man toward woman, having in direct object the establishment of an absolute tyranny over her. To prove this, let facts be submitted to a candid world.

4   He has never permitted her to exercise her inalienable right to the elective franchise.

5   He has compelled her to submit to laws, in the formation of which she had no voice.

6   He has withheld from her rights which are given to the most ignorant and degraded men—both natives and foreigners.

7   Having deprived her of this first right of a citizen, the elective franchise, thereby leaving her without representation in the halls of legislation, he has oppressed her on all sides.

He has made her, if married, in the eye of the law, civilly dead.   8

He has taken from her all right in property, even to the wages she earns.   9

He has made her, morally, an irresponsible being, as she can commit many 10 crimes with impunity, provided they be done in the presence of her husband. In the covenant of marriage, she is compelled to promise obedience to her husband, he becoming, to all intents and purposes, her master—the law giving him power to deprive her of her liberty, and to administer chastisement.

He has so framed the laws of divorce, as to what shall be the proper 11 causes, and in case of separation, to whom the guardianship of the children shall be given, as to be wholly regardless of the happiness of women—the law, in all cases, going upon a false supposition of the supremacy of man, and giving all power into his hands.

After depriving her of all rights as a married woman, if single, and the 12 owner of property, he has taxed her to support a government which recognizes her only when her property can be made profitable to it.

He has monopolized nearly all the profitable employments, and from those 13 she is permitted to follow, she receives but a scanty remuneration. He closes against her all the avenues to wealth and distinction which he considers most honorable to himself. As a teacher of theology, medicine, or law, she is not known.

He has denied her the facilities for obtaining a thorough education, all colleges being closed against her.   14

He allows her in Church, as well as State, but a subordinate position, claiming Apostolic authority for her exclusion from the ministry, and, with some exceptions, from any public participation in the affairs of the Church.   15

He has created a false public sentiment by giving to the world a different 16 code of morals for men and women, by which moral delinquencies which exclude women from society, are not only tolerated, but deemed of little account in man.

He has usurped the prerogative of Jehovah himself, claiming it as his right 17 to assign for her a sphere of action, when that belongs to her conscience and to her God.

He has endeavored, in every way that he could, to destroy her confidence 18 in her own powers, to lessen her self-respect, and to make her willing to lead a dependent and abject life.

Now in view of this entire disfranchisement of one-half the people of this 19 country, their social and religious degradation—in view of the unjust laws above mentioned, and because women do feel themselves aggrieved, oppressed, and fraudulently deprived of their most sacred rights, we insist that they have immediate admission to all the rights and privileges which belong to them as citizens of the United States.

In entering upon the great work before us, we anticipate no small amount 20 of misconception, misrepresentation, and ridicule; but we shall use every instrumentality within our power to effect our object. We shall employ agents, circulate tracts, petition the State and National legislatures, and endeavor to enlist the pulpit and the press in our behalf. We hope this Convention will be followed by a series of Conventions embracing every part of the country.

QUESTIONS FOR READING

1. Summarize the ideas of paragraphs 1 and 2. Be sure to use your own words.
2. What are the first three facts given by Stanton? Why are they presented first?
3. How have women been restricted by law if married or owning property? How have they been restricted in education and work? How have they been restricted psychologically?
4. What, according to Stanton, do women demand? How will they seek their goals?

QUESTIONS FOR REASONING AND ANALYSIS

5. What is Stanton's claim? With what does she charge men?
6. Most—but not all—of Stanton's charges have been redressed, however slowly. Which continue to be legitimate complaints, in whole or in part?

QUESTIONS FOR REFLECTION AND WRITING

7. Do we need a new declaration of sentiments for women? If so, what specific charges would you list? If not, why not?
8. Do we need a declaration of sentiments for other groups—children, minorities, the elderly, animals? If so, what specific charges should be listed? Select one group (that concerns you) and prepare a declaration of sentiments for that group. If you do not think any group needs a declaration, explain why.

THINGS PEOPLE SAY | NEIL DEGRASSE TYSON

An astrophysicist whose research interests include star formation and the structure of the Milky Way, Neil Tyson is director of the Hayden Planetarium in New York City. He is also one of today's most important figures in bringing science to the nonspecialist. He has been *Natural History* magazine's columnist, and since 2006 he has been the host of the PBS show *NOVAScienceNow*. A popular public speaker, Tyson is the author of nine books, including a collection of his essays. The following column from *Natural History* was originally published in the July/August 1998 issue.

PREREADING QUESTIONS Given your knowledge of the author and the title of his essay, what do you expect his subject to be? How often do you observe the physical universe and think about what you see?

1   Aristotle once declared that while the planets moved against the background stars, and while shooting stars, comets, and eclipses represented intermittent variability in the atmosphere and the heavens, the stars themselves were fixed and unchanging on the sky and that Earth was the center of all motion in the universe. From our enlightened perch, 25 centuries later, we chuckle at the folly of these ideas, but the claims were the consequence of legitimate, albeit simple, observations of the natural world.

Neil deGrasse Tyson with the "tools of his trade."

Aristotle also made other 2 kinds of claims. He said that heavy things fall faster than light things. Who could argue against that? Rocks obviously fall to the ground faster than tree leaves. But Aristotle went further and declared that heavy things fall faster than light things in direct proportion to their own weight, so that a 10-pound object would fall ten times faster than a 1-pound object.

Aristotle was badly mistaken. 3

To test him, simply release 4 a small rock and a big rock simultaneously from the same height. Unlike fluttering leaves, neither rock will be much influenced by air resistance and both will hit the ground at the same time. This experiment does not require a grant from the National Science Foundation to execute. Aristotle could have performed it but didn't. Aristotle's teachings were later adopted into the doctrines of the Catholic Church. And through the Church's power and influence Aristotelian philosophies became lodged in the common knowledge of the Western world, blindly believed and repeated. Not only did people repeat to others that which was not true, but they also ignored things that clearly happened but were not supposed to be true.

When scientifically investigating the natural world, the only thing worse 5 than a blind believer is a seeing denier. In A.D. 1054, a star in the constellation Taurus abruptly increased in brightness by a factor of a million. The Chinese astronomers wrote about it. Middle Eastern astronomers wrote about it. Native Americans of what is now the southwestern United States made rock engravings of it. The star became bright enough to be plainly visible in the daytime for weeks, yet we have no record of anybody in all of Europe recording the event. (The bright new star in the sky was actually a supernova explosion that occurred in space some 7,000 years earlier but its light had only just reached Earth.) True, Europe was in the Dark Ages, so we cannot expect that acute data-taking skills were common, but cosmic events that were "allowed" to happen were routinely recorded. For example, 12 years later, in 1066, what ultimately became known as Halley's comet was seen and duly depicted—complete with agape onlookers—in a section of the famous Bayeux tapestry, circa 1100. An exception indeed. The Bible says the stars don't change. Aristotle said the stars don't change. The Church, with its unmatched authority, declares the stars don't change. The population then falls victim to a collective delusion that was stronger than its members' own powers of observation.

6   We all carry some blindly believed knowledge because we cannot realistically test every statement uttered by others. When I tell you that the proton has an antimatter counterpart (the antiproton), you would need $1 billion worth of laboratory apparatus to verify my statement. So it's easier to just believe me and trust that, at least most of the time, and at least with regard to the astrophysical world, I know what I am talking about. I don't mind if you remain skeptical. In fact, I encourage it. Feel free to visit your nearest particle accelerator to see antimatter for yourself. But how about all those statements that don't require fancy apparatus to prove? One would think that in our modern and enlightened culture, popular knowledge would be immune from falsehoods that were easily testable.

7   It is not.

8   Consider the following declarations. The North Star is the brightest star in the nighttime sky. The Sun is a yellow star. What goes up must come down. On a dark night you can see millions of stars with the unaided eye. In space there is no gravity. A compass points north. Days get shorter in the winter and longer in the summer. Total solar eclipses are rare.

9   Every statement in the above paragraph is false.

10   Many people (perhaps most people) believe one or more of these statements and spread them to others even when a firsthand demonstration of falsehood is trivial to deduce or obtain. Welcome to my things-people-say rant:

11   The North Star is not the brightest star in the nighttime sky. It's not even bright enough to earn a spot in the celestial top 40. Perhaps people equate popularity with brightness. But when gazing upon the northern sky, three of the seven stars of the Big Dipper, including its "pointer" star, are brighter than the North Star, which is parked just three fist-widths away. There is no excuse.

12   And I don't care what else anyone has ever told you, the Sun is white, not yellow. Human color perception is a complicated business, but if the Sun were yellow, like a yellow lightbulb, then white stuff such as snow would reflect this light and appear yellow—a snow condition confirmed to happen only near fire hydrants. What could lead people to say that the Sun is yellow? In the middle of the day, a glance at the Sun can damage your eyes. Near sunset, however, with the Sun low on the horizon and when the atmospheric scattering of blue light is at its greatest, the Sun's intensity is significantly diminished. The blue light from the Sun's spectrum, lost to the twilight sky, leaves behind a yellow-orange-red hue for the Sun's disk. When people glance at this color-corrupted setting Sun, their misconceptions are fueled.

13   What goes up need not come down. All manner of golf balls, flags, automobiles, and crashed space probes litter the lunar surface. Unless somebody goes up there to bring them back, they will never return to Earth. Not ever. If you want to go up and not come down, all you need to do is travel at any speed faster than about seven miles per second. Earth's gravity will gradually slow you down but it will never succeed in reversing your motion and forcing you back to Earth.

Unless your eyes have pupils the size of binocular lenses, no matter your 14 seeing conditions and no matter your location on Earth, you will not resolve any more than about five or six thousand stars in the entire sky out of the 100 billion (or so) stars of our Milky Way galaxy. Try it one night. Things get much, much worse when the Moon is out. And if the Moon happens to be full, it will wash out the light of all but the brightest few hundred stars.

During the Apollo space program, while one of the missions was en route 15 to the Moon, a noted television news anchor announced the exact moment when the "astronauts left the gravitational field of Earth." Since the astronauts were still on their way to the Moon, and since the Moon orbits Earth, then Earth's gravity must extend into space *at least as far as the Moon.* Indeed, Earth's gravity, and the gravity of every other object in the universe, extends without limit—albeit with ever-diminishing strength. Every spot in space is teeming with countless gravitational tugs in the direction of every other object in the universe. What the announcer meant was that the astronauts crossed the point in space where the force of the Moon's gravity exceeds the force of Earth's gravity. The whole job of the mighty three-stage *Saturn V* rocket was to endow the command module with enough initial speed to just reach this point in space because thereafter you can passively accelerate toward the Moon— and they did. Gravity is everywhere.

Everybody knows that when it comes to magnets, opposite poles attract 16 while similar poles repel. But a compass needle is designed so that the half that has been magnetized "North" points to Earth's magnetic north pole. The only way a magnetized object can align its north half to Earth's magnetic north pole is if Earth's magnetic north pole is actually in the south and the magnetic south pole is actually in the north. Furthermore, there is no particular law of the universe that requires the precise alignment of an object's magnetic poles with its geographic poles. On Earth the two are separated by about 800 miles, which makes navigation by compass a futile exercise in northern Canada.

Since the first day of winter is the shortest "day" of the year, then every 17 succeeding day in the winter season must get longer and longer. Similarly, since the first day of summer is the longest "day" of the year, then every suc- ceeding day in the summer must get shorter and shorter. This is, of course, the opposite of what is told and retold.

On average, every couple years, somewhere on Earth's surface, the Moon 18 passes completely in front of the Sun to create a total solar eclipse. This event is more common than the Olympics, yet you don't read newspaper headlines declaring "a rare Olympics will take place this year." The perceived rarity of eclipses may derive from a simple fact: for any chosen spot on Earth, you can wait up to a half-millennium before you see a total solar eclipse. True, but lame as an argument because there are spots on Earth (like the middle of the Sahara Desert or any region of Antarctica) that have never, and will not likely ever, host the Olympics.

Want a few more? At high noon, the Sun is directly overhead. The Sun 19 rises in the east and sets in the west. The Moon comes out at night. On the equinox there are 12 hours of day and 12 hours of night. The Southern Cross is a beautiful constellation. All of these statements are wrong too.

20   There is no time of day, nor day of the year, nor place in the continental United States where the Sun ascends to directly overhead. At "high noon," straight vertical objects cast no shadow. The only people on the planet who see this live between 23.5 degrees south latitude and 23.5 degrees north latitude. And even in that zone, the Sun reaches directly overhead on only two days per year. The concept of high noon, like the brightness of the North Star and the color of the Sun, is a collective delusion.

21   For every person on Earth, the Sun rises due east and sets due west on only two days of the year: the first day of spring and the first day of fall. For every other day of the year, and for every person on Earth, the Sun rises and sets someplace else on the horizon. On the equator, sunrise varies by 47 degrees across the eastern horizon. From the latitude of New York City (41 degrees north—the same as that of Madrid and Beijing) the sunrise spans more than 60 degrees. From the latitude of London (51 degrees north) the sunrise spans nearly 80 degrees. And when viewed from either the Arctic or Antarctic circles, the Sun can rise due north and due south, spanning a full 180 degrees.

22   The Moon also "comes out" with the Sun in the sky. By invoking a small extra investment in your skyward viewing (like looking up in broad daylight) you will notice that the Moon is visible in the daytime nearly as often as it is visible at night.

23   The equinox does not contain exactly 12 hours of day and 12 hours of night. Look at the sunrise and sunset times in the newspaper on the first day of either spring or fall. They do not split the day into two equal 12-hour blocks. In all cases, daytime wins. Depending on your latitude, it can win by as few as seven minutes at the equator up to nearly half an hour at the Arctic and Antarctic circles. Who or what do we blame? Refraction of sunlight as it passes from the vacuum of interplanetary space to Earth's atmosphere enables an image of the Sun to appear above the horizon several minutes before the actual Sun has actually risen. Equivalently, the actual Sun has set several minutes before the Sun that you see. The convention is to measure sunrise by using the upper edge of the Sun's disk as it peeks above the horizon; similarly, sunset is measured by using the upper edge of the Sun's disk as it sinks below the horizon. The problem is that these two "upper edges" are on opposite halves of the Sun thereby providing an extra solar width of light in the sunrise/sunset calculation.

24   The Southern Cross gets the award for the greatest hype among all eighty-eight constellations. By listening to Southern Hemisphere people talk about this constellation, and by listening to songs written about it, and by noticing it on the national flags of Australia, New Zealand, Western Samoa, and Papua New Guinea, you would think we in the North were somehow deprived. Nope. Firstly, one needn't travel to the Southern Hemisphere to see the Southern Cross. It's plainly visible (although low in the sky) from as far north as Miami, Florida. This diminutive constellation is the smallest in the sky—your fist at

arm's length would eclipse it completely. Its shape isn't very interesting either. If you were to draw a rectangle using a connect-the-dots method you would use four stars. And if you were to draw a cross you would presumably include a fifth star in the middle to indicate the cross-point of the two beams. But the Southern Cross is composed of only four stars, which more accurately resemble a kite or a crooked box. The constellation lore of Western cultures owes its origin and richness to centuries of Babylonian, Chaldean, Greek, and Roman imaginations. Remember, these are the same imaginations that gave rise to the endless dysfunctional social lives of the gods and goddesses. Of course, these were all Northern Hemisphere civilizations, which means the constellations of the southern sky (many of which were named only within the last 250 years) are mythologically impoverished. In the North we have the Northern Cross, which is composed of all five stars that a cross deserves. It forms a subset of the larger constellation Cygnus the swan, which is flying across the sky along the Milky Way. Cygnus is nearly twelve times larger than the Southern Cross.

When people believe a tale that conflicts with self-checkable evidence it 25 tells me that people undervalue the role of evidence in formulating an internal belief system. Why this is so is not clear, but it enables many people to hold fast to ideas and notions based purely on supposition. But all hope is not lost. Occasionally, people say things that are simply true no matter what. One of my favorites is, "Wherever you go, there you are" and its Zen corollary, "If we are all here, then we must not be all there."

Source: Reprinted with permission from *Natural History*, July/August 1998. This article appears in Neil deGrasse Tyson's book *Death by Black Hole: And Other Cosmic Quandaries* (New York: W. W. Norton, 2007), pp. 291–297.

QUESTIONS FOR READING

1. What happened in 1054? Who wrote about the event? Who did not? What happened in 1066? Why did Europeans record this year's event?
2. What *kinds* of knowledge do we usually have to accept from experts? What *kinds* of falsehoods should we not hold on to?
3. Why do people believe that the sun is yellow? Or that it rises in the east and sets in the west?
4. How does Tyson account for people believing statements that conflict with evidence?

QUESTIONS FOR REASONING AND ANALYSIS

5. What does Tyson accomplish in his opening four paragraphs?
6. The author provides a list of well-known "truths" and then explains why each one is a false fact. Has he provided sufficient evidence to make his point? If not, why not?
7. What is Tyson's claim, the main point he wants to establish with readers?

8. Has Tyson convinced you that it is important to observe the natural world and use logic to test what we assume to be true? If not, why not?

9. What are some of the sources of false facts? Where does Tyson put most of the blame—on those who pass on false facts or those who embrace them by ignoring evidence to the contrary? Do you agree with his view on where to place the blame? Why or why not?

10. How many of Tyson's false facts did you believe to be true? Have you now adjusted your fact list? Are you sharing your new knowledge with family and friends? Reflect on your reactions to Tyson's essay.

Studying Some Arguments by Genre

Definition Arguments

READ: How does the cat respond to the big dog's questions?

REASON: Does the big dog expect the responses he gets to his questions? How do you know?

REFLECT/WRITE: What is a rhetorical question? What is the risk of using one?

"Define your terms!" someone yells in the middle of a heated debate. Although yelling may not be the best strategy, the advice is sound for writers of argument. People do disagree over the meaning of words. Although we cannot let words mean whatever we want and still communicate, we do recognize that many words have more than one meaning. In addition, some words carry strong connotations, the emotional associations we attach to them. For this reason, realtors never sell *houses;* they always sell *homes.* They want you to believe that the house they are showing will become the home in which you will feel happy and secure.

Many important arguments turn on the definition of key terms. If you can convince others that you have the correct definition, then you are well on your way to winning your argument. The civil rights movement, for example, really turned on a definition of terms. Leaders argued that some laws are unjust, that because it is the law does not necessarily mean it is right. Laws requiring separate schools and separate drinking fountains and seats at the back of the bus for blacks were, in the view of civil rights activists, unjust laws, unjust because they are immoral and as such diminish us as humans. If obeying unjust laws is immoral, then it follows that we should not obey such laws. And when we recognize that obeying such laws hurts us, then we have an obligation to act to remove unjust laws. Civil disobedience—illegal behavior to some—becomes, by definition, the best moral behavior.

Attorney Andrew Vachss has argued that there are no child prostitutes, only prostituted children. Yes, there are children who engage in sex for money. But, Vachss argues, that is not the complete definition of a prostitute. A prostitute chooses to exchange sex for money. Children do not choose; they are exploited by adults, beaten and in other ways abused if they do not work for the adult controlling them. If we agree with his definition, Vachss expects that we will also agree that the adults must be punished for their abuse of those prostituted children.

DEFINING AS PART OF AN ARGUMENT

There are two occasions for defining words as a part of your argument:

- You need to define any technical terms that may not be familiar to readers—or that readers may not understand as fully as they think they do. David Norman, early in his book on dinosaurs, writes:

  Nearly everyone knows what some dinosaurs look like, such as *Tyrannosaurus, Triceratops,* and *Stegosaurus.* But they may be much more vague about the lesser known ones, and may have difficulty in distinguishing between dinosaurs and other types of prehistoric creatures. It is not at all unusual to overhear an adult, taking a group of children around a museum display, being reprimanded sharply by the youngsters for failing to realize that a woolly mammoth was not a dinosaur, or—more forgivably—that a giant flying reptile such as *Pteranodon,* which lived at the time of the dinosaurs, was not a dinosaur either.

So what exactly is a dinosaur? And how do paleontologists decide on the groups they belong to?

Norman answers his questions by explaining the four characteristics that all dinosaurs have. He provides what is often referred to as a *formal definition.* He places the dinosaur in a class, established by four criteria, and then distinguishes this animal from other animals that lived a long time ago. His definition is not open to debate. He is presenting the definition and classification system that paleontologists, the specialists, have established.

- You need to define any word you are using in a special way. If you were to write: "We need to teach discrimination at an early age," you should add: "by *discrimination* I do not mean prejudice. I mean discernment, the ability to see differences." (*Sesame Street* has been teaching children this good kind of discrimination for many years.) The word *discrimination* used to have only a positive connotation; it referred to an important critical thinking skill. Today, however, the word has been linked to prejudice; to discriminate is to act on one's prejudice against some group. Writing today, you need to clarify if you are using the word in its original, positive meaning.

WHEN DEFINING *IS* THE ARGUMENT

We also turn to definition because we believe that a word is being used incorrectly or is not fully understood. Columnist George Will once argued that we should forget *values* and use instead the word *virtues*—that we should seek and admire virtues, not values. His point was that the term *values,* given to us by today's social scientists, is associated with situational ethics, or with an "if it feels good do it" approach to action. He wants people to return to the more old-fashioned word *virtues* so that we are reminded that some behavior is right and some is wrong, and that neither the situation nor how we might "feel" about it alters those truths. In discussions such as Will's the purpose shifts. Instead of using definition as one step in an argument, definition becomes the central purpose of the argument. Will rejects the idea that *values* means the same thing as *virtues* and asserts that it is virtue—as he defines it—that must guide our behavior. An extended definition *is* the argument.

STRATEGIES FOR DEVELOPING AN EXTENDED DEFINITION

Arguing for your meaning of a word provides your purpose in writing. But, it may not immediately suggest ways to develop such an argument. Let's think in terms of what definitions essentially do: They establish criteria for a class or category and then exclude other items from that category. (A pen is a writing instrument that uses ink.) Do you see your definition as drawing a line or as setting up two entirely separate categories? For example:

When does interrogation   become $\parallel$ torture?

One might argue that some strategies for making the person questioned uncomfortable are appropriate to interrogation (reduced sleep or comforts, loud noise). But, at some point (stretching on a rack or waterboarding) one crosses a line to torture. To define torture, you have to explain where that line is—and how the actions on one side of the line are different from those on the other side.

What are the characteristics of wisdom as opposed to knowledge?

Do we cross a line from knowledge to become wise? Many would argue that wisdom requires traits or skills that are not found simply by increasing one's knowledge. The categories are separate. Others might argue that, while the categories are distinct, one does need knowledge to also be wise.

Envisioning these two approaches supports the abstract thinking that defining requires. Then what? Use some of the basic strategies of good writing:

- *Descriptive details.* Illustrate with specifics. List the traits of a leader or a courageous person. Explain the behaviors that we find in a wise person, or the behaviors that should be called torture. Describe the situations in which liberty can flourish, or the situations that result from unjust laws. Remember to use negative traits as well as positive ones. That is, show what is *not* covered by the word you are defining.

- *Examples.* Develop your definition with actual or hypothetical examples. Churchill, Lincoln, and FDR can all be used as examples of leaders. The biblical Solomon is generally acknowledged as a good example of a wise person. You can also create a hypothetical wise or courteous person, or a person whose behavior you would consider virtuous.

- *Comparison and/or contrast.* Clarify and limit your definition by contrasting it with words of similar—but not exactly the same—meanings. For example, what are the differences between knowledge and wisdom or interrogation and torture? The goal of your essay is to establish subtle but important differences so that your readers understand precisely what you want a given word to mean. In an essay at the end of this chapter, Robin Givhan distinguishes among *glamour, charisma,* and *cool* as a way to develop her definition of *glamour.*

- *History of usage or word origin.* The word's original meanings can be instructive. If the word has changed meaning over time, explore these changes as clues to how the word can (or should) be used. If you want readers to reclaim *discrimination* as a positive trait, then show them how that was part of the word's original meaning before the word became tied to prejudice. Word origin—etymology—can also give us insight into a word's meaning. Many words in English come from another language, or they are a combination of two words. The words *liberty* and *freedom* can usefully be discussed by examining etymology. Most dictionaries provide some word origin information, but the best source is, always, the *Oxford English Dictionary.*

- *Use or function.* A frequent strategy for defining is explaining an item's use or function: A pencil is a writing instrument. A similar approach can give insight into more general or abstract words as well. For example, what do we have—or gain—by emphasizing virtues instead of values? Or, what does a wise person *do* that a non-wise person does not do?

- *Metaphors.* Consider using figurative comparisons. When fresh, not clichés, they add vividness to your writing while offering insight into your understanding of the word.

In an essay titled "Why I Blog," Andrew Sullivan, one of the Internet's earliest bloggers, uses many of these strategies for developing a definition of the term *blog:*

- *Word origin.* "The word *blog* is a conflation of two words: *Web* and *log.* . . . In the monosyllabic vernacular of the Internet, *Web log* soon became the word *blog.*"

- *One-sentence definition.* "It contains in its four letters a concise and accurate self-description: it is a log of thoughts and writing posted publicly on the World Wide Web."

- *Descriptive details.* "This form of instant and global self-publishing . . . allows for no retroactive editing. . . . [I]ts truth [is] inherently transitory."

- *Contrast.* "The wise panic that can paralyze a writer . . . is not available to a blogger. You can't have blogger's block."

- *Metaphors.* "A blog . . . bobs on the surface of the ocean but has its anchorage in waters deeper than those print media is technologically able to exploit."

These snippets from Sullivan's lengthy essay give us a good look at defining strategies in action.

GUIDELINES for Evaluating Definition Arguments

When reading definition arguments, what should you look for? The basics of good argument apply to all arguments: a clear statement of claim, qualified if appropriate, a clear explanation of reasons and evidence, and enough relevant evidence to support the claim. How do we recognize these qualities in a definition argument? Use the following points as guides to evaluating:

- **Why is the word being defined?** Has the writer convinced you of the need to understand the word's meaning or change the way the word is commonly used?

- **How is the word defined?** Has the writer established his or her definition, clearly distinguishing it from what the writer perceives to be objectionable definitions? It is hard to judge the usefulness of the writer's position if the differences in meaning remain fuzzy. If George Will is going to argue for using *virtues* instead of *values*, he needs to be sure that readers understand the differences he sees in the two words.

- **What strategies are used to develop the definition?** Can you recognize the different types of evidence presented and see what the writer is doing in his or her argument? This kind of analysis can aid your evaluation of a definition argument.

- **What are the implications of accepting the author's definition?** Why does George Will want readers to embrace *virtues* rather than *values*? Will's argument is not just about subtle points of language. His argument is also about attitudes that affect public policy issues. Part of any evaluation of a definition argument must include our assessment of the author's definition.

- **Is the definition argument convincing?** Do the reasons and evidence lead you to agree with the author, to accept the idea of the definition and its implications as well?

PREPARING A DEFINITION ARGUMENT

In addition to the guidelines for writing arguments presented in Chapter 4, you can use the following advice specific to writing definition arguments.

Planning

1. *Think:* Why do you want to define your term? To add to our understanding of a complex term? To challenge the use of the word by others? If you don't have a good reason to write, find a different word to examine.

2. *Think:* How are you defining the word? What are the elements/parts/steps in your definition? Some brainstorming notes are probably helpful to keep your definition concrete and focused.

3. *Think:* What strategies will you use to develop and support your definition? Consider using several of these possible strategies for development:
    - *Word origin or history of usage*
    - *Descriptive details*
    - *Comparison and/or contrast*
    - *Examples*
    - *Function or use*
    - *Metaphors*

Drafting

1. Begin with an opening paragraph or two that introduces your subject in an interesting way. Possibilities include the occasion that has led to your writing—explain, for instance, a misunderstanding about your term's meaning that you want to correct.

2. Do *not* begin by quoting or paraphrasing a dictionary definition of the term. "According to Webster . . ." is a tired approach lacking reader interest. If the dictionary definition were sufficient, you would have no reason to write an entire essay to define the term.

3. State your claim—your definition of the term—early in your essay, if you can do so in a sentence or two. If you do not state a brief claim, then establish your purpose in writing early in your essay. (You may find that there are too many parts to your definition to combine into one or two sentences.)

4. Use several specific strategies for developing your definition. Select strategies from the list above and organize your approach around these strategies. That is, you can develop one paragraph of descriptive details, another of examples, another of contrast with words that are not exactly the same in meaning.

5. Consider specifically refuting the error in word use that led to your decision to write your own definition. If you are motivated to write based on what you have read, then make a rebuttal part of your definition argument.

6. Consider discussing the implications of your definition. You can give weight and value to your argument by explaining the larger significance of your definition.

A CHECKLIST FOR REVISION ■·■·■·■·■·■·■·■·■·■·■·■·■·■·■·■·■·■·■

☐ Do I have a good understanding of my purpose? Have I made this clear to readers?

☐ Have I clearly stated my definition? Or clearly established the various parts of the definition that I discuss in separate paragraphs?

☐ Have I organized my argument, building the parts of my definition into a logical, coherent structure?

☐ Have I used specifics to clarify and support my definition?

☐ Have I used the basic checklist for revision in Chapter 4 (see p. 111)?   ■·■·■

STUDENT ESSAY

PARAGON OR PARASITE?

Laura Mullins

Do you recognize this creature? He is low maintenance and often
unnoticeable, a favorite companion of many. Requiring no special attention,
he grows from the soil of pride and rejection, feeding regularly on a diet
of ignorance and insecurity, scavenging for hurt feelings and defensiveness,
gobbling up dainty morsels of lust and scandal. Like a cult leader clothed in
a gay veneer, disguising himself as blameless, he wields power. Bewitching
unsuspecting but devoted groupies, distracting them from honest
self-examination, deceiving them into believing illusions of grandeur or, on
the other extreme, unredeemable worthlessness, he breeds jealousy, hate,
and fear; thus, he thrives. He is Gossip.

One of my dearest friends is a gossip. She is an educated, honorable,
compassionate, loving woman whose character and judgment I deeply admire
and respect. After sacrificially raising six children, she went on to study medicine
and become a doctor who graciously volunteers her expertise. How, you may be
wondering, could a gossip deserve such praise? Then you do not understand the
word. My friend is my daughter's godmother; she is my gossip, or *godsib,* meaning
sister-in-god. Derived from Middle English words *god,* meaning spiritual, and *sip/
sib/syp,* meaning kinsman, this term was used to refer to a familiar acquaintance,
close family friend, or intimate relation, according to the *Oxford English Dictionary.*
As a male, he would have joined in fellowship and celebration with the father
of the newly born; if a female, she would have been a trusted friend, a birth-
attendant or midwife to the mother of the baby. The term grew to include
references to the type of easy, unrestrained conversation shared by these folks.

As is often the case with words, the term's meaning has certainly
evolved, maybe eroded from its original idea. Is it harmless, idle chat,
innocuous sharing of others' personal news, or back-biting, rumor-spreading,

Attention-getting introduction.

Clever extended metaphor.

Subject introduced.

Etymology of gossip and early meanings.

Current meanings.

and manipulation? Is it a beneficial activity worthy of pursuit, or a deplorable danger to be avoided?

Good use of sources to develop definition.

In her article "Evolution, Alienation, and Gossip" (for the Social Issues Research Centre in Oxford, England), Kate Fox writes that "gossip is not a trivial pastime; it is essential to human social, psychological, and even physical well-being." Many echo her view that gossip is a worthy activity, claiming that engaging in gossip produces endorphins, reduces stress, and aids in building intimate relationships. Gossip, seen at worst as a harmless outlet, is encouraged in the workplace. Since much of its content is not inherently critical or malicious, it is viewed as a positive activity. However, this view does nothing to encourage those speaking or listening to evaluate or examine motive or purpose; instead, it seems to reflect the "anything goes" thinking so prevalent today.

Conversely, writer and high school English and geography teacher Lennox V. Farrell of Toronto, Canada, in his essay titled "Gossip: An Urban Form of Sorcery," presents gossip as a kind of "witchcraft . . . based on using unsubstantiated accusations by those who make them, and on uncritically accepting these by those enticed into listening." Farrell uses gossip in its more widely understood definition, encompassing the breaking of confidences, inappropriate sharing of indiscretions, destructive tale-bearing, and malicious slander.

Good use of metaphor to depict gossip as negative.

What, then, is gossip? We no longer use the term to refer to our children's godparents. Its current definition usually comes with derogatory implications. Imagine a backyard garden: you see a variety of greenery, recognizing at a glance that you are looking at different kinds of plants. Taking a closer look, you will find the gossip vine; inconspicuously blending in, it doesn't appear threatening, but ultimately it destroys. If left in the garden it will choke and then suck out life from its host. Zoom in on the garden scene and follow the creeping vine up trees and along a fence where two neighbors visit. You can overhear one woman saying to the other, "I know I should be the last to tell you, but your husband is being unfaithful to me." (Caption from a cartoon by Alan De la Nougerede.)

The current popular movement to legitimize gossip seems an excuse to condone the human tendency to puff-up oneself. Compared in legal terms, gossip is to conversation as hearsay is to eyewitness testimony; it's not credible. Various religious doctrines abhor the idea and practice of gossip. An old Turkish proverb says, "He who gossips to you will gossip of you." From the Babylonian Talmud, which calls gossip the three-pronged tongue, destroying the one talking, the one listening, and the one being spoken of, to the Upanishads, to the Bible, we can conclude that no good fruit is born from gossip. Let's tend our gardens and check our motives when we have the urge to gossip. Surely we can find more noble pursuits than the self-aggrandizement we have come to know as gossip.

Conclusion states view that gossip is to be avoided—the writer's thesis.

FOR ANALYSIS AND DEBATE

GLAMOUR, THAT CERTAIN SOMETHING | ROBIN GIVHAN

Robin Givhan is a graduate of Princeton and holds a master's degree in journalism from the University of Michigan. When she was fashion editor at the *Washington Post*, she won a Pulitzer Prize (2006) for criticism, the first time the prize has been awarded to a fashion writer. In 2010 she moved to *The Daily Beast* and *Newsweek*, but was laid off by these publications in December 2012, when *Newsweek* gave up print journalism. Givhan's coverage of the world of fashion frequently becomes a study of culture, as we see in the following column, published February 17, 2008, shortly before the 2008 Academy Awards show.

PREREADING QUESTIONS What is the difference between glamour and good looks? What famous people do you consider glamorous?

Glamour isn't a cultural necessity, but its usefulness can't be denied.   1

It makes us feel good about ourselves by making us believe that life can 2 sparkle. Glamorous people make difficult tasks seem effortless. They appear to cruise through life shaking off defeat with a wry comment. No matter how hard they work for what they have, the exertion never seems to show. Yet the cool confidence they project doesn't ever drift into lassitude.

Hollywood attracts people of glamour—as well as the misguided souls 3 who confuse it with mere good looks—because that is where it is richly rewarded. And the Academy Awards are the epicenter of it all. We'll watch the Oscars next Sunday to delight in the stars who glide down the red carpet like graceful swans or who swagger onto the stage looking dashing.

4   Of course, we'll watch for other reasons, too. There's always the possibility of a supremely absurd fashion moment or an acceptance speech during which the winner becomes righteously indignant—Michael Moore–style—or practically hyperventilates like Halle Berry. While Moore, a nominee, is not glamorous, he is compelling for the sheer possibility of an impolitic eruption. Berry isn't glamorous either, mostly because nothing ever looks effortless with her. (She has even expressed anguish over her beauty.) Mostly, though, we will watch in search of "old Hollywood" glamour. But really, is there any other kind?

5   Among the actors who consistently manage to evoke memories of Cary Grant or Grace Kelly are George Clooney and Cate Blanchett. There's something about the way they present themselves that speaks to discretion, sex appeal and glossy perfection. As an audience, we think we know these actors but we really don't. We know their image, the carefully crafted personality they display to the public. If they have been to rehab, they went quietly and without a crowd of paparazzi.

6   Their lives appear to be an endless stream of lovely adventures, minor mishaps that turn into cocktail party banter, charming romances and just enough gravitas to keep them from floating away on a cloud of frivolity.

7   These actors take pretty pictures because they seem supremely comfortable with themselves. It's not simply their beauty we're seeing; it's also an unapologetic pleasure in being who they are.

8   Oscar nominee Tilda Swinton has the kind of striking, handsome looks of Anjelica Huston or Lauren Bacall. But Swinton doesn't register as glamorous as much as cool. She looks a bit androgynous and favors the eccentric Dutch design team of Viktor & Rolf, which once populated an entire runway show with Swinton doppelgangers. Coolness suggests that the person knows

something or understands something that average folks haven't yet figured out. Cool people are a step ahead. Glamour is firmly situated in the now.

There's nothing particularly intimate about glamour, which is why it 9 plays so well on the big screen and why film actors who embody it can sometimes be disappointing in real life. Glamour isn't like charisma, which is typically described as the ability to make others feel important or special.

Neither quality has much to do with a person's inner life. Glamour is no 10 measure of soulfulness or integrity. It isn't about truth, but perception. *Redbook* traffics in truth. *Vogue* promotes glamour.

Although Hollywood is the natural habitat for the glitterati, they exist 11 everywhere: politics, government, sports, business. Tiger Woods brought glamour to golf with his easy confidence and his ability to make the professional game look as simple as putt-putt. Donald Trump aspires to glamour with his flashy properties and their gold-drenched decor. But his efforts are apparent, his yearning obvious. The designer Tom Ford is glamorous. The man never rumples.

In the political world, Barack Obama has glamour. Bill Clinton has cha-12 risma. And Hillary Clinton has an admirable work ethic. Bill Clinton could convince voters that he felt their pain. Hillary Clinton reminds them detail by detail of how she would alleviate it. Glamour has a way of temporarily making you forget about the pain and just think the world is a beautiful place of endless possibilities.

Ronald Reagan evoked glamour. His white-tie inaugural balls and 13 morning-coat swearing-in were purposefully organized to bring a twinkle back to the American psyche. George W. Bush has charisma, a.k.a. the likability factor, although it does not appear to be helping his approval rating now. Still, he remains a back-slapper and bestower of nicknames.

Charisma is personal. Glamour taps into a universal fairy tale. It's uncon-14 cerned with the nitty-gritty. Instead, it celebrates the surface gloss. And sometimes, a little shimmer can be hard to resist.

QUESTIONS FOR READING

1. How does glamour make us feel?
2. Where do we usually find glamour? Why?
3. Which celebrities today best capture Hollywood's glamour of the past?
4. What traits do the glamorous have?
5. Explain the differences among glamour, charisma, and cool.

QUESTIONS FOR REASONING AND ANALYSIS

6. Examine the opening three sentences in paragraph 12. What makes them effective?

7. What are the specific strategies Givhan uses to develop her definition?

8. What is Givhan's claim?

QUESTIONS FOR REFLECTION AND WRITING

9. Givhan asserts that glamour is in the present but "cool people are a step ahead." Does this contrast make sense to you? Why or why not?

10. Do we ever really know the glamorous, charismatic, and cool celebrities? Explain.

11. Some young people aspire to be cool. How would you advise them? What should one do, how should one behave, to be cool? Is "cool" a trait that we can "put on" if we wish? Why or why not?

1. In the student essay, Laura Mullins defines the term *gossip*. Select one of the following words to define and prepare your own extended definition argument, using at least three of the strategies for defining described in this chapter. For each word in the list, you see a companion word in parentheses. Use that companion word as a word that you contrast with the word you are defining. (For example, how does gossip differ from conversation?) The idea of an extended definition argument is to make fine distinctions among words similar in meaning.

   courtesy (manners)   hero (star)

   wisdom (knowledge)   community (subdivision)

   patriotism (chauvinism)   freedom (liberty)

2. Select a word you believe is currently misused. It can be misused because it has taken on a negative (or positive) connotation that it did not originally have, or because it has changed meaning and lost something in the process. A few suggestions include *awful, fabulous, exceptional* (in education), *propaganda*.

3. Define a term that is currently used to label people with particular traits or values. Possibilities include *nerd, yuppie, freak, jock, redneck, bimbo, wimp*. Reflect, before selecting this topic, on why you want to explain the meaning of the word you have chosen. One purpose might be to explain the word to someone from another culture. Another might be to defend people who are labeled negatively by a term; that is, you want to show why the term should not have a negative connotation.

CHAPTER 8

Evaluation Arguments

READ: What is the situation? Where are we?

REASON: Look at the faces; what do you infer to be the attitude of the participants?

REASON/WRITE: What is the photo's message?

"I really love Ben's Camaro; it's so much more fun to go out with him than to go with Gregory in his Volvo wagon," you confide to a friend. "On the other hand, Ben always wants to see the latest horror movie—and boy are they horrid! I'd much rather watch one of our teams play—whatever the season; sports events are so much more fun than horror movies!"

"Well, at least you and Ben agree not to listen to Amy Winehouse CDs. Her life was so messed up; why would anyone admire her music?" your friend responds.

CHARACTERISTICS OF EVALUATION ARGUMENTS

Evaluations. How easy they are to make. We do it all the time. So, surely an evaluation argument should be easy to prepare. Not so fast. Remember at the beginning of the discussion of argument in Chapter 3, we observed that we do not argue about personal preferences because there is no basis for building an argument. If you don't like horror movies, then don't go to them—even with Ben! However, once you assert that sporting events are more fun than horror movies, you have shifted from personal preference to the world of argument, the world in which others will judge the effectiveness of your logic and evidence. On what basis can you argue that one activity is more fun than the other? And, always more fun? And, more fun for everyone? You probably need to qualify this claim and then you will need to establish the criteria by which you have made your evaluation. Although you might find it easier to defend your preference for a car for dates, you, at least in theory, can build a convincing argument for a qualified claim in support of sporting events. Your friend, though, will have great difficulty justifying her evaluation of Winehouse based on Winehouse's lifestyle. An evaluation of her music needs to be defended based on criteria about music—unless she wants to try to argue that any music made by people with unconventional or immoral lifestyles will be bad music, a tough claim to defend.

In a column for *Time* magazine, Charles Krauthammer argues that Tiger Woods is the greatest golfer ever to play the game. He writes:

> How do we know? You could try Method 1: Compare him directly with the former greatest golfer, Jack Nicklaus. . . . But that is not the right way to compare. You cannot compare greatness directly across the ages. There are so many intervening variables: changes in technology, training, terrain, equipment, often rules and customs.
>
> How then do we determine who is greatest? Method 2: The Gap. Situate each among his contemporaries. Who towers? . . . Nicklaus was great, but he ran with peers: Palmer, Player, Watson. Tiger has none.

Krauthammer continues with statistics to demonstrate that there is no one playing now with Tiger who comes close in number of tournaments won, number of majors won, and number of strokes better in these events than the next player. He then applies the Gap Method to Babe Ruth in baseball, Wayne

Gretzky in hockey, and Bobby Fischer in chess to demonstrate that it works to reveal true greatness in competition among the world's best.

Krauthammer clearly explains his Gap Method, his basic criterion for judging greatness. Then he provides the data to support his conclusions about who are or were the greatest in various fields. His is a convincing evaluation argument.

These examples suggest some key points about evaluation arguments:

- **Evaluation arguments are arguments, not statements of personal preferences.** As such, they need a precise, qualified claim and reasons and evidence for support, just like any argument.

- **Evaluation arguments are about "good" and "bad," "best" and "worst."** These arguments are not about what we should or should not do or why a situation is the way it is. The debate is not whether one should select a boyfriend based on the kind of car he drives or why horror movies have so much appeal for many viewers. The argument is that sports events are great entertainment, or better entertainment than horror movies.

- **Evaluation arguments need to be developed based on a clear statement of the criteria for evaluating.** Winehouse won Grammys for her music—why? By what standards of excellence do we judge a singer? A voice with great musicality and nuance? The selection of songs with meaningful lyrics? The ability to engage listeners—the way the singer can "sell" a song? The number of recordings sold and awards won? All of these criteria? Something else?

- **Evaluation arguments, to be successful, may need to defend the criteria, not just to list them and show that the subject of the argument meets those criteria.** Suppose you want to argue that sporting events are great entertainment because it is exciting to cheer with others, you get to see thrilling action, and it is good, clean fun. Are sports always "good, clean fun"? Some of the fighting in hockey matches is quite vicious. Some football players get away with dirty hits. Krauthammer argues that his Gap Method provides the better criterion for judging greatness and then shows why it is the better method. Do not underestimate the challenge of writing an effective evaluation argument.

TYPES OF EVALUATION ARGUMENTS

The examples we have examined above are about people or items or experiences in our lives. Tiger Woods is the greatest golfer ever, based on the Gap Method strategy. Sports events are more fun to attend than horror movies. We can (and do!) evaluate just about everything we know or do or buy. This is one type of evaluation argument. In this category we would place the review—of a book, movie, concert, or something similar.

A second type of evaluation is a response to another person's argument. We are not explaining why the car or college, sitcom or singer, is good or great or the best. Instead, we are responding to one specific argument we have read (or listened to) that we think is flawed, flawed in many ways or in one significant way that essentially destroys the argument. This type of evaluation argument is called a rebuttal or refutation argument.

Sometimes our response to what we consider a really bad argument is to go beyond the rebuttal and write a counterargument. Rather than writing about the limitations and flaws in our friend's evaluation of Winehouse as a singer not to be listened to, we decide to write our own argument evaluating Winehouse's strengths as a contemporary singer. This counterargument is best described as an evaluation argument, not a refutation. Similarly, we can disagree with someone's argument defending restrictions placed by colleges on student file sharing. But, if we decide to write a counterargument defending students' rights to share music files, we have moved from rebuttal to our own position paper, our own argument based on values. Counterarguments are best seen as belonging to one of the other genres of argument discussed in this section of the text.

GUIDELINES for Analyzing an Evaluation Argument

The basics of good argument apply to all arguments: a clear statement of claim, qualified as appropriate, a clear explanation of reasons and evidence, and enough relevant evidence to support the claim. When reading evaluation arguments, use the following points as additional guides:

- **What is the writer's claim?** Is it clear, qualified if necessary, and focused on the task of evaluating?
- **Has the writer considered audience as a basis for both claim and criteria?** Your college may be a good choice for you, given your criteria for choosing, but is it a good choice for others? Qualifications need to be based on audience: College A is a great school for young people in need of B and with X amount of funds. Or: *The Da Vinci Code* is an entertaining read for those with some understanding of art history and knowledge of the Roman Catholic Church.
- **What criteria are presented as the basis for evaluation?** Are they clearly stated? Do they seem reasonable for the topic of evaluation? Are they defended if necessary?
- **What evidence and/or reasons are presented to show that the item under evaluation meets the criteria?** Specifics are important in any evaluation argument.
- **What are the implications of the claim?** If we accept the Gap Method for determining greatness, does that mean that we can never compare stars from different generations? If we agree with the rebuttal argument, does that mean that there are no good arguments for the claim in the essay being refuted?
- **Is the argument convincing?** Does the evidence lead you to agree with the author? Do you want to buy that car, listen to that CD, read that book, see that film as a result of reading the argument?

PREPARING AN EVALUATION ARGUMENT

In addition to the guidelines for writing arguments presented in Chapter 4, you can use the following advice specific to writing evaluation arguments.

Planning

1. **Think:** Why do you want to write this evaluation? Does it matter, or are you just sharing your personal preferences? Select a topic that requires you to think deeply about how we judge that item (college, book, CD, etc.).

2. **Think about audience:** Try to imagine writing your evaluation for your classmates, not just your instructor. Instead of thinking about an assignment to be graded, think about why we turn to reviews, for example. What do readers want to learn? They want to know if they should see that film. Your job is to help them make that decision.

3. **Think:** What are my criteria for evaluation? And, how will I measure my topic against them to show that my evaluation is justified? You really must know how you would determine a great singer or a great tennis player before you write, or you risk writing only about personal preferences.

4. **Establish a general plan:** If you are writing a review, be sure to study the work carefully. Can you write a complete and accurate summary? (It is easier to review a CD than a live concert because you can replay the CD to get all the details straight.) You will need to balance summary, analysis, and evaluation in a review—and be sure that you do not mostly write summary or reveal the ending of a novel or film! If you are evaluating a college or a car, think about how to order your criteria. Do you want to list all criteria first and then show how your item connects to them, point by point? Or, do you want the criteria to unfold as you make specific points about your item?

    To analyze a film, consider the plot, the characters, the actors who play the lead characters, any special effects used, and the author's (and director's) "take" on the story. If the "idea" of the film is insignificant, then it is hard to argue that it is a great film. Analysis of style in a book needs to be connected to that book's intended audience. Style and presentation will vary depending on the knowledge and sophistication of the intended reader. If, for example, you have difficulty understanding a book aimed at a general audience, then it is fair to say that the author has not successfully reached his or her audience. But if you are reviewing a book intended for specialists, then your difficulties in reading are not relevant to a fair evaluation of that book. You can point out, though, that the book is tough going for a nonspecialist—just as you could point out that a movie sequel is hard to follow for those who did not see the original film.

Drafting

1. Begin with an opening paragraph or two that engages your reader while introducing your subject and purpose in writing. Is there a specific occasion that has led to your writing? And what, exactly, are you evaluating?

2. Either introduce your criteria next and then show how your item for evaluation meets the criteria, point by point, through the rest of the essay; or, decide on an order for introducing your criteria and use that order as your structure. Put the most important criterion either first or last. It can be effective to put the most controversial point last.

3. If you are writing a review, then the basic criteria are already established. You will need some combination of summary, analysis, and evaluation. Begin with an attention-getter that includes a broad statement of the work's subject or subject category: This is a *biography* of Benjamin Franklin; this is a *female action-hero film*. An evaluation in general terms can complete the opening paragraph. For example:

> Dr. Cynthia Pemberton's new book, *More Than a Game: One Woman's Fight for Gender Equity in Sport*, is destined to become a classic in sport sociology, sport history, and women's studies.

4. The rest of the review will then combine summary details, analysis of presentation, and a final assessment of the work in the concluding paragraph. From the same review, after learning specifics of content, we read:

> The target audience for this book includes educators, coaches, athletes, and administrators at any level. Additionally, anyone interested in studying women's sports or pursuing a Title IX case will love this book.

5. Consider discussing the implications of your evaluation. Why is this important? Obviously for a book or film or art show, for example, we want to know if this is a "must read" or "must see." For other evaluation arguments, let us know why we should care about your subject and your perspective. Charles Krauthammer does not just argue that Tiger Woods is the greatest golfer ever; he also argues that his Gap Method is the best strategy for evaluation. That's why he shows that it works not just to put Woods ahead of Nicklaus but also to put other greats in their exalted place in other sports.

A CHECKLIST FOR REVISION

☐ Do I have a good understanding of my purpose? Have I made my evaluation purpose clear to readers?

☐ Have I clearly stated my claim?

☐ Have I clearly stated my criteria for evaluation—or selected the appropriate elements of content, style, presentation, and theme for a review?

☐ Have I organized my argument into a coherent structure by some pattern that readers can recognize and follow?

☐ Have I provided good evidence and logic to support my evaluation?

☐ Have I used the basic checklist for revision in Chapter 4? (See p. 111.)

STUDENT REVIEW

WINCHESTER'S ALCHEMY: TWO MEN AND A BOOK

Ian Habel

One can hardly imagine a tale promising less excitement for a general audience than that of the making of the *Oxford English Dictionary* (*OED*). The sensationalism of murder and insanity would have to labor intensely against the burden of lexicography in crafting a genuine page-turner on the subject. Much to my surprise, Simon Winchester, in writing *The Professor and the Madman: A Tale of Murder, Insanity, and the Making of the Oxford English Dictionary,* has succeeded in producing so compelling a story that I was forced to devour it completely in a single afternoon, an unprecedented personal feat.

The Professor and the Madman is the story of the lives of two apparently very different men and the work that brought them together. Winchester begins by recounting the circumstances that led to the incarceration of Dr. W. C. Minor, a well-born, well-educated, and quite insane American ex-Army surgeon. Minor, in a fit of delusion, had murdered a man whom he believed to have crept into his Lambeth hotel room to torment him in his sleep. The doctor is tried and whisked off to the Asylum for the Criminally Insane, Broadmoor.

The author then introduces readers to the other two main characters: the *OED* itself and its editor James Murray, a lowborn, self-educated Scottish philologist. The shift in narrative focus is used to dramatic effect. The natural assumption on the part of the reader that these two seemingly unrelated plots must eventually meet urges us to read on in anticipation of that connection. As each chapter switches focus from one man to the other, it is introduced by a citation from the *OED*, reminding us that the story is ultimately about the dictionary. The citations also serve to foreshadow and provide a theme for the chapter. For example, the *OED* definition of *murder* heads the first chapter, relating to the details of Minor's crime.

Winchester acquaints us with the shortcomings of seventeenth- and eighteenth-century attempts at compiling a comprehensive dictionary of the English language. He takes us inside the meetings of the Philological Society, whose members proposed the compilation of the dictionary to end all dictionaries. The *OED* was to include examples of usage illustrating every shade of meaning for every word in the English language. Such a mammoth feat would require enlisting thousands of volunteer readers to comb the corpus of English literature in search of illustrative quotations to be submitted on myriad slips of paper. These slips of paper on each word would in turn be studied by a small army of editors preparing the definitions.

It is not surprising that our Dr. Minor, comfortably tucked away at Broadmoor, possessing both a large library and seemingly infinite free time, should become one of those volunteer readers. After all, we are still rightfully assuming some connection of the book's two plot lines. Yet what sets Dr. Minor apart from his fellow volunteers (aside from the details of his incarceration) is the remarkable efficiency with which he approached his task. Not content merely to fill out slips of paper for submission, Minor methodically indexed every possibly useful mention of any word appearing in his personal library. He then asked to be kept informed of the progress of the work, submitting quotations that would be immediately useful to editors. In this way he managed to "escape" his cell and plunge himself into the work of contemporaries, to become a part of a major event of his time.

Minor's work proved invaluable to the *OED*'s staff of editors, led by James Murray. With the two plot lines now intertwined, readers face such questions as "Will they find out that Minor is insane?" "Will Minor and Murray ever meet?" and "How long will they take to complete the dictionary?" The author builds suspense regarding a meeting of Minor and Murray by providing a false account of their first encounter, as reported by the American press, only to shatter us with the fact that this romantic version did not happen. I'll let Winchester give you the answers to these questions, while working his magic on you, drawing you into this fascinating tale of the making of the world's most famous dictionary.

EVALUATING AN ARGUMENT: THE REBUTTAL OR REFUTATION ESSAY

When your primary purpose in writing is to challenge someone's argument rather than to present your own argument, you are writing a *rebuttal* or *refutation.* A good refutation demonstrates, in an orderly and logical way, the weaknesses of logic or evidence in the argument. Study the following guidelines to prepare a good refutation essay and then study the sample refutation that follows. It has been annotated to show you how the author has structured his rebuttal.

GUIDELINES for Preparing a Refutation or Rebuttal Argument

1. **Read accurately.** Make certain that you have understood your opponent's argument. If you assume views not expressed by the writer and accuse the writer of holding those illogical views, you are guilty of the straw man fallacy, of attributing and then attacking a position that the person does not hold. Look up terms and references you do not know and examine the logic and evidence thoroughly.

2. **Pinpoint the weaknesses in the original argument.** Analyze the argument to determine, specifically, what flaws the argument contains. If the argument contains logical fallacies, make a list of the ones you plan to discredit. Examine the evidence presented. Is it insufficient, unreliable, or irrelevant? Decide, before drafting your refutation, exactly what elements of the argument you intend to challenge.

3. **Write your claim.** After analyzing the argument and deciding on the weaknesses to be challenged, write a claim that establishes that your disagreement is with the writer's logic, assumptions, or evidence, or a combination of these.

4. **Draft your essay, using the following three-part organization:**

    a. *The opponent's argument.* Usually you should not assume that your reader has read or remembered the argument you are refuting. Thus at the beginning of your essay, you need to state, accurately and fairly, the main points of the argument to be refuted.

    b. *Your claim.* Next make clear the nature of your disagreement with the argument you are rebutting.

    c. *Your refutation.* The specifics of your rebuttal will depend on the nature of your disagreement. If you are challenging the writer's evidence, then you must present the evidence that will show why the evidence used is unreliable or misleading. If you are challenging assumptions, then you must explain why they do not hold up. If your claim is that the piece is filled with logical fallacies, then you must present and explain each fallacy.

MIND OVER MASS MEDIA | STEVEN PINKER

A professor of psychology at Harvard University, Steven Pinker is the author of significant articles and books on visual cognition and the psychology of language—his areas of research. These include *The Language Instinct* (2007) and *How the Mind Works* (2009). *Time* magazine has listed Pinker as one of the "100 most influential people in the world." His contribution to the ongoing debate over the impact of the Internet and social media was published on June 12, 2010.

PREREADING QUESTIONS Given Pinker's title and the headnote information, what do you expect him to write about? Can you anticipate his position—or will you have to read to discover it?

New forms of media have always caused moral panics: the printing press, newspapers, paperbacks and television were all once denounced as threats to their consumers' brainpower and moral fiber.

Attention-getting opening.

So too with electronic technologies. PowerPoint, we're told, is reducing discourse to bullet points. Search engines lower our intelligence, encouraging us to skim on the surface of knowledge rather than dive to its depths. Twitter is shrinking our attention spans.

But such panics often fail basic reality checks. When comic books were accused of turning juveniles into delinquents in the 1950s, crime was falling to record lows, just as the denunciations of video games in the 1990s coincided with the great American crime decline. The decades of television, transistor radios and rock videos were also decades in which I.Q. scores rose continuously.

1st point of refutation: Reality check, past and present.

For a reality check today, take the state of science, which demands high levels of brainwork and is measured by clear benchmarks of discovery. These days scientists are never far from their email, rarely touch paper and cannot lecture without PowerPoint. If electronic media were hazardous to intelligence, the quality of science would be plummeting. Yet discoveries are multiplying like fruit flies, and progress is dizzying. Other activities in the life of the mind, like philosophy, history and cultural criticism, are likewise flourishing, as anyone who has lost a morning of work to the Website *Arts & Letters Daily* can attest.

Critics of new media sometimes use science itself to press their case, citing research that shows how "experience can change the brain." But cognitive

2nd point: How the brain really works.

neuroscientists roll their eyes at such talk. Yes, every time we learn a factor skill the wiring of the brain changes; it's not as if the information is stored in the pancreas. But the existence of neural plasticity does not mean the brain is a blob of clay pounded into shape by experience.

6   Experience does not revamp the basic information-processing capacities of the brain. Speed-reading programs have long claimed to do just that, but the verdict was rendered by Wood Allen after he read *War and Peace* in one sitting: "It was about Russia." Genuine multitasking, too, has been exposed as a myth, not just by laboratory studies but by the familiar sight of an S.U.V. undulating between lanes as the driver cuts a deal on his cellphone.

7   Moreover, as the psychologists Christopher Chabris and Daniel Simons show in their new book *The Invisible Gorilla: And Other Ways Our Intuitions Deceive Us*, the effects of experience are highly specific to the experiences themselves. If you train people to do one thing (recognize shapes, solve math puzzles, find hidden words), they get better at doing that thing, but almost nothing else. Music doesn't make you better at math, conjugating Latin doesn't make you more logical, brain-training games don't make you smarter. Accomplished people don't bulk up their brains with intellectual calisthenics; they immerse themselves in their fields. Novelists read lots of novels, scientists read lots of science.

8   The effects of consuming electronic media are also likely to be far more limited than the panic implies. Media critics write as if the brain takes on the qualities of whatever it consumes, the informational equivalent of "you are what you eat." As with primitive peoples who believe that eating fierce animals will make them fierce, they assume that watching quick cuts in rock videos turns your mental life into quick cuts or that reading bullet points and Twitter turns your thoughts into bullet points and Twitter postings.

9   Yes, the constant arrival of information packets can be distracting or addictive, especially to people with attention deficit disorder. But distraction is not a new phenomenon. The solution is not to bemoan technology but to develop strategies of self-control, as we do with every other temptation in life. Turn off email or Twitter when you work, put away your BlackBerry at dinner time, ask your spouse to call you to bed at a designated hour.

3rd point: Control use and understand what makes us smart.

10   And to encourage intellectual depth, don't rail at PowerPoint or Google. It's not as if habits of deep reflection, thorough research and rigorous reasoning ever came naturally to people. They must be acquired in special institutions, which we call universities, and maintained with constant upkeep, which we call analysis, criticism and debate. They are not granted by propping a heavy encyclopedia on your lap, nor are they taken away by efficient access to information on the Internet.

11   The new media have caught on for a reason. Knowledge is increasing exponentially; human brainpower and waking hours are not. Fortunately, the Internet and information technologies are helping us manage, search and retrieve our collective intellectual output at different scales, from Twitter and previews to e-books and online encyclopedias. Far from making us stupid, these technologies are the only things that will keep us smart.

Source: *New York Times/International Herald Tribune*, June 12, 2010. Reprinted by permission of the author.

1. What is Pinker's subject? (Be precise.)
2. What happened to the crime rate during the 1990s?
3. What happened during the years of heavy TV use and the publication of rock videos?
4. What changes occur in the brain when we learn new information? What does not change?
5. What do people do to be successful in their fields?

6. What is Pinker's response to those who complain about the new electronic technologies? What is his claim?
7. What kinds of evidence does Pinker provide?

8. Pinker asserts that speed reading and multitasking have been shown to be myths. Is this idea new to you? Are you surprised? Do you believe that you can multitask successfully? If so, how would you seek to refute Pinker?
9. Is the author convincing in his refutation of those who argue that electronic technologies will make us stupid? If so, why? If not, why not?

FOR ANALYSIS AND DEBATE

CHRISTMAS-TREE TOTALITARIANS | THOMAS SOWELL

A former professor of economics with a PhD from the University of Chicago, Thomas Sowell is currently a Senior Fellow at the Hoover Institution at Stanford University. He is the author of numerous books and articles, including *Intellectuals and Society* (2009). The following column was posted December 25, 2012, on the *National Review Online.*

PREREADING QUESTIONS Does the title give you any clue as to the subject of Sowell's essay—beyond connecting it to its publication date? What might be his general subject or approach?

When I was growing up, an older member of the family used to say, "What 1 you don't know would make a big book." Now that I am an older member of the family, I would say to anyone, "What you don't know would fill more books than the *Encyclopaedia Britannica*." At least half of society's trouble come from know-it-alls, in a world where nobody knows even 10 percent of it all.

Some people seem to think that, if life is not fair, then the answer is to turn 2 more of the nation's resources over to politicians—who will, of course, then spend these resources in ways that increase the politicians' chance of getting reelected.

The annual outbursts of intolerance toward any display of traditional Christmas 3 scenes, or even daring to call a Christmas tree by its name, show that today's liberals are by no means liberal. Behind the mist of their lofty words, the totalitarian mindset shows through.

4   If you don't want to have a gun in your home or in your school, that's your choice. But don't be such a damn fool as to advertise to the whole world that you are in "a gun-free environment" where you are a helpless target for any homicidal fiend who is armed. Is it worth a human life to be a politically correct moral exhibitionist?

5   The more I study the history of intellectuals, the more they seem like a wrecking crew, dismantling civilization bit by bit—replacing what works with what sounds good.

6   Some people are wondering what takes so long for the negotiations about the "fiscal cliff." Maybe both sides are waiting for supplies. Democrats may be waiting for more cans to kick down the road. Republicans may be waiting for more white flags to hold up in surrender.

Thomas Sowell

7   If I were rich, I would have a plaque made up, and sent to every judge in America, bearing a statement made by Adam Smith more than two-and-a-half centuries ago: "Mercy to the guilty is cruelty to the innocent."

8   If someone wrote a novel about a man who was raised from childhood to resent the successful and despise the basic values of America—and who then went on to become president of the United States—that novel would be considered too unbelievable, even for a work of fiction. Yet that is what has happened in real life.

9   Many people say, "War should be a last resort." Of course it should be a last resort. So should heart surgery, divorce, and many other things. But that does not mean that we should just continue to hope against hope indefinitely that things will work out, somehow, until catastrophe suddenly overtakes us.

10   Everybody is talking about how we are going to pay for the huge national debt, but nobody seems to be talking about the runaway spending that created that record-breaking debt. In other words, the big spenders get political benefits from handing out goodies, while those who resist giving them more money to spend will be blamed for sending the country off the "fiscal cliff."

11   When Barack Obama refused to agree to a requested meeting with Israeli prime minister Benjamin Netanyahu—the leader of a country publically and repeatedly threatened with annihilation by Iran's leaders, as the Iranians move toward creating nuclear bombs—I thought of a line from the old movie classic *Citizen Kane*: "Charlie wasn't cruel. He just did cruel things."

12   There must be something liberating about ignorance. Back when most members of Congress had served in the military, there was a reluctance of politicians to try to tell military leaders how to run the military services. But,

now that few members of Congress have ever served in the military, they are ready to impose all sorts of fashionable notions on the military.

After watching a documentary about the tragic story of Jonestown, I was struck by the utterly unthinking way that so many people put themselves completely at the mercy of a glib and warped man, who led them to degradation and destruction. And I could not help thinking of the parallel with the way we put a glib and warped man in the White House.   13

There are people calling for the banning of assault weapons who could not define an "assault weapon" if their lives depended on it. Yet the ignorant expect others to take them seriously.   14

Source: *National Review Online*, December 25, 2012. Reprinted by permission of Thomas Sowell and Creators Syndicate, Inc. © 2012 Creators Syndicate, Inc.

QUESTIONS FOR READING

1. Who, in Sowell's view, are totalitarians?
2. Who are "politically correct moral exhibitionist[s]"?
3. What action leads the author to write that Obama does "cruel things"? What else does Sowell call Obama?

QUESTIONS FOR REASONING AND ANALYSIS

4. Sowell writes about Christmas trees, the fiscal cliff, Obama, guns, and the national debt; how do these topics connect to give Sowell his general subject?
5. What, then, is the author's claim? Do you see a general theme that unites the many issues Sowell includes?
6. How does the author develop and support his claim?
7. Examine Sowell's style and tone. How would you characterize his tone? Is his approach likely to be effective for his primary audience? Explain.

QUESTIONS FOR REFLECTION AND WRITING

8. Do you find any logical fallacies in Sowell's argument? If so, how would you challenge them?
9. Has Sowell supported his general claim and specific generalizations to your satisfaction? Why or why not?

1. Think about sports stars you know. Write an argument defending one player as the best in his or her field of play. Think about whether you want to use Krauthammer's "Method 1" or "Method 2" or your own method for your criteria. (Remember that you can qualify your argument; you could write about the best college football player this year, for example.)

2. If you like music, think about what you might evaluate from this field. Who is the best rock band? Hip-hop artist? Country-western singer? And so forth. Be sure to make your criteria for evaluation clear.

3. You have had many instructors—and much instruction—in the last 12+ years. Is there one teacher who is/was the best? If so, why? Is there a teaching method that stands out in your memory for the excellence of its approach? Find an evaluation topic from your educational experiences.

4. Select an editorial, op-ed column, letter to the editor, or one of the essays in this text as an argument with which you disagree. Prepare a refutation of the work's logic or evidence or both. Follow the guidelines for writing a refutation or rebuttal in this chapter.

5. What is your favorite book? Movie? Television show? Why is it your favorite? Does it warrant an argument that it is really good, maybe even the best, in some way or in some category (sitcoms, for example)? Write a review, following the guidelines for this type of evaluation argument given in this chapter.

CHAPTER 9

The Position Paper: Claims of Values

READ: Who are the speakers? What is the situation?

REASON: What is the point of the cartoon? What does Dana Summers, the cartoonist, want readers to think about?

REFLECT/WRITE: Why does this cartoon make a good opening for a chapter on arguments based on values?

As we established in Chapter 4, all arguments involve values. Evaluation arguments require judgment—thoughtful judgment, one hopes, based on criteria—but judgment nonetheless. If you believe that no one should spend more than $25,000 for a car, then you will not appreciate the qualities that attract some people to Mercedes. When one argues that government tax rates should go up as income goes up, it is because one believes that it is *right* for government to redistribute income to some degree: The rich pay more in taxes, the poor get more in services. When countries ban the importing of ivory, they do so because they believe it is *wrong* to destroy the magnificent elephant just so humans can use their ivory tusks for decorative items. (Observe that the word *magnificent* expresses a value.)

Some arguments, though, are less about judging what is good or best, or less about how to solve specific problems, than they are about stating a position on an issue. An argument that defends a general position (segregated schools are wrong) may imply action that should result (schools should be integrated), but the focus of the argument is first to state and defend the position. It is helpful to view these arguments, based heavily on values and a logical sequencing of ideas with less emphasis on specifics, as a separate type—genre—of argument. These claims of values are often called position papers.

CHARACTERISTICS OF THE POSITION PAPER

The position paper, or claim of values, may be the most difficult of arguments simply because it is often perceived to be the easiest. Let's think about this kind of argument:

- A claim based on values and argued more with logic than specifics is usually more general or abstract or philosophical than other types of argument. Greenpeace objects to commercial fishing that uses large nets that ensnare dolphins along with commercial fish such as tuna. Why? Because we ought not to destroy such beautiful and highly developed animals. Because we ought not to destroy more than we need, to waste part of nature because we are careless or in a hurry. For Greenpeace, the issue is about values—though it may be about money for the commercial fishermen.

- The position paper makes a claim about what is right or wrong, good or bad, for us as individuals or as a society. Topics can range from capital punishment to pornography to reducing the amount of trash we toss.

- Although a claim based on values is often developed in large part by a logical sequencing of reasons, support of principles also depends on relevant facts. Remember the long list of specific abuses listed in the Declaration of Independence (see pp. 156–59). If Greenpeace can show that commercial fisheries can be successful using a different kind of net or staying away from areas heavily populated by dolphins, it can probably get more support for its general principles.

- A successful position paper requires more than a forceful statement of personal beliefs. If we can reason logically from principles widely shared by our audience, we are more likely to be successful. If we are going to challenge their beliefs or values, then we need to consider the conciliatory approach as a strategy for getting them to at least listen to our argument.

GUIDELINES for Analyzing a Claim of Value

When reading position papers, what should you look for? Again, the basics of good argument apply here as well as with definition arguments. To analyze claims of values specifically, use these questions as guides:

- **What is the writer's claim?** Is it clear?
- **Is the claim qualified if necessary?** Some claims of value are broad philosophical assertions ("Capital punishment is immoral and bad public policy"). Others are qualified ("Capital punishment is acceptable only in crimes of treason").
- **What facts are presented?** Are they credible? Are they relevant to the claim's support?
- **What reasons are given in support of the claim?** What assumptions are necessary to tie reasons to claim? Make a list of reasons and assumptions and analyze the writer's logic. Do you find any fallacies?
- **What are the implications of the claim?** For example, if you argue for the legalization of all recreational drugs, you eliminate all "drug problems" by definition. But what new problems may be created by this approach? Consider more car accidents and reduced productivity for openers.
- **Is the argument convincing?** Does the evidence provide strong support for the claim? Are you prepared to agree with the writer, in whole or in part?

PREPARING A POSITION PAPER

In addition to the guidelines for writing arguments presented in Chapter 4, you can use the following advice specific to writing position papers or claims of value.

Planning

1. **Think:** What claim, exactly, do you want to support? Should you qualify your first attempt at a claim statement?
2. **Think:** What grounds (evidence) do you have to support your claim? You may want to make a list of the reasons and facts you would consider using to defend your claim.

3. **Think:** Study your list of possible grounds and identify the assumptions (warrants) and backing for your grounds.

4. **Think:** Now make a list of the grounds most often used by those holding views that oppose your claim. This second list will help you prepare counterarguments to possible rebuttals, but first it will help you test your commitment to your position. If you find the opposition's arguments persuasive and cannot think how you would rebut them, you may need to rethink your position. Ideally, your two lists will confirm your views but also increase your respect for opposing views.

5. **Consider:** How can I use a conciliatory approach? With an emotion-laden or highly controversial issue, the conciliatory approach can be an effective strategy. Conciliatory arguments include

   - the use of nonthreatening language,
   - the fair expression of opposing views, and
   - a statement of the common ground shared by opposing sides.

You may want to use a conciliatory approach when (1) you know your views will be unpopular with at least some members of your audience; (2) the issue is highly emotional and has sides that are "entrenched" so that you are seeking some accommodations rather than dramatic changes of position; (3) you need to interact with members of your audience and want to keep a respectful relationship going. The sample student essay on gun control (at the end of this chapter) illustrates a conciliatory approach.

Drafting

1. Begin with an opening paragraph or two that introduces your topic in an interesting way. Possibilities include a statement of the issue's seriousness or reasons why the issue is currently being debated—or why we should go back to reexamine it. Some writers are spurred by a recent event that receives media coverage; recounting such an event can produce an effective opening. You can also briefly summarize points of the opposition that you will challenge in supporting your claim. Many counterarguments are position papers.

2. Decide where to place your claim statement. Your best choices are either early in your essay or at the end of your essay, after you have made your case. The second approach can be an effective alternative to the more common pattern of stating one's claim early.

3. Organize evidence in an effective way. One plan is to move from the least important to the most important reasons, followed by rebuttals to potential counterarguments. Another possibility is to organize by the arguments of the opposition, explaining why each of their reasons fails to hold up. A third approach is to organize logically. That is, if some reasons build on the accepting of other reasons, you want to begin with the necessary underpinnings and then move forward from those.

4. Maintain an appropriate level of seriousness for an argument of principle. Of course, word choice must be appropriate to a serious discussion, but in addition be sure to present reasons that are also appropriately serious. For example, if you are defending the claim that music CDs should not be subject to content labeling because such censorship is inconsistent with First Amendment rights, do not trivialize your argument by including the point that young people are tired of adults controlling their lives. (This is another issue for another paper.)

5. Provide a logical defense of or specifics in support of each reason. You have not finished your task by simply asserting several reasons for your claim. You also need to present facts or examples for or a logical explanation of each reason. For example, you have not defended your views on capital punishment by asserting that it is right or just to take the life of a murderer. Why is it right or just? Executing the murderer will not bring the victim back to life. Do two wrongs make a right? These are some of the thoughts your skeptical reader may have unless you explain and justify your reasoning. *Remember:* Quoting another writer's opinion on your topic does not provide proof for your reasons. It merely shows that someone else agrees with you.

A CHECKLIST FOR REVISION

☐ Do I have a clear statement of my claim? Is it qualified, if appropriate?

☐ Have I organized my argument, building the parts of my support into a clear and logical structure that readers can follow?

☐ Have I avoided logical fallacies?

☐ Have I found relevant facts and examples to support and develop my reasons?

☐ Have I paid attention to appropriate word choice, including using a conciliatory approach if that is a wise strategy?

☐ Have I used the basic checklist for revision in Chapter 4 (see p. 111)?

STUDENT ESSAY

EXAMINING THE ISSUE OF GUN CONTROL

Chris Brown

The United States has a long history of compromise. Issues such as representation in government have been resolved because of compromise, forming some of the bases of American life. Americans, however, like to feel

> Introduction connects ambivalence in American character to conflict over gun control.

that they are uncompromising, never willing to surrender an argument. This attitude has led to a number of issues in modern America that are unresolved, including the issue of gun control. Bickering over the issue has slowed progress toward legislation that will solve the serious problem of gun violence in America, while keeping recreational use of firearms available to responsible people. To resolve the conflict over guns, the arguments of both sides must be examined, with an eye to finding the flaws in both. Then perhaps we can reach some meaningful compromises.

Student organizes by arguments for no gun control.

Gun advocates have used many arguments for the continued availability of firearms to the public. The strongest of these defenses points to the many legitimate uses for guns. One use is protection against violence, a concern of some people in today's society. There are many problems with the use of guns for protection, however, and these problems make the continued use of firearms for protection dangerous. One such problem is that gun owners are not always able to use guns responsibly. When placed in a situation in which personal injury or loss is imminent, people often do not think intelligently. Adrenaline surges through the body, and fear takes over much of the thinking process. This causes gun owners to use their weapons, firing at whatever threatens them. Injuries and deaths of innocent people, including family members of the gun owner, result. Removing guns from the house may be the best solution to these sad consequences.

1. Guns for protection.

Responding to this argument, gun advocates ask how they are to defend themselves without guns. But guns are needed for protection from other guns. If there are no guns, people need only to protect themselves from criminals using knives, baseball bats, and other weapons. Obviously the odds of surviving a knife attack are greater than the odds of surviving a gun attack. One reason is that a gun is an impersonal weapon. Firing at someone from 50 feet away requires much less commitment than charging someone with a knife and stabbing repeatedly. Also, bullet wounds are, generally, more severe than knife wounds. Guns are also more likely to be misused when a dark figure is in one's house. To kill with the gun requires only to point and shoot; no recognition of the figure is needed. To kill with a knife, by contrast, requires getting within arm's reach of the figure, and knowing, for sure, the identity of your presumed opponent.

There are other uses of guns, including recreation. Hunting and target shooting are valid, responsible uses of guns. How do we keep guns available for recreation? The answer is in the form of gun clubs and hunting clubs. Many are already established; more can be constructed. These clubs can provide recreational use of guns for responsible people while keeping guns off the streets and out of the house.

2. Recreational uses.

The last argument widely used by gun advocates is the constitutional right to bear arms. The fallacies in this argument are that the Constitution was written in a vastly different time. This different time had different uses for guns, and a different type of gun. Firearms were defended in the Constitution because of their many valid uses and fewer problems. Guns were mostly muskets, guns that were not very accurate beyond close range. Also, guns took more than 30 seconds to load in the eighteenth century and could fire only one shot before reloading. These differences with today's guns affect the relative safety of guns then and now. In addition, those who did not live in the city at the time used hunting for food as well as for recreation; hunting was a necessary component of life. That is not true today. Another use of guns in the eighteenth century was as protection from animals. Wild animals such as bears and cougars were much more common. Settlers, explorers, and hunters needed protection from these animals in ways not comparable with modern life.

3. Second Amendment rights.

Finally, Revolutionary America had no standing army. Defense of the nation and of one's home from other nations relied on local militia. The right to bear arms granted in the Constitution was inspired by the need for national protection as well as by the other outdated needs previously discussed. Today America has a standing army with enough weaponry to adequately defend itself from outside aggressors. There is no need for every citizen to carry a musket, or an AK-47, for the protection of the nation. It would seem, then, that the Second Amendment does not fully apply to modern society. While it justifies gun ownership, it is open to restrictions and controls based on the realities of today's world.

To reach a compromise, we also have to examine the other side of the issue. Some gun-control advocates argue that all guns are unnecessary and should be outlawed. The problem with this argument is that guns will still be available to those who do not mind breaking the law. Until an economically sound and feasible way of controlling illegal guns in America is found, guns cannot be totally removed, no matter how much legislation is passed. This means that if guns are to be outlawed for uses other than recreational uses, a way must be found to combat the illegal gun trade that will evolve. Tough criminal laws and a large security force are all that can be offered to stop illegal uses of guns until better technology is available. This means that, perhaps, a good resolution would involve gradual restrictions on guns, until eventually guns were restricted only to recreational uses in a controlled setting for citizens not in the police or military.

Both sides on this issue have valid points. Any middle ground needs to offer something to each side. It must address the reasons people feel they need guns for protection and allow for valid recreational use, but keep military-style guns off the street, except when in the hands of properly trained police officers. Time and money will be needed to move toward the removal of America's huge gun arsenal. But, sooner or later a compromise on the issue of gun control must be made to make America a safer, better place to live.

TO TRACK MY THIEF | DAVID POGUE

A graduate of Yale University with an interesting blend of study in music, English, and computer science, David Pogue writes a weekly column for the *New York Times* and a monthly column for *Scientific American*, focusing on technology issues. He has hosted *NOVA ScienceNow* shows on PBS and is a CBS News correspondent. Before becoming a columnist, he arranged and conducted a number of Broadway musicals and wrote a number of the books "for Dummies." The following column comes from the November 2012 issue of *Scientific American*.

PREREADING QUESTIONS Knowing that this is a technology column and considering the title, what do you expect Pogue's subject to be? What makes Pogue's title clever and catchy?

When I boarded an Amtrak train this summer, I had no idea what kind of ride I was in for.

Upon arrival at my home stop in Connecticut, I realized that my iPhone was missing. I still had hope, though. Apple's free Find My iPhone service uses GPS, Wi-Fi and cellular information to locate lost i-gadgets on a map. After a couple of days, Find My iPhone emailed me to announce that it had found my phone—a map revealed it to be at a house in Seat Pleasant, MD.

Well, great. How was I going to retrieve a phone five states away? On a nutty whim, I posted a note to my Twitter followers about my lost phone. "Find My iPhone shows it in MD. Anyone want to help me track it down? ADVENTURE!" And I included a map showing the green locator dot over a satellite image of a nondescript house.

Within an hour the quest to recover my phone was on blogs, Twitter, and even national newspapers and television shows. "Where's Pogue's phone?" became a high-tech treasure hunt.

Using the address provided by Find My iPhone, local police got involved. The homeowner confessed to stealing the phone—no doubt baffled as to how the police had known exactly how to find him. And a day later I had the phone back. (I decided not to press charges.)

To me, that was that. Modern tech + good old-fashioned police work = happy ending, right?

Not for everyone. Lots of people were disturbed by the affair. They saw my posting the thief's address as a gross violation of his privacy.

"Are there to be ANY limits in this country?" wrote one reader. "Mr. Pogue . . . not only . . . crowdsourced instant 'deputies,' giving [them] detailed maps of the device's location but got the police to go to that location. That location is someone's home. What's the presumption of privacy there?"

My initial thought was: "Wait a minute—we're expressing sympathy for the *thief?*" When you steal something, don't you risk giving up some rights? How was my Twitter post any different from the "wanted" posters of suspects' photographs that still hang in post offices?

Of course, the difference in this case is that I, not law enforcement, posted the map and began the chase. Does that constitute a breach of the thief's rights? Is this a slippery slope into a world where the Internet's citizens become digital vigilantes?

11   Those are tricky questions. Even when the government or law-enforcement agencies want to get cell location information, the law is not always clear-cut. Sometimes the police require a warrant to obtain such information from cell phone companies; in other instances, they do not. In my case, there's not even much law to guide us, says Chris Soghoian, a privacy researcher at Indiana University Bloomington. A bill proposed last year in Congress, nicknamed the "GPS Act," would have addressed "find my phone" services, saying that it's "not unlawful" for the owner of a stolen phone to use geolocation information to help an investigation.

12   It is possible, Soghoian says, that I violated some kind of state harassment or stalking statute. For the most part, however, both the legal and ethical ramifications of my crowdsourced phone quest are nothing but murk. It would have been better if I had been able to recover the phone without blasting a photograph of the guy's home to the Internet at large. It would have been better if he hadn't taken my phone at all or had responded to the "Reward if found" messages I sent to its screen. Yet combining the powers of geotracking and social networking seemed such an obvious tactic that, at the time, I hardly gave it a second thought.

13   In the end, maybe what society really needs is an app called Find My Moral Compass.

QUESTIONS FOR READING

1. What happened to the author on his train ride home?
2. What app found his phone?
3. What did he do with this information?

QUESTIONS FOR REASONING AND ANALYSIS

4. What sequence of thoughts and discussions did Pogue go through as he listened to others and reflected on his actions?
5. What is the ethical issue created by Pogue's actions?
6. What position does he reach on the issue? Does he offer a specific claim statement or imply one?

QUESTIONS FOR REFLECTION AND WRITING

7. How might we classify Pogue's essay, based on style and approach? Would you still assert that the author has presented an argument—one that explores an ethical issue created by modern technology? Why or why not? Explain.
8. If you had been one of the author's Twitter followers, how would you have responded to his "ADVENTURE"? Does Pogue need a moral compass, or did he act ethically? Be prepared to defend your view.
9. Does our digital world come with a loss of privacy? If so, is it worth the trade-off? Be prepared to discuss or write about this issue.

TRASH TALK: REFLECTIONS ON OUR THROWAWAY SOCIETY | GREGORY M. KENNEDY, SJ

The author of *An Ontology of Trash* (2007), Greg Kennedy is currently a student of theology at Regis College in Toronto, Canada. His essay originally appeared May 7, 2012, in *America*, a national weekly journal for Roman Catholics. He chose to modify the original article somewhat to reach out to this text's more diverse readership.

PREREADING QUESTIONS Knowing that the author is a Jesuit seminarian, would you necessarily expect his position on trash to be different from that of any other writer on this topic? How might his education and training influence his approach or writing style?

Every morning my colleague's desk captured my passing eye. Nestled 1 beneath the computer screen, between her cup of pens and a stapler, she kept her mid-morning snack. Sometimes it was two chocolates in gold foil, or a pair of sugar biscuits bound together in cellophane, sometimes rose-colored paper enveloping a candy from the Philippines. And always fruit. One day it was an apple, another an orange, a third day a banana. Regardless of the variety, the fruit was invariably as meticulously wrapped as its companion foodstuffs.

Now plastic wrap around an apple struck me as redundant. Plastic wrap 2 around a banana or orange still snug in its peel struck me as downright ridiculous. I could not help staring incredulously each morning at these doubly embedded specimens, but never gathered the gumption to query my colleague about her logic.

Why, I wondered, would a person spend time, energy, and money to 3 shroud a banana in plastic, which would later require more time, energy and money to get rid of? After all, the good Creator already outfitted the banana with an effective, protective cover. What purpose does that extra layer of petrochemical veneer serve?

By no means would my colleague stand alone in the dock before such 4 questions. Nearly every retailer and almost as many customers in this country suspect that no licit commercial transaction has occurred if, in the end, there isn't a bag, or a box, a bottle, or a blister pack to pitch into the garbage pail.

In *Gone Tomorrow: The Hidden Life of Garbage*, Heather Rogers estimates 5 that 80% of U.S. products, like plastic wrap, are discarded after a single use. Of course, it takes a special kind of person to use a banana more than once. Food, the quintessential consumer good, has become a Grade-A disposable in the overstocked market. A supersized portion of comestibles in this country does not receive even the fleeting honor of a single use. The average American household wastes a quarter of all the food it presumably worked hard to bring home. Add to that the other waste occurring along the entire length of the production and distribution line—from the farm to the supermarket deli—and the total percentage of food wasted before tasted approaches a shocking and shaming forty percent.

Except in rare instances, for example, pie-throwing contests, food is not 6 intentionally produced in order to be tossed. The same does not hold for food's innumerable, protective accessorizing. Of all municipal solid waste, the single largest share goes to containers and packaging at 30%. Juice boxes, polystyrene clamshells, tin cans, plastic this, that and the other thing—nary a bite comes to our lips that has not recently emerged from an artificial peel.

7　　At first glance, it may seem that the plastic cling wrap and the organic banana peel differ only chemically, since they share the same function: packaging. Ever since Aristotle, philosophers have looked to an object's putative purpose in seeking to define its particular essence. This technique often succeeds with manufactured objects, but always stumbles over natural things. Only the consumer conveniently regards the banana peel as packaging. From the standpoint of the banana tree, the peel plays a vital part in procreation. To the soil the peel means future nutrients and increased fertility.

8　　Irreducible to a single purpose, natural things exist as waste only temporarily and conditionally. When out one evening picking saskatoon berries, a friend expressed his anxiety to me about the coming nightfall. "If we don't pick these bushes clean, all their berries will go to waste." I conceded a limited truth to this statement. As far as our stomachs were concerned, the berries would not fulfill their function if they never reached our mouths.

9　　Had we consulted the bush and berries, however, we might have slowed our hurried harvest. With respect to reproduction, the berries existed as ingeniously designed aerial seed-distribution units. In boyishly biological terms: birds eat the berries, fly a while and poop out the seeds across all the various kinds of soils one hears about in parables. However, we, the civilized consumers, would, by eating the seeds, destine them to destruction in the sewage treatment plant. So where exactly was the waste, on the bush or in our plumbing?

10　　Plastic wrap does not enjoy this multiplicity of purpose, nor the redemptive ambiguity of "waste." Its design is much less intelligent. Once the wrap fulfills its single function, it is good for nothing. In fact, it is about as good *as* nothing, because it has no more to achieve. If function and essence do go together in manufactured objects, then a consumer item deprived of function will also be devoid of essence. It becomes waste unconditionally and forever, since it no longer serves any possible end.

11　　Since it was originally conceived and produced to lose its function after a single use, the object was in a sense already wasted even before it performed its purpose. So here we have an object that already existed as waste. Planned obsolescence, you could say, renders objects presently obsolete. Such absolute waste, waste considered from all possible angles, waste built right into the conception of an object, I philosophically classify as "trash."

12　　The word "trash" has a modern ring. The reality began littering history only after the Industrial Revolution, when the mass production of goods took off, leaving the ground piled up with discarded, worn out bags. Albert Borgmann, philosopher of technology at the University of Montana, locates the key to modern industry in its division of labor. This is standard history. What moves Borgmann's interpretation well beyond mediocrity is where he draws the most basic lines of division: not between human workers, but within technology itself.

The genius of modern technology, he demonstrates, lies in its unprece- 13 dented ability to split the product from its production. Consumers desire commodities, such as tasty food, amusing entertainment, easy transportation. Devices deliver these desirables. Their delivery advances toward perfection the closer they come to providing products in demand without demanding anything in return. Thus the perfect device remains completely hidden behind the convenience of the consumable commodity.

Convenience, the rock on which we have built the consumer world, relies 14 absolutely on the division between commodity and device. Digging your own potatoes is not terribly convenient, especially when compared to dashing into 7-11 for a sealed-fresh bag of salt-and-vinegar chips. A complex, technological and all but invisible industrial food system is the globalized device feeding our hunger for fast-food convenience items. Packaging, of course, is an essential ingredient for making food convenient.

As part of the device, packaging has a sole function: to deliver the com- 15 modity of food as safely and conveniently as possible. Its single function necessitates its single use. If the consumer had to fold the plastic wrap and bring it home for tomorrow's snack, or had to wash and dry the take-away cup in preparation for the next injection of java, or had to return the aluminum can to the cola company for refills, then these devices would be delivering their goods inconveniently. But by definition, the device can't make such demands; its whole point is to disappear. As soon as it has accomplished its mission of delivery, the packaging device exhausts the conditions of its existence. It is trash, pure and simple. Into the void of the trash or recycling bin it vanishes.

So the banana peel and the plastic wrap differ much more than just chemi- 16 cally. The peel, not limited to a single purpose, exists and functions within an integrated web of relationships. Each relationship lets it be in a unique way. The peel exists as waste only within a limited subset of its total interconnections.

The plastic wrap, on the other hand, was expressly designed to deliver just 17 one value: the protection of goods from air, dirt and germs. Once the food is gone then so goes the plastic's *raison d'etre*. The wrap has nothing left to live for; it is curled up and buried. Materially, the object has the same qualities as it had when it first spooled off the roll. But as far as the consumer is concerned, it has instantly become irredeemable waste. How many of us would entrust another sandwich to it? No, it simply must be trashed. It belongs nowhere in our consumer world.

We all know that, despite our worst intentions, the disposables we discard 18 do not really disappear. Yet we like to pretend that they do. As consumers we have precious little business with the trash we generate. Our elaborate system of garbage collection, incineration, disposal and recycling is a sophisticated device that delivers to most urban consumers the commodities of sanitation and cleanliness. Undoubtedly, swept streets and clean homes count as real blessings. But hiding our trash within the technological division of commodity and device allows us to consume without concerning ourselves about consequences.

19   And the consequences keep piling up. In spite of all our roused environmental consciousness and the de-materialization of the digital age, our quantity of trash compounds. According to the EPA, Americans generated 2.68 lbs of municipal solid waste per person per day in 1960. By 2010 that total had bloated to 4.43 lbs. The fatter the wedge we drive between the commodity and its device, the more trash we inevitably stuff into the gap.

20   We can and must do otherwise. Some years after WWII, French philosopher Jean-Paul Sartre said: "We were never more free than during German occupation." Sartre had a flair for paradox. Under occupation, every act took on significance; every act, no matter how prosaic, held out the chance for bravery and non-conformity. In a throw-away society, analogous opportunities prevail. Every shopping bag you refuse, every coffee cup you reuse, every piece of plastic you eschew is an act of freedom and conscience against our thoughtless slavery to trash.

Source: *America: The National Catholic Weekly*, May 7, 2012. Reprinted by permission of the author.

QUESTIONS FOR READING

1.   What percentage of food is wasted?
2.   What percentage of solid waste is composed of packaging? How does packaging's purpose differ from food's purpose?
3.   How does plastic covering differ from organic covering—such as the banana peel?
4.   What do modern consumers want? How does plastic packaging help to deliver this?

QUESTIONS FOR REASONING AND ANALYSIS

5.   Explain why plastic packaging is "trash" whereas organic "waste" is not.
6.   Our digital age has presumably resulted in less paper, and yet our volume of solid waste continues to increase. What—implies Kennedy—is contributing to the increased tonnage of trash?
7.   Review elements of style in Chapter 2 and then analyze Kennedy's writing, focusing on three characteristics that you select to study. How does his style contribute to his argument?

QUESTIONS FOR REFLECTION AND WRITING

8.   What specific suggestions for wasting less food and tossing less trash do you have to add to Kennedy's discussion? Explain and defend your suggestions. If you don't think that wasting food along the way or filling solid waste dumps are really that big a problem, prepare your rebuttal of Kennedy's argument.
9.   Kennedy concludes his essay by quoting Sartre. Explain Sartre's point and how Kennedy uses it to support his concluding point. Contemplate other ways in which we could use these ideas as guides to living.

1. Chris Brown, in the student essay, writes a conciliatory argument seeking common ground on the volatile issue of gun control. Write your own conciliatory argument on this issue, offering a different approach than Brown, but citing Brown for any ideas you borrow from his essay. Alternatively, write a counterargument of his essay.

2. There are other "hot issues," issues that leave people entrenched on one side or the other, giving expression to the same arguments again and again without budging many, if any, readers. Do not try to write on any one of these about which you get strongly emotional. Select one that you can be calm enough over to write a conciliatory argument, seeking to find common ground. Some of these issues include same-sex marriage, legalizing recreational drugs, capital punishment, mainstreaming students with disabilities, the use of torture to interrogate terrorists. Exclude abortion rights from the list—it is too controversial for most writers to handle successfully.

3. Other issues that call for positions based on values stem from First Amendment rights. Consider a possible topic from this general area. Possibilities include:

   Hate speech should (or should not) be a crime.

   Obscenity and pornography on the Internet should (or should not) be restricted.

   Hollywood films should (or should not) show characters smoking.

4. Consider issues related to college life. Should all colleges have an honor code—or should existing codes be eliminated? Should students be automatically expelled for plagiarism? Should college administrators have any control over what is published in the college newspaper?

CHAPTER 10

Arguments about Cause

READ: Who is the person in the ad? Why is she posed with the draped net?

REASON: What argument does the ad make? What visual strategies are used? What assumption about audience is made?

REFLECT/WRITE: Is the ad effective? Why or why not?

Because we want to know *why* things happen, arguments about cause are both numerous and important to us. We begin asking why at a young age, pestering adults with questions such as "Why is the sky blue?" and "Why is the grass green?" And, to make sense of our world, we try our hand at explanations as youngsters, deciding that the first-grade bully is "a bad boy." The bully's teacher, however, will seek a more complex explanation because an understanding of the causes is the place to start to guide the bully to more socially acceptable behavior.

As adults we continue the search for answers. We want to understand past events: Why was President Kennedy assassinated? We want to explain current situations: Why do so many college students binge drink? And of course we also want to predict the future: Will the economy improve if there is a tax cut? All three questions seek a causal explanation, including the last one. If you answer the last question with a yes, you are claiming that a tax cut is a cause of economic improvement.

CHARACTERISTICS OF CAUSAL ARGUMENTS

Causal arguments vary not only in subject matter but in structure. Here are the four most typical patterns:

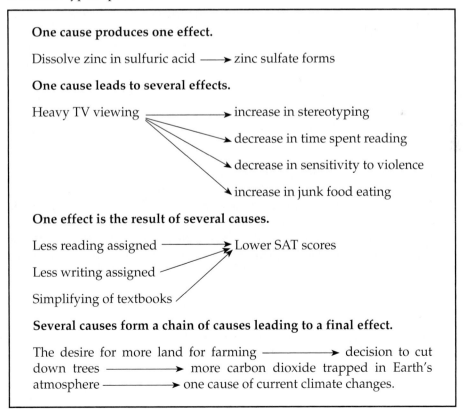

One cause produces one effect.

Dissolve zinc in sulfuric acid ⟶ zinc sulfate forms

One cause leads to several effects.

Heavy TV viewing ⟶ increase in stereotyping

decrease in time spent reading

decrease in sensitivity to violence

increase in junk food eating

One effect is the result of several causes.

Less reading assigned ⟶ Lower SAT scores

Less writing assigned

Simplifying of textbooks

Several causes form a chain of causes leading to a final effect.

The desire for more land for farming ⟶ decision to cut down trees ⟶ more carbon dioxide trapped in Earth's atmosphere ⟶ one cause of current climate changes.

These models lead to several key points about causal arguments:

- **Most causal arguments are highly complex.** Except for some simple chemical reactions, most arguments about cause are difficult, can involve many steps, and are often open to challenge. Even arguments based in science lead to shrill exchanges. Think, then, how much more open to debate are arguments about the worldwide economic downturn or arguments about human behavior. Many people think that "it's obvious" that violent TV and video games lead to more aggressive behavior. And yet, psychologists, in study after study, have not demonstrated conclusively that there is a clear causal connection. One way to challenge this causal argument is to point to the majority of people who do not perform violent acts even though they have watched television and played video games while growing up.

- **Because of the multiple and intertwined patterns of causation in many complex situations, the best causal arguments keep focused on their purpose.** For example, you are concerned with global warming. Cows contribute to global warming. Are we going to stop cattle farming? Not likely. Factories contribute to global warming. Are we going to tear down factories? Not likely—but we can demand that smokestacks have filters to reduce harmful emissions. Focus your argument on the causes that readers are most likely to accept because they are most likely to accept the action that the causes imply.

- **Learn and use the specific terms and concepts that provide useful guides to thinking about cause.** First, when looking for the cause of an event, we look for an *agent*—a person, situation, another event that led to the effect. For example, a lit cigarette dropped in a bed caused the house fire—the lit cigarette is the agent. But why, we ask, did someone drop a lit cigarette on a bed? The person, old and ill, took a sleeping pill and dropped the cigarette when he fell asleep. Where do we stop in the chain of causes?

  Second, most events do not occur in a vacuum with a single cause. There are *conditions* surrounding the event. The man's age and health were conditions. Third, we can also look for *influences.* The sleeping pill certainly influenced the man to drop the cigarette. Some conditions and influences may qualify as *remote causes. Proximate causes* are more immediate, usually closer in time to the event or situation. The man's dozing off is a proximate cause of the fire. Finally, we come to the *precipitating cause,* the triggering event—in our example, the cigarette's igniting the combustible mattress fabric. Sometimes we are interested primarily in the precipitating cause; in other situations, we need to go further back to find the remote causes or conditions that are responsible for what has occurred.

- **Be alert to the difference between cause and correlation.** First, be certain that you can defend your pattern of cause and effect as genuine causation, not as correlation only. Married people are better off financially, are healthier, and report happier sex lives than singles or cohabiting couples. Is this a correlation only? Or, does marriage itself produce these effects? Linda Waite is one sociologist who argues that marriage is the cause. Another example: Girls who participate in after-school activities are much less likely to get pregnant. Are the activities a cause? Probably not. But there are surely conditions and influences that have led to both the decision to participate in activities and the decision not to become pregnant.

An Example of Causal Complexity: Lincoln's Election and the Start of the Civil War

If Stephen Douglas had won the 1860 presidential election instead of Abraham Lincoln, would the Civil War have been avoided? An interesting question posed to various American history professors and others, including Waite Rawls, president of the Museum of the Confederacy. Their responses were part of an article that appeared in the *Washington Post* on November 7, 2010.

Obviously, this is a question that cannot be answered, but it led Rawls to discuss the sequence of causes leading to the breakout of the war. Rawls organizes his brief causal analysis around a great metaphor: the building and filling and then lighting of a keg of powder. Let's look at his analysis.

Existing Conditions

"The wood for the keg was shaped by the inability of the founding fathers to solve the two big problems of state sovereignty and slavery in the shaping of the Constitution."

More Recent Influences

1. "[T]he economics of taxes and the politics of control of the westward expansion were added to those two original issues as the keg was filled with powder."
2. "By the time of the creation of the Republican Party in 1856, the powder keg was almost full and waiting for a fuse. And the election of any candidate from the Republican Party—a purely sectional party—put the fuse in the powder keg, and the Deep South states seceded. But there was still no war."

Proximate Causes

"Two simultaneous mistakes in judgment brought the matches out of the pocket—the Deep South mistakenly thought that Lincoln, now elected, would not enforce the Union, and Lincoln mistakenly thought that the general population of the South would not follow the leadership" of the Deep South states.

Precipitating Causes

1. "Lincoln struck the match when he called the bluff of the South Carolinians and attempted to reinforce Fort Sumter, but that match could have gone out without an explosion."
2. "Lincoln struck a second, more fateful match, when he called for troops to put down the 'insurrection.' That forced the Upper South and Border States into a conflict that they had vainly attempted to avoid." (Reprinted by permission of Waite Rawls.)

Rawls concludes that the election of Lincoln did not start the war; it was only one step in a complex series of causes that led to America's bloodiest war. His analysis helps us see the complexity of cause/effect analysis.

Mill's Methods for Investigating Causes

John Stuart Mill, a nineteenth-century British philosopher, explained in detail some important ways of investigating and demonstrating causal relationships: commonality, difference, and process of elimination. We can benefit in our study of cause by understanding and using his methods.

1. **Commonality.** One way to isolate cause is to demonstrate that one agent is *common* to similar outcomes. For instance, twenty-five employees attend a company luncheon. Late in the day, ten report to area hospitals, and another four complain the next day of having experienced vomiting the night before. Public health officials will soon want to know what these people ate for lunch. Different people during the same twelve-hour period had similar physical symptoms of food poisoning. The common factor may well have been the tuna salad they ate for lunch.

2. **Difference.** Another way to isolate cause is to recognize one key *difference.* If two situations are alike in every way but one, and the situations result in different outcomes, then the one way they differ must have caused the different outcome.

   Studies in the social sciences are often based on the single-difference method. To test for the best teaching methods for math, an educator could set up an experiment with two classrooms similar in every way except that one class devotes fifteen minutes three days a week to instruction by drill. If the class receiving the drill scores much higher on a standard test given to both groups of students, the educator could argue that math drills make a measurable difference in learning math. But the educator should be prepared for skeptics to challenge the assertion of only one difference between the two classes. Could the teacher's attitude toward the drills also make a difference in student learning? If the differences in student scores are significant, the educator probably has a good argument.

3. **Process of elimination.** We can develop a causal argument around a technique we all use for problem solving: *the process of elimination.* When something happens, we examine all possible causes and eliminate them, one by one, until we are satisfied that we have isolated the actual cause (or causes).

   When the Federal Aviation Administration has to investigate a plane crash, it uses this process, exploring possible causes such as mechanical failure, weather, human error, or terrorism. Sometimes the process isolates more than one cause or points to a likely cause without providing absolute proof.

EXERCISE: Understanding Causal Patterns

From the following events or situations, select the one you know best and list as many conditions, influences, and causes—remote, proximate, precipitating—as you can think of. You may want to do this exercise with your class partner or in small groups. Be prepared to explain your causal pattern to the class.

1. Decrease in marriage rates in the United States
2. Arctic ice melt
3. Increase in the numbers of women elected to public office
4. High salaries of professional athletes
5. Increased interest in soccer in the United States
6. Comparatively low scores by U.S. students on international tests in math and science
7. Majority of 2012 U.S. Olympians were women

GUIDELINES for Analyzing Causal Arguments

When analyzing causal arguments, what should you look for? The basics of good argument apply to all arguments: a clear statement of claim, qualified if appropriate; a clear explanation of reasons and evidence; and enough relevant evidence to support the claim. How do we recognize these qualities in a causal argument? Use these points as guides to analyzing:

- **Does the writer carefully distinguish among types of causes?** Word choice is crucial. Is the argument that A and A alone caused B or that A was one of several contributing causes?

- **Does the writer recognize the complexity of causation and not rush to assert only one cause for a complex event or situation?** The credibility of an argument about cause is quickly lost if readers find the argument oversimplified.

- **Is the argument's claim clearly stated, with qualifications as appropriate?** If the writer wants to argue for one cause, not the only cause, of an event or situation, then the claim's wording must make this limited goal clear to readers. For example, one can perhaps build the case for heavy television viewing as one cause of stereotyping, loss of sensitivity to violence, and increased fearfulness. But we know that the home environment and neighborhood and school environments also do much to shape attitudes.

- **What reasons and evidence are given to support the argument?** Can you see the writer's pattern of development? Does the reasoning seem logical? Are the data relevant? This kind of analysis of the argument will help you evaluate it.

- **Does the argument demonstrate causality, not just a time relationship or correlation?** A causal argument needs to prove *agency*: A is the cause of B, not just something that happened before B or something that is present when B is present. March precedes April, but March does not cause April to arrive.

- **Does the writer present believable causal agents, agents consistent with our knowledge of human behavior and scientific laws?** Most educated people do not believe that personalities are shaped by astrological signs or that scientific laws are suspended in the Bermuda Triangle, allowing planes and ships to vanish or enter a fourth dimension.

- **What are the implications for accepting the causal argument?** If A and B clearly are the causes of C, and we don't want C to occur, then we presumably must do something about A and B—or at least we must do something about either A or B and see if reducing or eliminating one of the causes significantly reduces the incidence of C.
- **Is the argument convincing?** After analyzing the argument and answering the questions given in the previous points, you need to decide if, finally, the argument works.

PREPARING A CAUSAL ARGUMENT

In addition to the guidelines for writing arguments presented in Chapter 4, you can use the following advice specific to writing causal arguments.

Planning

1. **Think:** What are the focus and limits of your causal argument? Do you want to argue for one cause of an event or situation? Do you want to argue for several causes leading to an event or situation? Do you want to argue for a cause that others have overlooked? Do you want to show how one cause is common to several situations or events? Diagramming the relationship of cause to effect may help you see what you want to focus on.

2. **Think:** What reasons and evidence do you have to support your tentative claim? Consider what you already know that has led to your choice of topic. A brainstorming list may be helpful.

3. **Think:** How, then, do you want to word your claim? As we have discussed, wording is crucial in causal arguments. Review the discussion of characteristics of causal arguments if necessary.

4. **Reality check:** Do you have a claim worth defending in a paper? Will readers care?

5. **Think:** What, if any, additional evidence do you need to develop a convincing argument? You may need to do some reading or online searching to obtain data to strengthen your argument. Readers expect relevant, reliable, current statistics in most arguments about cause. Assess what you need and then think about what sources will provide the needed information.

6. **Think:** What assumptions (warrants) are you making in your causal reasoning? Are these assumptions logical? Will readers be likely to agree with your assumptions, or will you need to defend them as part of your argument? For example: One reason to defend the effects of heavy TV watching on viewers is the commonsense argument that what humans devote considerable time to will have a significant effect on their lives. Will your readers be prepared to accept this commonsense reasoning, or will they remain skeptical, looking for stronger evidence of a cause/effect relationship?

Drafting

1. Begin with an opening paragraph or two that introduces your topic in an interesting way. Lester Thurow in "Why Women Are Paid Less Than Men" writes:

    > In the 40 years from 1939 to 1979 white women who work full time have with monotonous regularity made slightly less than 60 percent as much as white men. Why?

    This opening establishes the topic and Thurow's purpose in examining causes. The statistics get the reader's attention.

2. Do not begin by announcing your subject. Avoid openers such as: In this essay I will explain the causes of teen vandalism.

3. Decide where to place your claim statement. You can conclude your opening paragraph with it, or you can place it in your conclusion, after you have shown readers how best to understand the causes of the issue you are examining.

4. Present reasons and evidence in an organized way. If you are examining a series of causes, beginning with background conditions and early influences, then your basic plan will be time sequence. Readers need to see the chain of causes unfolding. Use appropriate terms and transitional words to guide readers through each stage in the causal pattern. If you are arguing for an overlooked cause, begin with the causes that have been put forward and show what is flawed in each one. Then present and defend your explanation of cause. This process of elimination structure works well when readers are likely to know what other causes have been offered in the past. You can also use one of Mill's other two approaches, if one of them is relevant to your topic.

5. Address the issue of correlation rather than cause, if appropriate. After presenting the results of a study of marriage that reveals many benefits (emotional, physical, financial) of marriage, Linda Waite examines the question that she knows skeptical readers may have: Does marriage actually *cause* the benefits, or is the relationship one of *correlation* only—that is, the benefits of marriage just happen to come with being married; they are not caused by being married.

6. Conclude by discussing the implications of the causal pattern you have argued for, if appropriate. Lester Thurow ends by asserting that if he is right about the cause of the gender pay gap, then there are two approaches society can take to remove the pay gap. If, in explaining the causes of teen vandalism, you see one cause as "group behavior," a gang looking for something to do, it then follows that you can advise young readers to stay out of gangs. Often with arguments about cause, there are personal or public policy implications in accepting the causal explanation.

A CHECKLIST FOR REVISION ■·■·■·■·■·■·■·■·■·■·■·■·■·■·■·■·■

☐ Do I have a clear statement of my claim? Is it appropriately qualified and focused? Is it about an issue that matters?

☐ Have I organized my argument so that readers can see my pattern for examining cause?

☐ Have I used the language for discussing causes correctly, distinguishing among conditions and influences and remote and proximate causes? Have I selected the correct word—either *affect* or *effect*—as needed?

☐ Have I avoided the *post hoc* fallacy and the confusing of correlation and cause?

☐ Have I carefully examined my assumptions and convinced myself that they are reasonable and can be defended? Have I defended them when necessary to clarify and thus strengthen my argument?

☐ Have I found relevant facts and examples to support and develop my argument?

☐ Have I used the basic checklist for revision in Chapter 4 (see p. 111)?

FOR ANALYSIS AND DEBATE

WHY YOUR OFFICE NEEDS MORE BRATTY MILLENNIALS | EMILY MATCHAR

The author, a graduate of Yale University, is a freelance writer whose articles focus on culture, food, travel, and women's issues. Her first book is *Homeward Bound: The New Cult of Domesticity* (2013).

PREREADING QUESTIONS Who are the millennials? What do you think they might be able to contribute to the office?

1   Have you heard the one about the kid who got his mom to call his boss and ask for a raise? Or about the college student who quit her summer internship because it forbade Facebook in the office?

2   Yep, we're talking about Generation Y—loosely defined as those born between 1982 and 1999—also known as millennials. Perhaps you know them by their other media-generated nicknames: teacup kids, for their supposed emotional fragility; boomerang kids, who always wind up back home; trophy kids—everyone's a winner!; the Peter Pan generation, who'll never grow up.

3   Now this pampered, over-praised, relentlessly self-confident generation (at age 30, I consider myself a sort of older sister to them) is flooding the workplace. They'll make up 75 percent of the American workforce by 2025—and they're trying to change everything.

4   These are the kids, after all, who text their dads from meetings. They think "business casual" includes skinny jeans. And they expect the company president to listen to their "brilliant idea."

5   When will they adapt?

6   They won't. Ever. Instead, through their sense of entitlement and inflated self-esteem, they'll make the modern workplace adapt to them. And we should thank them for it. Because the modern workplace frankly stinks, and the changes wrought by Gen Y will be good for everybody.

Few developed countries demand as much from their workers as the United   7
States. Americans spend more time at the office than citizens of most other
developed nations. Annually, we work 408 hours more than the Dutch, 374 hours
more than the Germans and 311 hours more than the French. We even work 59
hours more than the stereotypically nose-to-the-grindstone Japanese. Though
women make up half of the American workforce, the United States is the only
country in the developed world without guaranteed paid maternity leave.

All this hard work is done for less and less reward. Wages have been stag-   8
nant for years, benefits shorn, opportunities for advancement blocked. While
the richest Americans get richer, middle-class workers are left to do more with
less. Because jobs are scarce and we're used to a hierarchical workforce, we
accept things the way they are. Worse, we've taken our overwork as a badge
of pride. Who hasn't flushed with a touch of self-importance when turning
down social plans because we're "too busy with work"?

Into this sorry situation strolls the self-esteem generation, printer-fresh   9
diplomas in hand. And they're not interested in business as usual.

The current corporate culture simply doesn't make sense to much of 10
middle-class Gen Y. Since the cradle, these privileged kids have been offered
autonomy, control and choices ("Green pants or blue pants today, sweetie?").
They've been encouraged to show their creativity and to take their extracurricular interests seriously. Raised by parents who wanted to be friends with
their kids, they're used to seeing their elders as peers rather than authority
figures. When they want something, they're not afraid to say so.

And what the college-educated Gen Y-ers entering the workforce want is 11
engaging, meaningful, flexible work that doesn't take over their lives. The
grim economy and lack of job opportunities don't seem to be adjusting their
expectations downward much, either. According to a recent AP analysis, more
than 53 percent of recent college grads are unemployed or underemployed,
but such numbers don't appear to keep these new grads from thinking their
job owes them something.

In a March MTV survey of about 500 millennials, called "No Collar 12
Workers," 81 percent of respondents said they should be able to set their own
hours, and 70 percent said they need "me time" on the job (compared with 39
percent of baby boomers). Ninety percent think they deserve their "dream
job." They expect to be listened to when they have an idea, even when they're
the youngest person in the room.

"Why do we have to meet in an office cross-country when we can call in 13
remotely via Skype?" asks Megan Broussard, a 25-year-old New Yorker who
worked at a large PR firm for three years before quitting to become a freelance writer and career adviser. "Why wouldn't my opinion matter as much as
someone else's who only has a few more years of experience than I do?"

These desires are not exactly radical. Who wouldn't want flexibility, auton- 14
omy and respect?

What's different, says Lindsey Pollak, the author of "Getting From College 15
to Career: Your Essential Guide to Succeeding in the Real World," is how Gen
Y-ers are asking for those things. Pollak, a consultant who advises companies
on how to deal with Gen Y, says these workers—at least, the well-educated

ones who can afford to make demands—want what everyone wants out of a job, they're just asking for it in a more aggressive way. "And they're the first ones to leave when they don't get it," Pollak says.

16   According to surveys, 50 percent of Gen Y-ers would rather be unemployed than stay in a job they hate. Unlike their child- and mortgage-saddled elders, many can afford to be choosy about their jobs, given their notorious reliance on their parents. After all, they can always move back in with Mom and Dad (40 percent of young people will move home at least once, per Pew research), who are likely to be giving them financial help well into their 20s (41 percent of Gen Y-ers receive financial support from their parents after college, according to research from Ameritrade).

17   In fact, it's possible that a bad economy can make being choosy even easier—if more people are struggling to find work and living at home, there's no stigma to it.

18   Nancy Sai, a 25-year-old who works at a nonprofit in Manhattan, spent a year living with her parents and working at a gas station while trying to snag her dream job. Her mom kept bugging her to look for something different— teaching! government! anything!—but Sai held firm. While it took her a year to find the ideal gig, she's glad she waited. Her job is meaningful, the office environment friendly and welcoming, her bosses forthcoming with feedback. Some of her friends have not been so lucky—one quit her job in politics when her boss refused to give her any time off.

19   "She couldn't separate her work life from her personal life at all," Sai says. "She quit without another job lined up. She said she felt the most liberated she had in two years."

20   Despite the recession, or perhaps because of it, corporations are eager to hire and retain the best, most talented Gen Y workers. "In this risky economic environment, the energy, insight and high-tech know-how of Gen Yers will be essential for all high-performing organizations," said a 2009 study on Gen Y from Deloitte, the professional services giant.

21   Companies are beginning to heed Gen Y's demands. Though flextime and job-sharing have been staples of the workforce for a few decades, they are becoming more accepted, even in rigid corporate culture, says Laura Schild-kraut, a career counselor specializing in the needs of Gen Y. There has also been a rise in new work policies, such as ROWE, or "results only work environment," a system in which employees are evaluated on their productivity, not the hours they keep. In a ROWE office, the whole team can take off for a 4 p.m. "Spider-Man" showing if they've gotten enough done that day.

22   Radical-sounding perks such as unlimited paid vacation—assuming you've finished your pressing projects—are more common among companies concerned with attracting and retaining young talent. By 2010, 1 percent of U.S. companies had adopted this previously unheard-of policy, largely in response to the demands of Generation Y.

23   The Deloitte study warns that, to retain Gen Y-ers, companies "must foster a culture of respect that extends to all employees, regardless of age or level in the organization." In other words: Treat your Gen Y workers nicely. But we should be treating everyone nicely already, shouldn't we?

Beyond that, Gen Y's demands may eventually help bring about the family- 24 friendly policies for which working mothers have been leading the fight. Though the Family and Medical Leave Act of 1993 afforded some protections for working parents, genuine flexibility is still a privilege of the lucky few, and parents who try to leave the office at 5:30 p.m. are often accused of not pulling their weight. Well, guess what? Now everybody wants to leave the office at 5:30. Because they've got band practice. Or dinner with their grandma. Or they need to walk their rescue puppy.

The American workplace has been transformed during economic upswings 25 and downturns. The weekend was a product of labor union demands during the relative boom of the early 20th century. The Great Depression led to the New Deal's Fair Labor Standards Act, which introduced the 40-hour workweek and overtime pay to most Americans. But now, workplace change is coming from unadulterated, unorganized worker pushiness.

So we could continue to roll our eyes at Gen Y, accuse them of being 26 spoiled and entitled and clueless little brats. We could wish that they'd get taken down a peg by the "school of hard knocks" and learn to accept that this is just the way things are.

But if we're smart, we'll cheer them on. Be selfish, Gen Y! Be entitled! 27 Demand what you want. Because we want it, too.

Source: *Washington Post*, August 19, 2012. Reprinted by permission of the author.

QUESTIONS FOR READING

1. What is the age range for millennials? What other term is used for this group?
2. How has this group been raised? How do they view their elders? Themselves?
3. What details describe the current middle-class work world in the United States?

QUESTIONS FOR REASONING AND ANALYSIS

4. What changes does Matchar want to see in the workplace?
5. What upbringing, according to the author, has caused the Gen Y-ers to hold their attitudes toward work?
6. What, then, is the author's claim? State it so that you have made a cause/effect statement.
7. What *kinds* of grounds does Matchar provide in support of her claim?

QUESTIONS FOR REFLECTION AND WRITING

8. Do you agree with the author that the Gen Y-ers' desired changes would be good for the workplace? Why or why not?
9. The descriptions of various generations are, of course, generalizations. (*You* might not be "bratty"!) Do you basically accept the characteristics of Gen Y-ers as described in the essay? And the upbringing that has shaped them? If you disagree, how would you challenge these generalizations? (Remember that these generalizations are not the author's alone; Matchar is expressing a widely shared analysis of this generation.)

"DARING TO DISCUSS WOMEN IN SCIENCE": A RESPONSE TO JOHN TIERNEY

CAROLINE SIMARD

Caroline Simard is a board member of the Ada Initiative and research consultant to the Anita Borg Institute for Women and Technology, at the Stanford University School of Medicine. She holds a PhD in communication and social science and works to find ways to increase the number of women and underrepresented minorities in science, technology, engineering, and mathematics (STEM), and business fields. Simard's essay, a response to an article by John Tierney, was posted at *Huffington Post*, June 9, 2010.

PREREADING QUESTIONS What type of argument do you anticipate, given the title and headnote information? What other type of argument should you anticipate, given the essay's location in this text?

1   On Monday [June 2010], John Tierney of the *New York Times* published a provocative article, "Daring to Discuss Women in Science," in which he argues that biology may be a factor to explain why women are not reaching high-level positions. He suggests that boys are innately more gifted at math and science and that the dearth of women in science may point to simple biological differences. If this is the case, why would we waste our time trying to get more women in science?

2   Mr. Tierney, let's indeed discuss women in science.

3   First, let me start by saying that I applaud the discussion—all potential explanations for a complex issue and all evidence need to be considered, even the ones that are not popular in the media or not "politically correct." I also believe that Larry Summer's now infamous comments about the possibility that biological differences account for the dearth of women scientists and technologists was, similarly, in the spirit of intellectual debate.

4   The problem with the biology argument that "boys are just more likely to be born good at math and science" isn't that it's not "politically correct"—it's that it assumes that we can take away the power of societal influences, which have much more solid evidence than the biology hypothesis. Tierney makes the point himself in his article—in order to provide evidence for biological differences, he cites a longitudinal Duke [University] study which shows that the highest achievers in SAT math tests (above 750), which counted 13 boys for every girl in the early 80s, became a ratio of 4 boys to 1 girls in 1991, "presumably because of sociocultural factors." Hmm, isn't this actual evidence that biology is not what is at play here? If it is possible to reduce the gender achievement gap in math by 3 thanks to "sociocultural factors," I rest my case. Sociocultural factors are indeed extremely powerful.

5   The Duke study also notes that the 4/1 achievement gap at the highest score hasn't changed in the last 20 years despite ongoing programs to encourage girls in math and science, whereas the highest achievers in writing ability (SAT above 700) shows a ratio of 1.2 girls for every boy, slightly favoring girls. However, if the premise is that boys are inherently "better" at math, and girls are inherently better at writing, why would the achievement gap be so large in math and negligible in writing? The stagnant 4 to 1 ratio is not evidence that there is an innate biological difference in math aptitude, but rather confirmation that persistent sociocultural barriers remain—that is, science and math are still thought of as male domains.

Research shows that math and science are [6] indeed thought of as stereotypically male domains. Project Implicit at Harvard University studied half a million participants in 34 countries and found that 70 percent of respondents worldwide have implicit stereotypes associating science with male more than with female. Years of research by Claude Steele and Joshua Aronson and their colleagues show that implicit stereotypes affect girls' performance in math—a phenomenon called "stereotype threat." When girls receive cues that "boys are better at math," their scores in math suffer. One study in a classroom setting showed that the difference in performance between boys and girls in math SAT scores was eliminated by simply having a mentor telling them that math is learned over time rather is "innate."

The problem is, girls are routinely getting the message that they don't [7] belong in math and science, further undermining their performance (and Mr. Tierney's article isn't exactly helping in changing the stereotype for the general public). The result of this implicit (unconscious) stereotype is that parents, teachers, and school counselors are less likely to encourage girls to pursue math and science than they are boys. These girls are then less likely to seek advanced math classes and would be unlikely, without those opportunities, to make it to the above 700 SAT math score regardless of ability.

Anecdotally, I had this experience with my daughter a couple of years ago. [8] At age 10, she had somehow decided that she wasn't good at math (despite being raised in a household with 2 PhDs). With her self-confidence plummeting, math homework became very painful in our household. When I dug deeper, I found that she mistakenly believed that you were either born with math ability or you weren't—that this was an innate biological ability as opposed to something you could learn, and that somehow she hadn't been "born with it." Once I actively dispelled that notion and provided her with additional mentoring, her math performance significantly improved. I never hear her say that she isn't good at math anymore, and her math homework is flawless.

The Duke article, and Tierney, raises an important question about prefer- [9] ence, however, that research suggests that boys are more interested in "things" and girls are more interested in "people" and thus gravitate towards fields reflecting that interest. In this research too, there is debate about what in this difference is "nature" versus "nurture"—there are powerful socialization forces at play. Regardless, we have to dispel the notion that science is only about "things" and not about people or somehow disconnected from all social relevance. Indeed, some of the most successful interventions to increase girls' interest in math and science have been to reframe the curriculum to provide examples and projects that are grounded in the interests of a diverse population of students. The EPICS program at Purdue University is a great example of grounding engineering disciplines in socially relevant contexts and has been shown to engage a diversity of students.

10   What we need, to put this debate to rest, is to replicate these findings in a country where science and math are not viewed as stereotypically male. The most recent cross-national comparison study, published in 2010 in *Psychological Bulletin* by Nicole Else-Quest and her colleagues and comparing 43 countries, shows that the achievement difference in math between girls and boys varies broadly across countries.

11   Their research shows that country-by-country variation is correlated with gender differences in self-confidence in math, which is compounded by stereotype threat. One of the strongest predictors of the gender gap in math achievement is a given country's level of gender equity in science jobs, consistent with socialization arguments: "if girls' mothers, aunts, and sisters do not have STEM careers, they will perceive that STEM is a male domain and thus feel anxious about math, lack the confidence to take challenging math courses, and underachieve on math tests."

12   Until girls stop getting the signal that math is for boys, the 4 to 1 gender gap in highest achievement categories of math and science will persist. This has nothing to do with innate ability.

13   Mr. Tierney, I look forward to your subsequent articles on this issue. Let's indeed dare to discuss women in science and continue to bring to bear the most relevant research on this issue.

Source: *HuffPostTech*, June 9, 2010. Reprinted by permission of the author.

QUESTIONS FOR READING

1. What is the occasion for Simard's posting? What is her topic?
2. What is Tierney's position on the issue?
3. What sociocultural factors are the causes of the gender gap in math and science, in Simard's view?

QUESTIONS FOR REASONING AND ANALYSIS

4. What is Simard's claim? (Try to state it with precision.)
5. What *kinds* of grounds does Simard present? What point about Tierney's warrant does the author want to make with the evidence she includes?
6. Examine Simard's style and tone; how do they help her argument?

QUESTIONS FOR REFLECTION AND WRITING

7. In the debate over women in science, there are two related assumptions: (1) Math ability is inborn and (2) Boys are innately better at math than girls. Have you heard either one—or both—of these views? Has Simard convinced you that the evidence challenges these ideas? Why or why not?
8. Why can stereotypes be a "threat"? How can ideas "threaten" us? Explain and illustrate to answer these questions.

1. Think about your educational experiences as a basis for generating a topic for a causal argument. For example: What are the causes of writer's block? Why do some apparently good students (based on class work, grades, etc.) do poorly on standardized tests? How does pass/fail grading affect student performance? What are the causes of high tuition and fees? What might be some of the effects of higher college costs? What are the causes of binge drinking among college students? What are the effects of binge drinking?

2. *Star Trek,* in its many manifestations, continues to play on television—why? What makes it so popular a series? Why are horror movies popular? What are the causes for the great success of the Harry Potter books? If you are familiar with one of these works, or another work that has been amazingly popular, examine the causes for that popularity.

3. The gender pay gap (see Figure 5.3 in Chapter 5) reflects earnings differences between all working men and all working women. It is not a comparison of earnings by job. What might be some of the causes for women continuing to earn less than men—in spite of the fact that more women than men now earn BA degrees? Consider what you know about women in the workforce who work full time. (The pay gap is also not about full- versus part-time work; both men and women work part time as well as full time.) Look at other graphics in Chapter 5 and think about what you have learned from Caroline Simard regarding women in STEM fields. Be prepared to discuss some causes of the pay gap or prepare an essay on the topic. (Be sure to qualify your claim as appropriate, based on what you know.)

CHAPTER 11

Presenting Proposals: The Problem/Solution Argument

READ: What is the subject of this cartoon?

REASON: How does the cartoon visualize the subject? What do you see between the primary sign and the "exit" sign?

REFLECT/WRITE: Toles illustrates a problem but not solutions. What have some states done to address the problem? What solutions can you suggest?

You think that there are several spots on campus that need additional lighting at night. You are concerned that the lake near your hometown is green, with algae floating on it. You believe that bikers on the campus need to have paths and a bike lane on the main roads into the college. These are serious local issues; you should be concerned about them. And, perhaps it is time to act on your concerns—how can you do that? You can write a proposal, perhaps a letter to the editor of your college or hometown newspaper.

These three issues invite a recommendation for change. And to make that recommendation is to offer a solution to what you perceive to be a problem. Public policy arguments, whether local and specific (lampposts or bike lanes), or more general and far-reaching (e.g., the federal government must stop the flow of illegal drugs into the country) can best be understood as arguments over solutions to problems. If there are only 10 students on campus who bike to class or only 200 Americans wanting to buy cocaine, then most people would not agree that we have two serious problems in need of debate over the best solutions. But, when the numbers become significant, then we see a problem and start seeking solutions.

Consider some of these issues stated as policy claims:

- The college needs bike lanes on campus roads and more bike paths across the campus.
- We need to spend whatever is necessary to stop the flow of drugs into this country.

Each claim offers a solution to a problem, as we can see:

- Bikers will be safer if there are bike lanes on main roads and more bike paths across the campus.
- The way to address the drug problem in this country is to eliminate the supply of drugs.

The basic idea of policy proposals looks like this:

Somebody	should (or should not)	do X – because:
(Individual, organization, government)		*(solve this problem)*

Observe that proposal arguments recommend action. They look to the future. And, they often advise the spending of someone's time and/or money.

CHARACTERISTICS OF PROBLEM/SOLUTION ARGUMENTS

- *Proposal arguments may be about local and specific problems or about broader, more general public policy issues.* We need to "think globally" these days, but we still often need to "act locally," to address the problems we see around us in our classrooms, offices, and communities.

- *Proposal arguments usually need to define the problem.* How we define a problem has much to do with what kinds of solutions are appropriate. For example, many people are concerned about our ability to feed a growing world population. Some will argue that the problem is not an agricultural one—how much food we can produce. The problem is a political one—how we distribute the food, at what cost, and how competent or fair some governments are in handling food distribution. If the problem is agricultural, we need to worry about available farmland, water supply, and farming technology. If the problem is political, then we need to concern ourselves with price supports, distribution strategies, and embargoes for political leverage. To develop a problem/solution argument, you first need to define the problem.

- *How we define the problem also affects what we think are the causes of the problem.* Cause is often a part of the debate, especially with far-reaching policy issues, and may need to be addressed, particularly if solutions are tied to eliminating what we consider to be the causes. Why are illegal drugs coming into the United States? Because people want those drugs. Do you solve the problems related to drug addicts by stopping the supply? Or, do you address the demand for drugs in the first place?

- *Proposal arguments need to be developed with an understanding of the processes of government, from college administrations to city governments to the federal bureaucracy.* Is that dying lake near your town on city property or state land? Are there conservation groups in your area who can be called on to help with the process of presenting proposals to the appropriate people?

- *Proposal arguments need to be based on the understanding that they ask for change—and many people do not like change, period.* Probably all but the wealthiest Americans recognize that our health-care system needs fixing. That doesn't change the fact that many working people struggling to pay premiums are afraid of any changes introduced by the federal government.

- *Successful problem/solution arguments offer solutions that can realistically be accomplished.* Consider Prohibition, for example. This was a solution to problem drinking—except that it did not work, could not be enforced, because the majority of Americans would not abide by the law.

GUIDELINES for Analyzing Problem/Solution Arguments

When analyzing problem/solution arguments, what should you look for? In addition to the basics of good argument, use these points as guides to analyzing:

- **Is the writer's claim not just clear but also appropriately qualified and focused?** For example, if the school board in the writer's community is not doing a good job of communicating its goals as a basis for its funding package, the writer needs to focus just on that particular school board, not on school boards in general.

- **Does the writer show an awareness of the complexity of most public policy issues?** There are many different kinds of problems with American schools and many more causes for those problems. A simple solution—a longer school year, more money spent, vouchers—is not likely to solve the mixed bag of problems. Oversimplified arguments quickly lose credibility.
- **How does the writer define and explain the problem?** Is the way the problem is stated clear? Does it make sense to you? If the problem is being defined differently than most people have defined it, has the writer argued convincingly for looking at the problem in this new way?
- **What reasons and evidence are given to support the writer's solutions?** Can you see how the writer develops the argument? Does the reasoning seem logical? Are the data relevant? This kind of analysis will help you evaluate the proposed solutions.
- **Does the writer address the feasibility of the proposed solutions?** Does the writer make a convincing case for the realistic possibility of achieving the proposed solutions?
- **Is the argument convincing?** Will the solutions solve the problem as it has been defined? Has the problem been defined accurately? Can the solutions be achieved?

Read and study the following annotated argument. Complete your analysis by answering the questions that follow.

WANT MORE SCIENTISTS? TURN GRADE SCHOOLS INTO LABORATORIES

PRIYA NATARAJAN

A professor in both the astronomy and physics departments at Yale University, Priya Natarajan is a theoretical astrophysicist. Her areas of investigation include black hole physics and gravitational lensing. Interested as well in enhancing general science literacy, Natarajan serves on the Advisory Board of NOVA ScienceNow, speaks at conferences, and writes newspaper articles. The following op-ed essay was published on February 5, 2012.

PREREADING QUESTIONS When you were in grade school, did you like to "discover things" in the natural world? How would you encourage early study of science?

"What's your major?" Ask a college freshman this question, and the answer may be physics or chemistry. Ask a sophomore or a junior, however, and you're less likely to hear about plans to enter the "STEM" fields—science, technology, engineering and mathematics. America's universities are not graduating nearly enough scientists, engineers and other skilled professionals to keep our country globally competitive in the decades ahead.

Author states problem.

And this is despite evidence such as a recent Center on Education and the Workforce report that forecasts skill requirements through 2018 and clearly shows the importance of STEM fields. The opportunities for those with just a high school education are restricted, it says—many high-paying jobs are open only to people with STEM college degrees.

States seriousness of problem.

A cause author will refute.

3   Still, as many as 60 percent of students who enter college with the intention of majoring in science and math change their plans. Because so many students intend to major in a STEM subject but don't follow through, many observers have assumed that universities are where the trouble starts. I beg to differ.

Author's solution.

4   I am a professor of astronomy and physics at Yale University, where I teach an introductory class in cosmology. I see the deficiencies that first-year students show up with. My students may have dexterity with the equations they're required to know, but they lack the capacity to apply their knowledge to real-life problems. This critical shortcoming appears in high school and possibly in elementary grades—long before college. If we want more Americans to pursue careers in STEM professions, we have to intervene much earlier than we imagined.

5   Many efforts are underway to get younger students interested in science and math. One example is the Tree of Life's online "treehouse" project, a collection of information about biodiversity compiled by hundreds of experts and amateurs. Students can use this tool to apply what they are learning in the classroom to the world around them. Starting early in children's education, we need to provide these types of engaging, interactive learning environments that link school curricula to the outside world.

Specific strategies for solving problem.

6   My own schooling is an example. Growing up in Delhi, India, I did puzzles, explored numbers and searched for patterns in everyday settings long before I ever saw an equation. One assignment I vividly remember asked us to find examples of hexagons. I eagerly pointed out hexagons everywhere: street tiles, leaves, flowers, signs, buildings. I was taught equations only after I learned what they meant and how to think about them. As a result, I enjoyed math, and I became good at it.

7   Not all American children have this experience, but they can. The Khan Academy, for example, has pioneered the use of technology to encourage unstructured learning outside the classroom and now provides teaching supplements in 36 schools around the country. For instance, recent reports describe a San Jose charter school using Khan's instructional videos in ninth-grade math classes to tailor lessons to each student's pace.

8   Perhaps more than English or history, STEM subjects require an enormous amount of foundational learning before students can become competent. Students usually reach graduate school before they can hope to make an original contribution. They can experiment in high school labs, but the U.S. schools' approach to math and science lacks, in large part, a creative element. We need to help students understand that math and science are cumulative

disciplines, and help them enjoy learning even as they gradually build a base of knowledge.

One way to do this is to encourage students to engage in self-guided or collaborative research projects—something the Internet has made much more feasible. An example from my own field is Zooniverse, a collection of experimental projects in which students can classify galaxies and search for new planets or supernovae using real data collected by NASA. Taking part in such explorations early will help students understand that science and math aren't just abstract equations, but tools we use to understand our world. By the time they get to college, they will have mastered the rhythm of the scientific method—learn, apply, learn, apply—and enjoy the process.

Six years ago, I had a student in an introductory cosmology class for non-science majors who had entered Yale as an economics major, a choice based primarily on pressure from his parents. After one summer researching gamma-ray bursts—the most energetic explosions in the universe—he is currently finishing up a PhD in physics at Berkeley. He was hooked by the opportunity to apply what he learned in the classroom to a challenging scientific problem. He loved the thrill of figuring something out.

Without firsthand experience of the scientific method and its eventual pay-off, students will continue to flock to other majors when their science and math courses become too demanding. If we want more scientists and engineers later, we need to teach children about the joys of hard work and discovery now.

Author states her claim.

Source: *Washington Post*, February 5, 2012. Reprinted by permission of the author.

QUESTIONS FOR READING

1. What are the STEM fields? Why are these fields important?
2. What percentage of college students planning to major in math or science end up changing fields?
3. What do many college students lack, leading them to have trouble in advanced STEM courses?

QUESTIONS FOR REASONING AND ANALYSIS

4. What is the problem Natarajan examines? What has caused this problem, in the author's view? What, then, is her claim?
5. How does the author support her claim?

QUESTIONS FOR REFLECTION AND WRITING

6. Few would question the reality of the problem Natarajan addresses; the issue is how to solve it. Do you agree that at least much of the cause rests with the early teaching of math and science? If yes, why? If no, why not?
7. From your experience, can you suggest other ways to improve early education in math and science?

PREPARING A PROBLEM/SOLUTION ARGUMENT

In addition to the guidelines for writing arguments presented in Chapter 4, you can use the following advice specific to defending a proposal.

Planning

1. **Think:** What should be the focus and limits of your argument? There's a big difference between presenting solutions to the problem of physical abuse of women by men and presenting solutions to the problem of date rape on your college campus. Select a topic that you know something about, one that you can realistically handle.

2. **Think:** What reasons and evidence do you have to support your tentative claim? Think through what you already know that has led you to select your particular topic. Suppose you want to write on the issue of campus rape. Is this choice due to a recent event on the campus? Was this event the first in many years or the last in a trend? Where and when are the rapes occurring? A brainstorming list may be helpful.

3. **Reality check:** Do you have a claim worth defending? Will readers care? Binge drinking and the polluting of the lake near your hometown are serious problems. Problems with your class schedule may not be—unless your experience reveals a college-wide problem.

4. **Think:** Is there additional evidence that you need to obtain to develop your argument? If so, where can you look for that evidence? Are there past issues of the campus paper in your library? Will the campus police grant you an interview?

5. **Think:** What about the feasibility of each solution you plan to present? Are you thinking in terms of essentially one solution with several parts to it or several separate solutions, perhaps to be implemented by different people? Will coordination be necessary to achieve success? How will this be accomplished? For the problem of campus rape, you may want to consider several solutions as a package to be coordinated by the counseling service or an administrative vice president.

Drafting

1. Begin by either reminding readers of the existing problem you will address or arguing that a current situation should be recognized as a problem. In many cases, you can count on an audience who sees the world as you do and recognizes the problem you will address. But in some cases, your first task will be to convince readers that a problem exists that should worry them. If they are not concerned, they won't be interested in your solutions.

2. Early in your essay define the problem—as you see it—for readers. Do not assume that they will necessarily accept your way of seeing the issue. You may need to defend your understanding of the problem before moving on to solutions.

3. If appropriate, explain the cause or causes of the problem. If your proposed solution is tied to removing the cause or causes of the problem, then you need to establish cause and prove it early in your argument. If cause is important, argue for it; if it is irrelevant, move to your solution.

4. Explain your solution. If you have several solutions, think about how best to order them. If several need to be developed in a sequence, then present them in that necessary sequence. If you are presenting a package of diverse actions that together will solve the problem, then consider presenting them from the simplest to the more complex. With the problem of campus rape, for example, you may want to suggest better lighting on campus paths at night plus an escort service for women who are afraid to walk home alone plus sensitivity training for male students. Adding more lampposts is much easier than getting students to take sensitivity classes.

5. Explain the process for achieving your solution. If you have not thought through the political or legal steps necessary to implement your solution, then this step cannot be part of your purpose in writing. However, anticipating a skeptical audience that says "How are we going to do that?" you would be wise to have precise steps to offer your reader. You may have obtained an estimate of costs for new lighting on your campus and want to suggest specific paths that need the lights. You may have investigated escort services at other colleges and can spell out how such a service can be implemented on your campus. Showing readers that you have thought ahead to the next steps in the process can be an effective method of persuasion.

6. Support the feasibility of your solution. Be able to estimate costs. Show that you know who would be responsible for implementation. Specific information strengthens your argument.

7. Show how your solution is better than others. Anticipate challenges by including reasons for adopting your program rather than another program. Explain how your solution will be more easily adopted or more effective when implemented than other possibilities. Of course, a less practical but still viable defense is that your solution is the right thing to do. Values also belong in public policy debates, not just issues of cost and acceptability.

A CHECKLIST FOR REVISION

☐ Do I have a clear statement of my policy claim? Is it appropriately qualified and focused?

☐ Have I clearly explained how I see the problem to be solved? If necessary, have I argued for seeing the problem my way?

☐ Have I presented my solutions—and argued for them—in a clear and logical structure? Have I explained how these solutions can be implemented and why they are better than other solutions that have been suggested?

☐ Have I used data that are relevant and current?

☐ Have I used the basic checklist for revision in Chapter 4? (See p. 111.)

FOR ANALYSIS AND DEBATE

POVERTY IN AMERICA: WHY CAN'T WE END IT?

PETER EDELMAN

A professor of law at Georgetown University, Peter Edelman is faculty director of the Center on Poverty, Inequality, and Public Policy at Georgetown and the author of numerous articles and books. His areas of specialty include constitutional law, legislation, and welfare law. His most recent book is *So Rich, So Poor: Why It's So Hard to End Poverty in America* (2012). The following essay appeared July 29, 2012 in the *New York Times*.

PREREADING QUESTIONS What percentage of Americans do you think live below the poverty line? Do you think the numbers are great enough to be considered a problem?

1   Ronald Reagan famously said, "We fought a war on poverty and poverty won." With 46 million Americans—15 percent of the population—now counted as poor, it's tempting to think he may have been right.

2   Look a little deeper and the temptation grows. The lowest percentage in poverty since we started counting was 11.1 percent in 1973. The rate climbed as high as 15.2 percent in 1983. In 2000, after a spurt of prosperity, it went back down to 11.3 percent, and yet 15 million more people are poor today.

3   At the same time, we have done a lot that works. From Social Security to food stamps to the earned-income tax credit and on and on, we have enacted programs that now keep 40 million people out of poverty. Poverty would be nearly double what it is now without these measures, according to the Center on Budget and Policy Priorities. To say that "poverty won" is like saying the Clean Air and Clean Water Acts failed because there is still pollution.

4   With all of that, why have we not achieved more? Four reasons: An astonishing number of people work at low-wage jobs. Plus, many more households are headed now by a single parent, making it difficult for them to earn a living income from the jobs that are typically available. The near disappearance of cash assistance for low-income mothers and children—i.e., welfare—in much of the country plays a contributing role, too. And persistent issues of race and gender mean higher poverty among minorities and families headed by single mothers.

5   The first thing needed if we're to get people out of poverty is more jobs that pay decent wages. There aren't enough of these in our current economy. The need for good jobs extends far beyond the current crisis; we'll need a full-employment policy and a bigger investment in 21st-century education and skill development strategies if we're to have any hope of breaking out of the current economic malaise.

6   This isn't a problem specific to the current moment. We've been drowning in a flood of low-wage jobs for the last 40 years. Most of the income of people in poverty comes from work. According to the most recent data available from the Census Bureau, 104 million people—a third of the population—have annual incomes below twice the poverty line, less than $38,000 for a family of three. They struggle to make ends meet every month.

This classic picture of poverty is old; sadly, as Edelman explains, poverty is still with us.

Half the jobs in the nation pay less than $34,000 a year, according to the Economic Policy Institute. A quarter pay below the poverty line for a family of four, less than $23,000 annually. Families that can send another adult to work have done better, but single mothers (and fathers) don't have that option. Poverty among families with children headed by single mothers exceeds 40 percent.

Wages for those who work on jobs in the bottom half have been stuck since 1973, increasing just 7 percent.

It's not that the whole economy stagnated. There's been growth, a lot of it, but it has stuck at the top. The realization that 99 percent of us have been left in the dust by the 1 percent at the top (some much further behind than others) came far later than it should have—Rip Van Winkle and then some. It took the Great Recession to get people's attention, but the facts had been accumulating for a long time. If we've awakened, we can act.

Low-wage jobs bedevil tens of millions of people. At the other end of the low-income spectrum we have a different problem. The safety net for single mothers and their children has developed a gaping hole over the past dozen years. This is a major cause of the dramatic increase in extreme poverty during those years. The census tells us that 20.5 million people earn incomes below half the poverty line, less than about $9,500 for a family of three—up eight million from 2000.

Why? A substantial reason is the near demise of welfare—now called Temporary Assistance for Needy Families, or TANF. In the mid-90s more than two-thirds of children in poor families received welfare. But that number has dwindled over the past decade and a half to roughly 27 percent.

One result: six million people have no income other than food stamps. Food stamps provide an income at a third of the poverty line, close to $6,300 for a family of three. It's hard to understand how they survive.

At least we have food stamps. They have been a powerful antirecession tool in the past five years, with the number of recipients rising to 46 million today from 26.3 million in 2007. By contrast, welfare has done little to counter the impact of the recession; although the number of people receiving cash assistance rose from 3.9 million to 4.5 million since 2007, many states actually reduced the size of their rolls and lowered benefits to those in greatest need.

Race and gender play an enormous part in determining poverty's continuing course. Minorities are disproportionately poor: around 27 percent of African-Americans, Latinos and American Indians are poor, versus 10 percent

of whites. Wealth disparities are even wider. At the same time, whites constitute the largest number among the poor. This is a fact that bears emphasis,
since measures to raise income and provide work supports will help more
whites than minorities. But we cannot ignore race and gender, both because
they present particular challenges and because so much of the politics of poverty is grounded in those issues.

15   We know what we need to do—make the rich pay their fair share of running the country, raise the minimum wage, provide health care and a decent
safety net, and the like. But realistically, the immediate challenge is keeping
what we have. Representative Paul Ryan and his ideological peers would slash
everything from Social Security to Medicare and on through the list, and would
hand out more tax breaks to the people at the top. Robin Hood would turn
over in his grave.

16   We should not kid ourselves. It isn't certain that things will stay as good as
they are now. The wealth and income of the top 1 percent grows at the
expense of everyone else. Money breeds power and power breeds more
money. It is a truly vicious circle.

17   A surefire politics of change would necessarily involve getting people in
the middle—from the 30th to the 70th percentile—to see their own economic
self-interest. If they vote in their own self-interest, they'll elect people who are
likely to be more aligned with people with lower incomes as well as with them.
As long as people in the middle identify more with people on the top than
with those on the bottom, we are doomed. The obscene amount of money
flowing into the electoral process makes things harder yet.

18   But history shows that people power wins sometimes. That's what happened in the Progressive Era a century ago and in the Great Depression as
well. The gross inequality of those times produced an amalgam of popular
unrest, organization, muckraking journalism and political leadership that
attacked the big—and worsening—structural problem of economic inequality.
The civil rights movement changed the course of history and spread into the
women's movement, the environmental movement and, later, the gay rights
movement. Could we have said on the day before the dawn of each that it
would happen, let alone succeed? Did Rosa Parks know?

19   We have the ingredients. For one thing, the demographics of the electorate are changing. The consequences of that are hardly automatic, but they
create an opportunity. The new generation of young people—unusually dis-
trustful of encrusted power in all institutions and, as a consequence, tending
toward libertarianism—is ripe for a new politics of honesty. Lower-income
people will participate if there are candidates who speak to their situations.
The change has to come from the bottom up and from synergistic leadership
that draws it out. When people decide they have had enough and there are
candidates who stand for what they want, they will vote accordingly.

20   I have seen days of promise and days of darkness, and I've seen them
more than once. All history is like that. The people have the power if they will
use it, but they have to see that it is in their interest to do so.

Source: *New York Times*, July 29, 2012. Reprinted by permission of the author.

QUESTIONS FOR READING

1. How many Americans live in poverty today?
2. What programs keep more from living in poverty?
3. What are the four causes Edelman lists that account for this poverty?
4. What solutions does Edelman present?

QUESTIONS FOR REASONING AND ANALYSIS

5. What is Edelman's claim? (State it as a problem/solution issue.)
6. One cause of poverty is the continued low incomes of women and minorities. Why, in examining solutions, does the author point out that extending aid will actually help more whites than minorities? What does he want readers to start thinking about?
7. Edelman makes clear that his call for some specific changes won't happen unless there is a more general change of attitude among voters. What change in thinking is essential in his view? Why?
8. Does the author believe that change is possible, that we could "win a war" on poverty? How optimistic does he seem to you?

QUESTIONS FOR REFLECTION AND WRITING

9. What numbers surprise you the most in this essay? Why?
10. Do you agree with Edelman that the change in attitude must come before the country will be able to decrease the numbers of poor in America? If you disagree, how would you rebut Edelman—that is, how can we reduce poverty without the attitude change?
11. Do you think that our poverty rate is a problem that we should address? Why or why not? Explain your position.

A MODEST PROPOSAL | JONATHAN SWIFT

For Preventing the Children of Poor People in Ireland from Being a Burden to Their Parents or Country, and for Making Them Beneficial to the Public

Born in Dublin, Jonathan Swift (1667–1745) was ordained in the Anglican Church and spent many years as dean of St. Patrick's in Dublin. Swift was also involved in the political and social life of London for some years, and throughout his life he kept busy writing. His most famous imaginative work is *Gulliver's Travels* (1726). Almost as well known is the essay that follows, published in 1729. Here you will find Swift's usual biting satire but also his concern to improve humanity.

PREREADING QUESTIONS Swift was a minister, but he writes this essay as if he were in a different job. What "voice" or persona do you hear? Does Swift agree with the views of this persona?

1   It is a melancholy object to those who walk through this great town[1] or travel in the country, where they see the streets, the roads, and cabin doors crowded with beggars of the female sex, followed by three, four, or six children, all in rags, and importuning every passenger for an alms. These mothers, instead of being able to work for their honest livelihood, are forced to employ all their time in strolling to beg sustenance for their helpless infants, who, as they grow up, either turn thieves for want of work, or leave their dear native country to fight for the pretender[2] in Spain or sell themselves to the Barbados.

Jonathan Swift

2   I think it is agreed by all parties that this prodigious number of children in the arms, or on the backs, or at the heels of their mothers, and frequently of their fathers, is in the present deplorable state of the kingdom a very great additional grievance; and therefore, whoever could find out a fair, cheap, and easy method of making these children sound and useful members of the commonwealth would deserve so well of the public as to have his statue set up for a preserver of the nation.

3   But my intention is very far from being confined to provide only for the children of professed beggars; it is of a much greater extent, and shall take in the whole number of infants at a certain age who are born of parents in effect as little able to support them as those who demand our charity in the streets.

4   As to my own part, having turned my thoughts for many years upon this important subject, and maturely weighed the several schemes of other projectors,[3] I have always found them grossly mistaken in the computation. It is true a child just dropped from its dam may be supported by her milk for a solar year with little other nourishment; at most not above the value of two shillings, which the mother may certainly get, or the value in scraps, by her lawful occupation of begging; and, it is exactly at one year that I propose to provide for them in such a manner as instead of being a charge upon their parents or the parish, or wanting food and raiment for the rest of their lives, they shall on the contrary contribute to the feeding, and partly to the clothing, of many thousands.

---

[1] Dublin.—Ed.

[2] James Stuart, claimant to the British throne lost by his father, James II, in 1688.—Ed.

[3] Planners.—Ed.

There is likewise another great advantage in my scheme, that it will pre- 5 vent those voluntary abortions, and that horrid practice of women murdering their bastard children, alas, too frequent among us, sacrificing the poor innocent babes, I doubt, more to avoid the expense than the shame, which would move tears and pity in the most savage and inhuman breast.

The number of souls in this kingdom being usually reckoned one million 6 and a half, of these I calculate there may be about two hundred thousand couples whose wives are breeders; from which number I subtract thirty thousand couples who are able to maintain their own children, although I apprehend there cannot be so many, under the present distress of the kingdom; but this being granted, there will remain a hundred and seventy thousand breeders. I again subtract fifty thousand for those women who miscarry, or whose children die by accident or disease within the year. There only remain a hundred and twenty thousand children of poor parents annually born. The question therefore is, how this number shall be reared and provided for, which, as I have already said, under the present situation of affairs, is utterly impossible by all the methods hereto proposed. For we can neither employ them in handicraft or agriculture; we neither build houses (I mean in the country) nor cultivate land. They can very seldom pick up a livelihood by stealing until they arrive at six years old, except where they are of towardly parts[4]; although I confess they learn the rudiments much earlier, during which time they can, however, be properly looked upon only as probationers, as I have been informed by a principal gentleman in the country of Cavan, who protested to me that he never knew above one or two instances under the age of six, even in the part of the kingdom renowned for the quickest proficiency in that art.

I am assured by our merchants that a boy or girl before twelve years old is 7 no saleable commodity; and even when they come to this age they will not yield above three pounds, or three pounds and a half a crown at most, on the exchange; which cannot turn to account either to the parents or the kingdom, the charge of nutriment and rags having been at least four times that value.

I shall now therefore humbly propose my own thoughts, which I hope will 8 not be liable to the least objection.

I have been assured by a very knowing American of my acquaintance in 9 London that a young healthy child well nursed is at a year old a most delicious, nourishing, and wholesome food, whether stewed, roasted, baked, or boiled; and I make no doubt that it will equally serve in a fricassee or ragout.

I do therefore humbly offer it to public consideration that of the hundred 10 and twenty-thousand children, already computed, twenty thousand may be reserved for breed, whereof only one fourth part to be males, which is more than we allow to sheep, black cattle, or swine; and my reason is that these children are seldom the fruits of marriage, a circumstance not much regarded by our savages, therefore one male will be sufficient to serve four females. That the remaining hundred thousand may at a year old be offered in sale to the persons of quality and fortune, through the kingdom, always advising the

---

[4] Innate abilities.—Ed.

mother to let them suck plentifully in the last month, so as to render them plump and fat for the table. A child will make two dishes at an entertainment for friends; and when the family dines alone, the fore or hind quarter will make a reasonable dish, and seasoned with a little pepper or salt will be very good boiled on the fourth day, especially in winter.

11   I have reckoned upon a medium that a child just born will weigh twelve pounds, and in a solar year if tolerably nursed increaseth to twenty-eight pounds.

12   I grant this food will be somewhat dear, and therefore very proper for landlords, who, as they have already devoured most of the parents, seem to have the best title to the children.

13   Infant's flesh will be in season throughout the year, but more plentiful in March, and a little before and after. For we are told by a grave author, an eminent French physician,[5] that fish being a prolific diet, there are more children born in Roman Catholic countries about nine months after Lent than at any other season; therefore reckoning a year after Lent, the markets will be more gutted than usual, because the number of popish infants is at least three to one in this kingdom; and therefore it will have one other collateral advantage, by lessening the number of Papists among us.

14   I have already computed the charge of nursing a beggar's child (in which list I reckon all cottagers, laborers, and four-fifths of the farmers) to be about two shillings per annum, rags included; and I believe no gentleman would repine to give ten shillings for the carcass of a good fat child, which, as I have said, will make four dishes of excellent nutritive meat, when he hath only some particular friend or his own family to dine with him. Thus the squire will learn to be a good landlord, and grow popular among his tenants; the mother will have eight shillings net profit, and be fit for work until she produces another child.

15   Those who are more thrifty (as I must confess the times require) may flay the carcass; the skin of which artificially dressed will make admirable gloves for ladies and summer boots for fine gentlemen.

16   As to our city of Dublin, shambles[6] may be appointed for this purpose, in the most convenient parts of it, and butchers we may be assured will not be wanting; although I rather recommend buying the children alive, and dressing them hot from the knife as we do roasting pigs.

17   A very worthy person, a true lover of his country, and whose virtues I highly esteem, was lately pleased in discoursing on this matter to offer a refinement upon my scheme. He said that many gentlemen of this kingdom, having of late destroyed their deer, he conceived that the want of venison might be well supplied by the bodies of young lads and maidens, not exceeding fourteen years of age nor under twelve, so great a number of both sexes in every county being now ready to starve for want of work and service; and these to be disposed of by their parents, if alive, or otherwise by their nearest relations. But with due deference to so excellent a friend and so deserving a patriot, I

---

[5] François Rabelais.—Ed.
[6] Butcher shops.—Ed.

cannot be altogether in his sentiments. For as to the males, my American acquaintance assured me from frequent experience that their flesh was generally tough and lean, like that of our school-boys, by continual exercise, and their taste disagreeable; and to fatten them would not answer the charge. Then as to the females, it would, I think with humble submission, be a loss to the public, because they soon would become breeders themselves; and besides, it is not probable that some scrupulous people might be apt to censure such a practice (although indeed very unjustly) as a little bordering upon cruelty; which, I confess, hath always been with me the strongest objection against any project, how wellsoever intended.

But in order to justify my friend, he confessed that this expedient was put 18 into his head by the famous Psalmanazar,[7] a native of the island Formosa who came from thence to London above twenty years ago, and in conversation told my friend that in his country when any young person happened to be put to death, the executioner sold the carcass to persons of quality as a prime dainty; and that in his time the body of a plump girl of fifteen, who was crucified for an attempt to poison the emperor, was sold to his Imperial Majesty's prime minister of state, and other great mandarins of the court, in joints from the gibbet, at four hundred crowns. Neither indeed can I deny that if the same use were made of several plump young girls in this town, who without one single groat to their fortunes cannot stir abroad without a chair, and appear at the playhouse and assemblies in foreign fineries which they never will pay for, the kingdom would not be the worse.

Some persons of a desponding spirit are in great concern about that vast 19 number of poor people who are aged, diseased, or maimed, and I have been desired to employ my thoughts what course may be taken to ease the nation of so grievous an incumbrance. But I am not in the least pain upon that matter, because it is very well known that they are every day dying and rotting by cold and famine, and filth and vermin, as fast as can be reasonably expected. And as to the younger laborers, they are now in almost as hopeful a condition. They cannot get work, and consequently pine away for want of nourishment to a degree that if at any time they are accidentally hired to common labor, they have not strength to perform it; and thus the country and themselves are in a fair way of being soon delivered from the evils to come.

I have too long digressed, and therefore shall return to my subject. I think 20 the advantages by the proposal which I have made are obvious and many, as well as of the highest importance.

For, first, as I have already observed, it would greatly lessen the number of 21 Papists, with whom we are yearly overrun, being the principal breeders of the nation as well as our most dangerous enemies; and who stay at home on purpose with a design to deliver the kingdom to the pretender, hoping to take their advantage by the absence of so many good Protestants, who have chosen rather to leave their country than stay at home and pay tithes against their conscience to an idolatrous Episcopal curate.

---

[7] A known imposter who was French, not Formosan as he claimed.—Ed.

22   Secondly, the poorer tenants will have something valuable of their own, which by law may be made liable to distress,[8] and help their landlord's rent; their corn and cattle being already seized, and money a thing unknown.

23   Thirdly, whereas the maintenance of a hundred thousand children, from two years old upwards, cannot be computed at less than ten shillings a piece per annum, the nation's stock will be thereby increased fifty thousand pounds per annum, besides the profit of a new dish introduced to the tables of all gentlemen of fortune in the kingdom who have any refinement in taste. And the money will circulate among ourselves, the goods being entirely of our own growth and manufacture.

24   Fourthly, the constant breeders, besides the gain of eight shillings sterling per annum by the sale of their children, will be rid of the charge of maintaining them after the first year.

25   Fifthly, this food would likewise bring great custom to taverns, where the vintners will certainly be so prudent as to procure the best receipts for dressing it to perfection, and consequently have their houses frequented by all the fine gentlemen, who justly value themselves upon their knowledge in good eating; and a skillful cook, who understands how to oblige his guests, will contrive to make it as expensive as they please.

26   Sixthly, this would be a great inducement to marriage, which all wise nations have either encouraged by rewards or enforced by laws and penalties. It would increase the care and tenderness of mothers towards their children, when they were sure of a settlement for life to the poor babes, provided in some sort by the public; to their annual profit instead of expense. We should soon see an honest emulation among the married women, which of them could bring the fattest child to the market. Men would become as fond of their wives during the time of their pregnancy as they are now of their mares in foal, their cows in calf, or sows when they are ready to farrow; nor offer to beat or kick them (as it is too frequent a practice) for fear of a miscarriage.

27   Many other advantages might be enumerated. For instance, the addition of some thousand carcasses in our exportation of barrelled beef, the propagation of swine's flesh, and improvement in the art of making good bacon, so much wanted among us by the great destruction of pigs, too frequent at our tables, which are no way comparable in taste or magnificence to a well-grown fat, yearling child, which roasted whole will make a considerable figure at a lord mayor's feast or any other public entertainment. But this and many others I omit, being studious of brevity.

28   Supposing that one thousand families in this city would be constant customers for infants' flesh, besides others who might have it at merry meetings, particularly weddings and christenings, I compute that Dublin would take off annually about twenty thousand carcasses, and the rest of the kingdom (where probably they will be sold somewhat cheaper) the remaining eighty thousand.

29   I can think of no one objection that will possibly be raised against this proposal, unless it should be urged that the number of people will be thereby

---

[8] Can be seized by lenders.—Ed.

much lessened in the kingdom. This I freely own, and it was indeed one princi-pal design in offering it to the world. I desire the reader will observe that I calculate my remedy for this one individual kingdom of Ireland and for no other that ever was, is, or I think ever can be upon earth. Therefore let no man talk to me of other expedients: of taxing our absentees at five shillings a pound: of using neither clothes nor household furniture except what is of our own growth and manufacture: of utterly rejecting the materials and instru-ments that promote foreign luxury: of curing the expensiveness or pride, van-ity, idleness, and gaming in our women: of introducing a vein of parsimony, prudence and temperance: of learning to love our country, wherein we differ even from Laplanders and the inhabitants of Topinamboo[9]: of quitting our ani-mosities and factions, nor act any longer like the Jews, who were murdering one another at the very moment their city was taken[10]: of being a little cau-tious not to sell our country and consciences for nothing: of teaching landlords to have at least one degree of mercy towards their tenants. Lastly, of putting a spirit of honesty, industry, and skill into our shopkeepers; who, if a resolution could now be taken to buy only our native goods, would immediately unite to cheat and exact upon us in the price, the measure, and the goodness, nor could ever yet be brought to make one fair proposal of just dealing, though often and earnestly invited to it.

Therefore I repeat, let no man talk to me of these and the like expedients, [30] till he hath at least a glimpse of hope that there will ever be some hearty and sincere attempt to put them in practice.

But as to myself, having been wearied out for many years with offering [31] vain, idle, visionary thoughts, and at length utterly despairing of success, I for-tunately fell upon this proposal, which, as it is wholly new, so it hath something solid and real, of no expense and little trouble, full in our own power, and whereby we can incur no danger in disobliging England. For this kind of com-modity will not bear exportation, the flesh being of too tender a consistence to admit a long continuance in salt, although perhaps I could name a country which would be glad to eat up our whole nation without it.

After all, I am not so violently bent upon my own opinion as to reject any [32] offer proposed by wise men, which shall be found equally innocent, cheap, easy, and effectual. But before something of that kind shall be advanced in contradiction to my scheme, and offering a better, I desire the author, or authors, will be pleased maturely to consider two points. First, as things now stand, how they will be able to find food and raiment for a hundred thousand useless mouths and backs. And secondly, there being a round million of crea-tures in human figure throughout this kingdom, whose whole subsistence put into a common stock would leave them in debt two million of pounds sterling, adding those who are beggars by profession to the bulk of farmers, cottagers, and laborers, with their wives and children who are beggars, in effect; I desire

---

[9] An area in Brazil.—Ed.

[10] Some Jews were accused of helping the Romans and were executed during the Roman siege of Jerusalem in A.D. 70—Ed.

those politicians who dislike my overture, and may perhaps be so bold to attempt an answer, that they will first ask the parents of these mortals whether they would not at this day think it a great happiness to have been sold for food at a year old in the manner I prescribe, and thereby have avoided such a perpetual scene of misfortunes as they have since gone through by the oppression of landlords, the impossibility of paying rent without money or trade, the want of common sustenance, with neither house nor clothes to cover them from the inclemencies of weather, and the most inevitable prospect of entailing the like or greater miseries upon their breed forever.

33   I profess, in the sincerity of my heart, that I have not the least personal interest in endeavoring to promote this necessary work, having no other motive than the public good of my country, by advancing our trade, providing for infants, relieving the poor, and giving some pleasure to the rich. I have no children by which I can propose to get a single penny, the youngest being nine years old, and my wife past childbearing.

QUESTIONS FOR READING

1. How is the argument organized? What is accomplished in paragraphs 1–7? In paragraphs 8–16? In paragraphs 17–19? In paragraphs 20–28? In paragraphs 29–33?

2. What specific advantages does the writer offer in defense of his proposal?

QUESTIONS FOR REASONING AND ANALYSIS

3. What specific passages and connotative words make us aware that this is a satirical piece using irony as its chief device?

4. After noting Swift's use of irony, what do you conclude to be his purpose in writing?

5. What can you conclude to be some of the problems in eighteenth-century Ireland? Where does Swift offer direct condemnation of existing conditions in Ireland and attitudes of the English toward the Irish?

6. What actual reforms would Swift like to see?

QUESTIONS FOR REFLECTION AND WRITING

7. What are some of the advantages of using irony? What does Swift gain by this approach? What are possible disadvantages in using irony? Reflect on irony as a persuasive strategy.

8. What are some current problems that might be addressed by the use of irony? Make a list. Then select one and think about what "voice" or persona you might use to bring attention to that problem. Plan your argument with irony as a strategy.

1. Think of a problem on your campus or in your community for which you have a workable solution. Organize your argument to include all relevant steps as described in this chapter. Although your primary concern will be to present your solution, depending on your topic you may need to begin by convincing readers of the seriousness of the problem or the causes of the problem—if your solutions involve removing those causes.

2. Think of a problem in education—K–12 or at the college level—that you have a solution for and that you are interested in. You may want to begin by brainstorming to develop a list of possible problems in education about which you could write—or look through Chapter 19 for ideas. Be sure to qualify your claim and limit your focus as necessary to work with a problem that is not so broad and general that your "solutions" become general and vague comments about "getting better teachers." (If one problem is a lack of qualified teachers, then what specific proposals do you have for solving that particular problem?) Include as many steps as are appropriate to develop and support your argument.

3. Think of a situation that you consider serious but that apparently many people do not take seriously enough. Write an argument in which you emphasize, by providing evidence, that the situation is a serious problem. You may conclude by suggesting a solution, but your chief purpose in writing will be to alert readers to a problem.

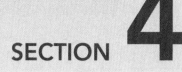

The Researched and Formally Documented Argument

CHAPTER 12

Locating, Evaluating, and Preparing to Use Sources

We do research all the time. You would not select a college or buy a car without doing research: gathering relevant information, analyzing that information, and drawing conclusions from your study. You may already have done some research in this course, using sources in this text or finding data online to strengthen an argument. Then you acknowledged your sources either informally in your essay or formally, following the documentation guidelines in this section. So, when you are assigned a more formal research essay, remember that you are not facing a brand-new assignment. You are just doing a longer paper with more sources, and you have this section to guide you to success.

SELECTING A GOOD TOPIC

To get started you need to select and limit a topic. One key to success is finding a workable topic. No matter how interesting or clever the topic, it is not workable if it does not meet the guidelines of your assignment. Included in those guidelines may be a required length, a required number of sources, and a due date. Understand and accept all of these guidelines as part of your writing context.

What Type of Paper Am I Preparing?

Study your assignment to understand the type of project. Is your purpose expository, analytic, or argumentative? How would you classify each of the following topics?

1. Explain the chief solutions proposed for increasing the Southwest's water supply.
2. Compare the Freudian and behavioral models of mental illness.
3. Find the best solutions to a current environmental problem.
4. Consider: What twentieth-century invention has most dramatically changed our personal lives?

Did you recognize that the first topic calls for a report? The second topic requires an analysis of two schools of psychology, so you cannot report on only one, but you also cannot argue that one model is better than the other. Both topics 3 and 4 require an argumentative paper: You must select and defend a claim.

Who Is My Audience?

If you are writing in a specific discipline, imagine your instructor as a representative of that field, a reader with knowledge of the subject area. If you are in a composition course, your instructor may advise you to write to a general reader, someone who reads newspapers but may not have the exact information and perspective you have. For a general reader, specialized terms and concepts need definition.

> **NOTE:** Consider the expectations of your readers. A research essay is not a personal essay. It is not about you; it is about a subject. Keep yourself in the background and carefully evaluate any use of the personal pronoun "I."

How Can I Select a Good Topic?

Choosing from assigned topics. At times students are unhappy with topic restriction. Looked at another way, your instructor has eliminated a difficult step in the research process and has helped you avoid the problem of selecting an unworkable topic. If topics are assigned, you will still have to choose from the list and develop your own claim and approach.

Finding a course-related topic. This guideline gives you many options and requires more thought about your choice. Working within the guidelines, try to write about what interests you. Here are examples of assignments turned into topics of interest to the student:

ASSIGNMENT	INTEREST	TOPIC
1. Trace the influence of any twentieth-century event, development, invention.	Music	The influence of the Jazz Age on modern music
2. Support an argument on some issue of pornography and censorship.	Computers	Censorship of pornography on the Internet
3. Demonstrate the popularity of a current myth and then discredit it.	Science fiction	The lack of evidence for the existence of UFOs

Selecting a topic without any guidelines. When you are free to write on any topic, you may need to use some strategies for topic selection.

- Look through your text's table of contents or index for subject areas that can be narrowed or focused.
- Look over your class notes and think about subjects covered that have interested you.
- Consider college-based or local issues.
- Do a subject search in an electronic database to see how a large topic can be narrowed—for example, type in "dinosaur" and observe such subheadings as *dinosaur behavior* and *dinosaur extinction.*
- Use one or more invention strategies to narrow and focus a topic:
  — Freewriting
  — Brainstorming
  — Asking questions about a broad subject, using the reporter's *who, what, where, when,* and *why.*

What Kinds of Topics Should I Avoid?

Here are several kinds of topics that are best avoided because they usually produce disasters, no matter how well the student handles the rest of the research process:

1. *Topics that are irrelevant* to your interests or the course. If you are not interested in your topic, you will not produce a lively, informative paper. If you select a topic far removed from the course content, you may create some hostility in your instructor, who will wonder why you are unwilling to become engaged in the course.
2. *Topics that are broad subject areas.* These result in general surveys that lack appropriate detail and support.
3. *Topics that can be fully researched with only one source.* You will produce a summary, not a research paper.
4. *Biographical studies.* Short undergraduate papers on a person's life usually turn out to be summaries of one or two major biographies.
5. *Topics that produce a strong emotional response in you.* If there is only one "right" answer to the abortion issue and you cannot imagine counterarguments, don't choose to write on abortion. Probably most religious topics are best avoided.
6. *Topics that are too technical for you* at this point in your college work. If you do not understand the complexities of the federal tax code, then arguing for a reduction in the capital gains tax may be an unwise topic choice.

WRITING A TENTATIVE CLAIM
OR RESEARCH PROPOSAL

Once you have selected and focused a topic, write a tentative claim, research question, or research proposal. Some instructors will ask to see a statement—from a sentence to a paragraph long—to be approved before you proceed. Others may require a one-page proposal that includes a tentative claim, a basic organizational plan, and a description of types of sources to be used. Even if your instructor does not require anything in writing, you need to write something for your benefit—to direct your reading and thinking. Here are two possibilities:

1. **SUBJECT:**   Computers

   TOPIC: The impact of computers on the twentieth century

   CLAIM: Computers had the greatest impact of any technological development in the twentieth century.

   RESEARCH
   PROPOSAL: I propose to show that computers had the greatest impact of any technological development in the twentieth century.

I will show the influence of computers at work, in daily living, and in play to emphasize the breadth of influence. I will argue that other possibilities (such as cars) did not have the same impact as computers. I will check the library's book catalog and databases for sources on technological developments and on computers specifically. I will also interview a family friend who works with computers at the Pentagon.

This example illustrates several key ideas. First, the initial subject is both too broad and unfocused (*What* about computers?). Second, the claim is more focused than the topic statement because it asserts a position, a claim the student must support. Third, the research proposal is more helpful than the claim only because it includes some thoughts on developing the thesis and finding sources.

2. Less sure of your topic? Then write a research question or a more open-ended research proposal. Take, for example, a history student studying the effects of Prohibition. She is not ready to write a thesis, but she can write a research proposal that suggests some possible approaches to the topic:

TOPIC:	The effect of Prohibition
RESEARCH QUESTION:	What were the effects of Prohibition on the United States?
RESEARCH PROPOSAL:	I will examine the effects of Prohibition on the United States in the 1920s (and possibly consider some long-term effects, depending on the amount of material on the topic). Specifically, I will look at the varying effects on urban and rural areas and on different classes in society.

PREPARING A WORKING BIBLIOGRAPHY

To begin this next stage of your research, you need to know three things:

- *Your search strategy.* If you are writing on a course-related topic, your starting place may be your textbook for relevant sections and possible sources (if the text contains a bibliography). For this course, you may find some potential sources among the readings in this text. Think about what you already know or have in hand as you plan your search strategy.
- *A method for recording bibliographic information.* You have two choices: the always reliable 3×5 index cards or a bibliography file in your personal computer.
- *The documentation format you will be using.* You may be assigned the Modern Language Association (MLA) format, or perhaps given a choice

between MLA and the American Psychological Association (APA) documentation styles. Once you select the documentation style, skim the appropriate pages in Chapter 14 to get an overview of both content and style.

A list of possible sources is only a *working* bibliography because you do not yet know which sources you will use. (Your final bibliography will include only those sources you cite—actually refer to—in your paper.) A working bibliography will help you see what is available on your topic, note how to locate each source, and contain the information needed to document. Whether you are using cards or computer files, follow these guidelines:

1. Check all reasonable catalogs and indexes for possible sources. (Use more than one reference source even if you locate enough sources there; you are looking for the best sources, not the first ones you find.)

2. Complete a card or prepare an entry for every potentially useful source. You won't know what to reject until you start a close reading of sources.

3. Copy (or download from an online catalog) all information needed to complete a citation and to locate the source. (When using an index that does not give all needed information, leave a space to be filled in when you actually read the source.)

4. Put bibliographic information in the correct format for every possible source; you will save time and make fewer errors. Do not mix or blend styles. When searching for sources, have your text handy and use the appropriate models as your guide.

The following brief guide to correct form will get you started. Illustrations are for cards, but the information and order will be the same in your PC file. (Guidelines are for MLA style.)

Basic Form for Books

As Figure 12.1 shows, the basic MLA form for books includes the following information in this pattern:

1. The author's full name, last name first.
2. The title (and subtitle if there is one) of the book, in italics (underlined in handwriting).
3. The facts of publication: the city of publication (followed by a colon), the publisher (followed by a comma), and the date of publication.
4. The publication medium—Print.

Note that periods are placed after the author's name, after the title, and at the end of the citation. Other information, when appropriate (e.g., the number of volumes), is added to this basic pattern. (See pp. 318–29 for many sample citations.) Include, in your working bibliography, the book's classification number so that you can find it in the library.

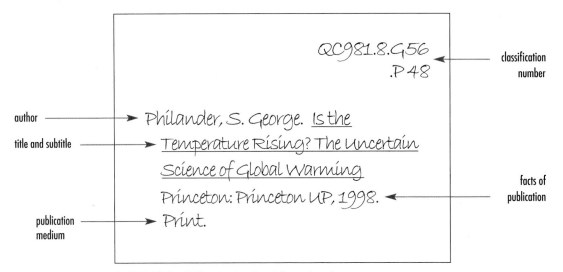

FIGURE 12.1 Bibliography Card for a Book

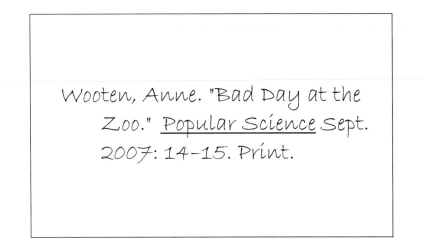

FIGURE 12.2 Bibliography Card for a Magazine Article

Basic Form for Articles

Figure 12.2 shows the simplest form for magazine articles. Include the following information, in this pattern:

1. The author's full name, last name first.
2. The title of the article, in quotation marks.
3. The facts of publication: the title of the periodical in italics (underlined in handwriting), the volume number (if the article is from a scholarly journal), the date (followed by a colon), and inclusive page numbers.
4. The publication medium—Print.

You will discover that indexes rarely present information in MLA format. Here, for example, is a source on problems with zoos, found in an electronic database:

BAD DAY AT THE ZOO.
Wooten, Anne. Popular Science, Sep2007, Vol. 271 Issue 3, p. 14–15, 2p.

If you read the article in the magazine itself, then the correct citation, for MLA, will look like that in the sample bibliography card in Figure 12.2. (Because *Popular Science* is a magazine, not a scholarly journal, you provide month and year but not volume and issue numbers.) However, if you obtain a copy of the article from one of your library's electronic databases, then your citation will need additional information to identify your actual source of the article:

Wooten, Anne. "Bad Day at the Zoo." *Popular Science* Sept. 2007: 14–15.
    Academic Search Complete. Web. 8 Sept. 2008.

Note that the medium of publication is now "Web," not "Print," and the name of the database is italicized as if it were a book containing the article.

> **NOTE:** A collection of printouts, slips of paper, and backs of envelopes is not a working bibliography! You may have to return to the library for missing information, and you risk making serious errors in documentation. Know the basics of your documentation format and follow it faithfully when collecting possible sources.

LOCATING SOURCES

All libraries contain books and periodicals and a system for accessing them. A library's *book collection* includes the general collection, the reference collection, and the reserve book collection. Electronic materials such as tapes and CDs will also be included in the general "book" collection. The *periodicals collection* consists of popular magazines, scholarly journals, and newspapers. Electronic databases with texts of articles provide alternatives to the print periodicals collection.

> **REMEMBER:** All works, regardless of their source or the format in which you obtain them—and this includes online sources—must be fully documented in your paper.

The Book Catalog

Your chief guide to books and audiovisual materials is the library catalog, usually an electronic database accessed from computer stations in the library or, with an appropriate password, from your personal computer.

One of the famous lions sitting in front of the New York Public Library.

In the catalog there will be at least four ways to access a specific book: the author entry, the title entry, one or more subject entries, and a keyword option. When you pull up the search screen, you will probably see that the keyword option is the default. If you know the exact title of the work you want, switch to the title option, type it in, and hit submit. If you want a list of all of the library's books on Hemingway, though, click on author and type in "Hemingway." Keep these points in mind:

- With a title search, do not type any initial article (a, an, the). To locate *The Great Gatsby,* type in "Great Gatsby."
- Use correct spelling. If you are unsure of spelling, use a keyword instead of an author or title search.
- If you are looking for a list of books on your subject, do a keyword or subject search.
- When screens for specific books are shown, either print screens of potential sources or copy all information needed for documentation—plus the call number for each book.

The Reference Collection

The research process often begins with the reference collection. You will find atlases, dictionaries, encyclopedias, general histories, critical studies, and biographies. In addition, various reference tools such as bibliographies and indexes are part of the reference collection.

Many tools in the reference collection once only in print form are now also online. Some are now only online. Yet online is not always the way to go. Let's consider some of the advantages of each of the formats:

Advantages of the Print Reference Collection

1. The reference tool may be only in print—use it.
2. The print form covers the period you are studying. (Most online indexes and abstracts cover only from 1980 to the present.)
3. In a book, with a little scanning of pages, you can often find what you need without getting spelling or commands exactly right.
4. If you know the best reference source to use and are looking for only a few items, the print source can be faster than the online source.

Advantages of Online Reference Materials

1. Online databases are likely to provide the most up-to-date information.
2. You can usually search all years covered at one time.
3. Full texts (with graphics) are sometimes available, as well as indexes with detailed summaries of articles. Both can be printed or e-mailed to your PC.
4. Through links to the Internet, you have access to an amazing amount of material. (Unless you focus your keyword search, however, you may be overwhelmed.)

Before using any reference work, take a few minutes to check its date, purpose, and organization. If you are new to online searching, take a few minutes to learn about each reference tool by working through the online tutorial.

A Word about Wikipedia

Many researchers go first to a general encyclopedia, in the past in print in the reference collection, today more typically online. This is not always the best strategy. Often you can learn more about your topic from a current book or a more specialized reference source—which your reference librarian can help you find. Both may give you additional sources for your project. If—or when—you turn to a general encyclopedia, make it a good one that is available online through your library. Some colleges have told their students that *Wikipedia* is not an acceptable source for college research projects.

Electronic Databases

You will probably access electronic databases by going to your library's home page and then clicking on the appropriate term or icon. (You may have found the book catalog by clicking on "library catalog"; you may find the databases by clicking on "library resources" or some other descriptive label.) You will need to choose a particular database and then type in your keyword for a basic

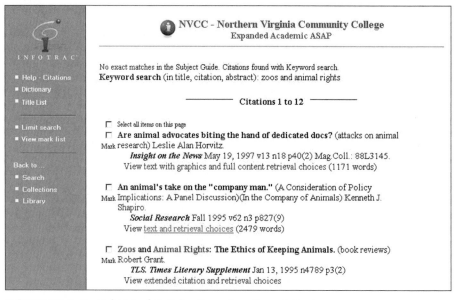

FIGURE 12.3 Partial List of Articles Found on Search Topic

search or select "advanced search" to limit that search by date or periodical or in some other way. Each library will create somewhat different screens, but the basic process of selecting among choices provided and then typing in your search commands remains the same. Figure 12.3 shows a partial list of articles that resulted from a keyword search for "zoos and animal rights."

GUIDELINES for Using Online Databases

Keep these points in mind as you use online databases:

- **Although some online databases provide full texts of all articles, others provide full texts of only some of the articles indexed.** The articles not in full text will have to be located in a print collection of periodicals.

- **Articles indexed but not available in full text often come with a brief summary or abstract.** This allows you to decide whether the article looks useful for your project. *Do not treat the abstract as the article. Do not use material from it and cite the author. If you want to use the article, find it in your library's print collection or obtain it from another library.*

- **The information you need for documenting material used from an article is not in correct format for any of the standard documentation styles.** You will have to reorder the information and use the correct style for writing titles. If your instructor wants to see a list of possible sources in MLA format, do not hand in a printout of articles from an online database.

- **Because no single database covers all journals, you may want to search several databases that seem relevant to your project.** Ask your reference librarian for suggestions of various databases in the sciences, social sciences, public affairs, and education.

The Internet

In addition to using electronic databases to find sources, you can search the Internet directly.

Keep in mind these facts about the Internet:

- The Internet is both disorganized and huge, so you can waste time trying to find information that is easily obtained in a library reference book or database.
- The Internet is best at providing current information, such as news and movie reviews. It is also a great source of government information.
- Because anyone can create a website and put anything on it, you will have to be especially careful in evaluating Internet sources. Remember that articles in magazines and journals have been selected by editors and are often peer reviewed as well, but no editor selects or rejects material on a personal website.

GUIDELINES for Searching the Web

The Internet will provide useful sources for many research projects. It will be much less useful than books or online databases for others. One task of the good researcher is to think about the best places to go to get the best material for a specific project. If you think the Internet will be useful for you, keep these general guidelines in mind to aid your research:

- Bookmark sites you expect to use often so that you do not have to remember a complex URL or do another Google search.
- Make your research terms as precise as possible to avoid getting overwhelmed with hits.
- If you are searching for a specific phrase, put quotation marks around the words. This will reduce the number of hits and lead to more useful sites. Example: "Rainforest depletion." Without the quotation marks, you will get lots of information about rainforests, but not necessarily about their depletion. You will also get information on the concept of depletion that has nothing to do with rainforests.
- Complete a bibliography card—including the date you accessed the source—for each separate site from which you take material (see Chapter 14 for documentation guidelines).

FIELD RESEARCH

Field research can enrich many projects. The following sections offer some suggestions.

Federal, State, and Local Government Documents

In addition to federal documents you may obtain through *PAIS* or *GPO Access*, department and agency websites, or the Library of Congress's good legislative site, *Thomas* (**http://thomas.loc.gov**), consider state and county archives, maps, and other published materials. Instead of selecting a national or global topic, consider examining the debate over a controversial bill introduced in your state legislature. Use online databases to locate articles on the bill and the debate and interview legislators and journalists who participated in or covered the debates or served on committees that worked with the bill.

You can also request specific documents from appropriate state or county agencies and nonprofit organizations. One student, given the assignment of examining solutions to an ecological problem, decided to study the local problem of preserving the Chesapeake Bay. She obtained issues of the Chesapeake Bay Foundation newsletter and brochures prepared by them advising homeowners about hazardous household waste materials that end up in the bay. Added to her sources were bulletins on soil conservation and landscaping tips for improving the area's water quality. Local problems can lead to interesting research topics because they are current and relevant to you and because they involve uncovering different kinds of source materials.

Correspondence

Business and government officials are usually willing to respond to written requests for information. Make your letter brief and well written. Either include a self-addressed, stamped envelope for the person's convenience or e-mail your request. If you are not e-mailing, write as soon as you discover the need for information and be prepared to wait several weeks for a reply. It is appropriate to indicate your deadline and ask for a timely response. Three guidelines for either letters or e-mails to keep in mind are:

1. Explain precisely what information you need.
2. Do not request information that can be found in your library's reference collection.
3. Explain how you plan to use the information. Businesses especially are understandably concerned with their public image and will be disinclined to provide information that you intend to use as a means of attacking them.

Use reference guides to companies and government agencies or their websites to obtain addresses and the person to whom your letter or e-mail should be sent.

Interviews

Some experts are available for personal interviews. Call or write for an appointment as soon as you recognize the value of an interview. Remember that interviews are more likely to be scheduled with state and local officials than with the president of General Motors. If you are studying a local problem, also consider leaders of the civic association with an interest in the issue. In many communities, the local historian or a librarian will be a storehouse of information about the community. Former teachers can be interviewed for papers on education. Interviews with doctors or nurses can add a special dimension to papers on medical issues.

If an interview is appropriate for your topic, follow these guidelines:

1. Prepare specific questions in advance.
2. Arrive on time, properly dressed, and behave in a polite, professional manner.
3. Take notes, asking the interviewee to repeat key statements so that your notes are accurate.
4. Take a tape recorder with you but ask permission to use it before taping.
5. If you quote any statements in your paper, quote accurately, eliminating only such minor speech habits as "you know's" and "uhm's." (See Chapter 14 for proper documentation of interviews.)
6. Direct the interview with your prepared questions, but also give the interviewee the chance to approach the topic in his or her own way. You may obtain information or views that had not occurred to you.
7. Do not get into a debate with the interviewee. You are there to learn.

Lectures

Check the appropriate information sources at your school to keep informed of visiting speakers. If you are fortunate enough to attend a lecture relevant to a current project, take careful, detailed notes. Because a lecture is a source, use of information or ideas from it must be presented accurately and then documented. (See Chapter 14 for documentation format.)

Films, DVDs, Television

Your library will have audiovisual materials that provide good sources for some kinds of topics. For example, if you are studying *Death of a Salesman,* view a videotaped version of the play. Also pay attention to documentaries on public television and to the many news and political talk shows on both public and commercial channels. In many cases transcripts of shows can be obtained from the TV station. Alternatively, tape the program while watching it so that you can view it several times. The documentation format for such nonprint sources is illustrated in Chapter 14.

Surveys, Questionnaires, and Original Research

Depending on your paper, you may want to conduct a simple survey or write and administer a questionnaire. Surveys can be used for many campus and local issues, for topics on behavior and attitudes of college students and/or faculty, and for topics on consumer habits. Explore surveymonkey.com for help administering an online survey. Simple ones are free! Remember: Surveying 50 of your Facebook friends will not produce a random sample. When writing questions, keep these guidelines in mind:

- Use simple, clear language.
- Devise a series of short questions rather than only a few that have several parts to them. (You want to separate information for better analysis.)
- Phrase questions to avoid wording that seeks to control the answer. For example, do *not* ask "Did you perform your civic duty by voting in the last election?" This is a loaded question.

In addition to surveys and questionnaires, you can incorporate some original research. As you read sources on your topic, be alert to reports of studies that you could redo and update in part or on a smaller scale. Many topics on advertising and television give opportunities for your own analysis. Local-issue topics may offer good opportunities for gathering information on your own, not just from your reading. One student, examining the controversy over a proposed new shopping mall on part of the Manassas Civil War Battlefield in Virginia, made the argument that the mall served no practical need in the community. He supported his position by describing existing malls, including the number and types of stores each contained and the number of miles each was from the proposed new mall. How did he obtain this information? He drove around the area, counting miles and stores. Sometimes a seemingly unglamorous approach to a topic turns out to be an imaginative one.

EVALUATING SOURCES, MAINTAINING CREDIBILITY

As you study your sources, keep rethinking your purpose and approach. Test your research proposal or tentative claim against what you are learning. Remember: You can always change the direction and focus of your paper as new approaches occur to you, and you can even change your position as you reflect on what you are learning.

You will work with sources more effectively if you keep in mind why you are using them. What you are looking for will vary somewhat, depending on your topic and purpose, but there are several basic approaches:

1. *Acquiring information and viewpoints firsthand.* Suppose that you are concerned about the mistreatment of animals kept in zoos. You do not want to just read what others have to say on this issue. First, visit a zoo, taking notes on what you see. Second, before you go, plan to interview at least one person on the zoo staff, preferably a veterinarian who can explain the zoo's guidelines for animal care. Only after gathering and thinking about these *primary sources* do you want to add to your knowledge by reading articles and books—*secondary sources.* Many kinds of topics require the use of both primary and secondary sources. If you want to study violence in children's TV shows, for example, you should first spend some time watching specific shows and taking notes.

2. *Acquiring new knowledge.* Suppose you are interested in breast cancer research and treatment, but you do not know much about the choices of

treatment and, in general, where we are with this medical problem. You will need to turn to sources first to learn about the topic. Begin with sources that will give you an overview, perhaps a historical perspective. Begin with sources that provide an overview of how knowledge and treatment have progressed in the last thirty years. Similarly, if your topic is the effects of Prohibition in the 1920s, you will need to read first for knowledge but also with an eye to ways to focus the topic and organize your paper.

3. *Understanding the issues.* Suppose you think that you know your views on illegal immigration, so you intend to read only to obtain some useful statistical information to support your argument. Should you scan sources quickly, looking for facts you can use? This approach may be too hasty. As explained in Chapter 3, good arguments are built on a knowledge of counterarguments. You are wise to study sources presenting a variety of attitudes on your issue so that you understand—and can refute—the arguments of others. *Remember: that with controversial issues often the best argument is a conciliatory one that presents a middle ground and seeks to bring people together.*

When you use facts and opinions from sources, you are saying to readers that the facts are accurate and the ideas credible. If you do not evaluate your sources before using them, you risk losing your credibility as a writer. (Remember Aristotle's idea of *ethos,* how your character is judged.) Just because they are in print does not mean that a writer's "facts" are reliable or ideas worthwhile. Judging the usefulness and reliability of potential sources is an essential part of the research process.

GUIDELINES for Evaluating Sources

Today, with access to so much material on the Internet, the need to evaluate is even more crucial. Here are some strategies for evaluating sources, with special attention to Internet sources:

- **Locate the author's credentials.** Periodicals often list their writers' degrees, current position, and other publications; books, similarly, contain an "about the author" section. If you do not see this information, check various biographical dictionaries (*Biography Index, Contemporary Authors*) or look for the author's website for information. For articles on the web, look for the author's e-mail address or a link to a home page. *Never use a web source that does not identify the author or the organization responsible for the material. Critical question:* Is this author qualified to write on this topic? How do I know?

- **Judge the credibility of the work.** For books, read how reviewers evaluated the book when it was first published. For articles, judge the respectability of the magazine or journal. Study the author's use of documentation as one measure of credibility. Scholarly works cite sources. Well-researched and reliable pieces in quality popular magazines will also make clear the sources of any statistics used or the credentials of any authority who is quoted. One good rule: Never use undocumented statistical information. Another judge of credibility is the quality of writing. Do not use sources filled with grammatical and mechanical errors. For web sources, find out what institution hosts the site. If you have not heard of the company or organization, find out more about it. *Critical question:* Why should I believe information/ideas from this source?

- **Select only those sources that are at an appropriate level for your research.** Avoid works that are either too specialized or too elementary for college research. You may not understand the former (and thus could misrepresent them in your paper), and you gain nothing from the latter. *Critical question:* Will this source provide a sophisticated discussion for educated adults?

- **Understand the writer's purpose.** Consider the writer's intended audience. Be cautious using works designed to reinforce biases already shared by the intended audience. Is the work written to persuade rather than to inform and analyze? Examine the writing for emotionally charged language. For Internet sources, ask yourself why this person or institution decided to have a website or contribute to a newsgroup. *Critical question:* Can I trust the information from this source, given the apparent purpose of the work?

- **In general, choose current sources.** Some studies published years ago remain classics, but many older works are outdated. In scientific and technical fields, the "information revolution" has outdated some works published only five years ago. So look at publication dates (When was the website page last updated?) and pass over outdated sources in favor of current studies. *Critical question:* Is this information still accurate?

PREPARING AN ANNOTATED BIBLIOGRAPHY

An annotated bibliography is a list of sources on a topic that includes a summary of each source. As part of your research process, you may be required to prepare either a partial or a complete annotated bibliography. Instructors include this assignment to keep you moving forward in your study of sources; it is a way of checking that you have found and read useful sources in good time to complete your project. Annotating each source also demands careful reading and analysis; it provides a check against skimming a source for some information without taking time to read and understand the context in which the information is presented and the author's position on the topic. You may find that your research paper is more focused and better written if you take the time to write a brief summary statement about each source you plan to use, even if an annotated bibliography is not required.

When preparing an annotated bibliography, list sources alphabetically and in correct MLA (or APA) format (see Chapter 14). Then, immediately after each citation, place a two-to-five-sentence summary of that source. Use hanging indentation, just as you would for your list of works cited at the end of your paper. *Warning: Do not confuse an annotated bibliography with a Works Cited list.* When you complete your research essay, list all sources used *without* the summaries.

A partial annotated bibliography follows, based on the sample student research essay in Chapter 13. Use this as your model.

Tell Us What You Really Are: The Debate over
Labeling Genetically Modified Food
Selected Annotated Bibliography
David Donaldson

MacDonald, Chris, and Melissa Whellams. "Corporate Decisions about Labeling

Genetically Modified Foods." *Journal of Business Ethics* 75.2 (2007): 181–89.

JSTOR. Web. 8 June 2011. MacDonald and Whellams examine the ethical obligation

of companies to label genetically modified foods. The authors explain that there is no

evidence that such products pose a health risk and that the FDA sees no reason to

require special labeling. The authors explain that such labeling would impose a hard-

ship on the companies preparing GM foods. Although the authors assert that they

do not necessarily oppose required labeling, they conclude that food companies are

not ethically obligated to voluntarily label GM foods.

U.S. Chamber of Commerce. "Precautionary Principle." U.S. Chamber of Commerce. 2011.

Web. 9 June 2011. The U.S. Chamber of Commerce has posted on its website a

statement regarding the "precautionary principle." The Chamber asserts that it has

always supported regulatory decisions based on good science and sound risk assessment.

The Chamber opposes the use of the "precautionary principle"—assume the worst and

regulate risks that are uncertain or unknown—as a guide for U.S. regulatory decisions.

U.S. Food and Drug Administration. "Bioengineered Foods." Statement of Robert E. Brackett to

the FDA. U.S. Food and Drug Administration. 12 July 2009. Web. 18 June 2011. Robert E.

Brackett's statement to the Senate Committee on Agriculture, Nutrition, and Forestry is a

lengthy, detailed review of the FDA's responsibilities in determining food safety in general and

its specific procedures for approving foods developed by hybridization and bioengineering.

Brackett explains that GM foods could conceivably create one of three problems: cause new

allergies, cause toxicity, or produce anti-nutrients (e.g., result in a decrease in Vitamin C). The

FDA has the power to screen new foods for all three potential problems and to disapprove or

require labeling, as appropriate. Brackett assures the Committee that the FDA works closely

with companies developing GM foods and that they carefully test for all three potential

problems to maintain a safe food supply for consumers.

CHAPTER 13

Writing the Researched Essay

You have agonized over your topic choice, searched for good sources, read and thought about your topic, seeking a way to put together a compelling argument—while not forgetting documentation. Whew! Don't rush now. Study this chapter's writing points and apply the guidelines to the writing of a convincing essay. Here are some general guidelines for studying sources.

GUIDELINES for Studying Sources

1. **Read first; take notes later.** First, do background reading, selecting the most general sources that provide an overview of the topic.

2. **Skim what appear to be your chief sources.** Learn what other writers on the topic consider the important facts, issues, and points of debate.

3. **Annotate photocopies**—do not highlight endlessly. Instead, carefully bracket material you want to use. Then write a note in the margin indicating how and where you might use that material.

4. **Either download Internet sources or take careful notes on the material.** Before preparing a note on content, be sure to copy all necessary information for documenting the material—including the date you accessed the website.

5. **Initially mark key passages in books with Post-Its.** Write on the Post-It how and where you might use the material. Alternatively, photocopy book pages and then annotate them. Be sure to record for yourself the source of all copied pages.

6. **As you study and annotate, create labels for source materials that will help you organize your essay.** For example, if you are writing about the problem of campus rape, you might label passages as: "facts showing there is a problem," "causes of the problem," and "possible solutions to the problem."

7. **Recognize that when you are working with many sources, note taking rather than annotating copies of sources is more helpful.** Notes, whether on cards or typed on separate sheets of paper, provide an efficient method for collecting and organizing lots of information.

AVOIDING PLAGIARISM

Documenting sources accurately and fully is required of all researchers. Proper documentation distinguishes between the work of others and your ideas, shows readers the breadth of your research, and strengthens your credibility. In Western culture, copyright laws support the ethic that ideas, new information, and wording belong to their author. To borrow these without acknowledgment is against the law and has led to many celebrated lawsuits. For students who plagiarize, the consequences range from an F on the paper to suspension from college. Be certain, then, that you know what the requirements for correct documentation are; accidental plagiarism is still plagiarism and will be punished.

> **NOTE:** MLA documentation requires precise page references for all ideas, opinions, and information taken from sources—except for common knowledge. Author and page references provided in the text are supported by complete bibliographic citations on the Works Cited page.

In sum, you are required to document the following:

- Direct quotations from sources
- Paraphrased ideas and opinions from sources
- Summaries of ideas from sources
- Factual information, except common knowledge, from sources

Understand that putting an author's ideas in your own words in a paraphrase or summary does not eliminate the requirement of documentation. To illustrate, consider the following excerpt from Thomas R. Schueler's report *Controlling Urban Runoff* (Washington Metropolitan Water Resources Planning Board, 1987: 3–4) and a student paragraph based on the report.

SOURCE

The aquatic ecosystems in urban headwater streams are particularly susceptible to the impacts of urbanization. . . . Dietemann (1975), Ragan and Dietemann (1976), Klein (1979) and WMCOG (1982) have all tracked trends in fish diversity and abundance over time in local urbanizing streams. Each of the studies has shown that fish communities become less diverse and are composed of more tolerant species after the surrounding watershed is developed. Sensitive fish species either disappear or occur very rarely. In most cases, the total number of fish in urbanizing streams may also decline.

Similar trends have been noted among aquatic insects which are the major food resource for fish. . . . Higher post-development sediment and trace metals can interfere in their efforts to gather food. Changes in water temperature, oxygen levels, and substrate composition can further reduce the species diversity and abundance of the aquatic insect community.

PLAGIARIZED STUDENT PARAGRAPH

Studies have shown that fish communities become less diverse as the amount of runoff increases. Sensitive fish species either disappear or occur very rarely, and, in most cases, the total number of fish declines. Aquatic insects, a major source of food for fish, also decline because sediment and trace metals interfere with their food-gathering efforts. Increased water temperature and lower oxygen levels can further reduce the species diversity and abundance of the aquatic insect community.

The student's opening words establish a reader's expectation that the student has taken information from a source, as indeed the student has. But where is the documentation? The student's paraphrase is a good example of plagiarism: an unacknowledged paraphrase of borrowed information that even collapses into copying the source's exact wording in two places. For MLA style, the author's name and the precise page numbers are needed throughout the paragraph. Additionally, most of the first sentence and the final phrase must be put into the student's own words or placed within quotation marks. The following revised paragraph shows an appropriate acknowledgment of the source used.

REVISED STUDENT PARAGRAPH TO REMOVE PLAGIARISM

In *Controlling Urban Runoff*, Thomas Schueler explains that studies have shown "that fish communities become less diverse as the amount of runoff increases" (3). Sensitive fish species either disappear or occur very rarely and, in most cases, the total number of fish declines. Aquatic insects, a major source of food for fish, also decline because sediment and trace metals interfere with their food-gathering efforts. Increased water temperature and lower oxygen levels, Schueler concludes, "can further reduce the species diversity and abundance of the aquatic insect community" (4).

What Is Common Knowledge?

In general, common knowledge includes

- undisputed dates,
- well-known facts, and
- generally known facts, terms, and concepts in a field of study when you are writing in that field

So, do not cite a source for the dates of the American Revolution. If you are writing a paper for a psychology class, do not cite your text when using terms such as *ego* or *sublimation*. However, you must cite a historian who analyzes the causes of England's loss to the Colonies or a psychologist who disputes Freud's ideas. *Opinions* about well-known facts must be documented. *Discussions* of debatable dates, terms, or concepts must be documented. When in doubt, defend your integrity and document.

USING SIGNAL PHRASES TO AVOID CONFUSION

If you are an honest student, you do not want to submit a paper that is plagiarized, even though that plagiarism was unintentional on your part. What leads to unintentional plagiarism?

- A researcher takes careless notes, neglecting to include precise page numbers on the notes, but uses the information anyway, without documentation.
- A researcher works in material from sources in such a way that, even with page references, readers cannot tell what has been taken from the sources.

Good note-taking strategies will keep you from the first pitfall. Avoiding the second problem means becoming skilled in ways to include source material in your writing while still making your indebtedness to sources absolutely clear to readers. The way to do this: Give the author's name in the essay. You can also include, when appropriate, the author's credentials ("According to Dr. Hays, a geologist with the Department of Interior, . . ."). These *introductory tags* or *signal phrases* give readers a context for the borrowed material, as well as serving as part of the required documentation of sources. *Make sure that each signal phrase clarifies rather than distorts an author's relationship to his or her ideas and your relationship to the source.*

GUIDELINES for Appropriately Using Sources

Here are three guidelines to follow to avoid misrepresenting borrowed material:

- **Pay attention to verb choice in signal phrases.** When you vary such standard wording as "Smith says" or "Jones states," be careful that you do not select verbs that misrepresent "Smith's" or "Jones's" attitude toward his or her own work. Do not write "Jones wonders" when in fact Jones has strongly asserted her views. (See pp. 294–95 for a discussion of varying word choice in signal phrases.)

- **Pay attention to the location of signal phrases.** If you mention Jones after you have presented her views, be sure that your reader can tell precisely which ideas in the passage belong to Jones. If your entire paragraph is a paraphrase of Jones's work, you are plagiarizing to conclude with "This idea is presented by Jones." Which of the several ideas in your paragraph comes from Jones? Your reader will assume that only the last idea comes from Jones.

- **Paraphrase properly.** Be sure that paraphrases are truly *in your own words*. To use Smith's words and sentence style in your writing is to plagiarize.

NOTE: Putting a parenthetical page reference at the end of a paragraph is not sufficient if you have used the source throughout the paragraph. Use introductory tags or signal phrases to guide the reader through the material.

EXERCISES: Acknowledging Sources to Avoid Plagiarism

1. The following paragraph (from Franklin E. Zimring's "Firearms, Violence and Public Policy" [*Scientific American*, Nov. 1991]) provides material for the examples that follow of adequate and inadequate acknowledgment of sources. After reading Zimring's paragraph, study the three examples with these questions in mind: (1) Which example represents adequate acknowledgment? (2) Which examples do not represent adequate acknowledgment? (3) In exactly what ways is each plagiarized paragraph flawed?

SOURCE

Although most citizens support such measures as owner screening, public opinion is sharply divided on laws that would restrict the ownership of handguns to persons with special needs. If the U.S. does not reduce handguns and current trends continue, it faces the prospect that the number of handguns in circulation will grow from 35 million to more than 50 million within 50 years. A national program limiting the availability of handguns would cost many billions of dollars and meet much resistance from citizens. These costs would likely be greatest in the early years of the program. The benefits of supply reduction would emerge slowly because efforts to diminish the availability of handguns would probably have a cumulative impact over time. (page 54)

STUDENT PARAGRAPH 1

One approach to the problem of handgun violence in America is to severely limit handgun ownership. If we don't restrict ownership and start the costly task of removing handguns from our society, we may end up with around 50 million handguns in the country by 2040. The benefits will not be apparent right away but will eventually appear. This idea is emphasized by Franklin Zimring (54).

STUDENT PARAGRAPH 2

One approach to the problem of handgun violence in America is to restrict the ownership of handguns except in special circumstances. If we do not begin to reduce the number of handguns in this country, the number will grow from 35 million to more than 50 million within 50 years. We can agree with Franklin Zimring that a program limiting handguns will cost billions and meet resistance from citizens (54).

STUDENT PARAGRAPH 3

According to law professor Franklin Zimring, the United States needs to severely limit handgun ownership or face the possibility of seeing handgun ownership increase "from 35 million to more than 50 million within 50 years" (54). Zimring points out that Americans disagree significantly on restricting handguns and that enforcing such laws would be very expensive. He concludes that the benefits would not be seen immediately but that the restrictions "would probably have a cumulative impact over time" (54). Although Zimring paints a gloomy picture of high costs and little immediate relief from gun violence, he also presents the shocking possibility of 50 million guns by the year 2040. Can our society survive so much fire power?

Clearly, only the third student paragraph demonstrates adequate acknowledgment of the writer's indebtedness to Zimring. Notice that the placement of the last parenthetical page reference acts as a visual closure to the student's borrowing. She then turns to her response to Zimring and her own views on the problem of handguns.

2. Read the following passage and then the three plagiarized uses of the passage. Explain why each one is plagiarized and how it can be corrected.

Original Text: Stanley Karnow, Vietnam, A History. The First Complete Account of Vietnam at War. New York: Viking, 1983, 319.

Lyndon Baines Johnson, a consummate politician, was a kaleidoscopic personality, forever changing as he sought to dominate or persuade or placate or frighten his friends and foes. A gigantic figure whose extravagant moods matched his size, he could be cruel and kind, violent and gentle, petty, generous, cunning, naïve, crude, candid, and frankly dishonest. He commanded the blind loyalty of his aides, some of whom worshipped him, and he sparked bitter derision or fierce hatred that he never quite fathomed.

a. LBJ's vibrant and changing personality filled some people with adoration and others with bitter derision that he never quite fathomed (Karnow 319).

b. LBJ, a supreme politician, had a personality like a kaleidoscope, continually changing as he tried to control, sway, appease, or intimidate his enemies and supporters (Karnow 319).

c. Often, figures who have had great impact on America's history have been dynamic people with powerful personalities and vibrant physical presence. LBJ, for example, was a huge figure who polarized those who worked for and with him. "He commanded the blind loyalty of his aides, some of whom worshipped him, and he sparked bitter derision or fierce hatred" from many others (Karnow 319).

3. Read the following passage and then the four sample uses of the passage. Judge each of the uses for how well it avoids plagiarism and if it is documented correctly. Make corrections as needed.

Original Text: Stanley Karnow, Vietnam, A History. The First Complete Account of Vietnam at War. New York: Viking, 1983, 327.

On July 27, 1965, in a last-ditch attempt to change Johnson's mind, Mansfield and Russell were to press him again to "concentrate on finding a way out" of Vietnam—"a place where we ought not be," and where "the situation is rapidly going out of control." But the next day, Johnson announced his decision to add forty-four American combat battalions to the relatively small U.S. contingents already there. He had not been deaf to Mansfield's pleas, nor had he simply swallowed the Pentagon's plans. He had waffled and agonized during his nineteen months in the White House, but eventually this was his final judgment. As he would later explain: "There are many, many people who can recommend and advise, and a few of them consent. But there is only one who has been chosen by the American people to decide."

a. Karnow writes that Senators Mansfield and Russell continued to try to convince President Johnson to avoid further involvement in Vietnam, "a place where we ought not to be" they felt. (327).

b. Though Johnson received advice from many, in particular Senators Mansfield and Russell, he believed the weight of the decision to become further engaged in Vietnam was solely his as the one " 'chosen by the American people to decide' "(Karnow 327).

c. On July 28, 1965, Johnson announced his decision to add forty-four battalions to the troops already in Vietnam, ending his waffling and agonizing of the past nineteen months of his presidency. (Karnow 357)

d. Karnow explains that LBJ took his responsibility to make decisions about Vietnam seriously (327). Although Johnson knew that many would offer suggestions, only he had "'been chosen by the American people to decide'" (Karnow 327). ■ ■

ORGANIZING THE PAPER

Armed with an understanding of writing strategies to avoid plagiarism, you are now almost ready to draft your essay. Follow these steps to get organized to write:

1. *Arrange notes (or your annotated sources) by the labels you have used and read them through.* You may discover that some notes or marked sections of sources now seem irrelevant. Set them aside, but do not throw them away yet. Some further reading and note taking may also be necessary to fill in gaps that have become apparent.

2. *Reexamine your tentative claim or research proposal.* As a result of reading and reflection, do you need to alter or modify your claim in any way? Or, if you began with a research question, what now is your answer to the question? Is, for example, TV violence harmful to children?

3. *Decide on the claim that will direct your writing.* To write a unified essay with a "reason for being," you need a claim that meets these criteria:

   • It is a complete sentence, not a topic or statement of purpose.

TOPIC:	Rape on college campuses.
CLAIM:	There are steps that both students and administrators can take to reduce incidents of campus rape.

- It is limited and focused.

UNFOCUSED:	Prohibition affected the 1920s in many ways.
FOCUSED:	Prohibition was more acceptable to rural than urban areas because of differences in values, social patterns, cultural backgrounds, and the economic result of prohibiting liquor sales.

- It establishes a new or interesting approach to the topic that makes your research meaningful.

NOT INVENTIVE:	A regional shopping mall should not be built next to the Manassas Battlefield.
INVENTIVE:	Putting aside an appeal to our national heritage, one can say, simply, that there is no economic justification for the building of a shopping mall next to the Manassas Battlefield.

4. *Write down the organization that emerges from your labels and grouping of sources, and compare this with your preliminary plan.* If there are differences, justify those changes to yourself. Consider: Does the new, fuller plan provide a complete and logical development of your claim?

DRAFTING THE ESSAY

Plan Your Time

How much time will you need to draft your essay? Working with sources and taking care with documentation make research paper writing more time-consuming than writing an undocumented essay. You also need to allow time between completing the draft and revising. Do not try to draft, revise, and proof an essay all in one day.

Handle In-Text Documentation as You Draft

The Modern Language Association (MLA) recommends that writers prepare their Works Cited page(s) *before* drafting their essay. With this important information prepared correctly and next to you as you draft, you will be less likely to make errors in documentation that will result in a plagiarized essay. Although you may believe that stopping to include parenthetical documentation as you write will cramp your writing, you really cannot try to insert the documentation after completing the writing. The risk of failing to document accurately is too great to chance. Parenthetical documentation is brief; listen to the experts and take the time to include it as you compose.

You saw some models of documentation in Chapter 12. In Chapter 14, you have complete guidelines and models for in-text (parenthetical) documentation and then many models for the complete citations of sources. Study the information in Chapter 14 and then draft your Works Cited page(s) as part of your preparation for writing.

Choose an Appropriate Writing Style

Specific suggestions for composing the parts of your paper follow, but first here are some general guidelines for research essay style.

Use the Proper Person

Research papers are written primarily in the third person *(she, he, it, they)* to create objectivity and to direct attention to the content of the paper. The question is over the appropriateness of the first person *(I, we)*. Although you want to avoid writing "as *you* can see," do not try to avoid the use of *I* if you need to distinguish your position from the views of others. It is better to write "I" than "it is the opinion of this writer" or "the researcher learned" or "this project analyzed." On the other hand, avoid qualifiers such as "I think." Just state your ideas.

Use the Proper Tense

When you are writing about people, ideas, or events of the past, the appropriate tense is the past tense. When writing about current times, the appropriate tense is the present. Both tenses may occur in the same paragraph, as the following paragraph illustrates:

> Fifteen years ago "personal" computers were all but unheard of. Computers were regarded as unknowable, building-sized mechanized monsters that required a precise 68 degree air-conditioned environment and eggheaded technicians with thick glasses and white lab coats scurrying about to keep the temperamental and fragile egos of the electronic brains mollified. Today's generation of computers is accessible, affordable, commonplace, and much less mysterious. The astonishing progress made in computer technology in the last few years has made computers practical, attainable, and indispensable. Personal computers are here to stay.

In the above example, when the student moves from computers in the past to computers in the present, he shifts tenses accurately.

When writing about sources, the convention is to use the present tense *even* for works or authors from the past. The idea is that the source, or the author, *continues* to make the point or use the technique into the present—that is, every time there is a reader. So, write "Lincoln selects the biblical expression 'Fourscore and seven years ago'" and "King echoes Lincoln when he writes 'five score years ago.'"

Avoid Excessive Quoting

Many students use too many direct quotations. Plan to use your own words most of the time for these good reasons:

- Constantly shifting between your words and the language of your sources (not to mention all those quotation marks) makes reading your essay difficult.
- This is your paper and should sound like you.
- When you take a passage out of its larger context, you face the danger of misrepresenting the writer's views.
- When you quote endlessly, readers may begin to think either that you are lazy or that you don't really understand the issues well enough to put them in your own words. You don't want to present either image to your readers.
- You do not prove any point by quoting another person's opinion. All you indicate is that there is someone else who shares your views. Even if that person is an expert on the topic, your quoted material still represents the view of only one person. You support a claim with reasons and evidence, both of which can usually be presented in your own words.

When you must quote, keep the quotations brief, weave them carefully into your own sentences, and be sure to identify the author in a signal phrase. Study the guidelines for handling quotations on pages 25–28 for models of correct form and style.

Write Effective Beginnings

The best introduction is one that presents your subject in an interesting way to gain the reader's attention, states your claim, and gives the reader an indication of the scope and limits of your paper. In a short research essay, you may be able to combine an attention-getter, a statement of subject, and a claim in one paragraph. More typically, especially in longer papers, the introduction will expand to two or three paragraphs. In the physical and social sciences, the claim may be withheld until the conclusion, but the opening introduces the subject and presents the researcher's hypothesis, often posed as a question. Since students sometimes have trouble with research paper introductions in spite of knowing these general guidelines, several specific approaches are illustrated here:

1. In the opening to her study of car advertisements, a student, relating her topic to what readers know, reminds readers of the culture's concern with image:

    Many Americans are highly image conscious. Because the "right" look is

    essential to a prosperous life, no detail is too small to overlook. Clichés about

    first impressions remind us that "you never get a second chance to make a

    first impression," so we obsessively watch our weight, firm our muscles, sculpt our hair, select our friends, find the perfect houses, and buy our automobiles. Realizing the importance of image, companies compete to make the "right" products, that is, those that will complete the "right" image. Then advertisers direct specific products to targeted groups of consumers. Although targeting may be labeled as stereotyping, it has been an effective strategy in advertising.

2. Terms and concepts central to your project need defining early in your paper, especially if they are challenged or qualified in some way by your study. This opening paragraph demonstrates an effective use of definition:

> William Faulkner braids a universal theme, the theme of initiation, into the fiber of his novel *Intruder in the Dust.* From ancient times to the present, a prominent focus of literature, of life, has been rites of passage, particularly those of childhood to adulthood. Joseph Campbell defines rites of passage as "distinguished by formal, and usually very severe, exercises of severance." A "candidate" for initiation into adult society, Campbell explains, experiences a shearing away of the "attitudes, attachments and life patterns" of childhood (9). This severe, painful stripping away of the child and installation of the adult is presented somewhat differently in several works by American writers.

3. Begin with a thought-provoking question. A student, arguing that the media both reflect and shape reality, started with these questions:

> Do the media just reflect reality, or do they also shape our perceptions of reality? The answer to this seemingly "chicken-and-egg" question is: They do both.

4. Beginning with important, perhaps startling, facts, evidence, or statistics is an effective way to introduce a topic, provided the details are relevant to the topic. Observe the following example:

> Teenagers are working again, but not on their homework. Over 40 percent of teenagers have jobs by the time they are juniors (Samuelson A22). And their jobs do not support academic learning since almost two-thirds of teenagers are employed in sales and service jobs that entail mostly carrying, cleaning, and wrapping (Greenberger and Steinberg 62–67), not reading, writing, and computing. Unfortunately, the negative effect on learning is not offset by improved opportunities for future careers.

Avoid Ineffective Openings

Follow these rules for avoiding openings that most readers find ineffective or annoying.

1. *Do not restate the title* or write as if the title were the first sentence in paragraph 1. It is a convention of writing to have the first paragraph stand independent of the title.

2. *Do not begin with "clever" visuals* such as artwork or fancy lettering.

3. *Do not begin with humor* unless it is part of your topic.

4. *Do not begin with a question that is just a gimmick, or one that a reader may answer in a way you do not intend.* Asking "What are the advantages of solar energy?" may lead a reader to answer "None that I can think of." A straightforward research question ("Is *Death of a Salesman* a tragedy?") is appropriate.

5. *Do not open with an unnecessary definition quoted from a dictionary.* "According to Webster, solar energy means . . ." is a tired, overworked beginning that does not engage readers.

6. *Do not start with a purpose statement:* "This paper will examine . . ." Although a statement of purpose is a necessary part of a report of empirical research, a report still needs an interesting introduction.

Compose Solid, Unified Paragraphs

As you compose the body of your paper, keep in mind that you want to (1) maintain unity and coherence, (2) guide readers clearly through source material, and (3) synthesize source material and your own ideas. Do not settle for paragraphs in which facts from notes are just loosely run together. Review the following discussion and study the examples to see how to craft effective body paragraphs.

Provide Unity and Coherence

You achieve paragraph unity when every sentence in a paragraph relates to and develops the paragraph's main idea. Unity, however, does not automatically produce coherence; that takes attention to wording. Coherence is achieved when readers can follow the connection between one sentence and another and between each sentence and the main idea. Strategies for achieving coherence include repetition of key words, the use of pronouns that clearly refer to those key words, and the use of transition and connecting words. Observe these strategies at work in the following paragraph:

> Perhaps the most important differences between the initiations of Robin
>
> and Biff and that experienced by Chick are the facts that Chick's epiphany does
>
> not come all at once and it does not devastate him. Chick
>
> learns about adulthood —and enters adulthood—piecemeal and with support.

His first eye-opening experience occurs as he tries to pay Lucas for dinner and

is rebuffed (15–16). Chick learns, after trying again to buy a clear conscience,

the impropriety and affront of his actions (24). Lucas teaches Chick how he

should resolve his dilemma by setting him "free" (26–27). Later, Chick feels out-

rage at the adults crowding into the town, presumably to see a lynching, then

disgrace and shame as they eventually flee (196–97, 210).

Coherence is needed not only within paragraphs but between paragraphs as well. You need to guide readers through your paper, connecting paragraphs and showing relationships by the use of transitions. The following opening sentences of four paragraphs from a paper on solutions to rape on the college campus illustrate smooth transitions:

¶ 3 Specialists have provided a number of reasons why men rape.

¶ 4 Some of the causes of rape on the college campus originate with the

colleges themselves and with how they handle the problem.

¶ 5 Just as there are a number of causes for campus rapes, there are a

number of ways to help solve the problem of these rapes.

¶ 6 If these seem like commonsense solutions, why, then, is it so difficult to

significantly reduce the number of campus rapes?

Without awkwardly writing "Here are some of the causes" and "Here are some of the solutions," the student guides her readers through a discussion of causes for and solutions to the problem of campus rape.

Guide Readers Through Source Material

To understand the importance of guiding readers through source material, consider first the following paragraph from a paper on the British coal strike in the 1970s:

The social status of the coal miners was far from good. The country

blamed them for the dimmed lights and the three-day workweek. They had

been placed in the position of social outcasts and were beginning to "con-

sider themselves another country." Some businesses and shops had even

gone so far as to refuse service to coal miners (Jones 32).

Who has learned that the coal miners felt ostracized or that the country blamed them? As readers we cannot begin to judge the validity of these assertions without some context provided by the writer. Most readers are put off by an unattached direct quotation or some startling observation that is documented correctly but given no context within the paper. Using signal phrases that identify the author of the source and, when useful, the author's credentials helps guide readers through the source material. The following revision of the paragraph above provides not only context but also sentence variety:

> The social acceptance of coal miners, according to Peter Jones, British correspondent for *Newsweek*, was far from good. From interviews both in London shops and in pubs near Birmingham, Jones concluded that Britishers blamed the miners for the dimmed lights and three-day workweek. Several striking miners, in a pub on the outskirts of Birmingham, asserted that some of their friends had been denied service by shopkeepers and that they "consider[ed] themselves another country" (32).

Select Appropriate Signal Phrases

When you use signal phrases, try to vary both the words you use and their place in the sentence. Look, for example, at the first sentence in the sample paragraph above. The signal phrase is placed in the middle of the sentence and is set off by commas. The sentence could have been written two other ways:

> The social acceptance of coal miners was far from good, according to Peter Jones, British correspondent for *Newsweek*.

OR

> According to Peter Jones, British correspondent for *Newsweek*, the social acceptance of coal miners was far from good.

Whenever you provide a name and perhaps credentials for your source, you have these three sentence patterns to choose from. Make a point to use all three options in your paper. Word choice can be varied as well. Instead of writing "Peter Jones says" throughout your paper, consider some of these verb choices:

Jones *asserts*	Jones *contends*	Jones *attests to*
Jones *states*	Jones *thinks*	Jones *points out*
Jones *concludes*	Jones *stresses*	Jones *believes*
Jones *presents*	Jones *emphasizes*	Jones *agrees with*
Jones *argues*	Jones *confirms*	Jones *speculates*

NOTE: Not all the words in this list are synonyms; you cannot substitute *confirms* for *believes*. First, select the verb that most accurately conveys the writer's relationship to his or her material. Then, when appropriate, vary word choice as well as sentence structure.

Readers need to be told how to respond to the sources used. They need to know which sources you accept as reliable and which you disagree with, and they need you to distinguish clearly between fact and opinion. Ideas and opinions from sources need signal phrases and then some discussion from you.

Synthesize Source Material and Your Own Ideas

A smooth synthesis of source material is aided by signal phrases and paren-thetical documentation because they mark the beginning and ending of mate-rial taken from a source. But a complete synthesis requires something more: your ideas about the source and the topic. To illustrate, consider the problems in another paragraph from the British coal strike paper:

> Some critics believed that there was enough coal in Britain to maintain enough power to keep industry at a near-normal level for thirty-five weeks (Jones 30). Prime Minister Heath, on the other hand, had placed the coun-try's usable coal supply at 15.5 million tons (Jones 30). He stated that this would have fallen to a critical 7 million tons within a month had he not declared a three-day workweek (Jones 31).

This paragraph is a good example of random details strung together for no apparent purpose. How much coal did exist? Whose figures were right? And what purpose do these figures serve in the paper's development? Note that the entire paragraph is developed with material from one source. Do sources other than Jones offer a different perspective? This paragraph is weak for several rea-sons: (1) It lacks a controlling idea (topic sentence) to give it purpose and direc-tion; (2) it relies for development entirely on one source; (3) it lacks any discussion or analysis by the writer.

By contrast, the following paragraph demonstrates a successful synthesis:

> Of course, the iridium could have come from other extraterrestrial sources besides an asteroid. One theory, put forward by Dale Russell, is that the iridium was produced outside the solar system by an exploding star (500). Such an explosion, Russell states, could have blown the iridium either off the surface of the moon or directly from the star itself (500–01), while also pro-ducing a deadly blast of heat and gamma rays (Krishtalka 19). This theory seems to explain the traces of iridium in the mass extinction, but it does not explain why smaller mammals, crocodiles, and birds survived (Wilford 220).
>
> So the supernova theory took a backseat to the other extraterrestrial theories: those of asteroids and comets colliding with the Earth. The authors of the

book *The Great Extinction,* Michael Allaby and James Lovelock, subtitled their

work *The Solution to . . . the Disappearance of the Dinosaurs.* Their theory: an

asteroid or comet collided with Earth around sixty-five million years ago, killing

billions of organisms, and thus altering the course of evolution (157). The fact

that the theory of collision with a cosmic body warrants a book calls for some

thought: Is the asteroid or comet theory merely sensationalism, or is it rooted

in fact? Paleontologist Leonard Krishtalka declares that few paleontologists

have accepted the asteroid theory, himself calling "some catastrophic theo-

ries . . . small ideas injected with growth hormone" (22). However,

other scientists, such as Allaby and Lovelock, see the cosmic catastrophic

theory as a solid one based on more than guesswork (10–11).

This paragraph's synthesis is accomplished by several strategies: (1) The paragraph has a controlling idea; (2) the paragraph combines information from several sources; (3) the information is presented in a blend of paraphrase and short quotations; (4) information from the different sources is clearly indicated to readers; and (5) the student explains and discusses the information.

You might also observe the different lengths of the two sample paragraphs just presented. Although the second paragraph is long, it is not unwieldy because it achieves unity and coherence. By contrast, body paragraphs of only three sentences are probably in trouble.

Write Effective Conclusions

Sometimes ending a paper seems even more difficult than beginning one. You know you are not supposed to just stop, but every ending that comes to mind sounds more corny than clever. If you have trouble, try one of these types of endings:

1.   Do not just repeat your claim exactly as it was stated in paragraph 1, but expand on the original wording and emphasize the claim's significance. Here is the conclusion of the solar energy paper:

     The idea of using solar energy is not as far-fetched as it seemed years

     ago. With the continued support of government plus the enthusiasm of

     research groups, environmentalists, and private industry, solar energy may

     become a household word quite soon. With the increasing cost of fossil fuel,

     the time could not be better for exploring this use of the sun.

2.   End with a quotation that effectively summarizes and drives home the point of your paper. Researchers are not always lucky enough to find the

ideal quotation for ending a paper. If you find a good one, use it. Better yet, present the quotation and then add your comment in a sentence or two. The conclusion to a paper on the dilemma of defective newborns is a good example:

> Dr. Joseph Fletcher is correct when he says that "every advance in medical capabilities is an increase in our moral responsibility" (48). In a world of many gray areas, one point is clear. From an ethical point of view, medicine is a victim of its own success.

3. If you have researched an issue or problem, emphasize your proposed solutions in the concluding paragraph. The student opposing a mall adjacent to the Manassas Battlefield concluded with several solutions:

> Whether the proposed mall will be built is clearly in doubt at the moment. What are the solutions to this controversy? One approach is, of course, not to build the mall at all. To accomplish this solution, now, with the re-zoning having been approved, probably requires an act of Congress to buy the land and make it part of the national park. Another solution, one that would please the county and the developer and satisfy citizens objecting to traffic problems, is to build the needed roads before the mall is completed. A third approach is to allow the office park of the original plan to be built, but not the mall. The local preservationists had agreed to this original development proposal, but now that the issue has received national attention, they may no longer be willing to compromise. Whatever the future of the William Center, the present plan for a new regional mall is not acceptable.

Avoid Ineffective Conclusions

Follow these rules to avoid conclusions that most readers consider ineffective and annoying.

1. *Do not introduce a new idea.* If the point belongs in your paper, you should have introduced it earlier.
2. *Do not just stop or trail off,* even if you feel as though you have run out of steam. A simple, clear restatement of the claim is better than no conclusion.
3. *Do not tell your reader what you have accomplished:* "In this paper I have explained the advantages of solar energy by examining the costs...." If you have written well, your reader knows what you have accomplished.

4. *Do not offer apologies or expressions of hope.* "Although I wasn't able to find as much on this topic as I wanted, I have tried to explain the advantages of solar energy, and I hope that you will now understand why we need to use it more" is a disastrous ending.

Choose an Effective Title

Give some thought to your paper's title since that is what your reader sees first and what your work will be known by. A good title provides information and creates interest. Make your title informative by making it specific. If you can create interest through clever wording, so much the better. But do not confuse "cutesiness" with clever wording. Review the following examples of acceptable and unacceptable titles:

VAGUE:	A Perennial Issue Unsolved
	(There are many; which one is this paper about?)
BETTER:	The Perennial Issue of Press Freedom Versus Press Responsibility
TOO BROAD:	Earthquakes
	(What about earthquakes? This title is not informative.)
BETTER:	The Need for Earthquake Prediction
TOO BROAD:	*The Scarlet Letter*
	(Never use just the title of the work under discussion; you can use the work's title as a part of a longer title of your own.)
BETTER:	Color Symbolism in *The Scarlet Letter*
CUTESY:	Babes in Trouble
	(The slang "Babes" makes this title seem insensitive rather than clever.)
BETTER:	The Dilemma of Defective Newborns

REVISING THE PAPER: A CHECKLIST

After completing a first draft, catch your breath and then gear up for the next step in the writing process: revision. Revision actually involves three separate steps: *rewriting*—adding or deleting text, or moving parts of the draft around; *editing*—a rereading to correct errors from misspellings to incorrect documentation format; and then *proofreading* the typed copy. If you treat these as separate steps, you will do a more complete job of revision—and get a better grade on your paper!

Rewriting

Read your draft through and make changes as a result of answering the following questions:

Purpose and Audience

☐ Is my draft long enough to meet assignment requirements and my purpose?

☐ Are terms defined and concepts explained appropriately for my audience?

Content

☐ Do I have a clearly stated thesis—the claim of my argument?

☐ Have I presented sufficient evidence to support my claim?

☐ Are there any irrelevant sections that should be deleted?

Structure

☐ Are paragraphs ordered to develop my topic logically?

☐ Does the content of each paragraph help develop my claim?

☐ Is everything in each paragraph on the same subtopic to create paragraph unity?

☐ Do body paragraphs have a balance of information and analysis, of source material and my own ideas?

☐ Are there any paragraphs that should be combined? Are there any very long paragraphs that should be divided? (Check for unity.)

Editing

Make revisions guided by your responses to the questions, make a clean copy, and read again. This time, pay close attention to sentences, words, and documentation format. Use the following questions to guide editing.

Coherence

☐ Have connecting words been used and key terms repeated to produce paragraph coherence?

☐ Have transitions been used to show connections between paragraphs?

Sources

☐ Have I paraphrased instead of quoted whenever possible?

☐ Have I used signal phrases to create a context for source material?

☐ Have I documented all borrowed material, whether quoted or paraphrased?

☐ Are parenthetical references properly placed after borrowed material?

Style

☐ Have I varied sentence length and structure?

☐ Have I avoided long quotations?

☐ Do I have correct form for quotations? For titles?

- ☐ Is my language specific and descriptive?
- ☐ Have I avoided inappropriate shifts in tense or person?
- ☐ Have I removed any wordiness, deadwood, trite expressions, or clichés?
- ☐ Have I used specialized terms correctly?
- ☐ Have I avoided contractions as too informal for most research papers?
- ☐ Have I maintained an appropriate style and tone for academic work?

Proofreading

When your editing is finished, prepare a completed draft of your paper according to the format described and illustrated below. Then proofread the completed copy, making any corrections neatly in ink. If a page has several errors, print a corrected copy. Be sure to make a copy of the paper for yourself before submitting the original to your instructor.

THE COMPLETED PAPER

Your research paper should be double-spaced throughout (including the Works Cited page) with 1-inch margins on all sides. Your project will contain the following parts, in this order:

1. *A title page,* with your title, your name, your instructor's name, the course name or number, and the date, neatly centered, if an outline follows. If there is no outline, place this information at the top left of the first page.
2. *An outline,* or statement of purpose, if required.
3. *The body or text of your paper.* Number all pages consecutively, including pages of works cited, using arabic numerals. Place numbers in the upper right-hand corner of each page. Include your last name before each page number.
4. *A list of works cited,* placed on a separate page(s) after the text. Title the first page "Works Cited." (Do not use the title "Bibliography.")

SAMPLE STUDENT ESSAY IN MLA STYLE

The following paper illustrates an argumentative essay using sources documented in MLA style.

Donaldson 1

David Donaldson

Professor Princiotto-Gorrell/Professor Stevens

English 203U—Research Process

7 July 2011

Tell Us What You Really Are: The Debate over

Labeling Genetically Modified Food

The decision to eat—or not to eat—genetically modified (GM) food is a

relatively new dilemma for consumers. People have been going to the grocery

store for years, and up until the mid-1990s there was little question as to what

they were buying. Consumers knew that when they picked up a tomato, that

product was in fact a tomato, not a tomato that had been spliced, or merged,

with the genes of some other organism in an attempt to get it to behave like

an entirely different fruit. There were most definitely food additives,

preservatives, and other questionable ingredients up until then, but before

1994, a tomato was still a tomato. Food additives, preservatives, potentially

allergenic ingredients, and possibly toxic ingredients must be labeled on each

product. Until GM food is proven to be safe it is essential that the federal

government also require labeling to denote the presence of genetically

modified organisms (GMOs). Safety is not the only factor in the GM food

debate. Religious and cultural concerns, as well as the consumer's freedom of

choice, must be considered when deciding whether to label GM foods.

The genetic modification of food is defined by MacDonald and

Whellams as "any change to the heritable traits of an organism achieved by

intentional manipulation" (181). Or, more specifically, defined by Sarah Kirby

as "the process of removing individual genes from one organism and

transplanting them into another organism," it is the basis of contemporary

bioengineering (352). Although there are scientists and government officials

who want to equate genetic modification with genetic hybridization, the

Provide last name
with page number
at top right of each
page.

Use heading on top
left when a separate
title page is not used.

Center title.

Indent paragraphs 5
spaces.

Double-space
throughout.

Clear opening leads
to student's thesis.

Key term defined.

Donaldson 2

definitions given for genetic modification do not match the definition of genetic hybridization.

It is true that plant and animal hybridization has been going on for a long time. That is how many of the flora and fauna here today were conceived. They did not just show up as they are today; rather, over time they evolved into what they are now due to progressive variations in their genes. As explained

by Gundorf and Huchingson, scientists used selective breeding to achieve a desired trait, or to suppress a trait deemed undesirable (233). Kirby expands on Gudorf and Huchingson's idea by adding that selective breeding was more natural since "it was restricted to two organisms that are able to breed together" (352). In "A Defense of the U.S. Position on Labeling Genetically Modified Organisms," Sally Kirsch adds that the United States Food and Drug Administration (FDA) even cites the longevity of selective breeding to justify their stance that nothing is wrong or unsafe about GM food (25).

Bioengineering has been seen as the answer to many of the environmental issues related to climate change, to help feed growing populations in developing countries. Scientists have created "drought resistant corn and soybeans," rice with increased nutrients, and "pest resistant plants" (Kirsch 21). However, for more cosmetic reasons, they have also created the FLAVR SAVR™ tomato. This tomato would eventually become the first GM food available to consumers. The *Gale Encyclopedia of Science* article "Plant Breeding" explains that it was not until 1992 that "a tomato with delayed ripening became the first genetically modified (GM) commercial food crop" (3375). Two years later, the company Calgene received approval from the FDA to sell their FLAVR SAVR™ tomatoes (Martineau 189). Kirsch notes that there was a lukewarm public greeting for Calgene's tomato, and the underwhelming sales further emphasized that the general public was apprehensive about GM food (21). However, in their article, "'Does Contain' vs. 'Does Not Contain': Does it Matter Which GMO Label is Used?" Crespi

Donaldson 3

and Marette argue that "Americans are much more accepting of GMOs than the rest of the world" (328).

This is no longer a process simply by which plants are being spliced with plant genes and animals are being spliced with animal genes. Today, bioengineers can create a plant that has been spliced with animal genes (Kirby 357). The health and safety results of the GM process are still relatively unknown as this technology is still new. The uncertainty of this process is fueling the public outcry for GMO labeling in the United States. Anne MacKenzie builds on Kirby's point, arguing that because consumers have become more knowledgeable about food and health, more concerned about the safety of the food supply, have developed a greater desire to know about how their food is made, and have mounted a growing distrust of biotech companies and the government, they want more information about what is going into their food (52).

The most noted possible health hazard linked to GM foods is the potential for new or heightened food allergies. MacKenzie, Gudorf and Huchingson, and Kirby all mention new food allergies as one of the more obvious reasons to require the mandatory labeling of GM food. MacKenzie states: "Allergenicity is an important consideration for foods derived through biotechnology because of the possibility of a new protein introduced into a food could be an allergen" (51). She adds that when a food such as soy, a common allergen, is used in the genetic modification process, "life-threatening" results are more likely to occur (51). Gudorf and Huchingson suggest that GM food could be held responsible for the increase in the number of people who have developed food-related allergies in the last decade (233). They also point out that, for example, people do not know specifically which peanut gene may spark their allergy (233). It could be the gene for color, the gene for oil production, or the gene that makes peanuts viable underground that contains the protein that sets off their allergy. If a

Student establishes difference between hybridization and genetic modification.

Here and below student examines possible problems with GM foods.

Donaldson 4

scientist wants to make a strawberry that grows underground, and inserts

that gene from the peanut into a strawberry's DNA, the same individuals who

are allergic to peanuts could now become allergic to that particular

strawberry (Gudorf and Huchingson 233).

Kirby acknowledges that GM foods may "set-off" allergies, but she adds

that genetic modification could also "produce dangerous toxins, increase

cancer risks, produce antibiotic-resistant pathogens, and damage food quality"

(359). Specifically related to allergies, Kirby explains that "people have never

before been exposed to several of the foreign proteins currently being

genetically spliced into foods" (360). Conversely, Robert Bracket, Director of

the Center for Food Safety and Applied Nutrition, testified before the FDA

that if the genetic modification process were to merge one organism with an

organism that is considered a common food allergen, soy, milk, egg, etc., then

that product would indeed be labeled as containing a common food allergen

as is required by law (FDA). Otherwise, Bracket says, "GM food is safe and

no different than its conventionally grown counterpart," which echoes the

FDA spokesman quoted by MacDonald and Whellams (FDA).

Aside from health concerns, there are also religious and cultural

motives that should be considered when deciding whether to label GM food.

Theologically speaking, Christianity does not necessarily reject GM food. In

"Some Christian Reflections on GM Food," Donald Bruce suggests that the

concern within Christianity is more a moral obligation to God's creation

rather than a dietary issue (119). However, multiple interpretations are

present. Genesis 1: 26–28 basically states that "Christian thinking has

generally seen intervention in the natural world as ordained by God in the

creation of ordinances that grant humans dominion over all the rest of

creation" (Bruce 119). Conversely, there are also Christians who think

that GM food is the result of humans "playing God in wrongly changing what

God has created" (Bruce 121). For Christians who believe that genetically

Donaldson 5

modifying food is wrong, mandatory labeling of GM food would guide them in their food choices.

For those of the Muslim or Jewish faith, GM food presents dietary concerns as well as potential moral objections. Ebrahim Moosa cites the splicing of animal genes into plants as one of the biggest worries Muslims face from GM food (135). He says that "a tomato containing a gene harvested from a flounder may not generate repugnance in an observant Muslim, since fish is permissible for adherents of this tradition, but a potato with a pig gene may well trigger visceral repugnance" (135). This is the same reason cited by Kirby (357). To emphasize his point, Moosa tells a story of Muhammad when he lived in Medina. In the story, Muhammad comes across farmers splicing different species of date-palm seedlings to increase their crop yields. Muhammad asks why they did it that way, and they reply: "That was the way they had always done it." The prophet then replies: "Well, perhaps, it would be better if you did not" (138). Kirby suggests that animal to plant genetic splicing is also the reason for those of the Jewish faith, or any vegetarian or vegan, to be concerned about the absence of mandatory GM food labeling (357). Peter Sand concurs, stating that providing consumers with information "irrespective of health concerns," such as labeling halal or kosher food, is essential in allowing consumers to have genuine freedom of choice (190).

Currently, although about "80% of processed food in the United States has a component from a genetically modified crop, a new survey finds that only 26% of Americans think they have ever eaten such food" (Krebs). This same United States Department of Agriculture (USDA) poll found that 94% of respondents felt that labeling items that contained GMOs would be a good idea (Krebs). This figure is up from a 2000 MSNBC poll that shows that "81% of people who responded were in favor of labeling genetically engineered products" (Kirsch 21). Kirsch follows that statement by confirming that the FDA and the biotech industry feel the opposite (21). Kirby repeats this view,

Current FDA position on GM foods.

l

Donaldson 6

adding that the FDA recognizes "no material difference in nutrition, composition, or safety between genetically modified food and food that has not been genetically modified" (qtd. in Kirby 353). Additionally, as long as the plant or animal that DNA is taken from and the plant or animal that the DNA is being spliced into are generally recognized as safe (GRAS), then the product is not subject to any sort of review prior to being released to consumers (Kirby 354). The FDA assumes that all products in the current food supply are GRAS. However, the current system does not take into account that the end result of tomato DNA and trout DNA is not simply a "tomato fish," but rather an entirely new entity that could bring with it unforeseen health risks ranging from food allergies to death.

Currently, according to Crespi and Marette, the United States has no mandatory GMO labeling requirement (328). Sand adds that the United States is not alone (187). He lists Canada and Argentina specifically, because combined the three countries are responsible for approximately 80% of the world's GM crops (187). Crespi and Marette add that much of the rest of the world currently recognizes the "precautionary principle," and the potentially deleterious effects of GMOs, and those governments do not want their citizens to be exposed to what might result from the consumption of GMOs (328).

To date, there have been no documented health risks related to GM foods. Proponents of GM food, such as the FDA, use this as the basis for their argument that GM foods pose no threat to consumers, and why mandatory labeling of GM food is unnecessary. An FDA spokesman says: "We have seen no evidence that the bioengineered foods now on the market pose any human health concerns or that they are in any way less safe than crops produced through traditional breeding" (qtd. in MacDonald and Whellams 184–185). While the tone throughout their article suggests that they disagree, MacDonald and Whellams argue that there is nothing unethical about GM foods that should result in mandatory labeling (184). Anne MacKenzie, the Associate Vice-

President of Science Evaluation for The Canadian Food Inspection Agency, concurs by saying that regulators have not yet noticed a "significant toxic or allergenic harm" (52). However, as stated by MacDonald and Whellams, many other countries choose to adopt the "precautionary principle" (185). This principle states that if something, like GM food, presents a potential threat to health or the environment, it is best to be cautious and to take action even if science hasn't demonstrated harmful effects (MacDonald and Whellams 185).

Because there may be serious, long-term negative implications on consumer health as a result of the continued consumption of GMOs, biotech companies, governments, and consumers should all be more wary of GM foods (MacDonald and Whellams 185). The "precautionary principle" is law in the European Union, as they consider unknown risk sufficient to require further study before approval. The United States takes the position that if something is not demonstrated to be harmful, then there is no problem in moving forward with implementation ("Precautionary Principle"). There is strong opposition from the United States's Chamber of Commerce to the Precautionary Principle; the Chamber argues that potential but unknown risk should not stand in the way of progress ("Precautionary Principle").

The United States currently operates under a voluntary labeling program (Sand 187), including labeling of foods with GMOs and those without GMOs. However, when Marion Nestle searched for labeling of foods with GMOs, she was not surprised that her search was unsuccessful. Nestle states: "Scientifically based or not, the motivation of the biotechnology companies for opposing labeling is obvious: if the foods are labeled as GM, you might choose not to buy them" (57). The FDA's voluntary labeling program for products that do not contain GMOs can be seen at the grocery store today in products that carry a GMO-free label. The question that remains is whether "GMO-free" labels offer consumers a fully informed choice.

Donaldson 8

The lack of a mandatory labeling system in the U.S. is not because no

Attempts to get GM
foods labeled.

one has tried. In 1999, Congressman Dennis Kucinich (D-OH) introduced into

Congress the "Genetically Engineered Food Right to Know Act" (Kirsch

26–27). The aim of this bill was to require food that contained GM material,

or was comprised of GM material, to be labeled as such (Kirsch 27). Kirby

explains that this bill would have required that "food produced with GM

material be labeled at each stage of the food production process," in order to

mitigate cross contamination (367). This bill would have made it necessary to

put a label on GM products that reads: "GENETICALLY ENGINEERED

UNITED STATES GOVERNMENT NOTICE: THIS PRODUCT CONTAINS A

GENETICALLY ENGINEERED MATERIAL OR WAS PRODUCED WITH A

GENETICALLY ENGINEERED MATERIAL" (Kirsch 27). Heather Carr adds

that Congressman Kucinich has introduced this bill into multiple sessions of

Congress, including as recently as 2010, never to make it out of committee.

Although support increased in the House of Representatives, it has never

been enough to move the bill through.

In 2000, Senator Barbara Boxer (D-CA) introduced a similar bill that

would have required a label stating: "GENETICALLY ENGINEERED. THIS

PRODUCT CONTAINS A GENETICALLY ENGINEERED MATERIAL"

(Kirsch 27). Like the House bill, this bill never came to fruition. The FDA

maintains that GM food is safe, and because of this, biotech companies say

that there is no need to liken their products to potentially dangerous

products (such as cigarettes or alcohol) with what resembles a warning label.

Anne MacKenzie disagrees with the biotech companies, arguing that

"consumers have a right to know" what they are eating, and how it was made

(50). She suggests that mandatory consumer-friendly labeling be used, but

that the labels should communicate in a way that does not mislead consumers

into thinking that GM food is any different from non-GM food (50–52). She

also asserts that the label "should not imply that the consumption of food

Donaldson 9

derived through biotechnology has implications for public health," since

currently there is no concrete evidence that GM food is either good or bad

for human consumption (52). MacDonald and Whellams proffer that if this

were done properly, it would be possible to label GM food while at the same

time addressing the biotech companies' concern that GM food labels would

"be seen as a warning" (183).

    While MacKenzie is in favor of mandatory labeling, Lars Bracht

Andersen remains apprehensive. Andersen, while supporting a consumer's

right to know, also understands the biotech industry's view that "mandatory

labeling, given predominantly negative consumer perceptions, is likely to

effectively remove GM foods from the market" (143). He argues for voluntary

labeling, stating that it would have the "least negative impact on the diversity of

the market" (143). However, since voluntary labeling alone seems unlikely to

protect consumers and provide adequate choice, mandatory labeling of GMO-

free products and of those products that contain GMOs is essential.

Student rejects voluntary labeling and repeats his thesis that GM foods need mandatory labeling.

Donaldson 10

Works Cited

Andersen, Lars Bracht. "The EU Rules on Labeling of Genetically Modified Foods: Mission Accomplished?" *European Food & Feed Law Review* 5.3 (2010): 136–43. *Academic Search Complete.* Web. 2 June 2011.

Bruce, Donald. "Some Christian Reflections on GM Food." *Boundaries: Religious Traditions And Genetically Modified Foods.* Ed. Conrad G. Brunk and Harold Coward. Albany: State U of New York P, 2009. Print.

Carr, Heather. "Genetically Engineered Organism Liability Act of 2010 H.R. 5579." *Eat Drink Better.* Important Media Network, 4 Aug. 2010. Web. 18 June 2011.

Clemmitt, M. "Global Food Crisis: What's Causing the Rising Prices?" *CQ Researcher* 18.24 (2008): 553–76. *CQ Researcher.* Web. 29 May 2011.

Crespi, John M., and Stephan Marette. "'Does Contain' vs. 'Does Not Contain': Does It Matter Which GMO Label Is Used?" *European Journal of Law and Economics* 16.3 (2003): 327–44. *SpringerLink.* Web. 12 June 2011.

Davison, John. "GM Plants: Science, Politics, and EC Regulations." *Plant Science* 178.2 (2010): 94–98. *ScienceDirect.* Web. 8 June 2011.

Gudorf, Christine E., and James E. Huchingson. *Boundaries: A Casebook in Environmental Ethics.* Washington D.C.: Georgetown UP, 2010. Print.

Kirby, Sarah. "Genetically Modified Foods: More Reasons to Label Than Not." *Drake Journal of Agricultural Law* 6.2 (2001): 351–68. *HeinOnline.* Web. 12 June 2011.

Kirsch, Sally R. "A Defense of the U.S. Position on Labeling Genetically Modified Organisms." *International and Comparative Environmental Law* 1.1 (2000): 21–28. *HeinOnline.* Web. 9 June 2011.

Krebs, Al. "New Poll—94% of Americans Want Labels on GE Food." *Organic Consumers Association.* Oct. 2003. Web. 9 June 2011.

MacDonald, Chris, and Melissa Whellams. "Corporate Decisions about Labeling Genetically Modified Foods." *Journal of Business Ethics* 75.2 (2007): 181–89. *JSTOR.* Web. 8 June 2011.

Continue to number pages consecutively.

Start a new page for Works Cited.

Double-space throughout.

List sources alphabetically.

Use hanging indentation.

Donaldson 11

Mackenzie, Anne A. "International Efforts to Label Food Derived Through
Biotechnology." *Governing Food: Science, Safety, and Trade.* Ed. Peter W. B.
Phillips and Robert Wolfe. Montreal: McGill–Queen's UP, 2001.
49–61. Print.

Martineau, Belinda. *First Fruit: The Creation of the Flavr Savr™ Tomato and the
Birth of Genetically Engineered Food.* New York: McGraw, 2001. Print.

Moosa, Ebrahim. "Genetically Modified Foods and Muslim Ethics." *Boundaries:
Religious Traditions and Genetically Modified Foods.* Ed. Conrad G. Brunk and
Harold Coward. Albany: State U of New York P, 2009. Print.

Nestle, Marion. *What to Eat.* New York: North Point, 2006. Print.

"Plant Breeding." *The Gale Encyclopedia of Science.* Ed. K. Lee Lerner and
Brenda Wilmoth Lerner. 4th ed. Vol. 4. Detroit: Gale, 2008. 3370–75.
Gale Virtual Reference Library. Web. 29 May 2011.

Sand, Peter H. "Labelling Genetically Modified Food: The Right to Know."
Review of European Community & International Environmental Law 15.2
(2006): 185–92. *Wiley Online Library.* Web. 9 June 2011.

U.S. Chamber of Commerce. "Precautionary Principle." U.S. Chamber of
Commerce, 2011. Web. 9 June 2011.

U.S. Food and Drug Administration. "Bioengineered Foods." Statement of
Robert E. Brackett to the FDA. U.S. Food and Drug Administration. 15
July 2009. Web. 18 June 2011.

Weasel, Lisa H. *Food Fray.* New York: AMACOM, 2009. Print.

CHAPTER 14

Formal Documentation: MLA Style, APA Style

In Chapter 12 you were shown, in sample bibliography cards, what information about a source you need to prepare the documentation for a researched essay. In Chapter 13 you were shown in-text documentation patterns as part of the discussion of avoiding plagiarism and writing effective paragraphs. The format shown is for MLA (Modern Language Association) style, the documentation style used in the humanities. APA (American Psychological Association) style is used in the social sciences. The sciences and other disciplines also have style sheets, but the most common documentation patterns used by undergraduates are MLA and APA, the two patterns explained in this chapter.

Remember that MLA recommends that writers prepare their Works Cited list—a list of all sources they have used—before drafting the essay. This list can then be used as an accurate guide to the in-text/parenthetical documentation that MLA requires along with the Works Cited list at the end of the essay. Heed this good advice. This chapter begins with guidelines for in-text documentation and then provides many models of full documentation for a Works Cited list.

> **REMEMBER:** Never guess at documentation! Always consult this chapter to make each in-text citation and your Works Cited page(s) absolutely correct.

As you now know, MLA documentation style has two parts: in-text references to author and page number and then complete information about each source in a Works Cited list. Because parenthetical references to author and page are incomplete—readers could not find the source with such limited information—all sources referred to by author and page number in the essay require the full details of publication in a Works Cited list that concludes the essay. General guidelines for in-text citations are given below.

> **NOTE:** You need a 100 percent correspondence between the sources listed in your Works Cited and the sources you actually cite (refer to) in your essay. Do not omit from your Works Cited any sources you refer to in your essay. Do not include in your Works Cited any sources not referred to in your paper.

GUIDELINES for Using Parenthetical Documentation

- **The purpose of documentation is to make clear exactly what material in a passage has been borrowed and from what source the borrowed material has come.**
- **Parenthetical in-text documentation requires specific page references for borrowed material—unless the source is not a print one.**

- **Parenthetical documentation is required for both quoted and paraphrased material and for both print and nonprint sources.**
- **Parenthetical documentation provides as brief a citation as possible consistent with accuracy and clarity.**

THE SIMPLEST PATTERNS OF PARENTHETICAL DOCUMENTATION

The simplest in-text citation can be prepared in one of three ways:

1. Give the author's last name (full name in your first reference to the writer) in the text of your essay and put the appropriate page number(s) in parentheses following the borrowed material.

   Frederick Lewis Allen observes that, during the 1920s, urban tastes spread

   to the country (146).

2. Place the author's last name and the appropriate page number(s) in parentheses immediately following the borrowed material.

   During the 1920s, "not only the drinks were mixed, but the company as well"

   (Allen 82).

3. On the rare occasion that you cite an entire work rather than borrowing from a specific passage, give the author's name in the text and omit any page numbers.

   Leonard Sax explains, to both parents and teachers, the specific ways in

   which gender matters.

   Each one of these in-text references is complete *only* when the full citation is placed in the Works Cited section of your paper:

   Allen, Frederick Lewis. *Only Yesterday: An Informal History of the Nineteen-*

      Twenties. New York: Harper, 1931. Print.

   Sax, Leonard. *Why Gender Matters*. New York: Random, 2005. Print.

The three patterns just illustrated should be used in each of the following situations:

1. The source referred to is not anonymous—the author is known.
2. The source referred to is by one author.
3. The source cited is the only work used by that author.
4. No other author in your list of sources has the same last name.

PLACEMENT OF PARENTHETICAL DOCUMENTATION

The simplest placing of an in-text reference is at the end of the sentence *before* the period. When you are quoting, place the parentheses *after* the final quotation mark but still before the period that ends the sentence.

During the 1920s, "not only the drinks were mixed, but the company as well"

(Allen 82).

> **NOTE:** Do not put any punctuation between the author's name and the page number.

If the borrowed material forms only a part of your sentence, place the parenthetical reference *after* the borrowed material and *before* any subsequent punctuation. This placement more accurately shows readers what is borrowed and what are your own words.

Sport, Allen observes about the 1920s, had developed into an obsession (66),

another similarity between the 1920s and the 1980s.

If a quoted passage is long enough to require setting off in display form (block quotation), then place the parenthetical reference at the end of the passage, *after* the final period. Remember: Long quotations in display form *do not* have quotation marks.

It is hard to believe that when he writes about the influence of science Allen

is describing the 1920s, not the 1980s:

> The prestige of science was colossal. The man in the street and the
> woman in the kitchen, confronted on every hand with new machines and
> devices which they owed to the laboratory, were ready to believe that
> science could accomplish almost anything. (164)

And to complete the documentation for all three examples:

Works Cited

Allen, Frederick Lewis. *Only Yesterday: An Informal History of the Nineteen-*

Twenties. New York: Harper, 1931. Print.

PARENTHETICAL CITATIONS OF COMPLEX SOURCES

Not all sources can be cited in one of the three patterns illustrated above, for not all meet the four criteria listed on p. 314. Works by two or more authors, for example, will need somewhat fuller references. Each sample form of in-text documentation given below must be completed with a full Works Cited reference, as shown above.

Two Authors, Mentioned in the Text

Richard Herrnstein and Charles Murray contend that it is "consistently . . . advantageous to be smart" (25).

Two Authors, Not Mentioned in the Text

The advantaged smart group forms a "cognitive elite" in our society (Herrnstein and Murray 26–27).

A Book in Two or More Volumes

Sewall analyzes the role of Judge Lord in Dickinson's life (2: 642–47).

OR

Judge Lord was also one of Dickinson's preceptors (Sewall 2: 642–47).

> **NOTE:** The number before the colon always signifies the volume number. The number(s) after the colon represents the page number(s).

A Book Listed by Title—Author Unknown

According to *The Concise Dictionary of American Biography*, William Jennings Bryan's 1896 campaign stressed social and sectional conflicts (117).

The *New York Times*' editors were not pleased with some of the changes in welfare programs ("Where Welfare Stands" 4: 16).

Always cite the title of the article, not the title of the journal, if the author is unknown. In the second example, the number before the page number is the newspaper's section number.

A Work by a Corporate Author

> A report by the Institute of Ecology's Global Ecological Problems Workshop
>
> argues that the civilization of the city can lull us into forgetting our
>
> relationship to the total ecological system on which we depend (13).

Although corporate authors may be cited with the page number within the parentheses, your writing will be more graceful if corporate authors are introduced in the sentence. Then only page numbers go in parentheses.

Two or More Works by the Same Author

> During the 1920s, "not only the drinks were mixed, but the company as well"
>
> (Allen, *Only Yesterday* 82).

> Frederick Lewis Allen contends that the early 1900s were a period of
>
> complacency in America (*The Big Change* 4–5).

> In *The Big Change*, Allen asserts that the early 1900s were a period of
>
> complacency (4–5).

If your list of sources contains two or more works by the same author, the fullest parenthetical citation includes the author's last name, followed by a comma, the work's title, shortened if possible, and the page number. If the author's name appears in the text—or the author and title both appear as in the third example above—omit these items from the parenthetical citation. When you have to include the title to distinguish among sources, it is best to put the author's name in the text.

Two or More Works in One Parenthetical Reference

> Several writers about the future agree that big changes will take place in
>
> work patterns (Toffler 384–87; Naisbitt 35–36).

Separate each author with a semicolon. But, if the parenthetical reference becomes disruptively long, cite the works in a "See also" note rather than in the text.

A Source Without Page Numbers

It is usually a good idea to name the nonprint source within your sentence so that readers will not expect to see page numbers.

> Although some still disagree, the *Oxford English Dictionary Online* defines
>
> global warming as "thought to be caused by various side-effects of modern
>
> energy consumption."

Complete Publication Information in Parenthetical Reference

At times you may want to give complete information about a source within parentheses in the text of your essay. Then a Works Cited list is not used. Use square brackets for parenthetical information within parentheses. This approach may be a good choice when you use only one source that you refer to several times. Literary analyses are one type of essay for which this approach to citation may be a good choice. For example:

> Edith Wharton establishes the bleakness of her setting, Starkfield, not just
>
> through description of place but also through her main character, Ethan,
>
> who is described as "bleak and unapproachable" (*Ethan Frome* [New York:
>
> Scribner's, 1911, Print] 3. All subsequent references are to this edition). Later
>
> Wharton describes winter as "shut[ting] down on Starkfield" and negating
>
> life there (7).

Additional-Information Footnotes or Endnotes

At times you may need to provide additional information that is not central to your argument. These additions belong in a content note. However, use these sparingly and never as a way of advancing your thesis. Many instructors object to content notes and prefer only parenthetical citations.

"See Also" Footnotes or Endnotes

More acceptable is the note that refers to other sources of evidence for or against the point to be established. These notes are usually introduced with "See also" or "Compare," followed by the citation. For example:

> Chekhov's debt to Ibsen should be recognized, as should his debt to other
>
> playwrights of the 1890s who were concerned with the inner life of their
>
> characters.[1]

---

[1] See also Eric Bentley, *In Search of Theater* (New York: Vintage, 1959) 330; Walter Bruford, *Anton Chekhov* (New Haven: Yale UP, 1957) 45.

PREPARING MLA CITATIONS FOR A WORKS CITED LIST

The partial in-text citations described and illustrated above must be completed by a full reference in a list given at the end of the essay. To prepare your Works Cited list, alphabetize, by author last name, the sources you have actually referred to and complete each citation according to the forms explained and illustrated in the following pages. The key is to find the appropriate model for each of your sources and then follow the model exactly. (Guidelines for formatting a finished Works Cited page are found on pp. 310–11.) But, you will make fewer errors if you also understand the basic pieces of information needed in citations and the order of that information.

Books require the following information, in the order given, with periods after each of the four major elements:

- Author, last name first.
- Title—and subtitle if there is one—in italics.
- Facts of publication: city of publication, followed by a colon, shortened publisher's name (Norton for W. W. Norton, for example), followed by a comma, and the year of publication, followed by a period.
- Medium of publication: Print.

Author	Title	Facts of Publication	Medium of Publication
Bellow, Saul.	*A Theft.*	New York: Viking-Penguin, 1989.	Print.

Forms for Books: Citing the Complete Book

A Book by a Single Author

Schieff, Stacy. *Cleopatra: A Life.* New York: Little, Brown, 2010. Print.

The subtitle is included, preceded by a colon, even if there is no colon on the book's title page.

A Book by Two or Three Authors

Adkins, Lesley, and Ray Adkins. *The Keys of Egypt: The Race to Crack the*

   Hieroglyph Code. New York: HarperCollins, 2000. Print.

Second (and third) authors' names appear in normal signature order.

A Book with More Than Three Authors

Baker, Susan P., et al. *The Injury Fact Book.* Oxford: Oxford UP, 1992. Print.

Use the name of the first person listed on the title page. The English "and others" may be used instead of "et al." Shorten "University Press" to "UP."

Two or More Works by the Same Author

Goodall, Jane. *In the Shadow of Man.* Boston: Houghton, 1971. Print.

---. *Through a Window: My Thirty Years with the Chimpanzees of Gombe.* Boston:

   Houghton, 1990. Print.

Give the author's full name with the first entry. For the second (and additional works), begin the citation with three hyphens followed by a period. Alphabetize the entries by the books' titles.

A Book Written Under a Pseudonym with Name Supplied

Wrighter, Carl P. [Paul Stevens]. *I Can Sell You Anything.* New York: Ballantine,

1972. Print.

An Anonymous Book

Beowulf: A New Verse Translation. Trans. Seamus Heaney. New York: Farrar,

2000. Print.

An Edited Book

Hamilton, Alexander, James Madison, and John Jay. *The Federalist Papers.* Ed.

Isaac Kramnick. New York: Viking-Penguin, 1987. Print.

Lynn, Kenneth S., ed. *Huckleberry Finn: Text, Sources, and Critics.* New York:

Harcourt, 1961. Print.

If you cite the author's work, put the author's name first and the editor's name after the title, preceded by "Ed." If you cite the editor's work (an introduction or notes), then place the editor's name first, followed by a comma and "ed."

A Translation

Schulze, Hagen. *Germany: A New History.* Trans. Deborah Lucas Schneider.

Cambridge: Harvard UP, 1998. Print.

Cornford, Francis MacDonald, trans. *The Republic of Plato.* New York: Oxford

UP, 1945. Print.

If the author's work is being cited, place the author's name first and the translator's name after the title, preceded by "Trans." If the translator's work is the important element, place the translator's name first, as in the second example above. If the author's name does not appear in the title, give it after the title. For example: By Plato.

A Book in Two or More Volumes

Spielvogel, Jackson J. *Western Civilization.* 2 vols. Minneapolis: West,

1991. Print.

A Book in Its Second or Subsequent Edition

> O'Brien, David M. *Storm Center: The Supreme Court and American Politics.*
>
> 2nd ed. New York: Norton, 1990. Print.

A Book in a Series

> Parkinson, Richard. *The Rosetta Stone.* British Museum Objects in Focus.
>
> London: British Museum, 2005. Print.

The series title—and number, if there is one—follows the book's title but is not put in italics.

A Reprint of an Earlier Work

> Twain, Mark. *Adventures of Huckleberry Finn.* 1885. Centennial Facsimile
>
> Edition. Introd. Hamlin Hill. New York: Harper, 1962. Print.

> Faulkner, William. *As I Lay Dying.* 1930. New York: Vintage-Random, 1964. Print.

Provide the original date of publication as well as the facts of publication for the reprinted version. Indicate any new material, as in the first example. The second example illustrates citing a reprinted book, by the same publisher, in a paperback version. (Vintage is a paperback imprint of the publisher Random House.)

A Book with Two or More Publishers

> Green, Mark J., James M. Fallows, and David R. Zwick. *Who Runs Congress?* Ralph
>
> Nader Congress Project. New York: Bantam; New York: Grossman, 1972. Print.

Separate the publishers with a semicolon.

A Corporate or Governmental Author

> California State Department of Education. *American Indian Education*
>
> *Handbook.* Sacramento: California Department of Education, Indian
>
> Education Unit, 1991. Print.

The Bible

> The Bible [Always refers to the King James Version.] Print.

> *The Reader's Bible: A Narrative.* Ed. with introd. Roland Mushat Frye. Princeton:
>
> Princeton UP, 1965. Print.

In the first example do not put the title in italics. Indicate the version if it is not the King James Version. Provide facts of publication for versions not well known.

Forms for Books: Citing Part of a Book

A Preface, Introduction, Foreword, or Afterword

> Sagan, Carl. Introduction. *A Brief History of Time: From the Big Bang to Black
> Holes.* By Stephen Hawking. New York: Bantam, 1988, ix–x. Print.

Use this form if you are citing the author of the Preface, Introduction, Foreword, or the like. Use an identifying word after the author's name and give inclusive page numbers for the part of the book by the author you are citing.

An Encyclopedia Article

> Ostrom, John H. "Dinosaurs." *McGraw-Hill Encyclopedia of Science and
> Technology.* 1957 ed. Print.

> "Benjamin Franklin." *Concise Dictionary of American Biography.* Ed. Joseph
> E. G. Hopkins. New York: Scribner's, 1964. Print.

Give complete publication facts for less well-known works or first editions.

One or More Volumes in a Multivolume Work

> James, Henry. *The Portrait of a Lady.* Vols. 3 and 4 of *The Novels and Tales of
> Henry James.* New York: Scribner's, 1908. Print.

A Work in an Anthology or Collection

> Hurston, Zora Neale. *The First One. Black Female Playwrights: An Anthology of
> Plays Before 1950.* Ed. Kathy A. Perkins. Bloomington: Indiana UP, 1989.
> 80–88. Print.

> Comstock, George. "The Medium and the Society: The Role of Television in
> American Life." *Children and Television: Images in a Changing Sociocultural
> World.* Ed. Gordon L. Berry and Joy Keiko Asamen. Newbury Park, CA:
> Sage, 1993. 117–31. Print.

Give inclusive page numbers for the particular work you have used.

An Article in a Collection, Casebook, or Sourcebook

> MacKenzie, James J. "The Decline of Nuclear Power." *engage/social* April 1986.
> Rpt. as "America Does Not Need More Nuclear Power" in *The
> Environmental Crisis: Opposing Viewpoints.* Ed. Julie S. Bach and Lynn Hall.
> Opposing Viewpoints Series. St. Paul: Greenhaven, 1986. 136–41. Print.

Many articles in collections have been previously published, so a complete citation needs to include the original facts of publication (excluding page numbers if they are not readily available) as well as the facts of publication for the collection. Include inclusive page numbers for the article used.

Cross-References

If you are citing several articles from one collection, you can cite the collection and then provide only the author and title of specific articles used, with a cross-reference to the editor(s) of the collection.

> Head, Suzanne, and Robert Heinzman, eds. *Lessons of the Rainforest.* San
>
> Francisco: Sierra Club, 1990. Print.

> Bandyopadhyay, J., and Vandana Shiva. "Asia's Forest, Asia's Cultures." Head
>
> and Heinzman 66–77. Print.

Forms for Periodicals: Articles in Journals and Magazines Accessed in Print

Articles from the various forms of periodicals, when read in their print format, require the following information, in the order given, with periods after each of the four major elements:

- Author, last name first.
- Title of the article, in quotation marks.
- Facts of publication: title of the journal (magazine or newspaper) in italics, volume and issue number *for scholarly journals only,* date followed by a colon and inclusive page numbers, and then a period.
- Medium of publication: Print.

The following models show the variations in the details of publication, depending on the type of publication.

Article in a Journal Paged by Year

> Brown, Jane D., and Carol J. Pardun. "Little in Common: Racial and Gender
>
> Differences in Adolescents' Television Diets." *Journal of Broadcasting and*
>
> *Electronic Media* 48.2 (2004): 266–78. Print.

Note that there is *no* punctuation between the title of the periodical and the volume number and date.

Article in a Journal Paged by Issue

> Lewis, Kevin. "Superstardom and Transcendence." *Arete: The Journal of Sport*
>
> *Literature* 2.2 (1985): 47–54. Print.

Provide both volume and issue number regardless of the journal's choice of paging.

Article in a Monthly Magazine

> Wegner, Mary-Ann Pouls. "Gateway to the Netherworld." *Archaeology* Jan./
>
> Feb. 2013: 50–53. Print.

Do not use volume or issue number. Cite the month(s) and year followed by a colon and inclusive page numbers. Abbreviate all months except May, June, and July.

Article in a Weekly Magazine

> Stein, Joel. "Eat This, Low Carbers." *Time* 15 Aug. 2005: 78. Print.

Provide the complete date, using the order of day, month, year.

An Anonymous Article

> "Death of Perestroika." *Economist* 2 Feb. 1991: 12–13. Print.

The missing name indicates that the article is anonymous. Alphabetize under D.

A Published Interview

> Angier, Natalie. "Ernst Mayr at 93." Interview. *Natural History* May 1997: 8–11. Print.

Follow the pattern for a published article, but add the descriptive label "Interview" (followed by a period) after the article's title.

A Review

> Whitehead, Barbara D. "The New Segregation." Rev. of *Coming Apart: The*
>
> *State of White America, 1960–2010,* by Charles Murrary. *Commonweal* 4
>
> May 2012. Print.

If the review is signed, begin with the author's name and then the title of the review article. Also provide the title of the work being reviewed and its author, preceded by "Rev. of." For reviews of art shows, videos, or computer software, provide place and date or descriptive label to make the citation clear.

Forms for Periodicals: Articles in Newspapers Accessed in Print

An Article from a Newspaper

> Arguila, John. "What Deep Blue Taught Kasparov—and Us." *Christian Science*
>
> *Monitor* 16 May 1997: 18. Print.

A newspaper's title should be cited as it appears on the masthead, excluding any initial article, thus *New York Times*, not *The New York Times*.

An Article from a Newspaper with Lettered Sections

Ferguson, Niall. "Rough Week, but America's Era Goes On." *Washington Post*

21 Sept. 2008: B1+. Print.

Place the section letter immediately before the page number without any spacing. If the paging is not consecutive, give the first page and the plus sign.

An Article from a Newspaper with a Designated Edition

Pereria, Joseph. "Women Allege Sexist Atmosphere in Offices Constitutes

Harassment." *Wall Street Journal* 10 Feb. 1988, eastern ed.: 23. Print.

Cite the edition used after the date and before the page number.

An Editorial

"Japan's Two Nationalisms." Editorial. *Washington Post* 4 June 2000: B6. Print.

Add the descriptive label "Editorial" after the article title.

A Letter to the Editor

Wiles, Yoko A. "Thoughts of a New Citizen." Letter. *Washington Post* 27 Dec.

1995: A22. Print.

Forms for Web Sources

Remember that the purpose of a citation is to allow readers to obtain the source you have used. To locate online sources, more information is usually needed than for printed sources. Include as many of the items listed below, in the order given here, as are relevant—and available—for each source. Take time to search a website's home page to locate as much of the information as possible. AND: Always include the date you accessed the source, as the web remains ever fluid and changing.

- Author (or editor, compiler, translator), last name first.
- Title of the work, in quotation marks if it is part of a site, in italics if it is a complete and separate work, such as an online novel.
- Facts of publication of the print version if the item was originally published in print.
- Title of the website, in italics—unless it is the same as item 2 above.
- Publisher or sponsor of the site (possibly a university, company, or organization).

- Date of publication. (If none is available, use n.d.)
- Medium of publication: Web.
- Your date of access: day, month, and year.

NOTE: MLA discourages the use of URLs as a way to access a web source. URLs invite errors by both writers and readers. A search for the title of the website is both faster and safer.

Study this annotated citation as a general model:

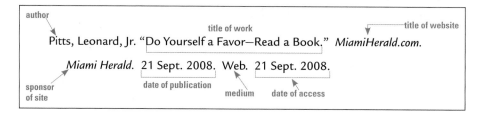

A Published Article from an Online Database

Shin, Michael S. "Redressing Wounds: Finding a Legal Framework to Remedy

Racial Disparities in Medical Care." *California Law Review* 90.6 (2002):

2047–2100. *JSTOR.* Web. 10 Sept. 2008.

Kumar, Sanjay. "Scientists Accuse Animal Rights Activists of Stifling Research."

British Medical Journal 23 Nov. 2002: 1192. *EBSCOhost.* Web. 12 Sept. 2008.

No posting date is used with databases of printed articles. Postings are ongoing.

An Article from a Reference Source

"Prohibition." *Encyclopaedia Britannica Online.* Encyclopaedia Britannica, 2007.

Web. 16 July 2008.

An Online News Source

Associated Press. "Parents: Work Hinders Quality Time with Kids." *CNN.com.*

Cable News Network. 31 July 2003. Web. 31 July 2003.

An Article in an Online Magazine

Kinsley, Michael. "Politicians Lie. Numbers Don't." *Slate.com.* Washington Post

Company. 16 Sept. 2008. Web. 21 Sept. 2008.

A Poem from a Scholarly Project

> Keats, John. "Ode to a Nightingale." *Poetical Works*. 1884. *Bartleby.com: Great*
>
> *Books*. Ed. Steven van Leeuwen. Web. 2 Oct. 2008.

Information from a Government Site

> United States Department of Health and Human Services. "The 2008 HHS
>
> Poverty Guidelines." 23 Jan. 2008. Web. 23 Sept. 2008.

Information from a Professional Site

> "Music Instruction Aids Verbal Memory." APA Press Release. Reporter: Agnes
>
> S. Chan. *APA Online*. American Psychological Association. 27 July 2003. Web.
>
> 16 Sept. 2008.

Information from a Professional Home Page or Blog

> Sullivan, Andrew. "America: The Global Pioneer of Torture." *The Daily Dish*.
>
> The Atlantic Monthly Group. 14 Sept. 2008. Web. 23 Sept. 2008.

For information from an untitled personal home page, use the label "Home page" (but not in italics or quotation marks).

Forms for Other Print and Nonprint Sources

The materials in this section, although often important to research projects, do not always lend themselves to documentation by the forms illustrated above. Follow the basic order of author, title, facts of publication, and medium of publication as much as possible. Add more information as needed to make the citation clear and useful to a reader.

An Article Published in Print and on CD or DVD

> Detweiler, Richard A. "Democracy and Decency on the Internet." *Chronicle of*
>
> *Higher Education* 28 June 1996: A40. *General Periodicals Ondisc. UMI-*
>
> *ProQuest*. Apr. 1997. CD.

A Work or Part of a Work on CD-ROM, DVD-ROM, Etc.

> Eseiolonis, Karyn. "Georgio de Chirico's *Mysterious Bathers*." *A Passion for Art:*
>
> *Renoir, Cezanne, Matisse and Dr. Barnes*. Corbis Productions, 1995. CD.

Kloss, William. "Donatello and Padua." *Great Artists of the Italian Renaissance*.

DVD. Chantilly, VA: The Teaching Company, 2004.

An Audio (or Video) from a Website

Vachss, Andrew. "Dead and Gone." Interview by Bill Thompson. Aired on *Eye*

on Books, 24 Oct. 2000. *The Zero*. Home page. Web. 25 Sept. 2008.

A Recording

Stein, Joseph. *Fiddler on the Roof*. Jerry Bock, composer. Original-Cast

Recording with Zero Mostel. RCA, LSO-1093. 1964. LP.

The conductor and/or performers help identify a specific recording.

Plays or Concerts

Mourning Becomes Electra. By Eugene O'Neill. Shakespeare Theater.

Washington, DC. 16 May 1997. Performance.

Principal actors, singers, musicians, and/or the director can be added as appropriate.

A Television or Radio Program

"Breakthrough: Television's Journal of Science and Medicine." PBS series

hosted by Ron Hendren. 10 June 1997. Television.

An Interview

Plum, Kenneth. Personal interview. 5 Mar. 2012.

A Lecture

Bateson, Mary Catherine. "Crazy Mixed-Up Families." Northern Virginia

Community College, 26 Apr. 1997. Lecture.

An Unpublished Letter or E-mail

Usick, Patricia. Message to the author. 26 June 2005. E-mail.

Maps and Charts

Hampshire and Dorset. Map. Kent, UK: Geographers' A–Z, n.d. Print.

Cartoons and Advertisements

Halleyscope. "Halleyscopes Are for Night Owls." Advertisement. *Natural
History* Dec. 1985: 15. Print.

United Airlines Advertisement. ESPN. 8 Aug. 2008. Television.

A Published Dissertation

Brotton, Joyce D. *Illuminating the Present Through Literary Dialogism: From the
Reformation Through Postmodernism.* Diss. George Mason U, 2002. Ann
Arbor: UMI, 2002. Print.

Government Documents

United States. Senate. Committee on Energy and Natural Resources.
Subcommittee on Energy Research and Development. *Advanced Reactor
Development Program: Hearing.* Washington: GPO, 24 May 1988. Print.

---. Environmental Protection Agency. *The Challenge of the Environment: A
Primer on EPA's Statutory Authority.* Washington: GPO, 1972. Print.

If the author is not given, cite the name of the government first followed by
the name of the department or agency. If you cite more than one document
published by the same government, use the standard three hyphens followed by a period. If you cite a second document prepared by the EPA, use
another three hyphens and period. Abbreviate the U.S. Government Printing
Office: GPO.

If the author is known, follow this pattern:

Geller, William. *Deadly Force.* U.S. Dept. of Justice National Institute of Justice
Crime File Study Guide. Washington: Dept. of Justice, n.d. Print.

Legal Documents

U.S. Const. Art. 1, sec. 3. Print.

The Constitution is referred to by article and section. Abbreviations are used.
Do not use italics.

When citing a court case, give the name of the case, the volume, name, and
page of the report cited, and the date. Italicize the name of the case in your text
but not in the Works Cited.

Turner v. Arkansas. 407 U.S. 366. 1972. Print.

AUTHOR/YEAR OR APA STYLE

The *author/year system* identifies a source by placing the author's last name and the publication year of the source within parentheses at the point in the text where the source is cited. The in-text citations are supported by complete citations in a list of sources at the end of the paper. Most disciplines in the social sciences, biological sciences, and earth sciences use some version of the author/year style. The guidelines given here follow the style of the *Publication Manual of the American Psychological Association* (6th ed., 2010).

APA Style: In-Text Citations

The simplest parenthetical reference can be presented in one of three ways:

1. Place the year of publication within parentheses immediately following the author's name in the text.

    In a typical study of preference for motherese, Fernald (1985) used an

    operant auditory preference procedure.

Within the same paragraph, additional references to the source do not need to repeat the year, if the researcher clearly establishes that the same source is being cited.

Because the speakers were unfamiliar subjects, Fernald's work eliminates the

possibility that it is the mother's voice per se that accounts for the preference.

2. If the author is not mentioned in the text, place the author's last name followed by a comma and the year of publication within parentheses after the borrowed information.

The majority of working women are employed in jobs that are at least

75 percent female (Lawrence & Matsuda, 1997).

3. Cite a specific passage by providing the page, chapter, or figure number following the borrowed material. *Always* give specific page references for quoted material.

- A brief quotation:

    Deuzen-Smith (1988) believes that counselors must be involved with clients and "deeply interested in piecing the puzzle of life together" (p. 29).

- A quotation in display form:

Bartlett (1932) explains the cyclic process of perception:

Suppose I am making a stroke in a quick game, such as tennis or cricket.

How I make the stroke depends on the relating of certain new experiences, most of them visual, to other immediately preceding visual experiences, and to my posture, or balance of posture, at the moment. (p. 201)

Indent a block quotation five spaces from the left margin, do not use quotation marks, and double-space throughout. To show a new paragraph within the block quotation, indent the first line of the new paragraph an additional five spaces. Note the placing of the year after the author's name, and the page number at the end of the direct quotation.

More complicated in-text citations should be handled as follows:

Two Authors, Mentioned in the Text

Kuhl and Meltzoff (1984) tested 4- to 5-month-olds in an experiment . . .

Two Authors, Not Mentioned in the Text

. . . but are unable to show preference in the presence of two mismatched

modalities (e.g., a face and a voice; see Kuhl & Meltzoff, 1984).

Give both authors' last names each time you refer to the source. Connect their names with "and" in the text. Use an ampersand (&) in the parenthetical citation.

More Than Two Authors

For works coauthored by three, four, or five people, provide all last names in the first reference to the source. Thereafter, cite only the first author's name followed by "et al."

> As Price-Williams, Gordon, and Ramirez have shown (1969), . . .

OR

> Studies of these children have shown (Price-Williams, Gordon, & Ramirez,
>
> 1969) . . .

THEN

> Price-Williams et al. (1969) also found that . . .

If a source has six or more authors, use only the first author's last name followed by "et al." every time the source is cited.

Corporate Authors

In general, spell out the name of a corporate author each time it is used. If a corporate author has well-known initials, the name can be abbreviated after the first citation.

FIRST IN-TEXT CITATION:	(National Institutes of Health [NIH], 1989)
SUBSEQUENT CITATIONS:	(NIH, 1989)

Two or More Works Within the Same Parentheses

When citing more than one work by the same author in a parenthetical reference, use the author's name only once and arrange the years mentioned in order, thus:

> Several studies of ego identity formation (Marcia, 1966, 1983) . . .

When an author, or the same group of coauthors, has more than one work published in the same year, distinguish the works by adding the letters *a, b, c,* and so on, as needed, to the year. Give the last name only once, but repeat the year, each one with its identifying letter; thus:

> Several studies (Smith, 1990a, 1990b, 1990c) . . .

When citing several works by different authors within the same parentheses, list the authors alphabetically; alphabetize by the first author when citing coauthored works. Separate authors or groups of coauthors with semicolons, thus:

> Although many researchers (Archer & Waterman, 1983; Grotevant, 1983;
>
> Grotevant & Cooper, 1986; Sabatelli & Mazor, 1985) study identity
>
> formation . . .

Personal Communication

Cite information obtained via interview, phone, letter, and e-mail communication.

> According to Sandra Haun (personal interview, September 7, 2008) . . .

Because readers cannot retrieve information from these personal sources, do *not* include a citation in your list of references.

APA STYLE: PREPARING A LIST OF REFERENCES

Every source cited parenthetically in your paper needs a complete bibliographic citation. These complete citations are placed on a separate page (or pages) after the text of the paper and before any appendices included in the paper. Sources are arranged alphabetically, and the first page is titled "References." Begin each source flush with the left margin and indent second and subsequent lines five spaces. Double-space throughout the list of references. Follow these rules for alphabetizing:

1. Organize two or more works by the same author, or the same group of coauthors, chronologically.

   Beck, A. T. (1991).

   Beck, A. T. (1993).

2. Place single-author entries before multiple-author entries when the first of the multiple authors is the same as the single author.

   Grotevant, H. D. (1983).

   Grotevant, H. D., & Cooper, C. R. (1986).

3. Organize multiple-author entries that have the same first author but different second or third authors alphabetically by the name of the second author or third and so on.

   Gerbner, G., & Gross, L.

   Gerbner, G., Gross, L., Jackson-Beeck, M., Jeffries-Fox, S., & Signorielli, N.

   Gerbner, G., Gross, L., Morgan, M., & Signorielli, N.

4. Organize two or more works by the same author(s) published in the same year alphabetically by title.

Form for Books

A book citation contains these elements in this form:

author	date	title	place of publication	publisher

Seligman, (M. E. P.) (1991). *Learned optimism.* New York: Knopf.

Authors

Give all authors' names, last name first, and initials. Separate authors with commas, use the ampersand (&) before the last author's name, and end with a period. For edited books, place the abbreviation "Ed." or "Eds." in parentheses following the last editor's name.

Date of Publication

Place the year of publication in parentheses followed by a period.

Title

Capitalize only the first word of the title and of the subtitle, if there is one, and any proper nouns. Italicize the title and end with a period. Place additional information such as number of volumes or an edition in parentheses after the title, before the period.

> Burleigh, N. (2007). *Mirage: Napoleon's scientists and the unveiling of Egypt.*

Publication Information

Cite the city of publication; add the state (using the Postal Service abbreviation) or country if necessary to avoid confusion; then give the publisher's name, after a colon, eliminating unnecessary terms such as *Publisher, Co.,* and *Inc.* End the citation with a period.

> Mitchell, J.V. (Ed.). (1985). *The ninth mental measurements yearbook.* Lincoln:
>
> University of Nebraska Press.
>
> National Institute of Drug Abuse. (1993, April 13). *Annual national high school*
>
> *senior survey.* Rockville, MD: Author.
>
> Newton, D. E. (1996). *Violence and the media.* Santa Barbara, CA: ABC-Clio.

Give a corporate author's name in full. When the organization is both author and publisher, place the word *Author* after the place of publication.

Form for Articles

An article citation contains these elements in this form:

author	date	title of article	title of journal

Changeaux, J.P. (1993). Chemical signaling in the brain. *Scientific American,*

volume 269, 58–62. page

Date of Publication

Place the year of publication for articles in scholarly journals in parentheses, followed by a period. For articles in newspapers and popular magazines, give the year followed by month and day (if appropriate).

> (1997, March).

Title of Article

Capitalize only the title's first word, the first word of any subtitle, and any proper nouns. Place any necessary descriptive information in square brackets immediately after the title.

> Scott, S. S. (1984, December 12). Smokers get a raw deal [Letter to the Editor].

Publication Information

Cite the title of the journal in full, capitalizing according to conventions for titles. Italicize the title and follow it with a comma. Give the volume number, italicized, followed by a comma, and then inclusive page numbers followed by a period. *If* a journal begins each issue with a new page 1, then also cite the issue number in parentheses immediately following the volume number. Do not use "p." or "pp." before page numbers when citing articles from scholarly journals; do use "p." or "pp." in citations to newspaper and magazine articles.

> Martin, C. L., Wood, C. H., & Little, J. K. (1990). The development of gender
>
> stereotype components. *Child Development, 61,* 1891–1904.
>
> Leakey, R. (2000, April/May). Extinctions past and present. *Time,* p. 35.

An Article or Chapter in an Edited Book

> Goodall, J. (1993). Chimpanzees—bridging the gap. In P. Cavalieri & P. Singer
>
> (Eds.), *The great ape project: Equality beyond humanity* (pp. 10–18). New
>
> York: St. Martin's.

Cite the author(s), date, and title of the article or chapter. Then cite the name(s) of the editor(s) in signature order after "In," followed by "Ed." or "Eds." in parentheses; the title of the book; the inclusive page numbers of the article or chapter, in parentheses, followed by a period. End with the city of publication and the publisher of the book.

A Report

> U.S. Merit Systems Protection Board. (1988). *Sexual harassment in the federal*
>
> *workplace: An update.* Washington, DC: U.S. Government Printing Office.

Form for Electronic Sources

As a minimum, an APA reference for any type of Internet source should include the following information: a document title or description, the date of publication, a way to access the document online, and, when possible, an author name.

When the Internet address (URL) is likely to be stable, you can cite that address. For example: www.nytimes.com. However, a good source that you find during your research may not be found later by your readers with the URL that you used. APA recommends, therefore, that such sources be documented with the item's DOI (digital object identifier) instead of its URL.

Do not place URLs within angle brackets (< >). Do not place a period at the end of the URL, even though it concludes the citation. If you have to break a URL at the end of a line, break only after a slash. Introduce the URL at the end of the citation this way: Retrieved from www.nytimes.com

DOIs are a series of numbers and letters that provide a link to a specific item, and this link does not change with time. Although DOIs are often on the first page of a document, they can, at times, be hard to locate. APA prefers that you always choose a source's DOI over its URL, if you can find it. Place the DOI at the end of the citation, and introduce the number thus: doi: [number]. Do not end the citation with a period.

Here are a few examples of citations for Internet sources:

Journal Article Retrieved Online, with DOI Information

Habernas, Jurgen. (2006). Political communication in media society.

Communication Theory 16(4), 411–426. doi: 10.1111/

j.1468-2885.2006.00280.x

Gardiner, K., Herault, Y., Lott, I., Antonarakis, S., Reeves, R., & Dierssen, M.

(2010). Down syndrome: From understanding the neurobiology to ther-

apy. Journal of Neuroscience 30(45), 14943–14945. doi: 10.1523/

JNEUROSCI.3728-10.2010

Electronic Daily Newspaper Article Available by Search

Schwartz, J. (2002, September 13). Air pollution con game. Washington Times.

Retrieved from http://www.washtimes.com

Journal Article Available from a Periodical Database

Note that no URL is necessary; just provide the name of the database.

Dixon, B. (2001, December). Animal emotions. Ethics & the Environment, 6(2),

22. Retrieved from Academic Search Premier database/EBSCOhost

Research Databases.

U.S. Government Report on a Government Website

U.S. General Accounting Office. (2002, March). Identity theft: Prevalence and

cost appear to be growing. Retrieved from http://www.consumer.gov/

idtheft/reports/gao-d02363.pdf

Cite a message posted to a newsgroup or electronic mailing list in the reference list. Cite an e-mail from one person to another *only* in the essay, not in the list of references.

SAMPLE STUDENT ESSAY IN APA STYLE

The following student essay illustrates APA style. Use 1-inch margins and double-space throughout, including any block quotations. Block quotations should be indented *five* spaces from the left margin (in contrast to the ten spaces required by MLA style). Observe the following elements: title page, running head, abstract, author/year in-text citations, subheadings within the text, and a list of references.

APA Style

Note placement of
running head and
page number.

Running Head: Depression and Marital Status 1

Sample title page
for a paper in
APA style.

The Relationship Between Depression and Marital Status

Carissa Ervine

Sociology of Mental Disorder: SOC 4714

Virginia Tech University

Depression and Marital Status 2

Abstract

Many studies have examined the relationship between mental disorders, specifically depression, and marital status. From the studies, several theories have developed to explain this relationship. An examination of the studies' findings and of the theories tested demonstrates that no one theory accounts for all patterns of marital status and mental health or disorder.

Papers in APA style usually begin with an abstract.

APA Style

Depression and Marital Status 3

Many studies have evaluated the relationship between mental disorders, more specifically depression, and marital status. These studies consistently find that people who are divorced or have never been married have more depressive symptoms than those who are married. This paper explores both the causes of and the theories that seek to explain these findings.

Definition and Description of Depression

Depression is a mood disorder in which individuals experience loss of interest or of pleasure in nearly all activities. They feel extreme sadness, despair, and hopelessness. These feelings lead to a lack of motivation to do simple, daily tasks. Many people with depression also have low self-esteem. According to the *Diagnostic and Statistical Manual of Mental Disorders* (DSM), a person must experience at least four of the symptoms listed in order to have depression: changes in appetite or weight, sleep, or psychomotor activity; decreased energy; feelings of worthlessness or guilt; difficulty concentrating or making decisions; or recurrent thoughts of death or suicide ideas or attempts.

Prevalence of Depression According to Marital Status

Throughout epidemiological research, studies have consistently shown that those who are married have fewer depressed symptoms than those who are not married (Kim & McKenry, 2005; Wade & Pevalin, 2004), and many studies have sought to find the reasons. Some think it is because marriage offers certain benefits; therefore, married people have better overall health and less depression (Kim & McKenry, 2002). When a marriage dissolves, so does that person's mental health. Marital disruption causes a significant increase in depression, even three years after a divorce (Aseltine & Kessler, 1993). It has also been found that people who are depressed before marriage have improved mental health once they are married (Lucas et al., 2003). Those who do get divorced have more depressive symptoms that may or may not disappear over time (Kim & McKenry, 2002; Lucas et al., 2003). Kim and McKenry (2002) demonstrate, though, that getting remarried after a divorce leads to a decrease in depressive symptoms.

Subheadings are often used in papers in the social sciences.

Depression and Marital Status 4

Studies have also evaluated whether people in marriages were happier because those who were not married, or who became divorced, got selected out of marriage due to psychological problems that make them undesirable partners. This idea is referred to as the social selection theory. Four years prior to getting divorced, people show higher rates of psychological problems than those who stayed married, although those who were widowed did not (Wade & Pevalin, 2004). People who get married and stay married have fewer depressive symptoms and better psychological well-being years before they ever got married (Lucas et al., 2003).

Some researchers assert that marriage itself is good for mental health, but that it is the quality of the marriage that matters. High marital stress causes depressive symptoms that tend to dissipate after divorce (Aseltine & Kessler, 1993; Johnson & Wu, 2002). Gove, Hughes, and Style (1983) demonstrated that marital quality and happiness are strong predictors of mental health. Actually, remaining unmarried can be more beneficial to one's psychological health than being in a continuously unhappy marriage.

Use ampersand within parentheses; use "and" in sentences.

Last, some studies suggest that marriage does not increase psychological well-being at all. These studies suggest that life satisfaction does change when major events ensue, and then people gradually adapt over time until their psychological health reaches their baseline (Lucas et al., 2003). Initially, people react strongly to both good and bad events, but as time passes, their emotional reactions lessen, and they return to normal (Lucas et al., 2003). Booth and Amato (1991) found that before a divorce occurs there is a rise in stress, but then stress levels return to normal two years after the divorce.

Evaluation of the Evidence

All these findings play some part in explaining why the married tend to have fewer depressive symptoms than their counterparts, but some studies were better conducted than others and used longitudinal data to explain

Depression and Marital Status 5

some of the differences found. The fact that married people have better health because they get benefits from marriage seems to be the best explanation. In many instances, the social selection perspective did not hold up. For example, some studies showed that the psychological health of divorced persons improved once they remarried (Johnson & Wu, 2002). If the selection perspective held, those who remarried would not likely experience a decrease in depressive symptoms. The selection perspective would support the idea that those selected out of marriage would not even be likely to remarry. Johnson and Wu's (2002) results consistently show that marriage is better for people because of the benefits they receive from it.

Frech and Williams (2007) found that those who were depressed before marriage had a decrease in depressive symptoms once they were married, supporting the idea that marriage offers benefits. This may occur because marriage provides economic and psychosocial benefits. Those who are married may have two incomes, resulting in less stress over financial matters. Marriage also offers day-to-day companionship, decreasing social isolation (Frech & Williams, 2007). These benefits do not support the fact that marital quality matters, because they are based on marital status per se.

Some researchers who favor the social selection theory believe that high rates of distress prior to a divorce indicate psychological problems in the individual (Wade & Pevalin, 2004), although this may not necessarily be the case. Higher stress levels are common in the years preceding a divorce. After all, divorce is not a discrete event; many problems lead up to it. Higher levels of distress in the years before a divorce may reflect anticipation of the marital disruption (Mastekaasa, 1995). While marriage can bring many benefits, the quality of the marriage is important. High stress levels because of an unhappy marriage are likely to explain the higher stress levels leading up to divorce.

Booth and Amato (1991) also found a pre-divorce rise in stress, but then they also found that levels of stress in the individuals return to normal two years after the divorce. While this finding does appear to challenge the selection perspective, it is not consistent with many other findings that marriage is better for psychological well-being. Johnson and Wu (2002) used the same waves of people in their study; they did not find that those remaining divorced experienced a decrease in depressive symptoms over time. Nor did satisfaction levels return to the original baselines after divorce. This difference in findings is likely to be caused by a difference in the number of times the participants were studied. Booth and Amato studied their respondents only every three years, whereas Johnson and Wu studied them more often. Johnson and Wu did not find that those remaining divorced experienced a decrease in depressive symptoms over time. Lucas (2005) argues that although some adaption does occur, normally it is not complete. Many people are likely to establish new baselines of psychological well-being that are slightly lower than they were before they were divorced (Lucas et al., 2003).

While many studies find fewer depressive symptoms in married people, discrepancies in explanations still exist. The strongest evidence indicates that married people have less depression because marriage offers many benefits and social supports that the unmarried do not have. But marital quality is just as important as marital status, and this can account for why distress levels go up right before divorce occurs. A bad marriage creates stress, and distress levels increase because of this, not because of poor psychological health that an individual brings to a marriage.

Review of Theories Relating to Marital Status and Depression

As noted, several theories explain why people who are married have better mental health than those who are not. First, the social selection theory asserts that those who are married have better psychological well-being than those who do not and that the unmarried have been "selected" out of marriage. That is, those who aren't married have more mental illness, such as depression, so they are not considered to be suitable mates (Johnson & Wu, 2002). These people either never marry or get married and then divorce. Their psychological characteristics predispose them to divorce (Mastekaasa, 1992).

The crisis theory asserts that having a divorce is a life crisis that temporarily changes mental health. People encounter many stressors while going through a divorce. One of these is the adjustment to role changes. Once the transition is completed, stress levels go down and psychological well-being returns to normal (Booth & Amato, 1991). Lucas et al. (2003) also found that after the marital transition of divorce, people adapted to their new set of circumstances. Depression went down and their psychological well-being returned.

Last, role theory asserts that the stress that the divorced experience is chronic. The new social role they must take on will cause them higher levels of distress because they have less social support, more economic responsibilities, and possibly more stress associated with raising children alone (Johnson & Wu, 2002). This theory also asserts that these chronic stress levels will not go down as long as the divorced remain single. If a divorced person decides to remarry, then his or her stress levels begin to dissipate because there are now fewer stressful roles to fulfill. The social causation perspective also ties into this. With fewer stressful roles to take on, married people can enjoy many of the benefits that marriage offers. When a marriage dissolves, however, they no longer have these benefits.

Evaluation of Theories

Role theory gives a good explanation of why married people have better psychological well-being and fewer depressive symptoms. It is well-known that stress increases the likelihood that someone will have a mental illness. It is also true that levels of depression increase when marital disruption occurs (Wade & Pevalin, 2004). The divorced are used to having a partner who can offer benefits such as greater financial security and a strong social network. With fewer resources to draw upon and more roles to take on, the divorced person is susceptible to depressive symptoms (Kim & McKerry, 2002). However, symptoms of distress and depression do decrease once a divorced person remarries and undergoes another role transition. With the new marriage, the

Depression and Marital Status 8

number of required roles decreases and the increased resources of the new marriage ease depression.

In contrast, crisis theory asserts that depressive symptoms and distress decrease with time after a divorce. But crisis theory does not seem to hold up, since studies demonstrate that marriage and remarriage increase psychological well-being. The fact that remarriage increases psychological well-being also contradicts the social selection perspective. If social selection did occur, people would be selected out from remarrying at all. None of these theories, however, effectively examines the effect of marital quality, an issue important to understanding the relationship between depression and marital status.

The best conclusion is that no one theory is complex enough to explain the relationship between marital status and mental health. It is likely that all theories have valid points and that the reason married people experience better mental health stems from a combination of causes. Further research should focus on finding a theory that can account for more, if not all, of the forces shaping the mental health of married people.

Depression and Marital Status 9

References

Aseltine, R. H., & Kessler, R.C. (1993). Marital disruption and depression in a
community sample. *Journal of Health and Social Behavior, 34,* 237–251.

Booth, A., & Amato, P. (1991). Divorce and psychological stress. *Journal of
Health and Social Behavior, 32,* 396–407.

Frech, A., & Williams, K. (2007). Depression and the psychological benefits of
entering marriage. *Journal of Health and Social Behavior, 48,* 149–163.

Gove, W. R., Hughes, M., & Style, B. S. (1983). Does marriage have positive
effects on the psychological well-being of the individual? *Journal of Health
and Social Behavior, 24,* 122–131.

Johnson, D. R., & Wu, J. (2002). An empirical test of crisis, social selection, and role
explanations of the relationship between marital disruption and
psychological distress: A pooled time-series analysis of four wave panel data.
Journal of Marriage and Family, 64, 211–224.

Kim, K. H., & McKenry, P. C. (2002). The relationship between marriage and
psychological well-being. *Journal of Family Issues, 23*(8), 885–911.

Lucas, R. E. (2005). Time does not heal all wounds: A longitudinal study of
reaction and adaption to divorce. *Psychological Science, 16*(12), 945–950.

Lucas, R. E., Clark, A. E., Georgellis, Y., & Diener, E. (2003). Reexamining
adaptation and the set point model of happiness: Reactions to changes
in marital status. *Journal of Personality and Social Psychology, 84*(3),
527–538.

Mastekaasa, A. (1992). Marriage and psychological well-being: Some evidence
on selection into marriage. *Journal of Marriage and the Family, 54,*
901–911.

Mastekaasa, A. (1995). Marital dissolution and subjective distress: Panel
evidence. *European Sociological Review, 11*(20), 173–185.

Wade, T. J., & Pevalin, D. J (2004). Marital transitions and mental health. *Journal
of Health and Social Behavior, 45,* 155–170.

Title the page "References."

Double-space throughout. In each citation, indent all lines, after the first, five spaces. Note APA style in placing dates.

For two or more sources by the same author, order by the year of publication.

A Collection of Readings

This section is divided into eight chapters, each on a current topic or set of interrelated issues open to debate. The chapters contain five or six articles, or a combination of articles and visuals, to remind us that complex issues cannot be divided into simple "for" or "against" positions. This point remains true even for the chapters on a rather specific topic. It is not sound critical thinking to be simply for or against any complicated public policy issue. No one is "for" or "against" protecting our environment, for example. The debate begins with restrictions on factories (raising costs), restrictions on car manufacturers, restrictions on energy use. It is when we get into these sorts of policy decisions, and ways of funding those decisions, that people have opposing viewpoints.

Questions follow each article to aid reading, analysis, and critical responses. In addition, each chapter opens with a visual both to enjoy and consider seriously as a contribution to the ideas in the chapter. Following each opening image is a brief introduction to the chapter and several general questions to focus your thinking as you read.

CHAPTER 15

The Media: Image and Reality

READ: What is the situation? Who speaks the lines?

REASON: Who, presumably, are the guys in suits sitting in front of the desk? Who, according to Wiley, must be controlling TV scheduling?

REFLECT/WRITE: What is Wiley's view of reality shows? Do you agree? Why or why not?

Although we may not agree with Marshall McLuhan that the medium itself IS the message, we still recognize the ways that the various media influence us, touching our emotions, shaping our vision of the world, altering our lives. The essays in this chapter explore and debate the effects of film and television, music and video games, advertising, and political speech on the ways we imagine the world and then construct our lives from those images. Surely we are influenced by media images, by the "reality" they reveal to us. The questions become how extensive is the influence, given the other influences in our lives, and what, if anything, can or should we do about it?

The chapter opens with a popular medium: the cartoon. Cartoons are not just a laugh; they present a view of life and seek to shape our thinking. Powerful messages also come to us in the print media—in the form of photographs and advertisements as well as from television, video games, movies, and the Internet.

PREREADING QUESTIONS

1. How "real" are "reality" shows? Does it matter if they are scripted?
2. How accurate is our press coverage? Do media outlets around the world "see" and show the same worldview to their viewers? How do bloggers offer another useful way of seeing our world?
3. How do films reflect our world and also shape our image of that world?
4. What do the various forms of music (jazz, rock, gangsta rap) tell us about ourselves and our world? What does your music preference tell us about you?
5. How does advertising shape our images of the world? How realistic are those images? Do we want ads to be "realistic"?
6. What standards of reliability, objectivity, and fairness should be set for the media? What, if any, distortions are acceptable because they make the story more compelling?

OF LOSERS AND MOLES: YOU THINK REALITY TV JUST WRITES ITSELF? | DERRICK SPEIGHT

Derrick Speight is, as he tells us in his essay, a reality TV writer based in Los Angeles, with a dozen TV series to his credit, as story writer or supervising story producer. His scoop on the reality of reality TV shows was published in the *Washington Post*, July 24, 2005.

PREREADING QUESTIONS Do you enjoy watching reality TV shows—or know people who do? Why do you—or they—like these shows? What are the reasons usually given for enjoying these types of TV shows?

1   A couple of summers ago, I found myself living out a high school fantasy. I was running across the hot white sands of a Mexican beach in Playa del

Carmen, chasing after stunning Playboy playmate Angie Everhart. As her bright orange bikini disappeared into the Caribbean surf, I closed my eyes and smiled—then quickly snapped back to reality. I was there as a writer for ABC's "Celebrity Mole: Yucatan," and my job was to find out what Everhart was saying about the show's other beauty, former MTV VJ Ananda Lewis. Would they be dueling divas, headed for a catfight by day's end? I needed to find out. So I sighed, put on the earpiece that picked up the two women's microphones, and began taking notes.

Reality TV writers like me are at the heart of a lawsuit filed by the Writers 2
Guild of America, West about two weeks ago. On behalf of 12 such scribes, the union is charging four reality production companies and four networks with unfair labor practices, including providing pay and benefits far below those earned by writers of traditional drama and sitcoms. The suit says a lot about the rise of reality TV, a formerly disreputable format that last year contributed half of the 20 top-rated shows on TV. But in hearing about it, I imagine that people across America were asking the same question members of my own family have voiced ever since I started down this career path: "How exactly do you *write* reality? Isn't it already real?"

Yes, Grandma, it is—in all its undigested, contextless, boring glory. What 3
I do is shape that mass into something that'll make viewers want to tune in week after week. Like a journalist, I sniff out what I *think* the story will be, then craft the interviews or situations that'll draw it out. Like a paperback writer, I'm all about highlighting character and plot. Simply put, drama is the pursuit of a goal, with obstacles. Both by developing promising story lines and by pulling out the zingy moments burned in hours upon hours of ho-hum footage, reality TV writers like me—who go under various titles, including story editor and story producer—create it. As I tell my family, having a reality TV show without writers would be like having a countertop of cake ingredients but no idea how to put them together. So, yes, I consider myself a writer.

My voyage into reality TV began by accident. Seven years ago, I was new 4
to Hollywood, and sure that I was destined to direct the next film version of *Superman.* But by the time I finished my first fresh-out-of-film-school internship with DreamWorks' Mark Gordon Productions, I was both slightly peeved about not meeting Steven Spielberg and badly in need of a paying job. Luckily, a friend of a friend was looking for production assistants to work on *World's Most Amazing Videos.* Hired for roughly $400 a week (and on top of the world about it), I was quickly promoted to logger—basically the guy who looks through all the footage and makes notes on what happens and when. That led to a job at a new company, Actual Reality Pictures, which would end up completely redirecting my career.

Actual Reality is the production company of Academy Award nominee 5
R. J. Cutler, whose documentary *The War Room* followed Bill Clinton's 1992 presidential campaign. The building was an intellectual hothouse, packed with scores of Ivy League grads who loved nothing more than to ruminate over the most minuscule story points. As we worked on Cutler's latest project, a docudrama about suburban Chicago teens called *American High,* staff meetings

were virtual master classes in narrative structure. Whole walls of multicolored index cards were dedicated to the deconstruction of an episode, inviting constant rearranging until the optimal narrative was found. And through it all, Cutler, the faintly aloof, greatly admired genius among us, wandered the office hallways yelling, "What's the story?!" My job was to rummage through film footage looking to answer that question. Apparently, our process worked: *American High* went on to win an Emmy.

6   After I left Actual Reality, I would never again encounter that type of intense, academic scrutiny of story structure. I had risen through the ranks, though, from logger to story assistant to story producer, overseeing other writers. So I ended up going to work on a whole slew of reality TV shows, both Nielsen-topping and not, including *The Bachelor, The Mole, The Surreal Life, The Benefactor* and *The Biggest Loser.* On every one of them, whether I was dealing with desperately weeping single gals or former parachute pant wearer MC Hammer, the main question was always the same: "What is the story?"

7   Some of the crafting of these shows took place on set, as on "Celebrity Mole: Yucatan." While filming is taking place, writers keep track of all the issues that may arise and anticipate which will yield the strongest narrative. Teams of us are on location, assigned to different characters. The uniform: a good pen, steno notepads, an audio monitoring device (to overhear comments and conversations), a digital watch, walkie-talkies and a comfortable pair of shoes—in case anyone takes off running. We typically stand within earshot of what's being filmed, noting mumbled quips, telling looks and memorable exchanges. At the end of the day, we all regroup, compare notes and decide which stories have evolved, or are evolving. These are the situations to which we'll pay particular attention, and in the days following, we'll make sure the right interview questions are asked to round out what appear to be the prominent stories. Like nonfiction writers, we do not script lines—but if we have a hunch, we ask the right questions to follow it up.

8   Preparation of this kind is, of course, half the battle, but the magic really happens after the filming is done, in post-production. In its one- to four-week scripting phase, the story producers pinpoint scenes, moments and interviews from a mountain of VHS tapes, then structure them to tell the strongest story. After it's approved by the executive producer, this script is given to an editor, who cuts it together. Six-day workweeks and long hours are expected—and get longer midway through editing, when a decision is invariably made to change the direction of the show. As story producers, the responsibility for that reshaping falls to us. Sometimes it's for the better, but sometimes it's for worse. *The Benefactor,* for example, began as an exciting, conceptually strong show led by billionaire Mark Cuban and dubbed the "Anti-Apprentice," to contrast with the Donald Trump hit. It was quickly mired by second guessing on all our parts, and we ended up giving in to some Trumpian gimmicks. In the end, the show floundered, suffering dismal ratings and was widely perceived as the very thing it was striving not to be . . . another *Apprentice.*

The current lawsuit isn't the Writer's Guild's first attempt to reach out to 9
reality TV crew members. Since this spring, they've been on a major campaign
to unionize, gathering up union authorization cards from over 1,000 writers,
editors and producers. Despite the many logistics associated with unionizing,
at the core, I believe the WGA's gesture to be quite complimentary: By their
actions, they are recognizing us as legitimate creative contributors, I like that.
It's also a sign that they expect reality TV to be more than just a passing fad.
Reality is evolving, and I look forward to its next chapter.

Source: *Washington Post*, July 24, 2005. Reprinted by permission of the author.

QUESTIONS FOR READING

1. Who has filed a lawsuit? What is their issue?
2. What do reality TV writers "do" for reality TV shows? What do they try to find?
3. What strategies do these writers use during the filming? After the filming?
4. What do the lawsuit and unionizing attempts suggest about the future of reality TV?

QUESTIONS FOR REASONING AND ANALYSIS

5. The author gives much information about his job. Is providing information his primary purpose—or not? If not, why does he give us all of the details?
6. If this is not primarily or exclusively informative, then what is Speight's claim?
7. What is effective about Speight's opening paragraph?
8. Why does he include the information in the second half of paragraph 8?

QUESTIONS FOR REFLECTION AND WRITING

9. Are you surprised to learn about reality TV writers—and their complex jobs? Why or why not?
10. Are you shocked or disappointed in reading this essay? Why might some be disappointed?
11. Although some never watch them, many people are "hooked" on reality TV. Why? What is the appeal? Would the appeal be less if viewers understood how these shows are constructed?

ZERO DARK THIRTY AND THE NEW REALITY OF REPORTED FILMMAKING | ANN HORNADAY

Hailing from Baltimore and a graduate of Smith College, Ann Hornaday is the chief
film critic for the *Washington Post*. She has been a freelance journalist and film critic
at the *Baltimore Sun*. Hornaday was a finalist in 2008 for a Pulitzer Prize in criticism.
Her study of *Zero Dark Thirty* was published December 13, 2012.

PREREADING QUESTIONS Have you seen this movie? If so, think about some of the film's issues. What issues do you think a film critic would examine?

1   Screenwriter Mark Baol and director Kathryn Bigelow were talking about their new movie, *Zero Dark Thirty*, and they were at a loss for words for what genre it belongs to. "Interpretive journalism?" Yuck.

2   "Docu-drama," Boal suggested.

3   "That term is so reductive," Bigelow countered.

4   "But in a sense, so is taking a urinal and saying, 'This is art,'" he said.

5   "That's 'found art,'" Bigelow replied, casting her vote for the term "reported film."

6   "'Reported film' is like 'found art' to me," she said definitely. "The event happens, then it's reported on, and then there's an imagistic version of that reportage."

7   *Zero Dark Thirty*, which opens in limited release next week [December 2012], hasn't even hit theaters and already it's touched a nerve, largely because it occupies such a strange new space in the cultural sphere. In many ways the film, about the 10-year manhunt for Osama bin Laden after the attacks of Sept. 11, 2001, hews to the classical lines of a tense procedural, as a CIA analyst, played by Jessica Chastain, systematically puts together a string of leads that finally convince her the al-Qaeda leader is living in a compound in Abbottabad, Pakistan.

8   But *Zero Dark Thirty* wasn't created in the conventional way, whereby filmmakers option a series of articles or a book about the event and then dramatize

Attack on bin Laden's compound.

it for the screen. Instead Boal, a former embedded journalist who wrote the Iraq war movie *In the Valley of Elah* and won an Oscar for Bigelow's *The Hurt Locker,* did his own reporting for *Zero Dark Thirty,* interviewing military and intelligence officials and operatives with intimate knowledge of the operations that resulted in bin Laden's death in May 2011.

Because of its unconventional provenance, *Zero Dark Thirty* is arriving on   9 the scene earlier than most feature-film accounts of recent history, subverting the usual rituals by which consensus is created, by journalists, politicians and pundits, and eventually by historians and purveyors of popular culture.

The upending of the opinion-making hierarchy has sent its denizens into   10 a swivet. When he got wind of the project, House Homeland Security Committee chief Peter T. King (R-N.Y.) called for investigations into Boal's access to classified information, expressing suspicion that *Zero Dark Thirty* would be a thinly veiled endorsement of President Obama in an election year. Obama, it turns out, is barely mentioned in the film, which has no obvious partisan ax to grind. But now Boal and Bigelow are under scrutiny for their depiction of torture, which some observers think is shown as yielding crucial, high-value information in bin Laden's eventual apprehension. (The film begins with a graphic scene of a prisoner being waterboarded, an episode that doesn't yield actionable intelligence directly but possibly weakens him enough to be manipulated later.)

As *Zero Dark Thirty* has begun to be screened in previews, it's become   11 something of a policy proxy, a vehicle for debate about Bush-era detainee pro- grams, "enhanced interrogation" techniques and black sites that were ignored or never fully entertained by many Americans at the time. As Boal and Bigelow gather critics' plaudits and awards (*Zero Dark Thirty* earned four Golden Globe nominations Thursday, including best film), the movie itself has entered a fasci- nating parallel conversation—part food fight for cable-news channels desper- ate for post-election fodder, part valuable (if belated) civic debate.

"So . . . @annhornaday making Zero Dark Thirty her #1 movie of the year   12 Makes her support torture and overall evil," read a message that appeared on my Twitter feed this week, while my email inbox filled with offers to interview think-tankers and other experts on torture (who haven't seen the movie). On the MSNBC show *Hardball,* host Chris Matthews asked New York film critic David Edelstein whether terrorism can be defeated by "playing by gentle- manly rules." Edelstein hesitated. "You're asking a film critic?" he inquired incredulously.

Well, yes. With *Zero Dark Thirty,* a medium that has always occupied a   13 liminal space—between art and entertainment, realism and spectacle, history and myth—has been pushed into yet one more indeterminate category, strad- dling journalism and drama. And it's asking viewers to develop a new set of standards by which to judge and process what's on-screen—not just in terms of aesthetic, moral and entertainment values, but as a means of processing events we haven't fully come to terms with, offering perhaps the first unifying narrative of a deeply contentious period.

14   "What are the cultural criteria that get applied to this?" Boal asked last week in New York, where he joined Bigelow for a lunchtime interview. "You know how to evaluate a book, if it's *The Looming Tower* or *The Green Zone*. There's this whole set of norms you can walk [them] through. And you know how to evaluate an article."

15   For his part, he said, he wants *Zero Dark Thirty* first and foremost to be evaluated as a movie. "Hopefully you view the work as what's on the screen. Then you go outside and see how it lines up with the rest of the world. But it should start with what the work creates within you, the emotional, intellectual, moral experience."

16   If he wants *Zero Dark Thirty* to be judged simply as a movie, then why did Boal go to the trouble to do so much original reporting? "Because it's new and it's cool and it's interesting," he said simply.

17   For her part, Bigelow—who won best picture and best director Oscars two years ago for *The Hurt Locker*, about a bomb technician in Iraq—*Zero Dark Thirty* provided her an opportunity to engage in the kind of visceral, immersive, action-driven filmmaking she's spent a career refining, often within the context of mostly male subcultures. The facts that Boal amassed regarding the bin Laden mission, she said, created "longitudinal and latitudinal guidelines" that she was "thrilled" to work with.

18   "You're working within these parameters that are kind of freeing and exciting," she said, because you're trying to bring something to life to the best of your ability and make it live and breathe and feel credible."

19   Much like *The Hurt Locker*, *Zero Dark Thirty* puts viewers right into the action, in this case a dizzying needle-in-a-haystack search for the courier who led the CIA to bin Laden, and later the SEAL raid, which is reenacted in virtually real time. But rather than engaging in we-got-him triumphalism, Bigelow allows for ambiguity, with conflicting emotions playing out on the faces of Chastain and co-star Jason Clarke, who plays an agency interrogator.

20   The torture scenes, while ugly and graphic, aren't presented in neat, ends-justify-means terms. It's the day-to-day tradecraft that's shown to be more important in the intelligence hunt, as CIA operatives use deception, misdirection and resources to pursue and woo their leads. (Perhaps the most crucial piece of information leading Chastain's character to bin Laden is a name that a colleague finds buried in old files; a crucial telephone number is obtained by buying a Lamborghini for a source.) If *Zero Dark Thirty* justifies anything, it's not torture but data mining, which might be sexy enough for *Moneyball* but not for *Hardball*.

21   If *Zero Dark Thirty* makes an editorial statement, Boal and Bigelow say, it's in an operative's line about "the big breaks and the little people who make them happen." In many ways, they're paying tribute to the kind of career officials and government bureaucrats that are so often ridiculed and scorned outside Washington. Like *Lincoln*, *Zero Dark Thirty* celebrates process, professionalism and continuity of government that transcends partisan bickering and policy changes.

22   "Bin Laden wasn't killed by superheroes," Boal said. "These are people doing their job, and in a sense that's extraordinary and in a sense it's not."

With luck, when audiences finally get to see *Zero Dark Thirty*, that nuance 23 won't be lost on them—even as they become swept up in the film's taut suspense (especially in the final 30 minutes). Rather than a simplistic, torture-good, terrorists-bad argument, they'll find an absorbing, richly textured portrayal of a pivotal chapter of American life, one that's not just clarifying but cathartic.

Is it problematic that, on the way to condensing a secret 10-year history 24 into a 2 1/2-hour film, *Zero Dark Thirty* takes some liberties with characters, timing and particular events? Will American viewers emerge feeling more ambivalent than certain about everything done on their behalf during the Bush administration and beyond? Are we willing—at the box office and through repeated viewing—to endorse *Zero Dark Thirty* as a metonym for the war on terror, the same way we've accepted *All the President's Men* as a symbolic catch-all for Watergate, which was a much larger and more complex episode than two dogged reporters bringing down a president?

We'd better be. In an era when legacy media are on the ropes and genu- 25 ine investigative reporting is becoming increasingly rare, journalism will surely keep migrating into other popular forms, creating a new audience of citizen-spectators. At least Boal hopes so: Earlier this week he announced plans to form Page One Productions, through which he'll work with reporters to create TV and feature films based on their stories.

"If news can be entertainment, which it is on certain cable channels, why 26 can't it be a two-way street?" he asked rhetorically when we met. "I can tell you that if movies don't do it, video games are certainly going to." Coming soon to a theater near you: "Unmanned Drone Strikes: The Movie." Grab some popcorn and let another argument begin.

QUESTIONS FOR READING

1. What is unconventional about the way the film was created?
2. What political debates have been connected to the film?
3. How does the scriptwriter want the movie to be judged?
4. What is Hornaday's perception of the movie's message?

QUESTIONS FOR REASONING AND ANALYSIS

5. Hornaday begins with debates by Boal and Bigelow over how to characterize *Zero Dark Thirty*. How does this opening aid the author's approach to the film?
6. Why is the problem of classification significant? What do we gain from classifying movies—and books and art works?
7. What is Hornaday's primary purpose in writing? What is her claim?

QUESTIONS FOR REFLECTION AND WRITING

8. What kinds of moviegoers will find this a useful guide? What moviegoers might be less helped by Hornaday? Why?

9. If you haven't seen the film, do these analyses and debates make you want to see it? Why or why not?

10. How did *Zero Dark Thirty* fare with the Oscar awards in February 2013? What were the reactions to the results regarding this film? Do some research and see how all of the issues and debates played out for *Zero Dark Thirty*.

WHAT'S UP DOC? A BLOODY OUTRAGE, THAT'S WHAT | KATHERINE ELLISON

A Pulitzer Prize–winning former foreign correspondent for Knight-Ridder Newspapers, Katherine Ellison is the author of four nonfiction books, including *The Mommy Brain: How Motherhood Makes Us Smarter* (2005) and *Buzz: A Year of Paying Attention* (2010). Her reaction to violent Internet cartoons appeared on October 23, 2005.

PREREADING QUESTIONS Do you use the Internet for "fun": games, porn, violent cartoons? Do you see any problems with such Internet sites?

1   The other day I found my 6-year-old son watching an Internet cartoon called "Happy Tree Friends."

2   Purple daisies danced, high-pitched voices sang and animals with heart-shaped noses waved cheerily. But then the music changed, and a previously merry green bear, wearing dog tags and camouflage, suffered an apparent psychotic breakdown.

3   *Crrrrrack!!* went the neck of a purple badger, as the bear snapped off its head. Blood splashed and continued flowing as the bear gleefully garroted a hedgehog, then finished off a whimpering squirrel already impaled on metal spikes by placing a hand grenade in its paw.

4   Joshua turned to me with a sheepish grin. He clearly had a sense that I wasn't happy about his new friends, but he couldn't have known what I was really thinking. Which was this: I'm a longtime journalist who reveres the First Amendment, and I live

in California's liberal bastion of Marin County. Yet I would readily skip my next yoga class to march with right-wing fundamentalists in a cultural war against "Happy Tree Friends."

Just when parents thought we knew who our electronic enemies were— the shoot-'em-up video games, the TVs hawking trans fats, the pedophile e-mail stalkers and teenage-boobs Web sites—here comes this new swamp-thing mass entertainment: the Internet "Flash cartoon," pared down to pure shock value. Its music and animation are tuned to the Teletubbies set—that's its "joke." Its faux warning, "Cartoon Violence: Not for Small Children or Big Babies" is pure come-on—for those who can read. And it's easy to watch over and over again, reinforcing its empathy-dulling impact. That makes it particularly harmful to young psyches, UCLA neuroscientist Marco Iacoboni told me, because children are prompted to copy what they see—especially what they see over and over again. "Not only do you get exposed and desensitized; you're primed, facilitated, almost invited to act that way," maintains Iacoboni, whose expertise in the brain dynamics of imitation makes him an outspoken critic of media mayhem.

"Happy Tree Friends" appears tailor-made to sneak under the radar of blocking software (which can't filter images), unless parents are somehow Internet-savvy enough to know about the site and specifically ban it in advance. And it's certainly suited for the kind of viral contagion that caught up with my 6-year-old, who learned of the site from his 9-year-old brother, who first saw it over the shoulder of a teenage summer camp counselor.

But the bottom line is, well, the bottom line. In its web-cartoon class, "Happy Tree Friends" is a humongous moneymaker, as irresistible to big advertisers as it is to 6-year-olds. At last count, the site was drawing 15 million unique viewers a month, reaping $300,000 or more in ads for each new episode. It recently snagged a place on cable TV, while spawning DVDs, trademark mints, T-shirts and, inevitably, a planned video game.

Internet cartoons had their defining moment with the hilarious "This Land Is Your Land" 2004 election-year parody, featuring George W. Bush calling John Kerry a "liberal wiener" and Kerry calling Bush a "right-wing nut job" to the famous Woody Guthrie tune. By then, the beaten-down Web ad industry was already starting to ride a dramatic recovery, thanks to burgeoning new content and the increasing prevalence of high-quality, high-speed connections. The trend has brought some truly interesting material—and also such savage fare as the graphic cartoon "Gonads & Strife" and another inviting you to repeatedly electrocute a gerbil in a light socket. The Bush-Kerry feature by some reports was the most popular cartoon ever. "Happy Tree Friends," now in its fifth, most successful, year [2005] may well be the most lucrative.

Its narrative is as primitive as its business plan. In every episode, the cute creatures are introduced, after which something awful happens to them, either by gruesome accident, or at the paws of the psychopathic bear. The wordless content appeals to a global audience, enhancing an already remarkably efficient delivery system for advertising. There's a running ad before each episode, while banners flash below and beside the cartoons.

10   The show itself reportedly began as a potential ad—ironically, *against* media violence according to Kenn Navarro, its co-creator. Navarro came up with the idea while designing an eight-second spot for an educational company, to illustrate what kids *shouldn't* be watching. Indeed, 30 years of extensive research underscores the link between TV violence and increased violent behavior among viewers. One study equates the impact as larger than that of asbestos exposure to cancer—a health risk that certainly moved our society to act. But try telling that to "Happy Tree Friends" Executive Producer John Evershed, CEO of Mondo Media in San Francisco.

11   Evershed, the father of three children, the youngest aged 2, told me during a phone conversation that he wouldn't let them watch "Happy Tree Friends." But then he argued that the cartoon wasn't really harmful. "It's like 'Tom & Jerry,'" he said. "I grew up on 'Tom & Jerry,' and I don't think I'm particularly aggressive."

12   Aggressive? AGGRESSIVE? Much as I'd like to, I can't fairly speak for Evershed on this point, but I certainly do worry about the impact on my children. As for "Tom & Jerry," I know "Tom & Jerry," and this is no "Tom & Jerry." "Tom & Jerry" never pulled knives or tore heads off or used someone's intestines to strangle a third party, just for starters.

13   "Tom & Jerry" also had creativity, with surprising plot twists and a richly emotive score. Most importantly, "Tom & Jerry" had a conscience. Routinely, Tom attacks Jerry and is punished for his aggression. In terms of human evolution, the 1940s classic is light-years ahead of "Happy Tree Friends," whose authors, Navarro and Rhode Montijo, have been quoted as saying, "If we are in a room brainstorming episodes and end up laughing at the death scene, then it's all good!"

14   Mad as I am, I'm actually not suggesting that the feds step in and ban this cartoon. The basic freedom of the Internet is too precious, and government censorship too risky and probably not even feasible. The current rules—restrictions on the major airwaves, but anything goes on the Web—will have to do.

15   But what about the big mainstream advertisers who've made "Happy Tree Friends" such a wild success? I was startled, while watching the cartoon, to see banner ads for companies including Toyota and Kaiser Permanente (which has a new campaign they call "Thrive." Thrive, indeed!). Consumers ought to be able to raise a stink, threaten a reputation, even wage boycotts in the face of such irresponsibility. But many Internet ads enjoy the escape clause of being random and ephemeral, as I found out when I called Hilary Weber, Kaiser's San Francisco–based head of Internet marketing. Weber said she couldn't even confirm that her company's ad had appeared.

16   "I can't replicate it," she said, adding that it would "take a lot of research" to establish whether Kaiser indeed had purchased such an ad. That, she explained, is because Kaiser, like many other big corporations,

buys bulk ads through third parties—saving money, yet relinquishing control over where the ads end up.

Weber said she was concerned about Kaiser's reputation and planned to 17 investigate further, yet declined to tell me the names of the third-party companies placing the firm's ads. So I then turned to Mika Salmi, CEO of Atom Shockwave, which manages the ads on "Happy Tree Friends." Salmi, on his cell phone, said he couldn't, with confidence, name the third-party companies with whom he contracts, though he thought one "might" be *Advertising*.com. But when I contacted Lisa Jacobson, *Advertising*.com's spokeswoman, she declined to name advertisers not already listed on her firm's Web page. "We actually don't think we're the best fit for this piece," Jacobson wrote me by e-mail. "You'll probably need to speak with companies like Kaiser and Toyota directly. But thanks for thinking of us . . ."

In our brief telephone conversation, Evershed told me he thinks parents 18 have the ultimate responsibility to shield their kids from media violence. In the abstract, I certainly agree with that, but I admit I sometimes wonder if I'm actually doing my kids a disservice by spending so much time and energy chasing them off the Internet, while coaching them in empathy, manners and the Golden Rule. Because if most of their peers, who lack the luxury of moms with time to meddle, are gorging on "Happy Tree Friends," it would probably serve them better to be trained to defend themselves with firearms and karate.

Still, for now at least, I refuse to be overwhelmed by the sheer magnitude 19 of what society expects from parents, with so little support in return.

So I'd like to offer just two public suggestions. Why can't summer camps 20 and afterschool programs more closely supervise Internet use? And why can't Kaiser and other big companies start crafting contracts that specifically stipulate that their ads never, ever end up on sites like "Happy Tree Friends"?

Meanwhile, I'm talking to other parents because the first step in this 21 peaceful war is to realize we're not alone. Together, we may even manage to subvert our culture's embrace of shock for shock's sake, one gory excess at a time.

Source: *Washington Post*, October 23, 2005. Reprinted by permission of the author.

QUESTIONS FOR READING

1. "Happy Tree Friends" is Ellison's primary example; what is her subject?
2. What is the problem with "Happy Tree Friends"? How does it differ from "Tom & Jerry"?
3. How did the author's 6-year-old discover the cartoon?
4. What did the author's research reveal about the website's advertisers?
5. What suggestions for change does Ellison propose?

QUESTIONS FOR REASONING AND ANALYSIS

6. What does Ellison *not* want to happen to the Internet? Why?

7. What is her claim?

8. In paragraph 18, Ellison writes that her sons might be better off with "firearms and karate" than encouragement in empathy and the Golden Rule. Does she really mean this? Why does she write it?

QUESTIONS FOR REFLECTION AND WRITING

9. Do you think that Ellison's suggestions will be helpful? Why or why not?

10. Should there be federal controls on Internet content? Why or why not?

11. If there are no controls, how will we protect youngsters from unhealthy sites? Or, should we not worry about protecting them? Explain and defend your position.

Sienna Walker

Professor Erik Nielson

FYS 100 Rap Music

12 September 2012

Big Pun's Prophesy

Like many rap artists in the late 1990s, Big Punisher, also known as "Big Pun," documented the challenges of life in the inner city. He did so most notably in his track titled "Capital Punishment" featuring Prospect, the New York City ghetto which he describes as a place of diminishing potential. Big Punisher depicts urban life as abandoned by an unjust political system, denying its responsibility to serve the people while systematically crushing opportunities for the city's disadvantaged residents, and he calls for the minority citizens to abandon governmental constraints by representing themselves through class action. The extended metaphor of capital punishment, the image of the judge, and various stylistic techniques including delivery and rhyme scheme, are the primary means by which Big Punisher expresses his criticism of the political system's failure to address the needs of the people and his encouragement of collective response from the inner city.

Walker 2

Big Punisher harshly criticizes the government and its policies from the start. In the third line, he claims that he has seen young citizens "led astray by the liars, death glorifiers observin' us," portraying "the Man," or any governmental authority, as dishonest and almost satanic. Additionally, from the first few lines of the first verse, the distinction between "they," presumably the establishment, and "us," the resilient minorities plagued by the struggles of street life, become apparent and will resurface throughout the track. Subsequently in the first verse, Big Pun rattles off the wrongs inflicted on his people, ranging from "purposely overtaxing" to "burning down the churches" to "million dollar bails," implying that the government is a ruthlessly oppressive and money hungry establishment that intentionally neglects its citizens. Last, the most explicit attacks come from lines such as "God 'f' the government and its fuckin' capital punishment" and the choral refrain, "disable the Republicans." Moreover, Big Punisher uses the death sentence to further depict the metaphorical death of opportunity for inner city dwellers at the hands of the tyrannical government.

One of the principal techniques Big Punisher employs in "Capital Punishment" is the metaphor of "death by gavel" to reinforce the idea that the governing system, by its employment of the death penalty, is deliberately suffocating street life. The repetition of the song's title "Capital Punishment" blankets the track. In both the chorus and the verses, the phrase is chanted over and over, inundating the audience's consciousness much like the death sentence would hang over the head of a guilty perpetrator. Big Punisher attacks capital punishment because, even today, it represents the utmost extent to which judicial law can be exercised. This acute judicial power juxtaposed with the raw powerlessness that pervades the inner city creates distance between the two parties as expectations on both ends fail to be met. In verse three, Big Punisher raps "the Man's claws are diggin' in my

Walker 3

back / I'm tryin' to hit him back," arguing that it is this almighty "Man," flexing his muscles in the courthouse and neglecting his supportive civic duties, who should be held responsible for a fair share of the overwhelming hardship in the streets. The image of claws in a human's back visually captures the minorities' struggles with the vicious, backstabbing authorities, represented much like a surprise attack where one opponent has an unfair advantage over another. These callous characterizations of the institution become more fully manifested through Big Punisher's use of the image of the judge.

The image of the judge adds to the theme of discriminatory punishment debilitating any urban prospects of success. Big Punisher does not limit the corruption to the streets, claiming "everybody gettin' they hustle on/judge singin' death penalty like it's his favorite fuckin' song." Instead, the way the lines are distinctly paired suggests that the "hustlin'" established on the streets seeps its way into the political system as well, corroding its responsibility to provide for its constituents. Furthermore, the judge is described with "the hammer in the palm, never shaky," also physically suggesting a rigid removal from the adversities of street life and underscoring Big Pun's previous indications of the intolerance of judicial discretion.

In addition to the content, Big Punisher's style, consisting of intricate rhyme schemes and fast-paced delivery, also contributes to the thematic prevalence of oppression which permeates the track. From the opening verse, the audience is exposed to Big Punisher's generous lyrical presentation, occasionally fitting 18 syllables in a single line. His breathless flow typifies the imaginable exhaustion of complying with the looming government, day in and day out. The institution's constant presence, "watching us close," may create the tendency to nervously rush out of view of the public eye, reminiscent of Big Punisher's fast-paced delivery. His rapid elocution can also be applied to the theme of the resiliency of the minority masses whose upbeat spirit cannot be

Walker 4

suppressed. What is more, Big Punisher raps, "I'm stressin' the issue here/ so we can cross the fiscal year/ tired of gettin' fired and hired as a pistoleer" in which the end and internal rhymes illustrate the complexity and inter-connectedness that characterize the government-citizen relationship. Similarly, the percussive emphasis on "fired" then "hired" within the larger end rhyme pattern beginning with "here," reflects the inner turmoil that inevitably accompanies corruption both in the streets and in the government. These stylistic sonic and literary devices serve to reinforce the underlying themes of "Capital Punishment."

However, in the midst of all the dark, oppressive policies imposed by the government, Big Punisher counters the idea of "the government tryin' to take out our sons" by declaring "we benefit the Earth with infinite worth." Although he accounts for the inevitable adversities of big city life with lines like "listen to me, shit is rough in the ghetto," his real aggression in the song is channeled not through accusing the government of its overbearing regulations and impossible standards, but through a forceful calling for change. Juxtaposed with the suicide of his cousin Juje who "lost it and turned on the oven," Big Punisher praises his sister who "just bought a home without a loan." Thus, he narrates the unbearable burdens of the deadly streets while raising up the success stories of his people, however infrequent. This praise also embraces Big Pun when he raps "we laid in the slums, made a cake out of crumbs." These examples pronounce the irrepressible ambition of the people. After considering that his people, or inner-city minorities, are entrepreneurial ("open our own labels") and charged ("my battery never die"), Big Punisher calls them to counteract.

Altogether, through the extended metaphor of the death penalty, the image of the unfazed judge, and various literary and sonic devices, Big Punisher describes the government as unjust and as targeted to bring about the demise of the project's masses. "Capital Punishment" renders the "Man"

Walker 4

incapable of serving inner-city residents and thus transfers the responsibilities

of the government from the authorities and into the hands of the people.

Big Punisher's call to action directed to those citizens living in the margins of

society may have implications beyond the ghetto and into the present, raising

the question of justice here and now.

. . .

Work Cited

Big Punisher, "Capital Punishment." *Capital Punishment.* Terror Squad, Loud

Records, 1998. MP3.

QUESTIONS FOR READING

1. What is Walker's subject?
2. What is Big Pun's attitude toward government?
3. How are inner-city minorities depicted?
4. What does Big Pun want his listeners to do?

QUESTIONS FOR REASONING AND ANALYSIS

5. What is Walker's purpose in writing? What is her claim?
6. What strategies does she analyze?
7. How does the death penalty serve as an extended metaphor?

QUESTIONS FOR REFLECTION AND DEBATE

8. Evaluate Walker's analysis: Is it specific? Is it clear? Does it connect elements of the rap song to the song's theme?
9. Do you like rap? If so, why? If not, why not?
10. Has rap made a contribution to modern music? If yes, how? If no, why not?

WORDS WE REMEMBER | FRANK LUNTZ

A graduate of the University of Pennsylvania with a doctorate in politics from Oxford University, Frank Luntz writes about, analyzes, and consults on the messages of advertising and politics. He appears frequently on television, is a political consultant running focus groups and doing polling, and has written several books on language, including *What Americans Really Want . . . Really* (2009) and *Words That Work: It's Not What You Say, It's What People Hear* (2007), from which the following excerpt is taken.

PREREADING QUESTIONS Given what you now know about the author—and the focus of this chapter—what "words" do you expect Luntz to examine?

"You talking to me?"

— *Taxi Driver*

"I'm going to make him an offer he can't refuse."

— *The Godfather*

"Here's looking at you, kid."

— *Casablanca*

"Rosebud."

— *Citizen Kane**

In a career spanning five decades, Larry King has interviewed quite literally thousands of celebrities, politicians, world leaders, and other famous and infamous individuals of note. But when I ask him to pick out the one interview out of those thousands he won't hesitate a second:

> I was with Martin Luther King, Jr., in 1961 when he was trying to integrate a hotel in Tallahassee, Florida. The hotel won't give him a room even though he has a reservation, and the police squad cars are coming because he's blocking the entrance. He knows he's going to be arrested. I'm there right next to him because I was invited there by his lawyer. So King sits down on this porch in front of this small twenty-room hotel. The owner of the hotel comes out, very straightforward but not belligerently, walks up to King and asks, *"What do you want?"* King says nothing, so the owner asks again in the same direct tone, *"What do you want?"* And Martin Luther King just looked up at him and said, *"My dignity."* And that word has stuck with me to this day.

That defines this chapter: words we remember. These are not the common words of common people. These are the political, corporate, and cultural words that have been burned into our brains. Some are serious, others frivolous. We may forget our passport or our license plate number, but this chapter is about the words that will always be with us. Forever.

"Great movie quotes become part of our cultural vocabulary." So said Jean Pickler Firstenberg, director and CEO of the American Film Institute, when in 2005 AFI released its list of the top 100 memorable movie lines. The jury assembled (made up of directors, actors, screenwriters, critics, historians, and others in the creative community) to select the top quotations was instructed to make their picks based on a quotation's "cultural impact" and legacy. It says something about American culture and priorities that a lot more of us can recite lines voiced in movies released fifty years ago than can tell you what our United States senator said this week, last week . . . ever.

When it comes to movie language, fiction is often more powerful than reality. Think about it. A lot more people know that Arnold Schwarzenegger delivered a defiant *"I'll be back"* (AFI rank #37) guarantee in the blockbuster film *The Terminator*

---

*"Let's get outta here" was the most common scripted line in all Hollywood productions. According to Filmsite.org, it was used at least once 84 percent of the time from the late 1930s through the mid 1970s. That said, it is the writers of these memorable lines, not the actors who spoke them, who deserve the credit.

than know that General Douglas MacArthur declared *"I shall return"* as he fled the Philippines from the advancing Japanese in that blockbuster military conflict World War II. Other than the infamous *"If it doesn't fit, you must acquit,"** no real court-room language is more immediately recognizable than the make-believe *"You can't handle the truth"* (#29) outburst by Jack Nicholson in the Aaron Sorkin-penned *A Few Good Men.* How many people know that *"Keep your friends close but your enemies closer"* from *The Godfather* (#58) is almost identical to what philosopher John Stuart Mill wrote 150 years ago and what Machiavelli advised almost 500 years ago? Surely not many.

5   My own favorite movie quote, *"What we've got here is failure to commu-nicate,"* from *Cool Hand Luke,* came in at #11—but for many businesses, it should be Number One. That clip, which ends in the unfortunate death of the Paul Newman character, is quoted and occasionally played at corporate retreats because it accurately sums up the reoccurring problem: listening to customers and understanding employees. Labor negotiations in particular have collapsed because of the failure to communicate. Wal-Mart even went so far as to shut down a store in Canada in early 2005 simply because company executives and local union leaders failed to properly communicate one anoth-er's positions. And the disastrous four-month strike of supermarkets in Southern California in 2004 is seen primarily as a result of labor leaders com-municating faulty information and corporate management communicating almost no information at all.

6   Then there's the Howard Beale character in the film classic *Network,* a movie that lays bare the never-ending pursuit of ratings and revenues. In the midst of an on-air nervous breakdown, he pleads with his viewers to "go to the window, open it, stick your head out and yell: 'I'm mad as hell, and I'm not going to take this anymore.' "That line ranks #19 on the AFI list, and it's on the lips of every disgruntled employee even today. Yet while it comes from a make-believe movie, the words have been coopted by very real political groups angry with the status quo. From Ross Perot's quixotic campaign in 1992 to the Freedom Alliance founded by Col. Oliver North, who actually named an April 2006 policy memo on immigration *"I'm Mad As Hell and I'm Not Going to Take It Anymore,"* that mad-as-hell language says exactly what you mean and means exactly what you say.

7   But those lines pale in impact to the top movie line of all time: *"Frankly, my dear, I don't give a damn,"* from *Gone with the Wind.* Short words, asser-tive tone, delivered spectacularly by Clark Gable and repeated countless times ever since. But in addition to being a classic movie quotation, *"Frankly, my dear . . ."* is also a perfect example of *words that work.* Though it seems tame

---

*If Robert Shapiro had his way, *"If it doesn't fit, you must acquit"* would never have entered the public lexicon. The most memorable phrase from the O. J. Simpson trial was delivered by Johnnie Cochran, but it wasn't spontaneous. In fact, they weren't even his words. They were written for him by another lawyer on the Simpson defense team, Gerald Uelmen, and Shapiro hated the phrase. "When I first heard it. I thought. 'Oh, God. I don't like that.' It's not something I would have been comfortable saying. But it worked for Cochran."

by today's standards, "I don't give a damn" was considered extreme profanity in the cultural context of 1939. It was debated, condemned, ridiculed . . . and it helped to expand the American lexicon in new directions.

Profanity continues to make a point even in today's coarsened lexicon. On the same day in 2004 that the Senate approved the Defense of Decency Act by a rather sizeable 99 to 1 vote, Vice President Dick Cheney told Vermont senator Patrick Leahy to *"go fuck yourself"* on the Senate floor. Guess which got more publicity. Two years later, at the 2006 G-8 Summit, George W. Bush whispered to British prime minister Tony Blair near an open microphone that *"what they need to do is get Syria to get Hezbollah to stop doing this shit and it's over"* in reference to the escalating military conflict between Israel and Hezbollah. The media pounced on that one word, all but ignoring the much more significant political statement. In a rare moment of exactness and candor, the *New York Times,* the *Washington Post,* and most major national newspapers gave readers the unedited version. This case was *"an exception,"* according to *Pittsburgh Post* executive editor David Shribman. *"The president was quoted in our paper and in others because the actual quote—the actual word—was incontrovertibly part of the story. Indeed, it was the story,"* said Mr. Shribman.[1] But as comedian George Carlin would sadly note, both words are still among the seven that still cannot be said on broadcast television. All four networks bleeped it out.*

Other entries in AFI's top 100 movie lines transcended their original celluloid delivery into fields of impact well beyond their initial intentions. *"Go ahead, make my day,"* #6 on the list, was delivered with clenched jaw by Clint Eastwood as Detective Harry Callahan in 1983's *Sudden Impact.* That same expression of bravado and supreme confidence gave way to George H. W. Bush's memorable *"Read my lips, no new taxes"* line at the 1988 Republican Convention and a surge in public support that propelled him from a seventeen-point deficit into an eight-point victory on election day. Bush the elder could have easily said that there won't be any additional taxes while he's in office.

Similarly, Bush the younger could have said that the terrorists who attacked the U.S. on 9/11 should either be captured or killed, but he didn't. Instead, he drew his inspiration from popular culture; his *"Dead or Alive"* comment about Osama bin Laden could have come right from a John Ford western. Even more memorable, *"Bring it on"* conveyed a swagger that would have made John Wayne proud. But those three simple words, *"bring it on,"* will also prove to be the worst three words of his entire presidency. Even former secretary of state Colin Powell admitted to me that those words made him cringe. It was unfortunate timing for Powell because he had worked feverishly and successfully to launch a $15 billion international HIV/AIDS relief program, one of the

8

9

10

---

*At the risk of losing a slot in the Conservative Book of the Month Club, the word *shit* also appeared in the *New York Times* on July 10, 1973, in the published transcript of the Watergate tape in which Nixon said, "I don't give a shit what happens. I want you to stonewall it, let them plead the Fifth Amendment, cover-up or anything else." But that word did not appear in the accompanying news stories about the tapes.

largest humanitarian relief efforts in American history. But at the White House press conference to announce the naming of a global AIDS coordinator and lay out the details of the program, a much different story emerged:

WORDS THAT *DON'T WORK*

Q: A posse of small nations, like Ukraine and Poland, are materializing to help keep the peace in Iraq, but with the attacks on U.S. forces and casualty rates rising, what does the administration do to get larger powers like France and Germany and Russia to join in?

BUSH: Well, first of all, you know, we'll put together a force structure that meets the threats on the ground. And we got a lot of forces there ourselves. And as I said yesterday, anybody who wants to harm American troops will be found and brought to justice.

There are some who feel like that if they attack us that we may decide to leave prematurely. They don't understand what they're talking about, if that's the case.

[*attempted interruption*]

Let me finish.

There are some who feel like that, you know, the conditions are such that they can attack us there. My answer is **BRING IT ON.** We got the force necessary to deal with the security situation.

---

11   For the first time in the *"War on Terror,"* Bush had the wrong words. Said Powell:

> "Looking at Bush as he was speaking, it's the kind of phrase that I immediately knew wouldn't translate or play well in Europe. It came across as sharp, arrogant, and frankly, it had that cowboy aspect to it that I knew wouldn't sound good to European cars."

12   It didn't sound good to American ears either. In my focus groups for MSNBC, even Republican women recoiled at the phrase. In a session I conducted for MSNBC in Ohio, one Republican mom said in a quivering but firm voice, *"I don't want them to bring it on. I don't want them to target our boys. That could have been my son over there."*

13   Those same words that proved so disastrous for President Bush offered an unparalleled opportunity for his opponent. In an incredible act of political jujitsu. Andrei Cherny, John Kerry's twenty-eight-year-old chief campaign speechwriter, captured that line and crafted an alternative refrain that challenged Bush to debate and defend his national security record, which took Kerry from boring presidential wannabe to dynamic frontrunner. But even though the partisan Democrat crowds loved it, Kerry eventually dropped it from his stump speech (and Cherny from the campaign) based on the faulty advice of campaign message-meister Bob Shrum who, according to *Newsweek*, thought that attack was too *"undignified"* and Cherny's suggested rhetoric too *"punchy."*

And now, a word from our sponsor . . . 14

> *"Two all-beef patties—special sauce—lettuce—cheese—pickles—onions—on a sesame seed bun."*
> *"Fly the friendly skies."*
> *"They're magically delicious."*
> *"Have it your way."*

Almost no adult in America would have the slightest trouble identifying 15
these advertising slogans, yet they were created decades ago. If you're a typical American today, you know these slogans—and the thousands like them—the way you know your own name. They are second nature, embedded deep within every one of us—part of the ambient noise of our lives, surrounding us like wallpaper, inescapable. Some are funny. Some are matter-of-fact. Some are genuinely annoying. The best are truly unforgettable.

See how long it takes you to name the last six presidents—if you can. Now 16
see how many of the following six top advertising slogans of the past forty years you can identify:[2]

1. *"Just do it"*
2. *"Tastes great, less filling"*
3. *"Where's the beef?"*
4. *"Let your fingers do the walking"*
5. *"Melts in your mouth, not in your hand"*
6. *"We bring good things to life"**

These short, innocuous bursts of words are actually more memorable than 17
the people who have occupied the most powerful position in the world, and they have convinced most of us, at one time or another in our lives, to buy one of the products they trumpet. Good advertising slogans and catchphrases are closely associated with their companies or products. But it is that rare combination of words, thoughts, and emotion that becomes an intrinsic part of the American idiom. And each of them abides by multiple rules of effective language. Think about it. . . .

"Just do it." has the values of simplicity, brevity, and is clearly 18
aspirational.

"Tastes great, less filling" has all three of those characteristics as well as a 19
fourth: novelty. "Wow," thought consumers. "Finally, a light beer with fewer calories and more drinkable."

"Where's the beef?" finally asked out loud in a humorous way the simple 20
rhetorical question that consumers had been thinking about for years.

"Let your fingers do the walking" is about as visual and relevant as you can 21
get. To this day, older Americans still remember this ad even though it hasn't run on television in decades.

---

* 1. Nike
  2. Miller Lite
  3. Wendy's
  4. Yellow Pages
  5. M&M's
  6. General Electric

22   *"Melts in your mouth, not in your hand"* is also about context and relevance. Finally, a chocolate candy that doesn't make a mess—and it earns its credibility every time you have one.

23   *"We bring good things to life"* is a simple definition of aspiration—a company that makes the good life possible for people like me. And the more one learned about GE products, the more credible the slogan became.

24   In fact, many of the most endearing homespun sayings began their lives as pitch lines for well-known products. For example, most people today don't realize that *"When it rains, it pours"* was popularized by Morton Salt in 1912 and was not something your great uncle with the bum knee came up with.[3] Some may remember that the phrase *"Loose lips sink ships"* comes from a World War II public service campaign.[4] But do you know the origins of the expression, *"Always a bridesmaid, never a bride"*? Would you believe it comes from a 1923 advertisement for Listerine?[5]

25   Tonight, when you're sitting at the dinner table, and someone states that they "can't believe they ate the whole thing," they'll be paraphrasing an Alka-Seltzer advertisement from the 1970s.[6] Or tomorrow morning, when you pick up the newspaper to see an analysis of what makes Americans tick, know that Chevy's *"heartbeat of America"* campaign has led to the resurgence of the phrase.[7]

26   Ad copy is conquering more and more of our brains' territory. A decade ago, popular Yale history professor Jaroslav Pelikan would regale his students with the tale of how, at the age of twelve, he had memorized Homer's *Odyssey*—in Greek.[8] Unfortunately, when they were twelve, most of his students were busy memorizing: *"Two-all-beef-patties-special-sauce-lettuce-cheese-pickles-onions-on-a-sesame-seed-bun."* Not exactly the language of *"wine-dark sea"* or *"rosy-fingered Dawn."*

27   Much of this advertising language saturation—and our subsequent ability to recall it—is involuntary. That's one of the definitions of words that work: We remember even when we're not trying. Not that we seek to ignore them. Effective commercial jingles are lodged in our memories every bit as indelibly as the Pledge of Allegiance or the childhood alphabet song—and often, not surprisingly, carry the same nostalgic power. Like the lyrics of the Bugs Bunny version of *The Barber of Seville* (my own personal favorite) or ABC's *Schoolhouse Rock* (*"Conjunction Junction, what's your function?"*—I bet you're singing it now), they hibernate for decades in some seldom-visited alcove of our minds—but it doesn't take much for them to awaken and burst back into our consciousness. Not that long ago I attended a performance of *The Barber of Seville* in Moscow. During the overture, I began to sing the Bugs Bunny lyrics quietly. Several Americans within earshot turned, smiled, and nodded knowingly. Like magic, these words are truly *part of us*, never to be forgotten.

28   There is no doubt that in the creation and dissemination of language, nothing in day-to-day life plays a more significant role than television. But the real question for those who seek to understand and then apply the power of words is whether television mirrors society or leads it. From television pioneer Norman Lear's perspective, his groundbreaking programming merely shined a bright light on words and situations that were all too familiar in real life, even if they had never been discussed on television. "There wasn't anything on *All in the Family* that

Do the words in this ad meet Luntz's guidelines for effective punch lines? Why or why not?

I didn't think one could hear in a schoolyard anywhere in the country. The accents would change, the inclination to certain phrases might change, but the basic sentiment was 'people speak,' 'ordinary folk talking.' You heard it either from the armchair from your favorite uncle or father or you heard it on the playground."*

29   Lear may claim that his characters reflected the words of the people, but his shows clearly pushed the language limit to the breaking point—and beyond. He enjoys telling the story about the first time *"son-of-a-bitch"* appeared on television:

> We did an episode of *Maude* where Walter comes close to committing some form of infidelity. The audience knows, and when Maude learns this at the very end, she embraces him and says "you son-of-a-bitch." That was the tagline.
>
> So I hear from the guy that runs Program Practices, and he says, "You're kidding Norman, you're not going to do that." We got into a long conversation about it, maybe a couple of conversations, and his argument to me was she could say something else just as successfully fitting and every bit as good. And I said. "Tell you what I'll do, Bill. You find it, you call me and tell me 'Norman, this is every bit as good,' and if you can look me in the eye on the telephone, metaphorically, and say 'I think it's as good,' I'll do it."
>
> So he called me in a day or so and said "Goddamn, I can't. I haven't found it." So he let me do it, and we did it, and nothing happened. The American public did not give a damn.

30   George Will may bemoan the dumbing down of America, but our frame of reference and common bond as Americans has become pop culture, not the classics.† We are much more likely to bond over an episode of *The Sopranos* than we are over a public reading of the *Federalist Papers*. Sadly, even the core democratic institutions and the people who gave birth to this country are less familiar to the next generation of American adults than the latest *American Idol/Survivor* phenomenon. In a poll of teenagers I conducted for the Constitution Center in Philadelphia a few years ago:

- Fewer than 2 percent of American teenagers knew that the man considered the father of the Constitution was James Madison, yet 90 percent knew that the male star of *Titanic* was Leonardo DiCaprio.

- Fewer than 2 percent of American teenagers could name then–Chief Justice William Rehnquist—yet 95 percent could tell you that the Fresh Prince of Bel Air was Will Smith.

- Fewer than 9 percent of American teenagers knew the name of the town where Abraham Lincoln lived for most of his adult life and which he represented in Congress (Springfield)—yet 75 percent knew the name of the town where Bart Simpson "lives" (Springfield).[9]

---

*From All in the Family to Maude, Good Times, and The Jeffersons, the shows Lear created in the 1970s had an incredible impact on the American psyche. His insistence that he only mirrored American culture is more a reflection of personal modesty than accuracy.

†I once invited Will to attend one of my focus groups to learn what's on the minds of the American voter. His response: "Heavens no. What makes you think I want to know what 'real people' are thinking?"

We know so much about things that don't really matter because we see ³¹ them on television—and therefore it matters to us—yet we are so remarkably ignorant about what should matter—our own national heritage, culture, and traditions—because no one ever explained why we should care. *Relevance* sells—and seeing it on television makes even the most obscure and trivial seem relevant.

Popular entertainment in general, and the thirty-second spot in particular, ³² need not be corrosive of the lexicon or the culture. Truth is, not all ads are bad. From the ads promoting Radio Free Europe that dramatically captured life behind the Iron Curtain in the 1960s to the infamous frying egg *"This is your brain; this is your brain on drugs"* in the 1980s and the fantastically successful *"Know when to say when"* campaign by Anheuser-Busch over the past decade, some promotional efforts have been enlightening, informative, and occasionally even influential.

And not all ads have to air hundreds of times for us to remember them. ³³ Two ads stand above all the rest for their impact, even though they were officially broadcast just once: the aforementioned "Daisy" spot that helped sink Barry Goldwater in 1964, and the infamous "1984" commercial for Apple that aired during that year's Super Bowl—forever connecting Hollywood production with Madison Avenue creativity. That spot, designed to introduce the much-anticipated Macintosh computer, was put together by the dream of award-winning director Ridley Scott and advertising powerhouse Chiat/Day—and *Advertising Age* named it the top spot of the decade.

Advertising certainly didn't start out to be corruptive or manipulative. The ³⁴ modern advertising age is said to have begun with the "creative revolution" touted by William Bernbach of the Doyle Dane Bernbach agency (DDB), who wrote, ambitiously, that: "good taste, good art, good writing can be good selling."[10]

DDB's 1959 campaign for Volkswagen, titled *"Think Small,"* was named ³⁵ by *Advertising Age* as the top ad campaign ever.[11] Just two words, brief and simple, but the contextual surprise signaled a new sophistication in American advertising, marking a subtle but influential shift in the way products would be sold from then on. The most memorable ads of the past fifty years as chosen by the industry itself do indeed rely on Bernbach's "good writing" equals "good selling" formulation.[12] And here's the pleasant surprise for family-oriented consumers: Almost all of the best of the best involve mainstream themes, everyday people, a positive outcome, and simple language. Among *Advertising Age's* top 100 ad campaigns of all time:

- Only eight involve sex.
- Only seven feature celebrities.
- Only four play on consumer fear and insecurities.[13]

The *idea* has primacy. Accessible language rules. ³⁶

37   The best advertising taglines abide by the Ten Rules of Effective Communication and are therefore easily remembered. In a recent national survey, the most recognized product and corporate taglines slogans included:

- *"You're in good hands,"* overtly visual, aspirational, and therefore not surprisingly recognized as Allstate's slogan by 87 percent of the American public.
- *"Like a Good Neighbor,"* again aspirational, and with a jingle written by Barry Manilow that enhances the memorability, recognized as State Farm's tagline by 70 percent.
- *"Always Low Prices. Always."* Overtly repetitive and unquestionably credible, Wal-Mart's tagline is identified by 67 percent.
- *"Obey Your Thirst,"* a relatively new tagline for Sprite, recognized by 35 percent of the population because of its novelty, twist of language, and visualization.
- *"Think Outside the Bun,"* Taco Bell's tagline, recognized by 34 percent, for reasons similar to Sprite's.
- *"i'm lovin' it,"* the latest and greatest for McDonald's, already at 33 percent despite being less than a year old, because it hits more than half of the rules: simplicity, brevity, credibility, aspiration, and relevance.
- *"What's in your wallet?"* the rhetorical question from Capital One that earns a 27 percent recognition level.[14]

MEMORABLE COMMERCIALS, JINGLES, AND WORDS THAT WORK
WRITTEN, PERFORMED, OR PRODUCED BY BARRY MANILOW

LANGUAGE	PRODUCT
"You deserve a break today"	McDonald's
"Like a good neighbor, State Farm is there"	State Farm Insurance
"I am stuck on Band-Aids . . ."	Band-Aids
"Grab a bucket of chicken"	KFC
"The most original soft drink ever"	Dr Pepper
"Give your face somethin' to smile about"	Stridex Medicated Pads
"Feelin' free"	Pepsi

---

38   These are all obviously attention-grabbing. The vast majority of advertising taglines—perhaps as high as 99 percent—never achieve widespread recognition or become part of the American lexicon because they lack creativity, simplicity, or relevance. For every jingle you can remember from childhood, or last year, you have probably forgotten a hundred of them. They simply didn't contain the words that work or the catchy tunes that last.

39   Curiously, it's not uncommon for companies to abandon incredibly successful slogans for new ones that flop. Someone needs to ask senior corporate

management at General Electric and the marketing whizzes at the various ad agencies why they found it beneficial to abandon *"We bring good things to life"* (recognized by 39 percent of Americans) in 2002 in favor of *"Imagination at work,"* which is recognized by a scant 5 percent?[15] Yes, imagination is important, vital, in the twenty-first century, but applying that imagination to everyday life is an even higher priority. Think about it: Do you have more respect for a company that is imagining the future, or making the future better for you personally?

Why did the U.S. Army jettison *"Be all that you can be,"* surely one of the 40 most widely known taglines in the world, for the rather odd and uninspiring *"An army of one"*? Especially when an "army," by definition, is more than one person. While it is understandable for an organization like the military to want to individualize and personalize what it does, that's just not a believable or credible selling point.

Why did Burger King replace its successful *"Have it your way"* slogan, 41 devised in 1974, with immediately forgettable taglines such as *"Best darn burger"* (1978), *"Burger King Town"* (1986), and the *"The Whopper says"* (2001), before finally returning to *"Have it your way"* in 2004?[16] When it comes to fast food, or "QSR" (Quick Service Restaurants) as those in the industry like to call themselves, individualizing and personalizing the product really does matter.

NOTES

1. *Pittsburgh Post-Gazette,* July 19, 2006, pg. C-1.
2. "Top 100 Advertising Campaigns," *Ad Age*
3. Ibid.
4. Ibid.
5. Ibid.
6. http://www.inthe70s.com/generated/commercials.shtml
7. http://www.inthe80s.com/tvcommercials/c.shtml
8. Directed Studies program, Yale University, autumn 1992.
9. Luntz Research "Constitutional Knowledge Survey," August 30, 1998.
10. *Ad Age,* "Top 100 Advertising Campaigns of the Century," by Bob Garfield.
11. Ibid.
12. Ibid.
13. Ibid.
14. Emergence Slogan Survey, *BusinessWeek,* Kiley, Oct. 2004.
15. Emergence Slogan Survey, *BusinessWeek,* Kiley, Oct. 2004.
16. "Ad Track," *USA Today,* May 23, 2005, by Michael McCarthy.

QUESTIONS FOR READING

1. What is Luntz's broad subject?
2. From what situations or "worlds" do Luntz's examples come?
3. What is the top movie line? (Do you know the line? Are you surprised?)
4. Why were George W. Bush's words memorable but not effective for him?
5. What are the general characteristics—Luntz's "rules"—of the clever phrases we remember?

QUESTIONS FOR REASONING AND ANALYSIS

6. What is Luntz's claim? How does he develop and support his claim?
7. In paragraph 31, the author asserts that what we see on TV we remember because it seems relevant to us, whereas what is really important we don't remember because no one has explained its relevance. Do you agree with these assertions? Is it correct to assert that no one has told us why we should care about politics, history, and culture?
8. Earlier in his book, Luntz gives 10 rules of successful writing. From this selection, how many rules can you find? From these rules, what can you conclude about the characteristics of ineffectual writing?

QUESTIONS FOR REFLECTION AND WRITING

9. How many of Luntz's memorable examples from film do you know? If you don't know many, do you think that you should see the films and become more culturally knowledgeable? Why or why not? If you don't recognize many of the ad slogans, do you think this is good (You don't watch too much TV!) or bad (You are not part of this shared culture.)? Explain your views.
10. Luntz makes a case for brevity as a mark of effective writing—in movie lines and ad slogans at any rate. Should brevity also be a guide for politicians? Do we want leaders to speak or write in "sound bites"? Ponder these questions.

CHAPTER 16

The Internet and Social Media: Their Impact on Our Lives

READ: Where is Rat? Why is he there?

REASON: What are the differences in Rat's poses as he reacts to the screen?

REFLECT/WRITE: What is the point of the story that the cartoon tells?

The influence of computers today—especially as a source of information and social interaction—is so great, and so complex, that it warrants a chapter's study. Virtually no one under 30 today turns first to a reference book. They "Google it." Meanwhile people of all ages, although most typically young people, spend many hours e-mailing, twittering, and posting on Facebook. The time we devote to these activities demands that we pause and think about the effects of such dramatic changes in our lives. Consider the following questions as you read and study the five essays in this chapter.

PREREADING QUESTIONS

1. Has e-mailing made us more—or less—productive?
2. Is Twitter a useful new form of communication—or a waste of time?
3. Is the Internet making us smarter—or interfering with the development of critical thinking?
4. What is the difference between having access to knowledge and being knowledgeable?
5. Should we fear the Internet's data mining—or ignore it as simply an advertising strategy?

I TWEET, THEREFORE I AM | PEGGY ORENSTEIN

Peggy Orenstein is a contributing writer to the *New York Times Magazine*, a popular speaker, and the author of several notable books concerning women's issues. Her latest is *Cinderella Ate My Daughter: Dispatches from the Front Lines of the New Girlie-Girl Culture* (2011). The following *New York Times Magazine* essay was published August 1, 2010.

PREREADING QUESTIONS On what expression—what philosophical statement—does Orenstein play with in her title? What does this play on words tell you about her anticipated audience?

1   On a recent lazy Saturday morning, my daughter and I lolled on a blanket in our front yard, snacking on apricots, listening to a download of E. B. White reading *The Trumpet of the Swan*. Her legs sprawled across mine; the

380

grass tickled our ankles. It was the quintessential summer moment, and a year ago, I would have been fully present for it. But instead, a part of my consciousness had split off and was observing the scene from the outside: this was, I realized excitedly, the perfect opportunity for a tweet.

I came late to Twitter. I might have skipped the phenomenon altogether, but I have a book coming out this winter, and publishers, scrambling to promote 360,000-character tomes in a 140-character world, push authors to rally their "tweeps" to the cause. Leaving aside the question of whether that actually boosts sales, I felt pressure to produce. I quickly mastered the Twitterati's unnatural self-consciousness: processing my experience instantaneously, packaging life as I lived it. I learned to be "on" all the time, whether standing behind that woman at the supermarket who sneaked three extra items into the express check-out lane (you know who you are) or despairing over human rights abuses against women in Guatemala.

Each Twitter post seemed a tacit referendum on who I am, or at least who I believe myself to be. The grocery-store episode telegraphed that I was tuned in to the Seinfeldian absurdities of life; my concern about women's victimization, however sincere, signaled that I also have a soul. Together they suggest someone who is at once cynical and compassionate, petty yet deep. Which, in the end, I'd say, is pretty accurate.

Distilling my personality provided surprising focus, making me feel stripped to my essence. It forced me, for instance, to pinpoint the dominant feeling as I sat outside with my daughter listening to E. B. White. Was it my joy at being a mother? Nostalgia for my own childhood summers? The pleasures of listening to the author's quirky, underinflected voice? Each put a different spin on the occasion, of who I was within it. Yet the final decision ("Listening to E. B. White's *Trumpet of the Swan* with Daisy. Slow and sweet.") was not really about my own impressions: it was about how I imagined—and wanted—others to react to them. That gave me pause. How much, I began to wonder, was I shaping my Twitter feed, and how much was Twitter shaping me?

Back in the 1950s, the sociologist Erving Goffman famously argued that all of life is performance: we act out a role in every interaction, adapting it based on the nature of the relationship or context at hand. Twitter has extended that metaphor to include aspects of our experience that used to be considered off-set: eating pizza in bed, reading a book in the tub, thinking a thought anywhere, flossing. Effectively, it makes the greasepaint permanent, blurring the lines not only between public and private but also between the authentic and contrived self. If all the world was once a stage, it has now become a reality TV show: we mere players are not just aware of the camera; we mug for it.

The expansion of our digital universe—Second Life, Facebook, MySpace, Twitter—has shifted not only how we spend our time but also how we construct identity. For her coming book, *Alone Together*, Sherry Turkle, a professor at M.I.T., interviewed more than 400 children and parents about their use of social media and cellphones. Among young people especially she found that the self was increasingly becoming externally manufactured rather than internally developed; a series of profiles to be sculptured and refined in response to public opinion. "On Twitter or Facebook you're trying to express something real about who you are," she explained. "But because you're also creating something for others' consumption, you find yourself imagining and playing to your audience more and more. So those moments in which you're supposed to be showing your true self become a performance. Your *psychology* becomes a performance." Referring to *The Lonely Crowd*, the landmark description of the transformation of the American character from inner- to outer-directed, Turkle added, "Twitter is outer-directedness cubed."

7   The fun of Twitter and, I suspect, its draw for millions of people, is its infinite potential for connection, as well as its opportunity for self-expression. I enjoy those things myself. But when every thought is externalized, what becomes of insight? When we reflexively post each feeling, what becomes of reflection? When friends become fans, what happens to intimacy? The risk of the performance culture, of the packaged self, is that it erodes the very relationships it purports to create, and alienates us from our own humanity. Consider the fate of empathy: in an analysis of 72 studies performed on nearly 14,000 college students between 1979 and 2009, researchers at the Institute for Social Research at the University of Michigan found a drop in that trait, with the sharpest decline occurring since 2000. Social media may not have instigated that trend, but by encouraging self-promotion over self-awareness, they may well be accelerating it.

8   None of this makes me want to cancel my Twitter account. It's too late for that anyway: I'm already hooked. Besides, I appreciate good writing whatever the form: some "tweeple" are as deft as haiku masters at their craft. I am experimenting with the art of the well-placed "hashtag" myself (the symbol that adds your post on a particular topic, like #ShirleySherrod, to a stream. You can also use them whimsically, as in, "I am pretending not to be afraid of the humongous spider on the bed. #lieswetellourchildren").

9   At the same time, I am trying to gain some perspective on the perpetual performer's self-consciousness. That involves trying to sort out the line between person and persona, the public and private self. It also means that the next time I find myself lying on the grass, stringing daisy chains and listening to E. B. White, I will resist the urge to trumpet about the swan.

Source: *New York Times Magazine*, August 1, 2010. Reprinted by permission of the author.

QUESTIONS FOR READING

1. Why did the author get into Twitter? How has tweeting affected her responses to experiences?

2. What, presumably, is Twitter's appeal for many users? How does this social medium actually produce the opposite of what users are seeking?

3. What is the difference between *person* and *persona*?

4. What is meant by the term *empathy*? What has happened to this trait among college students over the last thirty years?

QUESTIONS FOR REASONING AND ANALYSIS

5. Describe the essay's characteristics of style and tone.

6. Even though the "feel" of this essay may be personal, Orenstein still presents an argument. What is her claim? What does she want readers to know about Twitter?

QUESTIONS FOR REFLECTION AND WRITING

7. Is participation in social media like performing on a reality show? What is your response to this comparison?

8. Are there any advantages to trying on different personalities? What are the possible disadvantages?

9. As you read, consider: What other writers in this chapter suggest that the Internet and social media encourage the superficial, keep us from contemplation and insight? Do you agree with their analysis? If so, why? If not, why not?

THE NEW DIGITAL DIVIDE | SUSAN B. CRAWFORD

A specialist in communications law and privacy issues, Susan Crawford is a professor at the Benjamin N. Cardozo School of Law. She holds her BA and JD. degrees from Yale University. Before returning to teach at Cardozo, she was special assistant to President Obama for Science, Technology, and Innovation Policy. Her article on the digital divide appeared December 4, 2011.

PREREADING QUESTIONS To what kind of "digital divide" might the title refer? Do you think this might be a problem, at least in the author's view?

For the second year in a row, the Monday after Thanksgiving—so-called Cyber 1 Monday, when online retailers offer discounts to lure holiday shoppers—was the biggest sales day of the year, totaling some $1.25 billion and overwhelming the sales figures racked up by brick-and-mortar stores three days before, on Black Friday, the former perennial record-holder.

Such numbers may seem proof that America is, indeed, online. But they 2 mask an emerging division, one that has worrisome implications for our economy and society. Increasingly, we are a country in which only the urban and suburban well-off have truly high-speed Internet access, while the rest—the poor and the working class—either cannot afford access or use restricted wireless access as their only connection to the Internet. As our jobs, entertainment, politics and even health care move online, millions are at risk of being left behind.

Telecommunications, which in theory should bind us together, has often 3 divided us in practice. Until the late 20th century, the divide split those with phone access and those without it. Then it was the Web: in 1995 the Commerce Department published its first look at the "digital divide," finding stark racial, economic and geographic gaps between those who could get online and those who could not.

4   "While a standard telephone line can be an individual's pathway to the riches of the Information Age," the report said, "a personal computer and modem are rapidly becoming the keys to the vault." If you were white, middle-class and urban, the Internet was opening untold doors of information and opportunity. If you were poor, rural or a member of a minority group, you were fast being left behind.

5   Over the last decade, cheap Web access over phone lines brought millions to the Internet. But in recent years the emergence of services like video-on-demand, online medicine and Internet classrooms have redefined the state of the art: they require reliable, truly high-speed connections, the kind available almost exclusively from the nation's small number of very powerful cable companies. Such access means expensive contracts, which many Americans simply cannot afford.

6   While we still talk about "the" Internet, we increasingly have two separate access marketplaces: high-speed wired and second-class wireless. High-speed access is a superhighway for those who can afford it, while racial minorities and poorer and rural Americans must make do with a bike path.

7   Just over 200 million Americans have high-speed, wired Internet access at home, and almost two-thirds of them get it through their local cable company. The connections are truly high-speed: based on a technological standard called Docsis 2.0 or 3.0, they can reach up to 105 megabits per second, fast enough to download a music album in three seconds.

8   These customers are the targets for the next generation of Internet services, technology that will greatly enhance their careers, education and quality of life. Within a decade, patients at home will be able to speak with their doctors online and thus get access to lower-cost, higher-quality care. High-speed connections will also allow for distance education through real-time videoconferencing; already, thousands of high school students are earning diplomas via virtual classrooms.

9   Households will soon be able to monitor their energy use via smart-grid technology to keep costs and carbon dioxide emissions down. Even the way that wired America works will change: many job applications are already possible only online; soon, job interviews will be held by way of videoconference, saving cost and time.

10   But the rest of America will most likely be left out of all this. Millions are still offline completely, while others can afford only connections over their phone lines or via wireless smartphones. They can thus expect even lower-quality health services, career opportunities, education and entertainment options than they already receive. True, Americans of all stripes are adopting smartphones at break-neck speeds; in just over four years the number has jumped from about 10 percent to about 35 percent; among Hispanics and African-Americans, it's roughly 44 percent. Most of the time, smartphone owners also have wired access at home: the Pew Internet and American Life Project recently reported that 59 percent of American adults with incomes above $75,000 had a smartphone, and a 2010 study by the Federal Communications Commission found that more than 90 percent of people at that income level had wired high-speed Internet access at home.

But that is not true for lower-income and minority Americans. According 11 to numbers released last month by the Department of Commerce, a mere 4 out of every 10 households with annual household incomes below $25,000 in 2010 reported having wired Internet access at home, compared with the vast majority—93 percent—of households with incomes exceeding $100,000. Only slightly more than half of all African-American and Hispanic households (55 percent and 57 percent, respectively) have wired Internet access at home, compared with 72 percent of whites.

These numbers are likely to grow even starker as the 30 percent of 12 Americans without any kind of Internet access come online. When they do, particularly if the next several years deliver subpar growth in personal income, they will probably go for the only option that is at all within their reach: wireless smartphones. A wired high-speed Internet plan might cost $100 a month; a smartphone plan might cost half that, often with a free or heavily discounted phone thrown in.

The problem is that smartphone access is not a substitute for wired. The vast 13 majority of jobs require online applications, but it is hard to type up a résumé on a hand-held device; it is hard to get a college degree from a remote location using wireless. Few people would start a business using only a wireless connection.

It is not just inconvenient—many of these activities are physically impossi- 14 ble via a wireless connection. By their nature, the airwaves suffer from severe capacity limitations: the same five gigabytes of data that might take nine minutes to download over a high-speed cable connection would take an hour and 15 minutes to travel over a wireless connection.

Even if a smartphone had the technical potential to compete with wired, 15 users would still be hampered by the monthly data caps put in place by AT&T and Verizon, by far the largest wireless carriers in America. For example, well before finishing the download of a single two-hour, high-definition movie from iTunes over a 4G wireless network, a typical subscriber would hit his or her monthly cap and start incurring $10 per gigabyte in overage charges. If you think this is a frivolous concern, for "movie" insert an equally large data stream, like "business meeting."

Public libraries are taking up the slack and buckling under the strain. Nearly 16 half of librarians say that their connections are insufficient to meet patrons' needs. And it is hard to imagine conducting a job interview in a library.

In the past, the cost of new technologies has dropped over time, and 17 eventually many Americans could afford a computer and a modem to access a standard phone line. Phone service—something 96 percent of Americans have—was sold at regulated rates and the phone companies were forced to allow competing Internet access providers to share their lines.

But there is reason to believe this time is different. Today, the problem is 18 about affording unregulated high-speed Internet service—provided, in the case of cable, by a few for-profit companies with very little local competition and almost no check on their prices. They have to bear all the cost of infrastructure and so have no incentive to expand into rural areas, where potential customers are relatively few and far between. (The Federal Communications

Commission recently announced a plan to convert subsidies that once supported basic rural telephone services into subsidies for basic Internet access.)

19   The bigger problem is the lack of competition in cable markets. Though there are several large cable companies nationwide, each dominates its own fragmented kingdom of local markets: Comcast is the only game in Philadelphia, while Time Warner dominates Cleveland. That is partly because it is so expensive to lay down the physical cables, and companies, having paid for those networks, guard them jealously, clustering their operations and spending tens of millions of dollars to lobby against laws that might oblige them to share their infrastructure.

20   Cable's only real competition comes from Verizon's FiOS fiber-optic service, which can provide speeds up to 150 megabits per second. But FiOS is available to only about 10 percent of households. AT&T's U-verse, which has about 4 percent of the market, cannot provide comparable speeds because, while it uses fiber-optic cable to reach neighborhoods, the signal switches to slower copper lines to connect to houses. And don't even think about DSL, which carries just a fraction of the data needed to handle the services that cable users take for granted.

21   Lacking competition from other cable companies or alternate delivery technologies, each of the country's large cable distributors has the ability to raise prices in its region for high-speed Internet services. Those who can still afford it are paying higher and higher rates for the same quality of service, while those who cannot are turning to wireless.

22   It doesn't have to be this way, as a growing number of countries demonstrate. The Organization for Economic Cooperation and Development ranks America 12th among developed nations for wired Internet access, and it is safe to assume that high prices have played a role in lowering our standing. So America, the country that invented the Internet and still leads the world in telecommunications innovation, is lagging far behind in actual use of that technology.

23   The answer to this puzzle is regulatory policy. Over the last 10 years, we have deregulated high-speed Internet access in the hope that competition among providers would protect consumers. The result? We now have neither a functioning competitive market for high-speed wired Internet access nor government oversight.

24   By contrast, governments that have intervened in high-speed Internet markets have seen higher numbers of people adopting the technology, doing so earlier and at lower subscription charges. Many of these countries have required telecommunications providers to sell access to parts of their networks to competitors at regulated rates, so that competition can lower prices.

25   Meanwhile, they are working toward, or already have, fiber-optic networks that will be inexpensive, standardized, ubiquitous and equally fast for uploading and downloading. Many of those countries, not only advanced ones like Sweden and Japan but also less-developed ones like Portugal and Russia, are already well on their way to wholly replacing their standard telephone connections with state-of-the-art fiber-optic connections that will even further reduce the cost to users, while significantly improving access speeds.

26   The only thing close is FiOS. But, according to Diffraction Analysis, a research firm, it costs six times as much as comparable service in Hong Kong, five times as much as in Paris and two and a half times as much as in Amsterdam.

When it comes to the retail cost of fiber access in America, we do about as well as Istanbul.

The new digital divide raises important questions about social equity in an infor- 27 mation-driven world. But it is also a matter of protecting our economic future. Thirty years from now, African-Americans and Latinos, who are at the greatest risk of being left behind in the Internet revolution, will be more than half of our work force. If we want to be competitive in the global economy, we need to make sure every American has truly high-speed wired access to the Internet for a reasonable cost.

Source: *New York Times*, December 4, 2011. Reprinted by permission of the author.

QUESTIONS FOR READING

1. How has online access created a divide in our society?
2. Who are those with access? What groups are, in general, left out?
3. To what do those with wired high-speed connections have access?
4. What percentage of Americans have smartphones? What group of Americans have wired high-speed Internet access at home? What percentage have no Internet access?
5. What are the limitations of smartphones?

QUESTIONS FOR REASONING AND ANALYSIS

6. Explain how and where wired (cable) access is provided; why is this a problem?
7. How do our costs and availability compare to that in other countries? Why should this comparison bother us?
8. What is Crawford's claim? Where does she state it? What does she gain with her choice of placement?

QUESTIONS FOR REFLECTION AND WRITING

9. Has the author convinced you that the digital divide is a problem? Why or why not?
10. Do you agree with her solution? If so, why? If not, how would you refute Crawford's proposal?

DO NOT FEAR THE CYBERMIND | DANIEL M. WEGNER

A professor of psychology at Harvard University since 2000, Daniel Wegner studies the role of thought in self-control and social life. Two of his books include the textbook *Psychology* (2nd ed., 2011, with coauthors) and *The Illusion of Conscious Will* (2002). The following article, drawn from his research on transactive memory, was published August 5, 2012.

PREREADING QUESTIONS Given Professor Wegner's areas of research, to what do you expect the "cybermind" refers? Based on the title, what genre of argument do you expect?

1   The line that separates my mind from the Internet is getting blurry. This has been happening ever since I realized how often it feels as though I know something just because I can find it with Google. Technically, of course, I don't know it. But when there's a smartphone or iPad in reach, I know everything the Internet knows. Or at least, that's how it feels.

2   This curious feeling of knowing has settled over most of us. In a group, someone always seems to be "checking" something in the conversation, piping up with handy facts culled from a rapid consultation with the Great and Powerful Man Behind the Curtain. I've attended more than one nerdy party where *everyone* had a link open and we were all talking about things we didn't know until we were prompted by our conversation to look them up.

3   Who knew that the king of hearts was the only one without a mustache? Well, I did—as soon as I checked. The Web is always there, an ever present cloud of intelligence.

4   The desire to consult the Web is almost like an itch. This was illustrated empirically in an experiment that Betsy Sparrow, Jenny Liu and I reported in the journal *Science* last year. We asked people either a series of easy trivia questions or a series of hard ones, and then immediately checked to see if consulting the Web was on their minds.

5   To do this, we measured their reaction times as they tried quickly to name the colors in which various words—including computer-related words (like "computer" or "laptop" or "Google")—were printed. The idea, based on an established principle in psychology, was that if computer-related thoughts were on people's minds, computer-related words would interfere with color-naming. (For instance, it's harder to identify the color that your own name is printed in than the color of some random name.) And after the batch of hard questions, people did indeed seem to have computers on their minds: many became especially slow to name the colors of computer-related words. When we're faced with hard questions, we don't search our minds—we first think of the Web.

6   Has this computer dependency made people stupid? In a further study, our group looked into the effect of computer availability on memory. We asked people to type into a computer 40 factoids they had each just been given. (For example, French fries are originally from Belgium, not France.) Those who were told the computer would not record these facts tended often to remember the facts themselves. But those told that the computer would record everything were inclined promptly to forget them. Knowing we can fall back on our computers makes us fail to store information in our own memories.

7   How did this happen? How did we become so dependent on these gadgets? Some commentators on the growth of technology see this step as the beginning of a chilling new world in which we have uploaded everything we know quite out of our own heads, becoming fools in the bargain. Like those who feared the iron horse or the electric toothbrush, though, people with this neo-Luddité view of technology are quite likely to be left behind as the rest of us rush to keep plugged in. The more forward-looking view is to accept the role of the Web as a mind-expander and wonder not at the bad but at the good it can do us.

There's nothing wrong, after all, with having our minds expanded. Each   8
time we learn *who* knows something or *where* we can find information—
without learning *what* the information itself might be—we are expanding our
mental reach. This is the basic idea behind so-called transactive memory. In
1985, with my collaborators Toni Giuliano (who is also my wife) and Paula
Hertél, I wrote a paper introducing the idea of transactive memory as a way to
understand the group mind. We observed that nobody remembers everything.
Instead, each of us in a couple or group remembers some things personally—
and then can remember much more by knowing who else might know what we
don't. In this way, we become part of a transactive memory system.

Toni and I noticed not long after we were married that we were sharing mem-   9
ory duties. I remembered where car and yard things were, she remembered
where house things were, and we could each depend on the other to be an
expert in domains we didn't need to master. The car-washing sponge was a problem, as it was both a house thing and car thing—so naturally each of us thought
it was the other's job and we misplaced it. But usually, our transactive memory
worked fine, and we got things done together. Never once did we get our assignments confused and leave our daughter waiting at the curb at day care.

Groups of people commonly depend on one another for memory in this way—   10
not by all knowing the same thing, but by specializing. And now we've added our
computing devices to the network, depending for memory not just on people but
also on a cloud of linked people and specialized information-filled devices.

We have all become a great cybermind. As long as we are connected to   11
our machines through talk and keystrokes, we can all be part of the biggest,
smartest mind ever. It is only when we are trapped for a moment without our
Internet link that we return to our own humble little personal minds, tumbling
back to earth from our flotation devices in the cloud.

Source: *New York Times*, August 5, 2012. Reprinted by permission of the author.

QUESTIONS FOR READING

1. Who is the "Great and Powerful Man Behind the Curtain"?
2. Explain the author's experiment; what did it demonstrate?
3. What did subjects in the second experiment do? What did this experiment
    demonstrate?
4. Explain the term *neo-Luddite.*
5. What is a transactive memory system?

QUESTIONS FOR REASONING AND ANALYSIS

6. What does Wegner want to show by using his wife and himself as an example?
7. What is the author's claim?
8. What kinds of evidence does Wegner provide? How does he refute those who
    think the Internet is making us stupid?

QUESTIONS FOR REFLECTION AND WRITING

9. What is your reaction to Wegner's image of a great cybermind of which we are all a part?

10. Do you agree with the author's rebuttal of the neo-Luddites? If yes, why? If no, how would you refute Wegner?

THE DEATH OF THE CYBERFLÂNEUR | EVGENY MOROZOV

Originally from Belarus, Evgeny Morozov is a journalist who studies the social implications of technology. He writes a syndicated monthly column about the Internet for *Slate* and for some European newspapers and is a contributing editor to *Foreign Policy*. *The New Delusion: The Dark Side of Internet Freedom* was published in 2011 and updated with a new afterword in 2012. His article on the cyberflâneur appeared February 5, 2012.

PREREADING QUESTIONS What is a flâneur? (If you don't know the word, look it up.) What, then, would a *cyberflâneur* be?

1   The other day, while I was rummaging through a stack of oldish articles on the future of the Internet, an obscure little essay from 1998—published, of all places, on a Web site called *Ceramics Today*—caught my eye. Celebrating the rise of the "cyberflâneur," it painted a bright digital future, brimming with playfulness, intrigue and serendipity, that awaited this mysterious online type. This vision of tomorrow seemed all but inevitable at a time when "what the city and the street were to the Flâneur, the Internet and the Superhighway have become to the Cyberflâneur."

2   Intrigued, I set out to discover what happened to the cyberflâneur. While I quickly found other contemporaneous commentators who believed that flânerie would flourish online, the sad state of today's Internet suggests that they couldn't have been more wrong. Cyberflâneurs are few and far between, while the very practice of cyberflânerie seems at odds with the world of social media. What went wrong? And should we worry?

3   Engaging the history of flânerie may be a good way to start answering these questions. Thanks to the French poet Charles Baudelaire and the German critic Walter Benjamin, both of whom viewed the flâneur as an emblem of modernity, his figure (and it was predominantly a "he") is now firmly associated with 19th-century Paris. The flâneur would leisurely stroll through its streets and especially its arcades—those stylish, lively and bustling rows of shops covered by glass roofs—to cultivate what Honoré de Balzac called "the gastronomy of the eye."

4   While not deliberately concealing his identity, the flâneur preferred to stroll incognito. "The art that the flâneur masters is that of seeing without being caught looking," the Polish sociologist Zygmunt Bauman once remarked. The flâneur was not asocial—he needed the crowds to thrive—but he did not blend in, preferring to savor his solitude. And he had all the time in the world: there were reports of flâneurs taking turtles for a walk.

5   The flâneur wandered in the shopping arcades, but he did not give in to the temptations of consumerism; the arcade was primarily a pathway to a rich sensory experience—and only then a temple of consumption. His goal was to observe, to bathe in the crowd, taking in its noises, its chaos, its heterogeneity, its

cosmopolitanism. Occasionally, he would narrate what he saw—surveying both his private self and the world at large—in the form of short essays for daily newspapers.

It's easy to see, then, why cyberflânerie seemed such an appealing notion 6 in the early days of the Web. The idea of exploring cyberspace as virgin territory, not yet colonized by governments and corporations, was romantic; that romanticism was even reflected in the names of early browsers ("Internet Explorer," "Netscape Navigator").

Online communities like GeoCities and Tripod were the true digital arcades of 7 that period, trading in the most obscure and the most peculiar, without any sort of hierarchy ranking them by popularity or commercial value. Back then eBay was weirder than most flea markets; strolling through its virtual stands was far more pleasurable than buying any of the items. For a brief moment in the mid-1990s, it did seem that the Internet might trigger an unexpected renaissance of flânerie.

However, anyone entertaining such dreams of the Internet as a refuge for 8 the bohemian, the hedonistic and the idiosyncratic probably didn't know the reasons behind the disappearance of the original flâneur.

In the second half of the 19th century, Paris was experiencing rapid and 9 profound change. The architectural and city planning reforms advanced by Baron Haussmann during the rule of Napoleon III were particularly consequential: the demolition of small medieval streets, the numbering of buildings for administrative purposes, the establishment of wide, open, transparent boulevards (built partly to improve hygiene, partly to hamper revolutionary blockades), the proliferation of gas street lighting and the growing appeal of spending time outdoors radically transformed the city.

Technology and social change had an effect as well. The advent of street 10 traffic made contemplative strolling dangerous. The arcades were soon replaced by larger, utilitarian department stores. Such rationalization of city life drove flâneurs underground, forcing some of them into a sort of "internal flânerie" that reached its apogee in Marcel Proust's self-imposed exile in his cork-lined room (situated, ironically, on Boulevard Haussmann).

11   Something similar has happened to the Internet. Transcending its original playful identity, it's no longer a place for strolling—it's a place for getting things done. Hardly anyone "surfs" the Web anymore. The popularity of the "app paradigm," whereby dedicated mobile and tablet applications help us accomplish what we want without ever opening the browsér or visiting the rest of the Internet, has made cyberflânerie less likely. That so much of today's online activity revolves around shopping—for virtual presents, for virtual pets, for virtual presents for virtual pets—hasn't helped either. Strolling through Groupon isn't as much fun as strolling through an arcade, online or off.

12   The tempo of today's Web is different as well. A decade ago, a concept like the "real-time Web," in which our every tweet and status update is instantaneously indexed, updated and responded to, was unthinkable. Today, it's Silicon Valley's favorite buzz-word.

13   That's no surprise: people like speed and efficiency. But the slowly loading pages of old, accompanied by the funky buzz of the modem, had their own weird poetics, opening new spaces for play and interpretation. Occasionally, this slowness may have even alerted us to the fact that we were sitting in front of a computer. Well, that turtle is no more.

14   Meanwhile, Google, in its quest to organize all of the world's information, is making it unnecessary to visit individual Web sites in much the same way that the Sears catalog made it unnecessary to visit physical stores several generations earlier. Google's latest grand ambition is to answer our questions—about the weather, currency exchange rates, yesterday's game—all by itself, without having us visit any other sites at all. Just plug in a question to the Google homepage, and your answer comes up at the top of the search results.

15   Whether such shortcuts harm competition in the search industry (as Google's competitors allege) is beside the point; anyone who imagines information-seeking in such purely instrumental terms, viewing the Internet as little more than a giant Q & A machine, is unlikely to construct digital spaces hospitable to cyberflânerie.

16   But if today's Internet has a Baron Haussmann, it is Facebook. Everything that makes cyberflânerie possible—solitude and individuality, anonymity and opacity, mystery and ambivalence, curiosity and risk-taking—is under assault by that company. And it's not just any company: with 845 million active users worldwide, where Facebook goes, arguably, so goes the Internet.

17   It's easy to blame Facebook's business model (e.g., the loss of online anonymity allows it to make more money from advertising), but the problem resides much deeper. Facebook seems to believe that the quirky ingredients that make flânerie possible need to go. "We want everything to be social," Sheryl Sandberg, Facebook's chief operating officer, said on *Charlie Rose* a few months ago.

18   What this means in practice was explained by her boss, Mark Zuckerberg, on that same show. "Do you want to go to the movies by yourself or do you want to go to the movies with your friends?" he asked, immediately answering his own question: "You want to go with your friends."

The implications are clear: Facebook wants to build an Internet where watch- 19
ing films, listening to music, reading books and even browsing is done not just
openly but socially and collaboratively. Through clever partnerships with companies like Spotify and Netflix, Facebook will create powerful (but latent) incentives
that would make users eagerly embrace the tyranny of the "social," to the point
where pursuing any of those activities on their own would become impossible.

Now, if Mr. Zuckerberg really believes what he said about cinema, there is 20
a long list of films I'd like to run by his friends. Why not take them to see
Satantango, a seven-hour, black-and-white art-house flick by the Hungarian
auteur Bela Tarr? Well, because if you took an open poll of his friends, or any
large enough group of people, *Satantango* would almost always lose out to
something more mainstream, like *War Horse.* It might not be everyone's top
choice, but it won't offend, either—that's the tyranny of the social for you.

Besides, isn't it obvious that consuming great art alone is qualitatively dif- 21
ferent from consuming it socially? And why this fear of solitude in the first
place? It's hard to imagine packs of flâneurs roaming the streets of Paris as if
auditioning for another sequel to *The Hangover.* But for Mr. Zuckerberg, as he
acknowledged on *Charlie Rose,* "it feels better to be more connected to all
these people. You have a richer life."

It's this idea that the individual experience is somehow inferior to the col- 22
lective that underpins Facebook's recent embrace of "frictionless sharing,"
the idea that, from now on, we have to worry only about things we don't want
to share; everything else will be shared automatically. To that end, Facebook is
encouraging its partners to build applications that automatically share everything we do: articles we read, music we listen to, videos we watch. It goes
without saying that frictionless sharing also makes it easier for Facebook to
sell us to advertisers, and for advertisers to sell their wares back to us.

That might even be worth it if frictionless sharing enhanced our online experi- 23
ence; after all, even the 19th-century flâneur eventually confronted advertising
posters and murals on his walks around town. Sadly, frictionless sharing has the
same drawback as "effortless poetry": its final products are often intolerable. It's
one thing to find an interesting article and choose to share it with friends. It's quite
another to inundate your friends with everything that passes through your browser
or your app, hoping that they will pick something interesting along the way.

Worse, when this frictionless sharing scheme becomes fully operational, 24
we will probably read all our news on Facebook, without ever leaving its con-
fines to visit the rest of the Web; several news outlets, including the *Guardian*
and the *Washington Post,* already have Facebook applications that allow users
to read their articles without even visiting their Web sites.

As the popular technology blogger Robert Scoble explained in a recent 25
post defending frictionless sharing, "The new world is you; just open up
Facebook and everything you care about will be streaming down the screen."

This is the very stance that is killing cyberflânerie: the whole point of the flâ- 26
neur's wanderings is that he does not know what he cares about. As the German
writer Franz Hessel, an occasional collaborator with Walter Benjamin, put it, "in
order to engage in flânerie, one must not have anything too definite in mind."
Compared with Facebook's highly deterministic universe, even Microsoft's

unimaginative slogan from the 1990s —"Where do you want to go today?" — sounds excitingly subversive. Who asks that silly question in the age of Facebook?

27   According to Benjamin, the sad figure of the sandwich board man was the last incarnation of the flâneur. In a way, we have all become such sandwich board men, walking the cyber-streets of Facebook with invisible advertisements hanging off our online selves. The only difference is that the digital nature of information has allowed us to merrily consume songs, films and books even as we advertise them, obliviously.

Source: *New York Times*, February 5, 2012. Reprinted by permission of the author.

QUESTIONS FOR READING

1. What was the occasion for Morozov's essay?
2. What are the characteristics of the flâneur? When and where did he flourish?
3. What characteristics of the early Web led observers to expect the cyberflâneur to flourish?
4. What led to the demise of the flâneur?
5. How did the Internet change in ways not hospitable to the cyberflâneur?

QUESTIONS FOR REASONING AND ANALYSIS

6. What is "frictionless sharing"? Does Morozov think this is a good thing? Explain.
7. How is Facebook like Baron Haussmann? What seems to be the author's attitude toward Facebook?
8. What is Morozov's claim? What is his primary organizing strategy? How does it help him develop his argument?
9. Explain the author's image of us all as sandwich-board people.

QUESTIONS FOR REFLECTION AND WRITING

10. Do you want "everything to be social"? Why or why not?
11. Do you agree that many people today seem to fear solitude? Do you agree with Morozov that we should not fear it? Why or why not?
12. Which of Morozov's comparisons, images, or metaphors strikes you the most? Why?

FACEBOOK IS USING YOU | LORI B. ANDREWS

Lori Andrews is a professor of law at Chicago-Kent College of Law and director of the Institute for Science, Law and Technology. She has been involved in setting policies for genetic technologies and is recognized as an expert on developing technologies. Her ten nonfiction books include *Genetics: Ethics, Law and Policy* (2002; 2nd ed., 2006) and *I Know Who You Are and I Saw What You Did: Social Networks and the Death of Privacy* (2012). The following essay appeared on February 5, 2012.

PREREADING QUESTIONS Do you use Facebook? How can Facebook be using you?

Last week, Facebook filed docu- 1 ments with the government that will allow it to sell shares of stock to the public. It is estimated to be worth at least $75 billion. But unlike other big-ticket corporations, it doesn't have an inventory of widgets or gadgets, cars or phones. Facebook's inventory consists of personal data—yours and mine.

Facebook makes money by selling ad space to companies that want to reach 2 us. Advertisers choose key words or details—like relationship status, location, activities, favorite books and employment—and then Facebook runs the ads for the targeted subset of its 845 million users. If you indicate that you like cupcakes, live in a certain neighborhood and have invited friends over, expect an ad from a nearby bakery to appear on your page. The magnitude of online information Facebook has available about each of us for targeted marketing is stunning. In Europe, laws give people the right to know what data companies have about them, but that is not the case in the United States.

Facebook made $3.2 billion in advertising revenue last year, 85 percent of 3 its total revenue. Yet Facebook's inventory of data and its revenue from advertising are small potatoes compared to some others. Google took in more than 10 times as much, with an estimated $36.5 billion in advertising revenue in 2011, by analyzing what people sent over Gmail and what they searched on the Web, and then using that data to sell ads. Hundreds of other companies have also staked claims on people's online data by depositing software called cookies or other tracking mechanisms on people's computers and in their browsers. If you've mentioned anxiety in an e-mail, done a Google search for "stress" or started using an online medical diary that lets you monitor your mood, expect ads for medications and services to treat your anxiety.

Ads that pop up on your screen might seem useful, or at worst, a nui- 4 sance. But they are much more than that. The bits and bytes about your life can easily be used against you. Whether you can obtain a job, credit or insurance can be based on your digital doppelgänger—and you may never know why you've been turned down.

Material mined online has been used against people battling for child cus- 5 tody or defending themselves in criminal cases. LexisNexis has a product called Accurint for Law Enforcement, which gives government agents information about what people do on social networks. The Internal Revenue Service searches Facebook and MySpace for evidence of tax evaders' income and whereabouts, and United States Citizenship and Immigration Services has been known to scrutinize photos and posts to confirm family relationships or weed out sham marriages. Employers sometimes decide whether to hire people based on their online profiles, with one study indicating that 70 percent of recruiters and human resource professionals in the United States have rejected candidates based on data found online. A company called Spokeo gathers online data for employers, the public and anyone else who wants it. The company even posts ads urging "HR Recruiters—Click Here Now!" and asking women to submit their boyfriends' e-mail addresses for an analysis of their online photos and activities to learn "Is He Cheating on You?"

6   Stereotyping is alive and well in data aggregation. Your application for credit could be declined not on the basis of your own finances or credit history, but on the basis of aggregate data—what other people whose likes and dislikes are similar to yours have done. If guitar players or divorcing couples are more likely to renege on their credit-card bills, then the fact that you've looked at guitar ads or sent an e-mail to a divorce lawyer might cause a data aggregator to classify you as less credit-worthy. When an Atlanta man returned from his honeymoon, he found that his credit limit had been lowered to $3,800 from $10,800. The switch was not based on anything he had done but on aggregate data. A letter from the company told him, "Other customers who have used their card at establishments where you recently shopped have a poor repayment history with American Express."

7   Even though laws allow people to challenge false information in credit reports, there are no laws that require data aggregators to reveal what they know about you. If I've Googled "diabetes" for a friend or "date rape drugs" for a mystery I'm writing, data aggregators assume those searches reflect my own health and proclivities. Because no laws regulate what types of data these aggregators can collect, they make their own rules.

8   In 2007 and 2008, the online advertising company NebuAd contracted with six Internet service providers to install hardware on their networks that monitored users' Internet activities and transmitted that data to NebuAd's servers for analysis and use in marketing. For an average of six months, NebuAd copied every e-mail, Web search or purchase that some 400,000 people sent over the Internet. Other companies, like Healthline Networks Inc., have in-house limits on which private information they will collect. Healthline does not use information about people's searches related to H.I.V., impotence or eating disorders to target ads to people, but it will use information about bipolar disorder, overactive bladder and anxiety, which can be as stigmatizing as the topics on its privacy-protected list.

9   In the 1970s, a professor of communication studies at Northwestern University named John McKnight popularized the term "redlining" to describe the failure of banks, insurers and other institutions to offer their services to inner city neighborhoods. The term came from the practice of bank officials who drew a red line on a map to indicate where they wouldn't invest. But use of the term expanded to cover a wide array of racially discriminatory practices, such as not offering home loans to African-Americans, even those who were wealthy or middle class.

10   Now the map used in redlining is not a geographic map, but the map of your travels across the Web. The term Weblining describes the practice of denying people opportunities based on their digital selves. You might be refused health insurance based on a Google search you did about a medical

condition. You might be shown a credit card with a lower credit limit, not because of your credit history, but because of your race, sex or ZIP code or the types of Web sites you visit.

Data aggregation has social implications as well. When young people in poor neighborhoods are bombarded with advertisements for trade schools, will they be more likely than others their age to forgo college? And when women are shown articles about celebrities rather than stock market trends, will they be less likely to develop financial savvy? Advertisers are drawing new redlines, limiting people to the roles society expects them to play. 11

Data aggregators' practices conflict with what people say they want. A 2008 *Consumer Reports* poll of 2,000 people found that 93 percent thought Internet companies should always ask for permission before using personal information, and 72 percent wanted the right to opt out of online tracking. A study by Princeton Survey Research Associates in 2009 using a random sample of 1,000 people found that 69 percent thought that the United States should adopt a law giving people the right to learn everything a Web site knows about them. We need a do-not-track law, similar to the do-not-call one. Now it's not just about whether my dinner will be interrupted by a telemarketer. It's about whether my dreams will be dashed by the collection of bits and bytes over which I have no control and for which companies are currently unaccountable. 12

Source: *New York Times*, February 5, 2012. Reprinted by permission of the author.

QUESTIONS FOR READING

1. How many people use Facebook?
2. How does Facebook make most of its money?
3. What is a "digital doppelganger"?
4. How is "redlining" used today to describe Web activity?
5. What do studies reveal about our preferences with regard to the Internet's tracking and data collecting?

QUESTIONS FOR REASONING AND ANALYSIS

6. What kinds of information are being collected about us from our Internet use? What is the author's attitude toward Internet tracking?
7. What, then, is the claim of her argument?
8. How does Andrews develop and support her argument?

QUESTIONS FOR REFLECTION AND WRITING

9. Has Andrews convinced you that digital mining leads to more serious problems than tailored pop-up ads? Why or why not?
10. Do you agree with the author's solution to the problem she sees? If yes, why? If no, why not?

CHAPTER 17

Marriage and Gender Issues: The Debates Continue

READ: What happens in the cartoon? How does Marvin characterize the dog's attitude?

REASON: What attitude is reflected in the way the dog is drawn in the first frame in the bottom row? What attitude is reflected in the way the cat is drawn in the middle frame in the bottom row?

REFLECT/WRITE: What makes the cartoon a clever way of expressing the artist's opposition to stereotyping?

Six writers provide much for readers to debate and reflect upon in this chapter on marriage and gender issues. The writers examine the incredible—and in some cases still controversial—changes to the institution of marriage and—by extension—to the family. And that extension immediately takes us to gender issues, to debates over "who's up and who's down," men or women, and to changing views—and laws—regarding gay marriage and gay families. (About one-third of gay partnerships have one or more children, an important statistic in these discussions.)

Here are a few more interesting statistics relevant to the debates in this chapter: In 2010, according to a Gallup poll, for the first time more than 50 percent of Americans supported gay and lesbian relationships. And for the first time, more men than women supported gay partnerships, with the greatest shifts in support coming from both young adult men and older men.

Some of the writers in this chapter approach the changes in marriage and gender views—and their effects on our politics, our culture, and our personal lives—from a social science perspective; others take a more jocular or satiric approach. Some write from the perspective of research data; others develop arguments from emotion or from a legal perspective. Some express strongly held views; others seek common ground. But, whatever the writer's specific topic, or the basis for the argument, or the values expressed, all would agree that the changes of the past thirty years have had a profound effect on our lives. All would probably also agree that while some issues will continue to benefit from both research and reflection, the reality is that the United States has accepted gay partnerships and is on the way to providing legal status for these partnerships.

PREREADING QUESTIONS

1. Do you expect to have a career? To have a spouse and children? Should society support both men and women having these choices? If so, how?

2. What role, if any, should government and the courts have in defining marriage?

3. What has been meant by the "traditional family"? In what ways has the "family" been reshaped in the twenty-first century?

4. Do you have a position on gay marriage? On partnership recognition and rights? If you have a position, what is it, and what is its source?

5. Do you expect to live with someone prior to marriage? Do you think such arrangements will benefit the marriage that you assume will follow? Would it be a good idea to learn more about cohabiting?

6. Much has been written recently about women getting ahead at the expense of men; do you think this is the case? Would it be useful to look at some of the facts?

ABOLISH MARRIAGE | MICHAEL KINSLEY

A member of the bar with a law degree from Harvard, Michael Kinsley is a former editor of both *Harper's* and *The New Republic* and a former columnist for the *Washington Post*. He is the founding editor (1996) of *Slate*, the online magazine, and has been a cohost of CNN's *Crossfire*. He is currently a columnist for *Bloomberg View*. The following column appeared July 3, 2003.

PREREADING QUESTIONS What are the key issues in the debate over gay marriage? What are gay marriage proponents seeking? What are social conservatives seeking?

1   Critics and enthusiasts of *Lawrence v. Texas,* last week's Supreme Court decision invalidating state anti-sodomy laws, agree on one thing: The next argument is going to be about gay marriage. As Justice Antonin Scalia noted in his tart dissent, it follows from the logic of *Lawrence.* Mutually consenting sex with the person of your choice in the privacy of your own home is now a basic right of American citizenship under the Constitution. This does not mean that the government must supply it or guarantee it. But the government cannot forbid it, and the government also should not discriminate against you for choosing to exercise a basic right of citizenship. Offering an institution as important as marriage to male-female couples only is exactly this kind of discrimination. Or so the gay rights movement will now argue. Persuasively, I think.

2   Opponents of gay rights will resist mightily, although they have been in retreat for a couple of decades. General anti-gay sentiments are now considered a serious breach of civic etiquette, even in anti-gay circles. The current line of defense, which probably won't hold either, is between social toleration of homosexuals and social approval of homosexuality. Or between accepting the reality that people are gay, even accepting that gays are people, and endorsing something called "the gay agenda." Gay marriage, the opponents will argue, would cross this line. It would make homosexuality respectable and, worse, normal. Gays are welcome to exist all they want, and to do their inexplicable thing if they must, but they shouldn't expect a government stamp of approval.

3   It's going to get ugly. And then it's going to get boring. So we have two options here. We can add gay marriage to the short list of controversies—abortion, affirmative action, the death penalty—that are so frozen and ritualistic that debates about them are more like kabuki performances than intellectual exercises. Or we can think outside the box. There is a solution that ought to satisfy both camps, and may not be a bad idea even apart from the gay marriage controversy.

4   That solution is to end the institution of marriage. Or rather (he hastens to clarify, dear) the solution is to end the institution of government-sanctioned marriage. Or, framed to appeal to conservatives: End the government monopoly on marriage. Wait, I've got it: Privatize marriage. These slogans all mean the same thing. Let churches and other religious institutions continue to offer marriage ceremonies. Let department stores and casinos get into the act if they want. Let each organization decide for itself what kinds of couples it wants to offer marriage to. Let couples celebrate their union in any way they choose and consider themselves married whenever they want. Let others be free to consider them not married, under rules these others may prefer. And, yes, if three people want to get married, or one person wants to marry herself,

and someone else wants to conduct a ceremony and declare them married, let 'em. If you and your government aren't implicated, what do you care?

In fact, there is nothing to stop any of this from happening now. And a lot of it 5 does happen. But only certain marriages get certified by the government. So, in the United States we are about to find ourselves in a strange situation where the principal demand of a liberation movement is to be included in the red tape of a government bureaucracy. Having just gotten state governments out of their bed-rooms, gays now want these governments back in. Meanwhile, social-conservative anti-gays, many of them southerners, are calling on the government in Washington to trample states' rights and nationalize the rules of marriage, if necessary, to prevent gays from getting what they want. The Senate majority leader, Bill Frist of Tennessee, responded to the Supreme Court's *Lawrence* deci-sion by endorsing a constitutional amendment, no less, against gay marriage.

If marriage were an entirely private affair, all the disputes over gay mar- 6 riage would become irrelevant. Gay marriage would not have the official sanc-tion of government, but neither would straight marriage. There would be official equality between the two, which is the essence of what gays want and are entitled to. And if the other side is sincere in saying that its concern is not what people do in private but government endorsement of a gay "lifestyle" or "agenda," that problem goes away too.

Yes, yes, marriage is about more than sleeping arrangements. There are 7 children, there are finances, there are spousal job benefits such as health insur-ance and pensions. In all of these areas, marriage is used as a substitute for other factors that are harder to measure, such as financial dependence or devo-tion to offspring. It would be possible to write rules that measure the real fac-tors at stake and leave marriage out of the matter. Regarding children and finances, people can set their own rules, as many already do. None of this would be easy. Marriage functions as what lawyers call a "bright line," which saves the trouble of trying to measure a lot of amorphous factors. You're either married or you're not. Once marriage itself becomes amorphous, who-gets-the-kids and who-gets-health-care become trickier questions.

So, sure, there are some legitimate objections to the idea of privatizing 8 marriage. But they don't add up to a fatal objection. Especially when you con-sider that the alternative is arguing about gay marriage until death do us part.

Source: *Washington Post*, July 3, 2003. Reprinted by permission.

QUESTIONS FOR READING

1. What will the next argument be about? What ruling will bring on this argu-ment? What about the ruling invites the argument?

2. Who will win the argument, in Kinsley's view?

3. According to the author, where are we in the "tug-of-war" over gay rights? Where would allowing gay marriage put us in the battle?

4. What is the author's solution to end the argument?

5. What is ironic about gays fighting for the right to marry? What is ironic about conservatives seeking a constitutional amendment against gay marriage?

6. What problems would emerge if governments stopped sanctioning marriage altogether? Are these problems insurmountable, in the author's view?

QUESTIONS FOR REASONING AND ANALYSIS

7. What is Kinsley's claim? Where does he state it?

8. When Kinsley writes that the argument over gay marriage will "get boring," what does he mean? How does his comparison to kabuki performances or to debates over abortion or the death penalty illustrate his point here?

9. How does Kinsley seek to convince both sides of the argument that his solution should please them?

10. The author anticipates counterarguments in his last two paragraphs. How effective is his rebuttal?

11. Analyze the essay's tone. How serious do you think Kinsley is in presenting his solution to the argument over gay marriage? If he does not think his solution is viable, then why is he proposing it? What is his purpose in writing?

QUESTIONS FOR REFLECTION AND WRITING

12. What is your reaction to Kinsley's proposal? Is the best solution to get government out of certifying marriage? If we wanted to "think outside the box," could we solve the other problems—of finances, child custody, and so forth—if we wanted to? How would you support the proposal or challenge it?

13. How will this issue end—and when—in your view? Why?

MY BIG FAT STRAIGHT WEDDING | ANDREW SULLIVAN

British-born Andrew Sullivan graduated from Oxford and has a PhD from Harvard University. Writing for newspapers and magazines, he was editor of *The New Republic* in the 90s, is a columnist for *Time* magazine, and in 2000 started his blog, *The Daily Dish*, first attached to *Time* but now at the *Atlantic online*. Sullivan has written six books, including *The Conservative Soul* (2006) and *Same-Sex Marriage: Pro and Con* (2004). The following article appeared in the September 2008 issue of the *Atlantic*.

PREREADING QUESTIONS What is the "source" of Sullivan's title? How does his title suggest his topic?

1   What if gays were straight?

2   The question is absurd—gays are defined as not straight, right?—yet increasingly central to the debate over civil-marriage rights. Here is how California's Supreme Court put it in a key passage in its now-famous May 15 [2008] ruling that gay couples in California must be granted the right to marry, with no qualifications or euphemisms:

These core substantive rights include, most fundamentally, the opportunity of an individual to establish—with the person with whom the individual has chosen to share his or her life—an *officially recognized and protected family* possessing mutual rights and responsibilities and entitled to the same respect and dignity accorded a union traditionally designated as marriage.

What's notable here is the starting point of the discussion: an "individual." The individual citizen posited by the court is defined as prior to his or her sexual orientation. He or she exists as a person before he or she exists as straight or gay. And the right under discussion is defined as "the opportunity of an individual" to choose another "person" to "establish a family" in which reproduction and children are not necessary. And so the distinction between gay and straight is essentially abolished. For all the debate about the law in this decision, the debate about the terms under discussion has been close to nonexistent. And yet in many ways, these terms are at the core of the decision, and are the reason why it is such a watershed. The ruling, and the language it uses, represents the removal of the premise of the last generation in favor of a premise accepted as a given by the next.

The premise used to be that homosexuality was an activity, that gays were people who chose to behave badly; or, if they weren't choosing to behave badly, were nonetheless suffering from a form of sickness or, in the words of the Vatican, an "objective disorder." And so the question of whether to permit the acts and activities of such disordered individuals was a legitimate area of legislation and regulation.

But when gays are seen as the same as straights—as individuals; as normal, well-adjusted, human individuals—the argument changes altogether. The question becomes a matter of how we treat a minority with an involuntary, defining characteristic along the lines of gender or race. And when a generation came of age that did not merely grasp this intellectually, but knew it from their own lives and friends and family members, then the logic for full equality became irresistible.

This transformation in understanding happened organically. It began with the sexual revolution in the 1970s, and then came crashing into countless previously unaware families, as their sons and uncles and fathers died in vast numbers from AIDS in the 1980s and 1990s. It emerged as younger generations came out earlier and earlier, and as their peers came to see gay people as fellows and siblings, rather than as denizens of some distant and alien subculture. It happened as lesbian couples became parents and as gay soldiers challenged the discrimination against them. And it percolated up through the popular culture—from *Will & Grace* and *Ellen* to almost every reality show since *The Real World*.

7   What California's court did, then, was not to recognize a new right to same-sex marriage. It was to acknowledge an emergent cultural consensus. And once that consensus had been accepted, the denial of the right to marry became, for many, a constitutional outrage. The right to marry, after all, is, as the court put it, "one of the basic, inalienable civil rights guaranteed to an individual." Its denial was necessarily an outrage—and not merely an anomaly—because the right to marry has such deep and inalienable status in American constitutional law.

8   The political theorist Hannah Arendt, addressing the debate over miscegenation laws during the civil-rights movement of the 1950s, put it clearly enough:

> The right to marry whoever one wishes is an elementary human right compared to which "the right to attend an integrated school, the right to sit where one pleases on a bus, the right to go into any hotel or recreation area or place of amusement, regardless of one's skin or color or race" are minor indeed. Even political rights, like the right to vote, and nearly all other rights enumerated in the Constitution, are secondary to the inalienable human rights to "life, liberty and the pursuit of happiness" proclaimed in the Declaration of Independence; and to this category the right to home and marriage unquestionably belongs.

9   Note that Arendt put the right to marry before even the right to vote. And this is how many gay people of the next generation see it. Born into straight families and reared to see homosexuality as a form of difference, not disability, they naturally wonder why they would be excluded from the integral institution of their own families' lives and history. They see this exclusion as unimaginable— as unimaginable as straight people would if they were told that they could not legally marry someone of their choosing. No other institution has an equivalent power to include people in their own familial narrative or civic history as deeply or as powerfully as civil marriage does. And the next generation see themselves as people first and gay second.

10   Born in a different era, I reached that conclusion through more pain and fear and self-loathing than my 20-something fellow homosexuals do today. But it was always clear to me nonetheless. It just never fully came home to me until I too got married.

11   It happened first when we told our families and friends of our intentions. Suddenly, they had a vocabulary to describe and understand our relationship. I was no longer my partner's "friend" or "boyfriend"; I was his fiancé. Suddenly, everyone involved themselves in our love. They asked how I had proposed; they inquired when the wedding would be; my straight friends made jokes about marriage that simply included me as one of them. At that

first post-engagement Christmas with my in-laws, I felt something shift. They had always been welcoming and supportive. But now I was family. I felt an end—a sudden, fateful end—to an emotional displacement I had experienced since childhood.

The wedding occurred last August in Massachusetts in front of a small group 12 of family and close friends. And in that group, I suddenly realized, it was the heterosexuals who knew what to do, who guided the gay couple and our friends into the rituals and rites of family. Ours was not, we realized, a different institution, after all, and we were not different kinds of people. In the doing of it, it was the same as my sister's wedding and we were the same as my sister and brother-in-law. The strange, bewildering emotions of the moment, the cake and reception, the distracted children and weeping mothers, the morning's butterflies and the night's drunkenness: this was not a gay marriage; it was a marriage.

And our families instantly and for the first time since our early childhood 13 became not just institutions in which we were included, but institutions that we too owned and perpetuated. My sister spoke of her marriage as if it were interchangeable with my own, and my niece and nephew had no qualms in referring to my husband as their new uncle. The embossed invitations and the floral bouquets and the fear of fluffing our vows: in these tiny, bonding gestures of integration, we all came to see an alienating distinction become a unifying difference.

It was a moment that shifted a sense of our own identity within our psyches 14 and even our souls. Once this happens, the law eventually follows. In California this spring, it did.

QUESTIONS FOR READING

1. What, according to Sullivan, is the key term in California's Supreme Court ruling in favor of gay marriage? How does it change the debate about gay marriage?

2. How did the change in thinking develop?

3. What does the author view the court's decision as recognizing?

4. What does the institution of marriage offer?

5. How did Sullivan come to fully understand its significance?

QUESTIONS FOR REASONING AND ANALYSIS

6. Although Sullivan uses his own experience, this is not primarily a personal narrative. What kind of argument is it?

7. What is the author's claim?

8. What kind of evidence does he present? Explain his line of reasoning in your own words.

9. Have you experienced the same shift in thinking about gays from Sullivan's generation to those in their 20s? (Polls demonstrate the shift in attitude for the country as a whole.)

10. Would you have put the right to marry ahead of the right to vote as the more essential right? What is Hannah Arendt's basis for this view? If you disagree, how would you refute Arendt's position?

11. Has Sullivan given you a new way to think about gays and gay marriage? Is he convincing? If not, why not?

THE MYTH OF MALE DECLINE | STEPHANIE COONTZ

Stephanie Coontz has recently retired from Evergreen State College, where she taught history and family studies. She is the author of several books including *Marriage, a History: How Love Conquered Marriage* (2006), and *A Strange Stirring: The Feminine Mystique and American Women at the Dawn of the 1960s* (2012). The following article appeared September 30, 2012.

PREREADING QUESTIONS What male decline do you think the title refers to? Do you think there has been a male decline?

1   Scroll through the titles and subtitles of recent books, and you will read that women have become *The Richer Sex*, that *The Rise of Women Has Turned Men Into Boys,* and that we may even be seeing *The End of Men.* Several of the authors of these books posit that we are on the verge of a "new majority of female breadwinners," where middle-class wives lord over their husbands while demoralized single men take refuge in perpetual adolescence.

2   How is it, then, that men still control the most important industries, especially technology, occupy most of the positions on the lists of the richest Americans, and continue to make more money than women who have similar skills and education? And why do women make up only 17 percent of Congress?

3   These books and the cultural anxiety they represent reflect, but exaggerate, a transformation in the distribution of power over the past half-century. Fifty years ago, every male American was entitled to what the sociologist R. W. Connell called a "patriarchal dividend"—a lifelong affirmative-action program for men.

4   The size of that dividend varied according to race and class, but all men could count on women's being excluded from the most desirable jobs and promotions in their line of work, so the average male high school graduate earned more than the average female college graduate working the same hours. At home, the patriarchal dividend gave husbands the right to decide where the family would live and to make unilateral financial decisions. Male privilege even trumped female consent to sex, so marital rape was not a crime.

5   The curtailment of such male entitlements and the expansion of women's legal and economic rights have transformed American life, but they have

hardly produced a matriarchy. Indeed, in many arenas the progress of women has actually stalled over the past 15 years.

Let's begin by determining which is "the richer sex."   6

Women's real wages have been rising for decades, while the real wages of   7 most men have stagnated or fallen. But women's wages started from a much lower base, artificially held down by discrimination. Despite their relative improvement, women's average earnings are still lower than men's and women remain more likely to be poor.

Today women make up almost 40 percent of full-time workers in manage-   8 ment. But the median wages of female managers are just 73 percent of what male managers earn. And although women have significantly increased their representation among high earners in America over the past half-century, only 4 percent of the C.E.O.'s in *Fortune*'s top 1,000 companies are female.

What we are seeing is a convergence in economic fortunes, not female   9 ascendance. Between 2010 and 2011, men and women working full time year-round both experienced a 2.5 percent decline in income. Men suffered roughly 80 percent of the job losses at the beginning of the 2007 recession. But the ripple effect of the recession then led to cutbacks in government jobs that hit women disproportionately. As of June 2012, men had regained 46.2 percent of the jobs they lost in the recession, while women had regained 38.7 percent of their lost jobs.

The 1970s and 1980s brought an impressive reduction in job segregation   10 by gender, especially in middle-class occupations. But the sociologists David Cotter, Joan Hermsen and Reeve Vanneman report that progress slowed in the 1990s and has all but stopped since 2000. For example, the percentage of female electrical engineers doubled in each decade in the 1960s, 1970s and 1980s. But in the two decades since 1990 it has increased by only a single percentage point, leaving women at just 10 percent of the total.

Some fields have become even more gender-segregated. In 1980, 75 per-   11 cent of primary school teachers and 64 percent of social workers were women. Today women make up 80 and 81 percent of those fields. Studies show that as occupations gain a higher percentage of female workers, the pay for those jobs goes down relative to wages in similarly skilled jobs that remain bastions of male employment.

Proponents of the "women as the richer sex" scenario often note that in   12 several metropolitan areas, never-married childless women in their 20s now earn more, on average, than their male age-mates.

But this is because of the demographic anomaly that such areas have excep-   13 tionally large percentages of highly educated single white women and young, poorly educated, low-wage Latino men. Earning more than a man with less education is not the same as earning as much as an equally educated man.

Among never-married, childless 22- to 30-year-old metropolitan-area   14 workers with the same educational credentials, males out-earn females in every category, according to a reanalysis of census data to be presented next month at Boston University by Philip Cohen, a sociologist at the University of Maryland. Similarly, a 2010 Catalyst survey found that female M.B.A.'s were paid an average of $4,600 less than men in starting salaries and continue to be outpaced by men in rank and salary growth throughout their careers, even if they remain childless.

15   Among married couples when both partners are employed, wives earned an average of 38.5 percent of family income in 2010. In that year nearly 30 percent of working wives out-earned their working husbands, a huge increase from just 4 percent in 1970. But when we include all married-couple families, not just dual-earner ones, the economic clout of wives looks a lot weaker.

16   In only 20 percent of all married-couple families does the wife earn half or more of all family income, according to Professor Cohen, and in 35 percent of marriages, the wife earns less than 10 percent.

17   Once they have children, wives usually fall further behind their husbands in earnings, partly because they are more likely to temporarily quit work or cut back when workplace policies make it hard for both parents to work full time and still meet family obligations.

18   But this also reflects prejudice against working mothers. A few years ago, researchers at Cornell constructed fake résumés, identical in all respects except parental status. They asked college students to evaluate the fitness of candidates for employment or promotion. Mothers were much less likely to be hired. If hired, they were offered, on average, $11,000 less in starting salary and were much less likely to be deemed deserving of promotion.

19   The researchers also submitted similar résumés in response to more than 600 actual job advertisements. Applicants identified as childless received twice as many callbacks as the supposed mothers.

20   Much has been made of the gender gap in educational achievement. Girls have long done better in school than boys, and women have now pulled ahead of men in completing college. Today women earn almost 60 percent of college degrees, up from one-third in 1960.

21   The largest educational gender gap is among families in the top 25 percent of the earnings distribution, where women lead men by 13 percent in graduation rates, compared to just a 2 percent advantage for women from the lowest income families.

22   But at all income levels, women are still concentrated in traditionally female areas of study. Gender integration of college majors has stalled since the mid-1990s, and in some fields, women have even lost ground. Between 1970 and 1985, women's share of computer and information sciences degrees rose from 14 percent to 37 percent. But by 2008 women had fallen back to 18 percent.

23   According to the N.Y.U. sociologist Paula England, a senior fellow at the Council on Contemporary Families, most women, despite earning higher grades, seem to be educating themselves for occupations that systematically pay less.

24   Even women's greater educational achievement stems partly from continuing gender inequities. Women get a smaller payoff than men for earning a high school degree, but a bigger payoff for completing college. This is not because of their higher grade point averages, the economist Christopher Dougherty concludes, but because women seem to need more education

simply to counteract the impact of traditional job discrimination and traditional female career choices.

If the ascent of women has been much exaggerated, so has the descent of [25] men. Men's irresponsibility and bad behavior is now a stock theme in popular culture. But there has always been a subset of men who engage in crude, coercive and exploitative behavior. What's different today is that it's harder for men to get away with such behavior in long-term relationships. Women no longer feel compelled to put up with it and the legal system no longer condones it. The result is that many guys who would have been obnoxious husbands, behaving badly behind closed doors, are now obnoxious singles, trumpeting their bad behavior on YouTube.

Their boorishness may be pathetic, but it's much less destructive than the [26] masculine misbehavior of yore. Most men are in fact behaving better than ever. Domestic violence rates have been halved since 1993, while rapes and sexual assaults against women have fallen by 70 percent in that time. In recent decades, husbands have doubled their share of housework and tripled their share of child care. And this change is not confined to highly educated men.

Among dual-earner couples, husbands with the least education do as [27] much or more housework than their more educated counterparts. Men who have made these adjustments report happier marriages—and better sex lives.

One thing standing in the way of further progress for many men is the [28] same obstacle that held women back for so long: overinvestment in their gender identity instead of their individual personhood. Men are now experiencing a set of limits—externally enforced as well as self-imposed—strikingly similar to the ones Betty Friedan set out to combat in 1963, when she identified a "feminine mystique" that constrained women's self-image and options.

Although men don't face the same discriminatory laws as women did 50 [29] years ago, they do face an equally restrictive gender mystique.

Just as the feminine mystique discouraged women in the 1950s and 1960s [30] from improving their education or job prospects, on the assumption that a man would always provide for them, the masculine mystique encourages men to neglect their own self-improvement on the assumption that sooner or later their "manliness" will be rewarded.

According to a 2011 poll by the Pew Research Center, 77 percent of [31] Americans now believe that a college education is necessary for a woman to get ahead in life today, but only 68 percent think that is true for men. And just as the feminine mystique exposed girls to ridicule and harassment if they excelled at "unladylike" activities like math or sports, the masculine mystique leads to bullying and ostracism of boys who engage in "girlie" activities like studying hard and behaving well in school. One result is that men account for only 2 percent of kindergarten and preschool teachers, 3 percent of dental assistants and 9 percent of registered nurses.

The masculine mystique is institutionalized in work structures, according to [32] three new studies forthcoming in the *Journal of Social Issues*. Just as women who display "masculine" ambitions or behaviors on the job are often penalized, so are men who engage in traditionally female behaviors, like prioritizing family involvement. Men who take an active role in child care and housework at home are more likely than other men to be harassed at work.

33 Men who request family leave are often viewed as weak or uncompetitive and face a greater risk of being demoted or downsized. And men who have ever quit work for family reasons end up earning significantly less than other male employees, even when controlling for the effects of age, race, education, occupation, seniority and work hours. Now men need to liberate themselves from the pressure to prove their masculinity. Contrary to the fears of some pundits, the ascent of women does not portend the end of men. It offers a new beginning for both. But women's progress by itself is not a panacea for America's inequities. The closer we get to achieving equality of opportunity between the sexes, the more clearly we can see that the next major obstacle to improving the well-being of most men and women is the growing socioeconomic inequality within each sex.

Source: *New York Times*, September 30, 2012. Reprinted by permission of the author.

QUESTIONS FOR READING

1. Explain the term "patriarchal dividend." What advantages did it provide?
2. What are the specific ways that men outearn women?
3. Women get more BAs today than men. Why does this fact fail to lead to an economic advantage for women?
4. How has the behavior of married men changed for the better? What has happened to those men whose boorish behavior in the past continued into their marriages?
5. What does the author mean by a "masculine mystique"?

QUESTIONS FOR REASONING AND ANALYSIS

6. What is Coontz's claim? Where does she state it?
7. In general, what has changed for women economically? Why does this change fail to support the myth of male decline?
8. For what reasons does Coontz reject the notion of "male decline"? The author devotes less space to this part of the argument; is she convincing nonetheless? Explain.

QUESTIONS FOR REFLECTION AND WRITING

9. Has Coontz presented a convincing dismissal of the myth of male decline? If yes, what makes her argument compelling? If no, how would you refute her argument?
10. How does your experience correspond to Coontz's analysis of men's experiences today? Are boys who behave and study often bullied? Are men who want to devote more time to family often penalized in their careers? Should boys and men have to "prove" their masculinity? Reflect on these issues.

THE DOWNSIDE OF LIVING TOGETHER | MEG JAY

A clinical psychologist, Meg Jay is an assistant clinical professor at the University of Virginia who also has a private practice in Charlottesville. She specializes in "twentysomethings." She is the author of *The Defining Decade: Why Your Twenties Matter—and How to Make the Most of Them* (2012).

PREREADING QUESTIONS Are you cohabiting or do you picture yourself cohabiting in the future? If so, do you see this lifestyle as "convenient" or as "a logical step to marriage"?

At 32, one of my clients (I'll call her Jennifer) had a lavish wine-country wedding. By then, Jennifer and her boyfriend had lived together for more than four years. The event was attended by the couple's friends, families and two dogs. 1

When Jennifer started therapy with me less than a year later, she was looking for a divorce lawyer. "I spent more time planning my wedding than I spent happily married," she sobbed. Most disheartening to Jennifer was that she'd tried to do everything right. "My parents got married young so, of course, they got divorced. We lived together! How did this happen?" 2

Cohabitation in the United States has increased by more than 1,500 percent in the past half century. In 1960, about 450,000 unmarried couples lived together. Now the number is more than 7.5 million. The majority of young adults in their 20s will live with a romantic partner at least once, and more than half of all marriages will be preceded by cohabitation. This shift has been attributed to the sexual revolution and the availability of birth control, and in our current economy, sharing the bills makes cohabiting appealing. But when you talk to people in their 20s, you also hear about something else: cohabitation as prophylaxis. 3

In a nationwide survey conducted in 2001 by the National Marriage Project, then at Rutgers and now at the University of Virginia, nearly half of 20-somethings agreed with the statement, "You would only marry someone if he or she agreed to live together with you first, so that you could find out whether you really get along." About two-thirds said they believed that moving in together before marriage was a good way to avoid divorce. 4

But that belief is contradicted by experience. Couples who cohabit before marriage (and especially before an engagement or an otherwise clear commitment) tend to be less satisfied with their marriages—and more likely to divorce—than couples who do not. These negative outcomes are called the cohabitation effect. 5

Researchers originally attributed the cohabitation effect to selection, or the idea that cohabitors were less conventional about marriage and thus more open to divorce. As cohabitation has become a norm, however, studies have shown that the effect is not entirely explained by individual characteristics like religion, education or politics. Research suggests that at least some of the risks may lie in cohabitation itself. 6

As Jennifer and I worked to answer her question, "How did this happen?" we talked about how she and her boyfriend went from dating to cohabiting. Her response was consistent with studies reporting that most couples say it "just happened." 7

8   "We were sleeping over at each other's places all the time," she said. "We liked to be together, so it was cheaper and more convenient. It was a quick decision but if it didn't work out there was a quick exit."

9   She was talking about what researchers call "sliding, not deciding." Moving from dating to sleeping over to sleeping over a lot to cohabitation can be a gradual slope, one not marked by rings or ceremonies or sometimes even a conversation. Couples bypass talking about why they want to live together and what it will mean.

10   When researchers ask cohabitors these questions, partners often have different, unspoken—even unconscious—agendas. Women are more likely to view cohabitation as a step toward marriage, while men are more likely to see it as a way to test a relationship or postpone commitment, and this gender asymmetry is associated with negative interactions and lower levels of commitment even after the relationship progresses to marriage. One thing men and women do agree on, however, is that their standards for a live-in partner are lower than they are for a spouse.

11   Sliding into cohabitation wouldn't be a problem if sliding out were as easy. But it isn't. Too often, young adults enter into what they imagine will be low-cost, low-risk living situations only to find themselves unable to get out months, even years, later. It's like signing up for a credit card with 0 percent interest. At the end of 12 months when the interest goes up to 23 percent you feel stuck because your balance is too high to pay off. In fact, cohabitation can be exactly like that. In behavioral economics, it's called consumer lock-in.

12   Lock-in is the decreased likelihood to search for, or change to, another option once an investment in something has been made. The greater the setup costs, the less likely we are to move to another, even better, situation, especially when faced with switching costs, or the time, money and effort it requires to make a change.

13   Cohabitation is loaded with setup and switching costs. Living together can be fun and economical, and the setup costs are subtly woven in. After years of living among roommates' junky old stuff, couples happily split the rent on a nice one-bedroom apartment. They share wireless and pets and enjoy shopping for new furniture together. Later, these setup and switching costs have an impact on how likely they are to leave.

14   Jennifer said she never really felt that her boyfriend was committed to her. "I felt like I was on this multiyear, never-ending audition to be his wife," she said. "We had all this furniture. We had our dogs and all the same friends. It just made it really, really difficult to break up. Then it was like we got married because we were living together once we got into our 30s."

15   I've had other clients who also wish they hadn't sunk years of their 20s into relationships that would have lasted only months had they not been living together. Others want to feel committed to their partners, yet they are confused about whether they have consciously chosen their mates. Founding relationships on convenience or ambiguity can interfere with the process of claiming the people we love. A life built on top of "maybe you'll do" simply may not feel as dedicated as a life built on top of the "we do" of commitment or marriage.

The unfavorable connection between cohabitation and divorce does seem [16] to be lessening, however, according to a report released last month by the Department of Health and Human Services. More good news is that a 2010 survey by the Pew Research Center found that nearly two-thirds of Americans saw cohabitation as a step toward marriage.

This shared and serious view of cohabitation may go a long way toward [17] further attenuating the cohabitation effect because the most recent research suggests that serial cohabitators, couples with differing levels of commitment and those who use cohabitation as a test are most at risk for poor relationship quality and eventual relationship dissolution.

Cohabitation is here to stay, and there are things young adults can do to [18] protect their relationships from the cohabitation effect. It's important to discuss each person's motivation and commitment level beforehand and, even better, to view cohabitation as an intentional step toward, rather than a convenient test for, marriage or partnership.

It also makes sense to anticipate and regularly evaluate constraints that [19] may keep you from leaving.

I am not for or against living together, but I am for young adults knowing [20] that, far from safeguarding against divorce and unhappiness, moving in with someone can increase your chances of making a mistake—or of spending too much time on a mistake. A mentor of mine used to say, "The best time to work on someone's marriage is before he or she has one," and in our era, that may mean before cohabitation.

Source: Excerpted from Meg Jay, *The Defining Decade: Why Your Twenties Matter—and How to Make the Most of Them Now*. New York: Twelve, 2012. Reprinted by permission of the author.

QUESTIONS FOR READING

1. How popular has cohabiting become? What percentage of marriages will be preceded by cohabiting?
2. In the opinion of two-thirds of twentysomethings, what impact will cohabiting have on marriage or divorce?
3. How can cohabiting result in "lock-in"?
4. How has the connection between cohabitation and divorce recently changed?

QUESTIONS FOR REASONING AND ANALYSIS

5. What is Jay's claim? Where does she state it?
6. What does the author gain by starting with a specific example of a client and holding her claim until later?
7. What is the author's advice for protecting oneself from the "cohabitation effect"? Is this good advice for all couples at any stage in a relationship? Explain.

QUESTIONS FOR REFLECTION AND WRITING

8. Are you surprised by the "cohabitation effect"? Why or why not?

9. What is the most important idea in this article that you want to share with friends? Why?

10. Many young people today do more hooking up than long-term dating of one person. Could this new form of "dating" with so little commitment have the effect of leading to cohabitation with little commitment? Reflect on and be prepared to discuss these relationship patterns.

UN-HITCHING THE MIDDLE CLASS | KATHLEEN PARKER

A columnist since 1987, Kathleen Parker became nationally syndicated in 1995 when she joined the *Washington Post*. She is a regular commentator on *The Chris Matthews Show* and the author of *Save the Males: Why Men Matter, Why Women Should Care* (2008). The following column appeared December 15, 2012.

PREREADING QUESTIONS What does the title suggest about this column's subject? Does the context of the chapter help to clarify Parker's topic?

1 As politicians compete to prove who loves the middle class more, they're missing the elephant *and* the donkey in the room.

2   The middle class needs not just tax breaks and jobs but also marriage.

3   This is the finding of a new University of Virginia and Institute for American Values report, "The State of Our Unions," which tracks the decline of marriage among the nearly 60 percent of Americans who have high school but not college educations. This has far-reaching repercussions that are not only societal but economic as well. By one estimate cited in the report, which was written by five family scholars, the cost to taxpayers when stable families fail to form is about $112 billion annually— or more than $1 trillion per decade.

4   Obviously, marriage or the lack thereof isn't the only cause of our deficit spending, but neither is it irrelevant. Consider that in the 1980s, only 13 percent of children were born outside of marriage among moderately educated mothers. By the end of this century's first decade, the number had risen to 44 percent.

That we seem unfazed by these numbers suggests a lack of attention to the 5
reasons marriage matters in the first place. It isn't so that wedding planners can
bilk daydreamers out of $50 billion a year or so that bridezillas can have reality
TV shows. Marriage matters because children do best when raised in a stable
environment with two committed parents, exceptions not with standing.

For whatever reasons—a fear of appearing judgmental or hypocritical, 6
perhaps—no one makes a peep. Many of us, after all, have divorced. But this
fact doesn't mean that marriage is no longer important or that children's needs
have changed. Furthermore, this report isn't concerned with the well-
educated, who are typically better equipped to cope with dysfunction, financial or otherwise.

What happens to the other 60 percent? And what happens to a society 7
upon whose beneficence the offspring of these broken or never-formed families ultimately may depend? Why isn't anyone talking about this?

In the past, dramatic family changes have prompted calls to national 8
action. The Moynihan Report of 1965 focused attention on the alarming rise of
African American children born out of wedlock. In the 1990s, rising divorce
rates and single motherhood spawned a fatherhood movement and welfare
reform. Recently, same-sex marriage has dominated our interests.

The hollowing out of marriage in middle America cries out for similarly 9
impassioned action. As lead author Elizabeth Marquardt writes in the report:

> Marriage is not merely a private arrangement; it is also a complex social institu- 10
> tion. Marriage fosters small cooperative unions—also known as stable families—
> that enable children to thrive, shore up communities, and help family members to
> succeed during good times and to weather the bad times. Researchers are finding
> that the disappearance of marriage in Middle America is tracking with the disap-
> pearance of the middle class in the same communities, a change that strikes at the
> very heart of the American Dream.

Our current debate about the fiscal cliff and entitlement spending can't be 11
separated from the breakdown of marriage. In the absence of stable families,
economic and societal need increases. And while most good-hearted souls
wish to help those in distress, we are essentially plugging holes in leaky boats.
Shouldn't we build better boats?

The report's scholars suggest doing this with a series of federal and state 12
proposals. One is to change the tax and welfare system, which frequently
imposes financial penalties—up to 20 percent of family income—on low-
income couples who choose to marry.

Another suggestion is to triple the tax credit for children under age 3, 13
which would have the added benefit of encouraging married people to have
more children—much needed in the longer term to support the nation's elderly.

These are but two of many, which can be viewed online at stateofourunions 14
.org, along with an urgent plea that President Obama include some of these
thoughts in his State of the Union address next month [January 2013]. It insults
no one to encourage couples to marry before having children, thus making a
public as well as private commitment to love and care for them.

15   Perhaps most important, to ignore the marriage deficit among America's middle class is essentially to be complicit in perpetuating a society of winners and losers. Those born to married, well-educated parents are more likely to prosper, while those born to fragmented families are more likely to repeat the patterns of their parents.

16   There in is a national tragedy worthy of our attention.

QUESTIONS FOR READING

1. What publication has led to Parker's essay? Who was studied? What does the study reveal?
2. Why does Parker believe that marriage matters?
3. What has been the country's response to family changes in the past, according to the author? What seems to be occupying us today?
4. What are some of Parker's suggestions for addressing the problem?

QUESTIONS FOR REASONING AND ANALYSIS

5. What type (genre) of argument is this?
6. What is Parker's claim? State it to reveal the argument's genre.
7. What, for the author, is the necessary first step in response to the issue?
8. Has Parker presented a convincing argument? If you don't think so, how would you refute her?

QUESTIONS FOR REFLECTION AND WRITING

9. The study's authors assert that marriage is "a complex social institution," not just a "private arrangement." Sociologists would agree with this statement. Have you thought about marriage in this way? Does it make sense to you? If you agree, then do you accept Parker's conclusion that problems with marriage for one part of society are problems for all of us? If you disagree, how would you argue that this conclusion does not follow?
10. Parker asserts that to ignore this problem is for all of us to be "complicit in perpetuating a society of winners and losers." Do you accept the concept that if you are aware of a problem and fail to act, then you contribute to the consequences of that problem? Reflect on this concept.
11. Do we want a society in which there are winners and losers, and some of the losers are children who have to overcome problems not of their doing? Reflect on this issue as well—or prepare to write on this issue.

SUPREMACY CRIMES | GLORIA STEINEM

Editor, writer, and lecturer, Gloria Steinem has been cited in *World Almanac* as one of the twenty-five most influential women in America. She is the cofounder of *Ms.* magazine and of the National Women's Political Caucus and is the author of a number of books and many articles. The following article appeared in *Ms.* in the August/ September 1999 issue.

PREREADING QUESTIONS Who are the teens who commit most of the mass shootings at schools? Who are the adults who commit most of the hate crimes and sadistic killings? What generalizations can you make about these groups based on your knowledge from media coverage?

You've seen the ocean of television coverage, you've read the headlines: 1 "How to Spot a Troubled Kid," "Twisted Teens," "When Teens Fall Apart."

After the slaughter in Colorado that inspired those phrases, dozens of 2 copycat threats were reported in the same generalized way: "Junior high students charged with conspiracy to kill students and teachers" (in Texas); "Five honor students overheard planning a June graduation bombing" (in New York); "More than 100 minor threats reported statewide" (in Pennsylvania). In response, the White House held an emergency strategy session titled "Children, Violence, and Responsibility." Nonetheless, another attack was soon reported: "Youth With 2 Guns Shoots 6 at Georgia School."

I don't know about you, but I've been talking back to the television set, 3 waiting for someone to tell us the obvious: it's not "youth," "our children," or "our teens." It's our sons—and "our" can usually be read as "white," "middle class," and "heterosexual."

We know that hate crimes, violent and otherwise, are overwhelmingly 4 committed by white men who are apparently straight. The same is true for an even higher percentage of impersonal, resentment-driven, mass killings like those in Colorado; the sort committed for no economic or rational gain except the need to say, "I'm superior because I can kill." Think of Charles Starkweather, who reported feeling powerful and serene after murdering ten women and men in the 1950s; or the shooter who climbed the University of Texas Tower in 1966, raining down death to gain celebrity. Think of the engineering student at the University of Montreal who resented females' ability to study that subject, and so shot to death 14 women students in 1989, while saying, "I'm against feminism." Think of nearly all those who have killed impersonally in the workplace, the post office, McDonald's.

White males—usually intelligent, middle class, and heterosexual, or 5 trying desperately to appear so—also account for virtually all the serial, sexually motivated, sadistic killings, those characterized by stalking, imprisoning, torturing, and "owning" victims in death. Think of Edmund Kemper, who began by killing animals, then murdered his grandparents, yet was released to sexually torture and dismember college students and other young women until he himself decided he "didn't want to kill all the coeds in the world." Or David Berkowitz, the Son of Sam, who murdered some

Outdoor rally for Congresswoman Giffords where a mass shooting occurred.

women in order to feel in control of all women. Or consider Ted Bundy, the charming, snobbish young would-be lawyer who tortured and murdered as many as 40 women, usually beautiful students who were symbols of the economic class he longed to join. As for John Wayne Gacy, he was obsessed with maintaining the public mask of masculinity, and so hid his homosexuality by killing and burying men and boys with whom he had had sex.

6   These "senseless" killings begin to seem less mysterious when you consider that they were committed disproportionately by white, non-poor males, the group most likely to become hooked on the drug of superiority. It's a drug pushed by a male-dominant culture that presents dominance as a natural right; a racist hierarchy that falsely elevates whiteness; a materialist society that equates superiority with possessions; and a homophobic one that empowers only one form of sexuality.

7   As Elliott Leyton reports in *Hunting Humans: The Rise of the Modern Multiple Murderer*, these killers see their behavior as "an appropriate—even 'manly'—response to the frustrations and disappointments that are a normal part of life." In other words, it's not their life experiences that are the problem, it's the impossible expectation of dominance to which they've become addicted.

8   This is not about blame. This is about causation. If anything, ending the massive cultural cover-up of supremacy crimes should make heroes out of boys and men who reject violence, especially those who reject the notion of superiority altogether. Even if one believes in a biogenetic component of male aggression, the very existence of gentle men proves that socialization can override it.

Nor is this about attributing such crimes to a single cause. Addiction to 9 the drug of supremacy is not their only root, just the deepest and most ignored one. Additional reasons why this country has such a high rate of violence include the plentiful guns that make killing seem as unreal as a video game; male violence in the media that desensitized viewers in much the same way that combat killers are desensitized in training; affluence that allows maximum access to violence-as-entertainment; a national history of genocide and slavery; the romanticizing of frontier violence and organized crime; not to mention extremes of wealth and poverty and the illusion that both are deserved.

But it is truly remarkable, given the relative reasons for anger at injustice in 10 this country, that white, non-poor men have a near-monopoly on multiple killings of strangers, whether serial and sadistic or mass and random. How can we ignore this obvious fact? Others may kill to improve their own condition, in self-defense, or for money or drugs; to eliminate enemies; to declare turf in drive-by shootings; even for a jacket or a pair of sneakers—but white males addicted to supremacy kill even when it worsens their condition or ends in suicide.

Men of color and females are capable of serial and mass killing, and commit 11 just enough to prove it. Think of Colin Ferguson, the crazed black man on the Long Island Railroad, or Wayne Williams, the young black man in Atlanta who kidnapped and killed black boys, apparently to conceal his homosexuality. Think of Aileen Carol Wuornos, the white prostitute in Florida who killed abusive johns "in self-defense," or Waneta Hoyt, the upstate New York woman who strangled her five infant children between 1965 and 1971, disguising their cause of death as sudden infant death syndrome. Such crimes are rare enough to leave a haunting refrain of disbelief as evoked in Pat Parker's poem "jonestown": "Black folks do not/Black folks do not/Black folks do not commit suicide." And yet they did.

Nonetheless, the proportion of serial killings that are not committed by 12 white males is about the same as the proportion of anorexics who are not female. Yet we discuss the gender, race, and class components of anorexia, but not the role of the same factors in producing epidemics among the powerful.

The reasons are buried deep in the culture, so invisible that only by 13 reversing our assumptions can we reveal them.

Suppose, for instance, that young black males—or any other men of 14 color—had carried out the slaughter in Colorado. Would the media reports be so willing to describe the murderers as "our children"? Would there be so little discussion about the boys' race? Would experts be calling the motive a mystery, or condemning the high school cliques for making those young men feel like "outsiders"? Would there be the same empathy for parents who gave the murderers luxurious homes, expensive cars, even rescued them from brushes with the law? Would there be as much attention to generalized causes, such as the dangers of violent video games and recipes for bombs on the Internet?

As for the victims, if racial identities had been reversed, would racism 15 remain so little discussed? In fact, the killers themselves said they were targeting blacks and athletes. They used a racial epithet, shot a black male student in the head, and then laughed over the fact that they could see his brain. What if that had been reversed?

16   What if these two young murderers, who were called "fags" by some of the jocks at Columbine High School, actually had been gay? Would they have got the same sympathy for being gay-baited? What if they had been lovers? Would we hear as little about their sexuality as we now do, even though only their own homophobia could have given the word "fag" such power to humiliate them?

17   Take one more leap of the imagination: suppose these killings had been planned and executed by young women—of any race, sexuality, or class. Would the media still be so disinterested in the role played by gender-conditioning? Would journalists assume that female murderers had suffered from being shut out of access to power in high school, so much so that they were pushed beyond their limits? What if dozens, even hundreds of young women around the country had made imitative threats—as young men have done—expressing admiration for a well-planned massacre and promising to do the same? Would we be discussing their youth more than their gender, as is the case so far with these male killers?

18   I think we begin to see that our national self-examination is ignoring something fundamental, precisely because it's like the air we breathe: the white male factor, the middle-class and heterosexual one, and the promise of superiority it carries. Yet this denial is self-defeating—to say the least. We will never reduce the number of violent Americans, from bullies to killers, without challenging the assumptions on which masculinity is based: that males are superior to females, that they must find a place in a male hierarchy, and that the ability to dominate someone is so important that even a mere insult can justify lethal revenge. There are plenty of studies to support this view. As Dr. James Gilligan concluded in *Violence: Reflections on a National Epidemic*, "If humanity is to evolve beyond the propensity toward violence . . . then it can only do so by recognizing the extent to which the patriarchal code of honor and shame generates and obligates male violence."

19   I think the way out can only be found through a deeper reversal: just as we as a society have begun to raise our daughters more like our sons—more like whole people—we must begin to raise our sons more like our daughters—that is, to value empathy as well as hierarchy; to measure success by other people's welfare as well as their own.

20   But first, we have to admit and name the truth about supremacy crimes.

Source: *Ms.* magazine, August/September 1999. Reprinted by permission of the author.

QUESTIONS FOR READING

1.   What kinds of crimes is Steinem examining? What kinds of crimes is she excluding from her discussion?

2.   What messages, according to Steinem, is our culture sending to white, non-poor males?

3.   How does Elliott Leyton explain these killers' behavior?

4. What is the primary reason we have not examined serial and random killings correctly, in the author's view? What is keeping us from seeing what we need to see?

5. What do we need to do to reduce "the number of violent Americans, from bullies to killers"?

QUESTIONS FOR REASONING AND ANALYSIS

6. What is Steinem's claim? Where does she state it?

7. What is her primary type of evidence?

8. How does Steinem qualify her claim and thereby anticipate and answer counterarguments? In what paragraphs does she present qualifiers and counterarguments to possible rebuttals?

9. How does the author seek to get her readers to understand that we are not thinking soundly about the mass killings at Columbine High School? Is her strategy an effective one? Why or why not?

QUESTIONS FOR REFLECTION AND WRITING

10. Steinem concludes by writing that we must first "name the truth" about supremacy violence before we can begin to address the problem. Does this make sense to you? How can this be good advice for coping with most problems? Think of other kinds of problems that this approach might help solve.

11. Do you agree with Steinem's analysis of the causes of serial and random killings? If yes, how would you add to her argument? If no, how would you refute her argument?

Sports Talk—Sports Battles

THE COWARDLY LION

READ: What scene is depicted? Where are we? What details answer these questions?

REASON: Why is the lion hiding under the bench? Why are his eyes not really covered? What issues does the cartoon address?

RELFECT/WRITE: What is Wilkinson's view of the issue? Is he on target?

Sports, at all levels, offer us so much. Sports can be a great equalizer. Many successful football and basketball players started at public schools, won scholarships to college, and made it to careers in the NFL or NBA. Sports also bring diverse people together, playing in amateur competition or cheering on their local professional teams.

And yet, controversies of one kind or another are never far from the front pages. Millionaire professional players make the news for assault, for arranging dogfights, for cheating with drugs. Should we expect superstar players to be role models? Or, just great players whose skills—but not whose lifestyles—we admire? Some would argue that they make their money because we support their play; shouldn't they feel an obligation to give back to the community? Is there a cult of privilege for athletes, beginning in high school, that can feed arrogance and a sense of being above the "rules" that govern the behavior of most people?

We can also ask about the role of sports in college. Although the original idea may have been to build strong bodies as well as strong minds, the reality is that Division I football and basketball are big business, pulling in big bucks for the schools and giving 18-year-olds a national stage on which to perform. Should these players see some of the money they "earn" for their schools?

These are some of the questions that authors in this chapter explore. After remembering the excitement and joy of cheering for a winning team, or participating in a victory for one's school, consider the following questions as you study this chapter's six essays.

PREREADING QUESTIONS

1. Should the NCAA demand higher academic credentials for would-be college athletes and expect college players to carry typical course loads leading to graduation?

2. Should Division I football and basketball players be paid a salary in addition to their college scholarships?

3. How are women in sports faring since Title IX was enacted? Should we care?

4. How much "enhancement" of athletes is fair? Should doping be legalized?

5. Are young people with athletic ability given too many free passes on bad behavior?

THE LESSON OF PENN STATE | JOHN FEINSTEIN

One of the hosts of a CBS morning sports radio show and a commentator on the Golf Channel, John Feinstein is one of today's best-known sports commentators. He has written more than 20 books on a variety of sports and sports figures, including *A Good Walk Spoiled: Days and Nights on the PGA Tour* (1996) and *One on One: Behind the Scenes with the Greats in the Game* (2011). A regular writer for *Golf Digest* and the *Washington Post*, Feinstein expressed his views on the Penn State scandal on July 15, 2012.

PREREADING QUESTIONS What do you know about the Penn State scandal? What lessons would you emphasize?

1   When the University of North Carolina wanted to name its new arena after basketball Coach Dean Smith in 1986, Smith objected, saying that arenas shouldn't be named for coaches. He was talked into it by university officials, who said that it was what most alumni wanted. Smith has lived an exemplary life, but he was right: When you put someone's name on a building, you immortalize him.

2   The living shouldn't be immortalized. Joe Paterno was proof of that.

3   The report by former FBI director Louis Freeh on the Penn State scandal that rocked all of college athletics confirmed, as many feared, that Paterno, Penn State's Hall of Fame football coach, who had an NCAA Division I record 409 victories, was guilty of concealing the accusations of rape and child molestation made against his former assistant, Jerry Sandusky.

4   The Freeh report makes clear that those who rioted after Paterno was fired last year should be even more ashamed of themselves now. Paterno's legacy is no longer stained or tarnished—it is destroyed. Regardless of how many good things he did during his 62 years as a Penn State employee, the tragedy that he failed to stop overwhelms all the good he did.

5   But this tragedy should do something else, too: remind everyone involved in college athletics that *no* coach, regardless of how many games he wins, how many players he graduates or how much money he raises for the university, should be allowed to have the absolute power that Paterno wielded. Absolute power doesn't always corrupt absolutely, but it absolutely can corrupt.

6   Penn State certainly isn't the only school where a coach is the most powerful figure. Years ago, the president of the University of Oklahoma commented—perhaps half-jokingly—that he hoped to build a university worthy of the football program. Two years ago, when Ohio State's football team was being investigated for multiple NCAA violations, President Gordon Gee was asked whether he had considered firing Coach Jim Tressel. "Fire him?" Gee responded. "I just hope he doesn't fire *me*."

7   That's called kidding on the square. Only after it became clear that Tressel had been aware of many of the violations and covered them up was he finally removed. Even then, he was allowed to "resign."

8   Coaches who win championships are huge moneymakers for their schools. Winning teams lead to more admissions applications and, far more important, massive contributions from alumni and boosters. Whenever Duke University mounts a major fundraising campaign, the centerpiece is men's basketball Coach Mike Krzyzewski, who has won four national championships and is the winningest coach in men's college basketball history.

9   Krzyzewski's off-court record is at least as laudable as his on-court record. Virtually all of his players graduate and he has raised countless dollars for various charitable causes as well as Duke.

10   That's fine. But no college coach should be placed on the pedestal that Paterno was put on at Penn State. That pedestal is what prevented then-President Graham Spanier from stepping up in 2001, when a graduate

assistant coach told Paterno that he had seen Sandusky in a university shower sexually assaulting a 10-year-old boy. Instead of ruling that the *only* option was to notify authorities, Spanier and the university's athletic director allowed Paterno to dictate the school's course of action—which was no action at all.

Many, if not most, iconic coaches are accorded that status merely because 11 they win. Kentucky men's basketball Coach John Calipari has built his national championship program around players who turn pro after one year in college. He's not the only coach who recruits such "one-and-dones"; he just does it better than anyone. Calipari is easily the most powerful man in Kentucky. Very few people who follow Kentucky basketball care whether any of Calipari's players graduate. That will be the case as long as his teams continue to contend regularly for the national championship.

That shouldn't be true anywhere, but it is true almost everywhere, espe- 12 cially those places where a coach has won for many years.

College presidents love to talk about the importance of academics and 13 refer to football and basketball players as "student-athletes." They set themselves up as bastions of righteousness even as they let coaches run amok in the name of winning games and making money.

This is an opportunity for presidents to do something other than preen. 14 They should take steps to ensure that no coach can ever again have the absolute power Paterno wielded. They should stop giving coaches multimillion-dollar contracts. They should stop building statues and naming stadiums, arenas and basketball courts for them—especially while the coaches are still active. They should also stop asking them to raise funds. Tell them to coach their teams and try to see to it that their players graduate. Period.

Source: *Washington Post*, July 15, 2012. Reprinted by permission of the author.

QUESTIONS FOR READING

1. How did Paterno become proof that living people ought not to be "immortalized"?
2. Who did what at Penn State?
3. What status have some college coaches achieved? Why?
4. What do some coaches ignore in the quest for successful teams?

QUESTIONS FOR REASONING AND ANALYSIS

5. What, for Feinstein, is the lesson of Penn State; that is, what is his claim?
6. Where does he state it? What does he gain by his placement? How does he support his claim?
7. What specific recommendations does the author list as a way to keep a coach's power in check?

QUESTIONS FOR REFLECTION AND WRITING

8. Do you agree that some college football and basketball coaches have been allowed too much power? If yes, why? If no, why not?

9. Why did the Penn State situation develop? Who should be held accountable?

10. What suggestions do you have for changing the culture of winning at Division I colleges?

SHOW THEM THE MONEY | DONALD H. YEE

A graduate of UCLA and the University of Virginia School of Law, Donald Yee is a partner in Yee & Dubin Sports, a Los Angeles–based sports management firm representing many professional players and coaches. Yee is a frequent speaker on sports-related issues and is an adjunct professor of law at the University of Southern California. "Show Them the Money" was published August 22, 2010, in the Washington Post.

PREREADING QUESTIONS Are the NCAA rules too strict? Are they unrealistic?

1   The Church of College Football is about to open for services. It is perhaps the most passionate religion we have in this country, a seductive blend of our most popular sport and the romantic notion that the young athletes are playing for their schools, not for money.

2   Two championship coaches recently launched attacks on sports agents for allegedly defiling this house of worship by giving college players what the National Collegiate Athletic Association calls "impermissible benefits"—benefits that make those players pros and not amateurs. "The agents that do this, and I hate to say this, but how are they any better than a pimp?" Alabama's Nick Saban so memorably put it last month. "I have no respect for people who do that to young people. None." And Florida's Urban Meyer said that the problem is "epidemic right now" and that agents and their associates need to be "severely punished."

3   Yet, I suspect that virtually everyone in our industry—players, coaches, administrators, boosters, agents and fans—shed our naivete a long time ago. We know that the sole focus for many star college players is getting ready for pro ball, that coaches are looking for financial security on the backs of teenagers and that boosters enjoy the ego stroke that comes with virtually owning a piece of a team. There isn't anything inherently wrong with these goals, but there isn't anything "amateur" about the process, either.

4   And we know that while college football players aren't getting a W-2, they are getting paid to play the game. It's a straightforward

business transaction: You play for us, we give you a one-year scholarship, renewable at the head coach's discretion. In some cases, rules are broken by schools or other parties so that relatives and other associates of the players can be paid, too.

I've had the privilege of representing professional athletes and coaches ₅ for more than 20 years, and I've had a front-row seat to observe the NCAA's brand of amateurism. I've heard many times about events that would constitute NCAA rule violations—some were egregious, many weren't. Some athletes take money from agents, marketers or others simply because they are hungry (the scholarship is not always enough to buy food). Yes, there are some people out there with malicious agendas, but there are also many people who act in good faith with an allegiance to the integrity of the sport.

The primary culprit isn't the people around the game; it's the NCAA's ₆ legislated view of amateurism. It lacks intellectual integrity and is terribly unnecessary—particularly when better alternatives exist.

Two developments this spring demonstrate why the sham of amateurism ₇ should come to an end.

The Pacific-10 Conference's luring of teams from the Mountain West ₈ and Big 12 conferences, which caused some scrambling in June, had nothing to do with education or amateur sports. It really didn't have anything to do with football or its traditions, either. It had everything to do with money. Saddled with expiring television contracts, the Pac-10 wanted to get bigger so it could command larger contracts in its next round of negotiating and possibly launch its own TV network. With the addition of the University of Utah and the University of Colorado, the Pac-10's revenues will grow. Its coaches will make more money, and its players will get bigger and shinier facilities, fancier menus, cushier dorms, more stylish travel arrangements and other perks.

The average Pac-10 student will see none of this.   ₉

Around the same time as the realignment, the University of Southern ₁₀ California, home of one of the premier college football programs, suffered a major embarrassment when Reggie Bush, who starred at tailback for the Trojans in the mid-2000s, was found to have received lavish gifts from a sports marketer. According to the NCAA, Bush was, in effect, a pro while he was in college, and the university knew it. The NCAA concluded that USC demonstrated a "lack of institutional control" over its football program. The team received a two-year postseason ban, lost 30 scholarships over three seasons and vacated its victories from the period when Bush was deemed to have been ineligible—including the 2004 national championship season.

Bush is long gone, now an NFL millionaire. His former USC head coach, Pete ₁₁ Carroll, is long gone, also now an NFL millionaire. Many of the assistant coaches who were there at the time are gone as well, and also became millionaires (e.g. University of Washington head coach Steve Sarkisian). Some left and then came back as millionaires (e.g. new head coach Lane Kiffin). Left to suffer the penalties are the current players, many of whom were in middle school or high school when Bush played.

12   The controversy over USC continues: Are the findings accurate? Should Carroll have done more, earlier? Is the punishment excessive? The answers won't matter, because I have no doubt that Bush-like situations will continue to emerge throughout college football. This sort of thing has been going on for years, and the incentives to keep it up are too strong in the current system.

13   What needs to change is the entire attitude toward college football. This is the perfect time to implement an honest approach to the combination of big-time football and higher education, an approach that eliminates the NCAA's notion of amateurism. College football generates huge revenues, and there is plenty of money to create a win-win business model for players, coaches and universities. A big business deserves market-driven reform, free of hypocrisy. Here are 10 steps to accomplish that.

14   **1. All of the major football-playing universities should lease the rights to operate a commercial football program on behalf of the university to an independent, outside company.** For example, the University of Southern California would contract with USC Football Inc. Such leases would be open to bidding—schools such as Notre Dame, USC and Texas could generate massive revenue. USC football could look exactly as it does now, except USC Football Inc. would have paid for the right to operate it. The university and the company would share net profits from all revenue streams at a negotiated level. Can you imagine how much more revenue schools could garner if, for instance, they were allowed to sell more ad space on uniforms?

15   This would not be a new business structure for major universities; many already use similar arrangements for other ventures. For example, many major athletic departments now sell their marketing rights to outside companies, and the majority of schools (and the NCAA) contract with the Collegiate Licensing Company to market and license their trademarks.

16   Some universities would find that the marketplace doesn't have any interest in their programs. This means that business people think football is a money-loser for those schools. So those schools should drop football and allocate the money to their core objective: educating students.

17   **2. Each university's football corporation could create leagues, whether long- or short-term, with other corporations.** There wouldn't have to be any allegiance to geography, fan loyalties or tradition. For example, some of these leagues could be premised on budget size. To a large degree, this is already being done; it's called the BCS. A group of conferences formed the BCS, or Bowl Championship Series, and decided to exclude other conferences.

18   Or the football corporations could decide to avoid joining a league, simply scheduling games as a free agent. Again, this is hardly novel—Notre Dame has done it for years, and Brigham Young University is contemplating it now—so this arrangement would simply formalize and spread the practice.

19   **3. All of the players would be paid a salary, whatever the market would bear.** Players would no longer receive scholarships. Just as in the pros,

they would be paid based on their perceived value to their program. If an outstanding high school player is coveted, he should be allowed to experience the fruits of American capitalism. Prominent high school players entering college are no different than prominent college players entering the NFL—they can bring excitement and new revenue to a program. No one, for instance, can deny the excitement, revenue and attention that Bush brought to USC. The players would pay income taxes; the football corporations would pay Social Security taxes; 401(k) plans could be established.

USC Football Inc. would be free to recruit a player any way it wants, with [20] anything it wants, say, an iPhone and plane tickets for his parents. If a player feels misled in the recruiting process, he could sue for fraud. Each program would be reliant on the business acumen of its operators and subject to whatever profit-margin goal it chooses.

4. The corporations could offer a range of educational opportunities. [21] Academically gifted players could take regular university courses, if they could have gained admission on their own merit. Others may be more interested in vocational training or other specialty classes. Either way, average students would no longer lose a chance at admission because the university made an exception for an academically less qualified athlete. And athletes would have a broader array of course offerings. Some may even choose not to attend classes and simply focus on honing their football skills.

5. The NCAA can be eliminated, at least as it relates to football. Many [22] of its rules are archaic and frankly gibberish. The NCAA itself states that it does not have subpoena power, which is one way of admitting that enforcement of its rules is difficult.

6. Universities could scrap much of their athletic administrations, just [23] **as Vanderbilt University has done.** The chief executive of, say, USC Football Inc. would make decisions, and her mandate would be to ensure that the operation was self-sufficient—no student fees (or taxpayer dollars, in the case of a public university) would be used to subsidize the football program or facilities. Any profits flowing back to the university could go directly to support the general student body and faculty. As it stands now, large public universities across the country employ sizable staffs in their athletic departments; these public employees (including the coaches) are entitled to public benefits and pensions, which are a drain on public resources.

7. Congress and state legislatures wouldn't have to waste time inves- [24] **tigating or discussing the regulation of college football.** So long as these new corporations mind the same business laws that apply to Apple or General Electric, our representatives could devote their energies elsewhere.

8. Coaches could focus strictly on coaching. They would be employees [25] of the corporation, not the university. Lane Kiffin wouldn't have to worry about monitoring every player's vehicle of choice or whether a booster is buying meals for his quarterback. And Nick Saban wouldn't have to waste his time discussing "pimps." In this system, players could take money from agents or marketers because their amateurism wouldn't be at stake.

26   **9. Universities could focus on their core mission of educating students.** University presidents wouldn't have to waste their time monitoring a football program, and they wouldn't have to attend any more NCAA functions.

27   **10. Finally, this system would end the tiresome sports media discussions of whether this player or that player was paid.** We could say without any hint of sarcasm, speculation or cynicism that yes, he was.

Source: *Washington Post*, August 22, 2010. Reprinted by permission of the author.

QUESTIONS FOR READING

1. What is Yee's subject?
2. What two situations are used to illustrate the "sham of amateurism" in college football?
3. What would some colleges discover if they sought to lease their football program to an outside management firm?
4. What options would athletes have under an outside corporation system?
5. What advantage would Yee's recommendations have for both coaches and colleges?

QUESTIONS FOR REASONING AND ANALYSIS

6. What is Yee's claim? What is the core of his argument?
7. Examine the author's introduction. What makes it clever?
8. What does Yee gain by presenting his proposal in a list of ten points? What effect on readers does he seek with this strategy?
9. Is it possible to agree with Yee that there is a problem and still reject his proposals? Is it possible to accept some of his suggestions? If so, which ones? If not, why not?

QUESTIONS FOR REFLECTION AND WRITING

10. Do you agree that we "worship" college football? Is that an accurate account of the country's fall weekends? (Have you ever counted the number of televised games?)
11. Do you agree that, in spite of the romanticism surrounding college sports, most people are not naïve; most understand that it is big business and that NCAA rules are regularly ignored? If you disagree, how would you counter Yee? If you agree, then are you prepared to accept the author's proposals? Why or why not?
12. In what sense is it incorrect to say that college athletes are unpaid?
13. Is it right to ask college athletes to pretend to be students, if that is not their interest?

RATHER THAN PAY ATHLETES, SHOW THEM RESPECT

SALLY JENKINS

A sportswriter for the *Washington Post* for a number of years, Sally Jenkins left in 1990 to work at *Sports Illustrated* and write a number of books, mostly about sports figures. She has a book written with Dean Smith about his years in college basketball. In 2000 she published, with Lance Armstrong, *It's Not About the Bike: My Journey Back to Life.* Her 2007 book *The Real All Americans* narrates the story of Jim Thorpe and the football players of the Carlisle Indian School. In 2000 Jenkins returned to the *Post.* The following column appeared there on November 4, 2011.

PREREADING QUESTIONS What athletes is Jenkins probably writing about? How valuable is respect—for anyone?

You may have noticed that the people in college football are the tiniest bit obsessed with money, from light-fingered bowl executives to numb-voiced university presidents droning about "impermissible benefits" while pocketing seven figures. Alabama's $4 million coach, Nick Saban, looks like he should be cruising on a yacht sipping Bacardi to the soft throb of a marine engine. No wonder players are preoccupied with compensation, and the answer to every NCAA scandal or controversy lately amounts to, "Pay us." 1

Look, I *know* the money is indecent and the NCAA system is blatantly unfair to athletes. The Southeastern Conference made $1 billion last year, and it would be nice if some of that reached the players at No. 1 LSU and No. 2 Alabama, whose individual sweat gives Saturday's matchup its commercial value. But there seems to be a misconception that if we pry a couple thousand out of NCAA President Mark Emmert's personal wallet and hand it to Alabama running back Trent Richardson, that will make everything right. It won't. Though it would be satisfying. 2

Paying players isn't the answer—not because it's wrong or violates some creaking old amateur code, but because we have yet to devise a fair, feasible way that won't create more inequities, killing scholarships in other sports, not to mention creating regulatory nightmares and legal uncertainties. In the meantime, we have a much deeper, underlying problem to solve. What college athletes need from us, more than cash, is a fundamental shift in how we view them. 3

Pay them? We don't even respect them. 4

When you watch LSU and Alabama this weekend, ask yourself what you really think about the players on the field, underneath your admiration for their physical skill. Deep down. Do you really believe they belong at a university, or does some part of you think they're just muscled-up entertainers and users, fake students who don't think, read or aspire academically? 5

In 2007, Cal-Berkeley education professor Herbert D. Simons published a study of more than 500 college athletes entitled "The Athlete Stigma in Higher Education." Here is what he found: 62 percent of them experienced negative perceptions and stereotyping. Athletes reported that their professors made negative comments about jocks in class, as did fellow students. When they asked professors for leeway to meet their practice schedules, 61.5 percent were refused, or suspected or accused of cheating, compared to 6 percent of whites. 6

7   Generally, Simons concluded, athletes were perceived as having "low intelligence, little academic motivation, and receiving undeserved benefits and privileges," and treated as if they harmed the academic reputation of the university. Just 15 percent felt they were positively perceived.

8   Before we can sort out how to close the gap in pay, we have to close this gap in perception. We can start by treating athletes as if they're worth more than a licensing fee.

9   "There are some educational steps we could take that would be every bit as valuable, if not more, than trying to answer the problems with financial issues," says Derek Van Rheenen, an education researcher and director of Cal's Athletic Study Center who was an all-American soccer player.

10   When we watch Alabama and LSU, let's try a thought experiment. Take a moment, at some point during the game, to think about Trent Richardson as an intelligent man with his helmet off who is majoring in business with a 3.26 grade-point average, and carrying the expectations of his family back in a Pensacola, Fla., housing project. Think of the tension he must feel, barked at by coaches if he gets too distracted by books, yet sneered at by teachers if he falls asleep in class. Consider the 40 hours a week he puts into grueling physical practice and weightlifting, followed by film study and game-planning, an intellectual load comparable to any class he takes.

11   "It's an absolute skill to read the game, it requires cognitive and intellectual ability," Van Rheenen says. Players "are literally looking at cues and prompts, like an avid reader does. People don't give credit to athletes, because they think it's instinctive. It's not. It's cognitive."

12   When you watch players on both sides, imagine how it feels to do homework at midnight with head nodding and limbs throbbing from soreness or injury, a fatigue no one else understands. Yet despite this, they will graduate at a higher rate than their peers. The latest graduation success rate numbers for the 'Bama team was 69 percent last year; LSU's 77 percent, both considerably higher than the national rate for all students.

13   Unmotivated? Low intelligence? Harmful to academic integrity?

14   The dirty little secret of college sports is not that Richardson and his teammates are on the bottom rung in compensation, driven into an underground economy. It's that they are on the bottom rung of expectations. Too many NCAA presidents secretly believe they are unworthy of teaching, and should be grateful just to be on campus.

15   Ask yourself if one reason we jump at the idea of pay-for-play is because it sounds easier than actually educating them. Payment is a pain reliever; it would make some people, including athletes, feel a little better. But it's an Anacin solution, not a cure, and we need to think more creatively.

16   The real crux of what plagues college athletics is this: A relatively small number of high-profile athletes, isolated in two commercial sports, enjoy scholarships (and some extracurricular benefits) while having what we consider to be weak connections to their classrooms. Division I football and basketball have become so heavily commercialized and so demanding that we worry the value of a scholarship is not an equitable or genuine repayment-in-kind for athletes any more.

But why isn't enhancing their scholarship just as good an answer as hand- 17
ing them cash?

What if we gave them better tools and services, more academic credit 18
toward degrees, and more support and incentives?

Tony Smith, the captain of the Cal football team in 1992, received his PhD 19
in education and is now the superintendent of schools in Oakland. He suggests that instead of cash payouts we talk about putting licensing money from
jersey sales in an incentive fund that every graduating member of a team gets
an equal cut of. A small account might coax them toward a degree and help
them transition when they leave school.

Money can be a mark of respect—or not. It can also be a form of dismissal. 20
If you want a kid to feel less used, don't just pay him. Try honoring him.

QUESTIONS FOR READING

1. Why is paying college players a bad idea, in Jenkins's view?
2. What attitudes toward football players does the author think many people hold?
3. What did Simons's study of college athletes reveal about how they were perceived?
4. How do Alabama and LSU football players' graduation rates compare to those of college students in general?
5. What realities of Division I college football and basketball contribute to the perception that those who play are not likely to be serious students?

QUESTIONS FOR REASONING AND ANALYSIS

6. What type (genre) of argument is this? State Jenkins's claim in a way that makes its type clear.
7. In addition to showing more respect to college players, what other actions does Jenkins recommend? Do you agree with some—or all or none—of these solutions? Why?
8. The author suggests that paying the players might be an easy way to avoid seeking to teach and help the players, an easy way to paint over our attitudes toward the players. Do you agree with her analysis? Why or why not?

QUESTIONS FOR REFLECTION AND WRITING

9. What stats surprise you the most? Why?
10. Jenkins presents the views of an educator who argues that athletic prowess is not instinct as much as cognitive skill. Is this a new idea for you? Does it make sense? Why or why not?
11. Whose argument is more convincing, Yee's or Jenkins's? Why? Defend your choice.

WHERE HAVE ALL THE GOOD COACHES GONE?

MEGAN GREENWELL

A former reporter at the *Washington Post*, Megan Greenwell has been a sports columnist at *Good* magazine and is currently a senior editor at *ESPN the Magazine*. She is also the cofounder and editor of *Tomorrow* magazine. The following article was published July 29, 2012.

PREREADING QUESTIONS Have you played for coaches who were supportive and good role models? How important are good coaches for young players?

1   I once had a soccer coach who stalked the sideline in cowboy boots, snarling helpful commentary such as "Man up!" and "Don't be a sissy!" When I broke my arm diving for a ball during practice, he asked if I was going to "cry like a girl" or get back in position. Being a 14-year-old girl, I cried.

2   I have never played for anyone else who seemed to disdain girls quite like Coach Cowboy Boots, but he did have something in common with every other coach I had during 15 years of playing organized sports: a Y chromosome. From kindergarten rec-league soccer through two years of Division I college fencing, I never played for a female coach.

3   That puts me in good company. Female college athletes have never been less likely to have a female coach. The same trend holds in this [2012] summer's Olympics: Of the five sports in which the United States is fielding a women's team under a single head coach—basketball, field hockey, soccer, volleyball and water polo—only the soccer coach is a woman.

4   Surprised? After all, opportunities for female athletes have skyrocketed since Title IX prohibited gender-based discrimination in educational institutions

Allyson Felix wins the 200-meter race at the 2012 Olympics.

40 years ago this summer. More than 200,000 women play college sports today, compared with 16,000 in 1972. When the Olympics opened on Friday, the U.S. team included more female athletes than male ones for the first time.

And there's the dirty little secret of Title IX: Female coaches have become   5
a casualty of the same law that provided such huge benefits to female athletes. In 1972, more than 90 percent of the people coaching women's teams were women. Today, that number is 43 percent, according to data compiled by two retired Brooklyn College professors who have tracked the number of female college athletes and coaches in the United States since Title IX became law.

The explanation for the downward trend is as simple as it is discouraging.   6
By legitimizing women's sports, Title IX bestowed a new level of respect—and significantly higher salaries—on college coaching jobs, transforming them from passion projects for the most dedicated women's sports advocates to serious career paths. When she began her career at the University of Tennessee in 1974, legendary basketball coach Pat Summitt earned $250 a month. Before retiring at the end of last season, she drew a salary of more than $2 million.

As soon as salaries began to rise, more men became interested in jobs   7
coaching women, says Judy Sweet, a longtime athletics administrator who became the NCAA's first-ever female athletic director of a combined men's and women's program at the University of California at San Diego in 1975. Assistant coaches of men's teams saw a chance to be promoted faster by applying to head-coach jobs on the women's side. Job opportunities doubled for graduating male athletes who weren't going pro but wanted to stay in the game. Athletic directors, whose ranks have always been overwhelmingly male, increasingly hired other men for open positions.

The result has been a consistent decrease in the percentage of female   8
coaches. In 1987, the share of women's teams coached by women dipped below 50 percent for the first time. Since 2000, men have been hired for more than two-thirds of open jobs coaching women's teams.

"In too many cases, athletic directors take the easy way out," Sweet says.   9
"Instead of actively recruiting outside of their networks, they hire the people they already know, and their networks are likely to be male-dominated."

In other words, the institutional factors that have kept women out of   10
coaching in the Title IX era are the same ones that have kept them out of the ranks of executives and partners and board members. Study after study shows that men are more likely to hire other men across many professions, even when there are equally or better-qualified female candidates. That gradually discourages many women from applying for those positions, exacerbating the problem.

Meanwhile, women are almost never seriously considered for jobs   11
coaching men—not a single woman coaches male Division I athletes in a team sport—so the total proportion of female coaches is less than 20 percent. The percentage of female coaches increases slightly at schools where a woman heads the athletic department but remains under 50 percent.

When girls and young women don't have the chance to be coached by   12
women, they lose an opportunity to have strong female role models. Having exclusively male coaches sends female athletes the message that coaching jobs

aren't for them. And when athletic directors consistently hire men over similarly qualified women, they send the message that men make better leaders.

13   Because I never had a female coach, my female sports role models were exclusively athletes, from Florence Griffith Joyner to Brandi Chastain. I was 15 when Chastain scored the championship-winning penalty kick in the 1999 World Cup, then ripped off her jersey in celebration. Though I was no longer playing soccer, I wanted to be just like her.

14   Chastain says that aside from serving as mentors, female coaches show their athletes a viable career path in the sport to which they've dedicated their lives. After the Women's Professional Soccer league folded this year—the second failed attempt to create a U.S. pro league—coaching college teams is one of the only ways for retired players to make a living in the game. And though the best female basketball players can get by in the WNBA, where salaries range from $36,570 to $105,000, coaching offers a much more stable option. Title IX was just the first step toward legitimizing women's sports; fully leveling the playing field means giving women a chance to make their game their career.

15   "Ultimately, I hope that women stay in sports if they've played their whole life and gained all this experience," Chastain says. "I would hope that they would be able to share it."

16   Chastain, 44, had a roughly equal number of male and female coaches during her soccer career, but she knows that's increasingly rare for younger athletes. The generation gap is apparent among coaches as well—especially in basketball, the most prominent women's college sport, which has seen the percentage of female coaches drop from 79.4 to 59.5 percent in the Title IX era. The most prominent female college coaches—Summitt, Stanford's Tara VanDerveer and Rutger's C. Vivian Stringer, among others—are either retired or in the twilight of their careers. Although Summitt was replaced by a female assistant coach, the percentage of paid female assistant coaches has dropped in the past 20 years, weakening the pipeline.

17   Sweet and an alliance of women are trying to reverse the trend. In 2003, Celia Slater, then the women's basketball coach at Division II Lynn University in Boca Raton, FL, earned an NCAA sponsorship for a series of four-day workshops designed to boost female college coaches' leadership and communication skills as well as their networks. Last year, Slater and Sweet expanded the effort into the Alliance of Women Coaches, a professional-development group for coaches at any level that aims to increase the number of women in sports leadership.

18   But Sweet says she's not optimistic. "I wish I could say I think the numbers are about to stop going down, but the signs don't point that way," she says. "It requires breaking this cycle of male university presidents hiring male board members hiring male athletic directors hiring male coaches."

19   Qualified female candidates are out there, agrees Chastian, who volunteers as an assistant coach under her husband, Santa Clara University women's soccer coach Jerry Smith. Asked if she's considered becoming a professional coach, she sighs.

20   "I've put myself out there to U.S. Soccer and others several times, and I haven't heard back," she says. "I'm hoping it will happen at some point."

Source: *Washington Post*, July 29, 2012. Reprinted by permission of the author.

QUESTIONS FOR READING

1. What did all of the author's coaches have in common?

2. How many women play college sports today?

3. When Title IX was passed, what percentage of coaches of women's teams were women? What percentage of coaches of women's teams today are women? For all collegiate teams—men's and women's—what percentage do women coach?

4. What has caused the big shift to more male coaches?

QUESTIONS FOR REASONING AND ANALYSIS

5. What type (genre) of argument is this? What is Greenwell's claim? State it so that the argument type is clear.

6. What kinds of evidence does the author present?

7. Greenwell asks readers if we are surprised to learn how few female coaches there are. Are you surprised? What is ironic about the loss of female coaches during the Title IX era?

QUESTIONS FOR REFLECTION AND WRITING

8. Do you agree that the relatively small number of female coaches is a problem for female athletes—or for fairness in the workplace? If yes, why? If no, why not?

9. What has happened in college coaching is not unique. What other fields can you name that have seen an increase in male workers when incomes in those fields have increased?

10. What might be advantageous for both men and women when more men enter fields previously dominated by women? Are there also advantages to more women entering fields previously dominated by men? Ponder these questions and be prepared to discuss and write about them.

HOW TO GET DOPING OUT OF SPORTS | JONATHAN VAUGHTERS

Jonathan Vaughters biked professionally for ten years, set the record up Mount Ventoux, and was a member of Lance Armstrong's team. Now retired from competing, Vaughters is CEO and General Manager of Slipstream Sports, a sports management company and the Garmin-Sharp cycling team. He has also confessed to doping and was a key witness against Armstrong at the United States Anti-Doping Agency's hearings. His plea for keeping doping out of sports was published in the *New York Times* on August 12, 2012.

PREREADING QUESTIONS Do you think that anyone has the answer to controlling doping? Possibly a former professional cyclist?

Why does an athlete dope? I know why, because I faced that choice.   1

My life on a bike started in middle school. When the buzzer on my Goofy   2
clock snapped on at 5:30 a.m., I popped out of bed with excitement and

purpose. Rushing down the stairs, I stretched 20 some odd layers of still baggy spandex onto my 90-pound skeleton and flew out of the garage. Into the dark, freezing Colorado morning I rode. For the next 30 miles, I pushed my heart rate as high as it would go and the pedals as fast as they would go, giving various extremities frostbite and giving my parents cause to question my sanity.

3   These early rides make up many of my memories from my teenage years; the crashes, the adrenaline and the discipline of training every day. But the most vivid memory from those rides was how I dreamed.

4   As I sped through the neighborhoods of suburban Denver, my mind was anywhere but. I was climbing the great alpine passes of the Tour de France. Erased from my mind were the bullies at school, the money troubles at home and the sad fact that no one wanted to go to homecoming with me. I found escape in this dream, and when I returned to reality, I decided there was no amount of hard work, suffering, discipline and sacrifice that would keep me from achieving this dream. Determination didn't begin to describe what I felt inside. I felt destined.

5   Achieving childhood dreams is a hard road. I found that to be only truer as the years and miles passed. First, there is the physical effort of riding 20,000 miles a year for 10 straight years to even get within spitting distance of ever riding the Tour de France. Then comes the strain on your family as they try to support, or at least understand, such a singular focus. Next, the loss of friends and social contact. While most of my friends were at prom, I was in bed early for a race the next day. During graduation, I drove my mom's '78 Oldsmobile across the country to a race where I might get "noticed." And while most kids went on to college, I went to a cold-water apartment in Spain, hoping to make it big.

6   People who end up living their dreams are not those who are lucky and gifted, but those who are stubborn, resolute and willing to sacrifice. Now, imagine you've paid the dues, you've done the work, you've got the talent, and your resolve is solid as concrete. At that point, the dream is 98 percent complete but there is that last little bit you need to become great.

7   Then, just short of finally living your childhood dream, you are told, either straight out or implicitly, by some coaches, mentors, even the boss, that you aren't going to make it, unless you cheat. Unless you choose to dope. Doping can be that last 2 percent. It would keep your dream alive, at least in the eyes of those who couldn't see your heart. However, you'd have to lie. Lie to your mother, your friends, your fans. Lie to the world. This has been the harsh reality laid out before many of the most talented, hardest working and biggest dreaming athletes.

8   How much does that last 2 percent really matter? In elite athletics, 2 percent of time or power or strength is an eternity. It is the difference in time between running 100 meters in 9.8 seconds and 10 seconds. In swimming it's between first and ninth place in the 100-meter breaststroke. And in the Tour de France, 2 percent is the difference between first and 100th place in overall time.

9   To be clear, running a 9.8 (or faster), winning the 100-meter breaststroke or winning the Tour de France are all very possible and have been done

without doping. But it is also clear that winning isn't possible if antidoping regulations aren't enforced. If you just said no when the antidoping regulations weren't enforced, then you were deciding to end your dream, because you could not be competitive. It's the hard fact of doping. The answer is not to teach young athletes that giving up lifelong dreams is better than giving in to cheating. The answer is to never give them the option. The only way to eliminate this choice is to put our greatest efforts into antidoping enforcement. The choice to kiss your childhood dream goodbye or live with a dishonest heart is horrid and tearing. I've been there, and I know. I chose to lie over killing my dream. I chose to dope. I am sorry for that decision, and I deeply regret it. The guilt I felt led me to retire from racing and start a professional cycling team where that choice was taken out of the equation through rigorous testing and a cultural shift that emphasized racing clean above winning. The choice for my athletes was eliminated.

I wasn't hellbent on cheating; I hated it, but I was ambitious, a trait we, as 10 a society, generally admire. I had worked for more than half my life for one thing. But when you're ambitious in a world where rules aren't enforced, it's like fudging your income taxes in a world where the government doesn't audit. Think of what you would do if there were no Internal Revenue Service.

And think about the talented athletes who did make the right choice and 11 walked away. They were punished for following their moral compass and being left behind. How do they reconcile the loss of their dream? It was stolen from them. When I was racing in the 1990s and early 2000s, the rules were easily circumvented by any and all—and if you wanted to be competitive, you first had to keep up. This environment is what we must continuously work to prevent from ever surfacing again. It destroys dreams. It destroys people. It destroys our finest athletes.

As I watched the Olympics these past two weeks, I was a bit envious, as I 12 know that huge strides have been made by many since my time to rid sports of doping. Athletes have the knowledge and confidence that nowadays, the race can be won clean.

If the message I was given had been different, but more important, if the 13 reality of sport then had been different, perhaps I could have lived my dream without killing my soul. Without cheating. I was 15 years younger then, 15 years less wise. I made the wrong decision, but I know that making that right decision for future generations must begin by making the right choice realistic. They want to make the right choice. This is the lesson I have learned from young athletes and why I have made it my life's work to help make the right choice real.

They must know, without doubt, that they will have a fair chance by racing 14 clean. And for them to do that, the rules must be enforced, and the painful effort to make that happen must be unending and ruthless. Antidoping enforcement is 1,000 percent better than in my era of competition, and that brings me great satisfaction. But we must support these efforts even more.

Almost every athlete I've met who has doped will say they did it only 15 because they wanted a level playing field. That says something: everyone wants a fair chance, not more. So, let's give our young athletes a level playing field, without doping. Let's put our effort and resources into making sport fair, so that no athlete faces this decision ever again. We put so much emotion into marketing and idolizing athletes, let's put that same zeal into giving them what they really want: the ability to live their dreams without compromising their morals.

Source: *New York Times*, August 12, 2012. Reprinted by permission of the author.

QUESTIONS FOR READING

1. How important is it to improve just 2 percent in a highly competitive sport?
2. When the author was told he would not be successful unless he doped, what did he do?
3. Eventually, what did Vaughters end up doing?
4. What, according to Vaughters, do athletes say they want?

QUESTIONS FOR REASONING AND ANALYSIS

5. What is Vaughters's claim? What is the basic logic of his argument? (Add a "because clause" to his claim.)
6. The author asserts that we achieve our dreams only through hard work and discipline, not luck or ability. Is this true? Can you defend this assertion? If yes, how? If no, then why do we want to embrace the idea?
7. What does the author mean by a "level playing field"? How does he think this can be achieved? Do you agree?

QUESTIONS FOR REFLECTION AND WRITING

8. Vaughters implies that more rigorous testing will get doping out of sports. Can testing control all doping? If yes, how would you make this happen? If no, are there other strategies that could also help keep athletes from choosing enhancement drugs?
9. Personal essays can make effective arguments, but what potential problems must the authors overcome to be successful?

AFTER ARMSTRONG'S FALL, THE CASE FOR PERFORMANCE ENHANCEMENT | BRADEN ALLENBY

President's Professor and Lincoln Professor of Engineering and Ethics in the School of Sustainable Engineering at Arizona State University, Braden Allenby holds a PhD in Environmental Sciences from Rutgers University in addition to a law degree. He entered academia after 20 years as counsel to AT&T. He is the coauthor, with Daniel Serewitz, of *The Techno-Human Condition* (2011) and author of *Reconstructing Earth: Technology and Environment in the Age of Humans* (2005).

PREREADING QUESTIONS Is there a case for performance enhancement? How do you expect Allenby to develop his argument?

In the past month, cyclist Lance 1 Armstrong has been stripped of his seven Tour de France titles. His commercial sponsors, including Nike, have fled. He has resigned as chairman of Livestrong, the anti-cancer charity he founded. Why? Because the U.S. Anti-Doping Agency and the International Cycling Union say he artificially enhanced his performance in ways not approved by his sport and helped others on his team do the same.

This may seem like justice, but that's 2 an illusion. Whether Armstrong cheated is not the core consideration. Rather, his case shows that enhancement is here to stay. If everyone's enhancing, it's a reality that we should embrace.

Look at any sport. People are run- 3 ning, swimming and biking faster and farther; linemen are bulkier than ever; sluggers have bigger muscles and hit more home runs. This might be due to better nutrition. Perhaps it is a result of legally prescribed drugs. Heck, it might simply be because of better training. But illegal enhancement has never been more evident or more popular.

Moreover, enhancement science—pharmacology, nanotechnology, bio- 4 technology and genetics—is more sophisticated than ever. A recent *Nature* article, for example, discusses oxygen-carrying particles that could be inserted in athletes' blood and DNA therapies that could enhance muscle performance.

In an earlier time, rules limiting the use of such technology may have been 5 a brave attempt to prevent cheating. Now, they are increasingly ineffectual. Humans are becoming a design space. That athletes are on the cutting edge of this engineering domain is neither a prediction nor a threat. It is the status quo.

Get over it.   6

Professional athletes didn't always make big bucks, so when enhancement 7 techniques were primitive, the payoff wasn't necessarily worth the health risks. And with less demand, there were fewer nerds in fewer laboratories creating enhancement technologies. Anabolic steroids, for example, weren't developed until the 1930s. Can you imagine Babe Ruth using a low-oxygen chamber that simulated a high-altitude environment to increase his red-blood-cell count and improve his respiratory system's efficiency? That's just one new way a player can get an edge.

Today, the gap between superstar athletes and almost-stars is rapidly grow- 8 ing. The benefits of being at the top of your game—money, sponsors, cars, houses, movie careers, book deals and groupies—have never been clearer. After all, how many lucrative marketing contracts go to bronze medalists?

9   To perform consistently, 21st-century athletes enhance legally with better gear, specialized diets, physical trainers, vitamin B, and energy drinks and gels. Why not add drugs and other technologies to the list of legal enhancements, especially when most of us are enhancing our workplace concentration with a morning coffee or energy shot?

10   In my engineering and sustainability classes, I ask my students how many have played sports in high school or college. Usually, at least half raise their hands. Then I ask how many know people who enhanced illegally. The hands stay up, even if I limit the question to high school athletes. Enhancement—legal or illegal, according to confused, arbitrary and contradictory criteria—is pervasive. Indeed, surveys show that significant numbers of non-athletes, especially in high school and college, use steroids to try to improve their appearance rather than to augment their play on the field. This should not be surprising, given the popularity of other cosmetic-enhancement techniques such as discretionary plastic surgery, even among young people.

11   Armstrong's alleged doping in the Tour de France is just more evidence that human excellence is increasingly a product of enhancement.

12   Mischaracterizing a fundamental change in sports as merely individual violations of the rules has serious consequences. For example, this thinking has led to inadequate research on the risks of enhancement technologies, especially new ones. Why research something that can't be used? My anecdotal class surveys show that students have significant skepticism about the reported side effects of such treatments and drugs, as well as perceptions of bias among regulators against enhancement. As a result of such attitudes, there's a tendency to play down the risks of some technologies. Call it the "Reefer Madness" response—ignoring real risks because you think the danger is exaggerated. This is ignorance born of prohibition.

13   What should be done? Past a certain age, athletes should be allowed to use whatever enhancements they think appropriate based on objective data. Providing reliable information about the full range of technologies should become the new mission of a (renamed) Anti-Doping Agency, one not driven by an anti-enhancement agenda. It wouldn't have to be a free-for-all: Age limits and other appropriate regulations could limit dangerous enhancements for non-professionals; those that are too risky could be restricted or, yes, banned.

14   How? Perhaps the Food and Drug Administration could take over these duties from the Anti-Doping Agency, using its own calculus. Is the proposed enhancement technology effective? Does it hurt more than it helps? It's doubtful that a genetic enhancement, for example, would be allowed. The field is too new. However, some supplements such as creatine, alphalipoic acid and at least some currently banned steroids would probably be acceptable.

15   In professional sports, normal people do not compete normally. We watch athletes who are enhanced—through top-notch training, equipment and sometimes illegal substances—compete for our amusement. And, despite our sanctimonious claims that this is wrong, we like it that way. So we do athletes

a deep disservice by clinging to our whimsical illusion of reality at the cost of their livelihood. If we allow football players to take violent hits and suffer concussions so that we might be entertained, why not allow them to use substances that might cause them health problems? It's their decision.

If you yearn to watch "purer" athletes, check out a Division III football 16 game. Visit the minor league ballpark near you. Set up an amateur league. Better yet, train for a marathon sans enhancement.

But don't force the Tour de France to cling to outdated ideas of how ath- 17 letes pedaling for their professional lives should behave. Cyclists have enhanced, are enhancing now and will continue to enhance. In his stubborn refusal to admit guilt in the face of the evidence, maybe this is what Armstrong is trying to tell us.

Source: *Washington Post*, October 28, 2012. Reprinted by permission of the author.

QUESTIONS FOR READING

1. What are some of the ways that athletes are enhancing their performance?
2. How has enhancement science changed?
3. Why has enhancement become so appealing to athletes?
4. What is a consequence of continuing to try to stop illegal doping?
5. How are our expectations of professional athletes different from that of amateurs?

QUESTIONS FOR REASONING AND ANALYSIS

6. What is Allenby's claim? How does he defend and support it?
7. In two paragraphs, the author discusses some specifics of managing sports with enhancement rules lifted. First, how does this discussion aid his argument? Second, do his suggestions seem sensible and feasible? Why or why not?

QUESTIONS FOR REFLECTION AND WRITING

8. Allenby suggests that since everybody is doing it, we should "get over it" and accept the reality of enhancement. This is a pragmatic approach to the problem; are you content with a pragmatic approach to doping in sports? Why or why not?
9. To what extent are we, the spectators, to blame for illegal doping?
10. Why do we play (and watch) competitive sports? Be prepared to discuss or write about questions 9 and 10.

CHAPTER 19

America's Colleges: Issues and Concerns

To say that the issues in education are both numerous and serious is certainly an understatement. Clinton wanted to be the "education president." Bush had his No Child Left Behind initiative. Obama has his Race to the Top plan and continues to emphasize the need to give everyone an opportunity to attend college. And yet criticism continues amid only a few voices defending U.S. schools. America's best schools and colleges attract students from around the world. However, the variations in funding, facilities, teachers, and test scores from one school to another should be unacceptable to politicians and parents—and the students—who lose out to inferior schools.

The vast differences become noticeable at the college level. On the one hand, Harvard students such as Mark Zuckerberg drop out to form companies and become rich and famous, leaving some to argue that the most talented young people are wasting time in college classes and should, instead, be immediately funded to pursue their creative plans. On the other hand, up to one-third of the freshman class at many quality colleges is taking at least one remedial course, with the percentage higher at community colleges. The average completion time for a four-year degree is now six years, and the completion rate of those who start college is less than 50 percent. Do these numbers spell failure for a goal of universal education—or is college work inappropriate for a majority of people? If an undergraduate degree is an unrealistic standard for most people, then how do we compete in a global economy with a workforce requiring brainpower, not brawn?

These are questions in need of contemplation by all involved, including current undergraduates. The chapter begins its exploration by looking at the still-uneven access to college and then moves to a debate on the worth of college, given its costs. When we question the worth of a degree, we also are raising questions about what college is for, why it should—or should not—be valued. The chapter ends with authors examining two campus concerns, cheating on exams and speech-code restrictions that might be considered censorship. These concerns closely tie to the broader debate of what it means to have a college education.

PREREADING QUESTIONS

1. How do you account for the weak showing of U.S. students on international tests in math and science? Should we, as a nation, be concerned?

2. What are the biggest obstacles to getting into college?

3. What should students want to get from a college education? Do students, parents, and the business community have differing perceptions on the purpose of college? Should they?

4. Should the United States develop better vocational training and apprenticeship programs? If so, how?

5. Why do good students cheat in college?

6. Are speech codes and guidelines to control harassment forms of censorship? If so, is this okay, or is it a problem?

5 MYTHS ABOUT WHO GETS INTO COLLEGE

RICHARD D. KAHLENBERG

A senior fellow at the Century Foundation, Richard Kahlenberg is an expert on K–12 schooling. He is the author of four books on education and the editor of seven more, most recently *Rewarding Strivers: Helping Low-Income Students Succeed in College* (2010). His articles are widely published, and he is a frequent guest on TV talk shows. The following article appeared in the *Washington Post* on May 23, 2010.

PREREADING QUESTIONS In preparation for reading, glance at the five myths the author will examine. Which, if any, myths do you think are accurate? Even if there is just one that you thought was an accurate statement, is that sufficient reason to study Kahlenberg's analysis?

1   This spring, more than 3 million students will graduate from America's high schools, and more than 2 million of them will head off to college in the fall. At the top colleges, competition has been increasingly fierce, leaving many high school seniors licking their wounds and wondering what they did "wrong." But do selective colleges and universities do a good job of identifying the best and brightest? And is the concern about who gets into the best colleges justified?

2   **1. Admissions officers have figured out how to reward merit above wealth and connections.** A 2004 Century Foundation study found that at the most selective universities and colleges, 74 percent of students come from the richest quarter of the population, while just 3 percent come from the bottom quarter. Rich kids can't possibly be 25 times as likely to be smart as poor kids, so wealth and connections must still matter.

3   Leading schools have two main admissions policies that favor wealthy students. The more glaring of these is legacy preferences—an admissions boost for the children of alumni. Legacy preferences increase a student's chances of admission by, on average, 20 percentage points over non-legacies. Schools use such preferences on the theory that they increase donations from alumni, but new research by Chad Coffman questions that premise. Those universities that

These students enjoy one another and their beautiful campus.

have abandoned legacy preferences—or never used them—have plenty of alumni donors. Examples include Caltech, Texas A&M and the University of Georgia.

Less obvious is the role of the SAT, which was, when it was introduced in 1926, supposed to help identify talented students from across all schools and backgrounds. Instead, it seems to amplify the advantages enjoyed by the most privileged students. New research by Georgetown University's Anthony Carnevale and Jeff Strohl finds that the most disadvantaged applicants (those who, among other characteristics, are black, attend public schools with high poverty rates, come from low-income families and have parents who are high school dropouts) score, on average, 784 points lower on the SAT than the most advantaged students (those who, among other things, are white, attend private schools and have wealthy, highly educated parents). This gap is equivalent to about two-thirds of the test's total score range. If the SAT were a 100-yard dash, advantaged kids would start off 65 yards ahead before the race even began.

2. Disadvantages based on race are still the biggest obstacle to getting into college. More than race, it's class: The effects of racial discrimination are increasingly dwarfed by the impact of socioeconomic status. Take that 784-point difference in SAT scores between the most advantaged and the most disadvantaged students. All other things being equal, the researchers found that there was a 56-point difference between black and white students. Most of the rest of the gap was the result of socioeconomic factors. To truly even the playing field, the system would therefore need to provide a lot of affirmative action to economically disadvantaged students who beat the odds and a little bit of affirmative action based on race.

Yet colleges and universities today do the opposite: They provide substantial preferences based on race and virtually none based on class. According to researchers William Bowen, Martin Kurzweil and Eugene Tobin, at highly selective institutions, for students within a given SAT range, being a member of an underrepresented minority increases one's chance of admission by 28 percentage points. That is, a white student might have a 30 percent chance of admission, but a black or Latino student with a similar record would have a 58 percent chance of admission. By contrast, Bowen and his colleagues found, students from poor families don't receive any leg up in the process—they fare neither better nor worse than wealthier applicants.

3. Generous financial aid policies are the key to boosting socioeconomic diversity. In response to the growing scarcity of poor and working-class students on campus, roughly 100 universities and colleges have boosted financial aid in the past several years. But these programs have not been enough to change the socioeconomic profile of these schools' student bodies. At the University of North Carolina at Chapel Hill, for example, a generous financial aid program, the Carolina Covenant, was instituted in 2004. Under its terms, low-income students are not required to take out loans as part of their financial aid packages.

According to research by Edward B. Fiske, the program has been successful in accomplishing one important goal: boosting the graduation rate among low-income students. Traditionally, low-income and working-class students drop out at much higher rates than do higher-income students, as financial worries and jobs with long hours distract from their studies. Fiske found that the Carolina Covenant raised the four-year graduation rates of low-income students by almost 10 percent.

9   Yet the proportion of low-income students at UNC-Chapel Hill remained flat between 2003 and 2008, because the university has not given such students (those eligible for federal Pell grants, 90 percent of which go to students from families making less than $40,000 a year) any break in the admissions process. A few other institutions, including Amherst and Harvard, have begun to consider a student's socioeconomic status in their admissions decisions; these schools provide a promising example. At Harvard, the percentage of students receiving Pell grants has shot up from 9.4 percent in the 2003–2004 school year to 15 percent in the 2008–2009 school year.

10   **4. Selective colleges are too expensive and aren't worth the investment.** A selective institution with a large endowment may indeed be worth the money. The least selective colleges spend about $12,000 per student, compared with $92,000 per student at the most selective schools. Put another way, at the wealthiest 10 percent of institutions, students pay, on average, just 20 cents in fees for every dollar the school spends on them, while at the poorest 10 percent of institutions, students pay 78 cents for every dollar spent on them.

11   Furthermore, selective colleges are quite a bit better at retention: If a more selective school and a less selective school enroll two equally qualified students, the more selective school is much more likely to graduate its student. Future earnings are, on average, 45 percent higher for students who graduated from more selective institutions than for those from less selective ones, and the difference in earnings is widest among low-income students. And according to research by Thomas Dye, 54 percent of America's top 4,325 corporate leaders are graduates of just 12 institutions.

12   **5. With more students going to college, we're closer to the goal of equal opportunity.** The good news is that students are going to college at a higher rate than ever before; the bad news is that stratification is increasing at colleges and universities. Much as urban elementary and secondary schools saw white, affluent parents flee to suburban schools in the 1970s and 1980s, less selective colleges are now experiencing white flight. According to Carnevale and Strohl, white student representation declined from 79 percent to 58 percent at less selective and noncompetitive institutions between 1994 and 2006, while black student representation soared from 11 percent to 28 percent. American higher education is in danger of quickly becoming both separate and unequal.

Source: *Washington Post,* May 23, 2010. Reprinted by permission of the author.

QUESTIONS FOR READING

1.   What numbers demonstrate that selective colleges are not rewarding merit above wealth and connections? What two admissions policies favor the rich?

2. What is the biggest obstacle to getting into college? Why are racial minorities not the most disadvantaged in the college selection process?

3. Why has increased financial aid not changed the socioeconomic mix at most colleges? Which colleges have begun to consider socioeconomic status in the admissions process?

4. For what three reasons is the cost of highly selective colleges possibly worth the price?

5. In spite of the increase in the numbers of students attending college, why is this not a sign of equal opportunity in higher education?

QUESTIONS FOR REASONING AND ANALYSIS

6. What kind of evidence does Kahlenberg provide in support of each of his arguments counter to current views regarding college admissions?

7. What is the author's purpose in writing? To expose myths about changes in college admissions is, ultimately, to write what kind of argument? Write a claim statement that reveals Kahlenberg's purpose in writing.

8. Is the information convincing? Why or why not?

QUESTIONS FOR REFLECTION AND WRITING

9. Are you surprised by any of the statistics? If so, which ones? If not, why not?

10. To embrace the five myths about college admissions is to see American society going in what direction? Presumably we would agree that this direction is good for our society. So, if these myths don't hold up to the facts, then what should we be doing to correct this problem? What are your suggestions—or the suggestions implied in much of the essay—for making a college education more available to all who wish to attend?

WHAT'S A COLLEGE EDUCATION REALLY WORTH? NOT ENOUGH | NAOMI SCHAEFER RILEY

When an editor and writer for the *Wall Street Journal*, Naomi Riley covered education, religion, and culture. She is now a freelance writer who appears in a number of newspapers and on her blog. She is the author of *The Faculty Lounges: And Other Reasons You Won't Get the College Education You Pay For* (2011) and *'Til Faith Do Us Part: How Interfaith Marriage Is Transforming America* (2013). The following article appeared June 5, 2011.

PREREADING QUESTIONS Do you think a college education is worth the cost? If not, why are you in college?

Did Peter Thiel pop the bubble? That was the question on the minds of parents, 1 taxpayers and higher education leaders late last month when the co-founder of PayPal announced that he was offering $100,000 to young people who would stay out of college for two years and work instead on scientific and technological innovations. Thiel, who has called college "the default activity," told *USA Today* that "the pernicious side effect of the education bubble is assuming education [guarantees] absolute good, even with steep student fees."

2   He has lured 24 of the smartest kids in America and Canada to his Silicon Valley lair with promises of money and mentorship for their projects. Some of these young people have been working in university labs since before adolescence. Others have consulted for Microsoft, Coca-Cola and other top companies. A couple didn't even have to face the choice of putting off college—one enrolled in college at age 12 and, at 19, had left his PhD studies at Stanford to start his own company.

3   Of course, Thiel's offer isn't going to change the way most universities do business anytime soon. These 24 kids represent the narrowest swath of the country's college-bound youth. (Though it's important to note: When we talk about America having the greatest system of higher education in the world, these are the kind of people we're bragging about.)

4   There's not much reason to worry that this program is going to produce a nation of dropouts, contrary to the fears of some wags such as James Temple, a columnist for the *San Francisco Chronicle*. Temple called the premise of the fellowships "scary" and worried about the broader message they send. However, as a country, we are still creeping along toward President Obama's dream of universal higher education. Obama sees this not only as a way for all individuals to have the opportunity to reach their full potential but also as a key to the nation's ability to compete in the global marketplace.

5   But Thiel put a dollar figure on something that certain young people may already have suspected was true. A friend of mine whose son, a budding Internet entrepreneur, just graduated from Yale told me about a conversation that her son reported having with another somewhat successful start-up founder. The latter had dropped out of Harvard Law School to launch his business, and he advised my friend's son to drop out of Yale—venture capitalists would know that he was serious if he was willing to give up that Ivy League diploma. My friend was a little horrified, having already dropped somewhere around $200,000 on her son's education, but it does raise the question: For a smart kid from an upper-middle-class family who went to one of the top high schools in the country, and who already has a business going, what does a college diploma mean?

6   Colleges have long been engaged in an odd deal with students and their parents. Paying for a college education—or taking on a huge amount of debt to finance an education—is a transaction in which most of the buyers and most of the sellers have fundamentally different understandings of the product.

7   Think about it this way: Suppose I start a print newspaper tomorrow. I might think I'm selling excellent journalism, while my "readers" are actually using my product to line their birdcages. It might work out fine for a while. But the imbalance in this transaction would make it difficult to talk in general terms about improving the product or whether the product is worth what I'm charging. I might think I should improve my grammar and hire more reporters. My customers might want me to make the paper thicker.

In the college transaction, most parents think they're buying their kids a 8 credential, a better job and a ticket, economically speaking at least, to the American dream. Most college professors and administrators (the good ones, anyway) see their role as producing liberally educated, well-rounded individuals with an appreciation for certain kinds of knowledge. If they get a job after graduation, well, that's nice, too.

The students, for the most part, are not quite sure where they fit into this 9 bargain. Some will get caught up in what they learn and decide to go on to further education. But most will see college as an opportunity to have fun and then come out the other end of the pipeline with the stamp of approval they need to make a decent salary after graduation.

So does Thiel's offer suggest that a university diploma might be most use-10 ful lining a birdcage? Yes and no. He has certainly undermined the worth of a credential. But it is universities themselves that have undermined the worth of the education. It is to their detriment that they have done so, certainly, but it is to the detriment of students as well.

In the recent movie *The Social Network,* Mark Zuckerberg is shown devoting 11 endless hours in his room to computer programming. He goes to a few parties, but mostly he is engaged in his new business venture, "the Facebook." How is this possible, one might wonder? Was he flunking out of his classes? No. Thanks to the wonders of grade inflation and the lack of a serious core curriculum, it is possible to get through Harvard and a number of other high-price universities acing your computer science classes and devoting very little effort to anything else.

Colleges and universities have allowed their value to slip by letting students 12 call this an undergraduate education. There is no compelling understanding among students of why they are there. Studying is not how they spend even the bulk of their waking hours, and their classes seem random at best. They may spend Monday in "19th Century Women's Literature," Tuesday in "Animal Behavior" and Wednesday in "Eastern Philosophy," but these courses may bear little relation to any they took the previous semester or any they will take the next.

A 2010 report called "What Will They Learn?," published by the American 13 Council of Trustees and Alumni, an organization that emphasizes traditional education, surveyed the curricula of more than 700 colleges. About 4 percent require students to take a basic economics class. A little more than a quarter of the public institutions and only 5 percent of the private colleges and universities require a single broad survey course in American history or government. And only 61 percent of colleges and universities require students to take a college-level mathematics class.

General education requirements are no longer general at all. They are 14 absurdly specific. At Cornell, you can fill your literature and arts requirement with "Global Martial Arts Film and Literature." And at Northwestern, the math requirement can be fulfilled with "Slavonic Linguistics." It's little wonder that smart students think their time is better spent coding.

So yes, Zuckerberg was wasting his parents' money and his own time. Why 15 pay to be at Harvard if that's what you're going to do? Why not take a class on Dostoyevsky or the history of Christianity or astronomy or ancient history? You are surrounded by some of the most learned people in the world, and you are holed up in your dorm room typing code. (One could place some blame on the students, but it's hard to fault people for not knowing what they don't know.) Surely Thiel has the right idea when it comes to the Zuckerbergs of the world. And colleges have only themselves to blame if they lose some of these very smart young people to his fellowships.

16   Beyond the top tier, there are also gaping holes in higher education. Executives at U.S. companies routinely complain about the lack of reading, writing and math skills in the recent graduates they hire. Maybe they too will get tired of using higher education as a credentialing system. Maybe it will be easier to recruit if they don't have to be concerned about the overwhelming student debt of their new employees.

17   Employers may decide that there are better ways to get high school students ready for careers. What if they returned to the idea of apprenticeship, not just for shoemakers and plumbers but for white-collar jobs? College as a sorting process for talent or a way to babysit 18-year-olds is not very efficient for anyone involved. Would students rather show their SAT scores to companies and then apply for training positions where they can learn the skills they need to be successful? Maybe the companies could throw in some liberal arts courses along the way. At least they would pick the most important ones and require that students put in some serious effort. Even a 40-hour workweek would be a step up from what many students are asked to do now.

18   If tuition continues to rise faster than inflation, and colleges cannot provide a compelling mission for undergraduate education, we may move further away from Obama's vision of education and closer to Peter Thiel's.

Source: *Washington Post*, June 5, 2011. Reprinted by permission of the author.

QUESTIONS FOR READING

1. Who is Peter Thiel and what did he do?
2. How typical are the students working for Thiel?
3. What do parents think they are buying when they pay for college? What do professors believe their role to be? What do students think they should be doing?
4. What characteristics of college courses and general requirements does the author present?
5. What might employers prefer new hires to do instead of getting a college degree?

QUESTIONS FOR REASONING AND ANALYSIS

6. What is the problem Riley addresses? (Think about this.) What, then, is her claim?
7. What are her reasons? (Add a "because" clause to the claim.)
8. Riley develops an extended metaphor, beginning in paragraph 4. What is the metaphor and what is its point?
9. What kinds of grounds does the author present? How effective are the grounds in support of the claim?

10. What seem to be the implications of Riley's view? Who should drop out of the top schools? Who should attend college? Who should consider some other approach to a job?

11. Riley doesn't really blame the good professors for defining the purpose of college differently from parents; what does she blame colleges for? Do you agree with her complaint? Why or why not?

12. What, in your view, is the purpose of college? Why?

WHAT'S MORE EXPENSIVE THAN COLLEGE? NOT GOING TO COLLEGE | DEREK THOMPSON

A senior editor at *The Atlantic,* Derek Thompson oversees business articles for *TheAtlantic .com.* He has published in *Slate, Business Week,* and *The Daily Beast* and appears on radio and TV talk shows. His essay was published at *TheAtlantic.com* on March 27, 2012.

PREREADING QUESTIONS Given Thompson's focus on business issues, how do you expect him to develop this argument? Is there more than one way to define the "worth" of a college education?

If you want to feel optimistic about the state of things for unemployed, disengaged, and dissatisfied youths in America, here's a way. Spin a globe. Stop it with your finger. If you touch land, the overwhelming odds are that the young people in that country are doing much worse.

There are 1.2 billion people between 15 and 24 in the world, according to the International Youth Foundation's new *Opportunity for Action* paper. Although many of their prospects are rising, they are emerging from conditions of widespread poverty and lack of access to the most important means of economic mobility: education. In the Middle East and North Africa, youth unemployment has been stuck above 20 percent for the last two decades. And in the parts of the world where youth unemployment has been low, such as south and east Asia, young people are overwhelmingly employed in the agriculture sector, which leaves them vulnerable to poverty.

The report is a crackerjack box of interesting facts—e.g.: the probability that a 15-year-old Russian male will die before he is 60 is higher than 40 percent, the highest in Europe; among women 15 to 24 years old, only 15 percent are working in the Middle East—but some of the most surprising stats are the closest to home.

The IYF authors focus on the so-called "NEETs" in the United States and Europe. NEET stands for those Not Engaged in Employment/education, or Training. A 2012 U.S. study put the social cost per NEET youth at $37,450, when you factored in lost earnings, public health spending, and other factors. That brings the total cost of 6.7 million NEET American youths to $4.75 trillion, equal to nearly a third of GDP, or half of U.S. public debt.

Statistics like this are a good reminder that, even though college tuition is famously outpacing median incomes, there is still something more expensive than going to school. Very often, that is not going to school.

6   The NEET study's final number might be too high. It also might be too low. I can't say. But it's far from the only report identifying an astronomical cost to not going to college.

- The typical income gap between a college graduate and a high school dropout has never been higher. Today, college grads earn 80 percent more than people who don't go to high school.

- A 2009 McKinsey report estimated that if we raised our education performance to the level of Korea, we could improve the US economy by more than $2 trillion. (We could, in other words, add the GDP of Italy to our economy with education reform.)

- Yet another study from NBER estimated that the benefit of a good teacher over an average teacher could improve a student's future lifetime earnings by $400,000.

- Finally, a study from the Hamilton Project found that $100,000 spent on college at age 18 would yield a higher lifetime return than an equal investment in corporate bonds, U.S. government debt, or hot company stocks.

7   College has its skeptics, and the skeptics make good points. Does a four-year university make sense for every student? Probably not. Is the modern on-site college education necessarily the ideal means to deliver training after high school? Maybe not. Vocational training and community colleges deserve a place in this discussion. And we happen to be living through a quiet revolution in higher education.

8   Here are three quick examples. First, beginning this year, students at MITx can take free online courses offered by MIT and receive a credential for a price far less than tuition if they demonstrate mastery in the subject. Second, the University of Southern California is experimenting with online classrooms that connect students across the country in front of a single professor. Third, there's Western Governors University, a nonprofit, private online university that's spearheading the movement toward "competency-based degrees" that reward what students can prove they know rather than how many hours or credits they amass.

9   Some of these experiments will fail, and some will scale. What's important is that they offer higher ed and

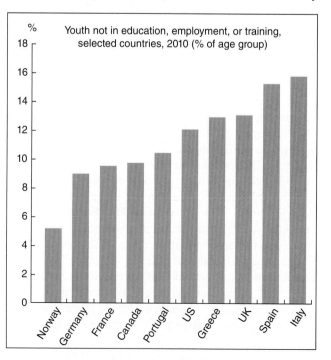

Youth not in education, employment, or training, selected countries, 2010 (% of age group)

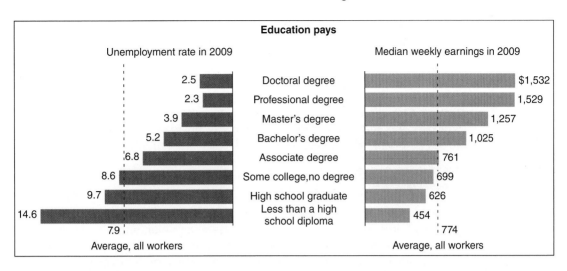

retraining that is cheap, creative, and convenient. If we can win the marketing war in neighborhoods blighted by NEETs and deliver a post-high school education to some of those 7 million young people who have disengaged with education and work, we will be spending money to save money.

Take out that globe one more time and give it a spin. I challenge you to 10 land on a region where education gains aren't translating to productivity and income gains. The highest-income countries have the highest rates of enroll-ment in secondary school and the smallest share of informal employment that is vulnerable to an economic downturn. *There is a cost to not educating young people. The evidence is literally all around us.*

Source: © 2012, The Atlantic Media Co. as first published in *The Atlantic* online, March 27, 2012. All rights reserved. Distributed by Tribune Media Services.

QUESTIONS FOR READING

1. How bad off are young people in the United States compared to other young people in the world?
2. What is the social cost to the United States of all the young people not engaged in either education or training?
3. How much can a good teacher improve lifetime earnings?
4. What are Thompson's three examples of big changes in education?

QUESTIONS FOR REASONING AND ANALYSIS

5. What is Thompson's claim? How does he develop and support his claim?
6. Is his support convincing? Why or why not?
7. How does he qualify his claim? How does this qualification aid his argument?

QUESTIONS FOR REFLECTION AND WRITING

8. What statistics surprise or impress you the most? Why?
9. Who has the more convincing argument—Riley or Thompson? Why? Defend your choice.

HELPING STUDENTS FIND THEIR PLACE IN THE WORLD

DANIELLE ALLEN

Holding a PhD in government from Harvard and one in classics from Cambridge University, Danielle Allen is a professor of social science at Princeton's Institute for Advanced Study. She serves on the boards of Princeton, the Mellon Foundation, and Amherst College. Among her books are *Why Plato Wrote* (2010) and *Talking to Strangers: Anxieties of Citizenship Since Brown v. Board of Education* (2004). The following article appeared on September 24, 2012.

PREREADING QUESTIONS What might Allen's helpful suggestions be? How do you expect college to help you?

1   Debates about the nature of higher education are often framed by the question of whether vocational elements or liberal arts elements should dominate in the curriculum. This is a mistake.

2   Human beings generally need to foster their development along four dimensions: They need to prepare themselves for bread-winning work; for civic and political engagement; for creative self-expression and world-making; and for rewarding relationships in spaces of intimacy and leisure. We can't do without the skills, knowledge and understanding that enable us to make a living. But neither can we do without a related set of competencies that help us understand who we are as human beings so that we can make reasonable choices about what, individually and collectively, we should do. How should we direct our creative capacities? What should be our shared political ideals and goals? What are the sources of satisfaction in private relationships?

3   When we consider education from the perspective of the collective, instead of the individual, and ask whether a citizenry generally is being educated as needed, there often seems to be a mismatch between what people choose to learn and the available jobs. The philosopher Plato seems to have been motivated by a similar frustration. He imagined a utopia ruled by a philosopher-king in which, from birth, everyone would be slotted into a particular occupational group and educated to excel to the highest degree within that occupation. Some would be farmers, some craftsmen and traders, some soldiers, and some political leaders. From a bird's-eye view, the state would know from an individual's birth who should be what.

4   Here and there we can see policy efforts that, in the name of efficiency, seek to apply to education the kinds of information that can be acquired from a bird's-eye view. For instance, Florida is reshaping its community college curriculum by setting up in particular areas degree programs in vocational specialties that labor demographers identify as undersupplied in that location. There is, of course, nothing wrong with putting real opportunities in front of people. But we don't want to craft an environment where people fail to come to their own understanding of what they should try to do because as a nation we are justifiably trying to increase the efficiency with which we match human capital to the labor market. For this reason, it is necessary to have a liberal arts element infused throughout the curriculum at all levels: in K-12 and community colleges as well as four-year colleges and universities.

Just as we should want to cultivate capacities for self-knowledge (to sup- 5 port vocational choices, among other reasons) we must also recognize that an element of self-knowledge includes being able to see how one's competencies connect to the diversity of methods available for self-support. One needs to understand oneself; one also needs to be able to see the vocational opportunities that are out there.

In our restructured world of work—which has a range of service jobs and 6 knowledge jobs that are not captured by the traditional professions and trades; where people will change areas of specialization multiple times over their working lives—simply seeing the opportunities is hard. To this end, the Mellon Foundation, on whose board I serve, has been supporting the placement of students who have earned PhDs in the humanities—people who have, in other words, committed themselves most fully to an education in the liberal arts— into non-academic jobs. The goal is to help those whose education has tipped more toward the liberal arts acquire the observational attunement necessary to see the range of occupational possibilities.

Human beings are not born complete; we make ourselves over the course 7 of our lives. Science confirms this. For all the power of genetics, from the moment of our birth culture has a huge impact on us, including even on which features of our genetic endowment come to the fore. We most fully realize our potential when we make ourselves—even if most commonly we can do this only with the help of others. Each of us is best positioned to be the expert on ourselves; this is why self-knowledge is so important. This is the reason we each have to find our own way in the world, rather than letting someone—for instance, a philosopher-king—place us once and for all in a particular position.

Our contemporary situation demands that we help our young people find 8 their way by marrying the cultivation of self-knowledge to a worldly capacity to see practical opportunities. This requires a curriculum that unifies liberal arts and vocational elements at all levels.

Source: *Washington Post*, September 24, 2012. Reprinted by permission of the author.

QUESTIONS FOR READING

1. In what four ways do we need to develop?
2. How did Plato imagine organizing society?
3. What can be lost in the name of efficiency?
4. What are some realities of today's world of work?
5. Who knows you best?

QUESTIONS FOR REASONING AND ANALYSIS

6. What, for Allen, is the wrong way to discuss higher education? What is the better way; that is, what is Allen's claim?
7. How does the author develop her argument? What are her grounds?
8. For Allen, what kind of education gives us the best chance of knowing ourselves? Do you agree? If yes, why? If no, how would you refute Allen?

9. Allen points out that today's new kinds of jobs don't fit neatly into traditional professional or trade categories. Is this a new idea for you? Does it make sense?

10. When you think of courses to take, do you think about what knowledge or skills you could acquire from those courses? If not, why not?

11. Do you think about what courses would enhance your knowledge of self? If not, why not?

WHY KIDS CHEAT AT HARVARD | HOWARD GARDNER

Howard Gardner is professor of cognition and education at the Harvard Graduate School of Education and senior director of the Harvard Zero Project, a project focused on creating performance-based assessments in education. The author of 28 books, he is best known for his theory of multiple intelligences. Among his many books are *Intelligence Reframed: Multiple Intelligences for the 21st Century* (1999) and *Truth, Beauty, and Goodness Reframed: Educating for the Virtues in the Era of Truthiness and Twitter* (2011). Dr. Gardner has been cited as one of the 100 most influential intellectuals in the world today. His article on Harvard student cheating appeared on September 7, 2012.

PREREADING QUESTIONS Why do you think that students at Harvard—or anywhere—cheat on exams and papers? Can we understand the motivation?

1   On August 27 [2012], approximately 1,600 freshmen arrived at Harvard College. Two days later, I had the pleasure of spending 90 minutes with 20 of these students. They impressed me with their intellect but also with their empathy and willingness to listen to and learn from one another. They were excited by the opportunity to be at Harvard; they used such superlatives that I joked to colleagues that in a few years, they would be so critical, if not cynical, they would have a hard time believing their earlier enthusiasm.

2   On August 30 [2012], I and many others learned of the university's largest cheating scandal in living memory. According to news reports, close to half of the 250 undergraduates in "Introduction to Congress" are being investigated for allegedly cheating on a final examination.

3   The fate of individual students is not yet known, but this event will clearly be a stain on Harvard's reputation as large and consequential as that suffered by the service academies in earlier decades.

4   Many wonder how this could have happened at "MGU" (man's greatest university). They will ask whether a large number of the same enthusiastic and loving students I met with last week might well, in a year or two, be part of a cheating scandal themselves. The answer, I fear, is yes.

5   I've been at Harvard for more than half a century—as an undergraduate, a graduate student, a researcher and, for almost three decades, a professor. I know the university well, and in many ways I love it. Yet almost 20 years ago I became concerned about the effect that market ways of thinking have on our society, particularly our young. Colleagues and I undertook a study of "good work." As part of that study, we interviewed 100 of the "best and brightest" students and spoke with them in depth about life and work.

6   The results of that study, reported in *Making Good*, surprised us. Over and over again, students told us that they admired good work and wanted to be good

The beautiful Harvard campus.

workers. But they also told us they wanted—ardently—to be successful. They feared that their peers were cutting corners and that if they themselves behaved ethically, they would be bested. And so, they told us in effect, "Let us cut corners now and one day, when we have achieved fame and fortune, we'll be good workers and set a good example." A classic case of the ends justify the means.

We were so concerned by the results that, for the past six years, we have 7 conducted reflection sessions at elite colleges, including Harvard. Again, we have found the students to be articulate, thoughtful, even lovable. Yet over and over again, we have also found hollowness at the core.

Two examples: In discussing the firing of a dean who lied about her academic 8 qualifications, no student supported the firing. The most common responses were "She's doing a good job, what's the problem?" and "Everyone lies on their resume." In a discussion of the documentary *Enron: the Smartest Guys in the Room,* students were asked what they thought of the company traders who manipulated the price of energy. No student condemned the traders; responses varied from caveat emptor to saying it's the job of the governor or the state assembly to monitor the situation.

One clue to the troubling state of affairs came from a Harvard classmate 9 who asked me: "Howard, don't you realize that Harvard has always been primarily about one thing—success?" The students admitted to Harvard these days have watched their every step, lest they fail in their goal of admission to an elite school. But once admitted, they begin to look for new goals, and being a successful scholar is usually not high on the list. What is admired is success on Wall Street, Silicon Valley, Hollywood—a lavish lifestyle that, among other things, allows you to support your alma mater and get the recognitions that follows.

As for those students who do have the scholarly bent, all too often they see 10 professors cut corners—in their class attendance, their attention to student work, and, most flagrantly, their use of others to do research. Most embarrassingly, when professors are caught—whether in financial misdealings or even plagiarizing others' work—there are frequently no clear punishments. If punishments ensue, they are kept quiet, and no one learns the lessons that need to be learned.

Whatever happens to those guilty of cheating, many admirable people are 12 likely to be tarred by their association with Harvard. That's the cost of being a flagship institution. Yet this scandal can have a positive outcome if leaders begin a searching examination of the messages being conveyed to our precious young people and then do whatever it takes to make those messages ones that lead to lives genuinely worthy of admiration.

Source: *Washington Post*, September 7, 2012. Reprinted by permission of the author.

QUESTIONS FOR READING

1. What is the occasion for Gardner's article?
2. What did the students Gardner interviewed 20 years ago say they admired? But, what did they want to be?
3. What did the students interviewed over the years think they might have to do to be successful?
4. What did Gardner conclude about his students as he continued to interview them?
5. What has Harvard "always been primarily about"?
6. What do the scholarly students often discover about professors?

QUESTIONS FOR REASONING AND ANALYSIS

7. Gardner is not reporting on the cheating incident; he is responding to it. What point does he want to make; that is, what is his claim?
8. How does the author develop and support his claim?
9. What does Gardner gain by telling readers of his long association with Harvard?

QUESTIONS FOR REFLECTION AND WRITING

10. Were you surprised by the students' responses to the fired dean and the Enron traders? Why or why not?
11. What values shape Gardner's definition of good students—or good professors? Do you agree with him? If yes, why? If no, how would you refute him?
12. Can cheating ever be justified—even if others do it? Explain your views on this issue.

THE CLOSED AMERICAN MIND | GEORGE WILL

A syndicated columnist since 1974, George Will is also the author of a number of books, including one about his great love—baseball. He is a regular participant in television talk shows of political analysis. The following column appeared December 2, 2012.

PREREADING QUESTIONS In what ways might the American mind be closed in the view of conservative Will? How will his discussion connect to the college campus?

1   In 2007, Keith John Sampson, a middle-aged student working his way through Indiana University-Purdue University Indianapolis as a janitor, was declared guilty of racial harassment. Without granting Sampson a hearing, the university administration—acting as prosecutor, judge and jury—convicted him of "openly reading [a] book related to a historically and racially abhorrent subject."

2   "Openly." "Related to." Good grief.

The book, *Notre Dame vs. the Klan,* celebrated the 1924 defeat of the Ku Klux 3
Klan in a fight with Notre Dame students. But some of Sampson's co-workers dis-
liked the book's cover, which featured a black-and-white photograph of a Klan rally.
Someone was offended, therefore someone else *must be* guilty of harassment.

This non sequitur reflects the right never to be annoyed, a new campus 4
entitlement. Legions of administrators, who now outnumber full-time faculty,
are kept busy making students mind their manners, with good manners understood as conformity to liberal politics.

Liberals are most concentrated and untrammeled on campuses, so look 5
there for evidence of what, given the opportunity, they would do to America.
Ample evidence is in *Unlearning Liberty: Campus Censorship and the End of
American Debate* by Greg Lukianoff, 38, a graduate of Stanford Law School who
describes himself as a liberal, pro-choice, pro-gay rights, lifelong Democrat who
belongs to "the notoriously politically correct Park Slope Food Co-Op in
Brooklyn" and has never voted for a Republican "nor do I plan to." But as president of the Foundation for Individual Rights in Education (FIRE), he knows that
the most common justifications for liberal censorship are "sensitivity" about
"diversity" and "multi-culturalism," as academic liberals understand those things.

In recent years, a University of Oklahoma vice president has declared that no 6
university resources, including e-mail, could be used for "the forwarding of political
humor/commentary." The College at Brockport in New York banned using the
Internet to "annoy or otherwise inconvenience" anyone. Rhode Island College prohibited, among many other things, certain "attitudes." Texas Southern University's
comprehensive proscriptions included "verbal harm" from damaging "assumptions" or "implications." Texas A&M promised "freedom from indignity of any
type." Davidson banned "patronizing remarks." Drexel University forbade "inappropriately directed laughter." Western Michigan University banned "sexism,"
including "the perception" of a person "not as an individual, but as a member of a
category based on sex." Banning "perceptions" must provide full employment for
the burgeoning ranks of academic administrators.

Many campuses congratulate themselves on their broad-mindedness 7
when they establish small "free-speech zones" where political advocacy can
be scheduled. At one point Texas Tech's 28,000 students had a "free-speech
gazebo" that was 20 feet wide. And you thought the First Amendment made
America a free-speech zone.

At Tufts, a conservative newspaper committed "harassment" by printing 8
accurate quotations from the Koran and a verified fact about the status of
women in Saudi Arabia. Lukianoff says that Tufts may have been the first
American institution "to find someone guilty of harassment for stating verifiable facts directed at no one in particular."

He documents how "orientation" programs for freshmen become propa- 9
ganda to (in the words of one orthodoxy enforcer) "leave a mental footprint on
their consciousness." Faculty, too, can face mandatory consciousness-raising.

In 2007, Donald Hindley, a politics professor at Brandeis, was found guilty of 10
harassment because when teaching Latin American politics he explained the origin of the word "wetbacks," which refers to immigrants crossing the Rio Grande.
Without a hearing, the university provost sent Hindley a letter stating that the

university "will not tolerate inappropriate, racial and discriminatory conduct." The assistant provost was assigned to monitor Hindley's classes "to ensure that you do not engage in further violations of the nondiscrimination and harassment policy." Hindley was required to attend "anti-discrimination training."

11   Such coercion is a natural augmentation of censorship. Next comes mob rule. Last year, at the University of Wisconsin-Madison, the vice provost for diversity and climate—really; you can't make this stuff up—encouraged students to disrupt a news conference by a speaker opposed to racial preferences. They did, which the vice provost called "awesome." This is the climate on an especially liberal campus that celebrates "diversity" in everything but thought.

12   "What happens on campus," Lukianoff says, "doesn't stay on campus" because censorship has "downstream effects." He quotes a sociologist whose data he says demonstrate that "those with the highest levels of education have the *lowest* exposure to people with conflicting points of view." This encourages "the human tendency to live within our own echo chambers." Parents' tuition dollars and student indebtedness pay for this. Good grief.

QUESTIONS FOR READING

1. What did student Keith Sampson experience at Indiana?
2. What are liberal concerns on campuses that can lead to what Will calls censorship?
3. What are "free-speech zones"?
4. What does Lukianoff mean by "downstream effects"?

QUESTIONS FOR REASONING AND ANALYSIS

5. What is Will's subject? What is his claim?
6. How does the author develop and support his claim?
7. Examine the evidence presented in paragraph 12; would you like to know more about the data? (When, where, and how the data were collected?)
8. Has Will presented a convincing argument? If yes, why? If no, why not?

QUESTIONS FOR REFLECTION AND WRITING

9. In paragraph 5, Will asserts that we can look to colleges to see what liberals would do to the country if they could. Does the comment belong in this essay, in your view, or does it seem a distraction? Explain your response.
10. Is it appropriate for colleges to establish rules about harassment? What about speech code guidelines? Explain your views.
11. What suggestions do you have for balancing a free exchange of ideas with a need to recognize the diversity of a campus community?

CHAPTER 20

The Environment: How Do We Sustain It?

READ: What situation is depicted? Who speaks to whom?

REASON: Who "hasn't noticed yet" and what has he failed to observe? What makes the cartoon clever?

REFLECT/WRITE: Explain the point of the cartoon.

In 2005 psychology professor Glenn Shean published a book titled *Psychology and the Environment*. Dr. Shean argues that we are behaving as if we have no environmental problems to face, and that therefore the biggest first step to solving problems related to environmental degradation is to make people aware of and concerned about the interconnected issues of climate change, the heavy use of fossil fuels, and species extinction. Because we are programmed to make quick decisions based on immediate dangers, we find it difficult to become engaged with dangers that stretch out into an indeterminate future. There is always tomorrow to worry about the polar bears or the increasing levels of CO_2 in the atmosphere, or the rapidly melting ice caps. And besides, who wants to give up a comfortable lifestyle because it might affect future life on this planet?

By 2008 even the Bush administration began to give voice to the concerns of environmentalists such as Dr. Shean. After much resistance, there seems to be a more widespread acceptance of climate change and the problems that it can cause, but even among those grudgingly on board there is still a debate as to the degree to which human actions are a major cause of the problems—as opposed to a recognition of periods of temperature increases and decreases that have been a part of the history of the planet. Why do we resist accepting responsibility for adding to the problem? Because to admit to being a cause means that we have to accept being part of the solution—we have to agree to change some of the things we are doing that are heating up the atmosphere. And here is where sacrifice and cost enter the picture. Do we expect factories to shut down? No, but regulations governing pollutants from their smokestacks will help the atmosphere—at a cost to doing business. Do we expect people to stop enjoying the beach? No, but we could have restrictions on building that destroys the barrier islands and marshlands protecting shorelines from erosion and destruction from storms. Do we expect people to stop driving cars? No, but the government could require manufacturers to build more fuel-efficient cars—at a cost to doing business.

And so, even though the conversation has changed somewhat since 2005, the debate continues over the extent to which human actions make a difference and then what should be done, at what cost, and at whose expense. In five articles and several visuals—including the one that opens this chapter—a variety of voices are heard on this debate.

PREREADING QUESTIONS

1. To whom do you listen primarily when you explore scientific questions? Scientists? Politicians? Religious leaders? What is the reasoning behind your choice?

2. How green is your lifestyle? Do you think it matters? Why or why not?

3. Does Dr. Shean describe you when he writes of those who are complacent about environment problems because there does not seem to be an immediate danger? If so, do you think you should reconsider your position? Why or why not?

4. If you accept that we have a problem, what solutions would you support? Reject? Why?

THE SIXTH EXTINCTION: IT HAPPENED TO HIM. IT'S HAPPENING TO YOU.

MICHAEL NOVACEK

Paleontologist Michael Novacek is senior vice president and provost of the American Museum of Natural History in New York City. Author of more than 200 articles and books, Novacek's most recent book is *Terra: Our 100-Million-Year-Old Ecosystem— and the Threats That Now Put It at Risk* (2008). "The Sixth Extinction" was published on January 13, 2008, in the *Washington Post.*

PREREADING QUESTIONS Who is the "Him" in Novacek's title? Is it ridiculous to suggest that *we* could be like *him?*

T. Rex in charge.

1 The news of environmental traumas assails us from every side—unseasonal storms, floods, fires, drought, melting ice caps, lost species of river dolphins and giant turtles, rising sea levels potentially displacing inhabitants of Arctic and Pacific islands and hundreds of thousands of people dying every year from air pollution. Last week brought more— new reports that Greenland's glaciers may be melting away at an alarming rate.

2 What's going on? Are we experiencing one of those major shocks to life on Earth that rocked the planet in the past?

3 That's just doomsaying, say those who insist that economic growth and human technological ingenuity will eventually solve our problems. But in fact, the scientific take on our current environmental mess is hardly so upbeat.

4 More than a decade ago, many scientists claimed that humans were demonstrating a capacity to force a major global catastrophe that would lead to a traumatic shift in climate, an intolerable level of destruction of natural habitats, and an extinction event that could eliminate 30 to 50 percent of all living species by the middle of the 21st century. Now those predictions are coming true. The evidence shows that species loss today is accelerating. We find ourselves uncomfortably privileged to be witnessing a mass extinction event as it's taking place, in real time.

5 The fossil record reveals some extraordinarily destructive events in the past, when species losses were huge, synchronous and global in scale. Paleontologists recognize at least five of these mass extinction events, the last

of which occurred about 65 million years ago and wiped out all those big, charismatic dinosaurs (except their bird descendants) and at least 70 percent of all other species. The primary suspect for this catastrophe is a six-mile-wide asteroid (a mile higher than Mount Everest) whose rear end was still sticking out of the atmosphere as its nose augered into the crust a number of miles off the shore of the present-day Yucatan Peninsula in Mexico. Earth's atmosphere became a hell furnace, with super-broiler temperatures sufficient not only to kill exposed organisms, but also to incinerate virtually every forest on the planet.

6   For several million years, a period 100 times greater than the entire known history of Homo sapiens, the planet's destroyed ecosystems underwent a slow, laborious recovery. The earliest colonizers after the catastrophe were populous species that quickly adapted to degraded environments, the ancient analogues of rats, cockroaches and weeds. But many of the original species that occupied these ecosystems were gone and did not come back. They'll never come back. The extinction of a species, whether in an incinerated 65-million-year-old reef or in a bleached modern-day reef of the Caribbean, is forever.

7   Now we face the possibility of mass extinction event No. 6. No big killer asteroid is in sight. Volcanic eruptions and earthquakes are not of the scale to cause mass extinction. Yet recent studies show that troubling earlier projections about rampant extinction aren't exaggerated.

8   In 2007, of 41,415 species assessed for the International Union for the Conservation of Nature (IUCN) Red List of Threatened Species, 16,306 (39 percent) were categorized as threatened with extinction: one in three amphibians, one quarter of the world's pines and other coniferous trees, one in eight birds and one in four mammals. Another study identified 595 "centers of imminent extinction" in tropical forests, on islands and in mountainous areas. Disturbingly, only one-third of the sites surveyed were legally protected, and most were surrounded by areas densely populated by humans. We may not be able to determine the cause of past extinction events, but this time we have, indisputably: We are our own asteroids.

9   Still, the primary concern here is the future welfare of us and our children. Assuming that we survive the current mass extinction event, won't we do okay? The disappearance of more than a few species is regrettable, but we can't compromise an ever-expanding population and a global economy whose collapse would leave billions to starve. This dismissal, however, ignores an essential fact about all those species: They live together in tightly networked ecosystems responsible for providing the habitats in which even we humans thrive. Pollination of flowers by diverse species of wild bees, wasps, butterflies and other insects, not just managed honeybees, accounts for more than 30 percent of all food production that humans depend upon.

10   What will the quality of life be like in this transformed new world? Science doesn't paint a pretty picture. The tropics and coral reefs, major sources of the planet's biological diversity, will be hugely debilitated. The 21st century may mark the end of the line for the evolution of large mammals and other animals that are now either on the verge of extinction, such as the Yangtze River dolphin, or, like the African black rhinoceros, confined to small, inadequately supportive habitats. And devastated ecosystems will provide warm welcome to all

those opportunistic invader species that have already demonstrated their capacity to wipe out native plants and animals. We, and certainly our children, will find ourselves largely embraced by a pest and weed ecology ideal for the flourishing of invasive species and new, potentially dangerous microbes to which we haven't built up a biological resistance.

Of course people care about this. Recent surveys show a sharp increase in concern over the environmental changes taking place. But much of this spike in interest is due to the marked shift in attention to climate change and global warming away from other environmental problems such as deforestation, water pollution, overpopulation and biodiversity loss. Global warming is of course a hugely important issue. But it is the double whammy of climate change combined with fragmented, degraded natural habitats—not climate change alone—that is the real threat to many populations, species and ecosystems, including human populations marginalized and displaced by those combined forces. 11

Still, human ingenuity, commitment and shared responsibility have great potential to do good. The IUCN Red List now includes a handful of species that have been revived through conservation efforts, including the European white-tailed eagle and the Mekong catfish. Narrow corridors of protected habitat now connect nature preserves in South Africa, and similar corridors link up the coral reefs of the Bahamas, allowing species in the protected areas to move back and forth, exchange genes and sustain their populations. Coffee farms planted near protected forests and benefiting from wild pollinators have increased coffee yields. New York's $1 billion purchase of watersheds in the Catskill Mountains that purify water naturally secured precious natural habitat while eliminating the need for a filtration plant that would have cost $6 to $8 billion, plus annual operating costs of $300 million. Emissions of polluting gases such as dangerous nitrogen oxides have leveled off in North America and even declined in Europe (unfortunately emissions of the same are steeply rising in China). Plans for reflective roofing, green space and increased shade to cool urban "heat islands" are at least under consideration in many cities. 12

These actions may seem puny in light of the enormous problem we face, but their cumulative effect can bring surprising improvements. Yet our recent efforts, however praiseworthy, must become more intensive and global. Any measure of success depends not only on international cooperation but also on the leadership of the most powerful nations and economies. 13

The first step in dealing with the problem is recognizing it for what it is. Ecologists point out that the image of Earth still harboring unspoiled, pristine wild places is a myth. We live in a human-dominated world, they say, and virtually no habitat is untouched by our presence. Yet we are hardly the infallible masters of that universe. Instead, we are rather uneasy regents, a fragile and dysfunctional royal family holding back a revolution. 14

The sixth extinction event is under way. Can humanity muster the leadership and international collaboration necessary to stop eating itself from the inside? 15

Source: *Washington Post*, January 13, 2008. Reprinted by permission of the author.

QUESTIONS FOR READING

1. What events suggest to scientists that we may be heading for another mass extinction?
2. What is the response of many to this "doomsaying" discussion?
3. How many mass extinctions has the Earth experienced? When was the last one and what happened then?
4. How do scientists describe the consequences of extinction No. 6?
5. What are the specific problems that combine to threaten a disastrous change in our environment?

QUESTIONS FOR REASONING AND ANALYSIS

6. What is the primary cause of a potential extinction No. 6? What, then, needs to be the primary source of the solutions? What, in the author's view, is the necessary first step?
7. In paragraph 12, Novacek describes some actions we have taken to address problems. What does he seek to accomplish by including this paragraph?
8. What is Novacek's claim? State it to reveal a causal argument.
9. Of the various consequences of extinction No. 6, listed in paragraph 10, what seems most frightening or devastating to you? Why?

QUESTIONS FOR REFLECTION AND WRITING

10. Novacek lists numbers and types of endangered species. Do these figures surprise you? Concern you? Why or why not?
11. In your experience, how widespread is the concern for environmental degradation? Do your friends and family discuss this issue? Do most dismiss the seriousness of the issue, as Novacek suggests?
12. Have you made changes to be kinder to the environment? If so, what have you done and what would you recommend that others do?
13. Do you agree with Novacek—or does he overstate the problem? If you agree, how would you contribute to his argument? If you disagree, how would you refute him?

TRUST ME, I'M A SCIENTIST | DANIEL T. WILLINGHAM

Why So Many People Choose Not to Believe What Scientists Say

A professor of psychology at the University of Virginia with a PhD in cognitive psychology from Harvard University, Daniel Willingham maintains a long list of interesting blogs at his university home page. He is the author of many articles and books, including *Why Don't Students Like School?* (2010) and *When Can You Trust the Experts: How to Tell Good Science from Bad in Education* (2012). The following article was published in May 2011.

A friend of mine has long held that a vaccination his son received as an infant 1
triggered his child's autism. He clings to this belief despite a string of scientific
studies that show no link between autism and vaccines. When the original
paper on such a link was recently discredited as a fraud, my friend's reaction
was that it will now be more difficult to persuade people of the dangers of
vaccination. He is not alone: nearly half of all Americans believe in the vaccine-
autism link or are unsure about it.

The paradox goes deeper. My friend insists that he trusts scientists—and 2
again, in this respect, he is like most Americans. In a 2008 survey by the
National Science Foundation, more respondents expressed "a great deal" of
confidence in science leaders than in leaders of any other institution except
the military. On public policy issues, Americans believe that science leaders
are more knowledgeable and impartial than leaders in other sectors of society,
such as business or government. Why do people say that they trust scientists
in general but part company with them on specific issues?

Many individuals blame the poor quality of science education in the U.S. If 3
kids got more science in school, the thinking goes, they would learn to appreciate scientific opinion on vaccines, climate, evolution and other policy issues.
But this is a misconception. Those who know more science have only a slightly
greater propensity to trust scientists. The science behind many policy issues is
highly specialized, and evaluating it requires deep knowledge—deeper than
students are going to get in elementary and high school science classes. A
more direct approach would be to educate people about why they are prone
to accept inaccurate beliefs in the first place.

Humans do seem to prize accuracy above all. We want our beliefs to be 4
accurate—to align with what is really true about the world—and we know that
science is a reliable guide to accuracy. But this desire to be accurate conflicts
with other motives, some of them unconscious. People hold beliefs to protect
important values, for example. Individuals who think of nature as sacred may
perceive genetic modification as morally wrong, regardless of its safety or
utility. People also hold beliefs that are rooted in their emotions. A flu
pandemic that can cause widespread death among the innocent may cause
feelings of fear and helplessness. One way to cope with those emotions is to
belittle warnings of a pandemic as improbable.

In reconciling our rational and irrational motives for belief, we have 5
become good at kidding ourselves. Because we want to see ourselves as
rational beings, we find reasons to maintain that our beliefs *are* accurate. One
or two contrarians are sufficient to convince us that the science is "controversial" or "unsettled." If people knew that other motives might compromise the
accuracy of their beliefs, most would probably try to be on their guard.

Asking science teachers to impart enough content to understand all the 6
issues may be unrealistic, but they might be able to improve people's appreciation for the accuracy of scientific knowledge. Through the study of the history
of science, students might gain an understanding both of their own motivations

for belief and of science as a method of knowing. If a student understands how a medieval worldview could have made a geocentric theory of the solar system seem correct, it is a short step to seeing similar influences in oneself.

7 Science history can also help students understand why scientific knowledge grows ever more accurate. It is easy for a non-scientist to dismiss an unpleasant conclusion as controversial on the grounds that scientists constantly change their minds: "First they say chocolate is bad for us, then it's good . . . they can't decide anything." By studying how new observations led to the revision of important theories, however, students see that scientists' readiness to change their beliefs to align with data is a source of great strength, not weakness, and why near consensus on issues such as global warming or vaccine safety is so impressive. Science may not be the only way of organizing and understanding our experience, but for accuracy it fares better than religion, politics and art. That's the lesson.

Source: *Scientific American*, May 2011. Reproduced with permission. Copyright © 2011 Scientific American, a division of Nature America, Inc. All rights reserved.

QUESTIONS FOR READING

1. How many Americans believe that vaccines cause autism?
2. What did the National Science Foundation study show about Americans' trust in scientists?
3. Does having more science knowledge increase trust in scientists?
4. Why do people seek reasons to reject scientific knowledge?
5. How can knowledge of science history increase trust in science?

QUESTIONS FOR REASONING AND ANALYSIS

6. What type (genre) of argument is this? Is it possible to categorize this argument in more than one genre?
7. What is Willingham's claim? State it to reveal the argument's genre.
8. How does the author develop and support his claim?
9. What is not the primary cause of distrust of science? What is the primary cause?
10. How would you describe the author's style and tone? How do they aid his argument?

QUESTIONS FOR REFLECTION AND WRITING

11. Does Willingham's analysis of human psychology make sense to you? If not, how would you explain the paradox of Americans' attitudes toward scientists?
12. How much knowledge of science history do you have? Is increasing this kind of knowledge at least part of the answer to trusting scientists? If yes, why? If no, why not?

GLOBAL WARMING IS JUST
THE TIP OF THE ICEBERG | JAMES R. LEE

Assistant professor at the American University School of International Service, Dr. Lee is also director of the Mandala Projects. These include the Trade and Environmental Database, the Inventory of Conflict and Environment, and the Global Classroom. He is currently working on a book related to the topic of the following essay, which appeared in the *Washington Post* on January 4, 2009.

PREREADING QUESTIONS If global warming is just the tip, what lies below the tip of the iceberg? What do you expect Lee to write about?

1   The Cold War shaped world politics for half a century. But global warming may shape the patterns of global conflict for much longer than that—and help spark clashes that will be, in every sense of the word, hot wars.

2   We're used to thinking of climate change as an environmental problem, not a military one, but it's long past time to alter that mindset. Climate change may mean changes in Western lifestyles, but in some parts of the world, it will mean far more. Living in Washington, I may respond to global warming by buying a Prius, planting a tree or lowering my thermostat. But elsewhere, people will respond to climate change by building bomb shelters and buying guns.

3   "There is every reason to believe that as the 21st century unfolds, the security story will be bound together with climate change," warns John Ashton, a veteran diplomat who is now the United Kingdom's first special envoy on climate change. "The last time the world faced a challenge this complex was during the Cold War. Yet the stakes this time are even higher because the enemy now is ourselves, the choices we make."

4   Defense experts have also started to see the link between climate change and conflict. A 2007 CNA Corp. report, supervised by a dozen retired admirals and generals, warned that climate change could lead to political unrest in numerous badly hit countries, then perhaps to outright bloodshed and battle. One key factor that could stoke these tensions is massive migration as people flee increasingly uninhabitable areas, which would lead to border tensions, greater demands for rescue and evacuation services and disputes over essential resources. With these threats looming, the U.N. Security Council held a precedent-setting debate on climate change in April 2007—explicitly casting global warming as a national security issue.

5   Global warming could lead to warfare in three different ways.

6   The first is conflict arising from scarcity. As the world gets hotter and drier, glaciers will melt, and the amount of arable land will shrink. In turn, fresh water, plants, crops and cattle and other domestic animals will be harder to come by, thereby spurring competition and conflict over what's left. In extreme examples, a truly desiccated ecosystem could mean a complete evacuation of a hard-hit region. And the more people move, the more they will jostle with their new neighbors.

7   Such displacement can arise either suddenly or slowly. The growth of the Sahara, for instance, took many millenniums; many thousands of years ago, people were slowly nudged out of the inland region of northern Africa and into such great river valleys as the Nile and the Niger. Over time, incremental but prolonged rises in sea levels will also gradually uproot hundreds of millions of people.

8   But sometimes the displacement happens with shocking speed: Just think of the deadly hurricanes Katrina and Rita, which together drove millions of people to suddenly leave Louisiana, Mississippi and Texas. As global warming and population growth increase, we could see far deadlier storms than Katrina. In 1991, a cyclone in Bangladesh displaced 2 million people and killed 138,000.

9   All this can lead to warfare when it's time for the displaced to find a new home. For most of human history, they could at least theoretically do so in unclaimed lands—a sort of territorial pressure valve whose existence tamped down conflict. But today, this reservoir of vacant turf no longer exists, except in the least hospitable parts of the planet. So when the displaced start eyeing currently inhabited areas, expect trouble—and the bigger the displacement, the bigger the fight.

10   The second cause of the coming climate wars is the flip side of scarcity: the problems of an increase in abundance. Suppose that global warming makes a precious resource easier to get at—say, rising temperatures in northern Canada, Alaska and Siberia make it easier to get at oil and gas resources in regions that had previously been too bone-chilling to tap. (A few degrees of change in temperature can transform a previously inhospitable climate.) But what happens if some tempting new field pops up in international waters

contested by two great powers? Or if smaller countries with murky borders start arguing over newly arable land?

Finally, we should also worry about new conflicts over issues of sovereignty 11 that we didn't need to deal with in our older, colder world. Consider the Northwest Passage, which is turning into an ice-free corridor from Europe to Asia during the summer months. Canada claims some portions of the route as its own sovereign waters, while the United States argues that these sections lie within international waters. Admittedly, it'd take a lot of tension for this to turn into a military conflict, but anyone convinced that the United States and Canada could never come to blows has forgotten the War of 1812. And not all this sort of resource conflict will occur between friendly countries.

Other kinds of territorial quarrels will arise, too. Some remote islands— 12 particularly such Pacific islands as Tuvalu, Kiribati, Tonga, the Maldives and many others—may be partially or entirely submerged beneath rising ocean waters. Do they lose their sovereignty if their territory disappears? After all, governments in exile have maintained sovereign rights in the past over land they didn't control (think of France and Poland in World War II). Nor are these new questions far away in the future. The first democratically elected president of the Maldives, Mohamed Nasheed, is already planning to use tourism revenue to buy land abroad—perhaps in India, Sri Lanka or Australia—to house his citizens. "We do not want to leave the Maldives, but we also do not want to be climate refugees living in tents for decades," he told Britain's *Guardian* newspaper.

The net result of these changes will be the creation of two geopolitical 13 belts of tension due to global warming, which will dramatically shape the patterns of conflict in the 21st century.

First, politics will heat up along what we might call the equatorial tension 14 belt, a broad swath of instability around the planet's center. This belt will creep southward, deeper into Africa, and extend far into central Asia.

Second, a new tension belt will develop around the polar circles. In the 15 short term, the main problems will arise in the Northern Hemisphere, but later in the 21st century, the area around the South Pole may also see increasing security strains as countries rush to claim and develop heretofore frozen areas. If the equatorial tension belt includes mostly poor, developing countries fighting over survival, the new polar tension belt will draw in wealthy, developed countries fighting over opportunity.

This is, admittedly, a glum view of the future. But we can still avoid the 16 new hot wars—or at least cool them down a bit. For starters, we should redouble our efforts to slow down global warming and undo the damage humanity has already done to the environment. Every little bit helps, so by all means, hassle your senator and recycle those bottles.

Beyond that, we need to get our heads around the idea that global warm- 17 ing is one of the most serious long-term threats to our national and personal security. For the next two decades or so, the climate will continue to change: Historic levels of built-up greenhouse gases will continue to warm the world— and spin it toward new patterns of conflict. So we need to do more than simply reverse climate change. We need to understand and react to it—ordinary people and governments alike—in ways that avoid conflict. Over the next few years, we may find that climate-change accords and peace treaties start to overlap more and more. And we may find that global warming is heating new conflicts up to the boiling point.

Source: *Washington Post*, January 4, 2009. Reprinted by permission of the author.

QUESTIONS FOR READING

1. What are the three ways that global warming can lead to war?
2. How can human displacement caused by global warming happen slowly? How can it come about quickly?
3. How can sovereignty issues be a result of global warming?
4. Where are the two geopolitical "belts of tension"?

QUESTIONS FOR REASONING AND ANALYSIS

5. What is Lee's claim? What evidence does he provide to support the seriousness of the problem?
6. Examine Lee's discussion of each cause; does he provide a convincing scenario for each possible source of conflict? Why or why not?
7. What type (genre) of argument is this? Where does Lee place most of his emphasis? Why? What does he provide in the final two paragraphs?

QUESTIONS FOR REFLECTION AND WRITING

8. Lee concedes that most of us see global warming as an environmental problem only—serious as that is. Is his warning of climate-change war a new idea for you? Does it make sense? (If you were a Maldives native, would Lee's argument seem more convincing?)
9. Most of the author's argument is given to explaining the problem—understandably. Can you add to his discussion of solutions? If recycling bottles won't stop immigrants from arid lands seeking new homes, what else do we need to do—as individuals and as a nation—to address the problems raised by Lee?

ON CLIMATE CHANGE, GOVERNMENT IS NOT THE ANSWER | ART CARDEN

Holding a PhD in economics from Washington University in St. Louis, Art Carden is assistant professor of economics at Samford University. He is also a senior research fellow with the Institute of Faith, Work, and Economics and a senior fellow with the Beacon Center of Tennessee. He has published in economics journals and magazines and is a regular contributor to *Forbes.com*. The following article on climate change appeared in the *Washington Examiner* on November 7, 2012.

PREREADING QUESTIONS What answers to the problems of climate change do you expect the author to suggest? Do you have answers to the problems of climate change?

Climate change is a textbook example of the economic case for government 1
intervention. In the language of an economics textbook, it involves a pretty
clear market failure created by the fact that my actions (emitting carbon dioxide) spill over onto non-consenting third parties.

Consider: I burn fossil fuels, to my own benefit. The climate changes. You 2
might also benefit if you own land in northern Canada, but you might be worse
off if you live in Miami or Bangladesh. How can you be compensated for the
harm I cause to benefit myself? On the face of it, there's a plausible case for
government involvement.

But in light of political responses to natural disasters and political out- 3
comes more generally, I'm included to think that political "solutions" are not
solutions at all. Consider how governments respond to natural disasters like
Hurricane Sandy. They openly defy the laws of the marketplace and impose
laws against price gouging. These laws in turn create shortages, which in turn
create unnecessary suffering.

Consider also the China-bashing that was on display in the recent presi- 4
dential election and the more general foreigner-bashing that is part and parcel
of the political scene. Such rhetoric and the policies based on it are at odds
with what economists left, right and center have known about trade for centuries. Trade creates wealth, and free trade among nations is a rising tide that
lifts all boats. In spite of this, few things are as unpopular as free trade (on the
Left) and open immigration (on the Right).

The rhetorical, cultural and political environment in which climate change 5
policy is made will never be one characterized by wise and benevolent leaders
seeking only the good of a populace consisting of recently enlightened New
Environmentalist Men and Women. People have all sorts of biases that warp
their political judgment, as Bryan Caplan has discussed in his book *The Myth
of the Rational Voter.*

With systematically biased voters, tangled webs of interest groups and 6
politicians who are all eager to cater to these biases and these interest groups,
the policies we get in the real world are likely to differ from the optimal policies that get discussed in the "externalities and public goods" lectures in
introductory economics classes by a pretty wide margin.

The lesson for climate change policy is dismal. Even if we agree that cli- 7
mate change is a problem, and even if we agree that climate change could
have very, very bad effects, ongoing research in "robust political economy" is
showing us that passing seemingly plausible ideas through the filters of political bias will give us something very different from the "solutions" we would
like to see.

How, then, should we address climate change? Adaptation is probably a 8
better strategy than prevention. Large-scale, top-down solutions are unlikely
to work, so the best way to proceed might be to recognize some of the key

insights of 2009 Nobel laureate Elinor Ostrom. Her work focused on how "bottom-up" solutions to resource management problems evolve. To translate it into the language of a bumper sticker you might have seen, "Think globally, act locally." Let's look for ways to devolve authority and to develop markets for goods and for risks that are not currently priced. Let's trust the initiative of innovative economic, social and cultural entrepreneurs rather than politicians.

Source: *Washington Examiner*, November 7, 2012. Reprinted with permission from the author.

QUESTIONS FOR READING

1. Why does it seem that government should seek solutions to climate change?
2. Why are political solutions not likely to be good ones? What are Carden's views of politicians and voters?
3. Does the author seem convinced that climate change is a serious problem?

QUESTIONS FOR REASONING AND ANALYSIS

4. What, exactly, is Carden refuting? What is his claim?
5. What alternative approach does he present?
6. What are the grounds for his rejection of government seeking solutions to climate change? Is his argument against government approach convincing? (Does he ever explain which governments—or should we assume that he means both federal and state governments?)
7. Does Carden demonstrate that the only two choices are government prevention or local adaptation? (Scientists have described the Arctic ice melt as faster than they had predicted years ago. Is "prevention" really an option?)

QUESTIONS FOR REFLECTION AND WRITING

8. Do you think that state and federal governments cope reasonably well with natural disasters such as Hurricane Sandy—keeping in mind what the word *disaster* means? Can communities and individuals cope better? (If you lost your home in a flood, would you be able to pay for a hotel room and, in a short time, find another home in which to live? Do most people have the resources to cope with disasters without government assistance?)
9. What suggestions do you have for managing our lives, individually and collectively, in a time of climate change that includes rising temperatures, rising sea levels, and more violent and unusual weather?

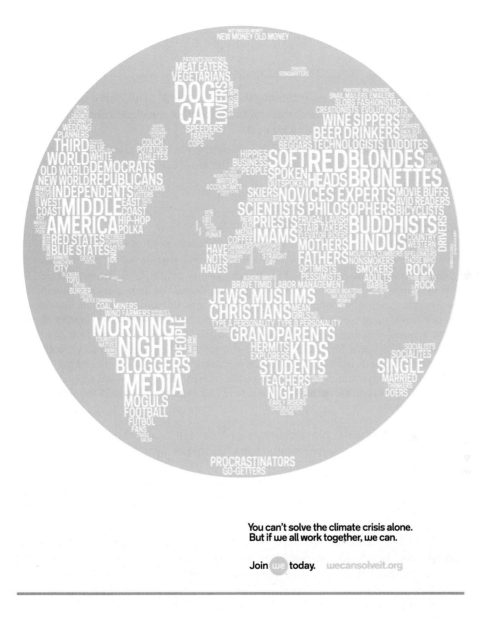

QUESTIONS FOR READING

1. What does the visual on this page represent?
2. What do the words in the visual communicate?

3. What is the ad's claim?

4. Does this ad's visual effectively support the claim? Why or why not?

5. Who has to work together to solve the climate crisis? (Think about this and also draw from your reading in this chapter.) Are all of the significant players likely to work together? Why or why not?

6. Does this ad catch your attention sufficiently for you to check out its website? For you to think about ways that you can help solve the climate problem? Why or why not?

THE COST OF CLIMATE INACTION
KRISTEN SHEERAN AND MINDY LUBBER

Formerly an associate professor at St. Mary's College of Maryland, Kristen Sheeran is now executive director of the Economics for Equity and the Environment Network (E3 Network), a group of economists concerned with environmental policy. Dr. Sheeran has published papers on economics in scholarly journals and addressed environmental issues in popular newspapers and magazines. Mindy Lubber, MBA, has been the regional administrator for the EPA and the founder/CEO of Green Century Capital Management. She is now president of Ceres, a national coalition of investors, environmental organizations, and other public interest groups working to incorporate sustainability into capital markets. Their article was published in the *Washington Post* on May 6, 2009.

PREREADING QUESTIONS   The authors' title might seem a bit cryptic; what "inaction" do you expect them to examine? And what are they likely to mean by "cost"?

1   Robert J. Samuelson's April 27 [2009] op-ed, "Selling the Green Economy," was way off the mark on the economics of tackling climate change. It was a call to bury our collective heads in the sand simply because the future involves uncertainty—exactly the opposite of what we need to do.

2   Samuelson argued that the cost of moving to a clean-energy economy is higher than advocates expect and that transition can't happen nearly fast enough to meet the ambitious goals proposed in the climate and energy bill sponsored by Reps. Henry Waxman (D-Calif.) and Edward Markey (D-Mass.).

3   But this assumes that all costs involved in mitigating climate change—and there will be costs—represent new costs, without acknowledging the massive error in our market system that equates the price of carbon emissions to zero. This fundamental error skews everything that follows, because if emitting carbon costs nothing on a balance sheet, all steps to reduce pollution count as "new costs."

4   The real cost of carbon emissions is far from zero. Each new scientific report brings proof of a changing climate that promises to disrupt agricultural patterns, set off a scramble for dwindling resources, raise sea levels, propel

population shifts and require massive emergency spending as we try to react to the growing crises. These are the costs of inaction.

A smart climate policy can create a mechanism to put the right price on 5 carbon, and rapid economic change will follow that firm price signal, along with reduced climate risks. Our work with more than 100 economists nationwide and at *RealClimateEconomics.org* demonstrates the weight of economic analysis supporting this point.

The failure to put a real price on carbon emissions also undermines 6 Samuelson's second point, that we cannot switch to clean energy technologies quickly. Many claim that these technologies will not work, at least in a cost-effective way, because we would already be using them if they did.

But we are not using them enough now because we have set the price of 7 carbon pollution at zero and have devoted most of our financial incentives to fossil fuel production to gas up our vehicles, heat our homes and power our factories. Acknowledging the climate crisis and pricing its risks correctly, instead of passing them on to our children, would produce an amazingly quick shift to new technologies and behaviors. We change habits when it makes economic sense to do so. Price matters.

Ultimately, households and businesses care more about their total energy 8 bill than costs per gallon or per kilowatt hour. Gas at $4 per gallon is cheaper in a car that gets 40 miles per gallon than $3-a-gallon gas in a clunker that gets 20 mpg. American entrepreneurial and research genius can move us to far greater energy efficiency quickly, using mostly existing technologies, when a carbon price rewards the effort.

The economic impacts on households, then, may not be as dramatic as 9 some warn. We can mobilize the political will for clean technologies and emissions reduction when, as economic research demonstrates, there is a visible payoff in jobs and strides in international competitiveness from these technologies.

And none of this is in conflict with the business community. Quite the 10 contrary. Consider Business for Innovative Climate and Energy Policy (BICEP), a coalition of nationally and globally known companies including Nike, Starbucks, Sun Microsystems, Timberland and Levi Strauss that the investor coalition Ceres coordinates. The heads of these companies believe that passing strong climate and energy legislation this year is in the interests of both the planet and their businesses.

Some BICEP businesses already see climate change affecting their supply 11 chains, manufacturing and international markets. Those are costs. These companies see strong climate and energy policy as pro-business because increased energy efficiency saves them money and clear price signals on carbon help them plan competitive strategies on a more level playing field.

The cost of inaction is high and could be catastrophic. But, contrary to claims, 12 the cost of switching to cleaner energy and dramatically lower emissions will spur competitive gains, cost far less and come much more quickly once we have set our goals, adjusted our incentives and corrected the market's false signals.

History shows that big changes often come in a rush, unforeseen by the 13 critics of the day. We believe that honest accounting for the reality of climate change will bring a convergence of effort and interests, triggering change on a scale that will, once again, alter the course of history.

Source: *Washington Post*, May 6, 2009. Reprinted by permission of Kristen Sheeran.

QUESTIONS FOR READING

1. Why do Sheeran and Lubber disagree with Robert Samuelson? What two points does Samuelson make? What, in the authors' view, does he ignore when making both points?
2. What are the climate disruptions listed by Sheeran and Lubber?
3. What can motivate households and businesses to embrace clean technologies and reduced emissions?
4. What is Ceres? What companies are part of BICEP?
5. What legislation do these companies support? Why do they support it?

QUESTIONS FOR REASONING AND ANALYSIS

6. Sheeran and Lubber use Samuelson's column as an occasion for writing, but their primary purpose is not simply to refute him. What is their claim? Where do they state it?
7. Explain, in your own words, the idea of carbon costs—and their effect on business decisions.
8. The authors conclude with a stirring belief in the possibility of significant change. Is their appeal an effective ending? Why or why not?

QUESTIONS FOR REFLECTION AND WRITING

9. Is the concept of carbon costs to business new to you? Does it make sense to factor in gas bills or spending for natural disasters as part of the costs of doing business? Why or why not?
10. Is the authors' focus on the costs of not responding to climate change an approach that works for you? If you are unmoved by Sheeran and Lubber's argument, how would you refute them?

CHAPTER 21

Laws and Rights: Gun Control and Immigration Debates

READ: What is the situation? Where are we?

REASON: Who speaks the lines? What is the speaker doing?

REFLECT/WRITE: What is amusing about the cartoon? What more serious point does Morin make?

The visuals and articles in this chapter explore and debate two current issues: gun control and immigration. In the spring of 2008, the Supreme Court, in a close decision, struck down the District of Columbia's ban on handguns. Some saw the decision as affirming the Second Amendment's guarantee of gun ownership to individuals. The Court, however, did not rule out all restrictions, and the several mass shootings since the ruling have led to a renewed interest in establishing further restrictions.

In his second inaugural address, President Obama asked Congress to pass not only reasonable gun restrictions but also immigration reform laws. His call comes after an Arizona law requiring police officers to check a person's status just because the person has done something to get police attention—including being part of a car collision that was not the "immigrant-looking" person's fault. Is this careful attention to illegal immigration, or is it harassment? Do states have the powers to enact such laws, or are immigration issues under federal control? This chapter raises these and other tough questions. Reflect on the following questions as a guide to your study of the current debates on gun control and immigration.

PREREADING QUESTIONS

1. What kinds of restrictions—if any—on guns will be consistent with the Supreme Court's 2008 ruling and the Second Amendment?
2. Is there any reason for citizens to own rapid-fire assault weapons?
3. Should the Arizona law be seen as a way to harass legal immigrants, thereby discouraging immigrants from settling in that state?
4. Is there any reason why young adults brought here illegally as children should be deprived of a college education or U.S. citizenship?
5. If you wanted to change any of the current laws on these issues to have them reflect your views, how would you go about trying to get your legislation passed?

GUN CONTROL? DREAM ON | KATHA POLLITT

Associate editor and columnist of *The Nation*, Katha Pollitt also contributes to other periodicals. Some of her essays are collected in *Reasonable Creatures: Essays on Women and Feminism* (1994), two volumes of poetry include *Antarctic Traveller* (1982), and *The Mind-Body Problem: Poems* (2009). Her successful collection, *Learning to Drive: And Other Life Stories*, was published in 2008. The following *Nation* column appeared August 8, 2012.

PREREADING QUESTIONS What does Pollitt's title tell you about her likely position on gun control? Which of the following opening statistics is the most arresting for you?

ONE NATION, UNDER GUNS There are 90 for every 100 Americans.	
Every year in the U.S. there are nearly:	Support for a ban on handguns has decreased in recent years . . .
30,000 gun deaths	60% in 1959
70,000 gun injuries	43% in 2011
20 instances of mass murder using guns	

Children led from Sandy Hook school after mass shooting.

Why am I even bothering to write about gun control? That was going to 1
be my opening sentence when this column was to be focused on the Aurora,
Colorado, movie-theater massacre: twelve people murdered and fifty-eight
wounded, some very severely, by James Holmes, demented neuroscience
graduate student. Then came the massacre at the Sikh temple in Oak Creek,
Wisconsin: six killed and three wounded, by Wade Michael Page, 40-year-old
white supremacist and leader of a racist hardcore band called End Apathy.
And even after this horrific crime, which the FBI is calling "domestic terrorism," my opening is the same: *Why am I even bothering to write about gun
control?* End apathy? Fat chance. If even the shooting of Gabrielle Giffords,
one of Congress's own, by Jared Loughner, another hyperarmed madman,
didn't move her pro-gun colleagues or their constituents, nothing will.

Remember the Million Mom March? In May 2000, 750,000 women gath- 2
ered on the National Mall to call for what are often referred to as "reasonable"
controls on guns, like background checks at gun shows and handgun registration (as opposed to "unreasonable" curbs like making it illegal to buy weapons intended to kill people—for example, handguns or AK-47s, let alone 6,000
rounds of ammunition on the Internet). Today you might as well stand on the
Mall and sing "Where Have All the Flowers Gone?"

The Million Mom March was loosely tied to the Gore campaign, and 3
Gore-Bush was the last election when Dems saw gun control as a potential vote
winner. Once Gore lost, Democrats fled the issue. For Democratic Party leaders
like Howard Dean (surprisingly, no friend to gun control) and Chuck Schumer,
restrictions on gun ownership interfered with the party's strategy of winning races
in red states by running macho pro-gun candidates like Jon Tester and Jim Webb
for the Senate, Brian Schweitzer for governor of Montana, or the host of conservative Blue Dog types who briefly swelled the ranks of Congressional Democrats.

So here we are today. Hours after the Sikh temple shooting, Nancy Pelosi 4
said she was "devastated" but foresaw no action on Capitol Hill. "The votes
aren't there," she lamented. Even in a Democratic Congress, she acknowledged, they might not be there, "because it takes a lot of votes to go down

that path." After the Aurora shooting, Obama spokesman Jay Carney emphasized controlling guns within the context of "existing law"—no easy task, given recent Supreme Court decisions upholding gun rights. Senator Frank Lautenberg, who has put forward a bill outlawing online ammunition sales—and recently refused to pull his amendment to the cybersecurity bill banning high-capacity ammunition clips—is the rare Dem on the national scene who hasn't given up. And Lautenberg is 88 years old.

5   In the absence of leadership at the national level, big-city police chiefs and mayors like Michael Bloomberg have tried to step into the breach. But with little support from the top and lacking an impassioned mass movement, to say nothing of money to combat the NRA's huge war chest, it's no wonder that gun control has shriveled into a Worthy Cause. According to Gallup, in 2011 only 26 percent of Americans favored a ban on handguns, down from a high of 60 percent way back in the dark ages of 1959. (Other polls show the country evenly divided but still unchanged by the recent mass murders.) Membership in the NRA has been increasing for decades and now stands at 4.3 million. As for the 30,000 annual gun deaths, 70,000 injuries and almost twenty mass murders a year? The ninety guns for every 100 Americans? It's something to wring your hands about, like sexting or obesity or plastic bags. Just another weird American thing.

6   Why is this? One reason is surely that guns have effectively become the emblem of the ongoing great white male right-wing freak-out. (Ladies might pack a pink pistol, but not an AK-47.) When Obama was elected, gun sales rose—quick, the Kenyan Muslim Communist is coming for our weapons! On NPR's *Diane Rehm Show*, John Velleco of Gun Owners of America seemed comfortable with the idea that someone might want an arsenal of assault weapons to protect his family from a home invasion. What home invasion would that be? And among the many foolish justifications for amassing high-powered weaponry is the delusion that you and your friends could outgun the government if you personally decided it had become a tyranny. That's almost as ridiculous as the notion that if everyone carried a gun, people would be safer. All those moviegoers in Aurora needed to make their misery complete was to have a bunch of freelancers shooting off their weapons in a dark theater.

7   The trouble is, as with so many aspects of conservatism—the anti-choice movement, the Tea Party, Ron Paul—"gun rights" supporters win on intensity and single-mindedness. We have common sense, but they have a master narrative: rugged individualism, patriotism and self-defense (which includes paranoid fantasies about threats from ordinary people in turbans whom they are too ignorant to realize are Sikhs, not Muslims . . . and obviously I'm not saying it would have been less horrific and more "understandable" if Page had attacked a mosque).

8   Of course, your average gun enthusiast is hardly tomorrow's Holmes or Loughner or Page—you have to be mentally ill to commit mass murder—but without a gun, it's difficult to kill and injure a whole crowd of people, no matter how much you'd like to. Gun advocates have devoted a great deal of ingenuity to trying to discredit this elementary point. And to the extent that gun-control supporters have become depressed and discouraged, they have succeeded.

Source: *The Nation*, August 8, 2012. Reprinted by permission of the author.

QUESTIONS FOR READING

1. What events have led to Pollitt's column?
2. Who used to work for more gun control? Why? And why did that support collapse?
3. How many gun deaths occur in the United States each year?
4. How does the author account for the country's focus on guns? What makes gun advocates successful?

QUESTIONS FOR REASONING AND ANALYSIS

5. What is Pollitt's claim? (Think about this; is there a precise claim statement anywhere?)
6. How does the author develop and support her argument? (What does she do first? Second? Third? See if you can find specific steps in the essay.)
7. How would you describe her tone? What elements of style help create that tone?
8. Who is Pollitt's audience? To what extent does her audience influence her approach and style?

QUESTIONS FOR REFLECTION AND WRITING

9. Do you agree with the author's analysis of the current situation in the gun debate? If yes, why? If no, why not?
10. What mass killing has taken place since this essay was published? How has it affected the gun debate? Would Pollitt be a little less depressed? Explain.

WE CAN'T AFFORD THE TRUE COST OF GUN CRIME | PETULA DVORAK

Petula Dvorak is a columnist for the *Washington Post.* Her column appeared on April 13, 2012.

PREREADING QUESTIONS When you read the essay's title, what "cost" do you expect the author to address? Does your expectation turn out to be accurate?

So let's say the human tragedy part of a shooting death isn't enough to 1 change your mind about gun control.

Maybe it's not the angle you want to take when talking about Trayvon 2 Martin, who may have been racially profiled but would still be alive today if George Zimmerman weren't a wannabe cop packing heat.

Or perhaps it's just bad luck that Amari Market-Purrel Perkins, a Prince 3 George's County first-grader, is dead because a fool living in his home stashed a gun in a Spider-Man backpack.

Sure, let's forget all that sad stuff. How about, instead, we talk about the 4 Benjamins, baby: What do guns in the wrong hands cost us?

Take a look at the massacre at Virginia Tech that occurred five years ago. 5 Put aside the loss of 32 lives, the devastation of 32 families, the permanent, emotional scarring of those who survived but were mentally or physically marred by the day one man unleashed all the demons in his head upon a university using a Walther P22 and a Glock 19.

6   What does allowing a mentally ill young man to legally buy two guns and an arsenal of magazines cost the rest of us in dollar terms?

7   About $48.2 million. That's according to the Center for American Progress, a liberal D.C. think tank that analyzed Seung Hui Cho's April 16, 2007, attack by sifting through the legal bills, university staffing costs, police costs, hospital bills and even autopsy receipts that kept piling up long after the candlelight vigils ended.

8   That $48.2 million tab for the two-hour shooting was picked up by local, state and federal taxpayers, the public university system, parents and students. That's a huge chunk of a state budget, and any other event that cost this much would get unblinking scrutiny.

9   "We have such a high demand in society for efficiency and careful use of tax dollars" that it made sense to look at such a tragedy through a fiscal lens, said Donna Cooper, a senior fellow with the economic policy team at the Center for American Progress and co-author of the cost study.

10   And yet, even after seeing the human tragedy and economic travesty that an assailant with guns can cause, crazy stuff is happening all around us to grant access to even more guns.

11   As if to spite the Virginia Tech community, the victims and their families on the eve of the anniversary of the massacre, Virginia opened the door and basically hung a "Welcome Back!" sign for gunrunners.

12   The state repealed its almost 20-year-old, commonsense law that limited people to purchasing just one handgun every 30 days.

13   That law clearly didn't stop Cho, who researched gun laws well and waited 32 days between his two gun purchases, but it does open the door for Virginia to become Guns R Us once again. Before the 30-day law was passed in 1993, Virginia was notorious for being the Northeast's major gun supplier. In New York in 1991, 40 percent of the weapons found at crime scenes were traced to the Old Dominion.

14   Come on—show me a society where guns mean less violence. Even Wyatt Earp figured that one out when he banned guns from his territory.

15   So why the sudden decision by the legislature to repeal this law and by Gov. Robert F. McDonnell (R) to sign the repeal? Did we hear a massive public outcry? Acknowledge the widespread pain and suffering of those who were unable to pursue life, liberty or happiness because they couldn't buy more than 12 guns a year?

16   My guess is that gun lobbyists fearing tighter regulations after a spike in murderous rampages began flying their flags, displaying their eagles and scaring the crud out of people.

17   Since the first modern-day mass killing—at a McDonald's in San Ysidro in 1984, where 40 people were shot and more than half of them died—there have been 15 similar killings over 23 years, according to the Center for American Progress report.

18   Now get this: In the five years since Virginia Tech, there have been 12.

19   I'm not seeing how making it easier to get a gun helps things, especially in Virginia.

The Founding Fathers were thinking of defending our land against the Redcoats when they wrote the Second Amendment. Suburban kids hopped up on years of *Grand Theft Auto;* 33-bullet magazines and semi-automatic killing machines; and a vigilante hell-bent on protecting a cul-de-sac from Skittles simply weren't in the mix. 20

So we need to work within that amendment to fit the world we live in today. 21

Most folks advocate commonsense proposals that can help keep guns out of the hands of dangerous people. 22

The Center for American Progress advocates full background checks on all gun transactions, including online and at gun shows. The group calls for clear standards and stronger compliance for reporting mental health issues to the National Instant Criminal Background Check System—which would have shown the gun dealer that Cho had recently been hospitalized for mental issues and should not have been eligible to buy his arsenal. 23

And they suggest outlawing high-capacity bullet magazines, which serve absolutely no purpose for any law-abiding gun owner. 24

If the struggle of former Arizona representative Gabrielle Giffords to recover from an attack by a crazed gunman, or the tears of Virginia Tech families and the daily loss of life to gun violence in America don't move you, just think cash. 25

A decade ago, doctors wrote in the *Journal of the American Medical Association* that gun violence was a public health crisis costing Americans more than $100 billion a year. 26

That's something we simply cannot afford. 27

QUESTIONS FOR READING

1. What does Dvorak mean when she writes: "Let's talk about the Benjamins"?
2. How much did the Virginia Tech massacre cost? Who paid the bills?
3. What law did Virginia recently change? How is this significant outside of Virginia?
4. How many mass murders have happened in the past five years?
5. What changes to improve safety are recommended by the Center for American Progress?

QUESTIONS FOR REASONING AND ANALYSIS

6. What is Dvorak's claim? Where does she state it?
7. How does the author develop and support her claim? Is she motivated to write only by the cost issue? Explain.
8. How does Dvorak anticipate gun supporters' use of the Second Amendment and seek to refute their counterargument?
9. Analyze Dvorak's style and tone; what strategies shape her style and create her tone?

10. The author wonders why gun owners need to buy more than twelve guns a year. Do you agree with her view? If so, why? If not, why not?

11. How do the proposals of the Center for American Progress compare to the changes in laws that President Obama has proposed? How has the Congress responded to these proposals? Do you agree with Congress's action? Why or why not?

12. Have you thought about the financial costs of gun deaths? Is this a useful approach to the issue? Why or why not?

"SENSELESS" IS NOT STUDYING GUN VIOLENCE | JAY DICKEY AND MARK ROSENBERG

Jay Dickey, an attorney and life member of the NRA, served in the House of Representatives (R, Arkansas) from 1993 to 2000. After leaving Congress, he led a consulting firm. Dr. Mark Rosenberg, a physician and public policy expert, was director of the National Center for Injury Prevention and Control at the U.S. Centers for Disease Control and Prevention from 1994 to 1999. Currently president and CEO of the Task Force for Global Health, Dr. Rosenberg is author or editor of several books, including *Violence in America: A Public Health Approach* (1991). Their article was published on July 29, 2012.

PREREADING QUESTIONS After reading about the two authors, are you surprised that they are coauthoring an article on gun control issues? Are you even more interested to see what they have to say together on this issue?

1   A few years ago, one of us came across a young woman who had just been hit by a car. She was the mother of two young children and one of Atlanta's star runners. I found her unconscious and bleeding profusely from a severe head injury. She died in my arms while I tried to resuscitate her.

2   Her death was tragic, but it wasn't "senseless." In scientific terms, it was explicable. The runner, who had competed in 15 marathons and broken many records, wore no lights or reflective vest in the early-morning darkness; she crossed the street within crosswalk lines that had faded to near-invisibility; there were no speed bumps on this wide, flat street to slow cars down.

3   Scientists don't view traffic injuries as "senseless" or "accidental" but as events susceptible to understanding and prevention. Urban planners, elected officials and highway engineers approach such injuries by asking four questions: What is the problem? What are the causes? Have effective interventions been discovered? Can we install these interventions in our community?

4   The federal government has invested billions to understand the causes of motor vehicle fatalities and, with that knowledge, has markedly reduced traffic deaths in the United States. Since the mid-1970s, research has inspired such interventions as child restraints, seat belts, frontal air bags, a minimum drinking age and motorcycle helmets. The National Highway Traffic Safety Administration estimates that 366,000 lives were saved through such efforts from 1975 to 2009.

Through the same scientific, evidence-based approach, our country has 5
made progress understanding and preventing violence. Once upon a time,
law-abiding citizens believed that violence generated by evil always had
existed and always would exist. By the mid-20th century, that sense of fatalism
was yielding to discoveries by social scientists, physicians and epidemiolo-
gists. Now a body of knowledge makes it clear that an event such as the mass
shooting in Aurora, Colo., was not a "senseless" occurrence as random as a
hurricane or earthquake but, rather, has underlying causes that can be understood and used to prevent similar mass shootings.

We also recognize different types of violence, including child abuse and 6
neglect, sexual assault, elder abuse, suicide and economically and politically
motivated violence. Like motor vehicle injuries, violence exists in a cause-and-
effect world; things happen for predictable reasons. By studying the causes of
a tragic—but not senseless—event, we can help prevent another.

Recently, some have observed that no policies can reduce firearm fatali- 7
ties, but that's not quite true. Research-based observations are available.
Child-proof locks, safe-storage devices and waiting periods save lives.

But it's vital to understand why we know more and spend so much more 8
on preventing traffic fatalities than on preventing gun violence, even though
firearm deaths (31,347 in 2009, the most recent year for which statistics are
available) approximate the number of motor vehicle deaths (32,885 in 2010).

From 1986 to 1996, the U.S. Centers for Disease Control and Prevention 9
(CDC) sponsored high-quality peer-reviewed research into the underlying
causes of gun violence. People who kept guns in their homes did not—despite
their hopes—gain protection, according to research published in the *New
England Journal of Medicine*. Instead, residents in homes with a gun faced a
2.7-fold greater risk of homicide and a 4.8-fold greater risk of suicide. The
National Rifle Association moved to suppress the dissemination of these
results and to block funding of future government research into the causes of
firearm injuries.

One of us served as the NRA's point person in Congress and submitted an 10
amendment to an appropriations bill that removed $2.6 million from the CDC's
budget, the amount the agency's injury center had spent on firearms-related
research the previous year. This amendment, together with a stipulation that
"None of the funds made available for injury prevention and control at the
Centers for Disease Control and Prevention may be used to advocate or promote gun control," sent a chilling message.

Since the legislation passed in 1996, the United States has spent about 11
$240 million a year on traffic safety research, but there has been almost no
publicly funded research on firearm injuries.

As a consequence, U.S. scientists cannot answer the most basic question: 12
What works to prevent firearm injuries?

We don't know whether having more citizens carry guns would decrease 13
or increase firearm deaths; or whether firearm registration and licensing would
make inner-city residents safer or expose them to greater harm. We don't
know whether a ban on assault weapons or large-capacity magazines, or

limiting access to ammunition, would have saved lives in Aurora or would make it riskier for people to go to a movie. And we don't know how to effectively restrict access to firearms by those with serious mental illness.

14 What we do know is that firearm injuries will continue to claim far too many lives at home, at school, at work and at the movies until we start asking and answering the hard questions. "Such violence, such evil is senseless," President Obama said last week. What is truly senseless is to decry these deaths as senseless when the tools exist to understand causes and to prevent these deadly effects.

15 We were on opposite sides of the heated battle 16 years ago, but we are in strong agreement now that scientific research should be conducted into preventing firearm injuries and that ways to prevent firearm deaths can be found without encroaching on the rights of legitimate gun owners. The same evidence-based approach that is saving millions of lives from motor-vehicle crashes, as well as from smoking, cancer and HIV/AIDS, can help reduce the toll of deaths and injuries from gun violence.

16 Most politicians fear talking about guns almost as much as they would being confronted by one, but these fears are senseless. We must learn what we can do to save lives. It is like the answer to the question: "When is the best time to plant a tree?" The best time to start was 20 years ago; the second-best time is now.

Source: *Washington Post*, July 29, 2012. Reprinted by permission of the authors.

QUESTIONS FOR READING

1. What event seems to have led to this essay?
2. What do the authors mean by "senseless"? What is it in contrast to?
3. What has research revealed about the relative safety of those with guns in their homes? What was the NRA's response to this research?
4. What legislation did Dickey sponsor and get passed in Congress?

QUESTIONS FOR REASONING AND ANALYSIS

5. What is the authors' claim? Where do they state it?
6. This essay has a relatively long introduction; what do the authors gain from their approach?
7. Analyze the essay's style and tone. Note especially the concluding paragraph; what makes it effective?

QUESTIONS FOR REFLECTION AND WRITING

8. This argument for research also represents a change of thinking for one of the authors. How does your knowledge of his change of heart—and his willingness to assert that he was wrong—affect your response to the essay? Explain.
9. Have the authors convinced you that firearm injuries are not senseless? If yes, why? If no, why not?

10. If you are convinced that we can understand the causes of firearm injuries, then are you prepared to embrace the conclusion that follows: We must do the research and find prevention strategies? If you reject the conclusion but accept the first step of the argument, how can you explain your unwillingness to follow the authors' logic? Be prepared to discuss these issues in class or think about preparing a counterargument.

IMMIGRATE, ASSIMILATE | AMY CHUA

A professor at Yale Law School since 2001, Amy Chua specializes in international business transactions, ethnic conflict, and globalization and the law. She is the author of *World on Fire* (2004) and *Day of Empire: How Hyperpowers Rise to Global Dominance—And Why They Fall* (2007). Her essay on immigration, published February 3, 2008, was a special to the *Washington Post*.

PREREADING QUESTIONS Given the title, where do you expect to find Chua on the immigration debate? Given her education and expertise, how do you expect her to support her argument?

If you don't speak Spanish, Miami really can feel like a foreign country. In any restaurant, the conversation at the next table is more likely to be in Spanish than English. And Miami's population is only 65 percent Hispanic. El Paso is 76 percent Latino. Flushing, N.Y., is 60 percent immigrant, mainly Chinese.   1

Chinatowns and Little Italys have long been part of America's urban landscape, but would it be all right to have entire U.S. cities where most people spoke and did business in Chinese, Spanish or even Arabic? Are too many Third World, non-English-speaking immigrants destroying our national identity?   2

For some Americans, even asking such questions is racist. At the other end of the spectrum, conservative talk-show host Bill O'Reilly fulminates against floods of immigrants who threaten to change America's "complexion" and replace what he calls the "white Christian male power structure."   3

But for the large majority in between, Democrats and Republicans alike, these questions are painful, and there are no easy answers. At some level, most of us cherish our legacy as a nation of immigrants. But are all immigrants really equally likely to make good Americans? Are we, as Samuel Huntington warns, in danger of losing our core values and devolving "into a loose confederation of ethnic, racial, cultural and political groups, with little or nothing in common apart from their location in the territory of what had been the United States of America"?   4

My parents arrived in the United States in 1961, so poor that they couldn't afford heat their first winter. I grew up speaking only Chinese at home (for every English word accidentally uttered, my sister and I got one whack of the chopsticks). Today, my father is a professor at Berkeley, and I'm a professor at Yale Law School. As the daughter of immigrants, a grateful beneficiary of America's tolerance and opportunity, I could not be more pro-immigrant.   5

Nevertheless, I think Huntington has a point.   6

7   Around the world today, nations face violence and instability as a result of their increasing pluralism and diversity. Across Europe, immigration has resulted in unassimilated, largely Muslim enclaves that are hotbeds of unrest and even terrorism. The riots in France late last year were just the latest manifestation. With Muslims poised to become a majority in Amsterdam and elsewhere within a decade, major West European cities could undergo a profound transformation. Not surprisingly, virulent anti-immigration parties are on the rise.

8   Not long ago, Czechoslovakia, Yugoslavia and the Soviet Union disintegrated when their national identities proved too weak to bind together diverse peoples. Iraq is the latest example of how crucial national identity is. So far, it has found no overarching identity strong enough to unite its Kurds, Shiites and Sunnis.

9   The United States is in no danger of imminent disintegration. But this is because it has been so successful, at least since the Civil War, in forging a national identity strong enough to hold together its widely divergent communities. We should not take this unifying identity for granted.

10   The greatest empire in history, ancient Rome, collapsed when its cultural and political glue dissolved, and peoples who had long thought of themselves as Romans turned against the empire. In part, this fragmentation occurred because of a massive influx of immigrants from a very different culture. The "barbarians" who sacked Rome were Germanic immigrants who never fully assimilated.

11   Does this mean that it's time for the United States to shut its borders and reassert its "white, Christian" identity and what Huntington calls its Anglo-Saxon, Protestant "core values"?

ANTI-IMMIGRANT MISTAKES

12   No. The anti-immigration camp makes at least two critical mistakes.

13   First, it neglects the indispensable role that immigrants have played in building American wealth and power. In the 19th century, the United States would never have become an industrial and agricultural powerhouse without the millions of poor Irish, Polish, Italian and other newcomers who mined coal, laid rail and milled steel. European immigrants led to the United States' winning the race for the atomic bomb.

14   Today, American leadership in the Digital Revolution—so central to our military and economic preeminence—owes an enormous debt to immigrant contributions. Andrew Grove (co-founder of Intel), Vinod Khosla (Sun Microsystems) and Sergey Brin (Google) are immigrants. Between 1995 and 2005, 52.4 percent of Silicon Valley startups had one key immigrant founder. And Vikram S. Pundit's recent appointment to the helm of Citigroup means that 14 CEOs of Fortune 100 companies are foreign-born.

15   The United States is in a fierce global competition to attract the world's best high-tech scientists and engineers—most of whom are not white Christians. Just this past summer, Microsoft opened a large new software-development center in Canada, in part because of the difficulty of obtaining U.S. visas for foreign engineers.

Second, anti-immigration talking heads forget that their own scapegoat- 16 ing vitriol will, if anything, drive immigrants further from the U.S. mainstream. One reason we don't have Europe's enclaves is our unique success in forging an ethnically and religiously neutral national identity, uniting individuals of all backgrounds. This is America's glue, and people like Huntington and O'Reilly unwittingly imperil it.

Nevertheless, immigration naysayers also have a point.   17

America's glue can be subverted by too much tolerance. Immigration 18 advocates are too often guilty of an uncritical political correctness that avoids hard questions about national identity and imposes no obligations on immigrants. For these well-meaning idealists, there is no such thing as too much diversity.

MAINTAINING OUR HERITAGE

The right thing for the United States to do—and the best way to keep 19 Americans in favor of immigration—is to take national identity seriously while maintaining our heritage as a land of opportunity. U.S. immigration policy should be tolerant but also tough. Here are five suggestions:

• Overhaul Admission Priorities.

Since 1965, the chief admission criterion has been family reunification. 20 This was a welcome replacement for the ethnically discriminatory quota system that preceded it. But once the brothers and sisters of a current U.S. resident get in, they can sponsor their own extended families. In 2006, more than 800,000 immigrants were admitted on this basis. By contrast, only about 70,000 immigrants were admitted on the basis of employment skills, with an additional 65,000 temporary visas granted to highly skilled workers.

This is backward. Apart from nuclear families (spouse, minor children, pos- 21 sibly parents), the special preference for family members should be drastically reduced. As soon as my father got citizenship, his relatives in the Philippines asked him to sponsor them. Soon, his mother, brother, sister and sister-in-law were also U.S. citizens or permanent residents. This was nice for my family, but frankly there is nothing especially fair about it.

Instead, the immigration system should reward ability and be keyed to the 22 country's labor needs, skilled or unskilled, technological or agricultural. In particular, we should significantly increase the number of visas for highly skilled workers, putting them on a fast track for citizenship.

• Make English the Official National Language.

A common language is critical to cohesion and national identity in an ethni- 23 cally diverse society. Americans of all backgrounds should be encouraged to speak more languages—I've forced my own daughters to learn Mandarin (minus the threat of chopsticks)—but offering Spanish-language public education to Spanish-speaking children is the wrong kind of indulgence. Native-language education should be overhauled, and more stringent English proficiency requirements for citizenship should be set up.

A Hispanic American shows his dual loyalties in march on Washington.

• Immigrants Must Embrace the Nation's Civic Virtues.

24   It took my parents years to see the importance of participating in the larger community. When I was in third grade, my mother signed me up for Girl Scouts. I think she liked the uniforms and merit badges, but when I told her that I was picking up trash and visiting soup kitchens, she was horrified.

25   For many immigrants, only family matters. Even when immigrants get involved in politics, they often focus on protecting their own and protesting discrimination. That they can do so is one of the great virtues of U.S. democracy. But a mind-set based solely on taking care of your own factionalizes our society.

26   Like all Americans, immigrants have a responsibility to contribute to the social fabric. It's up to each immigrant community to fight off an "enclave" mentality and give back to their new country. It's not healthy for Chinese to hire only Chinese, or Koreans only Koreans. By contrast, the free health clinic set up by Muslim Americans in Los Angeles—serving the entire poor community—is a model to emulate. Immigrants are integrated at the moment they realize that their success is intertwined with everyone else's.

• Enforce the Law.

27   Illegal immigration, along with terrorism, is the chief cause of today's anti-immigration backlash. It is also inconsistent with the rule of law, which, as any immigrant from a developing country will tell you, is a critical aspect of U.S. identity. But if we're serious about this problem, we need to enforce the law against not only illegal aliens, but also against those who hire them.

It's the worst of all worlds to allow U.S. employers who hire illegal aliens— 28 thus keeping the flow of illegal workers coming—to break the law while demonizing the aliens as lawbreakers. An Arizona law that took effect Jan. 1 tightens the screws on employers who hire undocumented workers, but this issue can't be left up to a single state.

• Make the United States an Equal-Opportunity Immigration Magnet.

That the 11 million to 20 million illegal Immigrants are 80 percent Mexican 29 and Central American is itself a problem. This is emphatically not for the reason Huntington gives—that Hispanics supposedly don't share America's core values. But if the U.S. immigration system is to reflect and further our ethnically neutral identity, it must itself be ethnically neutral, offering equal opportunity to Sudanese, Estonians, Burmese and so on. The starkly disproportionate ratio of Latinos—reflecting geographical fortuity and a large measure of lawbreaking—is inconsistent with this principle.

Immigrants who turn their backs on American values don't deserve to be 30 here. But those of us who turn our backs on immigrants misunderstand the secret of America's success and what it means to be American.

Source: *Washington Post*, February 3, 2008. Reprinted by permission of the author.

QUESTIONS FOR READING

1. What is Huntington's concern for America?
2. What has happened in some European cities? To several European countries? What causes internal conflict in Iraq?
3. What are the two mistakes of those who oppose immigration, in the author's view?
4. What are the author's suggestions for a tough immigration policy? State her five proposals in your own words.

QUESTIONS FOR REASONING AND ANALYSIS

5. Why does Chua provide her immigrant experience and family success story? As a part of her argument, what purpose does it serve?
6. What is clever about her concluding paragraph? How does it mirror the approach of her argument?
7. What is Chua's claim? Express her position as a problem/solution argument.
8. Look at Chua's five proposals. What kinds of grounds does she provide in support?
9. Is the author convincing? If so, what makes her argument effective? If not, why not?

QUESTIONS FOR REFLECTION AND WRITING

10. Chua asserts that the chief cause of anti-immigration attitudes is a combination of terrorism and illegal aliens. Do you agree with this assessment? If not, why not?

11. Where do you stand on immigration? In opposition? Embracing diversity? Or somewhere in the middle? Has Chua established a good argument for the middle ground? Why or why not?

12. Is there any specific proposal with which you disagree? If so, why? How would you refute Chua's defense of that proposal?

LEGAL, ILLEGAL | ROBERTO SURO

A professor of public policy and director of the Tomas Rivera Policy Institute at the University of Southern California, Roberto Suro is author or editor of several books on immigration, including *Writing Immigration: Scholars and Journalists in Dialogue* (2011). Suro is also active in the community, serving on the board of directors of an association of charities and as a trustee of a foundation supporting social science research. The following essay was published July 5, 2012.

PREREADING QUESTIONS Can you find any clues to Suro's essay from his title? What do you expect to discover?

1   A century ago, the immigrants from across the Atlantic included settlers and sojourners. Along with the many folks looking to make a permanent home in the United States came those who had no intention to stay, and who would make some money and then go home. Between 1908 and 1915, about 7 million people arrived while about 2 million departed. About a quarter of all Italian immigrants, for example, eventually returned to Italy for good. They even had an affectionate nickname, "uccelli di passaggio," birds of passage.

2   Today, we are much more rigid about immigrants. We divide newcomers into two categories: legal or illegal, good or bad. We hail them as Americans in the making, or brand them as aliens fit for deportation. That framework has contributed mightily to our broken immigration system and the long political paralysis over how to fix it. We don't need more categories, but we need to change the way we think about categories. We need to look beyond strict definitions of legal and illegal. To start, we can recognize the new birds of passage, those living and thriving in the gray areas. We might then begin to solve our immigration challenges.

3   Crop pickers, violinists, construction workers, entrepreneurs, engineers, home health-care aides and particle physicists are among today's birds of passage. They are energetic participants in a global economy driven by the flow of work, money and ideas. They prefer to come and go as opportunity calls them. They can manage to have a job in one place and a family in another.

4   With or without permission, they straddle laws, jurisdictions and identities with ease. We need them to imagine the United States as a place where they can be productive for a while without committing themselves to staying forever. We need them to feel that home can be both here and there and that they can belong to two nations honorably.

Civilian watches the border with Mexico, determined to spot illegals crossing the desert.

Imagine life with a radically different immigration policy: The Jamaican 5 woman who came as a visitor and was looking after your aunt until she died could try living in Canada for a while. You could eventually ask her to come back to care for your mother. The Indian software developer could take some of his Silicon Valley earnings home to join friends in a little start-up, knowing that he could always work in California again. Or the Mexican laborer who busts his back on a Wisconsin dairy farm for wages that keep milk cheap would come and go as needed because he could decide which dairy to work for and a bi-national bank program was helping him save money to build a better life for his kids in Mexico.

Accommodating this new world of people in motion will require new 6 attitudes on both sides of the immigration battle. Looking beyond the culture war logic of right or wrong means opening up the middle ground and understanding that managing immigration today requires multiple paths and multiple outcomes, including some that are not easy to accomplish legally in the existing system.

A new system that encourages both sojourners and settlers would not 7 only help ensure that our society receives the human resources it will need in the future, it also could have an added benefit: Changing the rigid framework might help us resolve the status of the estimated 11 million unauthorized migrants who are our shared legacy of policy failures.

Currently, we do not do gray zones well. Hundreds of thousands of people 8 slosh around in indeterminate status because they're caught in bureaucratic limbo or because they have been granted temporary stays that are repeatedly extended. President Obama created a paler shade of gray this summer by exercising prosecutorial discretion not to deport some young people who were brought to this country illegally as children. But these are exceptions, not rules.

9   The basic mechanism for legal immigration today, apart from the special category of refugee, is the legal permanent resident visa, or green card. Most recipients are people sponsored by close relatives who live in the United States. As the name implies, this mechanism is designed for immigrants who are settling down. The visa can be revoked if the holder does not show "intent to remain" by not maintaining a U.S. address, going abroad to work full time or just traveling indefinitely. Legal residents are assumed to be on their way to becoming Americans, physically, culturally and legally. After five years of living here, they become eligible for citizenship and a chance to gain voting rights and full access to the social safety net.

10   This is a fine way to deal with people who arrive with deep connections to the country and who resolve to stay. That can and should be most immigrants. But this mechanism has two problems: The nation is not prepared to offer citizenship to every migrant who is offered a job. And not everyone who comes here wants to stay forever.

11   It may have once made sense to think of immigrants as sodbusters who were coming to settle empty spaces. But that antique reasoning does not apply when the country is looking at a long, steep race to remain competitive in the world economy, particularly not when innovation and entrepreneurship are supposed to be our comparative advantage. To succeed, we need modern birds of passage.

12   The challenges differ depending on whether you are looking at the high end of the skills spectrum, the information workers or at low-skilled laborers.

13   A frequent proposal for highly skilled workers comes with the slogan, "Staple a green card to the diploma." That is supposed to ensure that a greater share of brainy international students remain in the United States after earning degrees in science and technology. But what if they are not ready for a long-term commitment? No one would suggest that investment capital or design processes need to reside permanently in one nation. Talent today yearns to be equally mobile. Rather than try to oblige smart young people from abroad to stay here, we should allow them to think of the United States as a place where they can always return, a place where they will spend part, not all, of their lives, one of several places where they can live and work and invest.

14   Temporary-worker programs are a conventional approach to meeting low-skilled labor needs without illegal immigration. That's what President George W. Bush proposed in 2004, saying the government should "match willing foreign workers with willing American employers." An immigrant comes to do a particular job for a limited period of time and then goes home. But such programs risk replacing one kind of rigidity with another. The relatively small programs currently in place don't manage the matchmaking very well. Competing domestic workers need to be protected, as do the migrant workers, and the

process must be nimble enough to meet labor market demand. Nobody really has pulled that off, and there is no reason to believe it can be done on a grand scale. Rather than trying to link specific migrants to specific jobs, different types of temporary work visas could be pegged to industries, to places or to time periods. You could get an engineering visa, not only a visa to work at Intel.

Both short-term visas and permanent residence need to be part of the 15 mix, but they are not the whole answer. Another valuable tool is the provisional visa, which Australia uses as a kind of intermediary stage in which temporary immigrants spend several years before becoming eligible for permanent residency. The U.S. system practically obliges visitors to spend time here without authorization when they've married a citizen, gotten a job or done something else that qualifies them to stay legally.

We also could borrow from Europe and create long-term permission to 16 reside for certain migrants that is contingent on simply being employed, not on having a specific job. And, legislation could loosen the definitions of permanent residency so that migrants could gain a lifetime right to live and work in the United States without having to be here (and pay taxes here) more or less continuously.

The idea that newcomers are either saints or sinners is not written 17 indelibly either in our hearts or in our laws. As the size of the unauthorized population has grown over the past 20 years or so, the political response has dictated seeing immigration policy through the stark lens of law enforcement: Whom do we lock up, kick out, fence off? Prominent politicians of both parties, including both presidential candidates, have engaged in macho one-upmanship when it comes to immigration. So, President Obama broke records for deportations. Mitt Romney, meanwhile, vows to break records for border security.

Breaking out of the either/or mentality opens up many avenues for managing future immigration. It could also help break the stalemate over the current population of unauthorized migrants. No election result will produce a Congress that offers a path to citizenship for everybody, but there is no support for total deportation, either.

If we accept that there are spaces between legal and illegal, then options 19 multiply.

Citizenship could be an eventual outcome for most, not all, people here 20 illegally, but everyone would get some kind of papers, and we can engineer a way for people to work their way from one status to another. The newly arrived and least attached could be granted status for a limited time and receive help with returning to their home countries. Others might be offered life-long privileges to live and work here, but not citizenship. We'd give the fullest welcome to those with homes, children or long time jobs.

By insisting that immigrants are either Americans or aliens, we make it 21 harder for some good folks to come and we oblige others to stay for the wrong reasons. Worse, we ensure that there will always be people living among us who are outside the law and that is not good for them or us.

Source: *Washington Post*, July 5, 2012. Reprinted by permission of the author.

QUESTIONS FOR READING

1. What, for Suro, was—and still is—a bird of passage?

2. How do we view these sojourners today?

3. How do immigrants typically come to the United States today? What are they expected to do?

4. What are the problems with this mechanism?

5. What are the two primary groups of sojourners? How does each group need to be accommodated?

QUESTIONS FOR REASONING AND ANALYSIS

6. What kind (genre) of argument is this? State Suro's claim to reveal the essay's argument type.

7. What approach to immigration issues is *not* the solution, in Suro's view? Why not? What are the problems with the current approach?

8. List the specific strategies Suro presents for handling various kinds of immigrants. Which ones will require new legislation?

9. What other problem will be easier to address once we agree to Suro's recommendations?

10. Analyze Suro's style and tone; how do they help his argument?

QUESTIONS FOR REFLECTION AND WRITING

11. Do you, in general, agree with Suro that seeing only two categories of immigrants is not the way to approach this issue? If yes, why? If no, why not?

12. Which of the author's specific proposals makes sense to you? Why?

13. Suro concludes that illegal immigrants are not good for either them or us. Why are illegals not good for us—we who are legal? Reflect on this question.

WHEN SOCIETIES COLLIDE: PART THREE: FINDING THE BEST FIT IMMIGRATION MODEL | PATRICIA B. STRAIT

Patricia Strait began her career as an air traffic controller in the U.S. Navy. She is currently on the faculty of the University of Richmond and serves as program chair of Human Resources and Leadership Studies. She has written articles in both English and Spanish on labor economics, immigration, and employee ethics. The following article, to be published in the *International Journal of Interdisciplinary Social Sciences*, will be the third and final of three connected articles that study immigration issues and problems.

PREREADING QUESTIONS What do you think you might learn from this in-depth sociological study of immigration? What differences from Chua's and Suro's essays can you anticipate?

INTRODUCTION AND REVIEW OF PARTS ONE AND TWO OF THE TRILOGY

In the first part of the trilogy (Strait, 2010), the sources which inform and shape immigration views were explored. The four major sources of information included the news media, government agencies, nongovernment organizations (NGOs), and scholarly journals. The news media was found to be the most prevalent and abundant source of information which influences perceptions regarding immigration, especially among the general public. The news media, which includes print, Internet, television and film, is primarily a profit-driven source which provides narratives which are structured in such a way as to be consumed quickly by the viewing public. The majority of the stories which appear in the news media emphasize two contrasting elements: One, the apprehension or transport of illegal immigrants, and two, upbeat stories of successful immigrant citizens. The stakeholders whose views are mostly commonly represented in the news media include primarily two groups: host populations who seek to protect their nations' borders and resources, and immigrant citizens who have earned residency via the "legitimate" immigration system.

The second source of information regarding immigration is government agencies which typically gather statistical information. Included in this group are agencies such as the US Census Bureau and the European Commission. Government agencies typically make this quantitative information available to the general public through their respective online databases. The information typically includes data on variables such as the number of immigrants, countries of origin, level of education, and place of residence. By comparing these variables across a period of time, patterns may be observed and geographic areas which have been particularly impacted by immigration may be identified. The information contained within these databases is used by primarily three groups: the public sector for the allocation of funds regarding government services, the private sector for marketing purposes, and politicians for identifying changing constituencies. The two stakeholder groups whose interests are represented most commonly by government agencies are the same two groups who are most likely to access the government databases, the host population and private enterprise.

The third source of information, nongovernment organizations, provides immigration information which is both extensive and contradictory. The stakeholder represented varies according to the mission of the NGO, its political orientation, and its source of funding. Although many NGOs claim to be nonpartisan, a sympathetic view toward one particular stakeholder or another can usually be detected. Examples of NGOs in the immigration arena include: the Pew Research Center, the Human Rights Watch, the Migration Policy Institute, the Center for Immigration Studies, and the CATO Institute. Each of these organizations represents a different place on the immigration debate continuum. Some NGOs are sympathetic to immigrants while others seek to protect the interests of host populations. It is also important to note that the research findings from NGOs are often contradictory.

Lastly, the information provided by scholarly journals typically comes in two categories: First, scholarly literature that explores the historic origins of diasporas, and second, population journals which investigate global shifts in demographics. Gabaccia (2000) represents the first category of researchers via her work concerning Italian transnational family economies. Other researchers such as Ong (1999; 2009) have introduced concepts such as "flexible citizenship" and the decreasing relevance of national borders. Fishkin (2005) has supported the idea that national borders have diminishing importance as more people become part of the global flow of talent. These researchers encourage stakeholders to question long-held assumptions regarding citizenship and national borders. In contrast, journals such as the *European Journal of Population, Population and Development Review,* and the *Journal of Population Research* tend to explore the shifting demographics between and within nations (Lee & Mason, 2009; Stalker, 2003). It is more difficult to detect the stakeholder whose interests are represented in scholarly journals as most researchers cultivate a detached scholarly perspective. Although it would appear that the information provided by these journals would be of interest to all stakeholders, it is probably other researchers who are most likely to access them due to the esoteric nature of the journals. The most important finding in Part One of the Trilogy was how strongly the information source influenced not only opinions, but the findings of the immigration research as well.

5   **Part Two of the Trilogy** (Strait, 2011) revealed ethical dilemmas which resulted when certain stakeholder groups were omitted from the immigration dialog. These ethical dilemmas included taxation of undocumented immigrants, expedited citizenship through military service, immigrant profiling, and the repatriation of undocumented immigrants to high risk environments.

6   **Taxation of Undocumented Immigrants:** As birth rates among host populations in industrialized nations continue to decline, social welfare programs have become more difficult to sustain as tax contributions to these programs have also declined. To make up this lost income, the tax revenue derived from immigrant populations has become an increasingly important revenue source for host countries. While some have expressed concern that more liberal immigration policies would result in a swelling underclass, current research has indicated that the size and composition of the underclass has remained the same through the years despite the recent increases in immigration (Griswold, 2009). The practice of collecting income taxes from illegal immigrants while denying them access to the services they are funding such as higher education, disability, and unemployment is viewed by many as controversial. In the meantime, however, destination nations continue to enjoy the economic benefits of cheap labor, reduced consumer costs, and additional tax revenues.

7   **Military Service as a Pathway to Citizenship:** Populating a nation's military with immigrants is far from a new government practice. Immigrants have been recruited to serve in the militaries of destination nations for centuries. In the case of the United States, the practice of using immigrants can be documented as far back as the Revolutionary War depending on how one wants to define the term *immigrant*. Other periods in which immigrants have been widely used in the world's militaries have included World I, World War II, the

Korean War, and Vietnam as well as the Persian Gulf Conflict, Somalia, Kosovo, Haiti and Panama. According to the US Senate, there are 114,601 foreign-born individuals serving in the US military as of June 2009 (Stock, 2009). The use of noncitizens continues to be common practice in other destination nations as well, especially in countries with low unemployment.

Repatriation of Immigrants to High Risk Environments: The flow of ille- 8 gal immigrants into the US, Spain and Italy continues despite these countries' attempts to re-enforce their coasts with both air and sea patrols. In addition, undocumented immigrants from Mexico and Central America are still arriving in the US via massive expanses of desert along the southwest border. In the year 2010, the state of Arizona experienced a record high number of deaths as 252 bodies were recovered along its borders (Medrano, 2010). Many other immigrants have died after being packed into trailers while being smuggled across the US border in conditions which lack both sanitary conditions and sufficient air to breathe (Hernandez, 2003). The United States, Spain and Italy are not the only countries of choice among undocumented immigrants and asylum seekers. Since the mid 1990s, Ireland has accepted 30,000 immigrants seeking asylum, the majority of them from Nigeria (Strieff, 2008). The nations of Sweden, England, and France are also popular among asylum seekers. For many destination nations whether to grant asylum or to repatriate asylum seekers to their countries of origin is often a difficult choice. Even within a single country, asylum decisions are often not consistent, but vary according to the area in which the immigrant entered the country as well as the immigrant's country of origin (Human Rights Watch 2002; 2003).

Immigrant Profiling for Purposes of Risk Management: The risk that 9 immigrants pose to destination nations is perceived to be two-fold. First is the terrorism risk as evidenced by the attacks of September 2001 in the US, Madrid in March 2004, London in July 2005, and Glasgow in June 2007. The second risk that immigrants are believed to pose is to the financial solvency of a host country's social programs such as healthcare, public education, transportation, and unemployment insurance. In any case, the attacks call into question the effectiveness of current profiling practices as a means of managing the terrorist risk. Many critics of the current profiling system are pushing governments to develop a strategy that would focus more on behaviors rather than demographic variables which often penalize innocent immigrants (Human Rights Watch 2005; 2007). Despite the headline grabbing events in England, Scotland, Spain, and the United States, the actual percentage of immigrants associated with terrorist activities is extremely small. Given the very few number of immigrants involved in terrorist activities, it appears the far greater risk that immigrants might pose to host nations is on their social welfare systems. Goodhart (2004), editor of the British publication *Prospect,* has made a compelling argument that immigrants pose a serious threat to a host country's economy by destroying the equilibrium of its social welfare system. Goodhart contends that social welfare systems that offer such services as health insurance, transportation, education, child care, and unemployment insurance are based on the common and equal needs of a homogenous society; a system in which all members contribute and carry a similar risk. Governments which have traditionally offered extensive social services such as Denmark, the Netherlands, and Sweden have had until recently homogenous populations which share a common history, language, religion and culture. The concern that many citizens have is that immigrants will draw upon the host population's social services disproportionately while at the same time contributing little to the tax base that funds these services.

PART THREE OF THE TRILOGY: TOWARD THE "BEST FIT" IMMIGRATION MODEL

10 The objective of this third and final part of the trilogy is to present three immigration models and demonstrate how a host country can determine the best fit immigration model for its circumstances. These models include: the Theory of Catalysts and Magnets, the Theory of Capitalism and Inequalities, and the Theory of Multiculturalism. The "best fit" model for a host country would be determined by an analysis of that country's history, culture, demographic and economic variables. The framework provided indicates that many of the immigration problems experienced by host countries today have been caused by failing to recognize the relevance of an immigration model's prerequisites thereby leading to the selection of an inappropriate immigration model. Below is an overview of the three immigration models followed by a description of the host country prerequisites. Host countries need to carefully review the prerequisites of each model in order to achieve the best fit and develop effective immigration policies.

11   **The Catalysts and Magnets Model:** This theory contends that host populations and immigrants are players in a global system of catalysts and magnets (Strait 2011; Shafir, 1995). Variables such as underperforming economies, wars, and natural disasters serve as catalysts which propel immigrants from their countries of origin. Host countries with robust economies and generous social welfare systems act as magnets. Immigrants are drawn to countries with strong magnets and over a period of two to three generations are absorbed into the host population.

12   **Best Fit for the Catalysts and Magnets Model:** In order for the Catalysts and Magnets Model to function properly, a host country must meet the following prerequisites:

- **Historical Prerequisites:** A historical pattern of sustained and intimate interactions with other cultures is an important prerequisite for the Catalysts and Magnets Model to succeed in a host nation. The host country's history should include a full integration of myriad ethnic groups and religions. Previous colonial powers such as the Netherlands, France, the UK, Portugal and Spain are not necessarily good candidates for the Catalysts and Magnets Model. This is especially true in cases where the colonial power never truly mixed with the native population of the colonized country. This segmentation of social groups is particularly relevant for former colonial powers that are currently experiencing "boomerang immigration" as former subjects migrate to the nation that colonized them.

- **Cultural Prerequisites:** The host population must be willing to socialize with, live along side, and ultimately intermarry with the immigrant population. In other words, the host country must have a social class structure which is permeable. Strong divisions between social classes and social norms which discourage intermarriage will make the adaptation of this model highly problematic. Intermarriage is an important vehicle for immigrants to be able to achieve full integration with the host population. The presence of well integrated immigrant citizens in the host nation is also important as they act as powerful facilitators to aid new immigrants who are facing challenges pertaining to the job market, culture, language, and religious practices of the host nation.

- **Demographic Prerequisites:** Immigrants should be able to fill existing gaps in the demographic profile for the host country. For instance, if the host country has a dearth of young workers between the ages of 18–35, then an immigrant population which predominately falls within that age category will be most beneficial to the host population. Birth rates are also an important factor. This is especially true when the host population has a low birth rate and an escalating number of people retiring. Immigrants who are able to fill vacancies in undermanned professions such as nursing, engineering, and the sciences are also beneficial to the host population and further support the Catalysts and Magnets Model.

- **Economic Prerequisites:** The economic environment which creates the most receptive environment for the Catalysts and Magnets Model is an environment in which the host nation has low unemployment modest inflation and steady GDP growth. Ideally, the host country would have an economic system in which all three sectors are active, the private sector to generate employment, the public sector to provide basic services, and the nonprofit sector to supply volunteers to assist immigrants. Most notably, the private sector must have the authority and flexibility to hire and dismiss workers as conditions dictate.

The Capitalism and Inequalities Model: The Theory of Capitalism and[13] Inequalities contends that capitalism by its very nature creates a shortage of host population workers at the lowest levels of employment, especially in labor intensive industries such as agriculture, construction, and food processing. This dearth of labor is caused by the host population becoming better qualified and moving up in the job market (Shafir, 1995; Strait, 2011). A capitalist system attracts immigrants both overtly and covertly in order to acquire the necessary labor to fill the void in labor intensive industries. In the Capitalism and Inequalities Model, the host and the immigrant populations never truly mix and intermarriage is unlikely. As immigrants retire or return to their countries of origin, more immigrants are needed to replace them. In the Capitalism and Inequalities Model, immigrants are not viewed as vested citizens and therefore are prohibited from accessing the host country's welfare system.

Best fit for the Capitalism and Inequalities Model: For the Capitalism[14] and Inequalities Model to function properly, a host country must meet the following prerequisites.

- **Historical Prerequisites:** A host country with a history of a homogenous population is well suited for the Capitalism and Inequalities Model. In order to bring immigrants in at strictly the lowest levels of employment, thus saving the better paying and more prestigious jobs for the host population, the host population must be insular in its practices. That is to say, that the host population would likely have a language which is not widely spoken by other populations, and its higher educational system would be primarily reserved for the host population. Countries which are more geographically isolated would also be a good fit for the Capitalism and Inequalities Model. For instance, countries which are far north, have a harsher climate or are surrounded by water make these countries less vulnerable to migration flows. Such isolation would also make it easier for the host country to monitor and control the arrival of new immigrants.

- **Cultural Prerequisites:** From a cultural perspective the host country would have values and practices which would be somewhat unique or specific to that country. This may include such things as a religious preference, views regarding the role of women, or the scope of government authority. The host country would also be of one mind regarding taxation, voting rights, and the environment. The best fit host country would have a rather closed social structure; thereby making it unlikely that the host and immigrant populations would intermarry.

- **Demographic Prerequisites:** From a demographic perspective, the best fit host nation would have an extremely low birth rate. The government and the private sector would partner to offer aggressive training and education programs which would allow the host population to move up the job ladder. The host nation would also need to have a high literacy rate.

- **Economic Prerequisites:** First and foremost from an economic perspective the ideal host country for this model would have a shortage of low skilled labor. National unemployment would be low. It would also be necessary to have a system of taxation which is perceived by the host population as fair and balanced. Access to financial aid from government programs would be restricted to the host population and no one group would be able to draw disproportionately on the welfare system. The government would have the support of the host population to enforce strict immigration control and would prohibit "chain migration," which occurs when immigrants bring over extended family members. All immigrant visas would have strict time limitations which could only be renewed if it served the best interest of the host population.

15   **The Multiculturalism Model:** The Multicultural Model of immigration contends that global migration is part of the natural order of the universe as the world becomes more mobile and interconnected. Multiculturalism is regarded as a phenomenon which in itself should be protected and valued. Multiculturalists believe that immigrants should not be forced to fully

assimilate or integrate with the host population but rather host countries should encourage and foster a pluralistic society. The mixing of various cultures, languages and religions is thought to create a more advanced and sophisticated society that is better prepared to compete in the global marketplace.

Best Fit for the Multicultural Model: For the Multicultural Model to succeed, the host country must meet the following prerequisites: 16

- **Historical Prerequisites:** For multiculturalism to be successful the host country must be able to articulate a clear vision regarding its founding principles, and have at least one powerful common denominator which unites the host population and all immigrant groups within its borders. Examples of compelling common denominators might include democracy or equal rights. The host nation would need to have a society with a long history of accepting people of many faiths and ethnic backgrounds, as well as a high tolerance for religious differences. A secular government with no undertones of favoritism toward a particular religion would also be an important prerequisite.

- **Cultural Prerequisites:** From a cultural perspective, the host nation would include a fluid social class structure in which an immigrant might easily move upward as more education and income are obtained. A secular education system would be of critical importance along with a curriculum which supports and encourages a transnational approach to education. Media and entertainment outlets would support a broad assortment of interests.

- **Demographic Prerequisites:** The demographic prerequisites would include a high tolerance for linguistic diversity while at the same time mandating one official language in public affairs. All groups would have equal access to educational institutions and equal protection under the law. A wide range of age groups would be needed in order to sustain pension programs. No one group would be allowed to draw upon government support programs disproportionately. The birth rate of the various ethnic groups would be equivalent across all ethnic groups allowing each group to grow proportionately with respect to the host population.

- **Economic Prerequisites:** Above all, the host country would have to have an economic and legal system which allows for the rapid creation of job opportunities. It would also allow businesses to "right size," which is to say increase or reduce their workforces as conditions dictate. Ideally, the host nation would have a pattern of low unemployment and modest inflation. The economic activity of the host nation would be diversified and would not rely on the government to create jobs. Taxes would also be low to increase disposable income and encourage consumption. NGOs would be active in supporting immigrant groups and helping them to assimilate. The influence of labor unions would be minimal in order to allow the private sector to set wages at a level that would permit businesses to develop products at competitive prices.

ANALYSIS AND DISCUSSION

17 Now that the immigration models and host country requirements have been described, it becomes clear why many host countries struggle to develop effective immigration policies. Symptoms of a mismatch between a host country and its current immigration model include such indicators as:

- An increasing number of violent attacks against immigrants and/or host populations
- Large numbers of unemployed immigrants
- The presence and growing influence of extremist groups
- Isolated and disenfranchised immigrant groups
- A growing sense of dislocation felt by the host population
- Disproportionate consumption of government aid by immigrant groups
- Highly segregated host and immigrant neighborhoods

18   **Notorious Mismatches:** Many EU nations such as the UK, France, Germany, the Netherlands, Sweden, and Norway have chosen Multiculturalism as their immigration model. Yet in each case, the leaders of these countries as well as other highly visible national figures have declared Multiculturalism a failure. Among these unlikely individuals are well-known human rights activist Hege Storhaug of Norway, Prime Minister David Cameron of the UK, German Chancellor Angela Merkel, former President Nicolas Sarkozy of France (the son of a Hungarian immigrant himself) and Swiss parliament member, Oskar Freysinger. Simply stated, Multiculturalism has failed in these countries because these countries do not possess the prerequisites required by the Multiculturalism Model. To begin with, there is no compelling common denominator which unites the disparate groups contained within their borders. Instead there is fragmentation regarding key values. Even the previously compelling ideals of democracy and religious freedom have not been values which have resonated with many of the immigrant groups which currently populate these host countries. In addition, the aforementioned countries do not have a long or consistent history of embracing people of different faiths and ethnic backgrounds. In contrast, they have actually had, until recently, fairly homogenous populations that have shared a common religion and language. Likewise, these countries do not have a permeable social structure in which an immigrant might easily mix with the host population. Lastly, several important economic prerequisites are also absent. With the exception of Germany, unemployment is nearing record levels within the EU. This fact combined with high taxes and stiff government regulations have discouraged the generation of new jobs in the private sector. Hiring, therefore, is slow and their economies are unable to absorb the steady influx of immigrants. The labor unions further hinder the private sector's ability to right size, and union salaries place an upward pressure on the price of goods and services, making them less competitive in the global marketplace especially against emerging economic contenders such as Brazil, China, and India. The final blow to Multiculturalism in many EU countries is the easy access to government support programs which has allowed certain immigrant groups

to draw disproportionately upon government subsidies. It is no wonder, then, that Multiculturalism has been declared a failure in much of Europe.

Which model then would be more appropriate for many of these EU [19] nations? Surprisingly, the answer appears to be the model of Capitalism and Inequalities. The irony is that capitalism is regarded by many EU citizens as part of the problem when in fact an analysis of their historical, cultural, demographic and economic variables calls for the Capitalism and Inequalities Model. That is to say that many EU countries have a history of slow job growth, powerful labor unions which tie the hands of the private sector to "right size," high unemployment, and easily accessible welfare programs.

In contrast, Australia, Canada and the US who have depended upon immi- [20] grants for the purposes of nation building have long utilized the Multicultural Immigration Model, although many now question whether the Multicultural Model is still appropriate for these countries as well. The reason that the Multicultural Model has succeeded for so long in these countries is that they are vast in size and provide numerous opportunities for immigrants. Other factors which helped to foster the success of the Multicultural Model in these countries have included low unemployment, minimal bureaucracy, rapid job creation, abundant resources, low taxes, fluid class structure, few unions, secular policies, a host population willing to intermarry with immigrants, and defining principles which have united the host population and immigrants. There is no question that the Multicultural Model is now under pressure in each of these three countries. The recent global recession and large scale illegal immigration have made their host populations wary of multiculturalism. The immigration model prerequisites described in this article appear to indicate that the Catalysts and Magnets Model may now be their more appropriate choice. For the Catalysts and Magnets Model to succeed in these countries, however, the host nations of Australia, Canada, and the US must be able to exert influence on both the catalysts and the magnets that create their immigration flows. In order to control the economic catalysts which drive immigrants from their native countries, these host nations must be willing to engage in direct foreign investment in order to provide immigrants with incentives to remain in their countries of origin. In order to control the magnets, three actions would be needed: punishment for employers who hire illegal immigrants, fine-tuning the visa process to allow for the acquisition of foreign temporary workers where and when needed, and restricting social welfare programs to permanent citizens. It is important to note that immigrants themselves can contribute to a mismatch or bad fit by choosing a host country that embraces a set of values that are incompatible with the immigrant's own beliefs or aspirations. For the immigrant to give himself the best chance of a good fit with a host nation, it is necessary for the immigrant to be fully informed of a host country's historical, demographic, cultural, and economic variables as well as the host country's immigration policies.

Immigration remains a contentious issue in all host nations, and significant [21] policy changes are slow to occur, especially during election years. It is important to clarify that one immigration model is not inherently better than another immigration model. The salient issue is that the host country's profile must be in sync with the model it has chosen. A host country which embraces an inappropriate immigration model is pursuing a dangerous path that can lead not only to social strife, but financial peril as well. A thorough understanding of the immigration models described herein and a careful analysis of a host country's variables should lead to more effective immigration policies for the 21st century.

REFERENCES

Fishkin, S. (2005). Crossroads of cultures: The transnational turn in American studies. *American Quarterly, 57* (1), 17–57.

Gabaccia, D. R. (2000). *Italy's Many Diasporas.* Seattle: University of Washington Press.

Goodhart, D. (2004, February). Too diverse? *Prospect.* Retrieved May 26, 2012, from http://www.carnegiecouncil.org/media/goodhart.pdf

Griswold, D. (2009). As immigrants move in, Americans move up. Cato Institute Report. Retrieved June 16, 2010, from http://www.cato.org/pub_display.php?pub_id=10650

Herandez, J. C. (2003). 18 illegal immigrants die in trailer in Texas. *Guadalajara Reporter.* Retrieved June 6, 2011, from http://guadalajarareporter.com/news-mainmenu-86/1996/18-illegal-immigrants-die-in-trailer-in-texas.html

Human Rights Watch. (2002). Discrecionalidad sin limites: La applicacion arbitaria de la ley Espanola de immigracion. Retrieved March 8, 2009, from http://books.google.com/Books?id=6iEpOQ9hwIMC&printsec=frontcover&source=gbs_ge_summary_R&cad=0#v=onepage&q&f=false

Human Rights Watch. (2003). Asylum seekers and refugees. Retrieved June 15, 2010, from http://hrw.org/legacy/un/chr59/refugees.htm

Human Rights Watch. (2005). Nota del ministerio de justicia de Espana al informe ?Sentando ejemplo? Medidas antiterroristas en Espana presentado por Human Rights Watch. Retrieved June 20, 2010, from http://www.hrw/org/spanish/docs/2005/02/15/ Spain10360.htm

Human Rights Watch. (2007). Espana: Las medidas antiterroristas vulneran los derechos basicos. Retrieved March 9, 2009, from http://hrw.org/spanish/docs/2005/01/27/ spain10075.htm

Human Rights Watch. (2009). World report. Retrieved June 19, 2010, from http://www.hrw/org/world-report-2009

Medrano, L. (2010). Border deaths for illegal immigrants hit record high in Arizona sector. *Christian Science Monitor.* Retrieved June 7, 2011, from http://www.csmonitor.com/USA/2010/1216/Border-deaths-for-illegal-immigrants-hit-record-high-in-Arizona-sector

Ong, A. (1999). *Flexible citizenship. The cultural logics of transnationality.* Durham and London: Duke University Press.

Shafir, G. (1995). *Immigrants and nationalists: Ethnic conflict and accommodation in Catalonia, The Basque country, Latvia, and Estonia.* Albany, NY: State University of New York Press.

Strait, P. B. (2010). When societies collide: An immigration trilogy. Part one: Stakeholder Identification through the synthesis of information. *International Journal of Interdisciplinary Social Sciences, 5* (5), 319–26.

Strait, P. B. (2011). When societies collide: A trilogy about immigration. Part two: Emerging ethical dilemmas in immigration. *International Journal of Interdisciplinary Social Sciences, 6* (2), 217–26.

Strait, P. B. (2011, August 28). Rising nationalism raises global tension. *Richmond Times Dispatch*. Retrieved from http://www.2.timesdispatch.com/news/commentary/2011/Aug/28/tdcomm03-rising-nationalism-raises-global-tension-ar-1267039/

Strieff, D. (2008, March 17). New Ireland changes go more than skin deep. *MSNBC Online News*. Retrieved May 9, 2009, from www.msnbc.com/id/23636868/from/TE

Stock, M. (2009). Essential to the fight: Immigrants in the military eight years after 9/11. *Immigration Policy Center*. Retrieved on June 7, 2011, from http://www.ilw.com/Articles/2009,1124-stock.pdf

Source: From *International Journal of Interdisciplinary Social Sciences*. In press. Reprinted by permission of the author.

QUESTIONS FOR READING

1. What are the four sources of information that shape views on immigration? What kinds of information does each source provide?

2. What ethical dilemmas were examined in part 2? What is the ethical dilemma found in each issue?

3. What are Strait's three immigration models? What is the idea behind developing the three models?

4. What characteristics of the host country are needed for a fit with the Catalysts and Magnets Model?

5. What characteristics of the host country are needed for a fit with the Capitalism and Inequalities Model?

6. What characteristics of the host country are needed for a fit with the Multiculturalism Model?

QUESTIONS FOR REASONING AND ANALYSIS

7. What is Strait's primary claim?

8. How is her argument more specifically applied to the United States?

9. Are Strait's three models supported by logic and reality, in your experience? If not, how would you refute her?

10. Do her analyses of and recommendations for the United States make sense to you? If not, in what specific ways would you disagree with her?

QUESTIONS FOR REFLECTION AND WRITING

11. What specifics in Strait's analysis surprise you the most? Why?

12. In paragraph 19, the author makes three specific recommendations for the United States to make the Catalysts and Magnets Model work. Do these recommendations seem logical to you? Do you think the United States is likely to accept them? Explain.

CHAPTER 22

America: Past, Present, Future

READ: Where are we? Who, in the photo, do you recognize?

REASON: What can you conclude about this gathering? (Think about critical events in the 21st century.)

REFLECT/WRITE: What feelings are captured in the photo? What makes the image arresting?

Thirteen years into the 21st century, we might be forgiven for harboring some uncertainty about the country's future. Although some have written of America's decline, we seem to have survived the recession better than many other countries and, as Thomas Friedman notes in this chapter, we are still the land of entrepreneurs, the country driving technological innovation. We also held elections in 2012 without violent demonstrations or fraud, actions all too often associated with elections in other parts of the world, as Zainab Chaudary points out. Fareed Zakaria, writing about the 2012 elections, sees decisions by a number of states as marks of the country's open-mindedness and acceptance of its diversity.

To borrow from Friedman, that's the good news. But, we still have some presence in Iraq, after years of an extremely costly war. We are still fighting in Afghanistan, and we surely must wonder if the effort will lead to a sustainable peace and a better society. Republicans and Democrats have wasted time, refusing to work together to solve budget and funding issues. Budget cuts are hurting public education at all levels, and far too many schools are failing to educate the next generation of workers. At times we find hatred and bigotry here, not just in trouble spots around the world, leaving writers such as Colbert King wondering when we will finally live up to the ideals expressed by Martin Luther King, Jr. How will the future judge us? Can we find ways to embrace what is good for the individual with what is good for all?

Some good news: Younger Americans are more concerned about the environment and far more accepting of diversity than older Americans. If young Americans will commit to becoming and staying informed and to participating in elections (older Americans vote in greater numbers than younger Americans in most elections) based on careful consideration of the candidates, there is hope that we can make ourselves anew and journey forward together, as so eloquently put by both Abraham Lincoln and Barack Obama.

You can begin by seeking out the authors in this text who have impressed you with the knowledge, wisdom, and perhaps calm approach to examining problems and offering solutions. Learn, and reflect on what you learn. Think about the kind of world you want to have for the rest of your life. You might also ask yourself: What can I do to make a difference?

SECOND INAUGURAL ADDRESS | ABRAHAM LINCOLN

A mostly self-educated country lawyer on the Western frontier, Abraham Lincoln (1809–1865) rose to become the sixteenth president of the United States. He first served in the Illinois State Legislature and one term in the U.S. House of Representatives before securing the Republican Party's nomination for president. He won the 1860 election by sweeping the North, his opposition to the spread of slavery resulting in few votes in the southern states. His moving appeals to the electorate won him reelection in spite of less moderate Republicans unhappy with him and those committed to secession wishing him dead. Six days after Robert E. Lee surrendered to General Grant, ending the Civil War, Lincoln was assassinated at Ford's Theater in Washington by Confederate supporter John Wilkes Booth. Scholars rank Lincoln as one of the top three greatest presidents, along with Washington and FDR. Lincoln delivered his brief but powerful address below at the swearing-in for his second term as president.

PREREADING QUESTIONS With the country still torn by war, Lincoln chose to speak only briefly; does this seem a wise and sensitive decision, or would you have wished for a longer discussion of the issues surrounding the war?

1   At this second appearing to take the oath of the presidential office, there is less occasion for an extended address than there was at the first. Then a statement, somewhat in detail, of a course to be pursued, seemed fitting and proper. Now, at the expiration of four years, during which public declarations have been constantly called forth on every point and phase of the great contest which still absorbs the attention, and engrosses the enerergies [sic] of the nation, little that is new could be presented. The progress of our arms, upon which all else chiefly depends, is as well known to the public as to myself; and it is, I trust, reasonably satisfactory and encouraging to all. With high hope for the future, no prediction in regard to it is ventured.

2   On the occasion corresponding to this four years ago, all thoughts were anxiously directed to an impending civil-war. All dreaded it—all sought to avert it. While the inaugural address was being delivered from this place, devoted altogether to *saving* the Union without war insurgent agents were in the city seeking to *destroy* it without war—seeking to dissol[v]e the Union, and divide effects, by negotiation. Both parties deprecated war; but one of them would *make* war rather than let the nation survive; and the other would *accept* war rather than let it perish. And the war came.

3   One eighth of the whole population were colored slaves, not distributed generally over the Union, but localized in the Southern part of it. These slaves constituted a peculiar and powerful interest. All knew that this interest was, somehow, the cause of the war. To strengthen, perpetuate, and extend this interest was the object for which the insurgents would rend the Union, even by war; while the government claimed no right to do more than to restrict the territorial enlargement of it. Neither party expected for the war, the magnitude of the duration, which it has already attained. Neither anticipated that the *cause* of the conflict might cease with, or even before, the conflict itself should cease. Each looked for an easier triumph, and a result less fundamental and astounding. Both read the same

Bible, and pray to the same God; and each invokes His aid against the other. It may seem strange that any men should dare to ask a just God's assistance in wringing their bread from the sweat of other men's faces; but let us judge not that we be not judged. The prayers of both could not be answered; that of neither has been answered fully. The Almighty has His own purposes. "Woe unto the world because of offences! For it must needs be that offences comes; but woe to that man by whom the offence cometh!" If we shall suppose that American Slavery is one of those offences which, in the providence of God, must needs come, but which, having continued through His appointed time, He now wills to remove, and that He gives to both North and South, this terrible war, as the woe due to those by whom the offence came, shall we discern therein any departure from those divine attributes which the believers in a Living God always ascribe to Him? Fondly do we hope—fervently do we pray—that this mighty scourge of war may speedily pass away. Yet, if God wills that it continue, until all the wealth piled by the bond-man's two hundred and fifty years of unrequited toil shall be sunk, and until every drop of blood drawn with the lash, shall be paid by another drawn with the sword, as was said three thousand years ago, so still it must be said, "the judgments of the Lord, are true and righteous altogether."

    With malice toward none; with charity for all; with firmness in the right, as 4 God gives us to see the right, let us strive on to finish the work we are in; to bind up the nation's wounds; to care for him who shall have borne the battle, and for his widow, and his orphan—to do all which may achieve and cherish a just, and a lasting peace, among ourselves, and with all nations.

QUESTIONS FOR READING

1. What is the great contest to which Lincoln refers?
2. Who chose to "make war"?
3. What cause does Lincoln give for the war?
4. How has the cause ceased while the war continues?
5. What guidelines for responding to the war's end does Lincoln establish?

QUESTIONS FOR REASONING AND ANALYSIS

6. In the long third paragraph, how does Lincoln explain why both sides in the war are suffering?
7. Analyze Lincoln's final paragraph—one long sentence: What elements of style do you find? What makes his oratory so powerful?

QUESTIONS FOR REFLECTION AND WRITING

8. Although admired perhaps second only to "The Gettysburg Address," too few have read this address. What surprised you the most in his "Second Inaugural"? Why?
9. What can today's leaders learn from Lincoln's speech? Explain.

YOUR MOST POWERFUL CURRENCY: YOUR VOTE

ZAINAB CHAUDARY

Holding a degree in political science from the University of Heidelberg, Zainab Chaudary is on the staff of Congressman Rush Holt (D-NJ). She is fluent in Urdu, German, and French. The focus of her work is with immigrant groups and immigration issues. At night she writes, using her blog, *The Momorist,* to reflect on life, on science and religion, past and present, human relationships, and probably politics as well. The following article appeared on altmuslimah.com November 1, 2012.

PREREADING QUESTIONS Do you value the privilege of voting? Do you actually vote in every election?

1   *As I write this, a brave young woman [Malala Yousafzai] sits in a hospital bed halfway across the world, recovering from a gunshot wound to the head that she received simply for speaking out, for using her young voice to bring about change on an issue that she felt demanded attention. The issue? The state of education for young girls and women in Swat, a conflict-ridden area in northern Pakistan beset with violence in the struggle between the right-wing Taliban and the more moderate-minded.*

2   I've listened to her story in anger and frustration, not only because of its tremendous injustice, but also because the story carries a slight twist of fate: the girl could have been me. I could have been a young woman gunned down for insisting to her right to an education in male-dominated Pakistan.

3   Of the many things I'm grateful to my parents for, perhaps the biggest one is this. Thirty years ago, they left behind family, friends, and a familiar way of life for the unknown, for the sole purpose of giving their baby daughter the very best opportunities and the chance to obtain an education and begin a career that was equal to that of any man. It's a story repeated across America time and time again, this tale of intrepid immigrants leaving their homes for the United States, a country of opportunity, diversity, and above all, choice.

4   The American political system makes the "American Dream" possible. Immigrants often leave behind countries where corruption is rampant and bribery is the norm, where citizens have no voice and no means of improving the state of their country, and where elections are rigged or despots rule on the basis of falsified vote counts (as in this instance in Iraq in 2002, when Saddam Hussein claimed to have won the elections by "100% of the vote"). To an ordinary citizen, bringing about change seems impossible in such a political system.

5   Yet so many of our first and second generation immigrants in the American-Muslim community take their vote for granted. Working in politics and promoting civic engagement, I have run into a mindset that is at best ambivalent to the electoral process and at worst vehemently opposed to political participation. In a year when American-Muslims are struggling with Islamophobia, egregious civil rights violations by the NYPD, and a dangerous misrepresentation of Muslims by the FBI, this voice is no longer a right we can take for granted—it is a necessity.

6   Women in our community in particular do see the importance of their vote. But this year's [2012] election hinges upon the female electorate. Despite the articles about the rise of women, both in the workforce and in the political sphere, women hold only 78 out of the 435 seats in the House of

Representatives and only 17 out of the 100 seats in the Senate, and women's issues are still being decided by the men in the room. Although women's issues loom large over the 2012 election—with debate on contraception, abortion rights, and decisions about women's health care decisions becoming more rancorous by the day—the gender gap in voting focuses more on issues such as education, the economy, and the size of government.

Perfection is elusive. Any country is a work in progress, and the key word here is "work." To foster change, one must *be* the vehicle for change. Malala Yousafzai lives in Pakistan, and fights for the right to an education, the right to make informed decisions in her life, and in her country. I live in the United States, where I'm still fighting for equal pay for women, the right to make decisions about my own body, and a domestic and foreign policy that is humane and just. There were women before us who fought for suffrage, and there are women in this day and age around the globe who are still battling for their basic rights as rational, intelligent human beings. We owe it to them. The female electorate must join the conversation and win a seat at the table with that best and most powerful currency of any democracy: their vote.

Source: *altmuslimah.com*, November 1, 2012. Reprinted by permission.

QUESTIONS FOR READING

1. For the author, what is important about Malala's story?
2. How does this country make the American Dream possible?
3. Which American citizens, especially, must embrace their right to vote?
4. How many women are now in the House of Representative and how many are in the Senate—after the 2012 election? (If you don't know, think about how to find this information online.)

QUESTIONS FOR REASONING AND ANALYSIS

5. What is Chaudary's claim? How does she develop and support her claim?
6. Do you find her essay compelling? If so, what makes it work? If not, why not?

QUESTIONS FOR REFLECTION AND WRITING

7. Women in the United States are better off than those in Pakistan; do they still have good reasons, in your view, to vote and get involved in politics? If yes, why? If no, why not?
8. What suggestions do you have for getting more young Americans engaged in politics?

DO YOU WANT THE GOOD NEWS FIRST? | THOMAS L. FRIEDMAN

The *New York Times* foreign affairs columnist, Thomas Friedman has won the Pulitzer Prize for Commentary three times. Friedman holds an MA in Modern Middle East Studies from Oxford University and is the author of several books, including *From Beirut to Jerusalem* (1989)—winner of the National Book Award for nonfiction—and *The World Is Flat: A Brief History of the 21st Century*—winner of the Goldman Sachs/Financial Times Business Book of the Year award. The following column appeared May 19, 2012.

PREREADING QUESTIONS Given what you know about the author's field of study and writing, what do you think the good news might be? What else can you expect to read about?

1   I've spent the last week traveling to two of America's greatest innovation hubs—Silicon Valley and Seattle—and the trip left me feeling a combination of exhilaration and dread. The excitement comes from not only seeing the stunning amount of innovation emerging from the ground up, but from seeing the new tools coming on stream that are, as Amazon.com's founder, Jeff Bezos, put it to me, "eliminating all the gatekeepers"—making it easier and cheaper than ever to publish your own book, start your own company and chase your own dream. Never have individuals been more empowered, and we're still just at the start of this trend.

2   "I see the elimination of gatekeepers everywhere," said Bezos. Thanks to cloud computing for the masses, anyone anywhere can for a tiny hourly fee now rent the most powerful computing and storage facilities on Amazon's "cloud" to test any algorithm or start any company or publish any book. Start-ups can even send all their inventory to Amazon, and it will do all the fulfillment and delivery—and even gift wrap your invention before shipping it to your customers.

3   This is leading to an explosion of new firms and voices. "Sixteen of the top 100 best sellers on Kindle today were self-published," said Bezos. That means no agent, no publisher, no paper—just an author, who gets most of the royalties, and Amazon and the reader. It is why, Bezos adds, the job of the company leader now is changing fast: "You have to think of yourself not as a designer but as a gardener"—seeding, nurturing, inspiring, cultivating the ideas coming from below, and then making sure people execute them.

4   The leading companies driving this trend—Amazon, Facebook, Microsoft, Google, Apple, LinkedIn, Zynga and Twitter—are all headquartered and listed in America. Facebook, which didn't exist nine years ago, just went public at a valuation of nearly $105 billion—two weeks after buying a company for $1 billion, Instagram, which didn't exist 18 months ago. So why any dread?

5   It's because we're leaving an era of some 50 years' duration in which to be a president, a governor, a mayor or a college president was, on balance, to give things away to people; and we're entering an era—no one knows for how long—in which to be a president, a governor, a mayor or a college president will be, on balance, to take things away from people. And if we don't make this transition in a really smart way—by saying, "Here are the things that made us great, that spawned all these dynamic companies"—and make sure that we're preserving as much of that as we can, this trend will not spread as it

should. Maybe we could grow as a country without a plan. But we dare not cut without a plan. We can really do damage. I can lose weight quickly if I cut off both arms, but it will surely reduce my job prospects.

What we must preserve is that magic combination of cutting-edge higher 6 education, government-funded research and immigration of high-I.Q. risk-takers. They are, in combination, America's golden goose, laying all these eggs in Seattle and Silicon Valley. China has it easy right now. It just needs to do the jobs that we have already invented, just more cheaply. America has to invent the new jobs—and that requires preserving the goose.

Microsoft still does more than 80 percent of its research work in America. 7 But that is becoming harder and harder to sustain when deadlock on Capitol Hill prevents it from acquiring sufficient visas for the knowledge workers it needs that America's universities are not producing enough of. The number of filled jobs at Microsoft went up this year from 40,000 to 40,500 at its campus outside Seattle, yet its list of unfilled jobs went from 4,000 to almost 5,000. Eventually, it will have no choice but to shift more research to other countries.

It is terrifying to see how budget-cutting in California is slowly reducing 8 what was once one of the crown jewels of American education—the University of California system—to a shadow of its old self. And I fear the cutting is just beginning. As one community leader in Seattle remarked to me, governments basically do three things: "Medicate, educate and incarcerate." And various federal and state mandates outlaw cuts in medicating and incarcerating, so much of the money is coming out of educating. Unfortunately, even to self-publish, you still need to know how to write. The same is happening to research. A new report just found that federal investment in biomedical research through the National Institutes of Health has decreased almost every year since 2003.

When we shrink investments in higher education and research, "we shoot 9 ourselves in both feet," remarked K.R. Sridhar, founder of Bloom Energy, the Silicon Valley fuel-cell company. "Our people become less skilled, so you are shooting yourself in one foot. And the smartest people from around the world have less reason to come here for the quality education, so you are shooting yourself in the other foot."

The Labor Department reported two weeks ago that even with our high 10 national unemployment rate, employers advertised 3.74 million job openings in March. That is, in part, about a skills mismatch. In an effort to overcome that, and help fill in the financing gap for higher education in Washington State, Boeing and Microsoft recently supported a plan whereby the state, which was cutting funding to state universities but also not letting them raise tuition, would allow the colleges to gradually raise rates and the two big companies would each kick in $25 million for scholarships for students wanting to study science and technology or health care to ensure that they have the workers they need.

This is not a call to ignore the hard budget choices we have to make. It's a 11 call to make sure that we give education, immigration and research their proper place in the discussion.

"Empowering the individual and underinvesting in the collective is our 12 great macro danger as a society," said the pollster Craig Charney. Indeed, it is. Investment in our collective institutions and opportunities is the only way to mitigate the staggering income inequalities that can arise from a world where Facebook employees can become billionaires overnight, while the universities that produce them are asked to slash billions overnight. As I've said, nations that don't invest in the future tend not to do well there.

QUESTIONS FOR READING

1. Why is it now easier to publish your own book or start your own business?
2. How has a company leader's job changed?
3. Which companies are creating these new trends in business?
4. What causes the "bad news"?
5. What do we need to preserve, in Friedman's view?
6. Why are there unfilled jobs even with high unemployment?

QUESTIONS FOR REASONING AND ANALYSIS

7. What is Friedman's claim? (It might help to see this as a problem/solution argument.)
8. How does the author develop and support his claim?
9. Friedman assumes that we are in a period of budget cuts. Is this an acceptable assumption? That is, can the author expect his readers to understand the current economic and political climate—and not have to provide support?

QUESTIONS FOR REFLECTION AND WRITING

10. Are you surprised by Friedman's list of what we need to preserve? Did you think that any of the three needed preserving? Explain your response.
11. Do you agree with Friedman that we must invest "in the collective," even in difficult economic times? Can society move forward only on the strength of a few very successful individuals? Ponder these issues—it is *your* future America.

THE EMERGING AMERICA | FAREED ZAKARIA

Holding degrees from Yale College and Harvard University, Indian American Fareed Zakaria is the host of CNN's international affairs program *GPS*, which is aired worldwide. On this program, Dr. Zakaria has interviewed heads of state as well as numerous intellectuals and business leaders. He is also an editor at *Time*, a columnist at the *Washington Post*, and the author of several books, including *The Future of Freedom* (2003) and *The Post-American World* (2008). The following column was published on November 9, 2012, just after the 2012 elections.

PREREADING QUESTIONS Would you describe America as "emerging"? What do you think Zakaria might emphasize in an essay with this title?

1 Growing up in India in the middle 1960s and 1970s, I always thought of America as the future. It was the place where the newest technology, the best

gadgets and the latest fads seemed to originate. Seemingly exotic political causes—women's liberation, gay rights, the fight against ageism—always seemed to get their start on the streets or in the legislatures and courts of the United States. Indians couldn't imagine embracing all American trends—in fact, some were rejected outright—because they were too edgy for a country like India. But we had a sneaking suspicion that today's weird California fad would become tomorrow's conventional practice.

For me, Tuesday's [2012] elections brought back that sense of America as the land of the future. The presidential race is being discussed as one that was "about nothing," with no message or mandate. But that's simply not true. Put aside the reelection of Barack Obama and consider what else happened this week: 2

Three states voted to legalize same-sex marriage, which is the civil rights cause of our times. One day we will look back and wonder how people could have been so willing to deny equal treatment under the law to a small minority—and Tuesday will stand as one of the most important moments marking the end of that cruelty. 3

Two other states voted to legalize some recreational use of marijuana, which will surely mark the beginning of the end of the war on drugs. This may be the most costly, distorting and futile war the United States has ever waged. Over the past four decades, we have spent $1 trillion to fight this "war" without reducing the price and availability of drugs in cities while also destroying our penal system. The United States has more than three times as many prisoners per capita as we had in 1980—and about 10 times as many prisoners as other rich countries, according to data from the Organization for Economic Cooperation and Development. In 2010, about 1.6 million Americans were arrested on drug charges, most for using marijuana, a drug that is no more dangerous than alcohol. 4

This week's votes indicate that Americans have begun rethinking those policies, perhaps moving toward ones that would deprive drug cartels of their huge profits and allow our police to focus on serious crimes. Ethan Nadelmann, an expert and advocate of such policies, notes that "even as the federal government persists with its failed drug war strategy, the United States has now emerged as the global leader in promoting more sensible policies with respect to marijuana." 5

Perhaps the most stunning shift this week came not in the passage of a ballot measure or law but in an exit-poll finding—one that might move us toward major legislation. When asked what should be done with the millions of illegal immigrants working in the United States, almost two-thirds of respondents wanted to grant them legal status. Four years ago, anti-immigrant voices were so loud that John McCain, the sponsor of a comprehensive and intelligent immigration reform bill, had to run away from his own handiwork when he campaigned for the White House. 6

There was no mandate for big government. On the contrary, voters—by a slim majority—told pollsters that government was doing too much. And they reelected a slew of Republican governors, many of whom have been competent and reform-minded in tackling the problems of their states. But in two rock-ribbed Republican states, Indiana and Missouri, voters rejected Senate candidates whose attitudes toward women were demeaning. 7

8   I hesitate to build a grand narrative out of all this, but the trend seems to be toward individual freedom, self-expression and dignity for all. This embrace of diversity—in every sense—is America's great gift to the world, one at which, since the days of J. Hector St. John de Crevecoeur and Alexis de Tocqueville, foreigners have marveled.

9   In 1990, the neoconservative writer Ben Wattenberg wrote a book titled *The First Universal Nation,* arguing that the United States was creating something unique in history, a nation composed of all colors, races, religions and creeds, all thriving in their individualism. That diversity, he wrote, was going to be America's greatest strength in the years ahead.

10   While Wattenberg's party, the GOP, has taken to looking at this new America with anxiety and fear, he was right. What the world saw this week was a picture of America at its best: edgy, experimental, open-minded—and brilliantly diverse.

QUESTIONS FOR READING

1.   What decisions did states make as part of the 2012 elections?

2.   How much has the United States spent on its drug war? What have been the results of this "war"?

3.   What attitudes were revealed in exit poles?

4.   What kind of nation are we creating, according to the author Wattenberg?

QUESTIONS FOR REASONING AND ANALYSIS

5.   What is Zakaria's claim? What grounds does he provide?

6.   Do you agree that the various state decisions and exit-poll views are significant? Why or why not?

QUESTIONS FOR REFLECTION AND WRITING

7.   Of the four election-day changes Zakaria presents, which one surprised you the most? Why?

8.   Some have written of America's decline in the world; Zakaria sees a country developing its uniqueness. Do you agree that the United States is becoming more open-minded and "brilliantly diverse"? If yes, why? If no, why not?

9.   Do you share Zakaria's enthusiasm for the changes revealed in the 2012 election? If yes, why? If no, why not?

WE STILL AREN'T GOOD ENOUGH | COLBERT I. KING

A Washington native, Colbert King has held a number of positions in the government, including special agent for the State Department, and in banking, including at the World Bank. King joined the *Washington Post* editorial board in 1990, began writing a weekly column in 1995, and became deputy editor of the editorial page in 2000. In 2003 he won a Pulitzer Prize for Commentary. He is a regular on the political talk show *Inside Washington*. The following column was published on January 19, 2013.

PREREADING QUESTIONS In what ways do you expect King to find the United States "not good enough"? Do you have issues in which you find the United States "not good enough"?

How fitting it is that this weekend's shabbat observance, which I plan to   1
share with the B'nai Tzedek Congregation in Potomac, coincides with two other weekend celebrations: Martin Luther King Jr. Day and the swearing-in of President Obama.

There is much to commemorate: the exodus to freedom from slavery in   2
Egypt; the life and legacy of America's foremost civil rights leader; and a changing United States that reelected its first black president.

But delve deep below this weekend's celebratory moments and consider   3
our world with introspection, and you might well be led to an observation that King made in 1954, one that still holds true.

In a sermon in Detroit, he said that you didn't have to look far to see that   4
something was basically wrong with our world.

Society, he said, has more knowledge today than people have had in any   5
period of human history, whether the topic is mathematics, science, social science or philosophy.

"The trouble isn't so much that we don't know enough," King preached, "but   6
it's as if we aren't good enough."

The trouble isn't so much that our scientific genius lags behind, he said,   7
but that our moral genius has not caught up.

Through our scientific advances, such as the building of jet aircraft that   8
can transect the globe, we have made the world a neighborhood, King said.

But morally, he said, we've failed to make it a brotherhood.   9

Examples abound.   10

Consider these words: "It is high time to assess how many [members of   11
parliament] and government members are of Jewish origin and who present a national security threat."

Do you think those evil thoughts were expressed during Adolf Hitler's   12
Third Reich? Marton Gyongyosi of the neo-Nazi Jobbik Party of Hungary spoke those words last fall.

The fire of anti-Semitism that reduced a once-thriving Hungarian Jewish   13
population to a third of its size still smolders. The smoke also rises in other parts of the world.

Some government leaders condemned Gyongyosi's remarks, belatedly.   14
But there are plenty of others, such as Iranian President Mahmoud Ahmadinejad, who belong in Gyongyosi's camp.

They remind us, just as King preached at the tender age of 29, that we still   15
aren't good enough. King declared that some things are right and some things are wrong, eternally and absolutely.

And there still exists one undeniable wrong that must be faced.   16

17   Despite scientific and technological advances that have taken us to places unthought of only a few years ago, in 2013 bigotry has global dimensions. It represents a moral challenge to the world.

18   King spoke of creating a worldwide fellowship that lifts concern "beyond one's tribe, race, class and nation." Embrace all mankind, he said.

19   Now that is a tough call for an American president, to move from national to ecumenical concerns.

20   Fixing the economy, rebuilding infrastructure, strengthening the middle class, managing the debt, protecting our homeland, defending the vulnerable and changing gun laws are presidential priorities that can't wait. They all cry out for action.

21   But bigotry is a global curse, a growing cancer on the world. Can America turn a blind eye to hatred?

22   Would that the questions stopped there.

23   Is hatred a popular subject for a reelected Barack Obama to address? The polls would probably say no.

24   *We have enough on our hands here at home,* is the common answer. *What do ethnic and religious rivalries have to do with us, anyway?*

25   Besides, is it good politics? The politicians probably would universally say no. There are no votes in taking on world hate.

26   But is it the right thing to do?

27   King would say yes.

28   Not because he believed that a word from the president of the United States would change the world.

29   But King might contend that the president of a racially, ethnically and religiously diverse nation founded on the principles of liberty and equal rights—however haltingly observed in the past—has an obligation to take sides against bigotry wherever it is found.

30   King wrote from his Birmingham jail cell that "injustice anywhere is a threat to justice everywhere."

31   "We are" he said, "caught in an inescapable network of mutuality, tied in a single garment of destiny. What ever affects one directly, affects all indirectly."

32   Bear this in mind as we gather this weekend to remember, rejoice and observe.

QUESTIONS FOR READING

1. What converging events seem fitting to King?
2. What is wrong with our world, in the view of Martin Luther King, Jr.? What do we have? What have we failed to do?
3. What is the author's primary example of bigotry and hatred?
4. What did Martin Luther King, Jr., think we need to act against injustice?

QUESTIONS FOR REASONING AND ANALYSIS

5. What is King's claim? How does he develop and support his claim?
6. King presents essentially one example of hatred and bigotry; should he catalogue more examples—or does he need just this one example to make his point? Explain.
7. How does the author connect the weekend's three events with the development of his argument? How does he refer again to the three events in his conclusion? (Did you notice and appreciate the unifying cleverness of King's strategy?)

QUESTIONS FOR REFLECTION AND WRITING

8. Do you agree with Martin Luther King, Jr.'s assertion that "injustice anywhere is a threat to justice everywhere"? If yes, why? If not, why not?
9. Do we have an obligation to "take sides against bigotry"—and hate—anywhere we find it in the world? Both Kings are asserting that we diminish ourselves morally when we see wrong and fail to act to eliminate it. What is your response to these ideas?

HOW THE FUTURE WILL JUDGE US | KWAME ANTHONY APPIAH

The son of a Ghanian lawyer and politician and British novelist, Appiah was educated in both Ghana and England. He holds a PhD in philosophy from Cambridge University, and, since 2002, he has held appointments in both the philosophy department at Princeton University and the university's Center for Human Values. Appiah is the author of many books, including *The Ethics of Identity* (2003) and *The Honor Code: How Moral Revolutions Happen* (2010). He is recognized as one of the world's most significant contemporary thinkers. His essay here was first published on September 26, 2010, in the *Washington Post*.

PREREADING QUESTIONS Given Appiah's areas of study and interest, what kinds of current problems do you think he will select for future judgment? What have we repudiated from our country's past?

Once, pretty much everywhere, beating your wife and children was 1 regarded as a father's duty, homosexuality was a hanging offense, and waterboarding was approved—in fact, invented—by the Catholic Church. Through the middle of the 19th century, the United States and other nations in the Americas condoned plantation slavery. Many of our grandparents were born in states where women were forbidden to vote. And well into the 20th century, lynch mobs in this country stripped, tortured, hanged and burned human beings at picnics.

2   Looking back at such horrors, it is easy to ask: What were people thinking?

3   Yet, the chances are that our own descendants will ask the same question, with the same incomprehension, about some of our practices today.

4   Is there a way to guess which ones? After all, not every disputed institution or practice is destined to be discredited. And it can be hard to distinguish in real time between movements, such as abolition, that will come to represent moral common sense and those, such as prohibition, that will come to seem quaint or misguided. Recall the book-burners of Boston's old Watch and Ward Society or the organizations for the suppression of vice, with their crusades against claret, contraceptives and sexually candid novels.

5   Still, a look at the past suggests three signs that a particular practice is destined for future condemnation.

6   First, people have already heard the arguments against the practice. The case against slavery didn't emerge in a blinding moment of moral clarity, for instance; it had been around for centuries.

7   Second, defenders of the custom tend not to offer moral counter-arguments but instead invoke tradition, human nature or necessity. (As in, "We've always had slaves, and how could we grow cotton without them?")

8   And third, supporters engage in what one might call strategic ignorance, avoiding truths that might force them to face the evils in which they're complicit. Those who ate the sugar or wore the cotton that the slaves grew simply didn't think about what made those goods possible. That's why abolitionists sought to direct attention toward the conditions of the Middle Passage, through detailed illustrations of slave ships and horrifying stories of the suffering below decks.

9   With these signs in mind, here are four contenders for future moral condemnation.

OUR PRISON SYSTEM

10   We already know that the massive waste of life in our prisons is morally troubling; those who defend the conditions of incarceration usually do so in non-moral terms (citing costs or the administrative difficulty of reforms); and we're inclined to avert our eyes from the details. Check, check and check.

11   Roughly 1 percent of adults in this country are incarcerated. We have 4 percent of the world's population but 25 percent of its prisoners. No other nation has as large a proportion of its population in prison; even China's rate is less than half of ours. What's more, the majority of our prisoners are non-violent offenders, many of them detained on drug charges. (Whether a country that was truly free would criminalize recreational drug use is a related question worth pondering.)

12   And the full extent of the punishment prisoners face isn't detailed in any judge's sentence. More than 100,000 inmates suffer sexual abuse, including rape, each year; some contract HIV as a result. Our country holds at least

25,000 prisoners in isolation in so-called supermax facilities, under conditions that many psychologists say amount to torture.

INDUSTRIAL MEAT PRODUCTION

The arguments against the cruelty of factory farming have certainly been [13] around a long time; it was Jeremy Bentham, in the 18th century, who observed that, when it comes to the treatment of animals, the key question is not whether animals can reason but whether they can suffer. People who eat factory-farmed bacon or chicken rarely offer a moral justification for what they're doing. Instead, they try not to think about it too much, shying away from stomach-turning stories about what goes on in our industrial abattoirs.

Of the more than 90 million cattle in our country, at least 10 million at any [14] time are packed into feedlots, saved from the inevitable diseases of over-crowding only by regular doses of antibiotics, surrounded by piles of their own feces, their nostrils filled with the smell of their own urine. Picture it—and then imagine your grandchildren seeing that picture. In the European Union, many of the most inhumane conditions we allow are already illegal or—like the sow stalls into which pregnant pigs are often crammed in the United States—will be illegal soon.

THE INSTITUTIONALIZED AND ISOLATED ELDERLY

Nearly 2 million of America's elderly are warehoused in nursing homes, [15] out of sight and, to some extent, out of mind. Some 10,000 for-profit facilities have arisen across the country in recent decades to hold them. Other elderly Americans may live independently, but often they are isolated and cut off from their families. (The United States is not alone among advanced democracies in this. Consider the heat wave that hit France in 2003: While many families were enjoying their summer vacations, some 14,000 elderly parents and grandparents were left to perish in the stifling temperatures.) Is this what Western modernity amounts to—societies that feel no filial obligations to their inconvenient elders?

Sometimes we can learn from societies much poorer than ours. My English [16] mother spent the last 50 years of her life in Ghana, where I grew up. In her final years, it was her good fortune not only to have the resources to stay at home, but also to live in a country where doing so was customary. She had family next door who visited her every day, and she was cared for by doctors and nurses who were willing to come to her when she was too ill to come to them. In short, she had the advantages of a society in which older people are treated with respect and concern.

Keeping aging parents and their children closer is a challenge, particularly [17] in a society where almost everybody has a job outside the home (if not across the country). Yet the three signs apply here as well: When we see old people who, despite many living relatives, suffer growing isolation, we know something is wrong. We scarcely try to defend the situation; when we can, we put it out of our minds. Self-interest, if nothing else, should make us hope that our descendants will have worked out a better way.

THE ENVIRONMENT

18   Of course, most transgenerational obligations run the other way—from parents to children—and of these the most obvious candidate for opprobrium is our wasteful attitude toward the planet's natural resources and ecology. Look at a satellite picture of Russia, and you'll see a vast expanse of parched wasteland where decades earlier was a lush and verdant landscape. That's the Republic of Kalmykia, home to what was recognized in the 1990s as Europe's first man-made desert. Desertification, which is primarily the result of destructive land-management practices, threatens a third of the Earth's surface; tens of thousands of Chinese villages have been overrun by sand drifts in the past few decades.

19   It's not as though we're unaware of what we're doing to the planet: We know the harm done by deforestation, wetland destruction, pollution, overfishing, greenhouse gas emissions—the whole litany. Our descendants, who will inherit this devastated Earth, are unlikely to have the luxury of such recklessness. Chances are, they won't be able to avert their eyes, even if they want to.

20   Let's not stop there, though. We will all have our own suspicions about which practices will someday prompt people to ask, in dismay: What were they thinking?

21   Even when we don't have a good answer, we'll be better off for anticipating the question.

Source: *Washington Post*, September 26, 2010. Reprinted by permission of the author.

QUESTIONS FOR READING

1. On what basis are current practices likely to be repudiated by future Americans? What three signs mark a practice for future condemnation?
2. How do the three signs suggest that our prison system is likely to be condemned?
3. What are the problems with our industrial meat production?
4. What in our work situations contributes to the isolation of the elderly? What happened to many older people in France in 2003?
5. How will the next generation have to react to the environment?

QUESTIONS FOR REASONING AND ANALYSIS

6. What is Appiah's claim? (You will need a complex statement that combines both a general idea and specific practices.)
7. How do Appiah's four practices illustrate his idea of the three warning signs?
8. What else does the author provide to defend his choice of the specific four practices?
9. Appiah is making some devastating judgments of people past and present. How would you describe his tone? How does his tone help him keep readers from feeling attacked or judged?

10. Has Appiah convinced you that the future will judge the four practices he discusses? Why or why not?

11. Did any of the four practices chosen by the author surprise you? If so, which one(s)? Why?

12. If you had been asked to select four current practices for condemnation, would you have included any of Appiah's? Why or why not? What other(s) would have been on your list? Why?

WE MADE OURSELVES ANEW, AND VOWED TO MOVE FORWARD TOGETHER | BARACK H. OBAMA

The forty-fourth president of the United States was born in Hawaii on August 4, 1961, to a white American mother and a black Kenyan father, while both were in college. After Obama attended Columbia College and Harvard Law School—where he became the first African American editor of the *Harvard Law Review*—Obama returned to Chicago to teach at the University of Chicago Law School and to practice civil rights law. Elected first to the Illinois State Senate, he was then, in 2004, elected to the U.S. Senate. In 2008 Obama became the first African American president of the United States. The following address was delivered at his second swearing in, January 21, 2013, following his reelection in 2012 to a second term as president.

PREREADING QUESTIONS Perhaps you heard the address, perhaps not; in either case, think about what issues you expect Obama to cover. Also pay attention to his style, his oratory.

Vice President Biden, Mr. Chief Justice, members of the United States Congress, distinguished guests, and fellow citizens:

Each time we gather to inaugurate a president, we bear witness to the 1 enduring strength of our Constitution. We affirm the promise of our democracy. We recall that what binds this nation together is not the colors of our skin or the tenets of our faith or the origins of our names.

What makes us exceptional, what makes us America, is our allegiance to 2 an idea articulated in a declaration made more than two centuries ago. We hold these truths to be self-evident, that all men are created equal. That they are endowed by their creator with certain unalienable rights, and among these are life, liberty and the pursuit of happiness.

Today we continue a never-ending journey to bridge the meaning of those 3 words with the realities of our time. For history tells us that while these truths may be self-evident, they've never been self-executing. That while freedom is a gift from God, it must be secured by his people here on Earth.

The patriots of 1776 did not fight to replace the tyranny of a king with the 4 privileges of a few, or the rule of a mob. They gave to us a republic, a government of and by and for the people. Entrusting each generation to keep safe our founding creed. And for more than 200 years, we have. Through blood drawn by lash, and blood drawn by sword, we noted that no union founded on the principles of liberty and equality could survive half-slave and half-free.

5   We made ourselves anew, and vowed to move forward together.

6   Together we determined that a modern economy requires railroads and highways to speed travel and commerce, schools and colleges to train our workers. Together we discovered that a free market only thrives when there are rules to ensure competition and fair play. Together we resolve that a great nation must care for the vulnerable and protect its people from life's worst hazards and misfortune.

7   Through it all, we have never relinquished our skepticism of central authority, nor have we succumbed to the fiction that all societies' ills can be cured through government alone. Our celebration of initiative and enterprise, our insistence on hard work and personal responsibility—these are constants in our character.

8   For we have always understood that when times change, so must we. That fidelity to our founding principles requires new responses to new challenges, that preserving our individual freedoms ultimately requires collective action.

9   For the American people can no more meet the demands of today's world by acting alone than American soldiers could have met the forces of fascism or communism with muskets and militias. No single person can train all the math and science teachers we'll need to equip our children for the future. Or build the roads and networks and research labs that will bring new jobs and businesses to our shores.

10   Now, more than ever, we must do these things together, as one nation and one people.

11   This generation of Americans has been tested by crises that steeled our resolve and proved our resilience. A decade of war is now ending.

12   And economic recovery has begun.

13   America's possibilities are limitless, for we possess all the qualities that this world without boundaries demands: youth and drive, diversity and openness, an endless capacity for risk and a gift for reinvention.

14   My fellow Americans, we are made for this moment and we will seize it, so long as we seize it together.

15   For we the people understand that our country cannot succeed when a shrinking few do very well and a growing many barely make it.

16   We believe that America's prosperity must rest upon the broad shoulders of a rising middle class. We know that America thrives when every person can find independence and pride in their work, when the wages of honest labor will liberate families from the brink of hardship.

17   We are true to our creed when a little girl born into the bleakest poverty knows that she has the same chance to succeed as anybody else because she is an American, she is free and she is equal not just in the eyes of God but also in our own.

18   We understand that outworn programs are inadequate to the needs of our time. So we must harness new ideas and technology to remake our

government, revamp our tax code, reform our schools, and empower our citizens with the skills they need to work hard or learn more, reach higher.

But while the means will change, our purpose endures. A nation that [19] rewards the effort and determination of every single American, that is what this moment requires. That is what will give real meaning to our creed.

We the people still believe that every citizen deserves a basic measure of [20] security and dignity. We must make the hard choices to reduce the cost of health care and the size of our deficit.

But we reject the belief that America must choose between caring for the [21] generation that built this country and investing in the generation that will build its future.

For we remember the lessons of our past, when twilight years were spent [22] in poverty and parents of a child with a disability had nowhere to turn. We do not believe that in this country freedom is reserved for the lucky or happiness for the few. We recognize that no matter how responsibly we live our lives, any one of us at any time may face a job loss or a sudden illness or a home swept away in a terrible storm. The commitments we make to each other through Medicare and Medicaid and Social Security, these things do not sap our initiative. They strengthen us.

They do not make us a nation of takers. They free us to take the risks that [23] make this country great.

We the people still believe that our obligations as Americans are not just [24] to ourselves, but to all posterity. We will respond to the threat of climate change, knowing that the failure to do so would betray our children and future generations.

Some may still deny the overwhelming judgment of science, but none can [25] avoid the devastating impact of raging fires, and crippling drought, and more powerful storms. The path toward sustainable energy sources will be long and sometimes difficult. But Americans cannot resist this transition. We must lead it.

We cannot cede to other nations the technology that will power new jobs [26] and new industries. We must claim its promise. That's how we will maintain our economic vitality and our national treasure, our forests and waterways, our crop lands and snow-capped peaks. That is how we will preserve our planet, commanded to our care by God. That's what will lend meaning to the creed our fathers once declared.

We the people still believe that enduring security and lasting peace do not [27] require perpetual war.

Our brave men and women in uniform tempered by the flames of battle [28] are unmatched in skill and courage.

Our citizens seared by the memory of those we have lost, know too well [29] the price that is paid for liberty. The knowledge of their sacrifice will keep us forever vigilant against those who would do us harm. But we are also heirs to those who won the peace, and not just the war. Who turn sworn enemies into the surest of friends. And we must carry those lessons into this time as well. We will defend our people, and uphold our values through strength of arms and the rule of law.

Obama greets troops in Afghanistan.

30   We will show the courage to try and resolve our differences with other nations peacefully. Not because we are naive about the dangers we face, but because engagement can more durably lift suspicion and fear.

31   America will remain the anchor of strong alliances in every corner of the globe. And we will renew those institutions that extend our capacity to manage crises abroad. For no one has a greater stake in a peaceful world than its most powerful nation. We will support democracy from Asia to Africa, from the Americas to the Middle East, because our interests and our conscience compel us to act on behalf of those who long for freedom. And we must be a source of hope to the poor, the sick, the marginalized, the victims of prejudice.

32   Not out of mere charity, but because peace in our time requires the constant advance of those principles that our common creed describes: tolerance and opportunity, human dignity and justice. We the people declare today that the most evident of truths—that all of us are created equal—is the star that guides us still, just as it guided our forebears through Seneca Falls and Selma and Stonewall; just as it guided all those men and women, sung and unsung, who left footprints along this great Mall, to hear a preacher say that we cannot walk alone, to hear a king proclaim that our individual freedom is inextricably bound to the freedom of every soul on Earth.

33   It is now our generation's task to carry on what those pioneers began, for our journey is not complete until our wives, our mothers and daughters can earn a living equal to their efforts.

34   Our journey is not complete until our gay brothers and sisters are treated like anyone else under the law, for if we are truly created equal, then surely the love we commit to one another must be equal as well.

Our journey is not complete until no citizen is forced to wait for hours to 35 exercise the right to vote.

Our journey is not complete until we find a better way to welcome the 36 striving, hopeful immigrants who still see America as a land of opportunity, until bright young students and engineers are enlisted in our workforce rather than expelled from our country.

Our journey is not complete until all our children, from the streets of 37 Detroit to the hills of Appalachia to the quiet lanes of Newtown, know that they are cared for and cherished and always safe from harm.

That is our generation's task, to make these works, these rights, these val- 38 ues of life and liberty and the pursuit of happiness real for every American.

Being true to our founding documents does not require us to agree on 39 every contour of life. It does not mean we all define liberty in exactly the same way or follow the same precise path to happiness.

Progress does not compel us to settle centuries-long debates about the 40 role of government for all time, but it does require us to act in our time.

For now, decisions are upon us and we cannot afford delay. We cannot 41 mistake absolutism for principle or substitute spectacle for politics, or treat name-calling as reasoned debate.

We must act. We must act knowing that our work will be imperfect. We 42 must act knowing that today's victories will be only partial, and that it will be up to those who stand here in four years—and 40 years, and 400 years hence—to advance the timeless spirit once conferred to us in a spare Philadelphia hall.

My fellow Americans, the oath I have sworn before you today, like the one 43 recited by others who serve in this Capitol, was an oath to God and country, not party or faction.

And we must faithfully execute that pledge during the duration of our 44 service. But the words I spoke today are not so different from the oath that is taken each time a soldier signs up for duty, or an immigrant realizes her dream.

My oath is not so different from the pledge we all make to the flag that 45 waves above and that fills our hearts with pride. They are the words of citizens, and they represent our greatest hope. You and I, as citizens, have the power to set this country's course. You and I, as citizens, have the obligation to shape the debates of our time, not only with the votes we cast, but the voices we lift in defense of our most ancient values and enduring ideas.

Let each of us now embrace with solemn duty, and awesome joy, what is 46 our lasting birthright. With common effort and common purpose, with passion and dedication, let us answer the call of history and carry into an uncertain future that precious light of freedom.

Thank you. God bless you. And may He forever bless these United States 47 of America.

Understanding Literature

The same process of reading nonfiction can be used to understand literature— fiction, poetry, and drama. You still need to read what is on the page, looking up unfamiliar words and tracking down references you don't understand. You still need to examine the context, to think about who is writing to whom, under what circumstances, and in what literary format. And, to respond fully to the words, you need to analyze the writer's techniques for developing ideas and expressing attitudes.

Although it seems logical that the reading process should be much the same regardless of the work, not all readers of literature are willing to accept that logic. Some readers want a work of literature to mean whatever they think it means. But what happened to the writer's desire to communicate? If you decide that a Robert Frost poem, for example, should mean whatever you are feeling when you read it, you might as well skip the reading of Frost and just commune with your feelings. Presumably you read Frost to gain some new insight from him, to get beyond just your vision and see something of human experience and emotion from a new vantage point.

Other readers of literature hesitate over the concept of *literary analysis,* or at least over the word *analysis.* These readers complain that analysis will "tear the work apart" and "ruin it." If you are inclined to share this attitude, stop for a minute and think about the last sports event you watched. Perhaps a friend explained: "North Carolina is so good at stalling to use up the clock; Duke will have to foul to get the ball and have a chance to tie the game." The game is being analyzed! And that analysis makes the event more fully experienced by those who understand at least some of the elements of basketball.

The analogy is clear. You, too, can be a fan of literature. You can enjoy reading and discussing your reading once you learn to use your active reading and analytic skills to open up a poem or story, and once you sharpen your knowledge of literary terms and concepts so that you can "speak the language" of literary criticism with the same confidence with which you discuss the merits of a full court press.

GETTING THE FACTS: ACTIVE READING, SUMMARY, AND PARAPHRASE

Let's begin with the following poem by Paul Dunbar. As you read, make marginal notes, circling a phrase you fancy, putting a question mark next to a difficult line, underscoring words you need to look up. Note, too, your emotional reactions as you read.

PROMISE | PAUL LAWRENCE DUNBAR

Born of former slave parents, Dunbar (1872–1906) was educated in Dayton, Ohio. After a first booklet of poems, *Oak and Ivy*, was printed in 1893, several friends helped Dunbar get a second collection, *Majors and Minors*, published in 1895. A copy was given to author and editor William Dean Howells, who reviewed the book favorably, increasing sales and Dunbar's reputation. This led to a national publisher issuing *Lyrics of Lowly Life* in 1896, the collection that secured Dunbar's fame.

I grew a rose within a garden fair,
And, tending it with more than loving care,
I thought how, with the glory of its bloom,
I should the darkness of my life illume;
And, watching, ever smiled to see the lusty bud   5
Drink freely in the summer sun to tint its blood.

My rose began to open, and its hue
Was sweet to me as to it sun and dew;
I watched it taking on its ruddy flame
Until the day of perfect blooming came,   10
Then hasted I with smiles to find it blushing red—
Too late! Some thoughtless child had plucked my rose and fled!

"Promise" should not have been especially difficult to read, although you may have paused a moment over "illume" before connecting it to "illuminate," and you may have to check the dictionary for a definition of "tint." Test your knowledge of content by listing all the facts of the poem. Pay attention to the poem's basic situation. Who is speaking? What is happening, or what thoughts is the speaker sharing? In this poem, the "I" is not further identified, so you will have to refer to him or her as the "speaker." You should not call the speaker "Dunbar," however, because you do not know if Dunbar ever grew a rose.

In "Promise" the speaker is describing an event that has taken place. The speaker grew a rose, tended to it with care, and watched it begin to bloom. Then, when the rose was in full bloom, some child picked the rose and took it away. The situation is fairly simple, isn't it? Too simple, unfortunately, for some readers who decide that the speaker never grew a rose at all. But when anyone writes, "I grew a rose within a garden fair," it is wise to assume that the writer means just that. People do grow roses, most often in gardens, and then the gardens are made "fair" or beautiful by the flowers growing there. Read first for the facts; try not to jump too quickly to broad generalizations.

As with nonfiction, one of the best ways to make certain you have understood a literary work is to write a summary or paraphrase. Since a summary condenses, you are most likely to write a summary of a story, novel, or play, whereas a paraphrase is usually reserved for poems or complex short passages. When you paraphrase a difficult poem, you are likely to end up with more words than in the original because your purpose is to turn cryptic lines into more ordinary sentences. For example, Dunbar's "Then hasted I with smiles" can be paraphrased to read: "Then, full of smiles, I hurried."

When summarizing a literary work, remember to use your own words, draw no conclusions, giving only the facts, but focus your summary on the key events in the story. (Of course the selecting you do to write a summary represents preliminary analysis; you are making some choices about what is important in the work.) Read the following short story by Kate Chopin and then write your own summary. Finally, compare yours to the summary that follows the story.

THE STORY OF AN HOUR | KATE CHOPIN

Now recognized as an important voice from nineteenth-century America, Kate Chopin (1851–1904) enjoyed popularity for her short stories from 1890 to 1900 and then condemnation and neglect for sixty years. She saw two collections of stories published—*Bayou Folk* in 1894 and *A Night in Acadie* in 1897—before losing popularity and critical acclaim with the publication of her short novel *The Awakening* in 1899, the story of a woman struggling to free herself from years of repression and subservience.

1 Knowing that Mrs. Mallard was afflicted with a heart trouble, great care was taken to break to her as gently as possible the news of her husband's death.

2 It was her sister Josephine who told her, in broken sentences; veiled hints that revealed in half concealing. Her husband's friend Richards was there, too, near her. It was he who had been in the newspaper office when intelligence of the railroad disaster was received, with Brently Mallard's name leading the list of "killed." He had only taken the time to assure himself of its truth by a second telegram, and had hastened to forestall any less careful, less tender friend in bearing the sad message.

3 She did not hear the story as many women have heard the same, with a paralyzed inability to accept its significance. She wept at once, with sudden, wild abandonment, in her sister's arms. When the storm of grief had spent itself she went away to her room alone. She would have no one follow her.

4 There stood, facing the open window, a comfortable, roomy armchair. Into this she sank, pressed down by a physical exhaustion that haunted her body and seemed to reach into her soul.

5 She could see in the open square before her house the tops of trees that were all aquiver with the new spring life. The delicious breath of rain was in the

air. In the street below a peddler was crying his wares. The notes of a distant song which some one was singing reached her faintly, and countless sparrows were twittering in the eaves.

There were patches of blue sky showing here and there through the clouds 6 that had met and piled one above the other in the west facing her window.

She sat with her head thrown back upon the cushion of the chair, quite 7 motionless, except when a sob came up into her throat and shook her, as a child who has cried itself to sleep continues to sob in its dreams.

She was young, with a fair, calm face, whose lines bespoke repression and 8 even a certain strength. But now there was a dull stare in her eyes, whose gaze was fixed away off yonder on one of those patches of blue sky. It was not a glance of reflection, but rather indicated a suspension of intelligent thought.

There was something coming to her and she was waiting for it, fearfully. 9 What was it? She did not know; it was too subtle and elusive to name. But she felt it, creeping out of the sky, reaching toward her through the sounds, the scents, the color that filled the air.

Now her bosom rose and fell tumultuously. She was beginning to recog- 10 nize this thing that was approaching to possess her, and she was striving to beat it back with her will—as powerless as her two white slender hands would have been.

When she abandoned herself a little whispered word escaped her slightly 11 parted lips. She said it over and over under her breath: "free, free, free!" The vacant stare and the look of terror that had followed it went from her eyes. They stayed keen and bright. Her pulses beat fast, and the coursing blood warmed and relaxed every inch of her body.

She did not stop to ask if it were or were not a monstrous joy that held her. 12 A clear and exalted perception enabled her to dismiss the suggestion as trivial.

She knew that she would weep again when she saw the kind, tender hands 13 folded in death; the face that had never looked save with love upon her, fixed and gray and dead. But she saw beyond that bitter moment a long procession of years to come that would belong to her absolutely. And she opened and spread her arms out to them in welcome.

There would be no one to live for her during those coming years; she 14 would live for herself. There would be no powerful will bending hers in that blind persistence with which men and women believe they have a right to impose a private will upon a fellow-creature. A kind intention or a cruel intention made the act seem no less a crime as she looked upon it in that brief moment of illumination.

And yet she had loved him—sometimes. Often she had not. What did it 15 matter! What could love, the unsolved mystery, count for in face of this possession of self-assertion which she suddenly recognized as the strongest impulse of her being!

"Free! Body and soul free!" she kept whispering. 16

Josephine was kneeling before the closed door with her lips to the key- 17 hole, imploring for admission. "Louise, open the door! I beg; open the door—you will make yourself ill. What are you doing, Louise? For heaven's sake open the door."

18   "Go away. I am not making myself ill." No; she was drinking in a very elixir of life through that open window.

19   Her fancy was running riot along those days ahead of her. Spring days, and summer days, and all sorts of days that would be her own. She breathed a quick prayer that life might be long. It was only yesterday she had thought with a shudder that life might be long.

20   She arose at length and opened the door to her sister's importunities. There was a feverish triumph in her eyes, and she carried herself unwittingly like a goddess of Victory. She clasped her sister's waist, and together they descended the stairs. Richards stood waiting for them at the bottom.

21   Someone was opening the front door with a latchkey. It was Brently Mallard who entered, a little travel-stained, composedly carrying his grip-sack and umbrella. He had been far from the scene of accident, and did not even know there had been one. He stood amazed at Josephine's piercing cry; at Richards' quick motion to screen him from the view of his wife.

22   But Richards was too late.

23   When the doctors came they said she had died of heart disease—of joy that kills.

Summary of "The Story of an Hour"

> Mrs. Mallard's sister Josephine and her husband's friend Richards come to tell her that her husband has been listed as killed in a train accident. They try to be gentle because Mrs. Mallard has a heart condition. She cries and then goes to her bedroom alone. She sits in an armchair and gazes out the open window. Her dull stare gives way to some new thought that she cannot push away. She whispers the word "free" and thinks about a future directed by herself. Responding to Josephine's pleas, she leaves the bedroom and sees Richards below—and then Mr. Mallard letting himself in the front door. Mrs. Mallard dies, and the doctors who attend her say she died of heart disease—of "joy that kills."

Note that the summary is written in the present tense. Brevity is achieved by leaving out dialogue and the details of what Mrs. Mallard sees outside her window and the future life she imagines. Observe that the summary is not the same as the original story. The drama and emotion are missing, details that help us to understand the story's ending.

Now for a paraphrase. Read the following sonnet by Shakespeare, looking up unfamiliar words and making notes. Remember to read to the end of a unit of thought, not just to the end of a line. Some sentences continue through several lines; if you pause before you reach punctuation, you will be confused. Write your own paraphrase, not looking ahead in the text, and then compare yours with the one that follows the poem.

SONNET 116 | WILLIAM SHAKESPEARE

Surely the best-known name in literature, William Shakespeare (1564–1616) is famous as both a dramatist and a poet. Rural Warwickshire and the market town of Stratford-on-Avon, where he grew up, showed him many of the character types who were to enliven his plays, as did the bustling life of a young actor in London. Apparently his sonnets were intended to be circulated only among his friends, but they were published nonetheless in 1609. His thirty-seven plays were first published together in 1623. Shakespeare's 154 sonnets vary, some focusing on separation and world-weariness, others on the endurance of love.

> Let me not to the marriage of true minds
> Admit impediments. Love is not love
> Which alters when it alteration finds,
> Or bends with the remover to remove.
> O, no! it is an ever-fixed mark   5
> That looks on tempests and is never shaken;
> It is the star to every wand'ring bark,
> Whose worth's unknown, although his height be taken.
> Love's not Time's fool, though rosy lips and cheeks
> Within his bending sickle's compass come;   10
> Love alters not with his brief hours and weeks,
> But bears it out even to the edge of doom.
>   If this be error and upon me proved,
>   I never writ, nor no man ever loved.

Paraphrase of "Sonnet 116"

I cannot accept barriers to the union of steadfast spirits. We cannot call love love if it changes because it discovers change or if it disappears during absence. On the contrary, love is a steady guide that, in spite of difficulties, remains unwavering. Love can define the inherent value in all who lack self-knowledge, though superficially they know who they are. Love does not lessen with time, though signs of physical beauty may fade. Love endures, changeless, eternally. If anyone can show me to be wrong in this position, I am no writer and no man can be said to have loved.

We have examined the facts of a literary work, what we can call the internal situation. But, as we noted in Chapter 2, there is also the external situation or context of any piece of writing. For many literary works, the context is not as essential to understanding as it is with nonfiction. You can read "The Story of an Hour," for instance, without knowing much about Kate Chopin, or the circumstances in which she wrote the story, although such information would enrich your reading experience. There is a body of information, however, that is important: the external literary situation. Readers should take note of these details before they begin to read:

- First, don't make the mistake of calling every work a "story." Make clear distinctions among stories, novels, plays, and poems.
- Poems can be further divided into narrative, dramatic, and lyric poems.
- A *narrative poem*, such as Homer's *The Iliad,* tells a story in verse. A *dramatic poem* records the speech of at least one character.
- A poem in which only one figure speaks—but clearly addresses words to someone who is present in a particular situation—is called a *dramatic monologue.*
- *Lyric poems,* Dunbar's "Promise" for example, may place the speaker in a situation or may express a thought or feeling with few, if any, situational details, but lyric poems have in common the convention that we as readers are listening in on someone's thoughts, not listening to words directed to a second, created figure. These distinctions make us aware of how the words of the poem are coming to us. Are we hearing a storyteller or someone speaking? Or, are we overhearing someone's thoughts?

> **REMEMBER:** Active reading includes looking over a work first and predicting what will come next. Do not just start reading words without first understanding what kind of work you are about to read.

Lyric poems can be further divided into many subcategories or types. Most instructors will expect you to be able to recognize some of these types. You should be able to distinguish between a poem in *free verse* (no prevailing metrical pattern) and one in *blank verse* (continuous unrhymed lines of iambic pentameter). (*Note:* A metrical line will contain a particular number—pentameter is five—of one kind of metrical "foot." The iambic foot consists of one unstressed syllable followed by one stressed syllable.) You should also be able to tell if a poem is written in some type of *stanza* form (repeated units with the same number of lines, same metrical pattern, and same rhyme scheme), or if it is a *sonnet* (always fourteen lines of iambic pentameter with one of two complex rhyme schemes labeled either "English" or "Italian"). You want to make it a habit to observe these external elements before you read. To sharpen your observation, complete the following exercise.

EXERCISE: Observing Literary Types and Using Literary Terms

1. After surveying this appendix, make a list of all the works of literature by primary type: short story, poem, play.

2. For each work on your list, add two more pieces of information: whether the author is American or British, and in what century the work was written. Why should you be aware of the writer's dates and nationality as you read?

3. Further divide the poems into narrative, dramatic, or lyric.

4. List as many of the details of type or form as you can for each poem. For example, if the poem is written in stanzas, describe the stanza form used: the number of lines, the meter, the rhyme scheme. If the poem is a sonnet, determine the rhyme scheme. (*Note:* Rhyme scheme is indicated by using letters, assigning *a* to the first sound and using a new letter for each new sound. Thus, if two consecutive lines rhyme, the scheme is *aa, bb, cc, dd,* and so on.)

SEEING CONNECTIONS: ANALYSIS

Although we read first for the facts and an initial emotional response, we do not stop there, because as humans we seek meaning. Surely there is more to "The Story of an Hour" than the summary suggests; emotionally we know this to be true. As with nonfiction, one of the best places to start analysis is with a work's organization or structure. Lyric poems will be shaped by many of the same structures found in essays: chronological, spatial, general to particular, particular to general, a list of particulars with an unstated general point, and so forth. In "Promise," Dunbar gives one illustration, recounted chronologically, to make a point that is left unstated. "Sonnet 116" contains a list of characteristics of love underscored in the conclusion by the speaker's conviction that he is right.

Analysis of Narrative Structure

In stories (and plays and narrative poems) we are given a series of events, in time sequence, involving one or more characters. In some stories, episodes are only loosely connected but are unified around a central character (Mark Twain's *Adventures of Huckleberry Finn,* for example). Most stories present events that are at least to some extent related causally; that is, action A by the main character leads to event B, which requires action C by the main character. This kind of plot structure can be diagrammed, as in Figure 1.

Figure 1 introduces some terms and concepts useful in analyzing and discussing narratives. The story's *exposition* refers to the background details

FIGURE 1 Plot Structure

needed to get the story started, including the time and place of the story and relationships of the characters. In "The Story of an Hour," a key detail of exposition is the fact that Mrs. Mallard has a heart condition. The *complication* refers to an event: Something happens to produce tension or *conflict*. In Chopin's story, the announcement of Mr. Mallard's death seems to be an immediate complication. But, after her initial tears, we do not see Mrs. Mallard dealing with this complication in the "typical" way. Instead, when she sits in her bedroom, she experiences a *conflict*. She struggles within herself. Why does she struggle? Why not just embrace the new idea that comes to her?

Although some stories present one major complication leading to a *climax* of decision or insight for the main character, many actually repeat the pattern, presenting several complications—each with an attempted resolution that causes yet another complication—until we reach the high point of tension, the *climax*. The action—or inaction—of the climactic moment leads to the story's *resolution* and ending.

These terms are helpful in analysis, even though some stories end abruptly, with little apparent resolution. A stark "resolution" is part of the modern writer's view of reality, that life goes on, with problems often remaining unresolved. A character in an unpleasant marriage continues in that marriage, perhaps ruefully, perhaps a bit wiser but no happier and unable to act to change the situation. What is the climactic moment in "The Story of an Hour"? How is the story resolved? What is significant about the doctors' explanation at the end? Are they correct?

Analysis of Character

An analysis of plot structure suggests to us that Mrs. Mallard is not in conflict over her husband's death. She is in conflict, initially, over her reaction to that death, but she resolves her conflict, only to have Mr. Mallard open the front door. Note the close connection between complication (event) and conflict (what the characters are feeling). Fiction requires both plot and character, events and players in those events. In serious literature the greater emphasis is usually on character, on what we learn about human life through the interplay of character and incident.

As we shift from plot to character, we can enhance our analysis by considering how writers present character. Writers will usually employ several techniques from the following list:

- Descriptive details. (Mrs. Mallard's heart condition. Josephine and Richards worry about her health.)
- Dramatic scenes. (Instead of telling, they show us. Much of "The Story of an Hour" is dialogue. When Mrs. Mallard is in her bedroom alone, we overhear her internal dialogue.)
- Contrast among characters. (Josephine assumes that Mrs. Mallard continues to be the distraught, bereft widow, whereas she is actually embracing

a future on her own. Note the contrast between the gentle, kind control of Mr. Mallard in their marriage and the way the control actually feels in his wife's experience of it.)

- Other elements in the work. (Names can be significant, or characters can become associated with significant objects, or details of setting can become symbolic. Note all of the specific details of events outside Mrs. Mallard's window. What, altogether, do they represent?)

Understanding character can be a challenge because we must infer from a few words, gestures, and actions. Looking at all of a writer's options for presenting character will keep us from overlooking important details.

Analysis of Elements of Style and Tone

All the elements, discussed in Chapter 2, that shape a writer's style and create tone can be found in literary works as well and need to be considered as part of your analysis. We can begin with Chopin's title. How much can happen in one hour? Well, the person we thought was dead is alive, and the "widow" ends up dead, quite a reversal of fortunes in such a short time. This situation is filled with irony. The doctors' misunderstanding of the cause of Mrs. Mallard's shock at the sight of her husband also adds irony to the story. The doctors express society's conventional thinking: Dear Mrs. Mallard is so happy that her husband is really alive that her heart cannot stand it. But is that really what shocks her into an early death?

Shakespeare's "Sonnet 116" develops the speaker's ideas about love through a series of metaphors. The rose in Dunbar's "Promise" is not a metaphor, though, because it is not part of a comparison. Yet, as we read the poem we sense that it is about something more serious than the nurturing and then stealing of one flower, no matter how beautiful. The poem's title gives us a clue that the rose stands for something more than itself; it is a symbol. Traditionally the red rose is a symbol of love. To tie the poem together, we will have to see how the title, the usual symbolic value of the rose, and specifics of the poem connect.

DRAWING CONCLUSIONS: INTERPRETATION

We have studied the facts of several works and analyzed their structures and other key elements. To reach some conclusions and shape our thinking into a coherent whole is to offer an interpretation of the work. At this point, readers can be expected to disagree somewhat, but if we have all read carefully and applied our knowledge of literature, differences should, most of the time, be ones of focus and emphasis. Presumably no one is prepared to argue that "Promise" is about pink elephants or "The Story of an Hour" about the Queen of England. Neither work contains any facts to support those conclusions.

What conclusions can we reach about "Promise"? A beautiful flower has been nurtured into bloom by a speaker who expects it to brighten his or her life. The title lets us know that the rose represents great promise. Has a rival stolen the speaker's loved one, represented symbolically by the rose? A thoughtless child would not be an appropriate rival for an adult speaker. In the context of this poem, the rose represents, more generally, something that the speaker cherishes in anticipation of the pleasure it will bring, only to lose that something.

What conclusions have you reached about "The Story of an Hour"? What is the real irony of the story? When Mr. Mallard, very much alive, opens the door to his home, what door does he shut for Mrs. Mallard?

WRITING ABOUT LITERATURE

When you are assigned a literary essay, you will usually be asked to write either an explication or an analysis. An *explication* presents a reading of a complex poem. It will combine paraphrase and explanation to clarify the poem's meaning. A *literary analysis* can take many forms. You may be asked to analyze one element in a work: character conflict, the use of setting, the tone of a poem. Or you could be asked to contrast two works. Usually an analytic assignment requires you to connect analysis to interpretation, for we analyze the parts to better understand the whole. If you are asked to examine the metaphors in a Shakespeare sonnet, for example, you will want to show how understanding the metaphors contributes to an understanding of the entire poem. In short, literary analysis is much the same as a style analysis of an essay. Thus the guidelines for writing about style discussed in Chapter 2 apply here as well.* Successful analyses are based on accurate reading, reflection on the work's emotional impact, and the use of details from the work to support conclusions.

Literary analyses can also incorporate material beyond the particular work. We can analyze a work in the light of biographical information or from a particular political ideology. Or we can study the social-cultural context of the work, or relate it to a literary tradition. These are only a few of the many approaches to the study of literature, and they depend on the application of knowledge outside the work itself. For undergraduates, topics based on these approaches usually require research. The student research essay at the end of the Appendix is a literary analysis. Alan examines Faulkner's *Intruder in the Dust* as an initiation novel. He connects his analysis to works by Hawthorne and Arthur Miller. What is taken from his research is documented and helps develop and support his own conclusions about the story.

To practice close reading, analysis, and interpretation of literature, read the following works. Use the questions after each work to aid your response.

---

* Remember: The guidelines for referring to authors, titles, and direct quotations—presented in Chapter 1—also apply.

TO HIS COY MISTRESS | ANDREW MARVELL

One of the last poets of the English Renaissance, Andrew Marvell (1621–1678) graduated from Cambridge University, spent much of his young life as a tutor, and was elected to Parliament in 1659. He continued in public service until his death. Most of his best-loved lyric poems come from his years as a tutor. "To His Coy Mistress" was published in 1681.

Had we but world enough, and time,
This coyness, lady, were no crime.
We would sit down, and think which way
To walk, and pass our long love's day.
Thou by the Indian Ganges' side   5
Shouldst rubies find; I by the tide
Of Humber would complain. I would
Love you ten years before the Flood,
And you should, if you please, refuse
Till the conversion of the Jews.   10
My vegetable° love should grow   *slowly vegetative*
Vaster than empires, and more slow;
An hundred years should go to praise
Thine eyes, and on thy forehead gaze;
Two hundred to adore each breast,   15
But thirty thousand to the rest;
An age at least to every part,
And the last age should show your heart.
For, lady, you deserve this state,
Nor would I love at lower rate.   20
    But at my back I always hear
Time's wingèd chariot hurrying near;
And yonder all before us lie
Deserts of vast eternity.
Thy beauty shall no more be found,   25
Nor in thy marble vault shall sound
My echoing song; then worms shall try
That long preserved virginity,
And your quaint honor turn to dust,
And into ashes all my lust.   30
The grave's a fine and private place,
But none, I think, do there embrace.
    Now therefore, while the youthful hue
Sits on thy skin like morning dew,
And while thy willing soul transpires   35
At every pore with instant fires,
Now let us sport us while we may,
And now, like amorous birds of prey,
Rather at once our time devour

40 Than languish in his slow-chapped power.
Let us roll all our strength and all
Our sweetness up into one ball,
And tear our pleasures with rough strife

45 Thorough° the iron gates of life.   *through*
Thus, though we cannot make our sun
Stand still, yet we will make him run.

QUESTIONS FOR READING, REASONING, AND REFLECTION

1. Describe the poem's external form.
2. How are the words coming to us? That is, is this a narrative, dramatic, or lyric poem?
3. Summarize the speaker's argument, using the structures *if, but,* and *therefore.*
4. What figure of speech do we find throughout the first verse paragraph? What is its effect on the speaker's tone?
5. Find examples of irony and understatement in the second verse paragraph.
6. How does the tone shift in the second section?
7. Explain the personification in line 22.
8. Explain the metaphors in lines 30 and 45.
9. What is the paradox of the last two lines? How can it be explained?
10. What is the idea of this poem? What does the writer want us to reflect on?

THE PASSIONATE SHEPHERD TO HIS LOVE
CHRISTOPHER MARLOWE

Cambridge graduate, Renaissance dramatist second only to Shakespeare, Christopher Marlowe (1564–1593) may be best known for this lyric poem. Not only is it widely anthologized, it has also spawned a number of responses by such significant writers as the seventeenth-century poet John Donne and the twentieth-century humorous poet Ogden Nash. For the Renaissance period the shepherd was a standard figure of the lover.

Come live with me and be my love,
And we will all the pleasures prove
That valleys, groves, hills, and fields,
Woods, or steepy mountain yields.

5 And we will sit upon the rocks,
Seeing the shepherds feed their flocks,
By shallow rivers to whose falls
Melodious birds sing madrigals.

And I will make thee beds of roses
And a thousand fragrant posies,   10
A cap of flowers, and a kirtle
Embroidered all with leaves of myrtle;

A gown made of the finest wool
Which from our pretty lambs we pull;
Fair lined slippers for the cold,   15
With buckles of the purest gold;

A belt of straw and ivy buds,
With coral clasps and amber studs:
And if these pleasures may thee move,
Come live with me, and be my love.   20

The shepherds' swains shall dance and sing
For thy delight each May morning:
If these delights thy mind may move,
Then live with me and be my love.

QUESTIONS FOR READING, REASONING, AND REFLECTION

1. Describe the poem's external structure.
2. What is the speaker's subject? What does he want to accomplish?
3. Summarize his "argument." How does he seek to convince his love?
4. What do the details of his argument have in common—that is, what kind of world or life does the speaker describe? Is there anything missing from the shepherd's world?
5. Would you like to be courted in this way? Would you say yes to the shepherd? If not, why?

THE NYMPH'S REPLY TO THE SHEPHERD | SIR WALTER RALEIGH

The renowned Elizabethan courtier, Sir Walter Raleigh (1552–1618) led a varied life as both a favorite of Queen Elizabeth and out of favor at court, as a colonizer and writer, and as one of many to be imprisoned in the Tower of London. In the following poem, Raleigh offers a response to Marlowe, using the nymph as the voice of the female lover.

If all the world and love were young,
And truth in every shepherd's tongue,
These pretty pleasures might me move
To live with thee and be thy love.

Time drives the flocks from field to fold   5
When rivers rage and rocks grow cold,

And Philomel becometh dumb;
The rest complains of cares to come.

The flowers do fade, and wanton fields
10   To wayward winter reckoning yields;
A honey tongue, a heart of gall,
Is fancy's spring, but sorrow's fall.

Thy gowns, thy shoes, thy beds of roses,
Thy cap, thy kirtle, and thy posies
15   Soon break, soon wither, soon forgotten,—
In folly ripe, in reason rotten.

Thy belt of straw and ivy buds,
Thy coral clasps and amber studs,
All these in me no means can move
20   To come to thee and be thy love.

But could youth last and love still breed,
Had joys no date nor age no need,
Then these delights my mind might move
To live with thee and be thy love.

QUESTIONS FOR READING, REASONING, AND REFLECTION

1. Describe the poem's external structure.
2. What is the context of the poem, the reason the speaker offers her words?
3. Analyze the speaker's argument, using *if* and *but* as your basic structure—and then the concluding, qualifying *but*.
4. What evidence does the speaker provide to support her argument?
5. Who has the more convincing argument: Marlowe's shepherd or Raleigh's nymph? Why?

IS MY TEAM PLOUGHING | A. E. HOUSMAN

British poet A. E. Housman (1859–1936) was a classicist, first a professor of Latin at University College, London, and then at the University of Cambridge. He spent the rest of his life at Trinity College, Cambridge. He is best known for his first volume of poetry, *A Shropshire Lad* (1896), a collection of crystal clear and deceptively simple verses that give expression to a world that has been lost—perhaps the innocence of youth.

"Is my team ploughing,
That I was used to drive

And hear the harness jingle
   When I was man alive?"

Ay, the horses trample,   5
   The harness jingles now:
No change though you lie under
   The land you used to plough.

"Is football playing
   Along the river shore,   10
With lads to chase the leather,
   Now I stand up no more?"

Ay, the ball is flying,
   The lads play heart and soul;
The goal stands up, the keeper   15
   Stands up to keep the goal.

"Is my girl happy,
   That I thought hard to leave,
And has she tired of weeping
   As she lies down at eve?"   20

Ay, she lies down lightly,
   She lies not down to weep:
Your girl is well contented.
   Be still, my lad, and sleep.

"Is my friend hearty,   25
   Now I am thin and pine,
And has he found to sleep in
   A better bed than mine?"

Yes, lad, I lie easy,
   I lie as lads would choose;   30
I cheer a dead man's sweetheart,
   Never ask me whose.

QUESTIONS FOR READING, REASONING, AND REFLECTION

1. Classify the poem according to its external structure.
2. Is this a narrative, dramatic, or lyric poem? How are we to read the words coming to us?
3. What is the relationship between the two speakers? What has happened to the first speaker? What has changed in the life of the second speaker?
4. What ideas are suggested by the poem? What does Housman want us to take from his poem?

TAXI | AMY LOWELL

Educated at private schools and widely traveled, American Amy Lowell (1874–1925) was both a poet and a critic. Lowell frequently read her poetry and lectured on poetic techniques, defending her verse and that of other modern poets.

> When I go away from you
> The world beats dead
> Like a slackened drum.
> I call out for you against the jutted stars
> 5 And shout into the ridges of the wind.
> Streets coming fast,
> One after the other,
> Wedge you away from me,
> And the lamps of the city prick my eyes
> 10 So that I can no longer see your face.
> Why should I leave you,
> To wound myself upon the sharp edges of the night?

QUESTIONS FOR READING, REASONING, AND REFLECTION

1. Classify the poem according to its external structure.
2. Is this a narrative, dramatic, or lyric poem?
3. Explain the simile in the opening three lines and the metaphor in the last line of the poem.
4. What is the poem's subject? What seems to be the situation in which we find the speaker?
5. How would you describe the tone of the poem? How do the details and the emotional impact of the metaphors help to create tone?
6. What is the poem's meaning or theme? In other words, what does the poet want us to understand from reading her poem?

THE ONES WHO WALK AWAY FROM OMELAS | URSULA K. LE GUIN

A graduate of Radcliffe College and Columbia University, Ursula K. Le Guin is the author of more than twenty novels and juvenile books, several volumes of poetry, and numerous stories and essays published in science fiction, scholarly, and popular journals. Her fiction stretches the categories of science fiction or fantasy and challenges a reader's moral understanding. First published in 1973, the following story, according to Le Guin, was inspired by a passage in William James's "The Moral Philosopher and the Moral Life" in which he asserts that we could not tolerate a situation in which the happiness of many people was purchased by the "lonely torment" of one "lost soul."

With a clamor of bells that set the swallows soaring, the Festival of Summer came to the city Omelas, bright-towered by the sea. The rigging of the boats in harbor sparkled with flags. In the streets between houses with red roofs and painted walls, between the old moss-grown gardens and under avenues of trees, past great parks and public buildings, processions moved. Some were decorous: old people in long stiff robes of mauve and gray, grave master workmen, quiet, merry women carrying their babies and chatting as they walked. In other streets the music beat faster, a shimmering of gong and tambourine, and the people went dancing, the procession was a dance. Children dodged in and out, their high calls rising like the swallows' crossing flights over the music and the singing. All the processions wound towards the north side of the city, where on the great water-meadow called the Green Fields boys and girls, naked in the bright air, with mudstained feet and ankles and long, lithe arms, exercised their restive horses before the race. The horses wore no gear at all but a halter without bit. Their manes were braided with streamers of silver, gold, and green. They flared their nostrils and pranced and boasted to one another; they were vastly excited, the horse being the only animal who has adopted our ceremonies as his own. Far off to the north and west the mountains stood up half circling Omelas on her bay. The air of morning was so clear that the snow still crowning the Eighteen Peaks burned with white-gold fire across the miles of sunlit air, under the dark blue of the sky. There was just enough wind to make the banners that marked the racecourse snap and flutter now and then. In the silence of the broad green meadows one could hear the music winding through the city streets, farther and nearer and ever approaching, a cheerful faint sweetness of the air that from time to time trembled and gathered together and broke out into the great joyous clanging of the bells.

Joyous! How is one to tell about joy? How describe the citizens of Omelas?

They were not simple folk, you see, though they were happy. But we do not say the words of cheer much any more. All smiles have become archaic. Given a description such as this one tends to make certain assumptions. Given a description such as this one tends to look next for the King, mounted on a splendid stallion and surrounded by his noble knights, or perhaps in a golden litter borne by great-muscled slaves. But there was no king. They did not use swords, or keep slaves. They were not barbarians. I do not know the rules and laws of their society, but I suspect that they were singularly few. As they did without monarchy and slavery, so they also got on without the stock exchange, the advertisement, the secret police, and the bomb. Yet I repeat that these were not simple folk, not dulcet shepherds, noble savages, bland utopians. They were not less complex than us. The trouble is that we have a bad habit, encouraged by pedants and sophisticates, of considering happiness as something rather stupid. Only pain is intellectual, only evil interesting. This is the treason of the artist: a refusal to admit the banality of evil and the terrible boredom of pain. If you can't lick 'em, join 'em. If it hurts, repeat it. But to praise despair is to condemn delight, to embrace violence is to lose hold of everything else. We have almost lost hold, we can no longer describe a happy man, nor make any celebration of joy. How can I tell you about the people of Omelas? They were not naïve and happy children—though their children were, in fact, happy. They were mature, intelligent, passionate adults whose lives were not wretched. O miracle! But I wish I could describe it better. I wish I could convince you. Omelas sounds in my words like a city in a fairy tale, long ago and far away, once upon a time. Perhaps it would be best if you imagined it as your own fancy bids, assuming it will rise to the occasion, for certainly I cannot suit you all. For instance, how about technology? I think that there would be no cars or helicopters in and above the streets; this follows from the fact that the people of Omelas are happy people. Happiness is based on a just discrimination of what is necessary, what is neither necessary nor destructive, and what is destructive. In the middle category, however—that of the unnecessary but undestructive, that of comfort, luxury, exuberance, etc.—they could perfectly well have central heating, subway trains, washing machines, and all kinds of marvelous devises not yet invented here, floating light-sources, fuelless power, a cure for the common cold. Or they could have none of that: it doesn't matter. As you like it. I incline to think that people from towns up and down the coast have been coming in to Omelas during the last days before the Festival on very fast trains and double-decked trams, and that the train station of Omelas is actually the handsomest building in town, though plainer than the magnificent Farmers' Market. But even granted trains, I fear that Omelas so far strikes some of you as goody-goody. Smiles, bells, parades, horses, bleh. If so, please add an orgy. If an orgy would help, don't hesitate. Let us not, however, have temples from which issue beautiful nude priests and priestesses already half in ecstasy and ready to copulate with any man or woman, lover or stranger, who desires union with the deep godhead of the blood, although that was my first idea. But really it would be better not to have any temples in Omelas—at least, not manned temples. Religion yes, clergy no. Surely the beautiful nudes can just wander about, offering themselves like divine soufflés to the hunger of the needy and the rapture of the flesh. Let them join the processions. Let tambourines be struck above the copulations, and the glory of desire be proclaimed upon the gongs, and (a not unimportant point) let the offspring of these delightful rituals be beloved and looked after by all. One thing I know there is none of in Omelas is guilt. But what else should there be? I thought that first there were no drugs, but that is puritanical. For those who like it, the faint insistent sweetness of *drooz* may perfume the ways of the city, *drooz* which first brings a great lightness and brilliance to the mind and limbs, and then after some hours a dreamy languor, and wonderful visions at last of the very arcana and inmost secrets of the Universe, as well as exciting the pleasure of sex beyond all belief; and it is not habit-forming. For more modest tastes I think there ought to be beer. What else, what else belongs in the joyous city? The sense of victory, surely, the celebration of courage. But as we did without clergy, let us do without soldiers. The joy built upon successful slaughter is not the right kind of joy; it will not do; it is fearful and it is trivial. A boundless and generous contentment, a magnanimous triumph felt not against some outer enemy but in communion with the finest and fairest in the souls of all men everywhere and the splendor of the world's summer; this is what swells the hearts of the people of Omelas, and the victory they celebrate is that of life. I really don't think many of them need to take *drooz*.

Most of the processions have reached the Green Fields by now. A marvelous smell of cooking goes forth from the red and blue tents of the provisioners. The faces of small children are amiably sticky; in the benign grey beard of a man a couple of crumbs of rich pastry are entangled. The youths and girls have mounted their horses and are beginning to group around the starting line of the course. An old woman, small, fat, and laughing, is passing out flowers from a basket, and tall young men wear her flowers in their shining hair. A child of nine or ten sits at the edge of the crowd, alone, playing on a wooden flute. People pause to listen, and they smile, but they do not speak to him, for he never ceases playing and never sees them, his dark eyes wholly rapt in the sweet, thin magic of the tune. 4

He finishes, and slowly lowers his hands holding the wooden flute. 5

As if that little private silence were the signal, all at once a trumpet sounds from the pavilion near the starting line: imperious, melancholy, piercing. The horses rear on their slender legs, and some of them neigh in answer. Soberfaced, the young riders stroke the horses' necks and soothe them, whispering, "Quiet, quiet, there my beauty, my hope." They begin to form in rank along the starting line. The crowds along the racecourse are like a field of grass and flowers in the wind. The Festival of Summer has begun. 6

Do you believe? Do you accept the festival, the city, the joy? No? Then let me describe this one more thing. 7

In a basement under one of the beautiful public buildings of Omelas, or perhaps in the cellar of one of its spacious private homes, there is a room. It has one locked door, and no window. A little light seeps in dustily between cracks in the boards, secondhand from the cobwebbed window somewhere across the cellar. In one corner of the little room a couple of mops, with stiff, clotted, foul-smelling heads, stand near a rusty bucket. The floor is dirt, a little damp to the touch, as cellar dirt usually is. The room is about three paces long and two wide: a mere broom closet or disused tool room. In the room a child is sitting. It could be a boy or a girl. It looks about six, but actually is nearly ten. It is feeble-minded. Perhaps it was born defective, or perhaps it has become imbecile through fear, malnutrition, and neglect. It picks its nose and occasionally fumbles vaguely with its toes or genitals, as it sits hunched in the corner farthest from the bucket and the two mops. It is afraid of the mops. It finds them horrible. It shuts its eyes, but it knows the mops are still standing there; and the door is locked; and nobody will come. The door is always locked; and nobody ever comes, except that sometimes—the child has no understanding of time or interval—sometimes the door rattles terribly and opens, and a person, or several people, are there. One of them may come in and kick the child to make it stand up. The others never come close, but peer in at it with frightened, disgusted eyes. The food bowl and the water jug are hastily filled, the door is locked, the eyes disappear. The people at the 8 door never say anything, but the child, who has not always lived in the tool room, and can remember sunlight and its mother's voice, sometimes speaks. "I will be good," it says. "Please let me out. I will be good!" They never answer. The child used to scream for help at night, and cry a good deal, but now it only makes a kind of whining, "eh-haa-eh-haa," and it speaks less and less often. It is so thin there are no calves to its legs; its belly protrudes; it lives on a half-bowl of corn meal and grease a day. It is naked. Its buttocks and thighs are a mass of festered sores, as it sits in its own excrement continually.

9   They all know it is there, all the people of Omelas. Some of them have come to see it, others are content merely to know it is there. They all know that it has to be there. Some of them understand why, and some do not, but they all understand that their happiness, the beauty of their city, the tenderness of their friendships, the health of their children, the wisdom of their scholars, the skill of their makers, even the abundance of their harvest and the kindly weathers of their skies, depend wholly upon this child's abominable misery.

10   This is usually explained to children when they are between eight and twelve, whenever they seem capable of understanding; and most of those who come to see the child are young people, though often enough an adult comes, or comes back, to see the child. No matter how well the matter has been explained to them, these young spectators are always shocked and sickened at the sight. They feel disgust, which they had thought themselves superior to. They feel anger, outrage, impotence, despite all the explanations. They would like to do something for the child. But there is nothing they can do. If the child were brought up into the sunlight out of that vile place, if it were cleaned and fed and comforted, that would be a good thing, indeed; but if it were done, in that day and hour all the prosperity and beauty and delight of Omelas would wither and be destroyed. Those are the terms. To exchange all the goodness and grace of every life in Omelas for that single, small improvement: to throw away the happiness of thousands for the chance of the happiness of one: that would be to let guilt within the walls indeed.

11   The terms are strict and absolute; there may not even be a kind word spoken to the child.

12   Often the young people go home in tears, or in a tearless rage, when they have seen the child and faced this terrible paradox. They may brood over it for weeks or years. But as time goes on they begin to realize that even if the child could be released, it would not get much good of its freedom: a little vague pleasure of warmth and food, no doubt, but little more. It is too degraded and imbecile to know any real joy. It has been afraid too long ever to be free of fear. Its habits are too uncouth for it to respond to humane treatment. Indeed, after so long it would probably be wretched without walls about it to protect it, and darkness for its eyes, and its own excrement to sit in. Their tears at the bitter injustice dry when they begin to perceive the terrible justice of reality, and to accept it. Yet it is their tears and anger, the trying of their generosity and the acceptance of their helplessness, which are perhaps the true source of

the splendor of their lives. Theirs is no vapid, irresponsible happiness. They know that they, like the child, are not free. They know compassion. It is the existence of the child, and their knowledge of its existence, that makes possible the mobility of their architecture, the poignancy of their music, the profundity of their science. It is because of the child that they are so gentle with children. They know that if the wretched one were not there snivelling in the dark, the other one, the flute-player, could make no joyful music as the young riders line up in their beauty for the race in the sunlight of the first morning of summer.

Now do you believe in them? Are they not more credible? But there is one 13 more thing to tell, and this is quite incredible.

At times one of the adolescent girls or boys who go to see the child, does 14 not go home to weep or rage, does not, in fact, go home at all. Sometimes also a man or woman much older falls silent for a day or two, and then leaves home. These people go out into the street, and walk down the street alone. They keep walking, and walk straight out of the city of Omelas, through the beautiful gates. They keep walking across the farmlands of Omelas. Each one goes alone, youth or girl, man or woman. Night falls; the traveler must pass down village streets, between the houses with yellow-lit windows, and on out into the darkness of the fields. Each alone, they go west or north, towards the mountains. They go on. They leave Omelas, they walk ahead into the darkness, and they do not come back. The place they go towards is a place even less imaginable to most of us than the city of happiness. I cannot describe it at all. It is possible that it does not exist. But they seem to know where they are going, the ones who walk away from Omelas.

Source: Copyright © 1973 by Ursula K. Le Guin; first appeared in *New Dimensions 3*, reprinted by permission of the author and the author's agent, Virginia Kidd.

QUESTIONS FOR READING, REASONING, AND REFLECTION

1. What is the general impression you get of the city of Omelas from the opening paragraph? To what senses does the author appeal?

2. Describe the people of Omelas. Are they happy? Do they have technology? Guilt? Religion? Soldiers? Drugs?

3. What shocking detail emerges about Omelas? On what does this ideal community thrive?

4. How do the children and teens respond to the locked-up child at first? How do they reconcile themselves to the situation? What do some residents do?

5. Can you understand the reason most residents accept the situation? Can you understand those who walk away? With which group do you most identify? Why?

6. On what does Le Guin want us to reflect? How would you state the story's theme?

TRIFLES | SUSAN GLASPELL

Born in Iowa, Susan Glaspell (1876–1948) attended Drake University and then began her writing career as a reporter with the *Des Moines Daily News*. She also started writing and selling short stories; her first collection, *Lifted Masks*, was published in 1912. She completed several novels before moving to Provincetown with her husband, who started the Provincetown Players in 1915. Glaspell wrote seven short plays and four long plays for this group, including *Trifles* (1916). The well-known "Jury of Her Peers" (1917) is a short-story version of the play *Trifles*. Glaspell must have recognized that the plot of *Trifles* was a gem worth working with in more than one literary form.

Characters
>   George Henderson, County Attorney
>   Henry Peters, Sheriff
>   Lewis Hale, A Neighboring Farmer
>   Mrs. Peters
>   Mrs. Hale

>   SCENE: *The kitchen in the now abandoned farmhouse of* JOHN WRIGHT, *a gloomy kitchen, and left without having been put in order—unwashed pans under the sink, a loaf of bread outside the bread-box, a dish-towel on the table—other signs of incompleted work. At the rear, the outer door opens and the* SHERIFF *comes in followed by the* COUNTY ATTORNEY *and* HALE. *The* SHERIFF *and* HALE *are men in middle life; the* COUNTY ATTORNEY *is a young man; all are much bundled up and go at once to the stove. They are followed by the two women—the* SHERIFF'*s wife first; she is a slight wiry woman, a thin nervous face.* MRS. HALE *is larger and would ordinarily be called more comfortable looking, but she is disturbed now and looks fearfully about as she enters. The women have come in slowly, and stand close together near the door.*

COUNTY ATTORNEY
[*Rubbing his hands.*] This feels good. Come up to the fire, ladies.

MRS. PETERS
[*After taking a step forward.*] I'm not—cold.

SHERIFF
[*Unbuttoning his overcoat and stepping away from the stove as if to mark the beginning of official business.*] Now, Mr. Hale, before we move things about, you explain to Mr. Henderson just what you saw when you came here yesterday morning.

COUNTY ATTORNEY
By the way, has anything been moved? Are things just as you left them yesterday?

SHERIFF

[*Looking about.*] It's just the same. When it dropped below zero last night I thought I'd better send Frank out this morning to make a fire for us—no use getting pneumonia with a big case on, but I told him not to touch anything except the stove—and you know Frank.

COUNTY ATTORNEY

Somebody should have been left here yesterday.

SHERIFF

Oh—yesterday. When I had to send Frank to Morris Center for that man who went crazy—I want you to know I had my hands full yesterday. I knew you could get back from Omaha by today and as long as I went over everything here myself—

COUNTY ATTORNEY

Well, Mr. Hale, tell just what happened when you came here yesterday morning.

HALE

Harry and I had started to town with a load of potatoes. We came along the road from my place and as I got here I said, "I'm going to see if I can't get John Wright to go in with me on a party telephone." I spoke to Wright about it once before and he put me off, saying folks talked too much anyway, and all he asked was peace and quiet—I guess you know about how much he talked himself; but I thought maybe if I went to the house and talked about it before his wife, though I said to Harry that I didn't know as what his wife wanted made much difference to John—

COUNTY ATTORNEY

Let's talk about that later, Mr. Hale. I do want to talk about that, but tell now just what happened when you got to the house.

HALE

I didn't hear or see anything; I knocked at the door, and still it was all quiet inside. I knew they must be up, it was past eight o'clock. So I knocked again, and I thought I heard somebody say, "Come in." I wasn't sure, I'm not sure yet, but I opened the door—this door [*indicating the door by which the two women are still standing*] and there in that rocker—[*pointing to it*] sat Mrs. Wright.
[*They all look at the rocker.*]

COUNTY ATTORNEY

What—was she doing?

HALE

She was rockin' back and forth. She had her apron in her hand and was kind of—pleating it.

COUNTY ATTORNEY

And how did she—look?

HALE

Well, she looked queer.

COUNTY ATTORNEY

How do you mean—queer?

HALE

Well, as if she didn't know what she was going to do next. And kind of done up.

COUNTY ATTORNEY

How did she seem to feel about your coming?

HALE

Why, I don't think she minded—one way or other. She didn't pay much attention. I said, "How do, Mrs. Wright, it's cold, ain't it?" And she said, "Is it?"—and went on kind of pleating at her apron. Well, I was surprised; she didn't ask me to come up to the stove, or to set down, but just sat there, not even looking at me, so I said, "I want to see John." And then she—laughed. I guess you would call it a laugh. I thought of Harry and the team outside, so I said a little sharp: "Can't I see John?" "No," she says, kind o' dull like. "Ain't he home?" says I. "Yes," says she, "he's home." "Then why can't I see him?" I asked her, out of patience. " 'Cause he's dead," says she. "*Dead?*" says I. She just nodded her head, not getting a bit excited, but rockin' back and forth. "Why—where is he?" says I, not knowing what to say. She just pointed upstairs—like that [*himself pointing to the room above*]. I got up, with the idea of going up there. I walked from there to here—then I says, "Why, what did he die of?" "He died of a rope around his neck," says she, and just went on pleatin' at her apron. Well, I went out and called Harry. I thought I might—need help. We went upstairs and there he was lyin'—

COUNTY ATTORNEY

I think I'd rather have you go into that upstairs, where you can point it all out. Just go on now with the rest of the story.

HALE

Well, my first thought was to get that rope off. It looked . . . [*Stops, his face twitches*] . . . but Harry, he went up to him, and he said, "No, he's dead all right, and we'd better not touch anything." So we went back downstairs. She was still sitting that same way. "Has anybody been notified?" said Harry. He said it business-like—and she stopped pleatin' of her apron. "I don't know," she says. "You don't *know?*" says Harry. "No," says she. "Weren't you sleepin' in the bed with him?" says Harry. "Yes," says she, "but I was on the inside."

"Somebody slipped a rope round his neck and strangled him and you didn't wake up?" says Harry. "I didn't wake up," she said after him. We must'a looked as if we didn't see how that could be, for after a minute she said, "I sleep sound." Harry was going to ask her more questions but I said maybe we ought to let her tell her story first to the coroner, or the sheriff, so Harry went fast as he could to Rivers' place, where there's a telephone.

COUNTY ATTORNEY

And what did Mrs. Wright do when she knew that you had gone for the coroner?

HALE

She moved from that chair to this one over here [*Pointing to a small chair in the corner*] and just sat there with her hands held together and looking down. I got a feeling that I ought to make some conversation, so I said I had come in to see if John wanted to put in a telephone, and at that she started to laugh, and then she stopped and looked at me—scared. [*The County Attorney, who has had his notebook out, makes a note.*] I dunno, maybe it wasn't scared. I wouldn't like to say it was. Soon Harry got back, and then Dr. Lloyd came, and you, Mr. Peters, and so I guess that's all I know that you don't.

COUNTY ATTORNEY

[*Looking around.*] I guess we'll go upstairs first—and then out to the barn and around there. [*To the Sheriff.*] You're convinced that there was nothing important here—nothing that would point to any motive.

SHERIFF

Nothing here but kitchen things.
[*The County Attorney, after again looking around the kitchen, opens the door of a cupboard closet. He gets up on a chair and looks on a shelf. Pulls his hand away, sticky.*]

COUNTY ATTORNEY

Here's a nice mess.
[*The women draw nearer.*]

MRS. PETERS

[*To the other woman.*] Oh, her fruit; it did freeze. [*To the Lawyer.*] She worried about that when it turned so cold. She said the fire'd go out and her jars would break.

SHERIFF

Well, can you beat the woman! Held for murder and worryin' about her preserves.

COUNTY ATTORNEY
I guess before we're through she may have something more serious than preserves to worry about.

HALE
Well, women are used to worrying over trifles.
[*The two women move a little closer together.*]

COUNTY ATTORNEY
[*With the gallantry of a young politician.*] And yet, for all their worries, what would we do without the ladies? [*The women do not unbend. He goes to the sink, takes a dipperful of water from the pail and pouring it into a basin, washes his hands. Starts to wipe them on the roller-towel, turns it for a cleaner place.*] Dirty towels! [*Kicks his foot against the pans under the sink.*] Not much of a housekeeper, would you say, ladies?

MRS. HALE
[*Stiffly.*] There's a great deal of work to be done on a farm.

COUNTY ATTORNEY
To be sure. And yet [*with a little bow to her*] I know there are some Dickson County farmhouses which do not have such roller towels.
[*He gives it a pull to expose its full length again.*]

MRS. HALE
Those towels get dirty awful quick. Men's hands aren't always as clean as they might be.

COUNTY ATTORNEY
Ah, loyal to your sex, I see. But you and Mrs. Wright were neighbors. I suppose you were friends, too.

MRS. HALE
[*Shaking her head.*] I've not seen much of her of late years. I've not been in this house—it's more than a year.

COUNTY ATTORNEY
And why was that? You didn't like her?

MRS. HALE
I liked her all well enough. Farmers' wives have their hands full, Mr. Henderson. And then—

COUNTY ATTORNEY
Yes—?

MRS. HALE

[*Looking about.*] It never seemed a very cheerful place.

COUNTY ATTORNEY

No—it's not cheerful. I shouldn't say she had the homemaking instinct.

MRS. HALE

Well, I don't know as Wright had, either.

COUNTY ATTORNEY

You mean that they didn't get on very well?

MRS. HALE

No, I don't mean anything. But I don't think a place'd be any cheerfuller for John Wright's being in it.

COUNTY ATTORNEY

I'd like to talk more of that a little later. I want to get the lay of things upstairs now.
[*He goes to the left, where three steps lead to a stair door.*]

SHERIFF

I suppose anything Mrs. Peters does'll be all right. She was to take in some clothes for her, you know, and a few little things. We left in such a hurry yesterday.

COUNTY ATTORNEY

Yes, but I would like to see what you take, Mrs. Peters, and keep an eye out for anything that might be of use to us.

MRS. PETERS

Yes, Mr. Henderson.
[*The women listen to the men's steps on the stairs, then look about the kitchen.*]

MRS. HALE

I'd hate to have men coming into my kitchen, snooping around and criticizing.
[*She arranges the pans under the sink which the Lawyer had shoved out of place.*]

MRS. PETERS

Of course it's no more than their duty.

MRS. HALE

Duty's all right, but I guess that deputy sheriff that came out to make the fire might have got a little of this on. [*Gives the roller towel a pull.*] Wish I'd thought of that sooner. Seems mean to talk about her for not having things slicked up when she had to come away in such a hurry.

MRS. PETERS

[*Who has gone to a small table in the left corner of the room, and lifted one end of a towel that covers a pan.*] She had bread set.
[*Stands still.*]

MRS. HALE

[*Eyes fixed on a loaf of bread beside the breadbox, which is on a low shelf at the other side of the room. Moves slowly toward it.*] She was going to put this in there. [*Picks up loaf, then abruptly drops it. In a manner of returning to familiar things.*] It's a shame about her fruit. I wonder if it's all gone. [*Gets up on the chair and looks.*] I think there's some here that's all right, Mrs. Peters. Yes—here; [*holding it toward the window*] this is cherries, too. [*Looking again.*] I declare I believe that's the only one. [*Gets down, bottle in her hand. Goes to the sink and wipes it off on the outside.*] She'll feel awful bad after all her hard work in the hot weather. I remember the afternoon I put up my cherries last summer.
[*She puts the bottle on the big kitchen table, center of the room. With a sigh, is about to sit down in the rocking-chair. Before she is seated realizes what chair it is; with a slow look at it, steps back. The chair which she has touched rocks back and forth.*]

MRS. PETERS

Well, I must get those things from the front room closet. [*She goes to the door at the right, but after looking into the other room, steps back.*] You coming with me, Mrs. Hale? You could help me carry them.
[*They go in the other room; reappear, Mrs. Peters carrying a dress and skirt, Mrs. Hale following with a pair of shoes.*]

MRS. PETERS

My, it's cold in there.
[*She puts the clothes on the big table, and hurries to the stove.*]

MRS. HALE

[*Examining the skirt.*] Wright was close. I think maybe that's why she kept so much to herself. She didn't even belong to the Ladies Aid. I suppose she felt she couldn't do her part, and then you don't enjoy things when you feel shabby. She used to wear pretty clothes and be lively, when she was Minnie Foster, one of the town girls singing in the choir. But that—oh, that was thirty years ago. This all you was to take in?

MRS. PETERS

She said she wanted an apron. Funny thing to want, for there isn't much to get you dirty in jail, goodness knows. But I suppose just to make her feel more natural. She said they was in the top drawer in this cupboard. Yes, here. And then her little shawl that always hung behind the door. [*Opens stair door and looks.*] Yes, here it is.

[*Quickly shuts door leading upstairs.*]

MRS. HALE

[*Abruptly moving toward her.*] Mrs. Peters?

MRS. PETERS

Yes, Mrs. Hale?

MRS. HALE

Do you think she did it?

MRS. PETERS

[*In a frightened voice.*] Oh, I don't know.

MRS. HALE

Well, I don't think she did. Asking for an apron and her little shawl. Worrying about her fruit.

MRS. PETERS

[*Starts to speak, glances up, where footsteps are heard in the room above. In a low voice.*] Mr. Peters says it looks bad for her. Mr. Henderson is awful sarcastic in a speech and he'll make fun of her sayin' she didn't wake up.

MRS. HALE

Well, I guess John Wright didn't wake when they was slipping that rope under his neck.

MRS. PETERS

No, it's strange. It must have been done awful crafty and still. They say it was such a—funny way to kill a man, rigging it all up like that.

MRS. HALE

That's just what Mr. Hale said. There was a gun in the house. He says that's what he can't understand.

MRS. PETERS

Mr. Henderson said coming out that what was needed for the case was a motive; something to show anger, or—sudden feeling.

MRS. HALE

[*Who is standing by the table.*] Well, I don't see any signs of anger around here. [*She puts her hand on the dish towel which lies on the table, stands looking down at table, one half of which is clean, the other half messy.*] It's wiped to here. [*Makes a move as if to finish work, then turns and looks at loaf of bread outside the breadbox. Drops towel. In that voice of coming-back to familiar things.*] Wonder how they are finding things upstairs. I hope she had it a little more red-up up there. You know, it seems kind of sneaking. Locking her up in town and then coming out here and trying to get her own house to turn against her!

MRS. PETERS

But Mrs. Hale, the law is the law.

MRS. HALE

I s'pose 'tis. [*Unbuttoning her coat.*] Better loosen up your things, Mrs. Peters. You won't feel them when you go out.

[*Mrs. Peters takes off her fur tippet, goes to hang it on hook at back of room, stands looking at the under part of the small corner table.*]

MRS. PETERS

She was piecing a quilt.

[*She brings the large sewing basket and they look at the bright pieces.*]

MRS. HALE

It's log cabin pattern. Pretty, isn't it? I wonder if she was goin' to quilt it or just knot it? [*Footsteps have been heard coming down the stairs. The Sheriff enters followed by Hale and the County Attorney.*]

SHERIFF

They wonder if she was going to quilt it or just knot it!

[*The men laugh, the women look abashed.*]

COUNTY ATTORNEY

[*Rubbing his hands over the stove.*] Frank's fire didn't do much up there, did it? Well, let's go out to the barn and get that cleared up.

[*The men go outside.*]

MRS. HALE

[*Resentfully.*] I don't know as there's anything so strange, our takin' up our time with little things while we're waiting for them to get the evidence. [*She sits down at the big table smoothing out a block with decision.*] I don't see as it's anything to laugh about.

MRS. PETERS

[*Apologetically.*] Of course they've got awful important things on their minds. [*Pulls up a chair and joins Mrs. Hale at the table.*]

MRS. HALE

[*Examining another block.*] Mrs. Peters, look at this one. Here, this is the one she was working on, and look at the sewing! All the rest of it has been so nice and even. And look at this! It's all over the place! Why, it looks as if she didn't know what she was about!
[*After she has said this they look at each other, then start to glance back at the door. After an instant Mrs. Hale has pulled at a knot and ripped the sewing.*]

MRS. PETERS

Oh, what are you doing, Mrs. Hale?

MRS. HALE

[*Mildly.*] Just pulling out a stitch or two that's not sewed very good. [*Threading a needle.*] Bad sewing always made me fidgety.

MRS. PETERS

[*Nervously.*] I don't think we ought to touch things.

MRS. HALE

I'll just finish up this end. [*Suddenly stopping and leaning forward.*] Mrs. Peters?

MRS. PETERS

Yes, Mrs. Hale?

MRS. HALE

What do you suppose she was so nervous about?

MRS. PETERS

Oh—I don't know. I don't know as she was nervous. I sometimes sew awful queer when I'm just tired. [*Mrs. Hale starts to say something, looks at Mrs. Peters, then goes on sewing.*] Well I must get these things wrapped up. They may be through sooner than we think. [*Putting apron and other things together.*] I wonder where I can find a piece of paper, and string.

MRS. HALE

In that cupboard, maybe.

MRS. PETERS

[*Looking in cupboard.*] Why, here's a bird-cage. [*Holds it up.*] Did she have a bird, Mrs. Hale?

MRS. HALE

Why, I don't know whether she did or not—I've not been here for so long. There was a man around last year selling canaries cheap, but I don't know as she took one; maybe she did. She used to sing real pretty herself.

MRS. PETERS

[*Glancing around.*] Seems funny to think of a bird here. But she must have had one, or why would she have a cage? I wonder what happened to it.

MRS. HALE

I s'pose maybe the cat got it.

MRS. PETERS

No, she didn't have a cat. She's got that feeling some people have about cats—being afraid of them. My cat got in her room and she was real upset and asked me to take it out.

MRS. HALE

My sister Bessie was like that. Queer, ain't it?

MRS. PETERS

[*Examining the cage.*] Why, look at this door. It's broke. One hinge is pulled apart.

MRS. HALE

[*Looking too.*] Looks as if someone must have been rough with it.

MRS. PETERS

Why, yes.
[*She brings the cage forward and puts it on the table.*]

MRS. HALE

I wish if they're going to find any evidence they'd be about it. I don't like this place.

MRS. PETERS

But I'm awful glad you came with me, Mrs. Hale. It would be lonesome for me sitting here alone.

MRS. HALE

It would, wouldn't it? [*Dropping her sewing.*] But I tell you what I do wish, Mrs. Peters. I wish I had come over sometimes when *she* was here. I—[*looking around the room*]—wish I had.

MRS. PETERS

But of course you were awful busy, Mrs. Hale—your house and your children.

MRS. HALE

I could've come. I stayed away because it weren't cheerful—and that's why I ought to have come. I—I've never liked this place. Maybe because it's down in a hollow and you don't see the road. I dunno what it is, but it's a lonesome place and always was. I wish I had come over to see Minnie Foster sometimes. I can see now—

[*Shakes her head.*]

MRS. PETERS

Well, you mustn't reproach yourself, Mrs. Hale. Somehow we just don't see how it is with other folks until—something comes up.

MRS. HALE

Not having children makes less work—but it makes a quiet house, and Wright out to work all day, and no company when he did come in. Did you know John Wright, Mrs. Peters?

MRS. PETERS

Not to know him; I've seen him in town. They say he was a good man.

MRS. HALE

Yes—good; he didn't drink, and kept his word as well as most, I guess, and paid his debts. But he was a hard man, Mrs. Peters. Just to pass the time of day with him—[*Shivers.*] Like a raw wind that gets to the bone. [*Pauses, her eye falling on the cage.*] I should think she would'a wanted a bird. But what do you suppose went with it?

MRS. PETERS

I don't know, unless it got sick and died.

[*She reaches over and swings the broken door, swings it again, both women watch it.*]

MRS. HALE

You weren't raised round here, were you? [*Mrs. Peters shakes her head.*] You didn't know—her?

MRS. PETERS

Not till they brought her yesterday.

MRS. HALE

She—come to think of it, she was kind of like a bird herself—real sweet and pretty, but kind of timid and—fluttery. How—she—did—change. [*Silence;*

then as if struck by a happy thought and relieved to get back to everyday things.] Tell you what, Mrs. Peters, why don't you take the quilt in with you? It might take up her mind.

MRS. PETERS

Why, I think that's a real nice idea, Mrs. Hale. There couldn't possibly be any objection to it, could there? Now, just what would I take? I wonder if her patches are in here—and her things.
[*They look in the sewing basket.*]

MRS. HALE

Here's some red. I expect this has got sewing things in it. [*Brings out a fancy box.*] What a pretty box. Looks like something somebody would give you. Maybe her scissors are in here. [*Opens box. Suddenly puts her hand to her nose.*] Why—[*Mrs. Peters bends nearer, then turns her face away.*] There's something wrapped up in this piece of silk.

MRS. PETERS

Why, this isn't her scissors.

MRS. HALE

[*Lifting the silk.*] Oh, Mrs. Peters—it's—
[*Mrs. Peters bends closer.*]

MRS. PETERS

It's the bird.

MRS. HALE

[*Jumping up.*] But, Mrs. Peters—look at it! Its neck! Look at its neck! It's all—other side *to.*

MRS. PETERS

Somebody—wrung—its—neck.
[*Their eyes meet. A look of growing comprehension, or horror. Steps are heard outside. Mrs. Hale slips box under quilt pieces, and sinks into her chair. Enter Sheriff and County Attorney. Mrs. Peters rises.*]

COUNTY ATTORNEY

[*As one turning from serious things to little pleasantries.*] Well ladies, have you decided whether she was going to quilt it or knot it?

MRS. PETERS

We think she was going to—knot it.

COUNTY ATTORNEY

Well, that's interesting, I'm sure. [*Seeing the bird-cage.*] Has the bird flown?

MRS. HALE

[*Putting more quilt pieces over the box.*] We think the—cat got it.

COUNTY ATTORNEY

[*Preoccupied.*] Is there a cat?
[*Mrs. Hale glances in a quick covert way at Mrs. Peters.*]

MRS. PETERS

Well, not now. They're superstitious, you know. They leave.

COUNTY ATTORNEY

[*To Sheriff Peters, continuing an interrupted conversation.*] No sign at all of anyone having come from the outside. Their own rope. Now let's go up again and go over it piece by piece. [*They start upstairs.*] It would have to have been someone who knew just the—
[*Mrs. Peters sits down. The two women sit there not looking at one another, but as if peering into something and at the same time holding back. When they talk now it is in the manner of feeling their way over strange ground, as if afraid of what they are saying, but as if they can not help saying it.*]

MRS. HALE

She liked the bird. She was going to bury it in that pretty box.

MRS. PETERS

[*In a whisper.*] When I was a girl—my kitten—there was a boy took a hatchet, and before my eyes—and before I could get there—[*Covers her face an instant.*] If they hadn't held me back I would have—[*Catches herself, looks upstairs where steps are heard, falters weakly*]—hurt him.

MRS. HALE

[*With a slow look around her.*] I wonder how it would seem never to have had any children around. [*Pause.*] No, Wright wouldn't like the bird—a thing that sang. She used to sing. He killed that, too.

MRS. PETERS

[*Moving uneasily.*] We don't know who killed the bird.

MRS. HALE

I knew John Wright.

MRS. PETERS

It was an awful thing was done in this house that night, Mrs. Hale. Killing a man while he slept, slipping a rope around his neck that choked the life out of him.

MRS. HALE

His neck. Choked the life out of him.
[*Her hand goes out and rests on the bird-cage.*]

MRS. PETERS

We don't know who killed him. We don't *know*.

MRS. HALE

[*Her own feeling not interrupted.*] If there'd been years and years of noth-ing, then a bird to sing to you, it would be awful—still, after the bird was still.

MRS. PETERS

[*Something within her speaking.*] I know what stillness is. When we home-steaded in Dakota, and my first baby died—after he was two years old, and me with no other then—

MRS. HALE

[*Moving.*] How soon do you suppose they'll be through, looking for the evidence?

MRS. PETERS

I know what stillness is. [*Pulling herself back.*] The law has got to punish crime, Mrs. Hale.

MRS. HALE

[*Not as if answering that.*] I wish you'd seen Minnie Foster when she wore a white dress with blue ribbons and stood up there in the choir and sang. [*A look around the room.*] Oh, I *wish* I'd come over here once in a while! That was a crime! That was a crime! Who's going to punish that?

MRS. PETERS

[*Looking upstairs.*] We mustn't—take on.

MRS. HALE

I might have known she needed help! I know how things can be—for women. I tell you, it's queer, Mrs. Peters. We live close together and we live far apart. We all go through the same things—it's all just a different kind of the same thing. [*Brushes her eyes, noticing the bottle of fruit, reaches out for it.*] If I was you I wouldn't tell her her fruit was gone. Tell her it *ain't*. Tell her it's all right. Take this in to prove it to her. She—she may never know whether it was broke or not.

MRS. PETERS

[*Takes the bottle, looks about for something to wrap it in; takes petticoat from the clothes brought from the other room, very nervously begins winding this around the bottle. In a false voice.*] My, it's a good thing the men couldn't hear us. Wouldn't they just laugh! Getting all stirred up over a little thing like a—dead canary. As if that could have anything to do with—with—wouldn't they *laugh*!

[*The men are heard coming downstairs.*]

MRS. HALE

[*Under her breath.*] Maybe they would—maybe they wouldn't.

COUNTY ATTORNEY

No, Peters, it's all perfectly clear except a reason for doing it. But you know juries when it comes to women. If there was some definite thing. Something to show—something to make a story about—a thing that would connect up with this strange way of doing it—

[*The women's eyes meet for an instant. Enter Hale from outer door.*]

HALE

Well, I've got the team around. Pretty cold out there.

COUNTY ATTORNEY

I'm going to stay here awhile by myself. [*To the Sheriff.*] You can send Frank out for me, can't you? I want to go over everything. I'm not satisfied that we can't do better.

SHERIFF

Do you want to see what Mrs. Peters is going to take in?

[*The Lawyer goes to the table, picks up the apron, laughs.*]

COUNTY ATTORNEY

Oh, I guess they're not very dangerous things the ladies have picked out. [*Moves a few things about, disturbing the quilt pieces which cover the box. Steps back.*] No, Mrs. Peters doesn't need supervising. For that matter, a sheriff's wife is married to the law. Ever think of it that way, Mrs. Peters?

MRS. PETERS

Not—just that way.

SHERIFF

[*Chuckling.*] Married to the law. [*Moves toward the other room.*] I just want you to come in here a minute, George. We ought to take a look at these windows.

COUNTY ATTORNEY

[*Scoffingly.*] Oh, windows!

SHERIFF

We'll be right out, Mr. Hale.

[*Hale goes outside. The Sheriff follows the County Attorney into the other room. Then Mrs. Hale rises, hands tight together, looking intensely at Mrs. Peters, whose eyes make a slow turn, finally meeting Mrs. Hale's. A moment Mrs. Hale holds her, then her own eyes point the way to where the box is concealed. Suddenly Mrs. Peters throws back quilt pieces and tries to put the box in the bag she is wearing. It is too big. She opens box, starts to take bird out, cannot touch it, goes to pieces, stands there helpless. Sound of a knob turning in the other room. Mrs. Hale snatches the box and puts it in the pocket of her big coat. Enter County Attorney and Sheriff.*]

COUNTY ATTORNEY

[*Facetiously.*] Well, Henry, at least we found out that she was not going to quilt it. She was going to—what is it you call it, ladies?

MRS. HALE

[*Her hand against her pocket.*] We call it—knot it, Mr. Henderson.

QUESTIONS FOR READING, REASONING, AND REFLECTION

1. Explain the situation as the play begins.

2. Examine the dialogue of the men. What attitudes about themselves—their work, their abilities, their importance—are revealed? What is their collective opinion of women?

3. When Mrs. Hale and Mrs. Peters discover the dead bird, what do they begin to understand?

4. What other "trifles" in the kitchen provide additional evidence as to what has happened?

5. What trifles can be seen as symbols? What do they reveal about Mrs. Wright's life and character?

6. What is the play about primarily? Is it a murder mystery? Does it speak for feminist values? Is it about not seeing—not really knowing—others? In a few sentences, state what you consider to be the play's dominant theme. Then list the evidence you would use to support your conclusion.

7. Is there any sense in which one could argue that Mrs. Wright had a right to kill her husband? If you were a lawyer, how would you plan her defense? If you were on the jury, what sentence would you recommend?

SAMPLE STUDENT LITERARY ANALYSIS

Alan Peterson

American Literature 242

May 5, 2010

Faulkner's Realistic Initiation Theme

William Faulkner braids a universal theme, the theme of initiation, into the fiber of his novel *Intruder in the Dust*. From ancient times to the present, a prominent focus of literature, of life, has been rites of passage, particularly those of childhood to adulthood. Joseph Campbell defines rites of passage as "distinguished by formal, and usually very severe, exercises of severance." A "candidate" for initiation into adult society, Campbell explains, experiences a shearing away of the "attitudes, attachments and life patterns" of childhood (9). This severe, painful stripping away of the child and installation of the adult is presented somewhat differently in several works by American writers.

One technique of handling this theme of initiation is used by Nathaniel Hawthorne in his story "My Kinsman, Major Molineaux." The story's main character, Robin, is suddenly awakened to the real world, the adult world, when he sees Major Molineaux "in tar-and-feathery dignity" (Hawthorne 528). A terrified and amazed Robin gapes at his kinsman as the large and colorful crowd laughs at and ridicules the Major; then an acquiescent Robin joins with the crowd in the mirthful shouting (Hawthorne 529). This moment is Robin's epiphany, his sudden realization of reality. Robin goes from unsophisticated rube to resigned cynical adult in one quick scene. Hawthorne does hold out hope that Robin will not let this event ruin his life, indeed that he will perhaps prosper from it.

A similar, but decidedly less optimistic, example of an epiphanic initiation occurs in Arthur Miller's play *Death of a Salesman*. Miller develops an initiation theme within a flashback. A teenaged Biff, shockingly confronted with Willy's infidelity and weakness, has his boyhood dreams, ambitions—his

Appropriate heading when separate title page is not used.

Center the title.

Double-space throughout.

Opening ¶ introduces subject, presents thesis, and defines key term—initiation.

Student combines paraphrase and brief quotations in definition.

Summary and analysis combined to explain initiation in Hawthorne's story.

Transition to second example establishes contrast with Hawthorne.

vision—shattered, leaving his life in ruins, a truth borne out in scenes in which
Biff is an adult during the play (1083–84, 1101). Biff's discovery of the vices
and shortcomings of his father overwhelms him. His realization of adult life is
a revelation made more piercing when put into the context of his naive and
overly hopeful upbringing. A ravaged and defeated Biff has adulthood wantonly
thrust upon him. Unlike Hawthorne's Robin, Biff never recovers.

¶ concludes with emphasis on contrast.

Transition to Faulkner's story by contrast with Hawthorne and Miller.

William Faulkner does not follow these examples when dealing with the
initiation of his character Chick in *Intruder in the Dust*. In Robin's and Biff's
cases, each character's passage into adulthood was brought about by
realization of and disillusionment with the failings and weaknesses of a male
adult playing an important role in his life. By contrast, Chick's male role
models are vital, moral men with integrity. Chick's awakening develops as he
begins to comprehend the mechanisms of the adult society in which he would
be a member.

Footnote first parenthetical reference to inform readers that subsequent citations will exclude the author's name and give only the page number.

Faulkner uses several techniques for illustrating Chick's growth into a
man. Early in the novel, at the end of the scene in which Chick tries to pay for
his dinner, Lucas warns Chick to "stay out of that creek" (Faulkner 16).[1] The
creek is an effective symbol: it is both a physical creek and a metaphor for the
boy's tendency to slide into gaffes that perhaps a man could avoid. The creek's
symbolic meaning is more evident when, after receiving the molasses, Chick
encounters Lucas in town. Lucas again reminds Chick not to "fall in no more
creeks this winter" (24). At the end of the novel, Lucas meets Chick in Gavin's
office and states: "you ain't fell in no more creeks lately, have you?" (241).
Although Lucas phrases this as a question, the answer is obvious to Lucas, as
well as to the reader, that indeed Chick has not blundered into his naive
boyhood quagmire lately. When Lucas asks his question, Chick's actual falling
into a creek does not occur to the reader.

---

1. Subsequent references to Faulkner's novel cite page numbers only.

Peterson 3

Another image Faulkner employs to show Chick growing into a man is
the single-file line. After Chick gets out of the creek, he follows Lucas into the
house, the group walking in single file. In the face of Lucas's much stronger
adult will, Chick is powerless to get out of the line, to go to Edmonds's house
(7). Later in the novel, when Miss Habersham, Aleck Sander, and Chick are
walking back from digging up the grave, Chick again finds himself in a single-file
line with a strong-willed adult in front. Again he protests, then relents, but
clearly he feels slighted and wonders to himself "what good that [walking
single file] would do" (130). The contrast between these two scenes
illustrates Chick's growth, although he is not yet a man.

Faulkner gives the reader other hints of Chick's passage into manhood.
As the novel progresses, Chick is referred to (and refers to himself) as a
"boy" (24), a "child" (25), a "young man" (46), "almost a man" (190), a "man"
(194), and one of two "gentlemen" (241). Other clues crop up from time to
time. Chick wrestles with himself about getting on his horse and riding away,
far away, until Lucas's lynching is "all over finished done" (41). But his growing
sense of responsibility and outrage quell his boyish desire to escape, to bury
his head in the sand. Chick looks in the mirror at himself with amazement at
his deeds (125). Chick's mother serves him coffee for the first time, despite
the agreement she has with his father to withhold coffee until his eighteenth
birthday (127). Chick's father looks at him with pride and envy (128–29).

Perhaps the most important differences between the epiphanic
initiations of Robin and Biff and that experienced by Chick are the facts that
Chick's epiphany does not come all at once and it does not devastate him.
Chick learns about adulthood—and enters adulthood—piecemeal and with
support. His first eye-opening experience occurs as he tries to pay Lucas for
dinner and is rebuffed (15–16). Chick learns, after trying again to buy a clear
conscience, the impropriety and affront of his actions (24). Lucas teaches

Note transition.

Note interpolation in
square brackets.

Good use of brief
quotations combined
with analysis.

Characteristics of
Chick's gradual
and positive ini-
tiation explained.
Observe coherence
techniques.

Chick how he should resolve *his* dilemma by setting him "free" (26–27). Later, Chick feels outrage at the adults crowding into the town, presumably to see a lynching, then disgrace and shame as they eventually flee (196–97, 210). As in most lives, Chick's passage into adulthood is a gradual process; he learns a little bit at a time and has support in his growing. Gavin is there for him, to act as a sounding board, to lay a strong intellectual foundation, to confirm his beliefs. Chick's initiation is consistent with Joseph Campbell's explanation: "all rites of passage are intended to touch not only the candidate, but also every member of his circle" (9). Perhaps Gavin is affected the most, but Chick's mother and father, and Lucas as well, are influenced by the change in Chick.

In *Intruder in the Dust,* William Faulkner has much to say about the role of and the actions of adults in society. He depicts racism, ignorance, resignation, violence, fratricide, citizenship, hope, righteousness, lemming-like aggregation, fear, and a host of other emotions and actions. Chick learns not only right and wrong, but that in order to be a part of society, of his community, he cannot completely forsake those with whom he disagrees or whose ideas he challenges. There is much compromise in growing up; Chick learns to compromise on some issues, but not all. Gavin's appeal to Chick to "just don't stop" (210) directs him to conform enough to be a part of the adult world, but not to lose sight of, indeed instead to embrace, his own values and ideals.

Student concludes by explaining the values Chick develops in growing up.

Peterson 5

Works Cited

Campbell, Joseph. *The Hero with a Thousand Faces*. Princeton: Princeton UP, 1949. Print.

Faulkner, William. *Intruder in the Dust.* New York: Random, 1948. Print.

Hawthorne, Nathaniel. "My Kinsman, Major Molineaux." 1832. *The Complete Short Stories of Nathaniel Hawthorne*. New York: Hanover/ Doubleday, 1959. 517–30. Print.

Miller, Arthur. *Death of a Salesman. 1949. An Introduction to Literature.* 9th ed. Eds. Sylvan Barnet, Morton Berman, and William Burto. Boston: Little, 1985. 1025–111. Print.

Paging is continuous.

Place Works Cited on separate page.

Double-space throughout.

Use hanging indentation.

SUGGESTIONS FOR DISCUSSION AND WRITING

1. Prepare an explication of either Amy Lowell's "Taxi" or Sir Walter Raleigh's "The Nymph's Reply to the Shepherd." You will need to explain both what the poem says and what it means—or what it accomplishes.

2. Analyze A. E. Housman's attitudes toward life and human relationships in "Is My Team Ploughing."

3. Analyze Mrs. Mallard's conflict, and decision about that conflict, as the basis for your understanding of the dominant theme in "The Story of an Hour."

4. You are Mrs. Wright's attorney (see *Trifles*, pp. 556–72). Write your closing argument in her defense, explaining why only a light sentence is warranted for Mrs. Wright. Select details from the play to support your assertions about Mrs. Wright's character and motivation.

5. Explain what you think are the most important ideas about community in Ursula K. Le Guin's "The Ones Who Walk Away from Omelas."

6. John Donne in "The Bait" and Ogden Nash in "Love Under the Republicans (or Democrats)" also have responses to Marlowe's "The Passionate Shepherd to His Love." Select one of these poems, find a copy, read and analyze it, and then evaluate its argument as a response to Marlowe's shepherd.

Photo Credits

Index